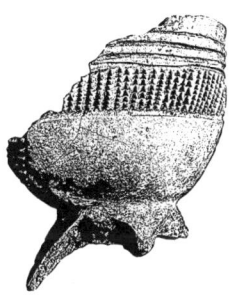

Social Constellations and Settlement Practice

CIVILIZATIONS OF THE WESTERN SUDAN

From the Atlantic to Lake Chad in the great grassland belt of the Sahel and dry savanna, the Western Sudan was home to remarkable cities, states, and alternative forms of complex society. Research has revealed cities without citadels and trading networks of great antiquity. The early history of complex society in the Western Sudan challenges our certainties that hierarchy and centralization were the drivers of social complexity, or that African cities and states drew their initial inspiration from Egypt or the Mediterranean.

YALE UNIVERSITY PUBLICATIONS IN ANTHROPOLOGY

EDITORIAL COMMITTEE

Richard L. Burger
Curatorial Editor-in-Chief
Charles J. MacCurdy Professor of Anthropology, Yale University
Chair, Council on Archaeological Studies
Curator of Anthropology, Peabody Museum of Natural History

Roderick J. McIntosh
Professor of Anthropology, Yale University
Curator-in-Charge of Anthropology, Peabody Museum of Natural History

Anne Underhill
Professor of Anthropology
Chair, Department of Anthropology, Yale University
Curator of Anthropology, Peabody Museum of Natural History

The Yale University Publications in Anthropology series, published by the Yale University Department of Anthropology and the Peabody Museum of Natural History at Yale University, is supported by the Theodore and Ruth Wilmanns Lidz Endowment Fund for Excellence in Scholarly Publications, dedicated to the dissemination of scholarly research and study of the world and its cultures.

The Yale University Publications in Anthropology series embodies the results of researches in the general field of anthropology directly conducted or sponsored by the Yale University Department of Anthropology and the Yale Peabody Museum of Natural History Division of Anthropology. Occasionally other manuscripts of outstanding quality that deal with subjects of special interest to the faculty of the Department of Anthropology may also be included.

Distributed by Yale University Press
NEW HAVEN AND LONDON

For quantity purchases or a complete list of available titles in this series visit
www.yalebooks.com or yalebooks.co.uk

Social Constellations and Settlement Practice

The Archaeology of Non-urban Complexity in Southeastern Burkina Faso

Daphne E. Gallagher

Number 96

Published by
the Yale University Department of Anthropology
and the Yale Peabody Museum of Natural History

Distributed by
Yale University Press
NEW HAVEN AND LONDON

Yale

YALE UNIVERSITY PUBLICATIONS IN ANTHROPOLOGY
NUMBER 96

Rosemary Volpe
Publications Manager

Sally H. Pallatto
Graphic Designer
Cover Design

Lauren H. Lee
Project Assistant

Index by Judy A. Hunt

Front cover: The sandstone cliffs of the Gobnangou escarpment in Burkina Faso. Photograph by Daphne E. Gallagher.

Back cover: Parkland savanna in the Maadaga Archaeological Survey study region in March 2006. Photograph by Daphne E. Gallagher.

Copyright © 2021 Yale University. All rights reserved.
This book may not be reproduced, in whole or in part, including illustrations, in any form (beyond that copying permitted by Sections 107 and 108 of the U.S. Copyright Law and except by reviewers for the public press), without the written permission of the publisher.

Peabody Museum of Natural History
Yale University
P. O. Box 208118
New Haven CT 06520-8118 USA
peabody.yale.edu

Distributed by Yale University Press
NEW HAVEN AND LONDON
www.yalebooks.com | yalebooks.co.uk

ISBN 978-0-913516-32-4
ISSN 1535-7082

Printed in the United States of America

Library of Congress Control Number: 2021931980

∞ This paper meets the requirements of ANSI/NISO Z39.48-1992 (Permanence of Paper).
10 9 8 7 6 5 4 3 2 1

Contents

- vi   List of Figures
- ix   List of Tables
- xi   Foreword
- xii   Preface

1	One	Generational Mobility and Complexity in Southeastern Burkina Faso
13	Two	Ethnoecology of Southeastern Burkina Faso
71	Three	The Maadaga Archaeological Survey: Methodologies and Relative Chronology
105	Four	Broad-spectrum Foragers of the Gobnangou: The Lithic Occupation
123	Five	Adopting Agriculture: The Pwoli Occupation
157	Six	Generational Mobility and Household Networks: The Siga Occupation
211	Seven	Indigo and the Escarpment: The Tuali Occupation
249	Eight	Situating the Archaeology of Southeastern Burkina Faso
261	Appendix A	Maadaga Archaeological Survey Site Catalog
293	Appendix B	Ceramic Tempers, Decorations, and Sherd Types
311	Appendix C	Ring Occupation Sites
315	Appendix D	Rock Art and Hidden Granary Sites

- 323   References
- 349   Index

Figures

Chapter One

2   figure 1.   Location of countries and extent of the Maadaga Archaeological Survey.
3   figure 2.   Approximate extent of the Gulmance kingdoms.

Chapter Two

18   figure 3.   Geology of the Volta Basin.
19   figure 4.   The Gobnangou escarpment in the Maadaga Archaeology Survey.
20   figure 5.   Major rivers and geographic features of southeastern Buskina Faso.
21   figure 6.   The Pendjari River in April 2006.
22   figure 7.   Odundo spring and pool in the Gobnangou escarpment.
23   figure 8.   The Koabu River as it flows away from the Gobnangou escarpment.
25   figure 9.   Soil map of southeastern Burkina Faso.
29   figure 10.   Average monthly annual rainfall and temperatures in Fada N'Gourma.
30   figure 11.   Local variability in annual rainfall along Gobnangou escarpment.
61   figure 12.   Parkland savanna in the Maadaga Archaeological Survey region.

Chapter Three

73   figure 13.   All recorded archaeological sites in Maadaga Archaeological Survey.
74   figure 14.   Sample field maps for documented sites.
76   figure 15.   Plowed and unplowed areas showing surface visibility differences.
77   figure 16.   Maadaga Archaeological Survey analytical zones for spatial analysis.
90   figure 17.   Examples of roulette decorations with associated sites.
94   figure 18.   Examples of dragged decorations with associated sites.
97   figure 19.   Examples of impressed decorations with associated sites.
99   figure 20.   Examples of applied decorations with associated sites.
102   figure 21.   Examples of Sherd Types 1 through 7.
103   figure 22.   Examples of Sherd Types 8 through 13 and 15.
104   figure 23.   Co-occurrence of sherd types in surface collections, excavation, and ethnohistorical record.

Chapter Four

106   figure 24.   Previously excavated sites with Middle Stone Age and geometric microlith assemblages.
109   figure 25.   Backed microliths from site MAS542 and an erosional area.
112   figure 26.   Lithic occcupation sites identified by Maadaga Archaeological Survey.

LIST OF FIGURES

116	FIGURE 27.	Plan of the MAS542 archaeological site.
117	FIGURE 28.	Profile of the stratigraphy of the MAS542 archaeological site.

CHAPTER FIVE

124	FIGURE 29.	Pwoli occupation sites identified by Maadaga Archaeological Survey.
126	FIGURE 30.	The MAS541 archaeological site.
126	FIGURE 31.	Associated AMS radiocarbon dates from the Pwoli occupation.
127	FIGURE 32.	Profiles of the stratigraphy of Unit E at site MAS541.
128	FIGURE 33.	Architectural features from Unit E at site MAS541.
129	FIGURE 34.	Iron objects from Unit E at site MAS541 and Unit A at site MAS502.3.
130	FIGURE 35.	Pwoli occupation ceramics from Unit E at site MAS541.
130	FIGURE 36.	Pwoli occupation sherds from Unit E at site MAS541.
141	FIGURE 37.	Profiles of the stratigraphy of Unit A at site MAS502.3.
144	FIGURE 38.	Pwoli occupation ceramics from Unit A at site MAS502.3.
145	FIGURE 39.	Pwoli occupation sherds from Unit A at site MAS502.3.

CHAPTER SIX

158	FIGURE 40.	Siga occupation sites identified by the Maadaga Archaeological Survey.
159	FIGURE 41.	Locations of Siga occupation sites mentioned in the text.
163	FIGURE 42.	Size distribution of Siga occupation sites.
164	FIGURE 43.	The MAS572 site cluster in relation to site MAS573.
164	FIGURE 44.	Profiles of the stratigraphy of units at sites MAS572.1 and MAS573.
165	FIGURE 45.	Features in Unit C at site MAS572.1.
166	FIGURE 46.	Profiles of stratigraphy of Unit B at site MAS780.
175	FIGURE 47.	Siga occupation ceramics Sherd Types 1 through 5.
176	FIGURE 48.	Siga occupation ceramics Sherd Types 6 through 10.
177	FIGURE 49.	Examples of Siga occupation ceramics Sherd Types 1 through 10.
178	FIGURE 50.	Siga occupation ceramics not assigned to sherd types.
179	FIGURE 51.	Ceramic assemblages at sites MAS572.1 and MAS573.
180	FIGURE 52.	Ceramic assemblage at site MAS780 showing different sherd types.
181	FIGURE 53.	Sherds from sites MAS572.1, MAS573, and MAS780 showing different sherd types.
186	FIGURE 54.	Diameter measurements of rim sherds of Siga occupation vessels.
190	FIGURE 55.	Pipe bowls from Siga occupation sites MAS573 and MAS848.
193	FIGURE 56.	Distribution of iron-working activities during the Siga occupation.
194	FIGURE 57.	Iron objects from Unit B at site MAS780.
194	FIGURE 58.	Iron bracelets from site MAS780.
201	FIGURE 59.	Ground stone objects from Siga occupation sites.
202	FIGURE 60.	Ground stone *hachettes* from Siga sites MAS572.2 and MAS643.
207	FIGURE 61.	Associated dates for datable items of the Siga occupation.

Chapter Seven

212	FIGURE 62.	Tuali-A occupation sites identified by Maadaga Archaeological Survey.
213	FIGURE 63.	Locations of Tuali-A occupation sites mentioned in the text.
214	FIGURE 64.	Size distribution of Tuali-A occupation sites.
218	FIGURE 65.	Tuali-A occupation ceramics.
219	FIGURE 66.	Tuali-A and Tuali-B occupation Sherd Types 11, 12, and 13.
223	FIGURE 67.	Pipes from Tuali-A sites MAS603, MAS948, MAS968, and MAS841.
224	FIGURE 68.	Distribution of iron-working activities during the Tuali-A occupation.
225	FIGURE 69.	Formal chipped stone tools from Tuali-A occupation sites.
226	FIGURE 70.	Tuali-B occupation sites identified by Maadaga Archaeological Survey.
227	FIGURE 71.	Locations of Tuali-B sites mentioned in the text.
233	FIGURE 72.	Tuali-B occupation ceramics Sherd Types 11 and 13.
235	FIGURE 73.	Distribution of iron-working and indigo dyeing during the Tuali-B occupation.
237	FIGURE 74.	Indigo dye pit features.

Chapter Eight

259	FIGURE 75.	Major roads, parks, and reserves in the Burkina-Benin-Niger border region.

Appendix C

313	FIGURE C.1.	Ring occupation ceramics Sherd Type 15 from site MAS863.

Appendix D

316	FIGURE D.1.	Rock art and hidden granary sites in the Gobnangou region.
317	FIGURE D.2.	Rock art sites MAS921 and MAS925.
318	FIGURE D.3.	Paintings at rock art site MAS925.
319	FIGURE D.4.	The rock art motifs at site MAS925.
319	FIGURE D.5.	Plan of hidden granary rockshelter MAS03 showing clay structures.
320	FIGURE D.6.	Structures at hidden granary rockshelter MAS03.

Tables

CHAPTER ONE
12 TABLE 1. Estimated dates for Maadaga Archaeological Survey occupations.

CHAPTER TWO
26 TABLE 2. Terminology of Gulmance soil classification.
27 TABLE 3. Terminology of Gulmance surface feature classification.
32 TABLE 4. Selected useful plant species of the Gobnangou region.
53 TABLE 5. African crops and plants likely cultivated prior to 1500 CE in the Gobnangou region.
57 TABLE 6. Crops introduced to the Gobnangou region since 1500 CE.
64 TABLE 7. Wild mammals found in environments of southeastern Burkina Faso.

CHAPTER THREE
81 TABLE 8. Temper size and vessel thickness in the Maadaga Archaeological Survey ceramic assemblage.
82 TABLE 9. Frequency of dominant pottery tempers.
86 TABLE 10. Frequency of types of surface treatments.
87 TABLE 11. Roulette decoration techniques identified in the ceramic assemblage.
91 TABLE 12. Dragged decoration techniques.
95 TABLE 13. Impressed decoration techniques.
98 TABLE 14. Applied decoration techniques.
100 TABLE 15. Summary of sherd types.

CHAPTER FOUR
110 TABLE 16. Gobnangou region Lithic occupation sites with formal chipped stone tools.
114 TABLE 17. Fauna identified from the Péntènga and Yobri rockshelters.
118 TABLE 18. Characteristic of chipped stone assemblages.

CHAPTER FIVE
131 TABLE 19. Characteristics of the ceramic assemblage from site MAS541.
132 TABLE 20. Ceramic decoration techniques in use at sites MAS541, MAS502.3, and MAS902.
136 TABLE 21. Iron, slag, and stone identified from Unit E at site MAS541.
137 TABLE 22. Fauna identified from Unit E at site MAS541.
139 TABLE 23. Estimated length of fishes from sites MAS541 and MAS502.3.
140 TABLE 24. Carbonized seeds and fruits from sites MAS541 and MAS502.3.

143 TABLE 25. Ceramic assemblage characteristics from sites MAS502.3 and MAS902.
146 TABLE 26. Iron, slag, and stone identified from Unit A at site MAS502.3.
148 TABLE 27. Fauna identified from Unit A at site MAS502.3.

CHAPTER SIX
160 TABLE 28. Characteristics of Siga single-component sites by confidence level.
162 TABLE 29. Siga ceramic assemblage characteristics by location and site size.
168 TABLE 30. Distribution of Siga sites by distance from the escarpment and Koabu.
170 TABLE 31. Ethnohistorical data on land use by Gulmance and Lele households.
172 TABLE 32. Characteristics of Siga single-component site ceramic assemblage.
173 TABLE 33. Ceramic decoration techniques in use at single-component Siga sites.
182 TABLE 34. Characteristics of ceramic assemblages from sites MAS780, MAS572.1, and MAS573.
183 TABLE 35. Ceramic decoration techniques in use at sites MAS780, MAS572.1, and MAS573.
192 TABLE 36. Evidence of smelting activity at Siga occupation sites.
196 TABLE 37. Iron, slag, and stone identified at sites MAS780, MAS572.1, and MAS573.
206 TABLE 38. Associated dates from different sources for the Siga occupation.

CHAPTER SEVEN
214 TABLE 39. Characteristics of Tuali-A single-component sites by confidence level.
215 TABLE 40. Tuali-A ceramic assemblage characteristics by location and site size.
216 TABLE 41. Distribution of Tuali-A sites by distance from the escarpment and Koabu.
220 TABLE 42. Characteristics of Tuali-A single-component site ceramic assemblage.
222 TABLE 43. Tuali-A ceramic decoration techniques in use at single-component sites.
228 TABLE 44. Characteristics of Tuali-B single-component sites by confidence level.
229 TABLE 45. Tuali-B ceramic assemblage characteristics by location and site size.
230 TABLE 46. Distribution of Tuali-B sites by distance from the escarpment and Koabu.
232 TABLE 47. Characteristics of Tuali-B single-component site ceramic assemblage.
234 TABLE 48. Tuali-B ceramic decoration techniques in use at single-component sites.
236 TABLE 49. Evidence of smelting and indigo dyeing activity at Tuali-B sites.

APPENDIX A
263 TABLE A.1. Catalog of sites documented by the Maadaga Archaeological Survey.

APPENDIX B
294 TABLE B.1. Frequency of temper combinations in the ceramic assemblage.
296 TABLE B.2. Common decorative groups identified in the ceramic assemblage.

APPENDIX C
312 TABLE C.1. Characteristics of Ring occupation sites.
312 TABLE C.2. Characteristics of the Ring occupation ceramic assemblage.
313 TABLE C.3. Decorations in use in the Ring occupation ceramic assemblage.

Foreword

The Yale University Publications in Anthropology Editorial Committee is delighted to welcome Dr. Daphne Gallagher's contribution to YUPA's Civilizations of the Western Sudan series. The monographs in this series are dedicated to chronicling new archaeological investigation that "challenges our certainties that hierarchy and centralization were the drivers of social complexity." Africa as a whole, and the Western Sudan in particular, is the locus of much innovative field research on what might be called alternative polities, (often) large territorial entities with socially, politically, and economically unified populations that manifest mechanisms of authority or power that defy older definitions of chiefdoms or states.

The archaeological terra incognita of the southern savanna of Burkina Faso is revealed as a dynamic settlement landscape of generational mobility (households move three to four times in a lifetime), where the authority of elites is reinforced by a politics of discouraged sedentarism. This landscape of abundant resources (especially water) might have been expected by a previous model of complex society to have encouraged high population densities and sedentarism. To the contrary, instead we have a "non-urban complexity" leading, by the twelfth to fourteenth centuries CE, to a consolidation of the Gulmance confederation out of previous local small-scale kingdoms. All this we now know from the skillful field investigation and analysis of, frankly, what earlier generations of archaeologists would have considered an interpretive nightmare: a dense, superficially homogeneous landscape of shallow domestic compounds utterly alien to the city-focused, high tell landscapes of the not-too-distant Niger River floodplains.

Intriguing questions remain, especially why agriculture was adopted so very late (well into the first millennium CE). Yet we welcome this volume as yet another reminder that we cannot always look at emerging social complexity as some kind of upward-trending "progressional" vector leading to cities or states.

Roderick J. McIntosh
Department of Anthropology, Yale University, and
Curator-in-Charge, Division of Anthropology,
Yale Peabody Museum of Natural History

Preface

The Maadaga Archaeological Survey was originally conceptualized as an archaeological investigation into a potentially late adoption of agriculture along the Gobnangou escarpment, a particularly rich microenvironmental zone in southeastern Burkina Faso. However, as we conducted our survey and catalogued an extraordinary number of ephemeral sites, the richness of the archaeological record shifted the project focus toward a broader consideration of the interplay between settlement patterns, political and social structures, and environment. This book explores the changing use of space evidenced through interpretation of this constellation of archaeological sites (a term whose use in the title reflects the ways sites of different ages combine to create the cultural landscape much like stars of different ages form constellations).

This project has been shaped by a body of postcolonial scholarship in multiple disciplines that has successfully challenged colonial views that savanna ecosystems were "marginal" and limited the range of economic, social, and political options available to communities. Instead, I emphasize the depth of knowledge and skill farmers use to sustainably cultivate their crops and argue that agricultural choices (including fallow timing, use of inputs, spatial relationships of fields and residences, and frequency of field and residence relocation) are shaped by cultural practice. This approach was further influenced by my participation in excavations at mounded archaeological sites in western Burkina Faso and conversations with farmers in both regions. The results of this research are evidence of the long-term resilience and flexibility of local agricultural practices at a moment when farmers face extraordinary challenges from rapid population growth and the accelerating effects of anthropogenic climate change.

The Maadaga Archaeological Survey would not have been possible without the support of Lassina Koté, of the Laboratory of Archaeology at the Université Ouaga 1 Professeur Joseph Ki-Zerbo (formerly the University of Ouagadougou), and the community of Maadaga. Koté's insights on every aspect of the project, from the practical to the theoretical, were invaluable, and I am especially grateful for his taking time to visit me in the field. At the Centre National de la Recherche Scientifique et Technologique, Vincent Sedogo and Eloi Bambara granted research permits for the project, and Oumarou Nao at the Ministry of Culture granted export permits for the faunal and botanical samples. K. Antoine Millogo and Jean-Baptiste Kiéthéga supported the project and, along with Koté, sponsored the participation of Marcel Zongo, a student at the University of Ouagadougou, who was an invaluable project member in the field. In Maadaga, our research was received with enthusiasm by the local community, including the hundreds of farmers who answered our questions and allowed us to walk, take collections, and in several cases excavate in their fields. Yao Guiré and his family were ambassadors for us with the local community and our frequent discussions greatly enriched the research. Finally, Diassibo "Zeze" Ouaba worked with us every day, acting as interpreter and guide. It is largely because of his investment and dedication that the project was successful.

The pilot season of fieldwork in 2004 was funded by the University of Michigan Center for Afroamerican and African Studies (CAAS–Africa Initiative) and the University of Michigan Museum of Anthropological Archaeology (UMMAA) James B. Griffin Fund. A National Science Foundation Archaeology Program Doctoral Dissertation Improvement Award (grant number BCS-0520615) provided the primary funding for the 2006 fieldwork in Burkina Faso, supplemented by additional funds from the University of Michigan Department of Anthropology. Additional post-field analyses were funded by the Richard I. Ford Endowment Fund for the Anthropological Study of Humans and the Environment (UMMAA), and the reanalyses for this book took place in the African Archaeology Lab at the University of Oregon. In Burkina Faso, the Tassin-Pelzer, Sommers, and LaDonne families generously provided lodging and support.

This book has its origins in my dissertation research, and I thank my committee at the University of Michigan (Richard Ford, Rebecca Hardin, Paul Berry, John Speth, and Henry Wright) as well as the rest of the UMMAA curators. At Michigan, my UMMAA and Africanist cohorts Liz Bridges, Anne Compton, Cameron Gokee, Amy Lawson, Amanda Logan, Dan Pugh, Kenny Sims, and Sudha Shah, along with the rest of the graduate students, supported me throughout the process. The sense of community among Michigan Anthropology students past and present remains one of the enduring strengths of the program.

The research presented here has evolved significantly during my time at the University of Oregon, where I am grateful for the support of the Robert D. Clark Honors College, African Studies Program, Department of the History of Art and Architecture, Department of Anthropology, and College of Arts and Sciences Dean's Office. At Oregon, A. B. Assensoh, Lowell Bowditch, Lindsay Braun, Alfredo Burlando, Liska Chan, Kara Clevinger, Larissa Ennis, Maria Escallon, Dennis Galvan, Sam Hopkins, Habib Iddrisu, Lamia Karim, Carson Keeble, Ana-Maurine Lara, Gyoung-Ah Lee, Becky Lindner, Madonna Moss, Jennifer O'Neal, Gabe Paquette, Carol Paty, Melissa Peña, Jenifer Presto, Miriam Rigby, Phil Scher, Lynn Stephen, Kirstin Sterner, Nelson Ting, Tim Williams, Stephen Wooten, and Kristin Yarris among others have been critical in helping me see this book through to completion. Melissa Graboyes deserves special mention for her encouragement, enthusiasm, and confidence in this project.

The undergraduate and graduate students at the University of Oregon who have embraced West African archaeology in the classroom and in the laboratory have been and continue to be a source of inspiration, among them Auschere Caufield, Mackenzie Clark, Jyhreh Johnson, Samantha McGee, Sophie Miller, Victoria Olajide, and Rory Walsh. Hayley Pratt-Stibich was my research assistant during the final stages of this project, and I am grateful for her efforts (as well as her memorable reproductions of Sherd Type 13 in iced gingerbread).

The suggestions and comments of the anonymous reviewers and from the editorial board of Yale University Publications in Anthropology, notably Richard Burger and Roderick McIntosh, have strengthened this work and I thank them for their time and support. This book has benefitted greatly from the care and attention to detail with which Rosemary Volpe shepherded it through the publication process.

I am grateful for the conversations I have had about African archaeology with

Hamady Bocoum, Louis Champion, Gerard Chouin, Mamadou Cissé, Fabrice Dabiré, Alioune Dème, Sirio Cannos Donnay, Barbara Eichhorn, Alexa Höhn, Stefanie Kahlheber, Daouda Keita, Léonce Ki, Richard Kuba, Chapuruhka Kusimba, Sibel Kusimba, Kevin MacDonald, Shawn Murray, Katharina Neumann, Christoph Pelzer, Lucas Petit, Annet Schmidt, and Ibrahima Thiaw, all of whom in some way shaped my thinking on this project. Rod McIntosh and Susan Keech McIntosh first introduced me to the possibilities of West African archaeology when I was a freshman in their courses at Rice University. For more than twenty years, they have encouraged and supported me as I have continued in the field.

Lastly, I would like to thank the Gallaghers, the Dueppens, the Griffallaghens, Amanda, Anna, Patrick, Simon, and Lester. Finally, Stephen Dueppen has been involved in this project from inception to fieldwork to analysis to writing. He walked every transect, talked over every aspect of the data, and read every draft of this manuscript. I am deeply grateful for his insights and support.

Daphne E. Gallagher
The Robert D. Clark Honors College
University of Oregon, Eugene

CHAPTER ONE

Generational Mobility and Complexity in Southeastern Burkina Faso

The relations between space, political strategies, and economic practices in precolonial West African states are poorly understood. The Gulmance kingdoms of eastern Burkina Faso exemplify these complexities, as they are characterized by a fluid landscape of generationally mobile households that are simultaneously anchored in different degrees of centralized control rooted in elite families. Unlike many of the often-discussed case studies of complexity in West Africa, the precolonial Gulmance kingdoms were not urbanized, and in that respect were similar to the precolonial kingdoms and states founded by related Gur-speaking populations to the west and south. In general, these polities have received only limited archaeological attention, as the archaeological signature of household compounds inhabited for only decades left ephemeral remains. However, the use of space by itself invokes differing concepts of power in relation to landscapes and provides an important counterpoint to discussions of space in complex societies research.

Recent archaeological scholarship has expanded recognition of the range of global diversity in complex societies, moving beyond models defining essential traits and opening the doors to comparative examination of polities rooted in different local or regional concepts of political economy, uses of space, and pathways of political action (e.g., R. J. McIntosh 1998, 2005, 2015; S. K. McIntosh 1999, 2020; Ogundiran 2002; Richard 2009, 2015, 2018; Dueppen 2012a, 2012b; Monroe 2013; Honeychurch 2014; Blanton 2016; Chirikure et al. 2017; Takezawa and Cissé 2017). One of the main goals of this book is to decouple simplistic links between residential mobility and agricultural practice in the West African savanna, since the fundamental nature of farming practice in this region was similar across societies with very different settlement patterns. Consequently, the specific spatial and residential organization of the agricultural landscape was not forced on populations by their ecosystem. Rather, the cultural dynamics of shifting individual residences, examined here as "generational mobility," were rooted in strong collective understandings of access and security afforded by complex sociopolitical settings.

I initiated the Maadaga Archaeological Survey (MAS) to examine the long-term histories of these practices through full-coverage survey in the Gobnangou region of southeastern Burkina Faso (Figure 1). The results of this research, which documented 517 archaeological sites in a 75 km² area, attest to the emergence of critical components

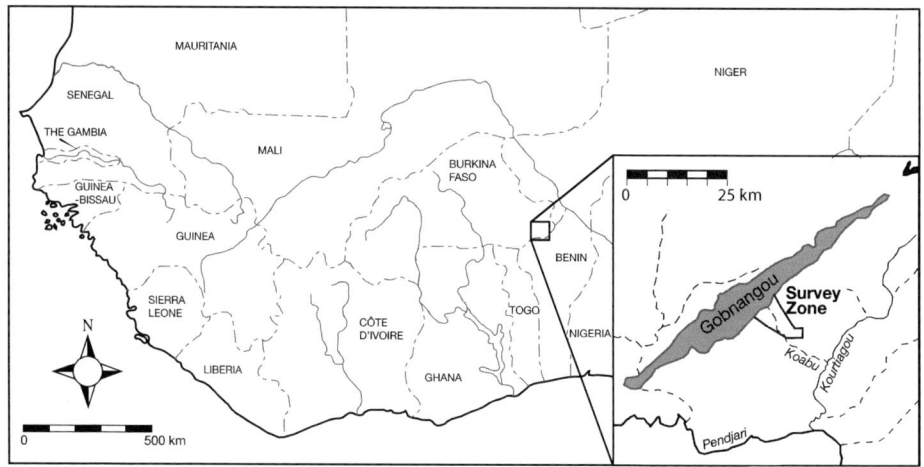

FIGURE 1. Location of countries and the extent of the Maadaga Archaeological Survey study region in West Africa.

of these sociospatial systems in the early second millennium CE. This shift toward generational mobility stood in stark contrast to the anchored sedentary farming households that had resulted in tell formation in the first millennium CE. As complex societies take many forms, the research presented throughout this book contributes an important case study that demonstrates how power, identity, craft production, agriculture, and residence articulate with concepts of space.

In this chapter, I contextualize the research project within the body of scholarship on Gulmance history and ethnography to make the case that the spatiopolitical landscape was not determined by the ecological setting, but rather represents a series of political choices in landscape use that emerged in the early second millennium CE.

Archaeology, History, and Ethnography of the Gulmance

This book is centered on territory in West Africa inhabited primarily by the Gulmance, who mostly reside in southeastern Burkina Faso and neighboring parts of northern Benin and western Niger (Figure 2). Gulmance is frequently written Gourmantche (also alternatively as Gourmantché, Gulimance, Gurmance, Gourma, Gurma, or Gulma) and can refer to the historical kingdoms, the language (Gulmancema), and the speakers of this language (*gulmanceba*) (see Madiéga et al. [1983] and Thiombiano-Ilboudo [2010:10–17] for discussions of the complex histories of these terms). "Gourma" and its variants are also frequently used to describe large geographical regions within the Niger Bend (the right bank of the Niger River). Today, most residents in territories formerly controlled by the Gulmance kingdoms consider themselves *gulmanceba*, although there was likely significantly more variability in the past (see the discussions in Richard and MacDonald [2015]). The MAS study region is also home to a small population descended from Hausa trading diasporas and seasonal Fulani pastoralists; however, Gulmancema is the primary language spoken, local schools are taught in French and Gulmancema, and traditional

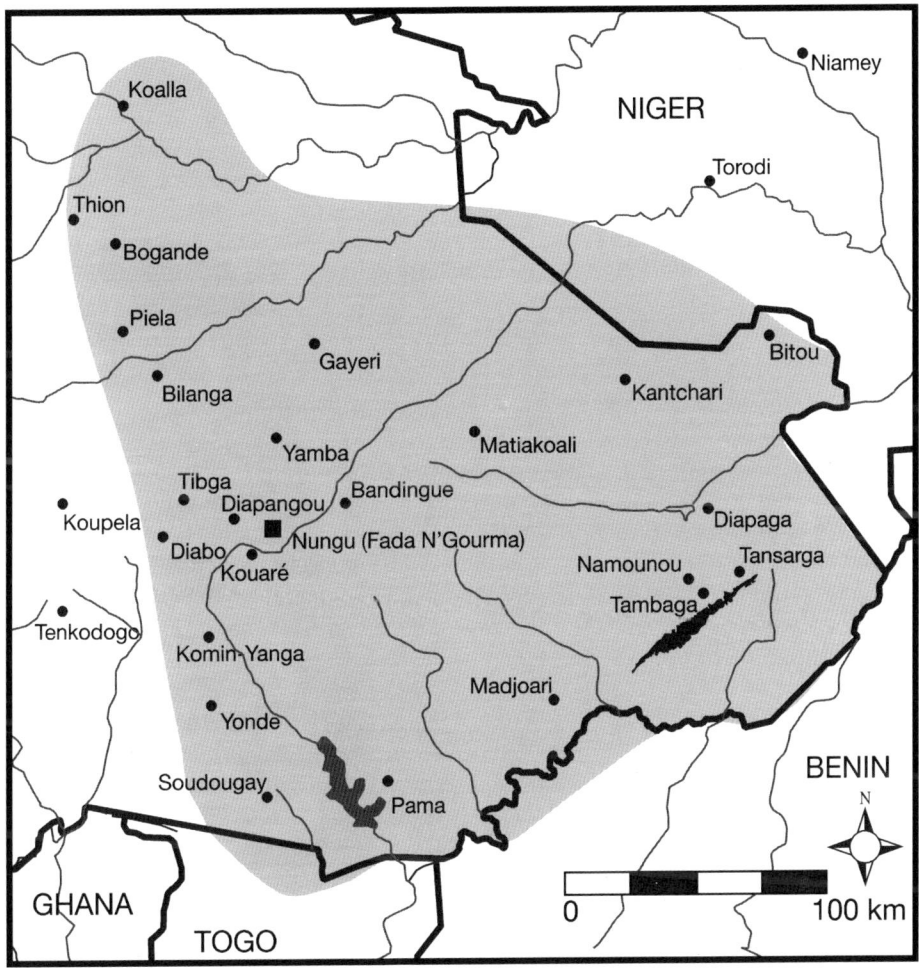

FIGURE 2. Approximate extent of the Gulmance kingdoms. Adapted from Chantoux (1966), Madiéga et al. (1983), and Thiombiano-Ilboudo (2010).

Gulmance *bado* (chiefs) retain significant authority in local communities.

At the time of colonial conquest, Gulmance territory was organized as what has been variously characterized as a hierarchical state (Chantoux 1966), a paramount chiefdom (Swanson 1985), a confederacy or federation of independent chiefdoms within a state-like larger political entity (Korbéogo 2013), or a collection of independent kingdoms that were never fully unified under a single ruler (Madiéga 1982, 2009). In spite of the disagreement over the precise nature of the political system, these scholars agree that the Gulmance had a very strong sense of common identity rooted not only in language and culture, but also in membership in this political structure. Conscious of calls in West African archaeology for nuanced approaches to state and sovereignty that emphasize process rather than category (see the discussions in S. K. McIntosh [1999] and Richard [2015, 2018]); in this book I will follow the preeminent Gulmance historian Y. Georges Madiéga (1982, 2009) in referring to these precolonial Gulmance political entities as kingdoms (*royaumes*), with recognition that their internal structures likely differed and that they may have been more or less cohesively joined in a confederacy at different times.

The history and ethnology of the Gulmance kingdoms are much less studied than those of their neighbors the Mossi, owing to colonial era decisions and a perception that the region was peripheral to major historical events (see discussions in Korbéogo [2013]). After early colonial documentation (e.g., Menjaud 1932), French ethnographer Michel Cartry conducted the first prolonged ethnographic research on the Gulmance (Cartry 1963, 1966, 1968, 1987; see also Balandier and Sautter 1963) and worked primarily in the Gobnangou region in partnership with an agronomist (Rémy 1967; see also Balandier and Sautter 1963). In the 1970s, Richard Swanson, an ethnologist raised by missionary parents in the Gobnangou region, carried out several seasons of fieldwork throughout the southern Gulmance region. Although, like Cartry, his primary academic interest was in symbolic representation (Swanson 1985), he also compiled a practical review of Gulmance agriculture for the United States Agency for International Development (Swanson 1979a, 1979b). In the late 1980s, German anthropologist Gudrun Geis-Tronich (1989, 1991) documented traditional material culture throughout the Gulmance region. More recently, Salif Titamba Lankoande (2008) has published a synthesis of regional history and ethnography, João Pedro Galhano Alves (2012) has written on Gulmance ethnoecology among populations near Park W, Niger, Emanuela Casti and colleagues (Casti and Yonkeu 2009; Casti 2015) have examined the cultural geography of the Gobnangou region, Gabin Korbéogo (2013) has carried out ethnographic research on the relations between natural resources and Gulmance political systems, and Alexis Kaboré (2018) has explored the interplay between mobility and fixed shrines and other ritual locations.

The Gulmance kingdoms made few appearances in the accounts of early Arab travelers or European explorers and remained largely unknown to Europeans before the twentieth century. During the colonial era, an uncritical synthesis of oral traditions was compiled by an administrator (Davy 1952) and later revised by a church official (Chantoux 1966). Their work, which emphasized dynastic succession, remained the master narrative on the kingdoms until the 1980s, when Madiéga, a Gulmance historian working in a framework inspired by Jan Vansina (1965), did extensive fieldwork and systematically reevaluated the oral historical record (Madiéga 1982, 2009; Madiéga et al. 1983). The results of his research are the foundation of contemporary scholarship on the Gulmance kingdoms. Additional oral histories have been collected by archaeologists, most notably the extensive work by Elise Foniyama Thiombiano-Ilboudo, who argues compellingly for the importance of integrating oral historical and archaeological data (Thiombiano-Ilboudo 2010:64).

Within the boundaries of the Gulmance kingdoms archaeological research has been more limited, with early work by Jean-Baptiste Kiéthéga documenting diverse sites, including many large iron-working installations throughout the region (Kiéthéga, Sidibé, and Bedaux 1993; Kiéthéga 2009). Aside from these broad-ranging exploratory surveys, most archaeological research in the Gulmance areas of Burkina Faso has focused on sites near Fada N'Gourma (Thiombiano-Ilboudo 2010, 2012a) or in the Gobnangou region in the southeast where, before the MAS project presented here, mid to late Holocene foraging sites had been the primary focus of research (see below). Even within the context of West Africa, where most areas could be considered understudied archaeologically, the Gulmance kingdoms are one of the least studied complex societies in West Africa. Even less is known about the history of the region before the founding of these kingdoms.

Gulmance Origins, Politics, and Space

Historians, drawing on collected oral traditions from multiple sources over the past century, have identified a variety of narratives about the origins of the Gulmance kingdoms that reflect the complex political histories of this region of West Africa (Chantoux 1966; Madiéga 1982, 2009). As suggested by Korbéogo (2013), these should not be considered contradictory, as they all invoke the arrival of leaders in land occupied by indigenous peoples who ultimately came together to create the *gulmanceba* and reflect different components of the deeper Gulmance past. These stories mediated the complex relationships between the Gulmance kingdoms and their neighbors, including the Mossi states. Although the Mossi speak a closely related Gur language and share many cultural features with the Gulmance, the differences in political structure between the two likely reflect a deep history of different models of leadership (see Izard 2003; Hien and Gomgnimbou 2009).

Most accounts agreed that the legendary warrior Jaba Lompo helped create the Gulmance by integrating local indigenous populations (the Tindamba, Taaba, Takamba, and Woba) with Bemba peoples who came from east of the Niger River. The various dates for the founding of these kingdoms differ and are largely derived through extrapolation of dynastic lists preserved in oral histories. Depending on the lengths assigned to reigns, Jaba Lompo's rule may have been as early as the twelfth or thirteenth century CE, although most historians place the founding of the Gulmance kingdoms later in the fifteenth or sixteenth century CE (see the discussions in Madiéga [1982], Madiéga et al. [1983], and Thiombiano-Ilboudo [2010]).

Foundational stories of the Gulmance kingdoms frequently invoke celestial origins for Jaba Lompo, describing him as descending from the heavens on horseback down a tamarind or baobab tree near Pama at the site of Kudiaboangu. In 2004 and 2006 several residents of Maadaga recounted stories of Jaba Lompo sailing up the Pendjari River shortly after this descent. As discussed in more detail by Korbéogo (2013) and Izard (2003), celestial origins helped establish distinct, unrelated foundations for the Gulmance and Mossi.

Other stories invoked the arrival of disgraced Bemba elites from Bornu, which in these accounts are also the origin point for the Mossi (Madiéga 1982). These knights intermarried with the descendants of Jaba Lompo and assimilated, adopting the local language. There are many interdictions related to the east in Gulmance culture that may reflect components of this story (for example, Gulmance elites did not travel east, habitations faced the west, and so on; see the discussions in Korbéogo [2013]). Lastly, there were accounts, primarily from the western margins of the Gulmance region near Mossi territories, that suggested a shared origin for the founding leaders of the Mossi and Gulmance. These characterized Jaba Lompo as the eldest son of Ouédraogo, the founder of the Mossi according to the Gambaga tradition, thus linking the Gulmance with the Mossi through kinship. Although most dynasties of the individual Gulmance kingdoms associated themselves directly with these origins, many also integrated unique, localized histories. For example, many stories describe some of the elites who founded the local dynasties of the Gobnangou region as Hausa in origin (Madiéga et al. 1983).

The oral histories of the early Gulmance kingdoms document diverse (and often different versions of) changing political alliances, including moments of unity in the face of outside threats, as well as internecine strife. The confederacy was ruled by the *Nunbado*, whose actual power over the other kingdoms varied through time, but who seems to have maintained a distinct title (leaders of other kingdoms or at lower levels held the titles of *batieba* or *bado*). Almost all accounts agreed that the peak of centralized political power occurred in the eighteenth century with the thirteenth dynasty rule of the *Nunbado* Yendabri and his establishment of a capital at Nungu (Fada N'Gourma). Shortly thereafter, the center once again weakened and at the time of colonial conquest the Gulmance kingdoms were fragmented.

In general, three strong themes emerge from the oral historical narratives. The first is cultural and linguistic assimilation, the second conflict with non-Gulmance populations to the north and south, and the third internal political fluidity. Although it is difficult to assess the precise timing and effects of most of the particular events, these general aspects of the political environment remained fairly consistent throughout the history of the Gulmance kingdoms.

Conflict with populations to the south (and north, though this was less relevant for the MAS project) was a common feature of almost every reign for which there is published oral historical data. Descriptions of these incursions range from organized campaigns (on both sides) to isolated raiding. In general, there were very few extended periods of minimal raiding and most of these corresponded to periods of lesser centralized control (which were perhaps not coincidentally the periods with less detailed descriptions). Overall, raiding from the south was portrayed as a constant concern or threat. This could have affected settlement decisions in the Gobnangou, which was located near the southern border.

Within the Gulmance kingdoms, absolute control from the *Nunbado* was rare, according to the oral histories, and usually limited to one or two consecutive reigns. It is particularly difficult to assess the historical role of the center in the governing of local populations. The *Nunbado* was primarily documented as interfering in the internal affairs of regional leaders in cases of succession, disputes with other leaders, or failure to pay tribute. However, the mores of day-to-day governance were for the most part absent from the oral historical narratives. Ultimately, the question of interest for this study was whether relative centralization and autonomy affected daily life within constituent kingdoms. Local people may have been insulated from these changes; however, periods of greater centralization could have brought benefits like larger-scale risk management and military support, as well as burdens such as increased agricultural production and military service.

It seems established that there was some sort of greater Gulmance political organization, yet the degree of centralization (or centralization in recent history) may have been overplayed. Madiéga and colleagues (1983:35) expanded on this theme:

> However, to observe the spirit of independence that prevailed at the level of certain dynasties, one can say that the idea of a *Nunbado*, supreme king of the Gulmance in the image of the Mogho Naba, emperor of the Mossi, dates in practice to the colonial period. There existed prior to the age of colonial French intervention independent dynasties…some of which even led bloody expeditions against the *diema* (kingdom) of the *Nunbado*. [*my translation*]

The assessment of Madiéga and colleagues is further supported by colonial history. In 1895, Germany signed treaties with the leaders of multiple kingdoms (Pama, Madjoari, and Kantchari) whose territories would have given them control over much of southeastern Burkina Faso and cut the French off from the Niger River. In contrast, France had only signed a treaty with the recently ousted *Nunbado* Bantchande. France's successful claims for the Gulmance region were therefore predicated on the existence of a centralized Gulmance polity in which the *Nunbado* held authority over the regional kingdoms.

Contemporary Gulmance political practices are deeply informed by these histories (Korbéogo 2013). Gulmance society is rooted in multiple lineages of different origins that control various sources of power in society. At the top is an elite class affiliated with the Thiombiano dynasty, from which local and regional leaders as well as the *Nunbado* derive. Leaders have authority over people and control the natural resources in their territory, including the trees, rocks, escarpments, water, and forest resources (Korbéogo 2013:64). Their central political role is spatially materialized; the leader's residence is placed in the center of the territory and his religious power is manifested by adjacent shrines (*bulo*) where he asserts divine power for the community. From this central position leaders assure the security of their territory.

In addition to political leaders, communities also have an earth priest (*tindano*), often drawn from the indigenous Tindamba lineage. The *tindano* maintains relations with natural forces and the ancestors in the community, sanctifies the earth, and works with the bado and council of elders on land issues, although he does not control access to the land or natural resources. Moreover, his power is limited by a widely held belief in Gulmance communities, also common elsewhere in Voltaic societies, that the earth cannot belong to anyone; it is considered unethical to refuse access to available farming land (Korbéogo 2013).

The Gulmance have historically lived in circular household compounds that were typically widely dispersed and surrounded by fields, although seminucleated settlements have become more common over the course of the nineteenth and twentieth centuries. Households moved every couple of decades and often shifted as much as several kilometers. Although movement occurred under the auspices and within the territory controlled by a leader, household independence in agricultural decision-making was at the core of Gulmance identity and shaped many aspects of the land tenure system. Within this land tenure system, mobility was a crucial "reset" mechanism; in cases like the Gobnangou region, where populations were tied to a single location by colonial authorities, complex webs of borrowed and lent land quickly developed and residents were forced to devise new mobile strategies to maintain access to land (Rémy 1967).

While the independent movement of Gulmance households seemed to some colonial outsiders to be random and unstructured, in practice it was institutionalized and politically sanctioned. As will be argued here (see the discussions in Chapter 2), there was no clear agro-ecological requirement for this settlement practice, as shown by its use throughout Gulmance territory, from the arid Sahelian margin in the north, to the rich wooded savannas and permanent watercourses of the Gobnangou in the southeast, to the leached, rocky soils and minimal surface water areas of the west.

The Politics of Movement

Systems of mobility are inherently enabled by mutual understandings of land rights. Residential mobilities can provide a social, economic and political reset button for community relations, as territory can be redistributed according to the changing needs of social groups (in particular generational differences in corporate group size), tensions between neighbors can be alleviated, and inequalities in soil quality can be addressed. Although mobility was not the only way to solve these problems, in the study region, Rémy (1967:37) noted that village relocation allowed the community of Yobri, without transferring land rights, to "periodically redo the spatial projection of social groups by the function of their quantitative and qualitative evolution." Yobri's history also illustrates the difficulty of maintaining Gulmance tenure traditions associated with frequent mobility in a context where colonial prohibitions restricted household movement, resulting in a complex, highly problematic layering of land claims leading to frequent disputes (Rémy 1967).

Larger sociopolitical characteristics and economic practices are indicated by generational mobility. First, a collective ethos of land access must have been shared that ensured households would have new land to move to when the need arose. This could imply the presence of larger-scale political structures for assuring access, a collective understanding in society that all households should have access to land, or both. Given their independent movement relative to one another, households in these systems must have been fairly independent economic units, largely responsible for their own agricultural labor and production.

Many of the characteristics of a system of generational mobility may in fact be indicators of sociopolitical complexity in the region, as smooth operation of the land system may imply the presence of structures to alleviate tensions in movement. Korbéogo (2013) has suggested that, in the Gulmance case, the dynamic movement of homesteads over time underwrote the power of political chiefs in the study region, because they controlled natural resources and each move allowed them to assert their power over access.

Among the ethnohistorical Gulmance, mobility was embedded in the political structure of the community and was intrinsic to the roles and rights of leaders. The relative power of the earth priest was lesser here than in other Voltaic societies, a point that was central to Korbéogo's (2013) analysis of Gulmance power and natural resources. He argued that the Gulmance practice of generational mobility itself tended to weaken the power of the earth priest (*tindano*) in the face of the political leader (*bado*), because the frequent resettling activated the territorial controls asserted by the *bado* and marginalized the importance of the earth shrine. Earth priests tended to have more power in more sedentary Mossi communities where conquering Mossi elites left in place pre-existing power relations but demanded output (Izard 1985, 2003; Skinner 1989; Simpore 2009). Korbéogo (2013) suggested that the assertion of power over natural resources in Gulmance communities resulted from a different foundation for social ranking, as elites increased their power in local settings at the expense of earth priests.

Within this view of place and space, Gulmance mobilities can be correlated with political processes, where movement of non-elite families regularly invoked activation of the power of the bado and reminded the community of their centrality to lifeways in assuring access to land and agricultural security. It has also been suggested that, given the low population densities and large numbers of wild animals in southeastern Burkina Faso, the spatial pattern that yields larger open spaces in dispersed communities may have aided in security since visibility was better over distances (Korbéogo 2013). The archaeological histories of these spatial practices are not well studied.

For the archaeologist, theorizing mobility provides a particularly distinct advantage for studying the ephemeral sites left by strategies like generational mobility. These sites often have few in situ features and little in the way of biological preservation. However, by focusing on the social and political context in which mobility takes place, it is possible to build upward from spatial practice, with its significant cultural variation.

Toward an Archaeology of Generational Mobility
The spatial and temporal dimensions of generational mobility offer unique challenges for archaeological interpretation. Much of the research on mobility has focused on un-

derstanding movements that took place on short timescales (such as seasonal rounds or transhumance) or on larger-scale processes of migration (e.g., Ames 1991; R. L. Kelly 1992; Sellet, Greaves, and Yu 2006; Barnard and Wendrich 2008; Beaudry and Parno 2013; Ashley, Antonites, and Fredriksen 2016). Many of the resulting correlates are of limited use for understanding generational mobility. Households moving on a decadal timescale are likely to invest in infrastructure and use less portable material culture in comparison to seasonally mobile populations, while migration occurs at a significantly broader spatial scale and frequently emphasizes processes of interaction between newly coresident populations. Consequently, archaeologists who focus on the mobility of agricultural populations emphasize the materialization of mobility itself; that is, evidence of occupation length and intensity of site use (e.g., Varien 1999; Berelov 2006).

At the level of the individual household, building, maintaining, and living in a residence creates a material record. The earthen architectural techniques commonly in use in the West African savanna require a high level of maintenance: yearly plastering and thatching, frequent reflooring, and often complete reconstruction (R. J. McIntosh 1974). If the residence was maintained for an extended period, the result was the creation of tell sites such as those common in western and northern Burkina Faso and eastern Mali (Lingané 1995; S. K. McIntosh 1995; Holl and Koté 2000; Bedaux et al. 2005; Koté 2007; Petit, Czerniewicz, and Pelzer 2011; Dueppen 2012a; Holl 2014; Huysecom et al. 2015). This effect can be seen in extreme form in the town of Djenné, Mali, where many earthen-brick houses have been occupied for hundreds of years; the ground surfaces of the interiors have moved upward as layers of floor were added, resulting in thresholds well above the street (S. K. McIntosh, Gallagher, and R. J. McIntosh 2003). Consequently, a coursed-earth or earthen-brick residence that was occupied for a longer period will leave a more robust archaeological deposit. Likewise, the location and density of trash can be direct indicators for intensity of occupation, although if household waste is deposited on fields rather than near the residence accurate data may not be available (Killion 1990; Graham 1994).

Similarly, mobility in space affects the nature of the archaeological record. Short-distance moves can either significantly accelerate tell formation or, in the case of the village drift, create extensive palimpsestic archaeological deposits (see examples in Agorsah [1985]; Lawson [2003]; Donnay [2016]). In contrast, long-distance moves to dispersed locations will create very ephemeral deposits, which are disproportionately affected by formation processes including deflation (Binford 1980, 1982; Schiffer 1987; Dunnell 1992). The distance moved also has a significant impact on the material culture of abandoned sites: heavy, easily replaceable items are more likely to be left behind, while smaller or more expensive items are likely to be moved (Graham 1994). However, choices regarding the transfer of material possessions may not be purely practical and are often culturally mediated, particularly in the case of a move spurred by the death of a household head, in which inheritance customs rather than distance may be the dominant factor. As part of lived experience, previous residence locations often remain significant both as activity areas and as social markers on the landscape (Sahlins 1957; Cameron and Tomka 1993; Stone 1996; Varien 1999).

The often ephemeral and deflated nature of cultural deposits in sites resulting from the practice of generational mobility complicates archaeological determinations of occupation length and frequency of movement. Given the lack of well-stratified deposits, chronological resolution is typically poor such that it is almost impossible to know which identified residential sites were occupied simultaneously or which of the previously occupied residences at a given time were known elements of the cultural landscape. However, the archaeological perspective is not as skewed as it might seem. It is possible to create a relative measure of site occupation length on the basis of shared depositional and post-depositional characteristics and the types and ranges of artifacts recovered. Moreover, if generational mobility continues over several centuries, one should expect a dense landscape or constellation of sites of different ages. Consequently, recognition of generational mobility requires a landscape approach rooted in full coverage survey.

Introduction to the Archaeological Case Study

The Gobnangou escarpment is a sandstone massif 100 km long by a maximum of 10 km wide, rising as much as 200 m above the surrounding savanna. Pocked with caves and canyons, it acts as an aquifer for the region and is drained by many small watercourses, a few of which remain into the late dry season. As a result, land at the base of the escarpment is particularly fertile and the diverse microenvironments created by both the escarpment itself and the soil diversity resulting from its position on the border between two major geological regions contain a wide variety of plant and animal communities (see Chapter 2 for a more detailed discussion of the natural environment of the Gobnangou). These features, combined with the availability of water, make it unsurprising that the Gobnangou supports much higher population densities than the surrounding savanna (Frank et al. 2001).

In 2004 and 2006, I directed the full coverage Maadaga Archaeological Survey that examined the catchment of the Koabu drainage (one of many with its headwaters in the escarpment). More than five hundred previously undocumented sites were recorded (most dating to within the last thousand years) and over 90% were small single-component scatters less than 50 cm deep (a complete inventory of sites is presented in Appendix A). However, the presence of a diversified pottery tradition and frequency of specialist activities such as iron smelting and (in more recent occupations) indigo cloth production indicate that these sites were part of a complex, economically integrated community.

The MAS built on the results of previous archaeological research in the region. In 1987, Goethe University Frankfurt and the University of Ouagadougou (now the Université Ouaga 1 Professeur Joseph Ki-Zerbo) began fieldwork there in hopes of identifying early agricultural sites. The project, which was part of a larger interdisciplinary effort on landscape ecology and cultural knowledge in the Burkinabe savanna, incorporated a large team of specialists, including botanists and geologists, and produced a significant literature on the geomorphology, ecology, and paleoenvironment of the region (Müller-Haude 1995; Küppers 1996). Over three seasons of fieldwork many sites were identified through opportunistic survey and three (Maadaga, Péntènga, and Kidikanbou) were excavated. The results were synthesized and published (Frank et al. 2001; see also Breunig and Wotzka 1991). Antoine Millogo of the University of Ouagadougou excavated at Yobri rockshelter in 1989 (K.A. Millogo 1993a, 1993b) and with Lassina Koté has documented rock art and hidden granary sites in the region (Millogo and Koté 2000; see Appendix D).

The German–Burkinabe team had originally planned a long-term regional project, but was disappointed by the preservation of the archaeological sites that were identified. The few rockshelter sites investigated were either heavily bioturbated (Péntènga rockshelter) or had no organic preservation (Maadaga rockshelter). The open-air sites were uniformly shallow and badly eroded, typical of those left by cultivators who move their residences frequently. Not only did these sites lack the long occupation sequences the German–Burkinabe team felt were necessary to closely examine change in agricultural practices, but a paleoecological reconstruction using charcoal from Péntènga rockshelter indicated that the local area was not heavily farmed until the relatively late date of 1100 CE (see Chapters 4 and 5). Given the fertility of the local landscape, these results were unexpected and suggested reasons other than environmental constraints determined early agricultural practice in the region. Because of these results, I initiated the MAS to study the development of agricultural practices and their social milieu from the late adoption of agriculture through the development of spatial and political practices associated with the Gulmance. The MAS identified evidence for three logistical strategies in use over the last several thousand years: chipped stone scatters in rockshelters and open-air locations likely left by mobile foragers, mounded sites resulting from multigenerational occupation by farmers in the later first millennium CE, and a dense landscape of ephemeral residential sites created by generationally mobile farmers from the early second millennium CE onward.

The following two chapters situate the archaeological project environmentally and methodologically. Chapter 2 examines the local and regional environmental setting, with particular attention to human interactions with natural resources and their effects on agricultural strategies. It unpacks the relations between farming strategies and mobility within the Gulmance system, arguing that this is one of many successful ways to structure agricultural practice in the West African savanna. Chapter 3 introduces the reader to the Maadaga Archaeological Survey, beginning with a description of the survey and excavation methodologies. It then provides an overview of the collected and excavated pottery assemblages and the identification of chronologically sensitive elements of the assemblage that enabled the seriation of individual site assemblages.

Although the German–Burkinabe project had developed a preliminary ceramic chronology for the Gobnangou region (Frank et al. 2001; Wotzka and Goedicke 2001), it relied predominantly on samples from the north side of the escarpment, emphasized occupation earlier than the second millennium CE, and had few points of concurrence with the ceramics recovered by the MAS project. Therefore, to place the identified sites within a chronological framework, I developed a local ceramic chronology consisting of three occupations: Pwoli, Siga, and Tuali (Table 1). The occupation names are drawn from Gulmancema locative particles that roughly translate, respectively, to "behind," "middle," and "in front." The use of the term "occupation" rather than the more common "phase" is meant to emphasize the preliminary nature of the sequence and allow for possible temporal overlap between the ceramic divisions. A full site catalog with assigned occupations and additional data on each site is included (Appendix A) along with additional technical data on the ceramic analysis (Appendix B).

The central section of the book presents a synthesis of the region's archaeology in separate chapters dedicated to the Lithic, Pwoli, Siga, and Tuali occupations. Each describes the archaeological data used to characterize the occupation, presents the results from spatial and material analyses, and contextualizes the occupation in the regional archaeological literature. Brief discussions of sites dating to within the last fifty years (Appendix C) and undated rock art and hidden granary sites (Appendix D) are included as well.

I begin the archaeological sequence with what I describe as the Lithic occupation (Chapter 4), a group of sites that includes not only Middle Stone Age and microlithic

TABLE 1. Estimated calendar dates for the occupations identified by the Maadaga Archaeological Survey.

Occupation	Number of assigned sites	Frequency
Lithic	6	ca. 6000 BCE–At least 650 CE
Pwoli	3	ca. 650–1050 CE
Siga	344	ca. 1050–1300/1650 CE
Tuali	134	ca. 1300/1650–1950 CE
Ring	19	ca. 1950 CE–Present

Late Stone Age sites, but also undated sites characterized by chipped stone assemblages. The Pwoli occupation (ca. 650–1050 CE) provided the earliest conclusive evidence for the use of domesticated plants and animals in the study region and was the only part of the sequence during which people created tell sites (Chapter 5). A dramatic shift in settlement pattern indicating generational mobility was first identified during the Siga occupation (ca. 1050–1300/1650 CE), when residents of the region produced hundreds of ephemeral sites that shared a highly diversified ceramic assemblage (Chapter 6). The subsequent Tuali occupation (ca. 1300/1650–1950 CE) was marked by a significant homogenization of the ceramic assemblage, accompanied by a general shift in the distribution of settlements toward the escarpment (Chapter 7). By the end of the Tuali occupation there is evidence for settlement nucleation and the creation of several indigo dyeing complexes composed of large plastered pits, perhaps indicating increasing involvement of the Gobnangou in interregional exchange systems.

The book concludes with a discussion that contextualizes the significance of the research along three primary axes (Chapter 8). First, I examine the value of the local sequence within its contributions to African archaeology, ranging from the late adoption of agriculture to the development of non-urban complexity and landscapes of power. Second, I critically engage the oral histories of Gulmance kingdoms, identifying potential points of alignment and articulation between them and the archaeological sequence. Finally, I discuss the significance of this work as a contribution to bodies of scholarship that are attempting to move beyond colonial and postcolonial narratives of environmental degradation and narrowly defined conceptualizations of complexity.

CHAPTER TWO

Ethnoecology of Southeastern Burkina Faso

Agricultural systems played central roles in the development and maintenance of complex societies in the savanna and Sahel zone of West Africa. In some areas, such as the Inland Niger Delta (S. K. McIntosh 1995; Murray 2005) and the Senegal River valley (Gallagher and Murray 2016; Gallagher, S. K. McIntosh, and Murray 2018), combinations of flood recession and rainfed agriculture allowed for year-round cropping and clear intensification strategies that historically supported very dense populations. However, away from these river valleys fairly similar extensive agricultural practices throughout the savanna region were associated with a remarkable variety of residential strategies, ranging from occupation of the same location for hundreds or even thousands of years (Holl and Koté 2000; Koté 2007; Dueppen 2012a; Holl 2014; Huysecom et al. 2015; Gallagher and Dueppen 2019) to frequently shifting household or community locations (A. Lawson 2003; Richard 2009, 2015, 2018; Donnay 2016). I argue that, given the great similarity in both environment and farming strategies, this diversity reflected cultural and political structures and histories rather than an ecological imperative. Understanding the development of complexity in the region requires scholars to unpack environmental narratives essentializing the relations between agriculture and residential strategies to build up to histories of sociospatial practice that ultimately supported the development of diverse precolonial complex political formations.

The dynamic nature of the savanna ecosystem has influenced a suite of traditional agricultural practices that buffer against unpredictable rainfall and mitigate low-fertility soils through a strong emphasis on field distribution and rotation (Pélissier 1966; Rémy 1967; Kowal and Kassam 1978; Swanson 1979a, 1979b; Baker 2000; Korbéogo 2013). Most farmers use two primary categories of fields for staple crops: permanent fields and rotating fields. Permanent fields, generally located near residences, are where early grain crops (such as fonio and rapidly maturing varieties of pearl millet and sorghum) are grown. They are closely managed to extend fertility and are more likely to be manured, mulched, and weeded. In contrast, the bulk of staple (and today cash) crops are grown in rotating fields. These can be as much as several kilometers from a residence. Crop succession is often used to extend field life and management is generally minimal. Instead, fields are cropped for four to seven years then left fallow for fifteen to twenty years or more.

Because long fallows require frequent reclearing of fields, colonial Europeans assumed that traditional farming strategies were environmentally destructive and unsustainable. They frequently tried to replace lower-yielding traditional agricultural practices with "modern" technologies and approaches, such as large-scale irrigation, intensive fertilization, higher-yielding crop varieties, and cash cropping (see the discussions in Fairhead and Leach [1996], Mortimore [1998], and Baker [2000]). As agronomists and ethnologists accumulated documentation on rainfall variability, soil fertility, and the hardiness of indigenous crops, they began to recognize the value of traditional methods that produced reliable yields in an unpredictable environment. An emphasis on modernization was replaced with an appreciation for the skill of local farmers in optimizing their methods to meet their needs under local climatic and environmental conditions. Studies of "perfected systems of cultivation" became common by the mid-twentieth century (e.g., Savonnet 1959; Pélissier 1966).

More recently, archaeological research has established the long-term sustainability of these methods and revealed the ability of West African farmers to cope with climate perturbations and unpredictability over hundreds to thousands of years. Evidence at sites ranging from large urban centers to small villages has established that, with the exception of sites on the Sahel margins that were particularly vulnerable to climate change, there is little evidence of environmental degradation or field exhaustion, indicating careful management of arable land and wild resources (e.g., Kahlheber 2004; Kahlheber and Neumann 2007; Dueppen 2012a; Höhn and Neumann 2012; Eichhorn and Neumann 2014; Huysecom et al. 2015; Gallagher, Dueppen, and Walsh 2016; Gallagher and Dueppen 2019).

Field Rotation and Household Mobility

In the ethnohistorical record, these sustainable cultivation practices were localized in relationship to residence and projected on the landscape in a variety of arrangements. The different distinct spatial organizations of built structures, field systems, and managed wooded savanna combined to create cultural landscapes that both reflected and enforced social, economic, religious, and political practices. For example, in parts of western Burkina Faso it was common for settlements to be highly clustered, with tightly packed room blocks creating a dense cultural space. Here, permanent fields surrounded the entire settlement, rather than individual households, and rotating fields were farther away, with access to sections of each field system enabled by the relations between households (Savonnet 1959; Capron 1973). In comparison, distributed settlement systems, like those historically used by the Tallensi, Tiv, or Mossi, were composed of dispersed household compounds, with permanent fields in a narrow band surrounding each and rotating fields and fallows often just beyond (Bohannan 1954; Prussin 1969; Rémy 1972).

Independent of the degree of nucleation or dispersion of households, frequency and distance of household movement over time and the effects of these movements on agricultural field locations affect the accumulation of the cultural landscape. The decision of any given household to abandon its old residence and construct a new one can result from multiple, particularistic factors. In general, moving tends to be a process that takes place at the household level; simultaneous relocation of an entire community is unusual, except in the face of natural disasters or other strong external stimuli (such as social or political instability). Moves within a given field system can be over short distances with the new compound located as little as 20 m from the previous residence. The effects of these moves on the macroscale spatial structure of the community are fairly minimal: in dispersed communities the move may be inconsequential, whereas in more nucleated communities the cumulative effect of individual moves can result in either tell formation or a gradual drift, such that the "old" abandoned town is contiguous with the "new" inhabited town (Agorsah 1985). In some cases, the drift may be intentional: in the Gambia, Lawson (2003:18) notes that Mandinka villages of up to one thousand individuals may gradually relocate to a new site (often as little as 1 km distant) on the death of a chief, a process that Lawson refers to as "serial sedentism." Similar processes, referred to as "shifting sedentism," are also known from the Casamance (Donnay 2016). In both locations, these practices have resulted in ephemeral archaeological sites.

In contrast, in some more dispersed settlement systems, such as those of the Gulmance, households regularly moved up to several kilometers, each time opening new fields or reclearing long abandoned fallows. Although over the long-term these societies were comparatively mobile, in practice residences were often inhabited for decades and farming strategies included both inputs in permanent fields and fallowing of rotating fields. As described above, in Gulmance communities residential movements of dispersed homesteads tend to occur every several decades, resulting in a constantly changing social landscape. Because of this practice of generational abandonment and movement of households, these societies created complex and extensive agricultural landscapes despite relying on the same general agricultural principles used by highly sedentary communities and households. From an archaeological perspective, the differences in mobility resulting from these regular moves are clear. However, it is important to keep in mind that over the course of an individual lifetime a resident of these communities might move only two to three times. This household-based mobility system is here discussed as "generational mobility" to recognize both the long-term cumulative effects of these strategies as well as the more sedentary lived experience.

The Anthropogenic Landscape

This chapter's focus is on the physical landscape, climate, ethnobiology, and agroecology of the Maadaga Archaeological Survey study region, and draws on the complementary perspectives offered by ecologists, botanists, agronomists, and anthropologists. Colonial ecologists working in West Africa were predominantly concerned with documenting the "natural" vegetation and consequently tended to characterize farming as a destructive force responsible for deforestation and desertification through uncontrolled burns and other practices that prevented vegetation from reaching its climax state (e.g., Stebbing 1935; Aubréville 1949; see the critical discussions in Swift [1996], Mortimore [1998], and Bassett and Crummey [2003]). These researchers assumed savannas followed a predictable regime of vegetation succession and consequently concluded that many southern savanna regions were "derived"; that is, they would have been forested had they not been farmed (e.g., Trochain 1940; Keay 1959; Hopkins 1974). While terms like "derived savanna" have remained in popular use, over the past forty years ecologists have significantly refined their understandings of savanna environments. Savannas are now understood to be dynamic, unpredictable, resilient systems driven by abiotic factors (e.g., Baker 2000). Adapted to extreme variation in rainfall, savanna vegetation communities have low resistance and can change easily into any number of stable states (Walker and Noy-Meir 1982). This can be seen particularly in savannas with higher levels of annual rainfall (greater than 700 mm), where the incidence of disturbance (notably from fire and herbivory) can substantially affect the levels of tree cover (Sankaran et al. 2005; Bond 2008; Staver, Archibald, and Levin 2011; Osborne et al. 2018). The result of these changing perspectives is a more nuanced framework for understanding the consequences of human activity, and in particular farming practices, on the local environment.

In contrast, colonial and immediately postcolonial agronomists focused on increasing the quantity and reliability of agricultural yields. Their papers often have an experimental tone, whether they are testing the efficacy of different types of fertilizer, documenting the water retention of soils, or trying to find the best method by which to encourage local farmers to take up the plow (e.g., Nye and Greenland 1960; Wills 1962). Agronomists are responsible for most of our knowledge of the soils and traditional crops of the West African savanna (Nye and Greenland 1960; Ahn 1970; Kowal and Kassam 1978), although their publications often include lengthy sections encouraging the adoption of cash cropping, plow agriculture, pesticides, and chemical fertilizers. More recent studies have a greater awareness of the savanna environments and cultural context, yet the emphasis remains on the practical concerns of agricultural production (e.g., NRC 1996, 2006, 2008; Bayala et al. 2015).

Finally, anthropologists in West Africa are interested in the ways in which agricultural practice was and is culturally constructed. In the 1960s, the influence of cultural materialism led to an explosion of research in West Africa and beyond that showed the efficacy, reliability, and resilience of traditional agricultural practice (e.g., Haswell 1953; Conklin 1954, 1963; Savonnet 1959; Pélissier 1966; Netting 1968). This work inspired a series of case studies documenting agrarian structures for West African groups within a cultural context (e.g., Clark and Haswell 1966; Rémy 1967, 1972; Barral 1968; Savonnet 1970, 1976). In spite of this overwhelming documentation, Baker (2000:67–69) notes that the importance of the cultural setting was largely ignored in the development literature for much of the twentieth century, although there are notable exceptions (e.g., Swanson 1979a, 1979b).

Over the past thirty years, the most effective research has integrated respect for local knowledge, an emphasis on practical data, and sophisticated understandings of ecosystem function. Projects are frequently interdisciplinary and contemporary scholars have combined advances from multiple literatures to transform understandings of environment and landscape use (e.g., Fairhead and Leach 1996; Mortimore 1998; Baker 2000; Bassett and Crummy 2003; Nacoulma et al. 2011; Iles 2016). All of these authors argue effectively for the sustainability of traditional practices, for the dynamism of the agricultural landscape, and for the importance of long-term perspectives in understanding the effects of farming on local environments.

Moreover, mobilities occur in landscapes that are sanctified spaces tied to divinities (including ancestors). Diverse ritual practices occur in both particular places that remain stable over time as well as in locations that change in response to activities (for example, opening fields; Cartry 1987; Korbéogo 2013; Kaboré 2018). The Gulmance political landscape is inscribed in space, in particular around the tombs of ranked elites (see Cartry 1987; Thiombiano-Ilboudo 2010) or places connected to ritual processes of chiefly succession, and is tied to the continual maintenance of ritual practices anchoring the community in chiefly compounds (Cartry 1987; Korbéogo 2013; Kaboré 2018).

The Environmental Setting

The Gobnangou escarpment and its forelands are characterized by diverse microenvironments ranging from rocky highlands to wooded savannas to gallery forests, and are notable for their complex local geology and variety of fauna and flora. Although baseline characteristics such as precipitation, groundwater, soils, geomorphology, temperature, day length, and many other factors affect the plants and animals (domesticated or wild) that flourish in the region, the landscape is likewise shaped by diverse cultural processes. These range from the macroscale (the designation of large areas as parks and reserves) to the microscale (the decision to leave an individual tree in place when clearing a field) and from the purposeful (the collection of firewood) and to the unintentional (the colonization of abandoned settlements by ruderal herbs). The result is an anthropogenic landscape that reflects the cumulative effects of millennia of human activity.

Here I draw on interdisciplinary perspectives to explore the limits and opportunities that the environmental setting of the Gobnangou provided for those who derived their subsistence and livelihood from its resources, and provide a context for social and political dynamics. The discussion begins with consideration of the geology, hydrology, soils, and climate, then moves to discussion of the vegetation and wild fauna. Throughout the focus is on human use of the landscape and the diverse range of choices available to local residents.

Geology

Central West Africa is an ancient landscape with no significant tectonic activity since the Precambrian (Sattran and Wenmenga 2002). The terrain is relatively flat and what relief exists is heavily eroded. In this landscape, the sheer cliffs of the Gobnangou escarpment dominate the surrounding terrain and are frequently referred to locally as "mountains" despite a maximal effective elevation of only 200 m (Müller-Haude 1995).

The Gobnangou escarpment is the northernmost of a series of sandstone outcrops and chains running along the border of two major geological formations: the Volta Basin and a vast peneplain known colloquially as the Mossi Plateau (Figure 3). The latter, which covers the bulk of Burkina Faso, is composed predominantly of a lateritic duracrust punctuated by hills and outcrops of metamorphic quartzites and volcanic rocks (Sattran and Wenmenga 2002).

The Gobnangou, however, lies within the narrow northern extension of the sedimentary Volta Basin. The cliffs themselves are an outcrop of the basal geological formation in the area, a fine-grained quartzitic sandstone known as the Dapaong–Boumbouaka Group (Sattran and Wenmenga 2002). The current form was created largely through erosion and both water and wind continue to modify the escarpment. In the plains surrounding the Gobnangou, this basal layer is overlain with 50 to 100 m of sedimentary horizons known collectively as the Pendjari or Oti Group. Significant members of this group include the tillites, dated to ca. 650 mya, which are indicative of glacial activity in the region, and the high quality cherts found in the Gobnangou that were deposited into areas scoured by these glaciers. This prime material for the manufacture of chipped stone tools may have attracted some of the earliest inhabitants in the region (see Chapter 4).

Today, the Gobnangou runs approximately 100 km northeast–southwest and reaches up to 10 km in width. Although cut by many canyons and valleys, some filled with sediment, the top of the escarpment is generally flat and rocky. In contrast, the edges of the formation range from sheer rock faces (with or without substantial talus slopes) to gradual

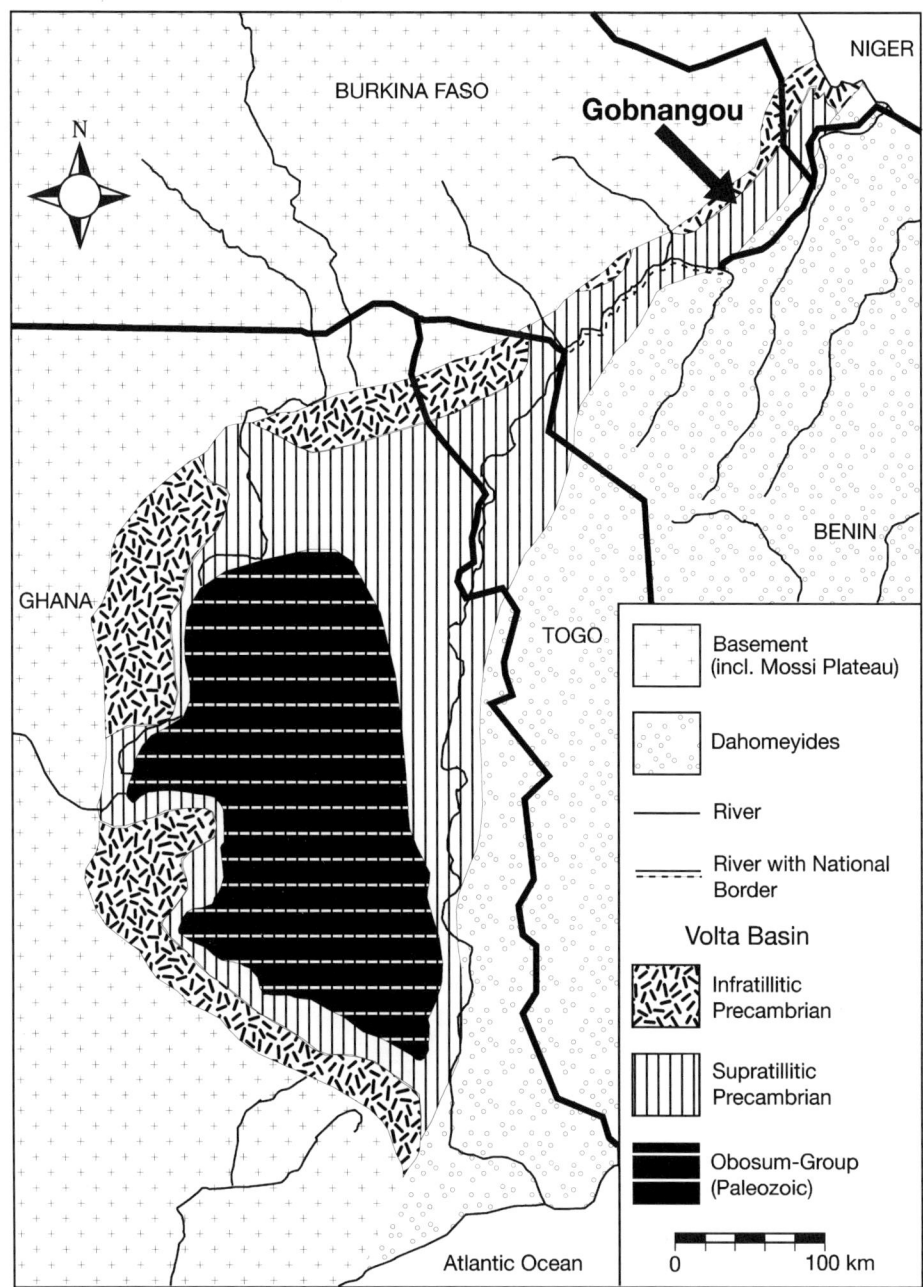

FIGURE 3. Geology of the Volta Basin. Redrawn from Frank et al. (2001).

slopes formed by large, stepped layers of sandstone. Small stack caves are common, both on the external faces and internal canyons of the formation. While the Gobnangou is striking as a physical landmark (see the discussions in Casti [2015]), its most significant geological role locally is as an aquifer.

The porous sandstone absorbs and stores water from the seasonal rains and con-

FIGURE 4. The Gobnangou escarpment in the Maadaga Archaeological Survey region.

sequently many of the small drainages originating in the escarpment run deep into the dry season (Müller-Haude 1995). The preponderance of vegetation around these channels throughout the year, even when not actively flowing, indicates subsurface moisture and many pools at the base of the escarpment are important sources of dry season water for both humans and animals. These high, dry season moisture levels of the Gobnangou result in important microenvironments within and around the escarpment. In contrast, the rapid, high-volume runoff of the rainy season creates flowing rivers that connect the escarpment to the resources of the Pendjari River system, while distributing alluvial sediments to the region.

The MAS study region is located along the south side of the Gobnangou. With the exception of a few canyons, the escarpment edge in the survey zone is composed of steep cliff faces pocked with several caves of different sizes and accessibility. In addition to several paths through the canyons, the escarpment faces are rugose and can be scaled in most areas. The cliff reaches its maximum height of around 150 m near the center of the survey region and descends to elevations as low as 20 to 30 m at the northern and southern limits (Figure 4).

Hydrology

The Gobnangou region is primarily within the Volta drainage system (Figure 5). Water from the escarpment descends through many small tributaries into the Pendjari River, which originates in the Atakora Mountains of Benin and flows from east to west approximately 20 to 30 km south of the survey zone before turning south (Hughes and Hughes 1992). Rainy season flooding peaks in September, when the river rises as much as 4 m and its floodplain can reach more than 5 km in width (in contrast to the dry season channel

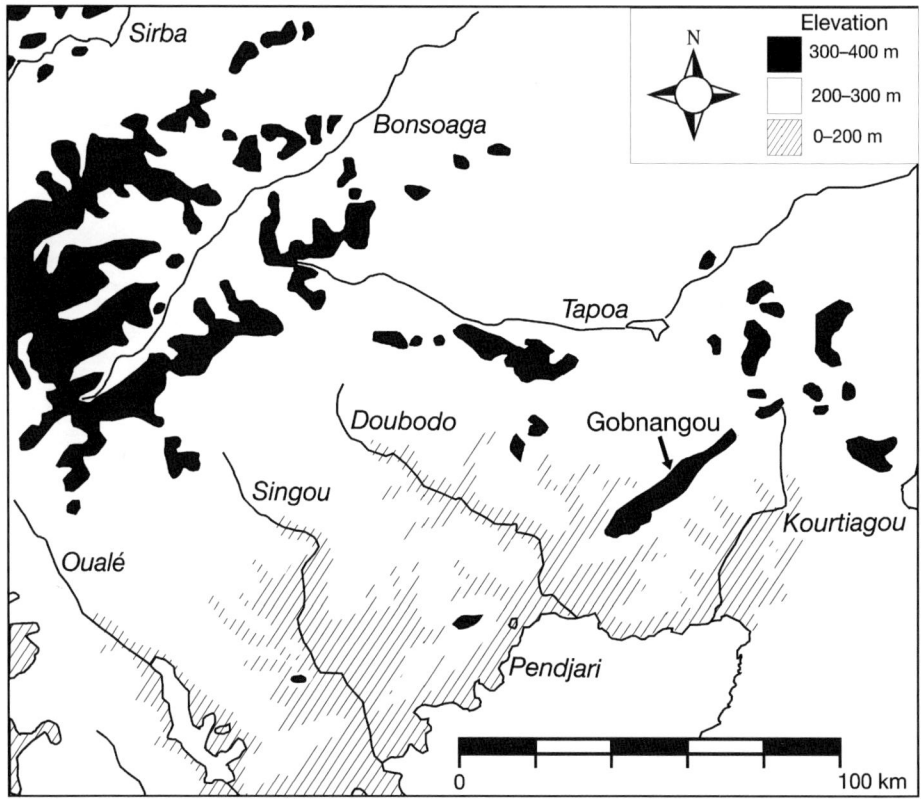

FIGURE 5. Major rivers and geographic features of southeastern Burkina Faso. Redrawn from Pigeonnière and Jomni (1998). The Tapoa, Bonsoaga, and Sirba Rivers drain to the Niger River. The other rivers drain to the Pendjari and ultimately to the Volta River.

width of less than 0.5 km) (Hughes and Hughes 1992; Figure 6). Like in most major permanent rivers in the region, the organisms that carry onchocerciasis (river blindness) and schistosomiasis (bilharzia) are endemic.

Although most drainages originating in the Gobnangou flow toward the Pendjari, those on the north and south sides of the escarpment follow very different paths. To the north, water from the escarpment flows into a wide, shallow channel that runs generally parallel to the cliff face. In the south, where the survey region is located, drainages flow perpendicularly from the escarpment for about 20 km before reaching the Kourtiagou, a major tributary of the Pendjari with its own relatively minor floodplain (Hughes and Hughes 1992). As a result, each primary drainage channel in the south has a smaller catchment. The channels of these southern drainages are for the most part narrower and deeper than their northern counterparts, perhaps indicative of faster flowing water; these streams deposit erosional sand from the Gobnangou along their paths.

As mentioned above, the Gobnangou acts as an aquifer for the region and water tables, particularly near the seasonal drainages, remain high year-round. Aside from a few pools at the base of the escarpment, surface water during the dry season is a rarity. Although major seasonal drainages may remain moist, particularly near the escarpment

Figure 6. The Pendjari River in April 2006.

where they are fueled by springs, they are generally reduced to a trickle and are easily crossed. As a result, despite the complexity of the drainage system, the dry season landscape is easily and rapidly traversed on foot.

During the rainy season, precipitation, runoff from the escarpment, and backflow from the rising waters of the Pendjari combine to fill the network of small drainages that dissect the landscape, as well as flood low-lying areas. In some cases these marshy lands are only covered with a few inches of water, just sufficient to smother the roots of non-aquatic plants. In other locations the water fills deep pools (often depressions running parallel to the banks of the primary seasonal drainages) that persist well into the dry season. When flowing, the drainages fill with river fish and other resources and are an easily accessible source of water. However, the drainages and flooded areas compartmentalize the landscape, significantly inhibiting ease of movement. According to current residents, travel times can triple in the summer months.

The survey region is organized around the catchment of one such primary seasonal drainage and its tributaries. The Koabu is a spring-fed stream originating in the escarpment. Throughout the year water emerges from a crack on top of the escarpment approximately 20 m from the edge of the cliff. It flows over the edge of the cliff (in the late dry season the waterfall can be reduced to a trickle) and fills a permanent pool known locally as Odundo (Figure 7). The primary channel of the Koabu originates from this pool and follows a shallow valley along the escarpment for approximately 500 m, passing through several smaller permanent pools before meandering south toward the Kourtiagou (Figure 8). Although during the winter months, the Koabu becomes a dry streambed within a few hundred meters of the escarpment, it has a clear stream cut, usually 2 to 3 m deep and 3 to 5 m wide. Near the escarpment, the channel is set in a wide valley with natural levees formed by the natural deposition of the heavier sand particles eroding from the escarpment. As the Koabu flows to the south, these levees become smaller and gradually disappear. Simultaneously, the parallel pools and flooded areas mentioned above become more

Figure 7. Odundo, a permanent spring and pool in the Gobnangou escarpment from which the Koabu originates, seen in April 2006.

FIGURE 8. The Koabu as it flows away (*arrows*) from the Gobnangou escarpment.

common; these are often characterized by thin surface layers of alluvial clay. In contrast to the Koabu itself, feeder drainages tend to be gently rounded valleys of various depths and widths that lack clear channels.

Soils and Mineral Resources

In general, savanna soils are known for their relatively low fertility. Without amendments most soils in the region can be farmed for only five to seven years, during which time farmers will rotate crops and intercrop grains and legumes to extend the life of the field. Soils are improved or maintained through the addition of manure and other fertilizers that are often applied to areas close to the residence, although it is rare that enough is available for anything other than gardens and crucial early season crops. Fields are commonly burned, which discourages weed growth and can rid the soil of pests and diseases (Moody 1974; Baker 2000). In savanna environments burning provides few fertility benefits, because any carbon, nitrogen, or sulfur in the vegetation is lost, not enough ash is produced to significantly change the soil pH, and the burned material does not decompose into humus (Nye and Greenland 1960; Ahn 1970; Kowal and Kassam 1978). Although considered labor intensive, mulching, whether with weeds pulled from the field or specifically collected and transported dry matter (such as grass or millet stalks) not only protects the soils from runoff, but also adds to humus content as the mulch decays; it may even attract termites, whose activity can enrich the soil (Slingerland and Masdewel 1996; Korbéogo 2015). Lastly, hoe cultivation itself offers certain advantages for the preservation of poor soils; by never completely clearing fields, farmers mitigate the effects of heavy downpours and the resulting runoff that removes essential nutrients (Pieri 1992).

Once fields have been exhausted, they are generally left fallow. This is the lowest-cost method for regenerating soil fertility and is preferred if adequate land is available.

Given the unpredictability of savanna environments (discussed below), the length of time a particular patch of exhausted land will take to regenerate varies. The most commonly cited period is around twenty years (e.g., Ahn 1970; Kowal and Kassam 1978), although the recovery time can depend on the reasons for abandonment of the field (pests, disease, weeds, soil nutrients, and erosion, among others) (Moody 1974; Kowal and Kassam 1978; Korbéogo 2013). Although the key remedy for soil regeneration is the accumulation of humus, the elimination of weeds may be a longer process (Nye and Greenland 1960).

On soil maps of eastern Burkina Faso, the bulk of the area immediately surrounding the Gobnangou escarpment is classified as pseudogleys (Boulet and Leprun 1969, as reproduced in Müller-Haude 1995; Pigeonnière and Jomni 1998; Figure 9). This catch-all classification for frequently waterlogged soils includes both tropical ferruginous soils and brown eutrophic soils. The latter, with their high organic content and rich chemical composition, are significantly better for agriculture than the eroded, low-nutrient tropical ferruginous soils that cover much of West Africa (Ahn 1970). However, in both cases regular inundation compacts the soil, restricting the flow of oxygen and affecting the ability of roots to penetrate the matrix. These diverse pseudogleys generally follow the same line as the geological limits of the Volta Basin, whereas to the northwest of the escarpment pockets of eutrophic brown soils are present among the dominant tropical ferruginous soils.

On the south side of the Gobnangou, Boulet, Leprun, and Müller-Haude differentiate a strip of soils 2 to 10 km wide along the base of the escarpment. These soils are heavily influenced by the composition of the escarpment itself. In the north near Kodjari, where the geological composition of the Gobnangou shifts from sandstone toward shale, there are pockets of vertisols (heavy, clayey soils). In the study region, however, the soils become significantly sandier as one approaches the escarpment, an effect exacerbated by the significant leaching of clay particles into the B horizon (subsoil). Better drainage near the escarpment is also apparent in the red color of the soils (indicative of air moving through the soil and oxidizing the free iron [Ahn 1970:9, 70]). Boulet and Leprun (1969) consider these a variant of tropical ferruginous soils.

These macroscale maps of necessity subsume significant variability and fail to account for local natural and anthropogenic processes that affect soil properties, including porosity, texture, drainage, and ultimately fertility. For example, the extension of sandy deposits along the path of the Koabu channel (mentioned above) is not apparent. The practical variability of local soils is reflected in two studies of Gulmance soil classification systems (Swanson 1979b; Müller-Haude 1995). Separated by sixteen years, Swanson's and Müller-Haude's studies are in many respects complementary. Swanson, a trained anthropologist, provides a general overview of the entire Gulmance region aimed primarily at agricultural development workers. Müller-Haude, a soil scientist, focused exclusively on the Gobnangou and coordinates the indigenous terms with analyses of the soil profiles. The differences in the terms they used likely reflect not only differential orthography, but also different dialects of Gulmancema. In general, Gulmance description of the landscape includes two cross-cutting sets of terminology: soil types (Table 2) are based on texture, color, and properties of the soils themselves; surface feature types (Table 3) emphasize slope and drainage, factors that can be as important for vegetation as composition (Ahn 1970:222).

As did Boulet and LePrun, the Gulmance classifications draw a distinction between the sandier, better-drained soils near the escarpment (*tinpienga, tinmoanga*) and the more compact, seasonally waterlogged soils farther downstream (*tinboanga, boanbala, baagu*).

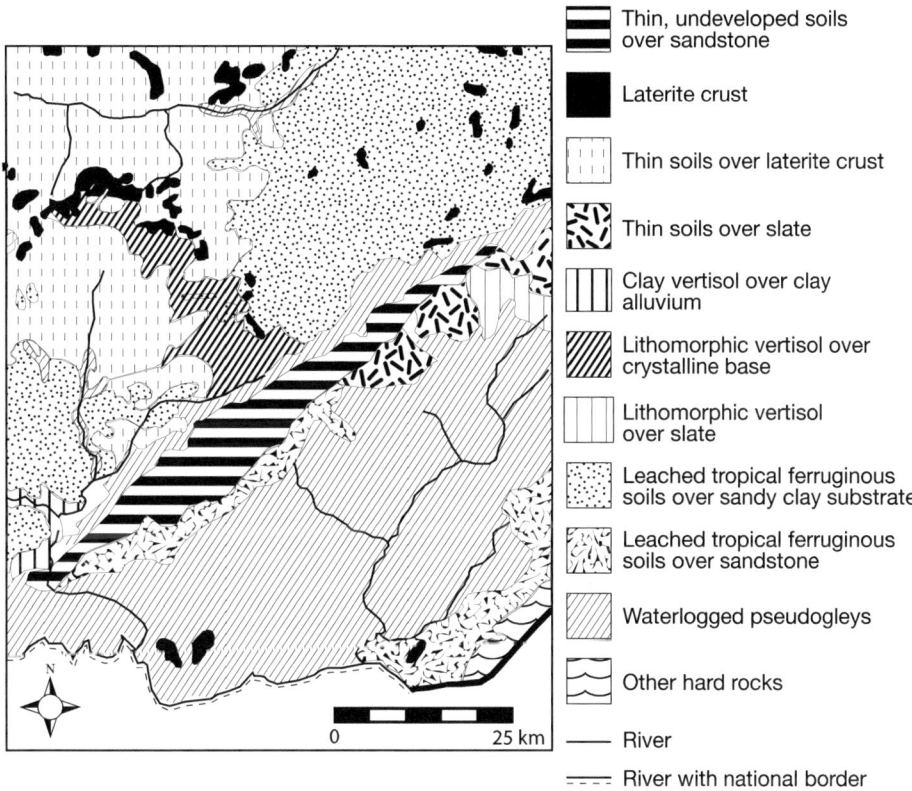

FIGURE 9. Soil map of southeastern Burkina Faso. Redrawn from Müller-Haude (1995) and based on Boulet and Leprun (1969).

However, the Gulmance terms point to the distinct functional effects of minor changes in slope, texture, and drainage. For instance, although both *boanbala* and *baagu* can be characterized as eutric fluvisols, the lack of standing water in *boanbala* results in different vegetation communities and higher agricultural potential.

Although soil type was not systematically recorded during the MAS project, it was apparent that, given the dynamic hydrology of the region, soils could differ considerably in their characteristics within very small areas. Whereas, in general, sand content and soil drainage decrease in proportion to distance from the escarpment, local variability on the scale of the individual agricultural field can significantly affect fertility and yield. Differences in vegetation communities on fallow and virgin land may likewise occur.

In addition to the different agricultural uses of the soils, several mineral resources in the region are commonly exploited. Clay (discussed in greater detail in Chapter 3) is found along the banks of most seasonal drainages and can usually be obtained from shallow deposits. Iron ore is also ubiquitous. The natural soils are very iron rich and easily form laterite deposits on both the surface and as a hardened subsurface bedrock. Although neither is a particularly high-quality ore, both can be smelted in traditional furnaces. Red ochre is also associated with iron deposits and easily obtained within the region. High-quality chert is more rare, but at least two deposits are known, one of which is slightly to

TABLE 2. Terminology of Gulmance soil classification.

Soil type[a]	Soil type[b]	FAO classification[c]	Description	Preferred crops[a]	Probable occurence in study region
Tinpienga	*Tinpienga*	Acrisol/Lixisol	Porous, light-colored, sandy	Late season pearl millet, peanut, early season pearl millet	Near the base of the escarpment
Tinmoanga	*Tinmuanga*	Rhodi-haplic Acrisol/Lixisol	Coarse, red; high clay content[a]; usually very sandy[b]	Late season pearl millet, sesame, cowpea	Near the base of the escarpment
Tinboanga	*Tinbuanli*	Dystric Planosol	Loamy with a high humus content, high moisture retention	Sorghum, kenaf, sweet potato, cowpea	Low-lying areas that do not flood, usually gentle depressions in the drainageway of a watershed
Tinanbiima	*Tintanbima*	Acrisol/Lixisol	Porous, sandy, very similar to *tinpienga*	Pearl millet, tuber, tuber, Bambara groundnut	Sandy levees along Koabu drainage (?)
Tinlubili, ligbali, buali-tinpia	*Tinlubili*	Ferric Lixisol	Dark and compact with high clay content	Sorghum, maize	Over lateritic crust (rare in study region)
Tancagi-boangu	*Tintancaga*	?	Lateritic, gravelly, red, dry out rapidly	Sorghum, maize, okra	Over lateritic crust (rare in study region)
Lilianli	*Lianli*	Salic Fluvisol	Salty	Late season pearl millet, cowpea, seasame	?
Obualigu, boalli	*Bolbuonli, tinbisimbili*	Vertisol, vertic Cambisol	Dark clay with high organic content	Salt lick for animals	?
			Dark, rich soil	Rice, dry season gardens	Over lateritic crust (rare in study region)

[a] Swanson (1979b)
[b] Müller-Haude (1995)
[c] United Nations Food and Agriculture Organization (FAO) soil groups as cited in Müller-Haude (1995)

TABLE 3. Terminology of Gulmance surface feature classification.

Surface feature type[a]	Surface feature type[b]	FAO classification[c]	Description	Probable occurence in study region
Fuanu			Drains center of a watershed; characterized by high soil moisture without flooding	Occurs in very thin strips along the Koabu and its feeders
Gbangbanli			High, often gently sloping land between two watersheds; requires frequent rainfall because of rapid runoff	Covers much of the study region
Jadouli	Tialu	Dystric Planosol	Fertile pockets of land on top of sandstone plateaus; generally very shallow	Located on the escarpment, outside the study region
Kpenbala			Floodplains of major rivers	Occurs along the Pendjari River south of the study region
Boanbala	Buanbalgu	Eutric Fluvisol	Land along the edge of streams, particularly in the lower reaches of a watershed	Land along the Koabu in the southern portion of the study region
Baagu	Baagu	Eutric Fluvisol	Seasonally inundated land with dark, heavy soils	Seasonally flooded pockets of land throughout the study region; often parallel to the Koabu
Ogbaanu	Gbanu	Eutric Fluvisol	Very flat land with little runoff	Does not occur in the study region
Tinbuooli			Small depressions where water drains and is absorbed	
Otialu			Flat surface with scattered laterite pebbles and little vegetation	Occurs in isolated locations along the southwestern edge of the study region
	Kpamkpagu	Stagnic Solonetz	High clay content and high absorption of sodium	At the edge of low-lying areas near Maadaga

[a] Swanson (1979b)
[b] Müller-Haude (1995)
[c] United Nations Food and Agriculture Organization (FAO) soil groups as cited in Müller-Haude (1995)

the south of the study region (see Chapter 4; Figure 24). There are no known sources of digestible mineral salts in or near the study region, although Küppers (1996) noted vegetation characteristic of salty soils in isolated pockets at the foot of the escarpment, notably near the contemporary towns of Maadaga and Yobri.

Climate

Temperature patterns in southeastern Burkina Faso are bimodal, although average monthly highs and lows fall within the fairly restricted ranges of 31 °C to 41 °C and 16 °C to 24 °C, respectively (Geis-Tronich 1991). Temperatures are at their maxima in late April and early May, shortly before the rains begin. They decrease throughout the monsoon season and daytime temperatures reach their lowest point of the year at the height of the rains in August. Although high temperatures rise in the early autumn before dipping slightly in midwinter, overnight lows decline steadily, reaching their lowest point of the year in January (Figure 10). On an interannual scale, the local effects of temperature on vegetation and agriculture are significantly less deterministic than those of rainfall.

Today the Gobnangou region likely receives on average 820 mm of rain a year, according to the rainfall at Maadaga from 1981 to 1990 (Küppers 1996) and consistent with longer records from Fada N'Gourma (Frank et al. 2001) and Pama (Rémy 1967). However, average precipitation figures for West Africa are often not representative of the rainfall in any given year. For example, annual rainfall at Fada N'Gourma from 1951 to 1985 ranged from 650 mm (1984) to 1,310 mm (1958). Nine years had less than 800 mm and twelve had more than 1,000 mm (Geis-Tronich 1991). These data incorporate the severe droughts of the late 1970s and 1980s, yet regional rainfall data from the early 1900s onward suggests that although this drought was particularly sustained, its intensity was well within the range of normal rainfall variation (Koechlin 1997).

In addition to interannual variability, an examination of detailed rainfall records for Tapoa Province from 1989 to 1992 reveals significant variability in the spatial distribution of rainfall (Figure 11; Office régional de développement [ORD] Diapaga as cited in Küppers 1996). As illustrated by the data for Maadaga and Logobou alone, towns 10 km apart regularly differ by more than 100 mm in their precipitation totals. Further complicating prediction for farmers, differences in rainfall totals are not consistent and this year's prime location can be next year's dry spot.

Equally critical, and also highly variable, are the commencement, distribution, duration, and termination of the rains (Kowal and Kassam 1978). For example, a short, intense rainy season that ends early can result in a less productive growing season than a smaller amount of precipitation distributed over more time. Likewise, an early rain followed by several weeks of drought can trick farmers into planting too soon and result in the loss of valuable seed. In the Gobnangou, where the rains usually start in the last weeks of May and end in late September or early October, the actual dates can vary by several weeks (Swanson 1979b; Küppers 1996). Likewise, the spatial variability discussed above affects the timing and distribution of rainfall as well (Küppers 1996).

Traditional farmers have several strategies available to them for buffering against unpredictable rainfall, including mulching to improve water retention (Lal 1974) and spacing fields over a large area (Savonnet 1970). One common method is the use of multiple varieties of multiple crops. Swanson (1979b) documented many varietals of staples, legumes, and other crop plants among the Gulmance. Many of the varieties were specifically developed and preserved to buffer against bad years; some prefer wet conditions, oth-

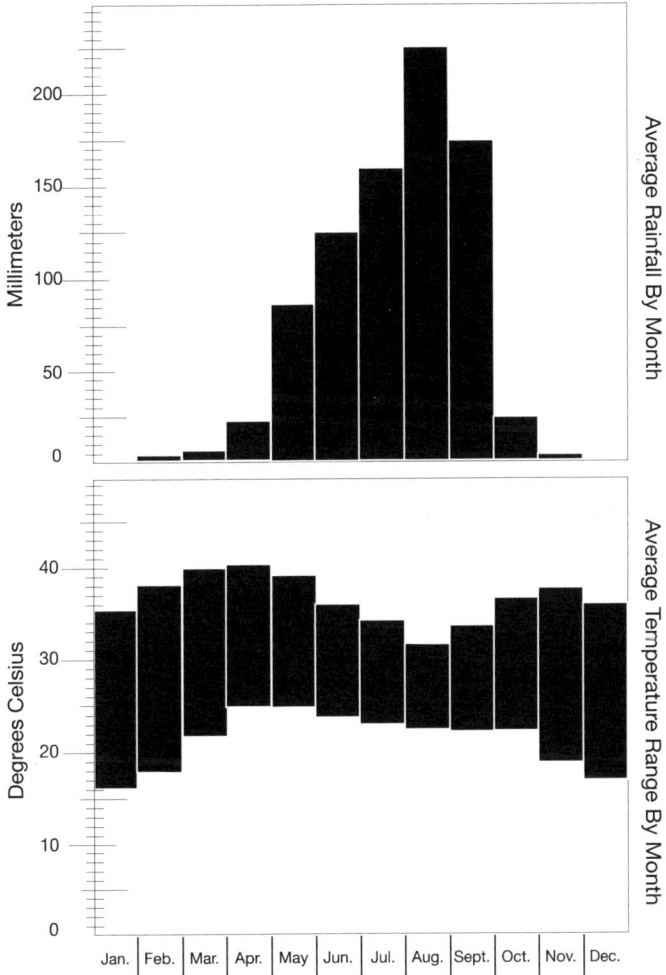

FIGURE 10. Average monthly annual rainfall (1935–1985, *top*) and temperatures (1935–1955, *bottom*) in Fada N'Gourma. Data from Frank et al. (2001) and Geis-Tronich (1991).

ers thrive in dry, and some require rain early, whereas others will produce well provided there is rain late in the season. Swanson (1979b) notes that farmers make an active effort to maintain the diversity of their seed stock, planting at least small quantities of most varieties available to them in most years.

Vegetation
The contemporary vegetation of the Gobnangou is an anthropogenic savanna typical of the Sudan zone. With the exception of useful species commonly protected when clearing fields, the forelands of the escarpment are largely devoid of mature trees and are instead dominated by farmland and shrubby fallows at various stages of maturity. The escarpment itself, in contrast, is home to many diverse plant communities that exploit the various microenvironments provided by its cracks, depressions, ravines, and rocky slopes. There

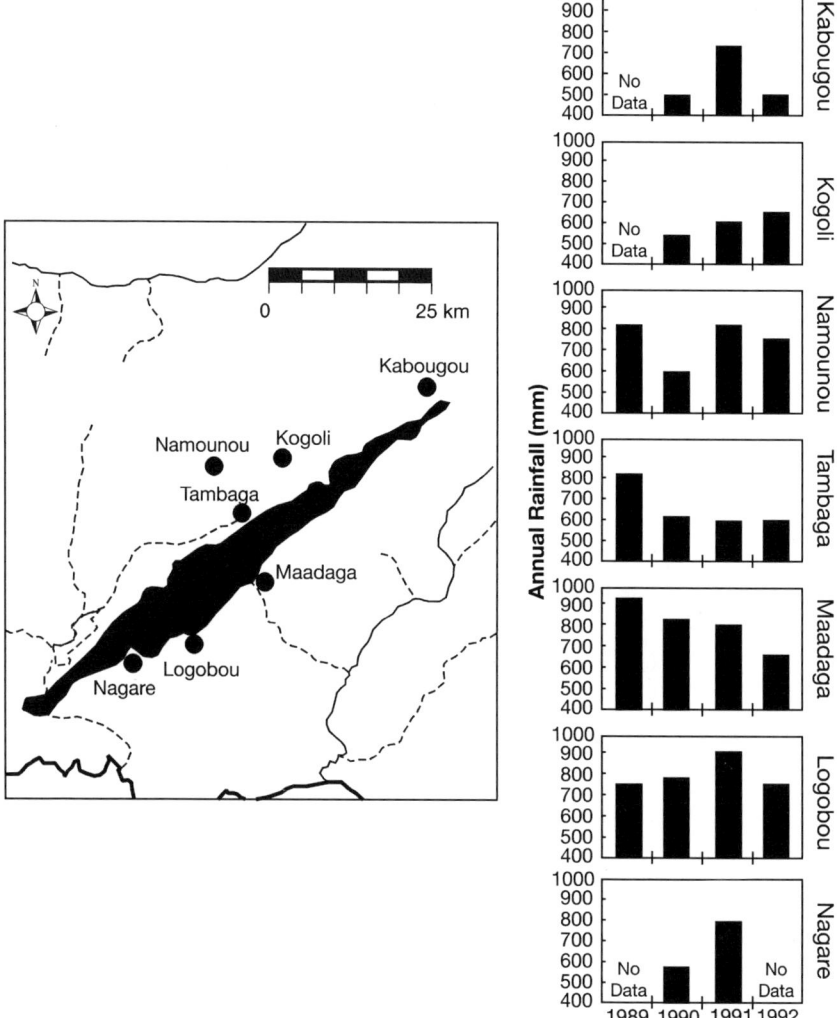

FIGURE 11. Local variability in annual rainfall from 1989 to 1992 in towns along the Gobnangou escarpment. Data from Küppers (1996).

are several excellent sources that provide detailed analyses of the biology of West African savanna ecosystems (e.g., Trochain 1940; Menaut and Cesar 1982; Walker and Noy-Meir 1982; Guinko 1984; Cole 1986; G. W. Lawson 1986; Sankaran et al. 2005; Staver, Archibald, and Levin 2011; Osborne et al. 2018), including some devoted specifically to southeastern Burkina Faso and its environs (Koster 1981; Küppers 1996; Casti and Yonkeu 2009; Nacoulma et al. 2011; O. Ouédraogo et al. 2011; M. Schmidt et al. 2013; I. Ouédraogo et al. 2014). This discussion will focus primarily on the distribution of economically useful plant species, and for that reason will use the botanical nomenclature from *The Useful Plants of West Tropical Africa* (Burkill 1985, 1994, 1995, 1997, 2000, 2004).

In practice, the range of wild plants used by local communities is extremely broad:

178 edible plants, 39 fiber plants, 19 dye plants, 31 construction woods, 49 firewoods, 168 fodder plants, as well as a broader selection of medicinal and miscellaneous use plants (Table 4; see a complete listing in Gallagher [2010:54–79]). As will be apparent in the discussion below, the vegetation of each microregion consists of multiple plant communities and these listings of necessity collapse significant variability.

Wild plants still play a significant role in the local diet and some species, notably shea (*Vitellaria paradoxa*) and locust bean (*Parkia biglobosa*), can be considered staples. Each is nutritionally rich. Shea butter is a solid vegetable fat of almost pure triglycerides. Locust beans contain 30% protein, 20% fat, and 12% sugar (NRC 2006). Both are storable in processed form. Leafy greens from trees such as baobab (*Adansonia digitata*) and herbaceous plants are an important component of sauces and, along with wild fruits, add significant variety, as well as essential vitamins and minerals, to the diet. Most of the high-value species in these categories are actively managed and may be cultivated if sufficient quantities do not grow naturally. Additional categories of plants, such as wild grains and tubers, are only minor components of the diet. They are consumed to maintain knowledge of their use in part, because they could be important in times of food shortage (see the discussions in Muller and Almedom [2008]). Wild plants are also valued for their medicinal properties or are used to treat and dye leather or cotton. Fibers are used to bind thatch roofs and make fish traps and nets. Incense, poisons, and adhesives are but a few of the additional elements of the regional ethnobotanical repertoire.

Availability of wood for fuel and construction is a significant factor for agricultural populations. Shrubs and young trees are often an adequate source for firewood, but the primary posts used for construction can require builders to seek out mature individuals with large, straight branches or trunks. Termite resistant species are particularly desirable, because posts need to last at least the lifetime of the building and are often reused in multiple successive structures. Multiple uses of a single species (for food, fuel, and construction) can put conflicting pressures on vegetation and consequently firewood preferences are notoriously variable and locally sensitive (Neumann 1999).

Fodder plants are primarily important during the dry season. The Gobnangou is well within the tsetse fly zone. Traditionally, resident livestock would have been primarily small populations of dwarf species tolerant of trypanosomiasis (sleeping sickness; see below). Although animal husbandry has expanded because of recent government spraying programs, the bulk of livestock in the region are still the herds brought south to forage by nomadic pastoralists during the dry season. Consequently, nutritious plants that stay green well into the dry season or are among the first to leaf in the spring are particularly valued, although the aquifer of the escarpment makes it a propitious place to graze throughout the winter months.

The Ecological Zones

The Gobnangou Escarpment
The Gobnangou escarpment is notable for the diversity of its flora (Thiombiano et al. 2010). The microenvironments created by rocky surfaces, soil pockets, canyons, and eroded slopes are home to diverse and unique plant communities. The presence of many springs that provide a steady supply of water deep into the dry season, particularly to plants in shaded canyons, exacerbates differences between the escarpment and its surrounding

TABLE 4. Selected useful plant species of the Gobnangou region. The species and their associations are compiled primarily from Küppers's (1996) analysis of the Gobnangou vegetation, supplemented by Koster (1982), Nacoulma et al. (2011), and Ouédraogoet al. (2011). Botanical nomenclature and ethnobotanical uses are from Burkill (1985, 1994, 1995, 1997, 2000, 2004), supplemented with several resources focused specifically on southeastern Burkina Faso (Geis-Tronich 1991; Witting and Martin 1995; Küppers 1996; Neumann 1999; Ouédraogo et al. 2014). When available, frequency in microenvironments is indicated as common (***), present (**), or rare (*); otherwise, presence (×) or absence only is indicated. Escarpment slopes (ES) include all species found on escarpment slopes, crevices, and ravines; highland savannas (HS) include species found on top of the escarpment in deeper soils; savannas (S) includes all species found in the minimally anthropogenic savannas of the parks and reserves; young fallows (YF) are those less than ten years old; old fallows (OF) are those more than ten years old and include heavily managed woodlands; and riverine (R) includes those species found in the gallery forests and floodplains surrounding major rivers. *Key to sources*: B, Burkill; GT, Geis-Tronich; K, Küppers; N, Neumann; O, Ouédraogo et al. 2014; WM, Witting and Martin.

Family (Subfamily)	Scientific name	Primary use	Part	Notes	Sources	Frequency in microenvironments					
						ES	HS	S	YF	OF	R
Leguminosae (Papilionoideae)	*Abrus puchellus* Wall.	Food	Plant	Stems used as sweetener	B						×
Leguminosae (Mimosoideae)	*Acacia dudgeoni* Craib	Food, construction, fodder	Gum, wood, leaf	Aromatic resin	B, O			*			
Leguminosae (Mimosoideae)	*Acacia macrostachya* Reichenb.	Food	Seeds	Seeds are cooked and consumed like beans	B	*	**			**	
Leguminosae (Mimosoideae)	*Acacia nilotica* (L.) Willd.	Food, dye, tanning and hide treatment, fodder	Young fruit, seed, fruit pods, leaf	Fruit edible when young; used to make a black dye; pods and seeds used in tanning	B, GT			×			×
Leguminosae (Mimosoideae)	*Acacia seyal* DC.	Food, construction	Gum, wood	Aromatic resin	B, GT			×			
Leguminosae (Mimosoideae)	*Acacia sieberiana* DC.	Fodder	Leaf	One of the last trees to drop its leaves	B, O			×			×

Continued

TABLE 4 CONTINUED

Family (Subfamily)	Scientific name	Primary use	Part	Notes	Sources	Frequency in microenvironments						
						ES	HS	S	YF	OF	R
Amaranthaceae	*Achyranthes aspera* L.	Potash	Wood	Entire plant is high in potash	B	***	*			*	×
Bombacaceae	*Adansonia digitata* L.	Food, fiber	Leaf, fruit, bark	Leaf is among the most common sauce ingredients; fruit pulp is often dried, powdered, and used as a sweetener	B, GT, O	*		*		*	×
Labiatae	*Aeollanthus pubescens* Benth.	Food	Leaf	Aromatic herb used as flavoring	B	*					
Leguminosae (Caesalpinioideae)	*Afzelia africana* Sm.	Food, construction, fodder	Unripe fruit, young leaves, aril, wood, leaf	Leaves are among the first to appear at the end of the dry season	B, K, N	**		*		*	×
Sapindaceae	*Allophylus africanus* P Beauv.	Food, firewood	Fruit, wood		B	**					
Liliaceae	*Aloe macrocarpa* var. *major* A. Berger	Food	Flower		B	*					

Continued

TABLE 4 CONTINUED

Family (Subfamily)	Scientific name	Primary use	Part	Notes	Sources	ES	HS	S	YF	OF	R
Leguminosae (Papilionoideae)	*Alysicarpus ovalifolius* (Schum. & Thonn.) J. Leonard	Fodder	Leaf		B		*		*	*	
Amaranthaceae	*Amaranthus spinosus* L.	Food	Leaf, flower	Introduced from Asia at an unknown point	B, WM		*				
Vitaceae	*Ampelocissus leonensis* (Hook. f.) Planch	Food	Fruit		B	*					
Gramineae	*Andropogon gayanus* Kunth	Matting, fodder	Culms, leaf	Long culms used for matting	B	***		x	**	**	x
Gramineae	*Andropogon pseudapricus* Stapf	Thatch	Culm	Frequently favored for thatching	B	*	**	x	***	***	
Annonaceae	*Annona senegalensis* Pers.	Food	Leaves, flowers, fruit	Flowers used as flavoring	B, O	**	**	**	**	**	x
Combretaceae	*Anogeissus leiocarpus* (DC.) Guill. & Perr.	Dye, construction, firewood, medicine	Leaf/bark, wood	Used to make a yellow-brown or red-brown dye	B, GT, N, O	*		**		**	x

Continued

TABLE 4 CONTINUED

Family (Subfamily)	Scientific name	Primary use	Part	Notes	Sources	Frequency in microenvironments					
						ES	HS	S	YF	OF	R
Moraceae	*Antaris africana* Engl.	Bark cloth	Bark	Very high quality bark cloth	B	**					
Balanitaceae	*Balanites aegyptiaca* (L.) Del.	Food, fodder	Fruit, leaf		B, O	*	*	**		**	×
Nyctaginaceae	*Boerhavia erecta* L.	Food	Leaf		B, WM		*			*	
Bombacaceae	*Bombax costatum* Pellegr. & Vuillet	Food, stuffing, fodder	Flowers, fruit, leaf	Flowers valued for creating mucilage in sauce; although not a traditional activity, fibers can be used for stuffing pillows and mattresses	B, GT, O	*	**	***		**	×
Palmae	*Borassus aethiopium* Mart.	Food, basketry	Fruit, sap, culm	Sap can be used to produce a palm wine	B, GT						×
Capparaceae	*Boscia angustifolia* A. Rich.	Food	Bark, fruit, seed	Bark pounded with cereals or added to soups; berries are bitter	B			*		*	×

Continued

TABLE 4 CONTINUED

Family (Subfamily)	Scientific name	Primary use	Part	Notes	Sources	Frequency in microenvironments						
						ES	HS	S	YF	OF	R
Gramineae	*Brachiaria lata* (Schumach.) CE Hubbard	Food, fodder	Seed, leaf	Seeds are eaten as a grain; leaves can be cut and dried; one of the earliest grasses to develop	B			x		*	x
Gramineae	*Brachiaria mutica* (Forssk.) Stapf	Fodder	Leaf	Considered one of the best tropical forage plants	B			x			x
Gramineae	*Brachiaria villosa* Vanderyst	Food, fodder	Seed, leaf	Seed eaten as grain	B	*	*	x	**	*	x
Euphorbiaceae	*Bridelia scleroneura* Mull.-Arg.	Food, firewood, medicine	Fruit, wood		B, O	**	*			*	
Leguminosae (Caesalpinioideae)	*Burkea africana* Hook.	Dye, firewood	Bark, wood	Used to make a black dye	B, N	**	***	***		**	x
Capparaceae	*Cadaba farinosa* Forssk.	Food	Leaf, bark	Pounded leaves are cooked in sauce or mixed with cereals	B			*			x
Leguminosae (Caesalpinioideae)	*Cassia sieberiana* DC.	Medicinal, firewood	Leaf, root, wood	Leaf and root are used as a purgative, diuretic, and febrifuge; charcoal used by Gulmance for smithing iron (GT)	B, GT, O	*		*		*	

Continued

TABLE 4 CONTINUED

Family (Subfamily)	Scientific name	Primary use	Part	Notes	Sources	Frequency in microenvironments					
						ES	HS	S	YF	OF	R
Amaranthaceae	*Celosia trigyna* L.	Medicinal	Leaf	Anti-helmitic	B	*			*		
Ulmaceae	*Celtis integrifolia* Lam.	Food, fodder	Leaf, young fruit	Leaf frequently used in sauce; fruit edible only when young	B	*					x
Gramineae	*Cenchrus biflorus* Roxb.	Fodder	Leaf	Only grazed when young (before spikes form)	B			x			
Pedaliaceae	*Ceratotheca sesamoides* Endl.	Food	Leaf, seed		B, WM		***	x			
Leguminosae (Caesalpinioideae)	*Chaemacrista mimosoides* (L.) Greene	Medicinal	Leaf	Used for dressing wounds	B	*	***	x	***	**	x
Gramineae	*Chloris pilosa* Schumach.	Fodder	Leaf		B	*	*		**		
Vitaceae	*Cissus populnea* Guill. & Perr.	Food	Mucilage, leaf, fruit		B	*	*			*	x
Capparidaceae	*Cleome gynandra* L.	Food	Leaf/root, seed	Leaf appreciated in sauces for its bitterness	B, WM						

Continued

TABLE 4 CONTINUED

Family (Subfamily)	Scientific name	Primary use	Part	Notes	Sources	Frequency in microenvironments					
						ES	HS	S	YF	OF	R
Capparaceae	*Cleome viscosa* L.	Food	Leaf, seed	Acrid leaf used in sauces; seeds used as a spice	B	*	*				x
Cochlospermaceae	*Cochlospermum tinctorium* A. Rich.	Dye	Root	Used to make a yellow-brown dye	B	*	***	x	*	**	
Combretaceae	*Combretum glutinosum* Perr.	Medicinal, construction, firewood, fodder	Wood, leaf		B, N, O	*	***	x		**	x
Combretaceae	*Combretum micranthum* G. Don	Medicinal, basketry, construction, firewood, fodder	Leaf, culm, wood	Leaf used as a diuretic, febrifuge, and digestive; culms are tough and pliable when young and are split to make large wicker baskets	B, GT, N, O	***	*	x			x
Combretaceae	*Combretum molle* R. Br.	Construction, firewood	Wood		B, N, O	*				*	
Combretaceae	*Combretum nigricans* Lepr.	Adhesive, firewood	Gum, wood		B, N, O	*	**	x		*	x

Continued

TABLE 4 CONTINUED

Family (Subfamily)	Scientific name	Primary use	Part	Notes	Sources	Frequency in microenvironments					
						ES	HS	S	YF	OF	R
Commelinaceae	*Commelina forskalaei* Vahl	Fodder	Leaf		B			×			
Burseraceae	*Commiphora africana* (A. Rich.) Engl.	Food, fodder	Resin, leaf	Aromatic resin known as African myrrh	B, O		*	×			×
Tiliaceae	*Corchorus tridens* Lam.	Food	Leaf	Leaf, stem, and flower can be dried for use in sauce	B, WM					*	
Capparaceae	*Crateva adansonii* DC.	Food	Leaf, fruit	Crushed and cooked in sauces	B, O						×
Rubiaceae	*Crossopteryx febrifuga* (Afzel.) Benth.	Medicinal, firewood	Bark, wood	Common febrifuge	B, O	*	*	*		**	×
Cyperaceae	*Cyperus esculentus* L.	Food	Tuber	Small tubers can be prepared fresh or roasted; its importance differs among ethnic groups	B						×
Gramineae	*Dactyloctenium aegyptium* (L.) P. Beauv.	Fodder	Leaf		B		*	×	**	*	

Continued

TABLE 4 CONTINUED

Family (Subfamily)	Scientific name	Primary use	Part	Notes	Sources	Frequency in microenvironments					
						ES	HS	S	YF	OF	R
Leguminosae (Caesalpinioideae)	*Daniella oliveri* (Rolfe) Hutch. & Dalz.	Food, medicinal, firewood	Resin, bark, wood	Aromatic resin; bark has various medical uses	B	***	*	×			×
Leguminosae (Caesalpinioideae)	*Detarium microcarpum* Guill. & Perr.	Food	Fruit		B, O	**	**	**		***	×
Leguminosae (Caesalpinioideae)	*Dialium guineense* Willd.	Food, firewood	Fruit, seed, wood		B						×
Ebenaceae	*Diospyros elliotii* (Hiern.) F White	Food	Fruit		B						×
Ebenaceae	*Diospyros mespiliformis* Hochst.	Food, construction	Fruit, wood		B, GT, N, O	***	*	*		*	×
Gramineae	*Echinochloa pyramidalis* (Lam.) Hitchc. & Chase	Food, fodder	Seed, salt, leaf	Palatable mineral salt can be made from the culm	B			×			×
Gramineae	*Eleusine indica* (L.) Gaertn.	Fodder	Leaf	Fodder is particularly high in nitrogen	B		*	×		*	
Gramineae	*Eragrostis pilosa* (L.) P Beauv.	Thatch	Culm		GT						

Continued

TABLE 4 CONTINUED

Family (Subfamily)	Scientific name	Primary use	Part	Notes	Sources	ES	HS	S	YF	OF	R
Gramineae	*Eragrostis tremula* Hochst. & Steud	Fodder	Leaf		B			×	*	*	
Euphorbiaceae	*Euphorbia unispina* N.E. Br.	Poison	Latex	Caustic latex commonly used in arrow poison	B			×			
Rubiaceae	*Feretia apodanthera* Del.	Fodder	Leaf	Dried leaves can be consumed as fodder	B, O	*	*	*			×
Moraceae	*Ficus glumosa* Del.	Food, dye, latex, bark cloth	Fruit, young leaf, bark, latex, leaf	Used to make a red dye; latex is high quality; not preferred for bark cloth	B, O	*	*	×			
Moraceae	*Ficus platyphylla* Del.	Food, tanning and hide treatment, latex	Leaf, bark, latex		B, O	*					×
Moraceae	*Ficus sycamorus* L. ssp. *gnaphalocarpa*	Food, medicinal	Young leaf, fruit	Fruit is the best of the *Ficus* sp.	B, O	*					
Thymelaeaceae	*Gnidia kraussiana* Meissner	Poison	Leaf, root	Leaf and root broadly used as poisons	B			×			×
Tiliaceae	*Grewia bicolor* Juss.	Food, fiber	Fruit		B, O	*	*	×		*	
Tiliaceae	*Grewia mollis* Juss.	Food, bows	Fruit, leaf, bark, wood	Wood used to make bows for hunting	B			×			×

Continued

TABLE 4 CONTINUED

Family (Subfamily)	Scientific name	Primary use	Part	Notes	Sources	Frequency in microenvironments					
						ES	HS	S	YF	OF	R
Tiliaceae	*Grewia villosa* Willd.	Food	Fruit		B	*					
Malvaceae	*Hibiscus asper* Hook.f.	Food	Fruit	Young fruit commonly used to thicken soups	B	**	*	×	*	**	
Euphorbiaceae	*Hymenocardia acida* Tul.	Firewood	Wood		B	*	*	*		*	
Convolvulaceae	*Ipomoea eriocarpa* R. Br.	Food	Leaf		B, WM	*			*		×
Leguminosae (Caesalpinioideae)	*Isoberlinia tomentosa* (Harms) Craib & Stapf	Food	Leaf		B	*					
Meliaceae	*Khaya senegalensis* (Desv.) A Juss.	Medicinal, construction, firewood, fodder	Bark, wood, leaf	Bark used as a febrifuge, emetic, and purgative; charcoal used by Gulmance for smithing iron (GT)	B, GT, O	**	*	*		*	×
Anacardiaceae	*Lannea acida* A. Rich.	Food	Young leaf, fruit, gum	Fruit may be dried and/or fermented to make an alcoholic beverage	B, O	**	**	*		*	

Continued

TABLE 4 CONTINUED

Family (Subfamily)	Scientific name	Primary use	Part	Notes	Sources	Frequency in microenvironments					
						ES	HS	S	YF	OF	R
Anacardiaceae	*Lannea microcarpa* Engl. & K. Krause	Food	Leaf, fruit, gum	Fruit may be dried and/or fermented to make an alcoholic beverage	B, GT, O	*	*	*		*	×
Asclepiadaceae	*Leptadinia hastata* (Pers.) Dec'ne	Food	Flower, leaf, shoot	Usually consumed cooked in sauces	B			×			×
Labiatae	*Leucas martinicensis* (Jacq.) R. Br.	Dye, insect repellant	Root	Used to make a yellow dye; plant is burned to repel mosquitoes	B		*		**	*	
Leguminosae (Papilionoideae)	*Lonchocarpus laxiflorus* Guill. & Perr.	Food, dye	Flower, fruit, leaf	Fruit can be dried and stored; used to make a blue dye	B	*		×			
Cyperaceae	*Mariscus alternifolius* Vahl.	Food	Rhizome	Fragrant rhizome used as a flavoring	B					*	×
Convolvulaceae	*Merremia pinnata* (Hochst. ex Choisy) Hallier f.	Fodder	Leaf		B	**	*				

Continued

TABLE 4 CONTINUED

Family (Subfamily)	Scientific name	Primary use	Part	Notes	Sources	Frequency in microenvironments						
						ES	HS	S	YF	OF	R
Rubiaceae	*Mitragyna inermis* (Willd.) O. Ktze.	Basketry, construction, medicinal	Culm, wood, leaf		B, GT, O		*	*		*	x
Moringaceae	*Moringa oleifera* Lam.	Food	Leaf, root, seed	Leaf has smell of mustard and is eaten raw and cooked; seeds eaten fried and used for their oil	B			x			x
Acanthaceae	*Nelsonia canescens* (Lam.) Spreng	Potash, fodder	Wood, leaf	Important salty fodder	B						x
Nymphaeaceae	*Nymphea lotus* L.	Food	Rhizome, calyx, seed	Rhizome eaten raw or cooked	B						x
Hydrocharitaceae	*Ottelia ulvifolia* (Planch) Walp.	Food	Fruit, leaf		B						x
Gramineae	*Oxytenanthera abyssinica* (A. Rich.) Munro	Furniture and fencing	Culm	Culms of this bamboo-like grass used for fencing and furniture	B	*					
Anacardiaceae	*Ozoroa insignis* Del.	Medicinal	Root	Febrifuge	B			x			
Gramineae	*Panicum subalbidum* Kunth	Food	Seed	Seeds eaten as grain	B	*	**	x			x

Continued

TABLE 4 CONTINUED

Family (Subfamily)	Scientific name	Primary use	Part	Notes	Sources	Frequency in microenvironments					
						ES	HS	S	YF	OF	R
Leguminosae (Mimosoideae)	*Parkia biglobosa* (Jacq.) Benth.	Food, dye	Fruit, seed	Storable vegetable butter made from fermented seed is a sauce base; used to make a black dye	B, GT, O	*		*		*	×
Gramineae	*Pennisetum pedicellatum* Trin.	Fodder	Leaf	Good fodder prior to flowering	B	**	***	×	***	***	×
Euphorbiaceae	*Phyllanthus reticularis* Poir.	Dye	Bark, root	Used to make a black or red dye	B			×			
Leguminosae (Caesalpinioideae)	*Piliostigma reticulatum* (DC.) Hochst.	Food, fiber, fodder	Fruit, bark, leaf	Pods edible when young; cordage is used for rainy season hut roofs, plunge basket frames, and stringing bows (GT)	B, GT, O	*	*	*		**	×
Leguminosae (Caesalpinioideae)	*Piliostigma thonningii* (Schum.) Milne-Redh.	Fiber, dye, firewood, fodder	Bark, bark root, wood, leaf	Used to make a red dye; charcoal used by Gulmance for smithing iron (GT)	B, GT	*	*	***		***	×

Continued

TABLE 4 CONTINUED

Family (Subfamily)	Scientific name	Primary use	Part	Notes	Sources	ES	HS	S	YF	OF	R
Caryophyllaceae	*Polycarpea* (three species)	Infusion	Leaf	Stimulating infusion drunk against fatigue	B		*	×			
Leguminosae (Mimosoideae)	*Prosopis africana* (Guill. & Perr.) Taub.	Food, construction, firewood	Seed, wood	Seeds are ground, fermented, and dried into cakes or sticks	B, N	*	*	**		**	
Meliaceae	*Pseudocedrela kotschyi* (Schweinf.) Harms	Dye, construction	Bark, wood	Used to make a brown dye	B, O					*	×
Leguminosae (Papilionoidea)	*Pterocarpus erinaceus* Poir.	Construction, fodder	Wood, leaf	One of the last trees to drop its leaves	B, K, O	**	*	***		**	×
Leguminosae (Papilionoidea)	*Pterocarpus lucens* Lepr.	Food, firewood	Leaf, wood	Charcoal used by Gulmance for smithing iron (GT)	B, GT						
Palmae	*Raphia sudanica* A. Chev.	Food	Fruit, sap	Sap can be used to produce a palm wine	B	*					×
Gramineae	*Rottboellia cochinensis* (Lour.) WD Clayton	Food, matting, fodder	Seed, culm, leaf	Culm may be used to make matting	B						×
Apocynaceae	*Saba senegalensis* (A. DC.) Pichon	Food, latex	Leaf, fruit, latex	Latex is usable but not high quality	B, O	*					

Continued

TABLE 4 CONTINUED

Family (Subfamily)	Scientific name	Primary use	Part	Notes	Sources	Frequency in microenvironments					
						ES	HS	S	YF	OF	R
Rubiaceae	*Sarcocephalus latifolius* (JE Sm.) EA Bruce	Medicinal	Bark	Common febrifuge	B, O	**		*		*	
Anacardiaceae	*Sclerocarya birrea* (A. Rich.) Hochst.	Food, construction	Fruit, wood	Fruit can be fermented to make an alcoholic beverage; fruit has oily, edible kernels	B, GT, O	*	*	*		*	
Polygalaceae	*Securidaca longepedunculata* Fres.	Fiber	Young shoots		B, O		*	*		*	
Euphorbiaceae	*Securinega virosa* (Roxb.) Baill.	Food, basketry, firewood	Fruit, culms, wood		B, GT	*	*	*	*	*	×
Leguminosae (Caesalpinioideae)	*Senna obtusifolia* (L.) Irwin & Barneby	Food	Young leaf, flower, seed	Young leaf and flower can be dried for use in sauce; roasted seeds can be used as a coffee substitute; introduced from the Americas at an unknown point	B, WM	*				*	
Gramineae	*Setaria pumila* (Poir.) Roem. & Schult.	Fodder	Leaf		B	**	**	×	***	**	×

Continued

TABLE 4 CONTINUED

Family (Subfamily)	Scientific name	Primary use	Part	Notes	Sources	Frequency in microenvironments					
						ES	HS	S	YF	OF	R
Bignoniaceae	*Stereospermum kunthianum* Cham.	Fodder, medicinal	Bark, root, leaf	Various	B, O	**	*	×	*	*	×
Apocynaceae	*Strophanthus sarmentosus* DC.	Poison	Seed	Seeds can be used as a poison	B	*					
Loganiaceae	*Strychnos spinosa* Lam.	Food, medicinal	Young leaf, fruit, plant	Young leaf commonly used in sauces; fruit is barely edible; has diverse medicinal uses	B, O	*	**	×		**	
Araceae	*Stylochiton lancifolius* Kotschy & Peyr.	Dye	Plant	Used to make a yellow dye	B				**		
Leguminosae (Caesalpinioideae)	*Tamarindus indica* L.	Food, dye, construction, fodder	Leaf, fruit, seed, bark, wood	Fruit can be eaten fresh, or dried and powdered; used to make a brown dye	B, O	*		*		*	×
Combretaceae	*Terminalia avicennoides* Guill. & Perr.	Dye, construction, firewood	Root, wood	Used to make a yellow dye; charcoal used by Gulmance for smithing iron (GT)	B, GT, N, O, WM			**		**	×
Combretaceae	*Terminalia macroptera* Guill. & Perr.	Construction, firewood	Wood		B			*		*	
Ulmaceae	*Trema orientalis* (L.) Blume	Fiber, firewood	Bark, wood	Bark yields a strong fiber used to make cordage	B	*	*				

Continued

TABLE 4 CONTINUED

Family (Subfamily)	Scientific name	Primary use	Part	Notes	Sources	ES	HS	S	YF	OF	R
Euphorbiaceae	*Uapaca togoensis* Pax	Food, firewood	Fruit, wood		B	*					
Malvaceae	*Urena lobata* L.	Food, fiber	Young leaf, seed, bast	Fatty seeds are added to stews	B	*		×			×
Sapotaceae	*Vitellaria paradoxa* Gaertn. f.	Food, construction, firewood	Seed, wood	Shea butter extracted from the kernel is a primary cooking oil; charcoal used by Gulmance for smelting iron (GT)	B, GT, O	**	*	***		***	×
Verbenaceae	*Vitex doniana* Sweet	Food	Young leaf, fruit	Fruit can be fermented to make an alcoholic beverage	B, GT, O	*	*				×
Leguminosae (Papilionoidea)	*Xeroderris stuhlmannii* (Taub.) Mendonca & EP Sousa	Medicinal	Bark, root	Vermifugal	B			**			
Olacaceae	*Ximenia americana* L.	Food, firewood	Fruit, seed, wood	Vegetable butter can be made from the seed	B, O	*	*	*		*	×
Rhamnaceae	*Ziziphus mauritiana* Lam.	Food	Fruit	Best of the *Ziziphus* sp. fruits; often dried, powdered, and made into sweets	B, O			×			

areas. Despite the generally hospitable conditions, the escarpment is not usually exploited as farmland. The thin and undeveloped soils maintain their fertility with the regular renewal of humus from wild vegetation, but if cleared would likely degenerate rapidly and recover slowly. Today, given the consequences of centuries of cultivation in the Gobnangou region, the lack of fallow plant communities further distinguishes the escarpment vegetation from that of its forelands.

Superficial soil layers on the high plateaus of the Gobnangou have resulted in the growth of several communities of savanna vegetation, the nature of which are strongly dependent on local sediment depth and fertility. Those on deeper soils are notable for their established communities of woody vegetation, which today stand in sharp contrast to the agricultural landscapes of the escarpment forelands. These include various edible tree and shrub species: *Bombax costatum,* whose flowers are frequently collected, dried, and sold in markets; *Ceratotheca sesamoides,* the leaves of which are harvested for sauces; *Acacia macrostachya* whose beans the Mossi collect and prepare in a way similar to domestic cowpeas; and a broad assortment of fruit trees, among them *Sclerocarya birrea* and *Detarium microcarpum.* There are aslo excellent firewoods, such as *Combretum glutinosum* and *Burkea africana.* The number and diversity of high-value fodder plants in the highland savannas also makes them favored areas for grazing.

The vegetation found on the slopes of the Gobnangou escarpment ranges from the woody shrubs of the gentle rocky talus to the hardy species that grow in the crevices of the sheer rock face. These plant communities are similar to those of the highlands in their species composition and diversity, but they tend to be significantly sparser and lack the coherency of the highland savannas. Thus, although more convenient for people living at the base of the escarpment, useful plants common in both regions are more easily exploited in bulk on the highlands.

The shaded canyons and ravines of the escarpment are characterized by lush vegetation. Relatively limited in their extent, these streambed environments are generally inappropriate for intensive use and are of greater importance during the dry season when they are one of the few sources of fresh greenery. Although the species composition has many similarities to the other plant communities of the escarpment, isolated examples of species characteristic of moister conditions are common. Additionally, both annual and perennial vegetation can achieve greater height in these environments.

Although fruit trees are most common among the edible plants, these environments are most important as a source of leafy vegetables. In addition to plants such as *Celtis integrifolia, Cissus populnea,* and *Senna obtusifolia* that are primarily used for their greens, species used primarily for their fruits (e.g., *Vitex doniana* and Lannea microcarpa) may be more valuable as sources of early or late vegetation. Likewise, although found in areas not as rich or diverse for grazing as the highland savannas, the available fodder plants take on greater importance during the dry season. Woody species such as *Daniella oliveri,* a rich source of construction and firewoods, could be rapidly depleted in these environments without careful management because of their limited extent. With other resources available, the drawbacks to removing the woody vegetation (such as increased evaporation and making the area less hospitable to wild animals) likely outweigh the benefits. Today, the woody vegetation in the escarpment streambeds, particularly those that are spring fed, is often protected. Finally, *Antaris africana,* the only plant in the region from which a high-quality bark cloth can be made, is found exclusively in these environments.

Minimally Anthropogenic Savannas

The forelands of the Gobnangou escarpment have been shaped by hundreds of years of cultivation. The effects of this cultivation have increased significantly over the last century due to the combined factors of increasing population, a greater emphasis on cash crops, and decreasing settlement mobility, as well as limitations on access to arable land resulting from the creation of large parks and reserves (Belemsobgo et al. 2010). The result has been a more intensive agricultural strategy in which more land is brought under cultivation and fallow periods are reduced. Consequently, contemporary surveys like Küppers's (1996) are of limited use in characterizing the lowland savanna vegetation of the Gobnangou during periods of less intensive cultivation.

Much of southeastern Burkina Faso, northern Benin, and southwestern Niger was set aside as parkland (Arly National Park, Pendjari National Park, and W of the Niger National Park) or partial reserves (Kourtiagou and Singou) in the 1930s. Most of the few remaining villages in these areas were relocated to outside park boundaries in the 1950s (Koster 1982; Casti and Yonkeu 2009; Belemsobgo et al. 2010; Kaboré 2018). Before the establishment of this parkland, these areas had low population densities and later were spared most of the effects of rapid population growth and agricultural expansion of the latter third of the twentieth century. Although not perfect replicas of earlier savanna landscapes, particularly given the use of controlled burning strategies designed to increase the visibility of game for tourists (Koster 1982) and the restriction of human activity (including limits on hunting, fishing, and the gathering of wild plants), national parks are the best available analog to these landscapes (Park W, Koster 1982; Arly, O. Ouédraogo et al. 2011).

Although parkland vegetation is similar in species composition to other areas (notably in the predominance of *Combretum* spp. as well as the presence of *Burkea africana* and *Terminalia* spp. variants), park vegetation is often significantly more robust, with canopy heights reaching 15 to 20 m. However, within the parks hardpans and other areas of shallow or rocky soils produce vegetation with heights closer to those of the Gobnangou escarpment. More significantly, the park savannas are frequently broken by patches of open grasslands characterized by species such as *Loudetia togoensis* and *Microchloa indica,* which are not favored for ungulate grazing. These grasslands differ from those on the escarpment highlands in overall species composition as well as in the presence of isolated shrubs.

Given their similarity, it is not surprising that the useful plants of the parks largely mirror those found on the escarpment. The greatest difference between the two zones is in fodder plants. The minimally anthropogenic savanna has a greater diversity of higher-quality fodders than the highland savannas and would be significantly better for grazing (perhaps in part accounting for the significant problems with illegal grazing in national parks [Koster 1982]). Additionally, the more robust woody vegetation is more desirable for construction use. The only significant food plant not found on the escarpment is the fast growing, heavily fruiting *Moringa olifera,* which is valued for its leaves and seeds.

Aside from these fairly marginal benefits (especially given the relative unimportance of livestock in the region), the close availability of minimally anthropogenic savanna would have added little diversity to the resources already available on the escarpment. The primary effect of this close availability would have been on ease of access and increased supply, particularly of mature trees.

Riverine Corridors
Although outside the survey region, the riparian environments along the Pendjari River, while in many respects similar to minimally anthropogenic savannas, include several species characteristic of Guinean forests (such as *Combretum paniculatum* and *Dialium guineense*). The riverine environment can be divided into three simplified zones characterized by the following vegetation: the aquatic plants of the river itself; the grasses, sedges, and other herbs that grow in its floodplain; and the gallery forests along the banks. These moisture-loving plants often extend from the Pendjari along its seasonal feeder drainages, particularly in areas where the water table is high. Today gallery forests abut the Gobnangou escarpment only within the confines of Arly National Park, although their current range has likely been restricted by intensive agricultural activity (see above).

Specialized Plant Communities
There are several specialized plant communities around the fringes of the Gobnangou. In most cases they differ from those in the areas already discussed in species distribution and frequency rather than in composition, yet they are important sources of variability. For example, in the northeastern area of the escarpment near Kodjari the composition of the flora is largely comparable to that of the adjacent highlands because of similarities in their soils created by the underlying slate bedrock. However, in the lowland slate community, *Crossopteryx febrifuga*, an important fever reducer, is dominant among the tree species.

Agriculture and Cultivated Plants

Located near the southern limit of the Sudanian savanna, residents of the Gobnangou historically grow a particularly diverse spectrum of crops (Tables 5 and 6). Rainfall totals are low enough that savanna crops like pearl millet can thrive, but also high enough that some forest crops, such as yams, can also be cultivated. Additionally, the different soils include the sandy, well-drained matrices preferred by legumes as well as waterlogged lowlands suitable for growing small crops of rice. The long growing season adds more flexibility. Swanson (1979b:35) notes that space and labor are often the limiting factors. As mentioned above, multiple varieties of almost every crop are grown. Intraspecies varietal differences not only act as a buffer against climatic uncertainty, they also help farmers space out the harvest over several months and mix preferred characteristics in the total harvest (such as storability, parasite resistance, and flavor). Significant effort is made to maintain varietal seed stocks (Swanson 1979b).

Spatial Distribution of Farming Activities
Farming activities in the region create patchy landscapes of permanent or long-term cultivation, shifting cultivation, fallows, and less modified savanna where wild resources predominate. Although often conceptualized as a series of rings emanating outward from the household or community (e.g., Pélissier 1966; Grove and Klein 1979; Okigbo 1984; Prudencio 1993), in practice different aspects of land use overlap, interlock, and intersect.

In the region today residents maintain year-round gardens along watercourses near escarpment springs. These gardens support cultivation of a broad range of vegetables and fruits that include a mix of indigenous vegetables such as okra and garden

TABLE 5. Crops of African origin and plants introduced before 1500 CE that are cultivated in the Gobnangou region. From Rémy (1967); Swanson (1979b); Geis-Tronich (1991); Küppers (1996); with additional information and botanical nomenclature from Burkill (1985, 1994, 1995, 1997, 2000, 2004) and the National Research Council Board on Science and Technology for International Development (NRC 1996, 2006, 2008). Gulmancema common names are from Swanson (1979b). *Key to sources*: B, Burkill; GT, Geis-Tronich; K, Küppers; NRC, National Research Council; R, Rémy; S, Swanson.

Family (Subfamily)	Scientific name	Common name			Primary useful part	Notes	References
		English	Gulmancema				
Gramineae	*Sorghum bicolor*	Sorghum	*Biadi, dimoandi*		Grain	Used not only as a starch, but also fermented to make the most common traditional alcohol (*daama*); at least twelve local varieties with different maturation rates and rainfall requirements	B, GT, K, NRC, R, S
Gramineae	*Pennisetum glaucum*	Pearl millet	*Diyue, dipiene*		Grain	Slightly less popular than sorghum, but can tolerate poor soils and drought; many varieties, including early and late maturing strains; difficult to store for multiple years	B, GT, K, NRC, R, S
Dioscoreaceae	*Dioscorea* spp.	Yam	*Anuga*		Root	Many varieties, most consumed in the pounded form known commonly as *fufu*; requires better soils and more agricultural labor than grains; Swanson notes high prices for grain in colonial period may have decreased yam cultivation	B, GT, S
Gramineae	*Oryza glaberrima*	African rice	*Muuli*		Grain	Local variety was grown on edges of waterlogged lowlands, but is now very rare; Swanson characterizes it as a hunger crop	B, NRC, R, S
Gramineae	*Digitaria exilis*	Fonio	*Imuaabi*		Grain	Currently grown in the far north of the Gulmance region; may have been supplanted in Gobnangou as an early crop by maize	B, GT, NRC, R, S
Leguminosae (Papilionoideae)	*Vigna unguiculata*	Cowpea	*Atuuna*		Seed	Most commonly consumed legume in the region; diverse preparations; at least eight local varieties; labor intensive and difficult to store	B, GT, K, NRC, R, S

Continued

TABLE 5 CONTINUED

Family (Subfamily)	Scientific name	Common name			Primary useful part	Notes	References
		English	Gulmancema				
Leguminosae (Papilionoideae)	*Vigna subterranea*	Groundnut	*Tiin-moana, tiin-piena, tiin-kpanga*		Seed	Diverse preparations; favors sandy soils near escarpment; can be stored for many years; many local varieties; has been supplanted in some areas by *Arachis hypogaea* (peanut)	B, GT, K, NRC, R, S
Malvaceae	*Abelmoschus esculentus*	Okra	*Imaani*		Fruit	Very common sauce ingredient; favored for mucilaginous qualities; some varieties are consumed fresh, others are sliced and dried for use during the winter and spring	B, GT, K, NRC, R, S
Malvaceae	*Hibiscus sabdariffa*	Roselle	*Tigoandi*		Fruit, calyx, seeds	Sour leaves and fleshy calyces common in sauces; iron-rich calyx can be dried for storage; seed may be used to make soumbala if *Parkia biglobosa* not available	B, GT, K, R, S
Solanaceae	*Solanum* sp.	African eggplant	*Akana*		Fruit	Small, egg-shaped fruits in many colors; easy to grow, although not particularly nutritious; consumed primarily in sauces	B, K, NRC, S
Liliaceae	*Allium* spp.	Onion	*Sualimasua*		Bulb	Uncertain when and how onions entered West Africa (some sources put the date at the fourteenth century CE); grown in gardens with irrigation	B, S
Lamiaceae	Possibly *Solenostemon rotundifolius*		*Apzala*		Root	Bush potato brought under cultivation in the Gobnangou region; possibly *Solenostemon rotundifolius*?	NRC, S
Amaranthaceae or Malvaceae	*Amaranthus* sp. or *Corchorus* sp.		*Anyinkpina*		Leaf	Cultivated version of a wild leafy green such as *Amaranthus* or *Corchorus*	S

Continued

TABLE 5 CONTINUED

Family (Subfamily)	Scientific name	Common name			Primary useful part	Notes	References
		English	Gulmancema				
Amaranthaceae or Malvaceae	*Amaranthus* sp. or *Corchorus* sp.		*Tikpankpandi*		Leaf	Cultivated version of a wild leafy green such as *Amaranthus* or *Corchorus*	S
Amaranthaceae or Malvaceae	*Amaranthus* sp. or *Corchorus* sp.		*Tinalifadi*		Leaf	Cultivated version of a wild leafy green such as *Amaranthus* or *Corchorus*	S
Cucurbitaceae	*Cucumis metuliferus*	Horned melon			Fruit	Eaten raw; can be stored at room temperature for up to six months	B, GT, K, NRC, S
Musaceae	*Musa* sp.	Banana, plantain	*Banane*		Fruit	Grown exclusively in gardens on seasonal drainages (needs year-round water); consumed primarily as fruit	B, S
Gramineae	*Saccharum officianarum*	Sugar cane	*Nasaali-kaanlo, kalakala*		Culm	Grown exclusively in gardens on seasonal drainages (needs year-round water); cut and chewed opportunistically; no local tradition of sugar refinement	B, GT, R, S
Gramineae	*Sorghum bicolor*	Sweet sorghum	*Kaanlo, kaano*		Culm	Sweet varieties are cut green for their stalk juice	B, GT, K, NRC, R, S
Palmae	*Elaeis guineensis*	Oil palm			Nut	Prefers moister climates than those of the study region; found only as isolated, cultivated specimens, particularly since *Vitellaria paradoxa* fills the same dietary niche	B, K
Pedaliaceae	*Sesamum orientale*	Sesame	*Ihen*		Seed	Oily seed usually consumed whole, cooked in porridge, or added to sauce; cultivation has expanded because of its value as a cash crop	B, GT, S

Continued

TABLE 5 CONTINUED

Family (Subfamily)	Scientific name	Common name			Primary useful part	Notes	References
		English	Gulmancema				
Malvaceae	*Gossypium* sp.	Cotton	*Kunkundi*		Fruit	Traditionally handspun, dyed with indigo, and woven in thin strips; indigenous varieties have been largely supplanted by commercial seed developed from American strains	B, GT, S
Leguminosae (Papilionoideae)	*Indigofera tinctoria*	Indigo	*Misiema*		Leaf	Branches, leaves, and flowers used to create a deep blue dye for cotton; cultivation has decreased with availability of commercial dyes	B, GT, S
Malvaceae	*Hibiscus cannabinus*	Kenaf	*Ibaligi*		Bark	Plants grown to the maximum possible height (often into the early dry season); stems soaked for several days, then stripped of bark to make a coarse, strong fiber resistant to rot	B, GT, S
Cucurbitaceae	*Lagenaria siceraria*	Calabash	*Otungu*		Fruit	Fruits have woody, impermeable shells used as containers; different varieties are used as bottles, bowls, ladles, etc.	B, GT, K, S
Cucurbitaceae	*Luffa cylindrica*	Loofah			Fruit	Uses include filtering liquids and consumption of the seed as a purgative; use of the fibrous vascular network as a sponge may be more recent	B, K
Unknown	Unknown		*Mibelima*			Small shrub used as a fish poison; cultivation forbidden under colonial rule; Swanson provides no information on scientific name	S

TABLE 6. Crops introduced to the Gobnangou region since 1500 CE. From Rémy (1967); Swanson (1979b); Geis-Tronich (1991); Küppers (1996); with additional information from Burkill (1985, 1994, 1995, 1997, 2000, 2004), Gallagher (2016), and the National Research Council Board on Science and Technology for International Development (NRC 2006). Gulmancema common names are from Swanson (1979b). *Key to sources*: B, Burkill; GT, Geis-Tronich; K, Küppers; NRC, National Research Council; R, Rémy; S, Swanson.

Family (Subfamily)	Scientific name	Common name — English	Common name — Gulmancema	Primary useful part	Introduced from	Notes	References
Gramineae	*Zea mays*	Maize	*Anuga*	Seed	Americas	Introduced to West Africa in the sixteenth century and has increased in popularity in recent years; primarily adopted as an early crop	B, GT, K, S
Convolvulaceae	*Ipomoea batatas*	Sweet potato	*Kuudiku, kuudiko*	Root	Americas	Sweet, starchy tuber usually used as a dietary supplement because it is difficult to store	B, GT, S
Euphorbiaceae	*Manihot esculentus*	Manioc	*Tangumbo, pangumbo, pangummo*	Root	Americas	Requires an elaborate leaching process to become edible; cultivation is currently expanding	B, GT, K, S
Dioscoreaceae	*Dioscorea esculenta*	Yam	*Anuga*	Root	Southeast Asia	Variety recently introduced to the region; has a relatively high yield, but not suitable for making fufu	B, K
Gramineae	*Oryza sativa*	Rice	*Muuli*	Seed	East Asia	Introduced by the French in 1952–1953 to expand local rice production	B, R, S
Leguminosae (Papilionoideae)	*Arachis hypogaea*	Peanut	*Tiina-namaga*	Seed	Americas	Favors sandy soils; often grown as a cash crop, but also used in local diets; occasionally used to make a roasted peanut oil	B, GT, K, S
Leguminosae (Papilionoideae)	*Vigna radiata*	Green gram		Seed	India	Recently introduced; grown on a very limited basis	B, K

Continued

TABLE 6 CONTINUED

Family (Subfamily)	Scientific name	Common name			Primary useful part	Introduced from	Notes	References
		English	Gulmancema					
Amaranthaceae	*Amaranthus hybridus*	Amaranth			Leaf	Americas	Grows spontaneously, but may also be cultivated; leaves are eaten fresh or in sauces; has hybridized with indigenous varieties	B, K, NRC
Cucurbitaceae	*Cucurbita pepo*	Squash	*Afela*		Fruit	Americas	Several varieties are commonly cultivated	B, GT, K, S
Solanaceae	*Capsicum annuum*	Chili pepper	*Ikambi*		Fruit	Americas	Used as flavoring	B, K
Solanaceae	*Capsicum fructescens*	Cayene pepper	*Ikambi*		Fruit	Americas	Used as flavoring	B, GT, K, S
Solanaceae	*Lycopersicum esculentum*	Tomato			Fruit	Americas	Common sauce ingredient; often grown in dry season gardens	B, K
Apiaceae	*Daucus carota* ssp. *sativa*	Carrot			Root	Europe	European garden vegetable introduced by colonial officials and missionaries	B, S
Apiaceae	*Lactuca sativa*	Lettuce			Leaf	Europe	European garden vegetable introduced by colonial officials and missionaries	B, S
Brassicaceae	*Brassica oleracea*	Cabbage			Leaf	Europe	European garden vegetable introduced by colonial officials and missionaries	B,
Anacardiaceae	*Mangifera indica*	Mango	*Maabu*		Fruit	India	Matures late in the dry season when it is one of the few fresh fruits available; introduced in nineteenth century	B, GT, K, S

egg; varieties that may have spread to the region in the fifteenth to seventeenth centuries, such as chili pepper; and plants that are recorded as twentieth-century introductions, such as cabbage and carrots (Swanson 1979b; Geis-Tronich 1991; Gallagher 2016). Interestingly, none of the researchers in the region have documented the presence of the indigenous melons (watermelon or *egusi*) *Citrullus* spp. and *Cucumis* spp. (Rémy 1967; Swanson 1979b; Geis-Tronich 1991; Küppers 1996). These gardens also include water-loving plants like sugar cane and oil palm, which are rarely found this far north in West Africa (Swanson 1979b; although see Champion and Fuller 2019). Swanson (1979b) notes that small crops of rice were occasionally planted in the past along the edges of some of the larger drainages.

Vegetables are grown during the rainy season in the close fields directly outside household compounds. These fields, which are often the most heavily fertilized with household waste and manure, are also used to grow early season staple crops that are among the first plants to fruit; consequently, these plantings often suffer greater losses to birds and other animals than late season crops (Swanson 1979b). Historically, tobacco was commonly planted in these fields once the early staple crops had been harvested (e.g., Rémy 1967; Prudencio 1993). Priority is also usually given to early season staple crops in fields located slightly farther from the household and significant effort may be put into weeding, maintaining soil fertility with manure or techniques such as burning of collected brush, and using soil conservation strategies such as mulching (Prudencio 1993). Yams, which may have been a staple in the past when the climate was more humid, are now grown primarily as a supplementary crop in close fields because they require more labor and higher-quality soils (Rémy 1967; Swanson 1979b).

Most of the harvest comes from late staple crops (millet and sorghum), which tend to be grown in fields farther from the household. Less energy is expended for these fields once the crop is planted; that is, the fields are rarely fertilized and often less frequently weeded. Successions of different major crop types are used on rotational bush fields (for example, sorghum–millet–cowpea; Swanson 1979a, 1979b), whereas for the distant shifting fields new land may be regularly cleared. Nonedible domesticates, including cotton, indigo, and roselle, were also grown.

Agricultural fields are not only used for cultivated plants. Edible wild species will often be left in place when found growing in fields. Several species of useful tree—notably *Acacia* spp., *Adansonia digitata*, *Vitellaria paradoxa*, *Lannea acida* and *L. microcarpa*, *Parkia biglobosa*, and *Tamarindus indicus*—are preserved when clearing fields, creating what is often referred to as a "park savanna" (Pullan 1974; Swanson 1979a, 1979b; Küppers 1996:13; Boffa 1999; Bayala et al. 2015; Figure 12). These trees are often the oldest and largest plants in the agricultural savanna and their visual dominance on the landscape belies their sparse distribution. Shea butter (*V. paradoxa*) and locust bean, or *nere* (*P. biglobosa*), can be considered staples and baobab (*A. digitata*) and tamarind (*T. indicus*) are significant elements of the diet. Because their productive lifespans can last hundreds of years (possibly thousands in the case of baobab), these trees are found in all stages of fallow in addition to in active agricultural fields.

Although the presence of these trees can negatively affect yields because of competition for water and nutrients, as well as from the effects of shade, economic trees are also beneficial for grain production (Pullen 1974; Boffa 1999; Assé and Lassoie 2011; Bayala et al. 2015). Trees can improve soil hydrology, fertility, erosion, and aeration and contribute leaf mulch, in addition to their other uses. Fields are likewise beneficial to the trees. As mature individuals with little competition, these trees often significantly out-produce the larger populations of fruit trees growing in the less fertile soils of the escarpment and are among the most economically valuable wild plants in the region (see the discussions in Gallagher, Dueppen, and Walsh [2016]).

Fallows and Fallow Vegetation

The soils of young fallows (one to three years from cultivation) are generally exhausted and have very little humus content. During the first few years of growth, the vegetation in these locations is dominated by nonwoody species that colonize open areas and thrive in low-nutrient conditions. As mentioned above, soils in the region recover slowly and although species composition changes, medium fallows (five to ten years from cultivation) are likewise dominated by nonwoody and grassy vegetation. Most of the plants found in these recovering fallow fields are of limited utility to humans and grazing is the primary activity. In young fallows, grain can be harvested from uniform stands of wild grasses such as *Brachiaria villosa* or *Dactyloctenium aegyptium,* but more frequently they are either used as fodder or cut for thatch. Medium fallows are still grazed, but the grasses (e.g., *Andropogon* spp.) shift toward species less amenable for human consumption. With the exception of trees left in place during cultivation, plants used for fruit, fiber, firewood, and construction are usually not yet mature enough to be exploited.

In the second and third decades of fallow, the vegetation matures and the community is dominated by a shrubby bush characterized by such plants as *Combretum* spp., *Piliostigma* spp., and *Terminalia* spp. Grazing is slightly improved with the addition of shrubs to the still extant grassy and other nonwoody species. In old fallows, food plants are still relatively rare compared with the highland savannas, although a few fruits and some leafy greens become available. However, in very old fallows (more than thirty years from cultivation), the assortment of mature edible plants, particularly trees and shrubs, increases significantly and begins to approach the diversity of options in highland and minimally anthropogenic savannas.

The woody vegetation in older fallows is most significant as a source of wood for construction and fuel. Several significant firewood species, notably *Anogeissus leiocarpus, Combretum glutinosum, Piliostigma thonningii,* and *Vitellaria paradoxa* (which in fallow fields are often too young to bear fruit), are common. Many of these can also be used for construction, although those in old fallows are more likely exploited for the slender poles that support granaries and temporary housing, as opposed to primary house posts that come from mature trees more commonly found in very old fallows and less anthropogenic landscapes.

Cultural Mediation of Farming Practice

Farmers across the African savanna rely on similar crop complexes in generally similar climate and soil conditions, resulting in broad commonalities in agricultural strategies (for example, maintenance of useful trees in fields, long fallows, and generally few inputs). Yet differences in land tenure rights, labor, mobility, and other factors result in dramatically different practices that can have long-term effects on the landscape (see the historical reviews in Lentz [2006, 2013]; also the discussions in M. Marchal [1983], Baker [2000], and Korbéogo [2013]). In the study region, Gulmance farming has been documented in detail by two scholars: Rémy (1967) focused his research on the community of Yobri, located at the base of the Gobnangou escarpment; Swanson (1979a, 1979b) surveyed Gulmance

FIGURE 12. Parkland savanna in the Maadaga Archaeological Survey study region in March 2006.

agriculture throughout eastern Burkina Faso. This discussion emphasizes the Gobnangou and draws primarily on these historical studies, thus it subsumes significant spatial and temporal variability in Gulmance farming practices. Although Gulmance farmers today maintain continuities with the organizational structures discussed, increasing land pressure and cotton farming are spurring changes in land tenure and labor.

According to Swanson and Rémy, Gulmance farmers in the mid to late twentieth century were committed cultivators who valued mobility and emphasized household independence in agricultural decision-making. Agricultural labor among the Gulmance was almost entirely performed by the household unit, with communal labor used only rarely for weeding or harvesting (Swanson 1979a, 1979b). Although all household members cultivated staple grains, additional crops were often highly gendered (for example, women cultivated okra and men cultivated yams). Like many cultivators who frequently move their fields, the Gulmance gained perpetual rights to land by clearing and farming it. Within this land tenure system, mobility acted as a crucial "reset" mechanism; in cases like the Gobnangou where populations were tied to a single location by colonial authorities, complex webs of borrowed and lent land quickly developed, and residents were forced to use new mobile strategies to maintain access to land (Rémy 1967).

A central element of Rémy's analysis is an explanation of the *kwadiegu*, or bush field, system, which both he and Swanson characterized as a recent innovation developed in response to attempts by colonial governments to encourage more sedentary agricultural practices. Although farmers maintained their residences in villages during the dry season, in the rainy season they moved to dispersed compounds close to their agricultural fields. The same *kwadiegu* was frequently used for multiple growing seasons and several farmers could locate their *kwadiegu* in the same general area, forming impromptu neighborhoods that dissolved when households moved to a new location. Both Rémy and Swanson assumed that before the colonial era households would have moved with their fields on a regular basis, resulting in a more dispersed landscape with less intensive impacts on any given location.

Fauna

Mammals, Reptiles, Amphibians, and Birds

The animals of the West African savanna range from species with generalized savanna adaptations to those restricted in their ecological requirements (Table 7). Aquatic species, like hippopotamus (*Hippopotamus amphibius*) or crocodile (*Crocodylus* spp. and *Osteolaemus* spp.), reside in permanent rivers or pools. The gallery forests along riverbanks tend to be home to diverse, often smaller, animals, including primates and many small antelopes. These forest ungulates tend to be solitary or live in pairs, unlike those in the savannas around the escarpment, which are often found in herds (Kingdon 2004). Many of these savanna species require water daily or every couple of days and cannot range too far from permanent water sources during the dry season. Finally, a few specialized species, such as the rock hyrax (*Procavia capensis*), are confined to rocky areas (Kingdon 2004). In practice, the mosaic nature of the savanna interspersed with gallery forest around the base of the Gobnangou is such that there was likely significant variability in the ways in which wild fauna interacted with human populations.

Most significantly for farmers, some wild animals feed on agricultural fields. Wild fowl often raid newly planted fields for seed during the early rainy season (Donkin 1991); small ungulates graze on the tender shoots of young crops (Kingdon 2004); and cane rats (*Thryonomys swinderianus*) will consume almost any grass (including millet), melons, and other vegetables at any stage of growth (Happold 1987; Estes 1991; Kingdon 2004). A patchwork layout of fields and savanna provides easy access to useful wild plants, but also provides habitat for these raiders, most of which favor littoral zones. Dry season gardens are often fenced to protect crops, but this strategy is not practical at a large scale and farmers and their families often reside near their fields during the growing season to protect them. Although destructive, these animals are also easy targets for garden hunting, a practice that provides a small, steady supply of meat (see the discussions in Dueppen [2012a] and Dueppen and Gallagher [2013]). Garden hunting often involves the use of traps, slings, and other expedient methods, in addition to more traditional bows and spears, and may be carried out by any member of the family. Such crop destruction is not limited to small animals, as larger ungulates and other animals such as elephants can feed on fields. Elephants damage fields simply by walking through them and are known to uproot orchards and other useful trees or damage branches and roots.

Many ungulate taxa in the region tend to avoid humans. Generally larger, these herd animals, including hartebeest (*Alcelaphus buselaphus*), roan antelope (*Hippotragus equinus*), buffalo (*Syncerus caffer*), and topi (*Damaliscus lunatus*), are usually far from human settlements (Estes 1991; Kingdon 1997) where they avoid competition for food with livestock and hunting pressure by humans. They are frequently hunted, primarily during the dry season when hunters are free from agricultural labor and animals are more easily located near water sources. Today they are rarely seen in the study region, preferring the large parks and reserves. Hunts have historically involved a variety of ritual practices and the animal products, both meat and hides, are important to local economies (Alves 2012).

The African savanna is home to an extraordinary diversity of carnivores. Although most avoid human settlements or are too small to cause problems, larger carnivores such as the cats, African hunting dogs (*Lycaon pictus*), and hyaenas (such as *Crocuta crocuta*) occasionally raid livestock and can endanger humans (Estes 1991). The meat of these animals is usually considered inferior, but they may be hunted for their hides or fur.

Fish and Shellfish

Like most rivers in West Africa, the Pendjari has a diverse and understudied population of fishes, although a recent survey identified at least 112 species from 59 genera, spread over 28 families (Moritz and Lalèyè 2018; see also Schwahn 2003). Distribution both in taxa and in size varies with seasonal changes in the depth and quality of water. During the dry season most fish are confined to the main channel of the Pendjari, with the occasional remnant pools along seasonal drainages limited to smaller individuals and taxa with tolerance for low-oxygen conditions, such as tilapia (Tilapiini) and *Clarias* catfish (Clariidae). During the wet season, a wider variety of fishes spawn throughout the network of seasonal drainages (including the Koabu), although some taxa still tend to inhabit the main drainages of the larger tributaries and the Pendjari itself (such as Nile perch, *Lates niloticus*). Fishing practices by communities are scheduled to take advantage of the changing fish distributions, ranging from deep-water fishing in main channels by boat, fishing in the floodplain for spawning fish during the floods, and the very common practice of catching fish trapped in residual pools at the end of the floods into the dry season. Technologies used differ with these strategies and include opportunistic line fishing, the use of nets, and the construction of small weirs and traps set in channels. Today, specialized dry-season fishing camps are common along the Pendjari River and preserved smoked fish is sold at local markets throughout the region. In addition to fish, freshwater bivalves are commonly collected at low-water in the late dry season.

Domestic Animals, Herding, and Pastoralism

Domestic animals are an integral part of socioeconomic systems in the region. They are intimately involved in agricultural systems, are used as social wealth, play central roles in rituals, guard property, and provide defense, in addition to being important food sources. In the contemporary cultural setting, with agricultural development projects and changing environmental conditions, the number of breeds and species present is expanding rapidly.

Goats (*Capra hircus*), and to a lesser extent sheep (*Ovis aries*), are historically the most common stock in the region. Herds were composed almost exclusively of dwarf varieties, selected for tolerance to trypanosomiasis and hardiness. Although their diets (primarily browse for goats and graze for sheep) are similar to those of other varieties, dwarf livestock are generally considered village animals and rarely stray far from settlements (Epstein 1971). While they significantly affect local vegetation, dwarf livestock tend to be kept in smaller numbers and consequently have a more minimal effect on environments than the larger Sahelian breeds common in less forested zones. Within the last century, given the combined effects of land clearance, governmental tsetse eradication programs, and environmental changes, increasing numbers of Fulani herders have moved into the region. As a result, there are two domesticated livestock production systems in place today: a residential, more sedentary program based around dwarf breeds and a nomadic, seasonal system that more significantly affects vegetation (Koster 1982).

Cattle (*Bos taurus*) follow essentially the same patterns as sheep and goat. Dwarf varieties have great antiquity in the region (see Dueppen 2012c), whereas the larger Sahelian breeds are newer additions primarily associated with nomadic Fulani herders. Additionally, Gulmance farmers have acquired larger breeds of cattle as animal traction and the use of oxen has become more popular (Swanson 1979b). Seasonality is important in

TABLE 7. Wild mammals larger than 1 kg found in various environments in southeastern Burkina Faso. Compiled from Kingdon (2004).

Scientific name	Common name	Size (kg)	Habitat					Diet
			Savanna grassland	Forest mosaic	Rocky slopes	Marsh or riverine	Raids fields	
Primates								
Cercopithecus patas	Patas monkey	7–25	x	x			x	Flowers, fruits, leaves, seeds; favors *Acacia* and *Balanites*
Cercopithecus tantalus	Tantalus monkey	5.5–9	x	x			x	Bark, buds, fruit, gum, roots, seeds, cultivated plants
Galago senegalensis	Senegal galago	0.11–0.30	x	x				Fruit, gum, invertebrates
Papio anubis	Olive baboon	11–50	x	x	x		x	Fruit, grass
Insectivores								
Atelerix albiventris	African hedgehog	0.25–1.6	x					Fruit, fungi, invertebrates, small vertebrates
Crocidura sp.	White-toothed shrew	0.1–0.4	x	x	x	x		Invertebrates, small vertebrates
Hares								
Lepus capensis	Cape hare	1–3.5	x				x	Grass, herbs
Lepus saxatilis	Scrub hare	1.5–4.5	x	x			x	Grass

Continued

TABLE 7 CONTINUED

Scientific name	Common name	Size (kg)	Habitat					Diet
			Savanna grassland	Forest mosaic	Rocky slopes	Marsh or riverine	Raids fields	
Rodents								
Cricetomys gambianus	Gambian rat, northern giant pouched rat	1–1.4	x	x			x	Fruit, leaves, nuts, roots
Hystrix cristata	Crested porcupine	12–27			x			Bark, fruit, roots
Thyronomys swinderianus	Marsh cane rat	4.5–8.8				x	x	Grass
Carnivores								
Acinonyx jubatus	Cheetah	35–65	x	x				Gazelle, impala, kob, springbok
Aonyx capensis	African clawless otter	12–34				x		Crabs, frogs
Atilax paludinosus	Marsh mongoose	2.2–5				x		Catfish, crabs, frogs, lungfish, mussels, snails
Canis adustus	Side-striped jackal	7.3–12	x					Omnivorous
Civettictis civetta	African civet	7–20		x		x		Omnivorous
Crocuta crocuta	Spotted hyaena	40–90	x					Carnivorous scavenger
Felis caracal	Caracal	12–19	x		x			Antelopes, birds, hares, hyraxes, small monkeys, rodents

Continued

TABLE 7 CONTINUED

Scientific name	Common name	Size (kg)	Habitat					Diet
			Savanna grassland	Forest mosaic	Rocky slopes	Marsh or riverine	Raids fields	
Felis serval	Serval	6–18	x	x		x		Birds, insects, small mammals, reptiles
Felis sylvestris	Wild cat	3–6.5	x	x				Birds, small mammals, mice, rats
Genetta genetta	Common genet	1.3–2.25	x					Fruit, invertebrates, small vertebrates
Genetta thierryi	Hausa genet	1.3–1.5	x					Invertebrates, rodents
Genetta tigrina	Blotched genet	1.2–3.1		x				Birds, invertebrates, frogs, reptiles, rodents
Herpestes ichneumon	Ichneumon mongoose	2.2–4.1				x		Birds, invertebrates, frogs, reptiles, rodents
Herpestes sanguinea	Slender mongoose	0.35–0.8	x	x	x			Birds, insects, frogs, reptiles, rodents
Ichneumia albicauda	White-tailed mongoose	2–5.2	x	x		x		Frogs, invertebrates, mice, reptiles
Ictonyx libyca	Zorilla	0.7–1.4	x					Invertebrates
Lutra maculicollis	Spot-necked otter	4–6.5				x		Crabs, fish, frogs, mollusks, other aquatics
Lycaon pictus	Wild dog	18–36	x	x				Mammals
Mellivora capensis	Ratel, honey badger	7–16	x	x				Omnivorous
Mungos gambianus	Gambian mongoose	1–2	x	x				Invertebrates, small vertebrates

Continued

TABLE 7 CONTINUED

Scientific name	Common name	Size (kg)	Habitat					Diet
			Savanna grassland	Forest mosaic	Rocky slopes	Marsh or riverine	Raids fields	
Mungos mungo	Banded mongoose	1.5–2.25	×	×				Beetle larvae, termites
Panthera leo	Lion	122–260	×	×	×	×		Medium-large mammals
Panthera pardus	Leopard	28–90	×	×	×			Birds, small to medium mammals
Vulpes pallida	Sand fox	2–3.6	×					Invertebrates, small vertebrates
Afrotheria								
Loxodonta africana	African elephant	2,200–6,300	×	×	×	×	×	Vegetation
Orycteropus afer	Aardvark	40–82	×	×				Ants, larvae, termites
Procavia capensis	Rock hyrax	1.8–5.5			×		×	Grass, herbs
Ungulates								
Alcelaphus buselaphus	Hartebeest	116–218	×	×				Grass, herbs
Cephalophus maxwelli	Maxwell's duiker	6–10		×				Fruits, herbs
Cephalophus rufilatus	Red-flanked duiker	6–14		×		×		Fruits, herbs
Cephalophus silvicultor	Yellow-backed duiker	45–80		×		×		Bark, berries, fruits, herbs, moss, seeds
Damaliscus lunatus	Topi	75–160	×			×		Grass

Continued

TABLE 7 CONTINUED

Scientific name	Common name	Size (kg)	Habitat					Diet
			Savanna grassland	Forest mosaic	Rocky slopes	Marsh or riverine	Raids fields	
Gazella rufifrons	Red-fronted gazelle	15–35	×					Grass, herbs, leaves, seeds
Giraffa camelopardalis	Giraffe	450–1930	×	×				Leaves; prefers *Acacia*, *Commiphora*, and *Terminalia*
Hippopotamus amphibius	Hippopotamus	510–3,200				×	×	Grass
Hippotragus equinus	Roan antelope	223–300	×	×				Grass, herbs, occasional shrubs
Kobus ellipsiprymnus	Waterbuck	160–300	×	×		×		Grass, reeds, rushes
Kobus kob	Kob	82–121	×	×		×		Grass
Ourebia ourebi	Oribi	12–22	×				×	Grass
Phacochoerus africanus	Common warthog	45–150	×	×		×	×	Grass, herbs
Redunca redunca	Bohor reedbuck	35–65	×	×		×	×	Grass, herbs
Sylvicapra grimmia	Common duiker	11–25.5	×	×			×	Fruits, leaves, shoots
Syncerus caffer	African buffalo	250–850	×	×				Grass, swamp vegetation
Taurotragus derbianus	Derby's eland	300–907	×					Grass, herbs, leguminous trees
Tragelaphus scriptus	Bushbuck	24–80	×	×			×	Grass, leguminous herbs, shrubs
Tragelaphus spekei	Sitatunga	40–130				×		Grass, herbs, shrubs

raising stock; during the rainy season livestock must be either penned or removed from farming zones to avoid the destruction of fields.

Sheep, goats, and cattle are all forms of storable and transferable wealth and are used in social transactions, although cattle are usually accorded greater prestige. With their higher social value, cattle are rarely slaughtered outside of special occasions (see Cartry 1987); sheep and goat are more commonly consumed and are a primary source of meat (Rémy 1967). Most dwarf breeds have limited use for dairy production and tend to stay close to settlements (Epstein 1971). During the dry season they fertilize nearby fields while feeding on the crop remnants; in the wet season they are more confined and their manure may be collected.

Chickens (*Gallus gallus*) and guinea fowl (*Numida meleagris*) are an important component of subsistence economies as a more day-to-day source of food. They feed themselves on seeds, bugs, and trash found near settlements and are an affordable, reliable, and low investment source of meat. Consequently, they are frequently consumed and are often used in ritual sacrifice (e.g., Tauxier 1912; Swanson 1985; Dueppen 2011).

Dogs (*Canis familiaris*), an extremely flexible species adapted to a variety of environments, are used for herding, guarding, and companionship. Their omnivorous diet is drawn mainly from scavenging at the edge of settlements (Epstein 1971). The keeping of donkeys (*Equus asinus*) and pigs (*Sus scrofa*) has expanded in recent years. Donkeys were primarily used for portage along trade routes and would have had difficulty in the Gobnangou because of their lack of trypanosomiasis tolerance. Pigs are omnivorous animals that can forage for food, including refuse, in human communities. Although not identified archaeologically, they are a common source of meat today in the Gobnangou, where there are few local taboos against their consumption and, similar to livestock, they can be used to accumulate wealth.

Climate and Vegetation Histories

The discussion to this point has been for the most part restricted to current and recent conditions in the region. However, the local environment has changed significantly over the past several thousand years, caused by a combination of natural and anthropogenic processes. The nature and extent of the latter are a focus of this work and discussed throughout the book. This section provides background on the natural processes of climate change and their overall effects on vegetation.

By using lake level chronologies, pollen cores, and other techniques, significant progress has been made toward documenting the timing and degree of dry and wet periods in West Africa (Maley and Vernet 2015; Nash et al. 2016; Lüning et al. 2018; Shanahan 2018). These studies have revealed significant variability across the region. For example, there is evidence for a humid phase at Lake Chad and in the Niger Bend region during late first millennium CE (Maley and Vernet 2015), yet the overall regional trend is one of increasing aridification (Nash et al. 2016). Lüning and colleagues (2018) suggest that the medieval climate anomaly in the early second millennium CE had different effects on precipitation in different parts of West Africa. These results show the importance of localized paleoclimate sequences, which in the Gobnangou region are provided by the charcoal excavated and identified by the German–Burkinabe team at the site of Péntènga rockshelter (Frank et al. 2001).

The earliest charcoal samples date to around 6100 cal BCE. They indicate a relatively high degree of woody plant cover and probably minimal human influence on the landscape.

Precipitation may have increased during the mid-Holocene (to approx. 900 to 1,200 mm per year), but not enough to drastically affect the vegetation and species composition of dry forests. Beginning around 3600 cal BCE, species composition changed and reflects a more arid climate, although species indicative of remnant dry forests remained. In addition, the appearance of more fire-resistant species and evidence of trauma in rings of larger trees indicate that brush fires became more common. Whether these were a side effect of less precipitation or intentionally set by humans is not yet known. The diverse savanna environment, including dry Guinean forests, remained fairly constant until at least 1100 CE (the end of the charcoal sequence), with no evidence for periods of significant aridification. This suggests that the escarpment contained sufficient moisture for pockets of dry Guinean forest to persist, likely in ravines and canyons, despite climate perturbations. More humid conditions in the late first millennium CE are also supported by the faunal record from site MAS541 (Dueppen and Gallagher 2013; see the discussions in Chapter 5).

More interesting than the species present are those that are conspicuously absent, notably *Combretum glutinosum*. This shrub, which is an excellent firewood, is particularly abundant in fields lying fallow. Other species indicative of agriculture or large fallows are also missing (e.g., *Guiera senegalensis* and *Annona senegalensis*). Thus, the charcoal sequence indicates that intensive farming occurred for the first time after 1100 CE.

Overall, vegetation zones in West Africa are generally delimited using rainfall isohyets and, historically, the advances and retreats of these zones accompanied transitions from dry to humid periods. The study region sits near the southern border of the Sudanian savanna. During humid optimums the vegetation would likely have been similar to that of Guinean forest. A comparison of the minimally anthropogenic savannas and the riverine forests (which contain Guinean elements) shows that, with a few exceptions, the differences would have been predominantly in species balance rather than composition (see Table 4).

Conclusion

The geology and hydrology of the Gobnangou region create diverse microenvironments and foster even higher species richness, making it an attractive location for human habitation. The main crops today are largely associated with savanna farming (for example, millet, sorghum, and cowpea), although the microenvironments also allow limited cultivation of forest crops. Although not ideal for most domesticated animals, given the presence of tsetse flies, some breeds are adapted to local conditions and the human diet can be supplemented with abundant wild game. All resources are nearby such that communities could easily access multiple zones, however the survey zone was defined to include multiple microenvironmental zones to more fully explore variability in the cultural landscape.

With their long-term knowledge of the parameters of effective food production in the savanna ecosystem, historical societies in West Africa have developed reliable economic strategies bridging the seasonal, annual, and interannual scales. What differs greatly throughout the region is the way in which these practices articulate with different residential and settlement system organizations. In the Gobnangou, the extensive nature of agriculture is today coupled with an extensive strategy of space rooted in intergenerational movements. As will be examined in subsequent chapters, this was not always the case in the archaeological record, reinforcing the need to focus on the complex dynamics between social and political influences and local ecologies on the development of cultural landscapes.

CHAPTER THREE

THE MAADAGA
ARCHAEOLOGICAL SURVEY
Methodologies and Relative Chronology

The Maadaga Archaeological Survey research program incorporated both full coverage survey and excavations. Although a large German–Burkinabe project had previously researched the study region, its survey in the late 1980s focused on the escarpment itself and areas along roads to the north. Its excavation program emphasized sites with assemblages characterized primarily by chipped stone (see the discussions in Chapter 4; Breunig and Wotzka 1991; Millogo 1993a; Millogo and Koté 2000; Frank et al. 2001). The MAS aimed to complement previous work by focusing its survey on a seasonal drainage extending south from the escarpment and by targeting (presumably agricultural) sites with large ceramic assemblages for excavation.

The surveyed area formed a triangle of approximately 75 km² and was anchored by the site of Maadaga rockshelter, located at the head of a large seasonal drainage. It was bounded on the northwest by the Gobnangou escarpment, on the south by the road from Kidikanbou to Paliboa, and on the north by the road from Maadaga to Paliboa. These boundaries were chosen to sample a variety of local microenvironmental zones and included the seasonal Koabu drainage, a seasonal lake, seasonally inundated marshy zones, sandy levees, uplands with different soil depths, a perennial spring, rockshelters, and both gently sloping and steep portions of the escarpment. Because the escarpment had been the primary focus of previous research, the orientation of the surveyed area facilitated the identification of sites farther from the cliff. The decreasing size of the survey zone as distance increased reflected both the catchment of the Koabu drainage and the practical difficulties of surveying areas farther from the escarpment without a vehicle. To increase the sample at a distance from the escarpment, we extended the survey area to the east near Paliboa.

Field research took place over the course of two seasons. A four-week pilot season in January and February 2004 included general reconnaissance, a preliminary survey, shovel testing, and excavations at one site. From March to June 2006 a more intensive eleven-week season carried out a full coverage survey and excavations at five sites.

Survey Methodologies

In 2004, the MAS conducted a small pilot survey program, documenting sites and taking opportunistic surface collections in seven survey blocks distributed throughout the drainage (total area 16 km^2). Between seasons we drew on the results of this initial survey to develop a systematic protocol for site definition, documentation, and surface collection adapted to the characteristics of the local archaeological record. Consequently, we revisited and redocumented all sites identified in 2004 during the 2006 fieldwork, with the exception of a few that lay outside the survey zone (see Appendix D). The data collected in 2004 was merged under the 2006 site numbers for the purposes of analysis.

The MAS carried out a full coverage survey of the study area in 2006, identifying 517 sites (Figure 13; Appendix A). The survey team consisted of a group of three to four individuals (Daphne Gallagher, Stephen Dueppen, Diassibo Ouaba, and Marcel Zongo) who walked more than 300 km of transects at 20 m spacing. Given the distributed nature of settlement in the region, many sites were located near currently occupied households. Over the course of the survey we interacted with hundreds of local residents who allowed us into their fields and provided valuable contextual information.

We recorded all sites with artifacts or indicators of cultural activity unless the remains were clearly derived from currently occupied or recently abandoned structures (defined as structures with standing architecture). We assigned each site a consecutive site number beginning with MAS500 (so as not to overlap with the numbering system used by the German–Burkinabe project) and gave clustered groups of distinct settlement locations (sites) the same primary number during survey (for example, MAS572.1, MAS572.2, and so on), because at the time we assumed that they represented different parts of a single site. Analyses indicated that these clusters were the result of diverse processes. Some may have been simultaneously occupied, but others may have resulted from practices such as building new houses adjacent to old ones or reoccupying older sites (which are seen locally as good locations for making earthen brick). At least five of the nine identified clusters included sites dating to multiple occupations. For these reasons clustered sites retain the linked numbers assigned during survey, but were treated as independent entities in the analysis.

For each site identified on survey, we documented the location using a GPS (Global Positioning System) device and systematically recorded the following information: soil color; soil texture; laterite pebble density; water sources within 200 m; the number, species, and size of trees on or near the site; sources of disturbance, including plowing, borrow pits, recent refuse, and termite mounds; types and densities of cultural artifacts, including ceramics, ground stone, slag, and chipped stone; and position relative to other sites and to significant natural features. We sketched a map of each site to scale (using pacing and 50 m measuring tapes) and estimated the depth of deposit (height above the natural surface) for each. As will be discussed in subsequent chapters, depth of deposit estimates proved highly unreliable as seemingly mounded sites were built on natural rises (for example, MAS541 had an estimated depth of 3.5 m and excavated cultural deposits of 1.2 m). Maps included not only site dimensions, but also the locations of significant features like in situ pots, artifact concentrations, useful trees, and borrow pits (Figure 14).

We took two surface collections at each site. First, we made a systematic collection of all surface artifacts within an arbitrary 5 by 5 m square to provide a representative and comparable sample, for which we chose locations with average object density and avoided unusually dense or sparse areas. Because of load limitations and the lack of pottery, we

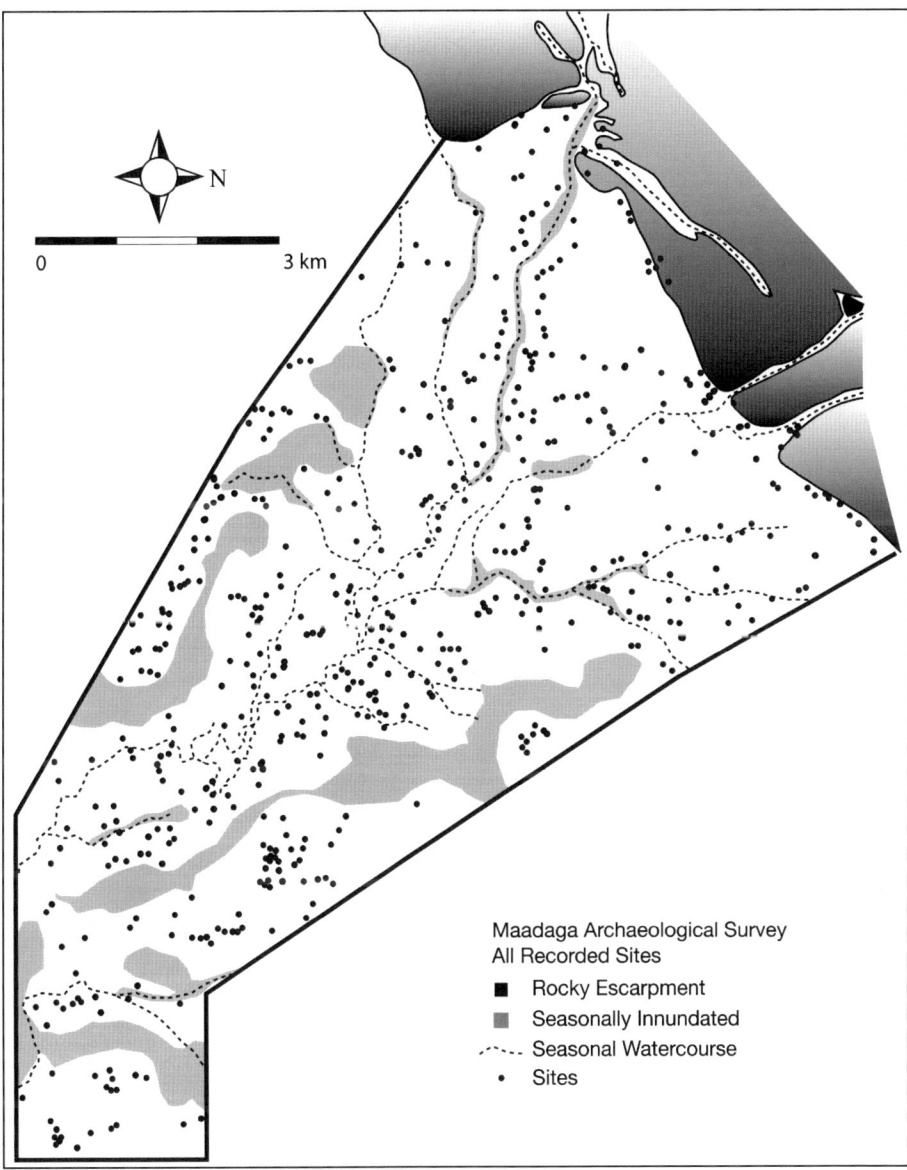

Figure 13. All recorded archaeological sites identified and documented by the Maadaga Archaeological Survey.

avoided placing systematic collections over slag heaps and iron furnaces. Second, carrying load and the limits of bicycle transport made multiple systematic collections at each site impractical, so we made a second opportunistic surface collection of any potentially diagnostic ceramic sherds (typically rims and decorated sherds) or unusual objects (such as polishing stones, pipes, and others). Large pieces of ground stone were typically recorded in place and not collected.

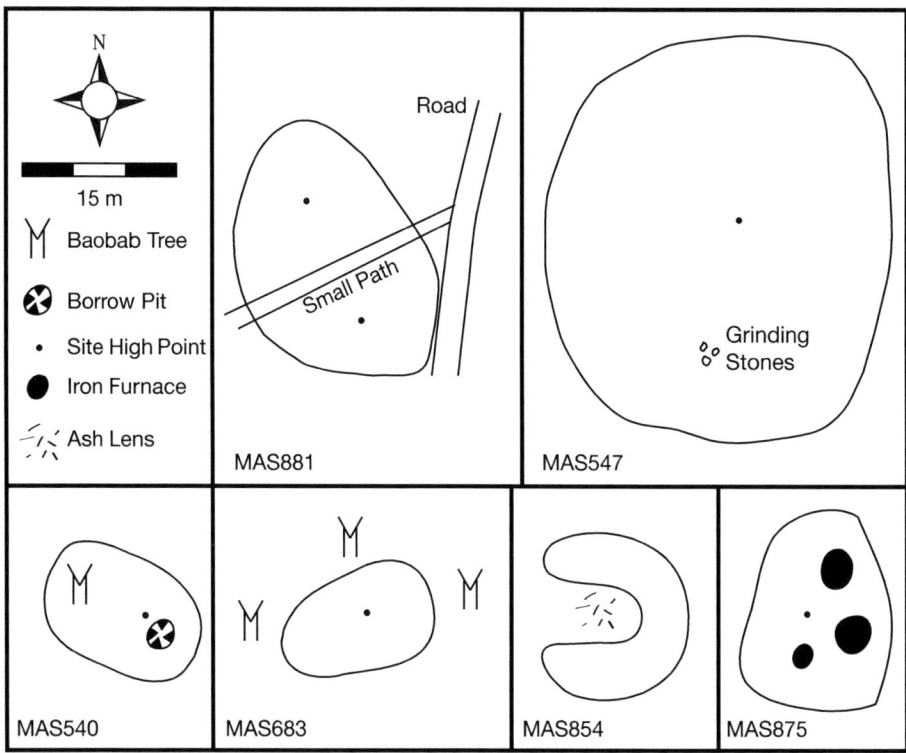

Figure 14. Sample field maps for documented sites.

Excavation Methodologies

In 2004, we dug shovel tests to investigate the depth of deposits for various categories of sites. Shovel tests in sites that were flat, including in the large surface lithic scatters near the base of the escarpment and at site MAS937 (Tuali occupation), found that even areas with dense surface materials had no subsurface deposits. In contrast, a shovel test at the mounded site of MAS541 (Pwoli occupation) revealed 60 cm of cultural deposits and did not reach sterile soil. Although the goal in 2004 was to identify sites for future excavation, we excavated site MAS542 (Lithic occupation), because it was eroding from a stream cut and we were concerned it would no longer exist by 2006.

Excavation was a significant component of fieldwork in 2006 and sites were chosen for the primary goal of developing a regional chronology that could be used to date the surface ceramics of sites identified during the survey. Consequently, we targeted five sites that had the greatest potential depth of deposit. Excavation was carried out by Gallagher, Dueppen, Ouaba, and individuals hired from households adjacent to each excavated site. Given the chronological focus, excavation units were small to maximize the number of sites that could be tested. We excavated sites in natural subdivisions within 10 cm arbitrary levels. We drew a map every 10 cm and assigned each identified cultural deposit an individual lot number. All sediment was screened using a 2 mm mesh, with the exception of flotation and radiocarbon samples, which we collected directly from the unit. The project did not excavate burials; when burials were identified in excavation units, they were pedestaled and the units subdivided. Full descriptions and analysis of excavation results are provided in Chapters 4 to 7.

We selected sites MAS541 (Unit E) and MAS502.3 (Unit A) for excavation for their particularly large size (3.5 m by 1,375 m² and 6.5 m by 7,200 m², respectively), visual appearance (coloring, texture, and shape) similar to tell sites in western Burkina Faso that contain several meters of stratified cultural deposits (e.g., Koté 2007; Dueppen 2012a; Holl 2014), and evidence for depth of deposit found in the 2004 shovel test at site MAS541. Although these sites did not yield the long sequences expected and their ceramic traditions were largely distinct from those identified during surface survey, the sites did contain more than 80 cm of cultural deposits, including preserved architecture, hearths, and floors.

Sites MAS572.1 (Unit C) and MAS573 (Unit D) also seemed to have depth of deposit, rising 2.0 and 1.75 m from the surface, respectively. These were much smaller mounds (600–1,100 and 800 m²). Despite dense surface artifacts, artifact frequency during excavation was very low and we found no organic remains (charcoal or animal bone). Likewise, we did not identify structures or floors in the extremely compact and hard sediment. Excavation units were terminated at 30 and 45 cm when it became physically impossible to dig because of soil hardness.

Finally, site MAS780 (Unit B) did not seem to have depth of deposit. However, the surface ceramic assemblage was particularly diverse and local residents reported finding rich subsurface deposits, including burials, when digging borrow pits. Our excavation unit likewise identified cultural deposits reaching 110 cm in depth, but they were mixed and had significant bioturbation. No in situ architecture or features were recovered.

Analysis of Spatial Data

Analysis of spatial data from the MAS posed several methodological problems. The preservation of sites in the region was affected by the dynamic geomorphological landscape. Both the Koabu and its tributaries have changed course several times and both destroyed and revealed previous habitations and activity areas. Sites near the Gobnangou escarpment, which were subject to both high-volume runoff and more intensive agriculture, seemed to be more poorly preserved. For example, in the areas within a few kilometers of the cliff base, where site density was low, Ouaba noted several locations where households occupied in the 1970s had vanished without a trace. Identification of sites was heavily affected by plowing, as sites were much more visible in recently farmed areas (Figure 15). For instance, new sites were identified during the 2006 survey because of newly plowed land in areas previously surveyed during 2004. Between 2004 and 2006 alone, rapid expansion of cotton farming brought an increasing percentage of land under cultivation in 2006, such that there were very few unplowed areas in the survey zone aside from inundated zones; 86% of identified sites had plowing noted as a source of disturbance. Finally, as will be discussed in detail throughout this book, most sites in the region were fairly brief occupations of only a few decades. Because most sites lacked directly datable material and ceramic phases persisted for several hundred years (see the discussions later in this chapter), it was impossible to determine precisely how many sites were occupied at any given time.

These combined factors created issues with using several standard modes of spatial

FIGURE 15. Plowed (*top*) and unplowed (*bottom*) areas in the survey zone, showing differences in the surface visibility of archaeological sites.

---

analysis, as most are predicated on simultaneous occupation. Clear broad spatial patterns were readily apparent in the data, suggesting changes over time in how households used space and positioned themselves within the landscape. To highlight these patterns, the study region was divided into two overlapping sets of zones to assess the relative locations of sites: Zones 1 through 7 tracked increasing distance from the escarpment and Zones A through C charted distance from the central Koabu drainage (Figure 16). Although both absolute numbers and density measurements of sites within individual zones were highly contingent given low chronological control and changes in topography (which affected both site preservation and surface visibility during the survey), it was possible to use the zones to compare major transformations in settlement strategies across occupations. Sites themselves had few spatial features and most simply consisted of a roughly circular scatter of artifacts.

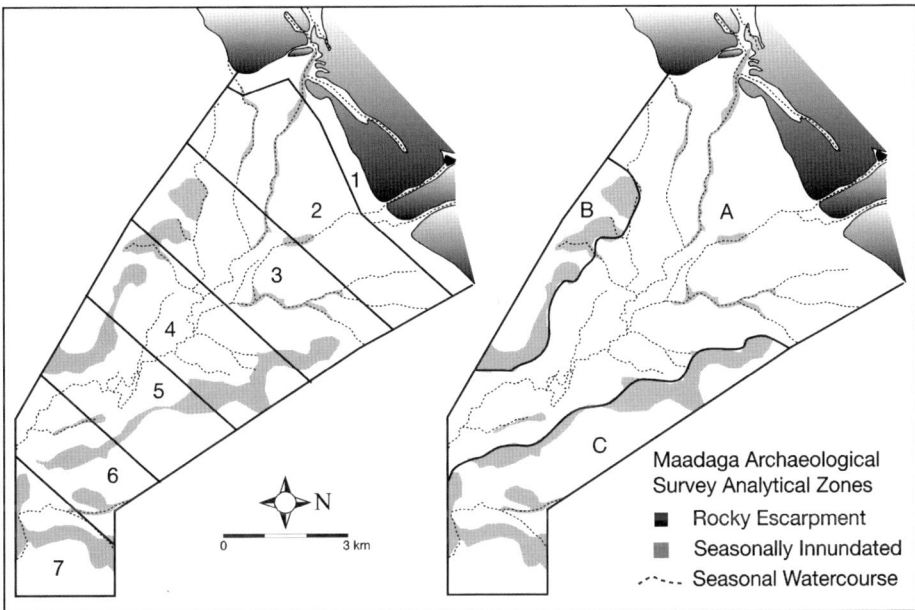

FIGURE 16. Maadaga Archaeological Survey analytical zones used for spatial analysis.

Analysis and Curation of Project Finds

All ceramic, stone, and metal-related artifacts from the project collected by survey and in excavations were documented in Burkina Faso and are stored in the Laboratory of Archaeology at the University of Ouagadougou, along with copies of all field notes, maps, drawings, and artifact recording sheets. Animal bone, flotation samples, and radiocarbon samples were exported for analysis in 2006 and returned in winter 2011 to the Laboratory of Archaeology for curation with the remainder of the collection. A small selection of radiocarbon samples was retained in the African Archaeology Lab at the University of Oregon for future dating.

All artifacts were counted, measured, and weighed. Selected artifacts were drawn, photographed, or both (Gallagher, Dueppen, and Zongo participated in the field analysis). Additional appropriate variables were documented for each class of object. For chipped stone ($N = 1,795$), other categories of data recorded for all collected artifacts included the type and color of stone and the presence of cortex. For flakes and formal tools, we documented bifacial and unifacial reduction, retouch, radial fissures, eraillure scars, and lipping. For cores we also noted directionality and evidence of bipolar flaking. For ground stone ($N = 128$), we recorded the stone type, shape, and likely function (such as basal grinding stone, handheld grinding stone, polishing stone, and *hatchette*). Internal and external vitrification was documented for tuyères ($N = 37$, ceramic tubes that provide air for iron-smelting furnaces). For rare finds such as pipes ($N = 7$), spindle whorls ($N = 1$), and iron objects ($N = 32$), we supplemented drawings and photographs with written descriptions. Finally, for ceramics ($N = 26,978$), the most numerous and temporally significant category of objects collected, we followed an attribute-based recording system (described in detail in the next section below). In all cases, field notes were a key component of analysis, because carrying load limits did not always allow for proportional opportunistic collection of objects other than ceramics, a bias that particularly affected heavy or bulky artifact classes such as ground stone, slag, and tuyères.

Flotation samples were sorted and seeds and fruits identified by Gallagher using published resources, notes and drawings made at the African Archaeobotany Laboratory at Goethe University (Frankfurt), and comparative collections at the University of Michigan Museum of Anthropological Archaeology (Ann Arbor, Michigan). Wood charcoal from the project has not yet been analyzed. Animal bone was identified by Dueppen using comparative collections at the University of Michigan Museum of Anthropological Archaeology, the Field Museum of Natural History (Chicago, Illinois), and the National Museum of Natural History at the Smithsonian Institution (Washington, DC) (see Dueppen and Gallagher 2013).

Ceramic Analysis: Methodological Considerations

Ceramic production and use is intricately interconnected with social and political practices, reflecting the complex identities held and expressed at the individual to the regional levels (Gosselain 2000, 2008, 2011; Haour et al. 2010; Cruz 2011; Guèye 2011; Insoll et al. 2011; Mayor 2011; Dueppen 2012a, 2015; Insoll, MacLean, and Kankpeyeng 2013; Richard and Macdonald 2015; M'Mbogori 2018). To understand the different choices involved, my analyses incorporate understandings drawn from a *chaîne opertoire* approach in outlining the nature of various stages in the life history of vessels. In doing so, I draw from the rich and growing body of ethnoarchaeological and archaeological research on potting in West Africa, which provides a strong socially rooted framework for discerning and interpreting recorded variables (see the references cited above; for material culture research in the Gulmance region specifically, see Geis-Tronich [1989, 1991]).

I considered several factors in developing the recording and analytical methods for the MAS assemblage. The primary goal in data recording was to document the sherds in such a way as to facilitate the creation of chronological and functional typologies, enable comparison of the project ceramics with other archaeological ceramic assemblages, and allow for examination of the social contexts of ceramic production, distribution, and use. Susan Keech McIntosh (1995) has argued persuasively for the use of individual attribute recording such that multiple modes of analysis can be used and typologies created from the same data set. This methodology is particularly effective when there is not an established typology in place, such that chronologically significant variables are not yet known, but also offers benefit for understanding variability that may be subsumed within defined types. Attribute-based recording is widely used by researchers in West Africa (see S. K. McIntosh 1995; Bedaux et al. 2005; Haour and Manning 2010; Mayor 2011; Dueppen 2012a; Gokee 2016; R. J. McIntosh, S. K. McIntosh, and Bocoum 2016; Haour 2019).

Previous work in southeastern Burkina Faso, northern Benin, and southwestern Niger has resulted in several ceramic typologies with little comparability between them. The German–Burkinabe research in the Gobnangou region used an intuitive typology that took into account several factors, including archaeological context in addition to the formal characteristics of the ceramics themselves (Breunig and Wotzka 1991; Frank et al. 2001; Wotzka and Goedicke 2001). The resulting groups were published with short descriptions, in some cases accompanied by drawings, and subsume a great deal of variability within each group. Thiombiano-Ilboudo's (2010) ceramic analyses from her research near Fada N'Gourma included images of individual vessels, direct comparisons with previous research (in particular, that of the Gobnangou projects), and collective characterization of the ceramics from individual excavation levels.

For ceramics from the Atakora Mountains and northern Gourma Plains of Benin, Petit (2005) used vessel form as the primary basis for ceramic description and provided summaries of the assemblages from different phases (see also N'Dah 2009). Vernet (1996) has also published basic descriptions of pottery from the southeastern region of Niger, accompanied primarily by illustrations of rim profiles. The Crossroads of Empires project in the Dendi region along the Niger and Mekrou Rivers in Benin has prioritized the publication of drawings and tables of original coding data (Haour et al. 2006, 2016; N'Dah 2009; Haour 2013, 2019; Haour et al. 2016).

Because the existing data on ceramics in the greater region is fragmented, we determined that an individual attribute analysis would provide the best opportunity for integration with the existing typologies, as well as for the identification of previously unknown vessel types and comparison across regions.

Overview of the Ceramic Assemblage

During the 2006 field season, 26,506 ceramic sherds were collected, 1,875 of which were from the five small excavations (Units A–E, at sites MAS502.3, MAS780, MAS572.1, MAS573, and MAS541, respectively). All ceramics from both survey and excavation were washed and individually recorded, with the exception of undecorated body sherds smaller than 4 cm^2, which we counted, weighed, and set aside ($n = 9,959$). For each of the remaining sherds ($n = 16,547$ for the primary study assemblage), we recorded the following data points: interior surface treatment; interior slip color and position; interior decoration; exterior surface treatment; exterior slip color and position; exterior decorations and positions; thickness; paste color; and temper inclusion types with their relative proportions and sizes. For rims, bases, and handles, we recorded firing conditions and interior and exterior diameters where possible. We drew all rims, bases, and handles (rim angle data was taken from drawings when needed), as well as selected body sherds. Representative sherds from all classes were photographed.

The small 2004 pilot assemblage ($n = 481$) was similarly recorded as described in detail above for 2006. However, because of inconsistencies in the coding between the two seasons, these sherds could not be fully integrated into the significantly larger 2006 assemblage. Therefore, although these data were considered when assessing the chronology of particular sites, they are not included in the quantified summaries below.

Paste

Potting clay is widely available in the Gobnangou region. Clay deposits are found along the banks of seasonal streams and high-quality clays are often available at a depth of 1 m or less (Geis-Tronich 1991:411). According to Geis-Tronich, twentieth-century Gulmance potters differentiated clays according to color; most of the clay available in the Gobnangou region was considered black clay, *u yoagboanu*. Dark gray because of its high proportion of magnesium oxide, black clay is often naturally interspersed with mica particles. Red clay, *u yoagpienu,* is available to the north of the escarpment; this clay is derived from Birimian deposits and can range from yellow-red to brown-red, depending on its proportion of iron oxide (Geis-Tronich 1991:412). However, both red and black clay produce fired vessels of a similar pale orange-red color (Geis-Tronich 1991:412) and were consequently difficult to distinguish archaeologically. Small quantities of mica were noted in the paste of almost all locally made pots available for purchase at the Nampuansiga market in 2004 and 2006. In comparison, as discussed in the next section, mica was uncommon in the archaeological assemblage.

Temper

Although some clays in the Gobnangou region are naturally tempered with sand, quartz, or mica, these were usually supplemented with added tempers such as grog (crushed pottery), crushed quartz or feldspar, and potentially additional mica. The archaeological assemblage was extraordinarily varied in its temper composition.

We assessed the temper of each sherd on a fresh break using a hand lens. In recording, we distinguished between dominant temper(s), regularly present temper(s), and sparse temper(s). The latter, usually isolated occurrences, were likely not intentionally added, but rather small pieces accidentally mixed in with other temper or naturally occurring in the clay. We recorded the average size of each temper type using the following categories: small (less than 1 mm^2), medium (less than 2 mm^2), and large (more than 2 mm^2). Across the assemblage temper size was statistically correlated with vessel thickness (see Table 8), suggesting that pastes were mixed with particular vessels in mind.

We identified the following six major classes of temper in the archaeological ceramics.

Grog

Crushed pottery was the most frequently occurring temper in the archaeological ceramics.

Quartz

This category referred to crushed pieces of quartz rather than silicate sand. Quartz veins are common in the Gobnangou escarpment, and quartz was the primary temper in pottery available for sale at the Nampuansiga market in 2004 and 2006. Frank and colleagues (2001) and Wotzka and Goedicke (2001) noted the presence of feldspar as well as quartz as a common temper in archaeological pottery from the region. Because the two are visually similar at the magnification we used, it is possible that some tempers recorded as quartz were actually feldspar. In the Fada N'Gourma area, quartz both occurs naturally in clays and is added as an intentional temper (Thiombiano-Ilboudo 2010:287).

Mica

Although mica occurs naturally in some of the local clay sources, twentieth-century potters sometimes added additional mica to create a particularly glittery effect (Geis-Tronich 1991). In comparing contemporary local pottery with archaeological pottery, the mica content in mica-dominant pots recovered during archaeological survey was significantly higher than naturally occurs in currently used clay sources.

TABLE 8. Temper size and vessel thickness of pottery in the Maadaga Archaeological Survey ceramic assemblage.

Temper size	Frequency	Percentage of assemblage	Mean vessel thickness (mm)
Small	1,364	8.3	8.9
Medium	14,121	86.3	11.0
Large	863	5.4	21.7

LATERITE

Small laterite pebbles were found almost exclusively in large vessels. These could have been intentionally added as temper or could be evidence of the use of less finely processed clays for these vessels.

ORGANICS

Organic material was only present in some large vessels. This suggests a degree of long-term consistency with Geis-Tronich's (1991) observation that organic temper was most commonly used for large constructions such as clay granaries and rarely used in pottery. Organic temper is also rare in the Fada N'Gourma region (Thiombiano-Ilboudo 2010:287).

SLAG

Crushed pieces of slag are known as a temper from areas on the forest margin (Stahl et al. 2008), but are less frequent in savanna areas to the northeast (S. K. McIntosh 1995; Mayor 2011; Dueppen 2012a). Slag was an infrequently used temper locally.

OTHER TEMPERS

Fine sand was not recorded, because its presence could not be reliably identified with a hand lens, although Geis-Tronich (1991) found its use by contemporary Gulmance potters to be virtually ubiquitous. Additionally, one heavily weathered undecorated sherd from excavations at site MAS502.3 had what seemed to be bone or shell temper.

SUMMARY

The study assemblage included 184 unique combinations of the type, size, and frequency of temper. To streamline the analysis, temper size was separated from the type and frequency designations (Table 8) and two summary codes were given to each sherd to indicate presence or absence. The first included only those tempers designated as dominant (18 categories) and the second those designated as dominant or regularly present (32 categories) (Tables 9 and B.1).

Grog was by far the most common temper, followed by quartz. Additional combinations of temper, notably those with mica, were used in specialized circumstances. Despite Geis-Tronich's (1991) identification of naturally micaceous clay as the predominant potting clay of the Gobnangou region and our observation of that clay in use in 2004 and 2006, only about 5% of sherds had mica as a regularly occurring or dominant temper (the percentage increased insignificantly if sherds with sparse mica were included). As M'Mbogori (2018) has noted, technical properties and convenience are not the only fac-

TABLE 9. Frequency of dominant pottery tempers in the Maadaga Archaeological Survey ceramic assemblage.

Temper field code	Dominant tempers	Frequency	Percentage of assemblage
2	Grog	10,193	61.6
3	Quartz	5,406	32.7
14	Quartz–mica	563	3.4
8	Grog–quartz	221	1.3
4	Mica	82	0.5
1	Organics	23	0.1
7	Grog–laterite	14	0.1
5	Laterite	7	<0.1
6	Slag	1	<0.1
9	Grog–organic	4	<0.1
10	Grog–mica	8	<0.1
11	Grog–slag	1	<0.1
13	Grog–quartz–mica	4	<0.1
14	Grog–quartz–laterite	2	<0.1
15	Quartz–mica–slag	5	<0.1
16	Quartz–organic	1	<0.1
17	Mica–laterite	1	<0.1
18	No dominant temper	8	<0.1

tors in clay selection and there are several possible explanations for why these micaceous deposits were likely less frequently exploited in the past. The micaceous clay may have been reserved for specific uses, there may have simply been other, more convenient clay sources, or pottery may have been made in other areas with different clays and traded to the study region. We attempted to identify clay sources in use by comparing the paste color of oxidized vessels within temper groups; however, all recorded paste colors (light brown, brown, gray, and orange) occurred in similar proportions irrespective of temper and are likely more indicative of firing conditions than clay source.

The preponderance of temper diversity, and in particular the number and variety of common temper formulas, was most likely a result of potters manufacturing their clays in small, hand-mixed batches. None of the more infrequent temper categories correlated with any particular vessel form or decorative scheme.

Vessel Form

Today most ceramics in the Gobnangou region are hand built using combinations of drawing, molding, and coiling techniques. Two typical examples of twentieth-century Gulmance vessel construction were provided by Geis-Tronich (1989). In the first, the building of a water jar in Tanbaga on the north side of the Gobnangou escarpment, the potter used a shallow concave mold made of fired clay or termite loam into which a thick lump of clay was pressed using a pestle. The potter then drew the clay up to form the sides while rotating the pot in the mold to smooth the sides and maintain a rounded shape. After drying, a donut of clay was applied around the small mouth, then drawn upward to create an elongated, slightly flared neck. In the second case, the building of a cooking pot in Kantchari, 90 km north of the surveyed area, the potter began by molding a flat piece of clay over the convex base of a fired pot. The clay was cut to make a hemisphere, removed from the mold, and left to dry. The dried hemispheres were placed in a sand pile to steady them and the upper portion of the pot was added using a coil technique. The coils were smoothed and shaped by the potter by hand and with a hard seedpod (*Piliostigma* sp.). The neck of the vessel could be built in the same way or drawn as described above. There is no record of Gulmance potters using the slow wheel techniques favored to the west (Frank 1998; LaViolette 2000; Mayor et al. 2005; Mayor 2011), although this does not exclude their use in the past.

There was little conclusive evidence for vessel formation techniques in the archaeological assemblage. A few of the thicker sherds from larger pots had visible coils, but in most cases their presence or absence could not be determined. Many of the flaring rims on jars had seams, indicating that they were most likely later additions to the body of the pot, as described above. Many pots were not perfectly round, with estimated diameters differing by as much as several centimeters at different points along the lip. Although this is typical for flares, it was also the case for simple rims and could indicate that the slow wheel was also not used in the past.

Geis-Tronich (1991:139–160) described twentieth-century ceramic assemblages and divided vessels into four local categories: *cancanli*, *sanli*, *bobli*, and *cuali*. Thiombiano-Ilboudo (2010:285) uses the terms *lisanli*, *libobili*, and *likwali*, respectively, for the latter three. Although Geis-Tronich did not provide a detailed functional analysis, *cancanli* (open subhemispherical bowls) and *sanli* (open hemispherical bowls) were generally used for serving; *bobli* (open jars) and *cuali* (restricted jars) were used for cooking, water transport and storage, and fermentation. In the early twentieth century, vessels' forms and functions were likely significantly more varied. By the time of Geis-Tronich's study commercially manufactured plastic and metal vessels had become commonplace and usurped many of the roles previously fulfilled by ceramics and gourds. During the 2004 and 2006 seasons, *libobli* and *likwali* were the most common vessel forms for sale at the Nampuansiga market. We frequently observed large *libobli* in active use for brewing and water storage in exterior courtyard spaces.

Only a few archaeological vessels with complete profiles were located on survey. Much of the vessel form information from the assemblage was derived from dissociated rim and base sherds. In general, there was significant variability in the rim assemblage and, although there were trends in vessel form, attempts to categorize sherds into distinct compartmentalized vessel or rim forms were not successful. A typology of vessels and rims would have subsumed significant variability, required arbitrary division of continuous variation, or resulted in a vast proliferation of types most of which would have contained one to three examples. The many small rims (less than 4 cm^2)—approximately one-third of the total rim sample—further complicated efforts, as did the similarities between the upper portions of jars with long flared necks and slightly flared open bowls and beakers.

Although rim and vessel forms could not be generally typologized, it was possible to identify a few regularly occurring forms and, in conjunction with other variables, use them to develop the sherd types described below. These rim and vessel forms are described here in general terms and each broad category incorporates significant variability. They do not account for the full variability in the assemblage.

Jars with Flared Necks
These are spheroid or ovoid jars with slightly constricted throats and flaring necks (as described above). These jars were present in a variety of shapes and sizes. Flares could range from 1.5 to 15 cm depending on the type and size of jar. An analysis of flare length and exterior rim angle found a fairly continuous distribution of flare length and a concentration of rim angles from 90° to 145°.

Jars or Bowls with Everted Necks
These vessels had short, strongly everted necks. The neck length ranges from 1.5 to 5.5 cm and exterior rim angles were concentrated between 155° and 170°. No large vessel fragments with these rims were recovered and these may be associated with jars, slightly restricted bowls, or both.

Large Open Vessels with Vertical Sides
These vessels, likely large storage bowls or jars, had large diameters (mostly between 35 and 50 cm) and thick walls that descended almost vertically. They often had square rims and sometimes had a thickened, pinched rim.

Simple Open Bowls
Open bowls were typically represented by fragments too small to be used to differentiate hemispherical and subhemispherical vessels.

Double Simple Open Bowls
These hourglass-shaped vessels all had at least one hemispherical or hemi-ovoid bowl. The basal bowl was in some cases a functional and size equivalent. In others there was a smaller, less finished pedestal base. There was no stem or similar feature in the middle. These vessels were difficult to distinguish from simple open bowls when only a small fragment was present.

Open Beakers
These open ovoid vessels with gently flaring sides were in a range of sizes, with diameters from 10 to 44 cm.

Small Jars with Out-turned Lips
Rims with out-turned lips occurred exclusively on smaller vessels, most with diameters under 35 cm.

Overall, vessels with restricted openings were very rare. Even when slightly restricted forms were present, they had broad flared rims such that the restriction was at the neck. Carinated vessels (found to the east and west, including in the Fada N'Gourma region [Thiombiano-Ilboudo 2010] and in the Dendi region [Haour et al. 2019]) were absent from the MAS assemblage.

Bases were predominantly rounded, but pedestal bases (mentioned above), ring bases, and cylindrical or button feet were also identified. With the exception of the pedestal bases, none of the other base techniques have been associated with any vessel form.

Surface Treatment

Identification of patterning in surface treatment posed particular problems. More than 40% of recorded sherds were weathered such that their original surface treatment could not be determined. This is unsurprising given that 88.9% of the study assemblage was collected from the surface. An additional 25% had space-filling decorations that obscured any surface treatment applied before decoration.

There are three stages in the construction of a vessel at which different surface treatments are usually applied. Self-slipping (smoothing with a slurry of particularly fine clay) and burnishing of either the self-slip or the primary fabric often occurs immediately after vessel construction. In contrast, red-slipping with a slurry of ground hematite and burnishing of that surface usually occurs after any decoration has been applied and the vessel has been dried. Finally, a thin external layer of clay mixed with finely crushed rock (referred to here as "roughing") may be applied, usually to the base. According to Geis-Tronich (1989), this step followed the application of slip. The latter two conditions held true archaeologically, as there were no cases in the study assemblage of decoration cut through slip or of slip over roughing. Slips were likely applied with fingers or a piece of cloth, and burnishing done with a piece of wood, the hard seedpod of *Piliostigma* sp., or a smooth quartz stone similar to those recorded by Geis-Tronich (1991) and collected at sites MAS552, MAS582, and MAS957. Burnishing serves a dual function; not only is it aesthetic, but it also helps the slip bind to the dried clay body (Rice 2015:163). The function of roughing is unknown, but given that it was confined to the base of vessels it likely adds stability or reduces wear, or both.

Among those sherds not recorded as weathered or decorated, self-slipping was the most common surface treatment (Table 10). Only 32% of self-slipped sherds were burnished; however, burnishing of self-slipped sherds was almost five times as common in excavation contexts as in surface contexts. This could reflect either different practices during the Pwoli occupation (which was represented almost exclusively in excavation contexts) or the effects of exposure and weathering on the preservation of burnished self-slipped sherds. In contrast, 74% of red-slipped sherds were burnished. Among this group, burnishing was not disproportionately found on sherds from excavation. The application of roughing does not have substantial time depth, as archaeological examples of the technique are only from the most recently occupied sites.

Decoration

The archaeological assemblage had a particularly diverse set of decoration techniques, despite the fact that only 28% of assemblage sherds were decorated. Recording of decoration involved noting each individual technique (defined as use of a specific tool in a specific way) used on the sherd. We recorded relationships between decoration techniques, as well as the position of the decoration on the sherd. All rim sherds, as well as examples of each technique and particularly complex composite decorations, were drawn.

We identified sixty-seven decoration techniques in use in the assemblage. These could be divided according to the tool used (cord, wood, finger, and so on) or the marks on the vessel (space-filling, lines, and others), but given the *chaîne opertoire* approach of this analysis they were categorized on the basis of the motion or technique used to make the

TABLE 10. Frequency of types of surface treatments in the Maadaga Archaeological Survey ceramic assemblage.

Surface treatment	Frequency	Percentage of assemblage	Percentage of sherds with preserved surface ($n = 5,596$)
Indeterminate (weathered)	6,913	41.9	—
Indeterminate (decorated)	3,997	24.2	—
Self-slipped	2,035	12.3	36.4
Self-slipped, burnished	997	6.0	17.8
Red-slipped	631	3.8	11.3
Red-slipped, burnished	1,759	10.7	31.4
Roughing applied	174	1.1	3.1

impressions. *Roulette* decorations are the patterns produced by rolling an object, in this case a carved wooden cylinder, a twisted, knotted, or braided cord, or a folded or braided strip, across the surface of the vessel to produce a zone of decoration (Table 11; Figure 17). *Dragged* decorations are those in which an object, most frequently a wooden stylus or carved comb, was impressed in the wet clay and dragged to create lines or a pattern (Table 12; Figure 18). *Impressed* decorations are those in which an object was pressed into the surface of the clay, then lifted without lateral movement (Table 13; Figure 19). *Applied* decorations are those in which a piece of clay was shaped and joined to the vessel surface, creating a protruding decoration (Table 14; Figure 20). Forty-four decoration techniques occurred on fewer than twenty sherds (less than 0.5% of the decorated assemblage) and twenty-four of these were found on fewer than five sherds. Interestingly, many of the decorations common at previously studied sites in the Gobnangou region dating from the fourth millennium BCE through the first millennium CE, including vertical bands or zones of rocker comb and angular incised patterns (Wotzka and Goedicke 2001), were either absent or very rare in the ceramic assemblage recovered by the MAS.

To facilitate analysis of the decorations, I created seventeen decorative groups, which encompassed more than 80% of decorated sherds (Table B.2). These groups served two purposes. First, they isolated the most frequent decorative techniques (for example, knotted or twisted cord roulette) and lumped together minor variations on the same technique (such as plastic ridges). Second, and more importantly, they allowed for the analytical combination of sherds representing different parts of common complex combinations of decorations (for example, channel comb in conjunction with parallel channels or incised shapes with space-filling comb impressions and folded strip roulettes). As will be seen below, some decoration groups were clustered tightly around specific tempers and thicknesses, which proved significant for developing a typology. In contrast, groups (primarily roulettes) with highly variable temper and vessel thickness represented decoration techniques that were used in a variety of settings.

TABLE 11. Roulette decoration techniques identified in the Maadaga Archaeological Survey ceramic assemblage ($N = 4{,}569$). See also Figure 17.

Technique	Field code	Description	Number of sherds	Percentage of decorated sherds	Notes
Twisted cord	Cord 2	Twisted cord roulette in a variety of sizes; may also include unrecognized braided strip roulette	2,566	56.16	Arazi and Manning (2010); Mayor (2010); S. K. McIntosh (1995), Twine 6; Dueppen (2012a), Twine 2; Haour et al. (2019), rc-1
Braided cord	Cord 1	Braided cord roulette	235	5.14	McIntosh and Guèye (2010); S. K. McIntosh (1995), Twine 10; Dueppen (2012a), Twine 4; Haour et al. (2019), rct-1
Folded strip	Cord 3	Folded strip roulette with minimal offset	158	3.46	Haour and Keita (2010); S. K. McIntosh (1995), Twine 4; Dueppen (2012a), Twine 3, Twine 22; Haour et al. (2019), rfp-1; Petit (2005), common in northern Benin throughout Iron Age
Braided strip	Cord 4	Braided strip roulette with comparatively wide spacing between rows; rarely, applied in two directions to create diamond pattern	134	2.93	Mayor (2010); see Appendix B, Sherd Type 3
Twisted knotted cord	Cord 5	Twisted knotted cord roulette; may have one knot or multiple knots	94	2.06	Arazi and Manning (2010); Haour et al. (2019), rc-3; see Appendix B, Sherd Type 4
Braided strip	Cord 6	Braided strip roulette; often alternately braided to create a chevron pattern	79	1.73	Mayor (2010); Dueppen (2012a), Twine 6; chevron similar to S. K. McIntosh (1995), Twine 12; Haour et al. (2019), rfp-3

Continued

TABLE 11 CONTINUED

Technique	Field code	Description	Number of sherds	Percentage of decorated sherds	Notes
Folded strip	Cord 9	Folded strip roulette with significant offset	47	1.03	Haour and Keita (2010); S. K. McIntosh (1995), Twine 5; Dueppen (2012a), Twine 7, Twine 22; Haour et al. (2019), rfp-1
Possible folded strip	R1	Closely spaced ovals or hexagons in low relief; likely made with a large, loose folded strip roulette	30	0.66	Haour and Keita (2010); possibly Haour et al. (2019), rfp-1c?
Possible cord wrapped	Cord 8	Short sections of cord in multiple directions; irregular cord wrapped roulette is a likely candidate	27	0.59	Livingstone Smith et al. (2010); MacDonald and Manning (2010)
Twisted cord	Cord 7	Loosely twisted cord roulette with multiple beads in each impression	23	0.5	Arazi and Manning (2010); S. K. McIntosh (1995), Twine 7; Dueppen (2012a), Twine 10
Carved wooden	TDC	Wooden roulette of angular patterns made from parallel lines	19	0.42	See Appendix B, Sherd Type 13; Geis-Tronich (1991); Haour et al. (2019), rbt
Folded strip	Cord 15	Folded strip roulette with ovals almost end-to-end	11	0.24	Haour and Keita (2010)
Carved wooden	VC	Horizontal rows of raised V-shaped impressions	10	0.22	Haour et al. (2019), rbt; see Appendix B, Sherd Type 13
Twisted cord	Cord 13	Twisted cord with a second wrapped twisted cord to create alternating thick and thin rows	5	0.11	Arazi and Manning (2010); Hurley (1979), Cord 42

Continued

TABLE 11 CONTINUED

Technique	Field code	Description	Number of sherds	Percentage of decorated sherds	Notes
Braided(?) strip	Cord 10	Braided strip roulette with double raised ovals	4	0.09	Mayor (2010); Dueppen (2012a), Twine 9. Possibly knotted strip roulette? See Soper (1985, fig. 5); Haour et al. (2019), rfp-2
Unknown	Cord 16	Very small raised interlocking pattern	4	0.09	
Cord wrapped	MLI	Fill of small pointed ovate impressions with similar alignment	2	0.04	
Cord wrapped	Cord 11	Long, linear cord impressions made with an untwisted fiber wrapped on a core	2	0.04	MacDonald and Manning (2010); S. K. McIntosh (1995), Twine 14
Carved wooden	R2	Raised boxes in offset parallel rows	1	0.02	Dueppen (2012a), Roulette 10
Carved wooden	R3	Large impressed squares	1	0.02	
Carved wooden	R4	Toothed line in parallel rows	1	0.02	Dueppen (2012a), Roulette 2
Carved wooden	R5	Double-toothed, almost wavy lines in parallel rows	1	0.02	Dueppen (2012a), Roulette 4

Firing

Twentieth-century Gulmance potters fired clay using an open-air technique (Geis-Tronich 1989). Pots were piled on a pallet of dried branches, then covered with wood and more branches. The pile was lit and allowed to burn through the night. The fired pots were removed the next morning. This technique was consistent with those frequently used in neighboring regions. There is no evidence in the present or past of construction of the brick kilns occasionally found in the Voltaic region to the west (Frank 1998; Dueppen 2012a).

This type of bonfire firing is known for its variability in atmosphere. Most sherds (66%) had oxidized exteriors and interiors with a blackened core. According to Rice (2015),

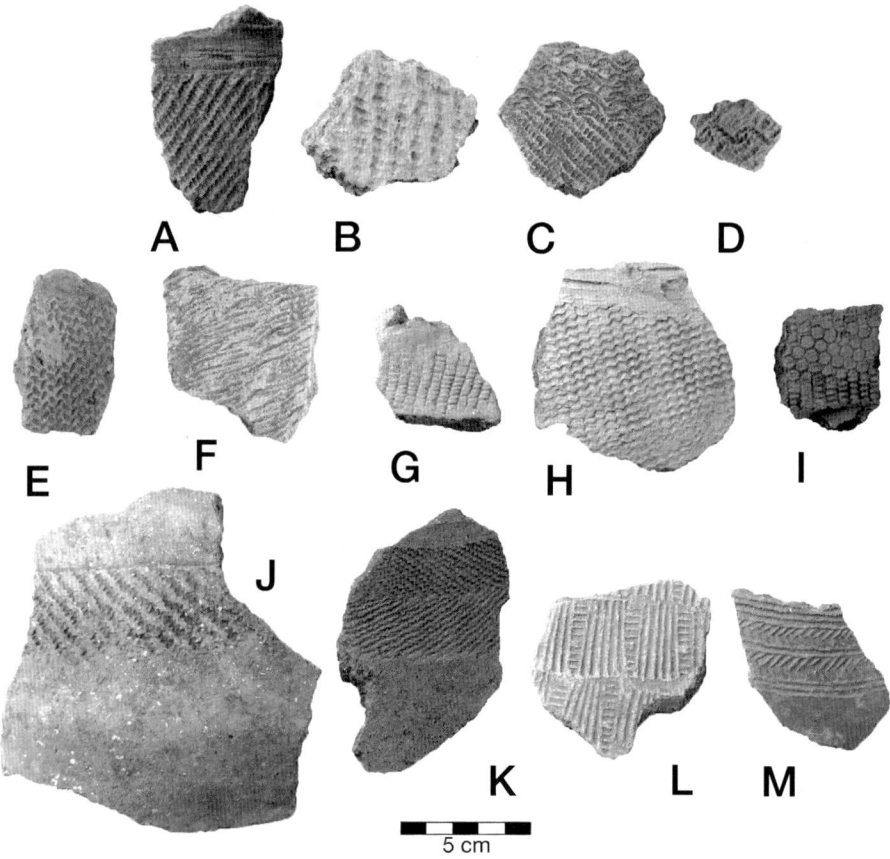

Figure 17. Examples of roulette decorations with associated sites. **A, B,** Twisted cord roulettes (Cord 2, MAS875; Cord 9, MAS502.3). **C, D,** Twisted knotted cord roulettes (Cord 5, MAS530, MAS780). **E,** Braided cord roulette (Cord 1, MAS616). **F,** Possible cord wrapped roulette (Cord 8, MAS572.1). **G, H,** Folded strip roulette (Cord 3, MAS513; Cord 9, MAS844). **I,** Possible folded strip roulette (R1 with Cord 3, MAS524). **J, K,** Braided strip roulettes (Cord 4, MAS505; Cord 6, MAS645). **L, M,** Carved wooden roulettes (TDC, MAS937; VC, MAS863). See also Table 11.

this phenomenon is caused by a charring of organic matter in the clay. (The organic matter is not necessarily a temper, but rather the humus, rootlets, and fibers common in surface and shallow sedimentary clays such as those found in the study region.) Under high temperatures or with particularly porous clays the carbonaceous material can completely oxidize, leaving no black residue. Cases of full oxidization in the assemblage (23%) were no more common among coarse-tempered sherds than fine-tempered sherds and were likely from firings in which higher temperatures were achieved. Likewise, fully reduced sherds (11%) may have been from lower temperature areas of a firing. However, complete blackening could also be the result of the intentional creation of a reducing atmosphere at the end of firing (Rice 2015:177). There were only a few cases where a similar technique may have been used, primarily with some of the earlier ceramic types.

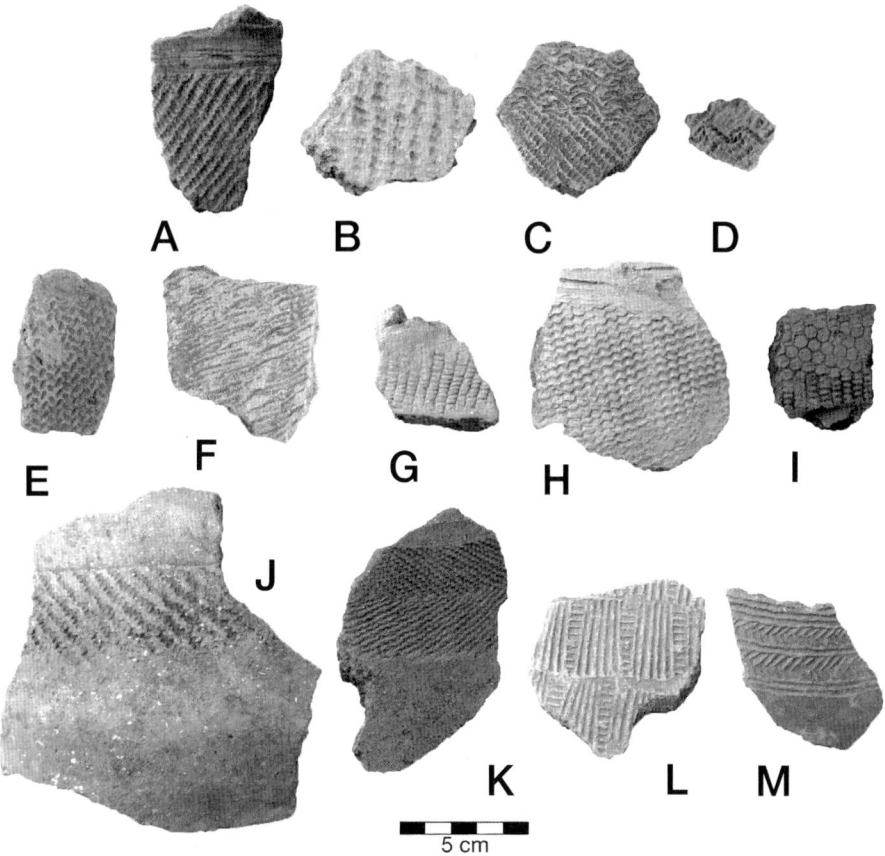

TABLE 12. Dragged decoration techniques identified in the Maadaga Archaeological Survey ceramic assemblage (N = 4,569). See also Figure 18.

Technique	Field code	Description	Number of sherds	Percentage of decorated sherds	Notes
Parallel channels	PC	Evenly spaced parallel channels; may or may not be made with a comb	311	6.81	
Channel	CH	Single straight channel of any direction or width; usually made with a stylus; ca. 1–3 mm wide	275	6.02	
Lip channel	LIPCH	Channel on the lip of the pot	55	Rims only	Geis-Tronich (1991) described this technique as produced with a leaf rib by twentieth-century Gulmance potters
Channel comb (single)	CC	Comb used to create short (<5 mm) parallel incisions within a channel; usually occurs in parallel rows	47	1.03	See Appendix B, Sherd Type 5
Semicircular channel	SC	Arching channel in a semicircular shape	30	0.66	
Dragged comb	DC	Comb dragged lightly across the vessel surface resulting in shallow, irregular channels	27	0.59	
Multiple triangular channels	MCT	Nested arrangements of channels in a triangle or chevron motif	21	0.46	
Other channels	IC	A specific arrangement of channels that does not fall into a different category; individually drawn	17	0.37	
Channel comb (double)	TC	Similar to CC, except two sets of short channels are made in opposing directions	15	0.33	See Appendix B, Sherd Type 5
Triangular channel	CT	Single channel used to create a triangle or chevron motif	11	0.24	
Cross-hatched incisions	XI	Incisions in a regular, space-filling cross-hatched pattern	10	0.22	Haour et al. (2019), sx
Diagonal incisions	DI	Rows of short diagonal incisions; incisions are generally less than 10 mm long	9	0.2	Petit (2005) identified this technique at Tchikandou-I (early second millennium CE)

Continued

TABLE 12 CONTINUED

Technique	Field code	Description	Number of sherds	Percentage of decorated sherds	Notes
Incisions	I	Incisions made with a sharp instrument that slices the clay	9	0.2	
Gouges	G	Short, deep, wide channels; usually in rows	7	0.15	
Multiple arching channels	MAC	Sets of roughly parallel, fairly wide arching channels that have a close origin point and expand outward	7	0.15	Wotzka and Goedicke's (2001) Group 10 has several sherds with this technique, all with quartz, feldspar, or laterite tempers; Wotzka and Goedicke identified this decoration only at open air sites near Kantchari
Incisions	MI	Multiple incisions with no consistent pattern	7	0.15	
"Ladder" channels	LC	Two closely spaced parallel channels with evenly spaced vertical lines running between them	4	0.09	Petit (2005) identified this technique at Tchikandou-I (early second millennium CE)
Cross-hatched channels	XC	Channels in a regular, space-filling cross-hatched pattern	4	0.09	
Channels	MCH	Multiple channels with no consistent pattern	3	0.07	
Banded dragged comb	BDC	Comb dragged a very short distance between channels	2	0.04	Petit (2005) identified this technique at Tchikandou-I (early second millennium CE)
Swirling dragged comb	SDC	Comb with four to five teeth dragged lightly in an open swirling pattern	2	0.04	
Vertical fill	VF	Fill pattern made of short (5–10 mm) vertical channels; although all have the same orientation, they are not horizontally aligned	1	0.02	

Ceramic Typology and Chronology

Defining Sherd Types

The creation and use of typologies has long been the subject of fierce archaeological debate (see the reviews and discussions in Whallon and Brown [1982], Adams and Adams [1991], Wylie [2002], Roberts and Vander Linden [2011], Ashley and Grillo [2015], and Rice [2015]). What has emerged is a consensus that the definition of a set of types must be accompanied by an explicit accounting of the methods used to create the types and their intended purpose, as well as consideration of variability both within and between types.

The goal of the study typology was to identify sherds from similar vessels to facilitate the chronological control of the ephemeral short-occupation sites that dominated the region. For this reason, very tight typological definitions were used to minimize the possibility of conflating similar ceramics from different phases of occupation. The methodology used in developing these types was essentially a cluster analysis focused on temper, vessel thickness, rim form, surface treatment, and decoration, with type definitions created by looking for cases of concordance among at least three of the five categories. Therefore, the resulting types cannot be equated one-to-one with vessels (thus their designation as *sherd types*), because different parts of a single vessel (rim, shoulder, or base) could fall into different sherd types.

Overall, 1,149 sherds (7% of the study assemblage and 25% of decorated sherds) were assigned to fifteen types (Sherd Types 1 to 15; Table 15; Figures 21 and 22). Detailed descriptions are given for each sherd type (Appendix B), including variability within each type, regional similarities, and analysis of other untyped and typed sherds in the assemblage that could derive from the same vessels. In addition, each sherd type is discussed in more detail (see Chapters 6 and 7) in the context of the full ceramic assemblage from the associated occupation.

The absolute number of typed sherds was low, but a clear correlation cannot be drawn between the percentage of sherds in the assemblage that was typed and the percentage that came from vessels represented by typed sherds. Often only specific parts of a vessel provided the necessary information to assign a sherd to a category. For example, Sherd Type 2 designations were only made when the rim and the decoration zone were present; however, using an almost complete example, as much as 75% of the vessel surface area fell below the decoration line. The effect was even more extreme on large vessels, such as those represented by Sherd Types 8 and 9.

Seriation of the Site Ceramic Assemblages

Through a contextualized consideration of typed ceramics, I divided sites identified by the MAS into five major occupations according to material assemblages: Lithic, Pwoli, Siga, Tuali, and Ring. Tuali was further divided into Tuali-A and Tuali-B variants. I used the term "occupation" rather than "phase" intentionally as, because of weak chronological control in the assemblages, it is possible these divisions reflected variability in activities or populations as well as change through time.

Although intended to aid in developing a ceramic chronology, seriation of the types described above presented several challenges. First, only thirteen typed sherds were recovered from below the plow zone in excavation contexts. Although many of these sherds were very small (raising concerns that they could have originated in earlier occupations, as archaeological sites are often used as a source of pre-mixed fabric for earthen bricks), these

FIGURE 18. Examples of dragged decorations with associated sites. **A,** Parallel channels (PC, MAS844). **B, C,** Channel comb (double TC, MAS572.7; single CC, MAS502.3). **D,** Banded dragged comb (BDC, MAS513). **E,** Swirling dragged comb (SDC, MAS775). **F,** Ladder channels (LC, MAS592.1). **G,** Multiple arching channels (MAC, MAS902). **H,** Multiple triangular channels (MCT, MAS511). **I,** Cross-hatched incisions (XI, MAS868). See also Table 12.

deposits had been subject to less mixing than those from the surface and provided a starting point for identifying elements of a contemporary assemblage. At site MAS780, Sherd Types 1, 2, 3, 4, and 5 were represented in the subsurface deposits. Notably, excavations at sites MAS502.3 and MAS541 yielded no typed sherds below the plow zone.

For the surface collections, despite the large overall size of the assemblage, the sample from any given site tended to be small (mean of 32 individually recorded sherds) and consequently, many site assemblages either lacked typed sherds completely ($n = 100$) or had only one typed sherd present ($n = 170$). Only 242 sites had multiple types, and a mere 100 of these had more than two types occurring together. A simple chi-square analysis was used to determine those types that co-occurred significantly (Figure 23).

TABLE 13. Impressed decoration techniques identified in the Maadaga Archaeological Survey ceramic assemblage (N = 4,569). See also Figure 19.

Technique	Field code	Description	Number of sherds	Percentage of decorated sherds	Notes
Space-filling comb impressions	FCI	Fill of dense comb impressions in a generally rectilinear pattern	52	1.14	See Appendix B, Sherd Type 1
Pinched rim	RP	Rim treatment in which the edge is extruded and formed by pinching between two fingers, resulting in a series of adjoining facets	22	Rims only	See Appendix B, Sherd Type 8
Braided cord impressions	IB	Braided cord lifted and impressed in rows	20	0.44	
Space-filling rocker comb	SCOR	Dense, unevenly applied rocker comb that creates a space-filling pattern	11	0.24	Wotzka and Goedicke (2001), Groups 1 and 2 have dense rocker comb on quartz-tempered sherds; Haour et al. (2019), Peig-B
Triangular impressions	TB	Triangular impressions, possibly created using the end of a stylus	6	0.13	
Circular impressions	CI	Solid impressed circles	5	0.11	
Rocker comb	COR	Rocker comb, impressed design made by pivoting the comb across the surface	5	0.11	
Curved comb impressions	CCI	Impressed semicircular comb	4	0.09	Haour et al. (2019), PeigIC
Comb impressions	COI	Impressed comb, typically in a row	3	0.07	
Fingernail impressions	FI	Impressed fingernail or thumbnail	3	0.07	

Continued

TABLE 13 CONTINUED

Technique	Field code	Description	Number of sherds	Percentage of decorated sherds	Notes
Angular impressions	HC	Angular, L-shaped impressions, likely made with a wedge-shaped stylus	3	0.07	
Finger impressions	TH	Impressed thumb or fingers	3	0.07	
Cord wrapped stick impressions	Cord 12	Impressed cord wrapped stick	2	0.04	MacDonald and Manning (2010)
Pivoted twisted cord impressions	Cord 14	Impressed twisted cord pivoted in a zigzag pattern	1	0.02	
Impressed comb with H-shaped teeth	IHC	Impressed comb with H-shaped teeth	1	0.02	

These data were then used to develop clusters of roughly contemporary ceramics. Notably, these clusters are not perfectly sequenced phases, but rather points of commonality that can overlap and include many spatial and temporal variations. These clusters will likely be significantly refined as more research is completed in southeast Burkina Faso and surrounding regions.

The clusters based on sherd types are as follows:
—*Siga Occupation*: Sherd Types 1, 2, 3, 4, 5, 6, with Sherd Types 7, 8, 9, and 10 also present.
—*Tuali Occupation*: Sherd Types 11, 12, and 14, with Sherd Types 9, 13, and 15 also present.

Attribution of Sites to Occupations

The ceramic clusters provided a crucial starting point for seriating the site assemblages; however, these clusters had only a limited utility for typing those sites with few or rare examples of typed sherds. Although most of the sites recorded were nominally single component, they were subject to intrusive ceramics that both predate and postdate the primary occupation. In the former case, ceramics could drift from earlier sites to later sites through a variety of means, such as by erosion, being tossed by farmers plowing fields, and being used as slingshot ammunition (observed while on survey), not to mention the effects of digging into older sites to make earthen bricks. New residences were often located near archaeological sites, because households exploited the same water sources, used the archaeological deposits as building material, took advantage of the rich soils often around sites from trash decomposition, and may have claimed ancestral rights to established useful trees and rejuvenated agricultural fields. Even if an archaeological site was not the primary trash disposal zone for a more recent residence, it is always

Figure 19. Examples of impressed decorations with associated sites. **A**, Space-filling comb with semicircular channels and dragged comb (FCI, SC, DC, MAS772.1). **B**, Space-filling rocker comb (SCOR, MAS550). **C**, Pinched rim (RP, MAS616). **D**, Angular impressions (HC, MAS524). See also Table 13.

---

possible that a new ceramic vessel could break near an older site on the way to visit a neighbor or to work in a field.

Consequently, in evaluating the site assemblages for assignation to an occupation, I used a holistic qualitative approach. The notes and maps for each site were referenced to identify possible sources of disturbance, particularly the presence of currently occupied compounds, as well as factors that could skew composite site data, such as clear evidence of a fragmented large jar on the surface. The ceramic assemblage was examined in detail, with attention not only to typed sherds, but also to the distribution of individual attributes, including temper and decoration techniques. Although these latter aspects did not pattern categorically, there were some trends at sites with little evidence of disturbance and high concentrations of sherds typed to one of the two primary clusters. The Siga occupation tended to have very diverse decoration techniques and mixed temper profiles that included grog-, quartz-, and mica-dominant sherds. In contrast, the Tuali occupation tended toward high proportions of quartz temper and few decorated sherds with a limited set of techniques. Sites with concentrations of Sherd Type 15 had particular spatial features and ceramic assemblage characteristics and it soon became apparent that these

TABLE 14. Applied decoration techniques identified in the Maadaga Archaeological Survey ceramic assemblage (N = 4,569). See also Figure 20.

Technique	Field code	Description	Number of sherds	Percentage of decorated sherds	Notes
Ridge with finger impressions (double)	R2T	Plastic ridge with two parallel rows of deep thumb or finger impressions (pinching?) running along it	139	3.04	See Appendix B, Sherd Type 9
Ridge	PR	Plastic ridge, often with a square profile	27	0.59	See Appendix B, Sherd Type 9
Ridge with finger impressions (single)	PRT	Plastic ridge with a row of deep thumb or finger impressions running along it	14	0.31	See Appendix B, Sherd Type 9
Ridge with gouges	PRG	Plastic ridge with evenly spaced vertical gouges	12	0.26	See Appendix B, Sherd Type 9
Plastic button	PB	Applied circular plastic button	11	0.24	
Small ridge	MR	Small plastic ridge with triangular cross section	6	0.13	
Small ridge with gouges	MRG	Small plastic ridge with evenly spaced gouges	2	0.04	

should be separated from the Tuali occupation (and assigned to the Ring occupation). No typed sherds were recovered from excavation at sites MAS541 and MAS502.3. These sites were assigned to their own occupation (Pwoli), as were sites without ceramic assemblages (Lithic).

Even with this attention to detail, uncertainty in the assignment of any individual site to temporal group(s) was inevitable given the available data and I assigned sites to specific occupations at a high or low level of confidence. Some sites with small or ambiguous assemblages, or both, were not assigned to any occupation.

Although there were a few exceptions, most multicomponent sites (n = 38) did not seem to be reoccupations. Most frequently, they were used as trash dumps for currently occupied compounds, resulting in significant mixing of their ceramic assemblages. In some cases, the sites had been destroyed with the potential mixing of multiple distinct sites, whereas in other cases older sites may have been used as borrow pits for constructing a new residence. The only examples of stratified multicomponent sites were those assigned to the Pwoli occupation, two of which had evidence of Siga occupation on the surface. Thus, although it may seem intuitive that multicomponent sites would have been the

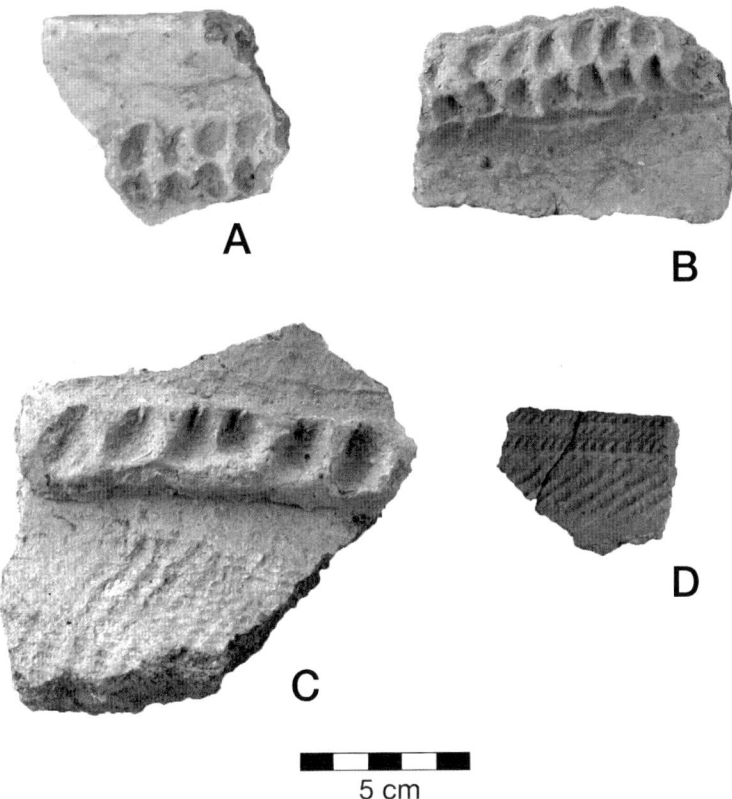

FIGURE 20. Examples of applied decorations with associated sites. **A, B,** Ridge with double finger impressions (R2T, MAS635, MAS661). **C,** Ridge with single finger impressions (PRT, MAS521). **D,** Small ridge with gouges with twisted cord roulette (MRG, Cord 2, MAS525). See also Table 14.

most informative, their complex postdepositional processes made them among the most difficult to interpret. Consequently, as a group they were among the least useful sites for understanding the characteristics of a given occupation.

Defining a Local Occupation Sequence

The methodologies applied to the ceramic assemblage resulted in the definition of five occupations in the study region. Forty-three sites, including two rock art sites (Appendix D), were not assigned to an occupation.

Lithic Occupation
Sites assigned to the Lithic occupation ($n = 6$; see Chapter 4) had no or very few ceramics. Several rockshelter sites in the Gobnangou with large geometric microlith assemblages also had sizeable ceramic assemblages (Millogo 1993a; Frank et al. 2001), but no sites identified by the MAS with evidence of a significant focus on chipped stone technologies had more than a few ceramics present.

TABLE 15. Summary of sherd types. For detailed descriptions, see Appendix B for sherd types and Table B.2 for decoration groups. For decoration field codes, see Tables 11–14. See also Figures 21 and 22.

Sherd type	Number of sherds	Number of sites	Primary temper	Vessel form	Mean thickness (mm)	Mean exterior diameter (cm)	Surface treatment	Decoration	Sampling
1	38	29	Quartz	Round jars with flaring necks	10	20.5	Self-slip	Zoned decoration with incisions, space filling comb impressions, parallel channels, and folded strip roulette (Decoration Group C, all sherds)	Rim, body
2	83	75	Grog	Gently flared beakers	10.3	22.4	Mixed, often polished	Twisted and braided cord roulettes (Decoration Groups G and H, sherds with correct rim only)	Rim
3	88	70	Mica, quartz	Unknown	11.3	n/a	n/a	Braided strip roulette (Decoration Group J, all sherds with correct temper)	Body
4	164	107	Grog	Open bowls or jars	9.6	28.3	Self-slip or lightly applied red slip	Twisted knotted cord roulette with twisted cord roulette (Decoration Group D, all sherds; Decoration Group H, sherds with correct rim only)	Rim, body
5	144	98	Grog	Open, possibly double bowls	8.6	20.2	Red slip	Channel comb with parallel channels (Decoration Group B, all sherds)	Rim, body
6	86	69	Grog	Cup-like pedestal base	n/a	15.6	Red slip	Channels, parallel channels	Base
7	11	11	Grog	Squat pedestal base	n/a	13.1	Red slip	None	Base

Continued

TABLE 15 CONTINUED

Sherd type	Number of sherds	Number of sites	Primary temper	Vessel form	Mean thickness (mm)	Mean exterior diameter (cm)	Surface treatment	Decoration	Sampling
8	17	17	Grog	Large open jars or basins	17.8	43.9	Mixed, often burnished	Pinched rim (RP)	Rim
9	175	118	Grog, laterite	Large open jars or basins	18.9	42.6+	Self-slip	Large plastic ridges sometimes with twisted cord roulette (Decoration Group A, all except miniridges)	Rim, body
10	49	45	Grog	Lug handle for unknown vessel shape	n/a	n/a	Mixed	None	Handle
11	93	78	Quartz	Jars with flaring necks	11.8	27.3	Self-slip or red slip	None	Rim, neck
12	18	16	Quartz	Jars with flaring necks	9.5	n/a	n/a	Braided strip roulette (Decoration Group K, sherds with correct rim or neck only)	Rim, neck
13	26	18	Quartz	Unknown	10.2	n/a	Red slip	Carved wooden roulettes with TDC and VC patterns (Decoration Group E, all sherds)	Body
14	166	54	Quartz	Rounded base	13	n/a	Roughing	None	Body
15	19	15	Quartz	Vessels with flaring necks	11.1	29.6	Red slip	Lip channels (LIPCH)	Rim

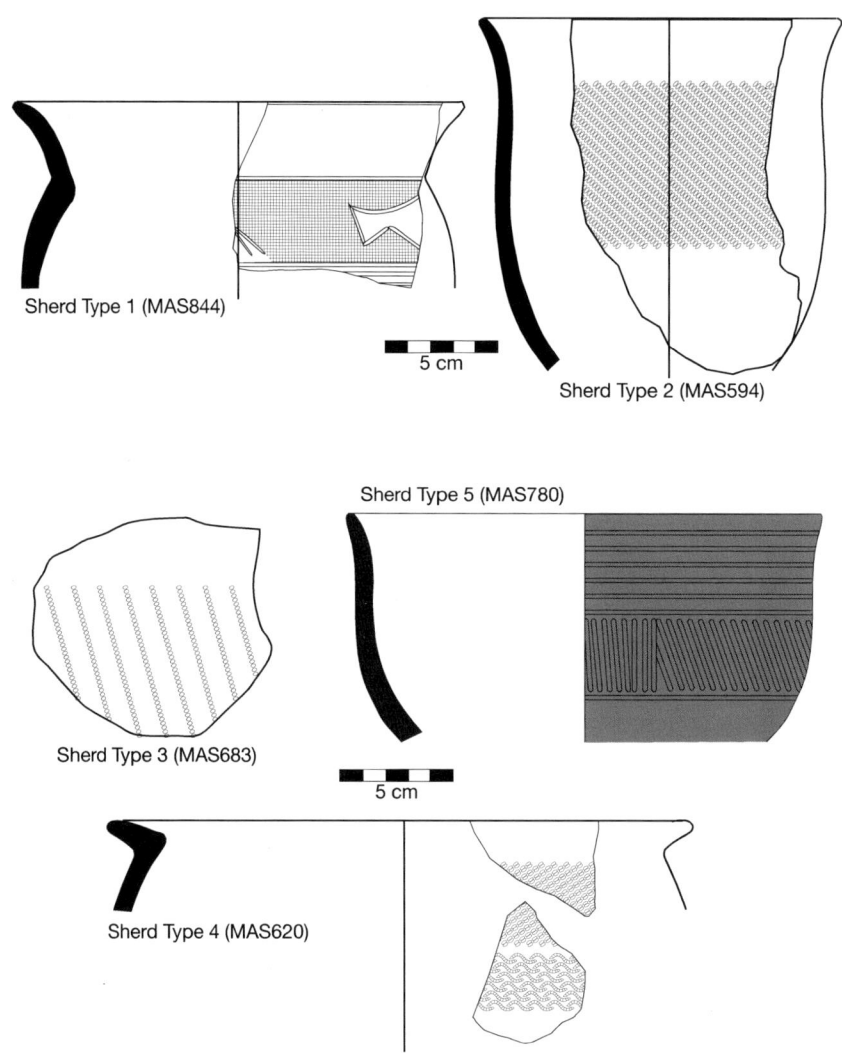

Figure 21. Examples of Sherd Types 1 through 7, with associated sites. See also Table 15.

Pwoli Occupation

The Pwoli occupation ($n = 3$; see Chapter 5) was primarily identified through excavation. Pwoli occupation ceramic assemblages had no typed sherds and high numbers of thin, burnished sherds with a variety of lightly applied decorations.

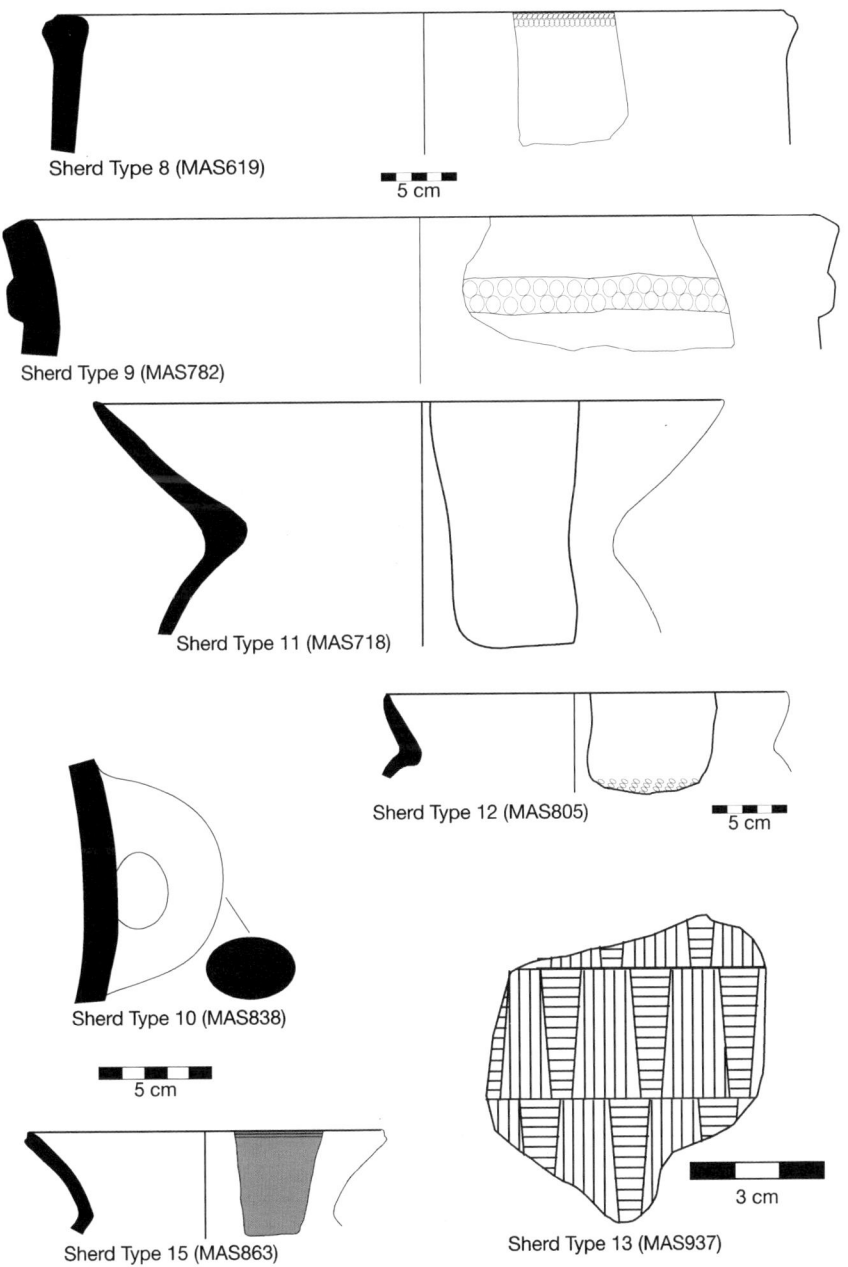

FIGURE 22. Examples of Sherd Types 8 through 13 and 15, with associated sites. See also Table 15.

Siga Occupation

Sites assigned to the Siga occupation ($n = 344$; see Chapter 6) were characterized by the presence of Sherd Types 1, 2, 3, 4, 5, and 6, with Sherd Types 7, 8, 9, and 10 also frequently present. The ceramic assemblages at these sites had different tempers, forms, vessel thick-

2	y												
3	y	y											
4	y	xy	xy										
5	xy	xy	xy	xy									
6			x	x	x								
7			x										
8													
9							x						
10		x			x								
11													
12										x			
13										a			
14										ax	x	a	
15						x				a		a	a
Type	1	2	3	4	5	6	7	8	9	10	11	12	13	14

FIGURE 23. Co-occurrence of sherd types in surface collections (**x**, significant at $p < 0.01$ using both Pearson and Fisher tests of chi square values), excavation (**y**, subsurface deposits at MAS780), and the ethnohistorical record (**a**, Gulmance pottery assemblages in Geis-Tronich [1991]).

ness, and decoration, reflecting both the diversity of sherd types present and the frequent occurrence of rare decorations and forms. Typically, more than 30% of sherds were decorated.

Tuali Occupation

Sites assigned to the Tuali occupation ($n = 134$; see Chapter 7) were characterized by the presence of Sherd Types 11, 12, 13, and 14. Once initial assignments were made, it was clear that the Tuali occupation could be split into Tuali-A assemblages (Sherd Types 9, 11, 12, and 14) and Tuali-B assemblages (Sherd Types 11, 12, 13, and 14). Both Tuali assemblages had low levels of decoration (less than 20%) and were dominated by quartz temper, but these patterns were more pronounced in the Tuali-B assemblage.

Ring Occupation

Ring occupation sites ($n = 19$; see Appendix C) were characterized by Sherd Type 15, with the occasional presence of Sherds Types 11 and 14. Many ring sites were clearly among the most recently abandoned sites (likely within the past fifty years) and tended to have comparatively little pottery. The small assemblages included large amounts of red-slipped sherds, very little decoration, and almost exclusively quartz temper. Overall, Ring sites were a small, transitional sample toward current occupation patterns.

The next four chapters present holistic discussions of the archaeological record for the Lithic, Pwoli, Siga, and Tuali occupations.

CHAPTER FOUR

Broad-spectrum Foragers of the Gobnangou
The Lithic Occupation

With its rich microenvironment, the Gobnangou escarpment and its forelands have been a favorable location for human habitation for the past several thousand years. Oliver Davies first recorded lithic scatters near the Gobnangou during a mid-century driving tour of the region (Davies 1967). These surface sites were characterized by microliths made of high-quality chert that likely derived from sources near the escarpment (Davies 1967). Although his description of the region was brief, Davies did send a small collection of unretouched chert flakes and debitage to the Archaeology Laboratory (Laboratoire de Préhistoire et Protohistoire) at what was then the Institut Français de l'Afrique Noire (now IFAN Cheikh Anta Diop), Dakar, Senegal (I examined this collection, labeled H.V. 57-31, in winter 2005). Large-scale archaeological research first occurred in the Gobnangou region in the late 1980s, when Goethe University Frankfurt and the University of Ouagadougou began a large, interdisciplinary project there (Breunig and Wotzka 1991; Millogo 1993a, 1993b; Müller-Haude 1995; Küppers 1996; Millogo and Koté 2000; Frank et al. 2001; Wotzka and Goedicke 2001).

Attracted by the diversity of microlithic tools known to exist in the Gobnangou, which suggested a lengthy forager occupation, the German–Burkinabe project hoped to isolate the transition from foragers to sedentary agricultural economies (Frank et al. 2001). Because of the deflated nature of the open-air agricultural sites that were identified, rockshelter and lithic sites were the primary focus of excavation (Figure 24). The project's research pushed the Gobnangou sequence possibly thousands of years earlier than previously suspected. Although poor organic preservation and the frequency of mixed deposits limited the reliability of absolute dating and site interpretation, this research provided most of the data available on early occupations in the region. The Maadaga Archaeological Survey did not locate any new stratified rockshelter sites in the limited section of escarpment surveyed, but did identify several previously undocumented open-air lithic scatters, one of which, site MAS542, we studied further through mapping and excavation of two small units.

Despite the patchy nature of evidence for foragers in the region and the challenges of dating the identified sites, an exploration of these data is crucial to understanding the history of subsistence strategies in the region. The early Gobnangou sequence can cur-

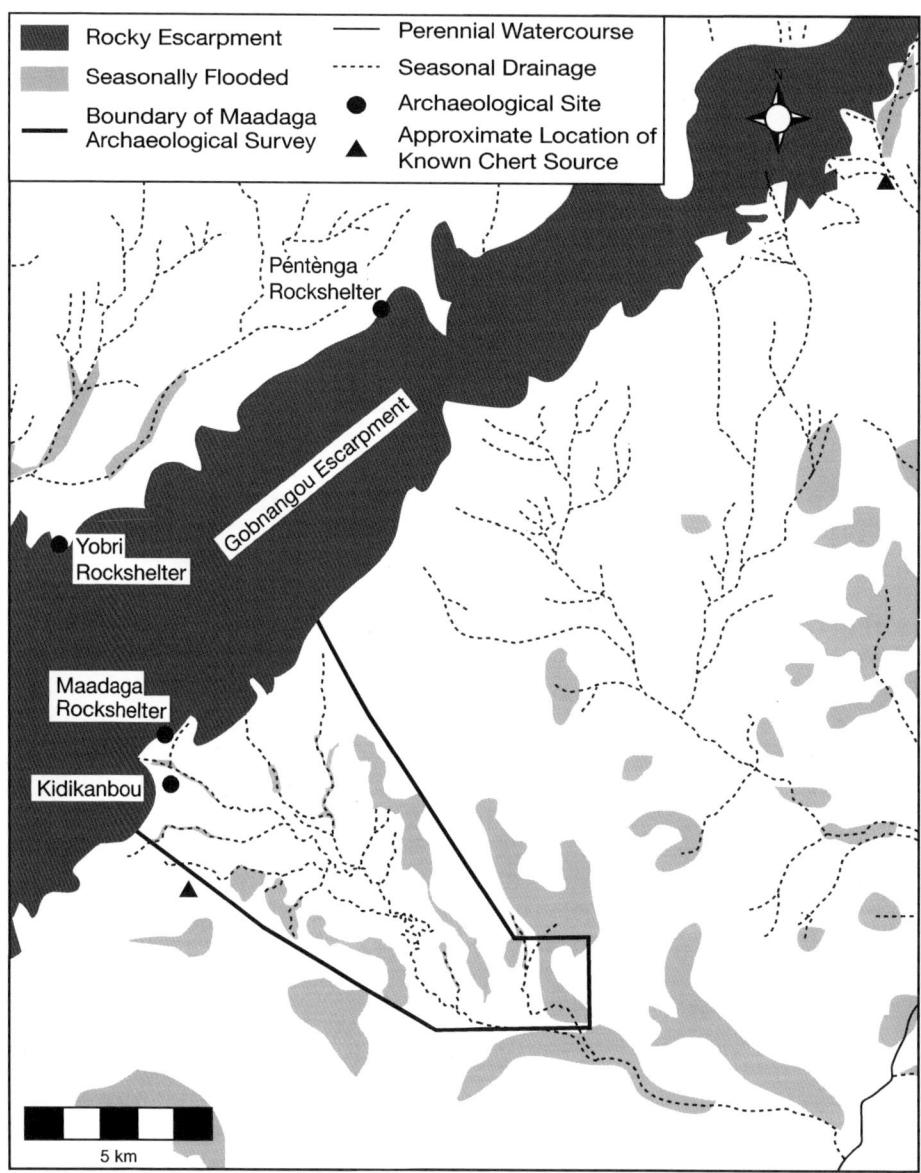

FIGURE 24. Archaeological sites with Middle Stone Age and geometric microlith assemblages excavated by Frank and colleagues (2001) and Millogo (1993a).

rently be divided into an undated occupation characterized by Mode 3 lithic technologies (according to J. Desmond Clark's [1969] widely used typology) largely lacking ceramics and a better-understood occupation of (Mode 5) microlith-using broad-spectrum mobile foragers starting by at the latest the mid-Holocene. Foragers likely continued to inhabit the region through at least the first millennium CE and possibly beyond.

Seeking the Middle Stone Age

Maadaga rockshelter is the site of the oldest identified archaeological deposits in southeastern Burkina Faso, a claim that rests almost exclusively on the recovery of a collection of chipped stone tools attributed to the Middle Stone Age (MSA) from the basal level of a small excavation unit. The MSA in West Africa includes most of the last 150,000 years and is generally thought to have terminated around the Pleistocene–Holocene transition (ca. 11,000 BCE; see reviews in Scerri et al. [2016, 2017], Chevrier et al. [2018], and Allsworth-Jones [2019]). Scholars working in other regions of Africa where Pleistocene occupations are a major focus of research increasingly favor the use of independent chronological frameworks such as the global marine isotope record (e.g., Barham and Mitchell 2008), yet the term MSA remains widespread in the West African literature. Its continued use, however, is less the result of conservatism and more an indication of the paucity of identified archaeological sites and research.

In 1989 and 1990, the German–Burkinabe Project conducted excavations at Maadaga rockshelter, the largest known shelter in the Gobnangou escarpment (Breunig and Wotzka 1991:172–176; Frank et al. 2001:134–140). Three excavation units were placed along a transect across the inside of the shelter, covering a total of 14 m² and reaching up to 1.9 m in depth; in the largest and deepest unit (trench 89/8) deposits were divided into five distinct layers. Below a loose, mixed surface matrix, the team excavated increasingly consolidated and rocky deposits until forced to stop before reaching bedrock. Although Layers 2 through 4 were not fully analyzed, Layer 5 (1.10 to 1.90 m with a total excavated volume of 1.6 m³) contained many stone artifacts characteristic of a Mode 3 lithic industry.

In total, 3,632 stone artifacts were recovered, most of which were made of quartzite or quartzitic sandstone. Cores were generally irregular, although Levallois cores were present. Scrapers, notched pieces, denticulates, and truncated flakes were the only retouched tools identified and these were both rare and lacked standardization. These types of Mode 3 flake tool artifacts are generally considered characteristic of MSA deposits in West Africa. For example, in the MSA deposits at Ounjougou, Mali (150,000–30,000 BP), local sandstone was also a common raw material and many of the same techniques were in use. However, there were also many significant differences. For example, residents of Ounjougou more frequently used discoidal techniques and bifacial flaking (Soriano et al. 2010; Chevrier et al. 2018). To the south in the Atakora Mountains of northern Benin, Petit (2005:27–48) identified several undated open-air scatters of irregular Mode 3 industries and one undated rockshelter with a Mode 3 component that he attributed to the MSA.

Mode 3 industries are typical of MSA sites in West Africa, but use of Mode 3 techniques is not sufficient evidence to support a Pleistocene occupation. Mode 3 techniques have been documented as persisting well into the late Holocene, although at later sites these flake tools were typically found in combination with other technologies (MacDonald and Allsworth-Jones 1994). Indeed, Millogo (1993a) noted a similar Mode 3 assemblage in the basal layers of his excavations at Yobri rockshelter (only 5 km from Maadaga rockshelter). His deposits were mixed with undecorated ceramics, which, if not intrusive, could indicate a later date for Mode 3 industries in the Gobnangou specifically. However, at Maadaga rockshelter no ceramics were recovered from below Layer 2 and even in Layer 2 the excavators considered them intrusive.

With the comparison between the Maadaga rockshelter Layer 5 assemblage and lithics from the few other MSA sites in West Africa published at the time (e.g., Allsworth-

Jones 1987), combined with the absence of microliths and pottery, Frank and colleagues (2001) felt they had sufficient evidence to attribute this assemblage to the MSA, although the similarities or lack thereof with the Yobri assemblage were not addressed. Unfortunately, direct dating of the assemblage was virtually impossible, because no organic remains, hearths, or other burned locations were identified during excavations of Layers 3 to 5 at the Maadaga rockshelter. The absence of these classes of evidence also prevented any characterization of economic activity. It is likely because of the lack of a secondary line of evidence for MSA occupation that Maadaga rockshelter has not been included in several recent reviews of the West African MSA (e.g., Chevrier et al. 2018; Allsworth-Jones 2019).

Given the rarity of stratified MSA sites in West Africa, the limitations of the Maadaga rockshelter deposits are unfortunate. Although the late Pleistocene archaeological record for sub-Saharan West Africa is extremely sparse, MSA populations in West Africa were likely no smaller than MSA populations in other mild climates. A reliance on organic tools (such as fiber), a paucity of deep rockshelters, and a lack of focused research are more plausible explanations for the meager archaeological record. In southeastern Burkina Faso, MSA layers have not been found at any other excavated rockshelters and our 2004 and 2006 surveys identified no Mode 3 assemblages at rockshelters or open-air sites. For the present, the MSA remains an intriguing, poorly understood prelude to the Gobnangou sequence.

Geometric Microliths in the Gobnangou Region

Aside from the few exceptions already discussed, lithic assemblages in the Gobnangou region were characterized by backed geometric microliths (Clark's [1969] Mode 5), an industry often associated with Late Stone Age foragers (Figure 25). However, in practice geometric microliths were used in West Africa throughout the Holocene at sites with and without ceramics, with and without plant and animal domesticates, and with and without iron tools (e.g., MacDonald 1997; Huysecom et al. 2009; N'Dah 2009; Gokee 2016; Watson 2017, 2018). In the Gobnangou region, geometric microliths initially appeared by 3600 BCE at the latest and were found at sites throughout the sequence (Table 16; Figure 26). These included sites with only microlithic tools and production debris, sites dominated by microlithic industries but with associated ceramics and ground stone, and sites at which microliths (and chipped stone generally) were a small component of the artifact assemblage. This chapter is primarily concerned with the first two categories; the third group will be discussed in subsequent chapters.

The most well-dated of these sites, Péntènga rockshelter (Frank et al. 2001), contained early layers with exclusively microlithic deposits and later layers with a mix of microliths and ceramics. Similar to the first part of the Péntènga sequence, four open-air sites with assemblages composed exclusively of chipped stone have been identified in erosional contexts and two, Kidikanbou (Frank et al. 2001) and MAS542, have been excavated; additional areas have been identified as possible talus slopes for rockshelters no longer in existence. In contrast, Yobri rockshelter (Millogo 1993a), with its mix of ceramics and microliths, had more in common with the later Péntènga deposits. Four additional sites identified by the MAS have ambiguous assemblages with either ceramic components or temporally mixed deposits. Péntènga, Kidikanbou, and Yobri have been fully published, therefore results from these excavations will only be summarized briefly here. Sites identified and recorded by the MAS, including the excavated site MAS542, will be discussed in more detail.

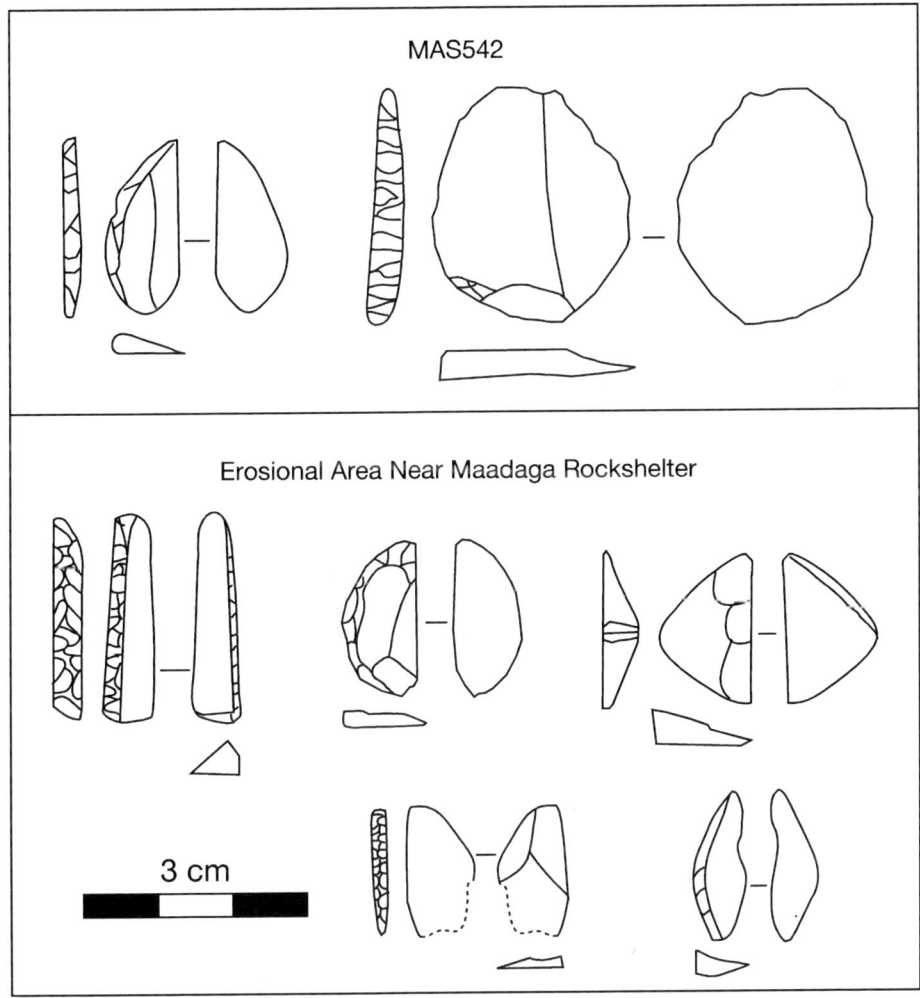

FIGURE 25. Backed microliths from site MAS542 (*top*) and an erosional area near Maadaga rockshelter at the Gobnangou escarpment (*bottom*).

Péntènga Rockshelter

The site of Péntènga rockshelter (Frank et al. 2001:150–170) is located near the upper edge of the Gobnangou escarpment adjacent to a large sandstone boulder, which likely formed an overhang before breaking away from the cliff face. Excavation of a 6 m² unit to a depth of 1.86 m found a loose sandy matrix with ceramics, charcoal, animal bones, and microlithic tools. Refitting of pot sherds and comparison of thermoluminescence (TL) dates from the pottery with radiocarbon dates on the charcoal yielded clear evidence of mixed deposits, although the unit could be divided into four temporal strata: ca. 6600–5450 cal BCE, ca. 3600 cal BCE, ca. 820–570 cal BCE, and ca. 150–1250 cal CE. The earliest set of dates came from charcoal in the lowest levels of the stratigraphy. These early deposits included microliths and ceramics, but because the ceramics were TL dated to 3600 cal BCE, Frank and colleagues (2001) assumed that they were intrusive. Several of the microliths,

TABLE 16. Gobnangou region Lithic occupation sites and those where formal chipped stone tools were recovered. Chipped stone was also identified as a minor artifact class at an additional 225 sites dated to the Pwoli, Siga, and Tuali occupations. Assigned level of confidence is given as high (H) or low (L).

Site name	Size of chipped stone assemblage	Number of formal tools	Description of chipped stone assemblage	Other artifact classes present	Occupation (confidence level)
Maadaga Rockshelter (Layer 5)	3,632	34?	Quartzitic sandstone flakes, cores, and debitage; retouched scrapers, denticulates, notched pieces, and truncated flakes	None	Middle Stone Age*
Kidikanbou	6,426	1,489	Microliths (57% of formal tools), flakes, blades, cores, hammerstones, debitage; majority of assemblage is chert	None	Lithic*
MAS542	273	2	Chert flakes, debitage, and cores (multidirectional and unidirectional); less than 10% quartz debitage and flakes	None	Lithic (H)
MAS867	15	0	Chert flakes and cores; several pieces of unworked chert	None	Lithic (H); Siga (L)
MAS947	52	0	Chert flakes and debitage; less than 5% quartz debitage; one piece unworked chert	None	Lithic (H)
MAS723	21	0	Chert flakes and debitage; less than 5% quartz flake	Ceramics (very few)	Lithic (L)
MAS864	30	0	Chert flakes and debitage; less than 10% quartz debitage	Ceramics (very few)	Lithic (L); Siga (L)
MAS907	28	2	Chert tools, flakes and debitage; less than 10% quartz debitage	Ceramics (very few)	Lithic (L); Siga (L)
MAS638	7	1	Chert tool, flakes, and debitage	Ceramics	Tuali-A (L), possible earlier component
MAS573	2	1	Chert tool and debitage	Ceramics, ground stone, slag	Siga (H)
MAS926	12	1	Chert tool and debitage; less than 10% quartz debitage	Ceramics	Siga (H)

Continued

TABLE 16 CONTINUED

Site name	Size of chipped stone assemblage	Number of formal tools	Description of chipped stone assemblage	Other artifact classes present	Occupation (confidence level)
MAS935	6	1	Chert tool, flakes, and debitage; 50% quartz debitage	Ceramics, ground stone, slag (high levels, possible furnace)	Siga (H)
MAS689	8	1	Chert tool, flakes, and debitage; one piece unworked chert	Ceramics, ground stone, slag	Tuali-A (H)
MAS705.2	2	1	Chert tool and debitage	Ceramics, ground stone	Tuali-A (H)
MAS755	1	1	One formal chert tool	Ceramics, ground stone, slag	Tuali-A (H)
MAS800	2	1	One formal tool and one piece unworked chert	Ceramics, ground stone, slag	Tuali-A (H)
MAS880	1	1	Chert tool	Ceramics	Tuali-B (H)

* Frank et al. (2001)

however, had been burned, which could indicate association with the charcoal. The identified charcoal assemblage from Péntènga rockshelter indicated that forests (which included the species *Anogeissus leiocarpus, Allophylus* sp., and *Pterocarpus* cf. *erinaceus*) grew in the sandy soils at the base of the escarpment, whereas savanna species such as *Terminalia* sp. were common on the slopes.

The lithic assemblage at Péntènga rockshelter was typical of the Gobnangou region: backed geometric microliths dominated the formal tool assemblage, with crescents and micropoints by far the most common forms, followed by trapezes and triangles. As is to be expected, about 95% of the assemblage was composed of unretouched debitage, including a small percentage of blades and bladelets.

Direct TL dating of the pottery (predominantly quartz-tempered open vessels with simple rims and rocker comb decoration) recovered in layers with a microlith assemblage generally similar to that from the earlier layers yielded dates from the second to third millennium BCE. As discussed below, pottery was a common element of mid-Holocene forager toolkits throughout West Africa. Ceramic vessels were particularly useful for tasks that required boiling, such as cooking grains or rendering vegetal fats (Stahl 1993; Rice 1999).

Roughly contemporary with the described pottery, the species composition in the identified charcoal changed to reflect a more arid climate, although species indicative of remnant forests remained. In addition, the appearance of more fire-resistant species and evidence of trauma-affected rings in larger trees indicated that brush fires became more common. Whether these were a side effect of less precipitation or intentionally set by hu-

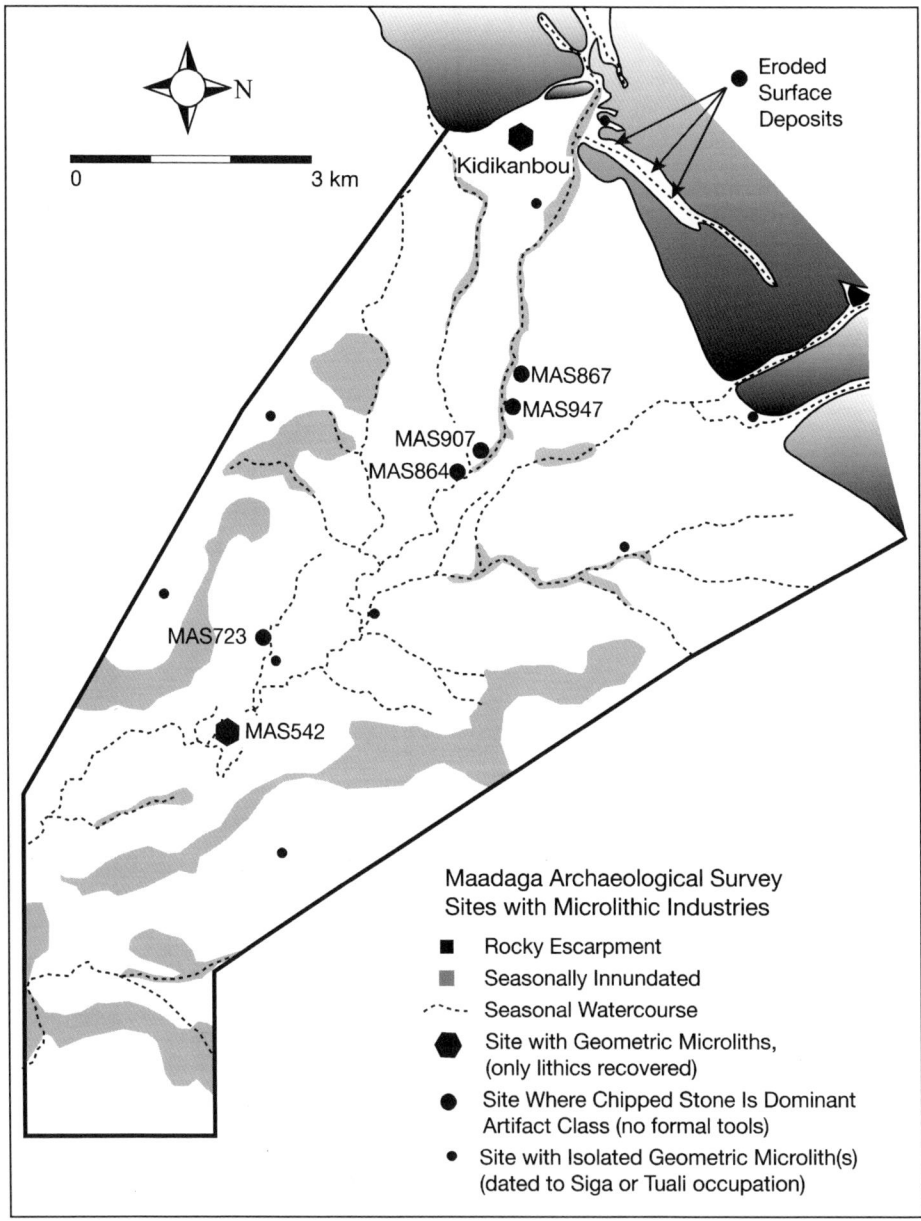

FIGURE 26. Lithic occupation sites identified by the Maadaga Archaeological Survey.

mans is not yet known. The diverse savanna environment, including dry forests, remained fairly constant through the Pwoli occupation.

The animal bone assemblage of Péntènga rockshelter provided unique evidence for subsistence practices associated with Mode 5 technologies in Burkina Faso (Frank et al. 2001; see also the discussions in Dueppen and Gallagher [2013]). The fauna in spits containing both microliths and early pottery showed a broad-spectrum hunting and collecting strategy of locally available resources, with a particular emphasis on aquatic resources such as fish, freshwater mollusks, and aquatic reptiles, almost all of which could have been caught or collected in the seasonal pools and drainages near the base of the escarpment (Table 17). The larger mammals, notably oribi and hartebeest, could have been found in the savannas surrounding the escarpment. Péntènga's fauna were generally consistent with a wet season and early dry season occupation of the site, when the fish and other aquatic resources would have been plentiful in the floodplain near the base of the escarpment (Dueppen and Gallagher 2013). Wild grasses ripen at this time of year, perhaps accounting for the presence of pottery at this site.

Yobri Rockshelter

From 1989 to 1990, Millogo (1993a) excavated five 1 by 1 m units at the rockshelter site of Yobri. These units uncovered a rich cultural deposit with a mixed lithic industry, including Mode 5 elements. The microlith assemblage was dominated by crescents and micropoints, although retouched flake tools were also present. Ceramics were common throughout the deposit and, aside from the microlithic component, Millogo considered the site otherwise comparable to the site of Rim in northwestern Burkina Faso (Andah 1978, 1980). A preliminary analysis of the animal bone identified a range of mammals and what seemed to be a greater focus on larger mammals (see Table 17). Although some freshwater mollusks were identified, the residents of Yobri did not emphasize aquatic resources like the residents of Péntènga. In particular, Millogo noted the lack of fish remains. The seasonality of the site may have differed significantly from Péntènga, perhaps reflecting use during the dry season, when water sources were reduced and large mammals clustered toward the escarpment.

Kidikanbou

Kidikanbou was a dense open-air scatter of microliths located about 300 m southeast of the Gobnangou cliff face near Maadaga rockshelter (Frank et al. 2001:141–149). The deposit was bioturbated by small animals and possibly eroded. Over 6,000 chert artifacts were recovered from 10 m² excavated to a depth of around 0.6 m, although the artifacts may have originally been on a sloping surface that was subsequently buried. Geometric microliths were unusually frequent ($n = 838$, 13% of the total assemblage, as compared with 2.5% at Péntènga). Fragmentary microliths were also unusually common for the region (36% of the total microlith population). Micropoints and triangles dominated the assemblage, with crescents and trapezes present in much smaller numbers. The site could not be dated because of a lack of organic preservation. Frank and colleagues (2001) interpreted Kidikanbou as a hunting camp where broken points were removed from shafts and replaced with new microliths, thus accounting for both the high percentage of fragmentary examples and the high numbers of formal tools. If a hunting camp, Kidikanbou's location on the edge of the escarpment could indicate that it was a dry-season occupation taking advantage of animals clustering near water sources at that time.

Site MAS542

Site MAS542 was located in an erosional gully near the main channel of the Koabu (Figure 27). The site was immediately notable for the large numbers of chert flakes clustered near the base of the gully wall. Given the site's vulnerability to further erosion, the MAS made large surface collections in 2004 and cut an excavation unit (Unit 1) into the side of the gully in an attempt to identify the primary lithic strata. We placed an additional small test unit on the opposite gully wall to estimate the original slope of the strata (Unit 2). In

TABLE 17. Fauna identified from the Péntènga and Yobri rockshelters. Faunal remains from below the rockfall at Péntènga (seventh to first millennia BCE, spits 11 to 21) were identified by W. van Neer (Frank et al. 2001:177) and are given as the number of identified specimens (NISP). Faunal remains at Yobri were identified by E. Desclaux and L. Jourdan (Millogo 1993a:131) and are given as present (×) or absent (—).

Category	Common name	Scientific name	Péntènga (NISP)	Yobri
Small bovid	Oribi	*Ourebia ourebi*	2	—
	Unidentified small bovid		19	—
Medium bovid	Unidentified medium bovid		6	×
Large bovid	Roan antelope	*Hippotragus equinus*		×
	Hartebeest or topi	*Alcelaphus buselaphus* or *Damaliscus* sp.	1	—
	Unidentified large bovid		5	×
Suid	Warthog	*Phacochoerus africanus*	2	×
Primate	Unidentified primate			×
Carnivore	Domestic dog or jackal	*Canis* sp.	3	—
Hyrax	Hyrax	*Procavia* sp.	7	—
Large rodent	Porcupine	Hystricidae		×
	Cane rat	*Thryonomys swinderianus*	4	—
	Gambian rat	*Cricetomys gambianus*	4	—
	Unidentified large rodent			×
Small rodent	Gerbil	*Gerbalis* sp.	3	—
	Unidentified small rodent		9	×
Avian	Unidentified raptor			×
	Small passeriform bird		1	—
Reptile	Crocodile	*Crocodylus* sp. (*C. cataphractus* or *C. niloticus*) or *Osteolaemus* sp.	7	—
	Monitor lizard	*Varanus* sp. (*V. niloticus* or *V. exanthematicus*)	9	—
	Unidentified small lizard		7	×
	Python	*Python* sp.	26	—
	Unidentified snake		1	×
	Mud turtle	*Pelusios adansonii*	3	—
	Unidentified turtle		30	×

Continued

TABLE 17 CONTINUED

Category	Common name	Scientific name	Péntènga (NISP)	Yobri
Amphibian	Frog or toad	*Anura* sp.	26	—
	Unidentified frog or toad			×
Freshwater bivalve	Bivalve	*Aspatharia dahomeyensis*	16	—
	Unidentified bivalve			×
Freshwater mollusk	Snail	*Lanistes varicus*	82	—
Fish	Tilapia	Tilapiini	1	—
	Synodontis catfish	*Synodontis* sp.	2	—
	Clarias catfish	*Clarias* sp.	38	—
	Lungfish	*Protopterus* sp.	28	—
	Bichir	*Polypterus* sp.	5	—
	Knifefish	*Gymnarchus niloticus*	1	—
Land snail	Land snail (large)		27	—
	Land snail (medium)		2	—
	Land snail (small)		3	—
	Land snail		—	×

2006, the MAS revisited the site and took additional surface collections of newly exposed artifacts. Only lithic artifacts were recovered; there were no datable materials.

Both excavation units were topped with a loose gray, sandy matrix mixed with matted dried vegetal material (Figure 28). This layer was significantly thicker in Unit 2, probably due to the denser brush growing on this part of the site. Below the loose surface materials, the deposit was a very compact hard yellow sediment with many small ferrous inclusions.

Only seventy-seven lithic artifacts were recovered during excavation, none of which had evidence of retouching. Unit 1 had a clear concentration of lithics between 60 and 75 cm depths (34 of 51 total artifacts). Only three artifacts were recovered above these strata. Below them all artifacts recovered were located at the erosional edges of the unit and may have originated from this lens. Despite the apparent constrained nature of the lithic assemblage, close examination of the profiles revealed no differentiation between the artifact-bearing stratum and sterile deposits. Excavations in Unit 2 ($n = 24$ artifacts) indicated that the lithic stratum was present at approximately the same absolute elevation. Artifacts from deeper strata in Unit 2 may have fallen into the unit, as it was difficult to control the loose surface layer during excavation.

Excavation and surface assemblages had the same characteristics and were presumed to have originated from the same deposit, therefore a summary of the lithic data for site MAS542 is presented holistically (Table 18). More than 90% of collected artifacts were gray chert, about half of which had visible cortex. No pieces of unworked raw material were recovered, but the five chert cores were small (between 3 and 6 cm maximum length) and multidirectional. Flakes were exclusively unifacial and generally long and broad (averaging

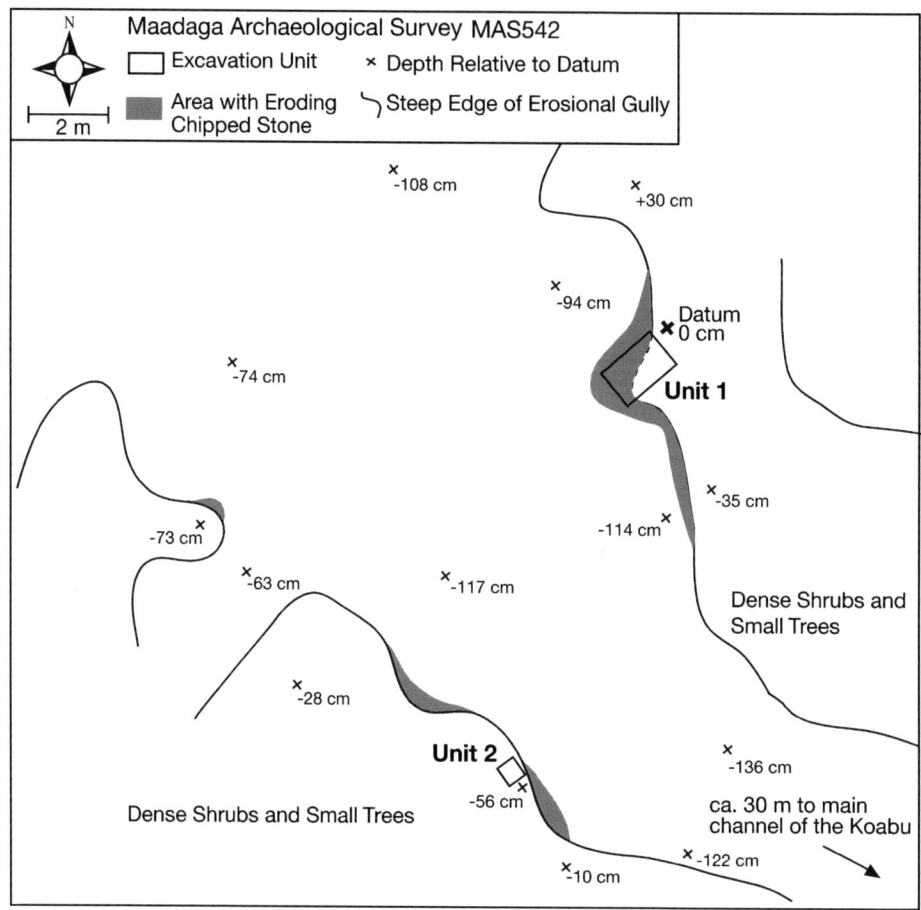

FIGURE 27. Plan of the MAS542 archaeological site.

33 mm in length and typically too wide to be considered blades). The two formal tools, both collected from the surface, included a crescent and a scraper (see Figure 25).

Eroded Surface Deposits near Maadaga Rockshelter

Maadaga rockshelter is located at the mouth of a small valley that runs parallel to the Gobnangou escarpment. The valley extends about 400 m along the primary channel of the Koabu, terminating at a spring-fed waterfall (Odundo; see Figure 7), and is bordered on the south by a sandstone outcrop. The escarpment face forming the north edge is pocked with small rockshelters, most of which were filled in with termite nests and none of which had in situ deposits. In 2004, survey along the base of the escarpment in this valley revealed ubiquitous surface scatters of lithics extending past Maadaga rockshelter and along the foot of the cliff. Three 50 by 50 cm shovel tests in the densest of these scatters confirmed them as exclusively surface features. Given the degree of fluvial activity in the region, we assumed they were erosional deposits that may have originated from the talus slopes of the rockshelters. Although little could be learned from their context, they did provide a point of comparison for the MAS542 and Kidikanbou assemblages, both of which had a significantly higher percentage

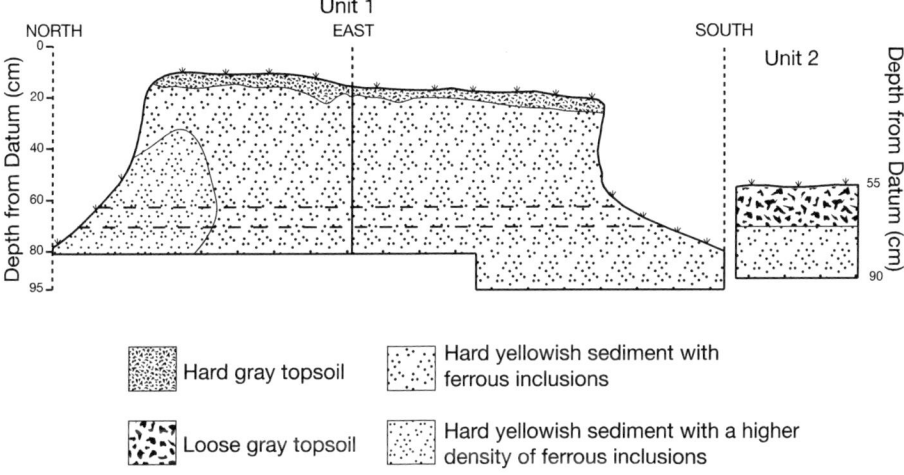

FIGURE 28. Profile of the stratigraphy of the MAS542 archaeological site. Stratum with the highest density of chipped chert was located from 60 to 75 cm below the datum in Unit 1 (*dotted lines*). This stratum was not visibly different from the surrounding matrix.

of chert. Visually, the flakes at site MAS542 were longer and broader than those recovered near the escarpment, an impression confirmed by measurements on intact flakes (see Table 18). As at site MAS542, formal tools were rare, although a backed bladelet and backed geometric microliths (crescents and triangles) were recovered (see Figure 25).

Additional Identified Lithic Sites

The MAS identified two surface scatters composed exclusively of chipped stone. Both MAS867 and MAS947 were located on sandy ridges along the Koabu and had assemblages comprised almost entirely of gray chert. However, surface collections from site MAS867 consisted primarily of cores and pieces of unworked raw material with only a few flakes. In contrast, the site MAS947 assemblage consisted primarily of debitage, including pieces of different sizes, pieces with and without cortex, and many measurable flakes. No cores were recovered, and only a few thin pieces of unworked raw material were identified. No formal tools or retouched flakes were found at either site.

Three sites, MAS723, MAS864, and MAS907, had surface assemblages consisting primarily of chipped stone, but also had surface ceramics in very low densities that could reflect either use of both technologies or a later reoccupation of the same area. The chipped stone at all three sites was primarily chert with a minor quartz component and consisted entirely of debitage and flakes; no cores or unworked raw material were recovered. Two broken tools with possible retouch were recovered from site MAS907. The ceramics at all three sites were infrequent and small with few decorations (MAS723: 4 sherds, 15 g, no decorations; MAS864: 5 sherds, 25 g, no decorations; MAS907: 10 sherds, 40 g, one decorated with semicircular channels). The mix of tempers indicated that these sherds aligned with the Siga occupation rather than with the primarily quartz-tempered early ceramic tradition from Péntènga rockshelter. Consequently, these sites were most likely either Siga occupation activity areas or multicomponent sites; that is, a later Siga use of the same space.

Chipped stone was also recovered from 225 sites dating to Pwoli, Siga, and Tuali occupations. Although in most cases only a few isolated pieces of debitage or flakes were

TABLE 18. Characteristics of chipped stone assemblages collected at sites identified by the Maadaga Archaeological Survey.

Artifacts	MAS542		Surface near Maadaga rockshelter		MAS867, MAS947		MAS723, MAS864, MAS907		All other sites (n = 234)	
	Number	Percentage	Number	Percentage	Number	Percentage	Number	Percentage	Number	Percentage
Type of chipped stone artifact										
Chipped stone	273	100	819	100	67	100	79	100	557	100
Chert	248	90.8	351	42.8	64	95.5	73	92.4	523	93.9
Quartz	25	9.2	469	57.2	3	4.5	6	7.6	34	6.1
Formal tools	2	0.7	6	0.7	0	0	2	0.3	9	1.6
Artifacts with cortex	137	50.1	337	41.1	49	73.1	62	78.4	422	75.8
Flakes										
Number of measurable flakes	62		92		11		9		66	
Average flake length (mm)	33		22		37		23		28	

present, these sites accounted for a majority of formal tools recovered from the region (see Table 16; see also Chapter 7; Figure 69). It is currently unknown whether these tools were manufactured at the sites where they were found or simply collected from older sites in the region. Chipped stone has been documented at agricultural sites throughout West Africa and chert could be preferred for tasks ranging from starting fires (two Siga iron furnace sites, MAS849 and MAS929, had some of the highest densities of chipped stone identified at sites with significant ceramic components) to hide scraping (e.g., Dueppen and Gokee 2014; Gokee 2016).

Dating Microlithic Industries

Dating of the sites dominated by chipped stone assemblages was tentative at best, as Maadaga rockshelter, Kidikanbou, MAS542, MAS867, MAS947, MAS723, MAS864, and MAS907 all had no organic remains. Worked chert flakes encased in laterite duracrust were observed near Maadaga rockshelter. Unfortunately, this stone matrix, which is the result of erosion and leaching processes that leave heavier ferrous elements in place, can form in as little as a few hundred years. Although there are reliable radiocarbon dates for Péntènga rockshelter (the 6500–5500 cal BCE date is based on five individually dated samples from three strata), their association with the microlithic assemblage must be considered tentative given the issues of stratigraphic integrity at the site, and it is possible that the microliths do not predate the ceramics (ca. 3600 cal BCE). However, the sixth millennium BCE date is bolstered by a similar date for microlithic industries in the greater region from RB 99-24, a site 115 km to the southeast of the study region along the Pendjari River in northern Benin, dated to 5480–5330 cal BCE (6440 ± 40 bp) (N'Dah 2009:182).

Association with ceramics was also difficult to use as a chronological indicator, because ceramics in West Africa significantly predate fully agricultural economies and in some cases microlithic industries. Several clearly preceramic Mode 5 sites are known in West Africa (e.g., Davies 1967; Andah 1978, 1980; Vernet 1996; MacDonald 1997; Petit 2005; N'Dah 2009; Fontana et al. 2010), but the samples are small and widely spaced. To date, the earliest ceramics identified in sub-Saharan West Africa are from the tenth millennium BCE levels at Ounjougou, where they were found first in association with bifacial flake tools and then with geometric microliths beginning around 8100 BCE (Huysecom et al. 2009). By the fourth millennium BCE, ceramics were present in Cameroon (Shum Laka; Lavachery 2001), Nigeria (Konduga; Wotzka and Goedicke 2001), Mali (Korounkorokalé; MacDonald 1997), and Ghana (Bosumpra; Oas, D'Andrea, and Watson 2015), as well as at Péntènga rockshelter. At most of these sites, pottery was a secondary artifact class in assemblages dominated by geometric microliths, as was the case at the Péntènga and Yobri rockshelters. Finally, in western and northern Burkina Faso early microlithic industries were often associated with polished stone *hachettes*, axes, and adzes (e.g., Andah 1978; Millogo and Koté 2000; Fontana et al. 2010). Similarly, Davies found polished adzes in conjunction with microliths between Arly and Pama (see the notes accompanying IFAN Ch. A. Diop collection H.V. 57-31). In the MAS, polished stone *hachettes* were recovered from Pwoli, Siga, and Tuali occupation sites, but none were found at sites with substantial chipped stone assemblages.

Whereas in other parts of sub-Saharan Africa there are identifiable temporal and spatial patterns in the microlithic industries themselves (e.g., Lombard et al. 2012; Mitchell 2017), in West Africa there are currently no known chronologically significant indicators that could be used to date the Gobnangou lithic assemblages. Likewise, no chronologically significant patterns have been noted for the Gobnangou itself: geometric microliths from throughout the sequence fall well into the range of variation present in the large samples from Péntènga and Kidikanbou. At Péntènga and neighboring sites, Wotzka and Goedicke (2001) identified chronologically significant patterns in the ceramics. Unfortunately, these early styles were not identified at any sites in the MAS area.

Overall, caution is necessary in interpreting sites MAS542, MAS867, MAS947, MAS723, MAS864, and MAS907. Given the evidence at Péntènga for microlithic industries from at the latest the fourth millennium BCE (and likely the sixth to seventh millennia BCE) and the mid to late first millennium CE dates for the adoption of agriculture in the region (see Chapter 5), it seems clear that there was at minimum several thousand years of occupation in the Gobnangou region by mobile foraging populations that used microlithic industries.

At the same time, microlithic industries continued through the first and into the second millennium CE. It is possible that foraging populations persisted in the region even as farming became more common during the Pwoli, Siga, and Tuali occupations. However, the prominence of micropoints in the assemblages could indicate an earlier date for some of the lithic sites that were identified. In southern Africa, where there has been more extensive research, although chipped stone tools remained important for particular tasks (notably scraping), the use of backed microliths in particular declined as iron arrowheads became available (see the discussions in Lombard et al. [2012] and Forssman [2015]). This also may have been the case in West Africa, as the foraging inhabitants of Korounkorokalé (west of Bamako, Mali) continued to rely on chipped stone industries after the introduction of iron smelting technology, yet replaced stone points with iron ones (MacDonald 1997).

It is also possible that some of the Lithic sites represent activity areas associated with the Pwoli, Siga, or Tuali occupations. Chipped stone was commonly recovered from the surface of Pwoli, Siga, and Tuali sites, although not in the densities found at Lithic sites. Clearly, this was considered a useful technology for agricultural populations in the region even if at this time chipped stone cannot be linked to specific tasks.

Mobility and Hunting Practices: Implications of Geometric Microlith Use

Aside from the limited faunal, botanical, and ceramic record at the Péntènga and Yobri rockshelters (both of which had significant stratigraphic mixing), there was very little data other than the geometric microlith industry from which to directly characterize foraging populations near the Gobnangou escarpment. Despite the lack of in situ deposits in the study region, research on better-documented microlithic industries in other parts of Africa can be used as a base from which to speculate about the possible economic strategies of early foragers in the region.

Backed microliths are often assumed to have been hafted into composite tools, particularly arrows, a practice well documented in the ethnographic and ethnohistorical record (see the discussions in Bousman [2005] and Goldstein and Shaffer [2017]). Prehistoric examples of hafting were documented at Makwe, Zambia, where mastic traces were found on geometric microliths (Phillipson 1976). Phillipson posited the presence of a variety of hafted tools, including chisels, arrow barbs, scrapers, and cutting implements, as well as the use of unhafted backed points and scrapers. Additional studies on microliths from Egypt, Kenya, and South Africa have confirmed that a variety of types, including crescents, were used for scraping and cutting tasks, often without hafting (e.g., Becker and Wendorf 1993; Binneman 1997; Binneman and Mitchell 1997; Goldstein and Shaffer 2017). To date, no microscopic use-wear analysis has been carried out on any microliths from the Gobnangou region.

Sites in the Gobnangou region did reveal some significant differences in the distribution of microlithic tool types. Although micropoints were a major component of the assemblage at all sites with large samples of formal tools, crescents were the second most common type at the two rockshelter sites to the north of the escarpment. In contrast, at Kidikanbou crescents were only a minor component of the assemblage and triangles were the second most common by a large margin. These differences could be functional, although microlith shapes rarely map directly to function. Given that Yobri and Péntènga shared an emphasis on crescents, whereas the faunal evidence reflected distinct foraging strategies, the differences between these two sites and Kidikanbou may reflect stylistic differences between the north and south sides of the escarpment (see the discussions on microlith style in Hiscock, Clarkson, and Mackay [2011]).

Regardless of their specific use, backed microliths are strongly associated with a wide range of hunting activities (Lombard and Parsons 2008; Pargeter 2011; Forssman 2015). Shaw (1985) originally posited that microliths were associated with savanna adaptations requiring greater mobility, whereas Holocene Mode 3 industries (such as at Iwo Eleru, Nigeria, and Shum Laka, Cameroon) were a forest phenomenon. However, even if one sets aside the Gobnangou case (on the forest-savanna margin), Holocene macrolithic industries are now widely known in the northern savanna (MacDonald and Allsworth-Jones 1994; Huysecom et al. 2004), whereas microlithic industries have been identified in southern Ivory Coast and Ghana (Davies 1967; Chenorkian 1983). If anything, the decoupling of lithic modes from ecological zones throws into sharper relief the question of why some groups used Mode 3 flakes while others used Mode 5 microliths.

A recent trend has been to suggest that microlithic industries were associated with more mobile settlement systems, because their efficient use of raw material would have been advantageous both for decreasing loads and increasing the time between visits to raw material sources (Barham and Mitchell 2008). Unlike much of West Africa, where quartz or quartzite chipped stone industries were the norm, the Gobnangou escarpment region had many outcrops of fine-grained chert. In a brief survey, Müller-Haude (1995) identified chert sources south of present-day Kidikanbou and near Kodjari. There were almost certainly additional sources and thus conservation of raw material would likely not have been necessary. It is also possible that cobbles of chert may have been available in the various drainages extending from the escarpment, although none were seen during the survey.

The frequency of cortex is often used as a proxy measure for distance from the raw material source. However, among sites in the survey region with large assemblages, the most distant from known chert sources (MAS542) actually had a higher percentage of cortex than closer sites. This indicates that access to sources within the region was not difficult. Examination of the sizes of flakes, cores, and unworked raw material at sites MAS542, MAS867, MAS947, MAS723, MAS864, and MAS907, as well as across all lithic artifacts recovered from all occupation phases, also found no evidence that distance from lithic sources affected flaking industries within the study region (although within the survey zone maximal distance from sources was less than 10 km, which may not have been sufficient to show variance). The role of mobility in influencing the use of microlithic industries is consequently uncertain in the Gobnangou, because lithic and faunal data indicated that at least some sites may have been part of a seasonal cycle. It is unknown, however, whether the cycle would have taken social groups far from the escarpment during certain seasons, as different sites along the escarpment may represent different seasons. Given the broad-spectrum adaptation at Péntènga, the need for long-distance mobility would seem unlikely.

Ambrose (2002), drawing on South African data, has proposed an alternate interpretation of Mode 5 industries: he suggested that they could indicate more predictable resource patterns (see also the discussion in Mitchell [2017]). Because microlithic composite tools are both more complex and more specialized, their use could indicate advance knowledge of tasks to be performed (whether through networks or stable environments). In the Gobnangou case, this hypothesis was potentially supported by the excessive number of fragmentary microliths at Kidikanbou, which Frank and colleagues (2001) attributed to the repair of hunting implements. Bousman (2005) suggested that this phenomenon could be indicative of low resource stress. In his study of the Robberg Mode 5 industry in South Africa, he argued that during periods of high resource scarcity, hunters were more likely to keep their hafted weapons in excellent repair, replacing complete microliths more frequently. Conversely, during times of abundance, hunters would have followed a time-minimization strategy and only repaired their weapons once microliths actually broke. Although Bousman's model (which was reinforced by multiple lines of evidence in the Robberg case) articulates well with a reconstruction of the Gobnangou as a relatively rich microenvironment, more supporting data would be necessary to evaluate this hypothesis for the Gobnangou.

Inherent in Bousman's model was the assumption that microlith breakage resulted from use. Since the publication of the analyses of the large microlith assemblages at Péntènga and Kidikanbou (Frank et al. 2001), there have been increasing efforts to distinguish fractures resulting from microlith use from those created during manufacture or by post-depositional processes (e.g., Close and Sampson 1998; Lombard and Pargeter 2008; Pargeter 2011; Pargeter and Bradfield 2012; Forssman 2015; Goldstein and Shaffer 2017). According to these studies, while the snap fractures that would create fragmentary microliths can result from use (e.g., Goldstein and Shaffer 2017), they can also result from a range of other processes, making them difficult to interpret. Microliths can break during manufacture (e.g., Close and Sampson 1998; Goldstein and Shaffer 2017), a possibility that Frank and colleagues (2001) dismiss as the primary cause, given the high percentage of broken microliths. More significantly, post-depositional trampling (e.g., Pargeter 2011; Pargeter and Bradfield 2012) also results in significant breakage, a process that could potentially account for the higher incidence of snap fractures at the open-air site of Kidikanbou than at the less accessible Péntènga.

Overall, the Gobnangou escarpment is a rich environmental zone with diverse resources that has been occupied by humans for many millennia. Owing to the limited economic data, our understanding of the nature of these sites is tentative, but current evidence does suggest that sites with microlithic technologies could have been occupied by mobile, broad-spectrum foragers. The diverse microenvironments, accessibility of raw materials, and permanent water sources of the escarpment would have allowed foragers to stay in the region year-round, a possibility supported by the different resources exploited at Yobri, Péntènga, and possibly Kidikanbou. The presence of pottery at some sites, but not others, could reflect caching for seasonal use or the presence of logistical base camps. At the same time, there was little evidence for sedentary occupation (such as hearth complexes, large middens, architectural improvements, and so on), suggesting that foraging groups in the region remained fairly mobile.

CHAPTER FIVE

Adopting Agriculture
The Pwoli Occupation

The Pwoli occupation (ca. 650–1050 CE) was represented by a small group of sites with the current earliest direct evidence for use of domesticated resources and agricultural strategies in southeastern Burkina Faso. Previous archaeological investigations of the Gobnangou escarpment by the German–Burkinabe project indicated a late adoption of agriculture in the region. As discussed in the previous chapter, the project's excavations of rockshelter and open-air sites around the escarpment in the late 1980s and early 1990s found no direct evidence for cultivation of domesticates. Charcoal profiles from the Péntènga rockshelter indicated the continuing presence of dry forests through the end of the sequence at 1100 CE and little evidence of taxa typically associated with agricultural fallows (Frank et al. 2001). Overall, the team's results pointed to the presence of seasonally mobile ceramic-using foragers with a broad-spectrum economy beginning around the mid-Holocene and continuing through the first millennium CE.

The German–Burkinabe excavations were largely confined to the escarpment itself, leaving open the possibility that first millennium CE agricultural populations were centered in areas with deeper soils farther downstream. The Maadaga Archaeological Survey, with its survey zone oriented perpendicular to the escarpment, offered the opportunity to test whether the patterns observed at the Péntènga and Yobri rockshelters were representative of the greater region. As described in this chapter, we did recover mid to late first millennium CE evidence for use of domesticated resources and the adoption of agriculture. This relatively late adoption of agriculture provided an opportunity to examine the experimentation integral to the incorporation of domesticates, beginning a trajectory that would ultimately lead toward the development of larger-scale farming societies in the early second millennium CE Siga occupation. These changes were accompanied by significant shifts in mobility, material culture, and likely societal organization.

This chapter discusses data from excavation of two mounded sites located along the Koabu drainage, MAS541 and MAS502.3 (Figure 29). Pwoli ceramic assemblages occurred primarily in subsurface deposits and were identified at a low-confidence level on the surface at site MAS902. Dating primarily to the last three centuries of the first millennium CE, Pwoli occupation sites were inhabited by sedentary iron-using communities

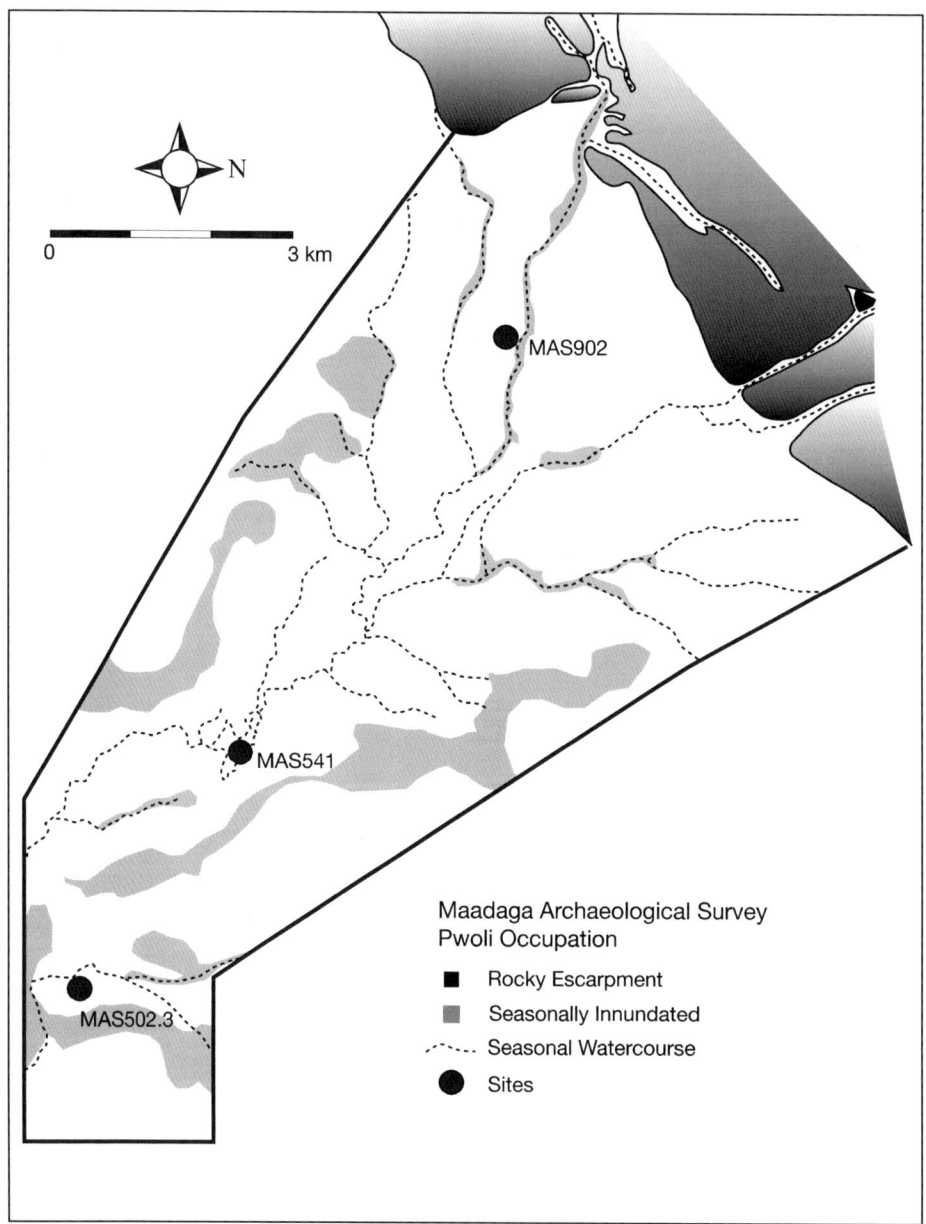

Figure 29. Pwoli occupation sites identified by the Maadaga Archaeological Survey.

that were slowly incorporating the use of plant and animal domesticates and shifting from long-distance logistical expeditions to more localized economic practices associated with increased social anchoring. These widely spaced agricultural homesteads likely had highly localized impacts on the environment, and were unlikely to have significantly altered the general landscape around the Gobnangou during this era.

Excavations at Site MAS541

Site MAS541 is a large mound that sits near a seasonal pool slightly over 200 m from the current banks of the Koabu (Figure 30). The site rises at least 4 m above the surrounding landscape and comprises an area of over 1,300 m². The surface of MAS541 is covered with a dense layer of laterite pebbles mixed with pottery and fragmented animal bone.

Excavation and Stratigraphic Summary

In 2004, the MAS dug a small shovel test into the surface at the mound peak at site MAS541 to determine the depth of the archaeological deposits. Although we recovered few artifacts, we did obtain a datable sample from an intact ash lens over 4 cm thick at 20 to 25 cm depth. This sample (Figure 31), taken from the profile to ensure its integrity, resulted in an accelerator mass spectrometry (AMS) radiocarbon date at a 2-sigma range of 890–1025 cal CE (Beta-195018, 1070 ± 40 bp), calibrated with OxCal v. 4.3.2 (Bronk Ramsey 2017) using IntCal13, the Northern Hemisphere atmospheric curve (Reimer et al. 2013). In 2006, we excavated a 1 by 2 m unit (Unit E at site MAS541) in twenty-seven stratigraphic units to a depth of 125 cm using the methodologies described in Chapter 3. Unit E contained multiple layers of architecture and for analysis was divided into five analytical units (AU; Figure 32).

ANALYTICAL UNIT 5: NATURAL BASE

Site MAS541 was originally established on a natural rise composed of sticky, heavy, and homogenous gray clay. The clay in AU5 (stratigraphic levels E25 to E27) did not contain any cultural materials, although we did encounter some insect disturbance. We considered the few sherds recovered from these levels intrusive.

ANALYTICAL UNIT 4: SERIES OF STRUCTURES

The intact, largely undisturbed deposits in AU4 contain three successive construction episodes (Figure 33). Although no walls have survived, preserved floors were found, most of which had lipping at the edges consistent with an association with architecture. Given the lack of brick preservation and the comparatively soft texture of the fill, a coursed-earth building technique was likely in use.

The earliest floor (Structure 1; stratigraphic levels E19, E21, E23–E24) had been dug at least 10 cm into the natural clay and covered most of the unit. The floor, made of orange clay with laterite pebbles, was applied in even 0.5 to 1.0 cm thick laminae up to a maximum thickness of 4 cm. Later floor layers did not reach the full extent of the original floor and the surface was thinner toward the edges of the structure. The curvature of the southern edge of the floor indicated a round structure 3.4 m in diameter, although floor lipping in the northern profile suggested either an interior feature or an unusual structure shape. No artifacts were found on the floor and there was a vertical burned surface in the southeastern part of the unit. However, no clear relationship between the burned feature and the floor could be established.

Above Structure 1 we found a semicircular burned feature about 60 cm in diameter that extended into the west profile (stratigraphic levels E14, E18, E20, E22). The feature had loose sediment, ash, and charcoal on the convex side (south) and the concave side (north) was a 6 cm vertical burned edge. The nature of this feature is as yet undetermined, but it was 10 cm above the floor of Structure 1 and not in association with any identifiable

FIGURE 30. The MAS541 archaeological site seen from the east.

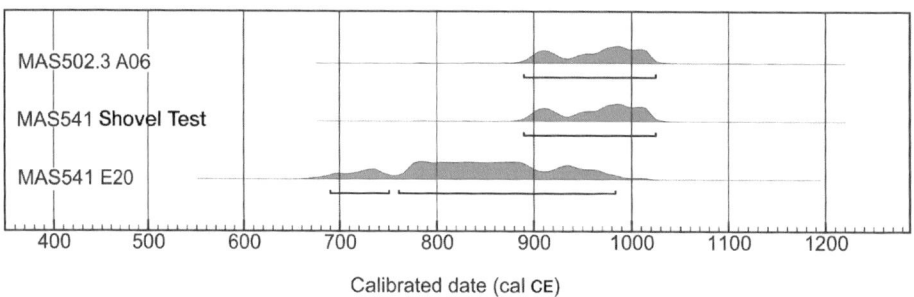

FIGURE 31. Associated AMS radiocarbon dates of carbonized wood for the Pwoli occupation. Dates were calibrated with OxCal v. 4.3.2 (Bronk Ramsey 2017) using IntCal13, the Northern Hemisphere atmospheric curve (Reimer et al. 2013). Samples are from Unit A (Beta-224995) at site MAS502.3, and Unit E (Beta-224996) and the 2004 shovel test (Beta-195018) at site MAS541 (Beta Analytic, USA).

surface. A radiocarbon sample from this feature yielded a date at the 2-sigma range of 690–983 cal CE (Beta-224996, 1180 ± 60 bp; see Figure 31).

Like Structure 1, Structure 2 (stratigraphic levels E12, E13, E15–E17) had an orange pebble and clay floor applied in multiple laminae that lipped up 8 cm at the edge, although again the later layers did not cover the full extent of the original floor. The area outside the floor was a clay fill with ashy spots and clumps of burned earth mixed in. There was a broken large iron spear in the southern part of the unit at approximately the same level (Figure 34).

Structure 3 (stratigraphic levels E08, E09, E11) was located in the southeastern corner of the unit. Like Structures 1 and 2, it had orange clay floors with multiple laminae that lipped up at the edges. However, unlike the earlier structures, Structure 3 had two distinct reflooring episodes separated by a 10 cm fill identical to the surrounding matrix. There was a small grinding stone fragment on the surface of the lower floor. A yellow clay and pebble surface in the northern part of the unit was found at the same depth as the lower floor. Un-

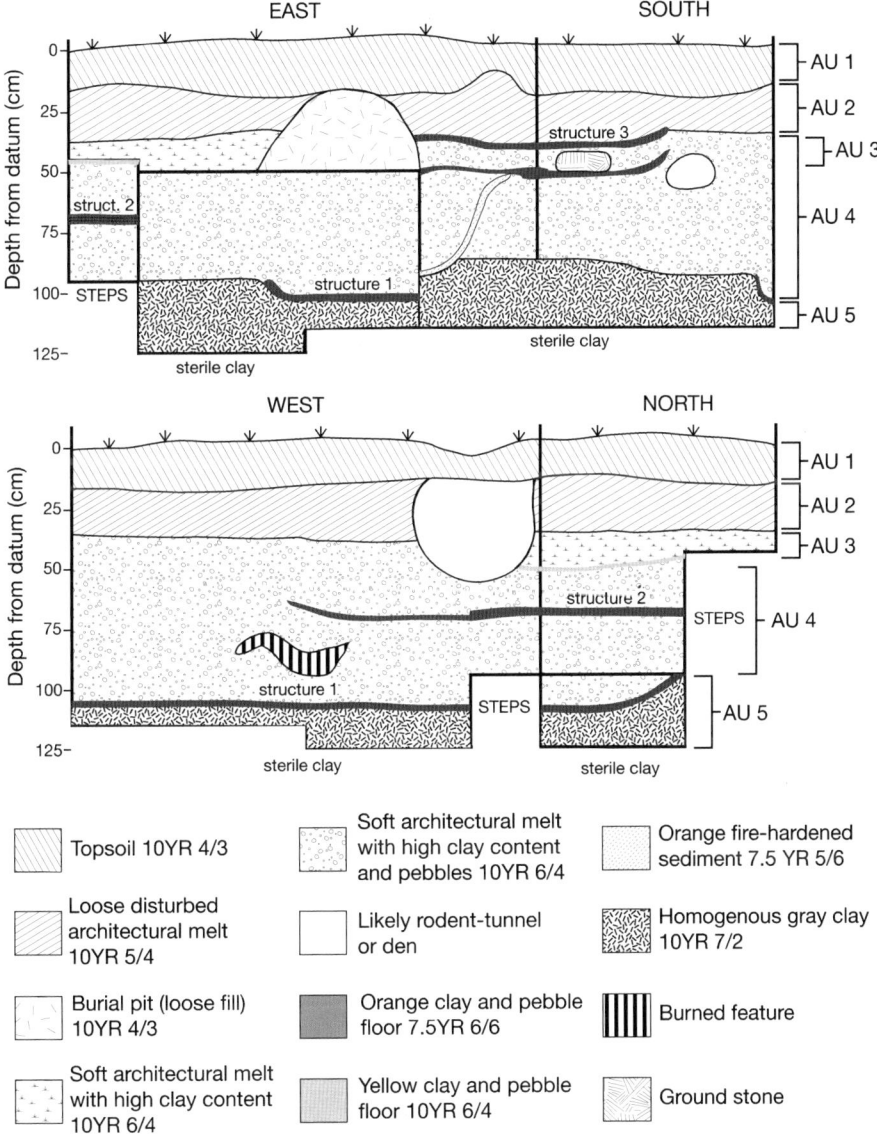

FIGURE 32. Profiles of the stratigraphy of Unit E at site MAS541, showing analytical unit (AU) divisions. Soil color designations are from Munsell Color (2009).

like the structure floors, the yellow layer was of uneven thickness and did not have a smooth top. This may be an exterior or expedient surface associated with the structure.

ANALYTICAL UNIT 3: DOMESTIC SPACE AND
CULTURAL FILL WITH SIGNIFICANT INTRUSIVE DISTURBANCE
The layer of cultural fill in AU3 (stratigraphic levels E06–E07, E10) was directly above

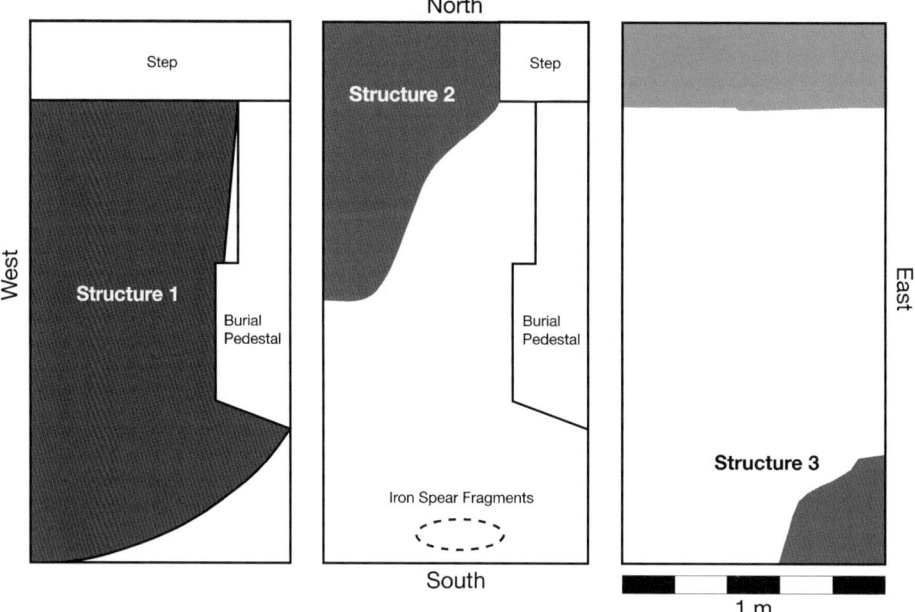

FIGURE 33. Architectural features of the three construction episodes found in Unit E at site MAS541. *From left,* Structure 1 at 110 cm, Structure 2 at 70 cm, and Structure 3 at 45 cm below datum.

Structure 3, but was heavily disturbed by rodent activity and a burial pit. When we reached about 55 cm depth (near the base of this layer), we pedestaled the space and left the burial undisturbed.

ANALYTICAL UNIT 2: CULTURAL FILL WITH SIGNIFICANT INTRUSIVE DISTURBANCE
The layer of cultural fill in AU2 (stratigraphic levels E03–E05) was not associated with any features. Although below the plow zone, it was heavily disturbed by rodent activity and the burial pit in AU3.

ANALYTICAL UNIT 1: DISTURBED TOPSOIL
This analytical unit (AU1; stratigraphic levels E01, E02) includes the surface and topsoil. Fully plowed, it had a coarser texture than the rest of the unit and significantly higher artifact densities, which was likely due to significant deflation.

Material Culture Analyses
Excavations at site MAS541 yielded 566 ceramics. We collected an additional 142 sherds from the surface of the site outside the boundaries of Unit E (Figures 35 and 36; Table 19). Some ceramics associated with the Siga occupation (including Sherd Types 2 and 10 and sherds with micaceous temper) were recovered from the surface of the site and may have been intrusive in the top levels of excavation (AU1 and AU2). However, even in the mixed surface assemblage the characteristics of the Pwoli assemblage were evident and distinct from those of single component Siga occupation sites. Aside from the sherds associated

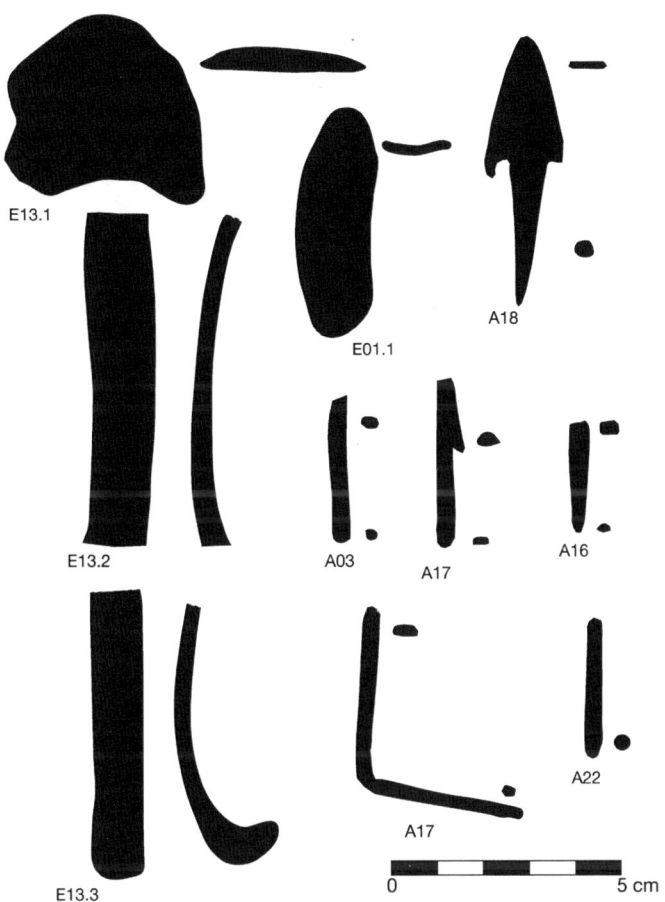

FIGURE 34. Iron objects from Unit E at site MAS541 (*at left*) and Unit A at site MAS 502.3 (*at right*), with excavation levels.

with the Siga occupation, no stratigraphic patterns could be identified within the ceramic assemblage.

Site MAS541 ceramics were characterized by grog and quartz tempers (occasionally used in combination), burnished vessel surfaces, infrequent use of red slip, and diverse, lightly impressed decorations that were either zoned or only applied to a limited set of vessels. Most of the sherds recovered were very fragmented (67% were smaller than 4 cm²), suggesting that most were from secondary contexts. It is possible they were incorporated into the coursed earth that was likely used to build the walls of the structures, which could indicate an even older occupation near the site. The level of fragmentation also made it difficult to determine vessel forms, although the thin mean wall thickness (9.6 mm) could indicate smaller vessels. Of the fifty-five rims from excavation (the largest are depicted in Figure 35), only five had measurable diameters. These were all under 25 cm, supporting a trend in the assemblage toward small vessels (Table 19).

Twisted cord roulette (Cord 2) was by far the most frequent decoration (seen in

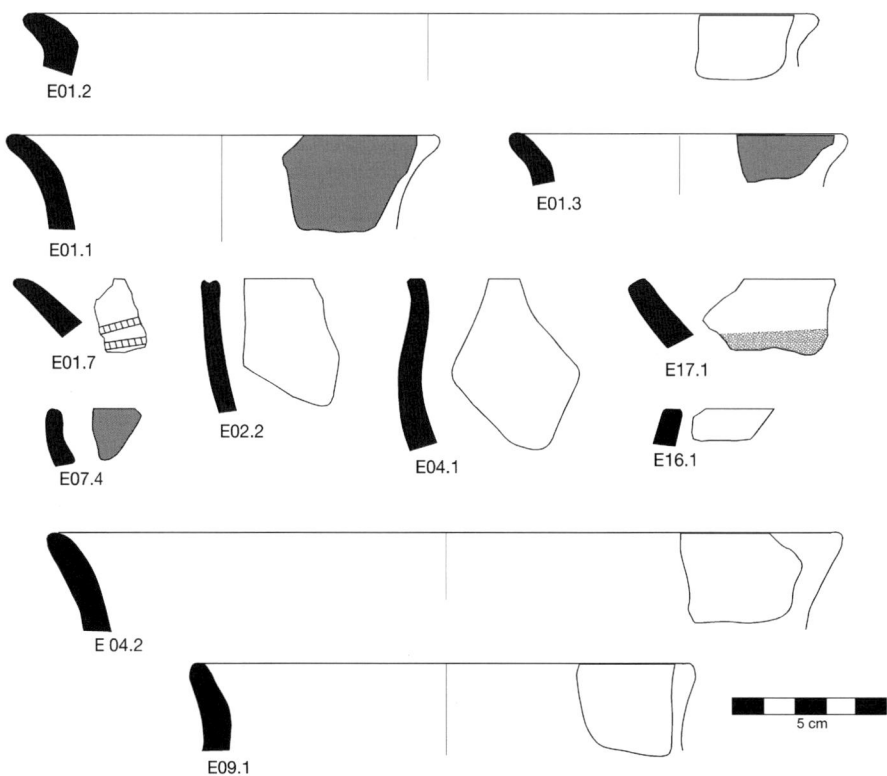

FIGURE 35. Pwoli occupation ceramics from Unit E at site MAS541, with excavation levels.

FIGURE 36. Pwoli occupation sherds from Unit E at site MAS541, with excavation levels.

TABLE 19. Characteristics of the ceramic assemblage from Unit E and surface collections at site MAS541.

Description	Analytical units					
	AU5	AU4	AU3	AU2	AU1	Surface
Depth from datum (cm)	105–125	50–105	40–50	20–40	0–20	n/a
Excavated volume (m^3)	0.22	0.84	0.2	0.4	0.4	n/a
Total number of sherds (N)	4	149	56	142	528	248
Number of sherds per cubic meter (N/m^3)	18	177	280	355	1,320	n/a
Total mass of sherds (g)	107	1,174	339	838	3,185	3,307
Mass of sherds per cubic meter (g/m^3)	486	1,398	1,695	2,095	7,963	n/a
Number of individually recorded sherds	4	149	56	97	260	142
Percentage of sherds with:						
Grog temper	75.0	62.4	62.5	73.1	61.9	62.2
Quartz temper	25.0	35.6	28.6	23.7	34.2	31.7
Grog and quartz temper	0.0	2.0	7.1	3.1	3.8	2.8
Mica temper	0.0	0.0	1.8	0.0	3.8	1.4
Self-slip, burnished	75.0	49.7	41.1	54.6	51.5	3.5
Red slip, burnished	0.0	4.7	7.1	6.1	5.8	2.1
Decoration	0.0	14.8	12.5	16.5	13.8	29.6
Number of decoration techniques	0	11	3	7	12	10
Number of decoration techniques per 100 sherds	0	7.4	5.3	7.2	4.6	7.0
Mean sherd thickness (mm)	15.2	9.3	9.6	9.4	9.8	11.7
Vessel diameters (cm)	n/a	15	n/a	24	24, 13, 10	28, 15

36% of decorated sherds) with the remaining decorated sherds divided among twenty-one different techniques (Table 20). Of these, folded strip roulettes, channels, and comb impressions were the most common in secure Pwoli occupation contexts. The unknown roulette Cord 16 was the only decoration technique unique to site MAS541; the four examples came from the topsoil, possibly from the same vessel. Even though all other decoration techniques were also used in subsequent occupations, the versions from

TABLE 20. Ceramic decoration techniques in use during the Pwoli and Siga occupations at sites MAS541, MAS502.3, and MAS902 by analytical unit (AU) and surface collected sherds. For full descriptions of decoration techniques see Tables 11–14.

Analytical unit	MAS541			MAS502.3			MAS902	Total number of sherds			Field code
	AU3, AU4, AU5	AU2, AU1	Surface	AU2, AU3	AU1	Surface	Surface				
Occupation	Pwoli	Pwoli/Siga	Pwoli/Siga	Pwoli	Pwoli/Siga	Pwoli/Siga	Pwoli/Siga	Pwoli	Pwoli/Siga	All sites	
Total number of sherds (N)	209	357	142	103	309	69	77	312	954	1,266	
Decoration technique											
Twisted cord roulette	7	22	26	22	16	8	19	29	91	120	Cord 2
Folded strip roulette	5	2	—	6	2	—	—	11	4	15	Cord 9
Parallel channels	1	2	—	7	4	2	3	8	11	19	PC
Channels	1	4	1	5	2	—	1	6	8	14	CH
Folded strip roulette	2	—	2	2	2	1	4	4	9	13	Cord 3
Dragged comb	—	2	2	3	—	—	1	3	5	8	DC
Space-filing rocker comb	3	1	—	—	—	—	1	3	2	5	SCOR
Possible folded strip roulette	2	—	—	1	—	—	—	3	—	3	R1

Continued

TABLE 20 CONTINUED

Analytical unit	MAS541			MAS502.3			MAS902	Total number of sherds			Field code
	AU3, AU4, AU5	AU2, AU1	Surface	AU2, AU3	AU1	Surface	Surface				
Occupation	Pwoli	Pwoli/Siga	Pwoli/Siga	Pwoli	Pwoli/Siga	Pwoli/Siga	Pwoli/Siga	Pwoli	Pwoli/Siga	All sites	
Space-filling comb impressions	1	—	—	2	—	—	—	3	—	3	FCI
Circular impression	—	—	—	2	—	—	—	2	—	2	CI
Braided strip roulette	—	4	—	1	1	—	1	1	6	7	Cord 4
Braided strip roulette	—	—	3	1	—	3	—	1	6	7	Cord 6
Lip channel	—	1	—	1	—	—	2	1	3	4	LIPCH
Folded strip roulette	—	—	2	1	—	—	—	1	2	3	Cord 15
Braided cord impression	1	—	—	—	—	1	—	1	1	2	IB
Twisted cord roulette	—	—	—	1	—	1	—	1	1	2	Cord 7
Plastic button	—	—	—	1	—	—	1	1	1	2	PB
Cord wrapped roulette	1	—	—	—	—	—	—	1	—	1	MLI
Braided cord roulette	—	1	1	—	3	—	—	—	5	5	Cord 1
Multiple arching channels	—	—	1	—	—	—	4	—	5	5	MAC
Unknown roulette	—	4	—	—	—	—	—	—	4	4	Cord 16

Continued

TABLE 20 CONTINUED

Analytical unit	MAS541			MAS502.3			MAS902	Total number of sherds			Field code
	AU3, AU4, AU5	AU2, AU1	Surface	AU2, AU3	AU1	Surface	Surface				
Occupation	Pwoli	Pwoli/Siga	Pwoli/Siga	Pwoli	Pwoli/Siga	Pwoli/Siga	Pwoli/Siga	Pwoli	Pwoli/Siga	All sites	
Semicircular channel	—	2	—	—	—	1	—	—	3	3	SC
Other channel	—	1	—	—	—	—	2	—	3	3	IC
Multiple triangular channels	—	—	1	—	—	1	—	—	2	2	MCT
Triangular channel	—	—	—	—	—	2	—	—	2	2	CT
Gouges	—	—	—	—	—	—	2	—	2	2	G
Comb impression	—	1	—	—	—	—	—	—	1	1	COI
Diagonal incisions	—	—	—	—	1	—	—	—	1	1	DI
Twisted knotted cord roulette	—	—	—	—	1	—	—	—	1	1	Cord 5
Channel comb (single)	—	—	—	—	—	1	—	—	1	1	CC
Cross-hatched channels	—	—	—	—	—	1	—	—	1	1	XC
Fingernail impressions	—	—	—	—	—	—	1	—	1	1	FI
Carved wooden roulette	—	—	—	—	—	—	1	—	1	1	R4
Pivoted twisted cord impressions	—	—	—	—	—	—	1	—	1	1	Cord 14

MAS541 tended to be smaller and more gently impressed or rouletted on the vessels, creating a distinct visual appearance.

In addition to ceramics, we recovered ground stone, chert, slag, and iron objects from site MAS541 (Table 21). A white sandstone ground stone fragment (a 6 by 10 cm triangle) with no central grinding area was visible in the profile resting on the lower floor of Structure 3. It seemed to be a basal grinding stone remnant. Its position between floors could indicate a period of abandonment between reflooring episodes or the inclusion of debris in the fill. A polished piece of red ochre, recovered from AU4, could mean that ceramics were made on site, although given the low frequency of red slip in the ceramic assemblage, it may have been used for other purposes. Fifteen pieces of chipped stone were collected in the systematic surface collection at the site and two were recovered from Unit E topsoil deposits. However, in secure Pwoli contexts only a gray chert flake and a small piece of quartz debitage were recovered.

Three large pieces of iron (two shaft fragments and a flat point, likely from the same object) were recovered from a trash deposit outside Structure 2 (see Figure 34). Finally, we found two very small pieces of slag (totaling 33 g) in the topsoil. We observed no other slag on the site surface.

Faunal and Botanical Analyses

Excavations at site MAS541 recovered a rich faunal assemblage of 759 specimens, 193 of which could be identified to size class or taxon, with the majority from wild species (Table 22). Dueppen analyzed the assemblage (using the methodologies and collections described in Chapter 3); results have been previously reported in Dueppen and Gallagher (2013), along with detailed ecological discussions of the identified fauna that are drawn on for this discussion (Dueppen and Gallagher 2013, table 2). Within the assemblage, Dueppen identified a much wider array of taxa in AU1 (which accounted for half the identifiable bone) than found in earlier stratigraphic levels. Bovids occurred in greater frequency in AU1 (49%) than in AU4 (23%) and fish were much more frequent in AU4 (21% compared with 6% in AU1). These two trends were statistically significant ($p < 0.01$) and could represent strategic subsistence shifts; however, the range of taxa present was largely similar and it is possible that delicate fish bones did not preserve as well as more robust bovid bones in the deflated and disturbed topsoil deposits of AU1. Conversely, AU4 samples were mostly from interior locations and the bones recovered were universally small, such that fish could be disproportionately represented in these contexts.

Overall, the faunal assemblage was very diverse and suggested a wide range of hunting techniques used to exploit multiple ecological niches. Cane rat, common duiker, and patas monkey are all found near the site and in agricultural fields. Cane rats in particular favor the margins of marshy areas and frequently raid crops (Happold 1987:152). With their large size (up to 9 kg), they were commonly consumed historically. Significantly larger animals such as roan antelope, hartebeest, and topi may also have lived near the site, but would have been more difficult to hunt or trap opportunistically. The presence of a yellow-backed duiker was particularly interesting. This is a solitary animal that favors dense forests in significantly wetter environments (yet may move into forested zones along riverine strips in the savanna). Yellow-backed duikers were not known in southeastern Burkina Faso in the historical era even along main river channels (Happold 1987; Estes 1991; Kingdon 1997). Even during the wetter environment of the first millennium CE, they would have been much more likely to be found along a major river such as the Pendjari.

TABLE 21. Iron, slag, and stone identified from Unit E at site MAS541. For stone, an asterisk (*) indicates a measurement in a fragmented direction.

Analytical unit	Stratigraphic level	Category	Material	Description	Length (cm)	Width (cm)	Height (cm)	Weight (g)
—	Surface (sys)	Chipped stone	Chert	Fourteen debitage pieces with cortex	1–5	—	—	14
—	Surface (sys)	Chipped stone	Chert	Flake with cortex	1.8*	—	—	3
AU1	E01	Chipped stone	Chert	Debitage with cortex	<1	—	—	1
AU1	E01	Chipped stone	Quartz	Debitage	1–2	—	—	1
AU1	E01	Iron	Iron	Flat leaf-shaped piece	4.8	2	0.2	8
AU1	E01	Sandstone	White sandstone	Five small fragments with no worked surface	—	—	—	23
AU1	E11	Possible ochre	Red stone (laterite or ochre)	Amorphous lump with polished exterior	3.4	4.9	3	82
AU4	E13	Iron	Iron	Wide flat shaft fragment, curved at the end	6	1.1	0.4	13
AU4	E13	Iron	Iron	Wide flat shaft fragment	7.3	1	0.4	14
AU4	E13	Iron	Iron	Flat, very roughly triangular with rounded top	4.4	3.6	0.5	24
AU4	E23	Chipped stone	Quartz	Debitage with cortex	1–2	—	—	2
AU4	E23	Chipped stone	Chert	Flake with cortex	2.7	—	—	6
AU4	E profile	Ground stone	White sandstone	Basal grinding stone fragment, isosceles triangle shape	10.5*	6*	5	404

TABLE 22. Fauna identified from Unit E at site MAS541. Faunal remains are given as the number of identified specimens (NISP). Analysis by S. Dueppen (Dueppen and Gallagher 2013).

Category	Common name	Scientific name	Analytical units (NISP)				
			AU3	AU2	AU1	AU4	Total
Very small bovid	Unidentified very small bovid		2	2	—	—	4
Small bovid	Common duiker	*Sylvicapra grimmia*	1	—	—	—	1
	Unidentified small bovid		13	1	1	5	20
Medium bovid	Yellow-backed duiker	*Cephalophus sylvicultor*	2	—	—	—	2
	Unidentified medium bovid		10	2	1	1	14
Large bovid	Roan antelope	*Hippotragus equinus*	—	2	—	—	2
	Hartebeest or topi	*Alcelaphus buselaphus* or *Damaliscus* sp.	4	2	—	—	6
	Unidentified large bovid		20	10	3	4	37
Primate	Patas monkey	*Erythrocebus patas*	1	—	—	—	1
Large rodent	Cane rat	*Thryonomys swinderianus*	14	14	—	7	35
Small rodent	Gerbil	*Gerbalis* sp.	—	5	—	—	5
Avian	Chicken or guinea fowl	*Gallus* sp. or *Numida* sp.	1	—	—	4	5
	Probable domestic chicken (eggshell)		—	2	—	2	4
	Probable francolin or guinea fowl (eggshell)		1	—	—	—	1
	Unidentified galliform		2	1	—	2	5
Reptile	Crocodile	*Crocodylus* (*C. cataphractus* or *C. niloticus*) or *Osteolaemus* sp.	2	—	—	—	2
	Monitor lizard	*Varanus* sp. (*V. niloticus* or *V. exanthematicus*)	5	2	—	1	8
	Python	*Python* sp.	1	—	—	—	1
	Senegalese flapshell turtle	*Cyclanorbis senegalensis*	—	1	—	—	1
	Unidentified turtle		2	1	—	—	3

Continued

TABLE 22 CONTINUED

Category	Common name	Scientific name	Analytical units (NISP)				
			AU3	AU2	AU1	AU4	Total
Amphibian	Frog or toad	*Anura* sp.	—	—	—	1	1
Freshwater bivalve	Bivalve	*Chambardia* sp. or *Spathopsis* sp.	2	2	—	1	5
	Unidentified bivalve		17	—	—	4	21
Fish	Tilapia	Tilapiini	1	2	—	1	4
	Synodontis catfish	*Synodontis* sp.	—	1	—	3	4
	Clarias catfish	*Clarias* sp.	3	3	—	2	8
	Auchenoglanis catfish	*Auchenoglanis* sp.	1	—	—	—	1
	Nile perch	*Lates niloticus*	—	—	—	2	2
	Unidentified catfish		1	—	—	1	2
Land snail	Land snail (large)	*Achatina* sp.	1	—	1	2	4
Total identified			107	53	6	43	209
Total identified to size class			45	15	5	10	75
Total identified to taxon			62	38	1	33	134

There was no evidence for domesticated cattle, sheep, or goats at site MAS541, but residents of the site likely kept domesticated chickens. Although a secure identification of chicken (as opposed to other galliform birds) could not be made from the skeletal elements that were preserved, eggshell provided supporting evidence that they were present (see Dueppen 2011).

The aquatic species at site MAS541 indicated exploitation of seasonal drainages, pools, and inundated areas near the site, as well as fishing in the larger main channels of more distant rivers. Most reptiles and amphibians, including crocodiles and monitor lizards, were likely available near the site in the wet season. Several of the identified fish species, including *Clarias* spp. and tilapia, can survive the lower-oxygen waters of seasonal channels and floodplains and are frequently trapped as waters recede at the end of the rainy season. However, larger individuals of these taxa may favor the deeper water of the main river channels.

In contrast, Nile perch, *Synodontis* sp., *Auchenoglanis* sp., and the Senegalese flapshell turtle more frequently favor deep channels with higher oxygen levels (Table 23). Even with the higher water levels of the moister climate during occupation of the site, these taxa were likely caught in the Pendjari River (25 km away), in the Kourtiagou River (13 km away), or both, rather than in the Koabu and its feeder drainages.

TABLE 23. Estimated length of fishes from Unit E at site MAS541 and Unit A at site MAS502.3.

Site	Analytical unit	Taxon	Estimated length (cm)					
			0–10	10–20	20–30	30–40	40–50	50–60
MAS541	AU1	Clariidae	1	—	1	1	—	—
		Tilapiini	—	1	—	—	—	—
	AU3	Clariidae	—	—	—	—	—	1
		Tilapiini	—	—	2	—	—	—
		Synodontis sp.	—	1	—	—	—	—
	AU4	Clariidae	—	—	—	—	—	1
		Tilapiini	—	—	—	1	—	—
		Lates niloticus	—	—	—	2	—	—
		Synodontis sp.	—	—	—	2	—	—
MAS502.3	AU2	Tilapiini	—	1	—	—	—	—
	AU3	Clariidae	—	—	1	1	—	—
		Tilapiini	—	—	1	—	—	—

In contrast to the rich animal bone assemblage, botanical samples from site MAS541 yielded few identifiable remains (Table 24). The most common were seed coat fragments of baobab (*Adansonia digitata*), which were present in every level. A single domestic pearl millet (*Pennisetum glaucum*) grain was recovered from the lowest levels of the unit. Other seeds recovered could only be identified at the tribe or family level (Amaranthaceae, Gramineae, Paniceae, and Malvaceae), all of which have many diverse herbaceous members.

Excavations at Site MAS502.3

Site MAS502.3 is a large mound perched on the edge of a broad, shallow seasonal drainage. Its highest area is at least 4 m above the agricultural plain to the south and the drop off to the north is a steep 6 to 7 m into the drainage. The site is part of a cluster of several mounds along this drainage, all of which had surface ceramic assemblages that were characteristic of the Siga occupation.

Excavation and Stratigraphic Analysis

In 2006, we excavated a 2 by 2 m unit (Unit A) on the highest part of site MAS502.3. Siga elements of the assemblage were in general confined to the topsoil, although some may have migrated into the lower layers of the unit through intrusive deposits (several burial

TABLE 24. Carbonized seeds and fruits identified from Unit E at site MAS541 and Unit A at site MAS502.3, given as present (×) or absent (—). Botanical nomenclature from Burkill (1985, 1994, 1995, 1997, 2000, 2004).

		Excavation unit				
		MAS541			MAS502.3	
	Analytical unit	AU4	AU3	AU2	AU3	AU2
	Number of samples	9	2	2	5	4
	Total volume of soil floated (L)	17	4	4	9	8
Family	Scientific name					
Gramineae	*Pennisetum glacum*	×	—	—	—	—
Bombacaceae	*Adansonia digitata*	×	×	×	×	×
Aizoaceae	*Trianthema portulacastrum*	—	—	—	—	×
Amaranthaceae	Unidentified	×	—	—	—	—
Cyperaceae	*Scleria* sp.	—	—	—	×	—
Gramineae	Paniceae	×	—	—	—	—
Gramineae	Unidentified	—	×	—	×	×
Leguminosae	Papilionoidae A Type	—	—	—	×	×
Leguminosae	Unidentified	—	—	—	—	×
Malvaceae	*Sida* sp.	×	—	—	—	—
Molluginaceae	*Glinus* sp.	—	—	—	—	×

pits) and bioturbation (rodent dens). Because of this extensive disturbance, Unit A could only be divided into three analytical units (Figure 37).

Natural Base
Site MAS502.3 was founded on a lateritic outcrop. The duricrust (stratigraphic level A23) at the base of the excavation unit was rough and uneven, with many small pockets of cultural deposits. In the eastern half of the unit this surface was encountered at only 65 cm depth, although it stepped down to 80 cm in the west. There was a burial pit, oriented northeast-southwest in the east-center of the unit, set into the duricrust. The burial was not excavated.

Analytical Unit 3: Occupation and Cultural Fill
Directly above the bedrock was a cultural layer (AU3; stratigraphic levels A13, A15–A22), in which the only identifiable feature was a burned ring of soil in the east profile. It seemed to have a dark ashy interior, but very little carbon was recovered. This possible hearth location was set into the laterite duricrust. To the north and northwest of this feature there was a thin layer of pure ash, resting below a larger deposit of ashy material with high densities of animal bone. At least two burial pits cut through this level; in both cases the unexcavated burials seemed to have been interred on the bedrock.

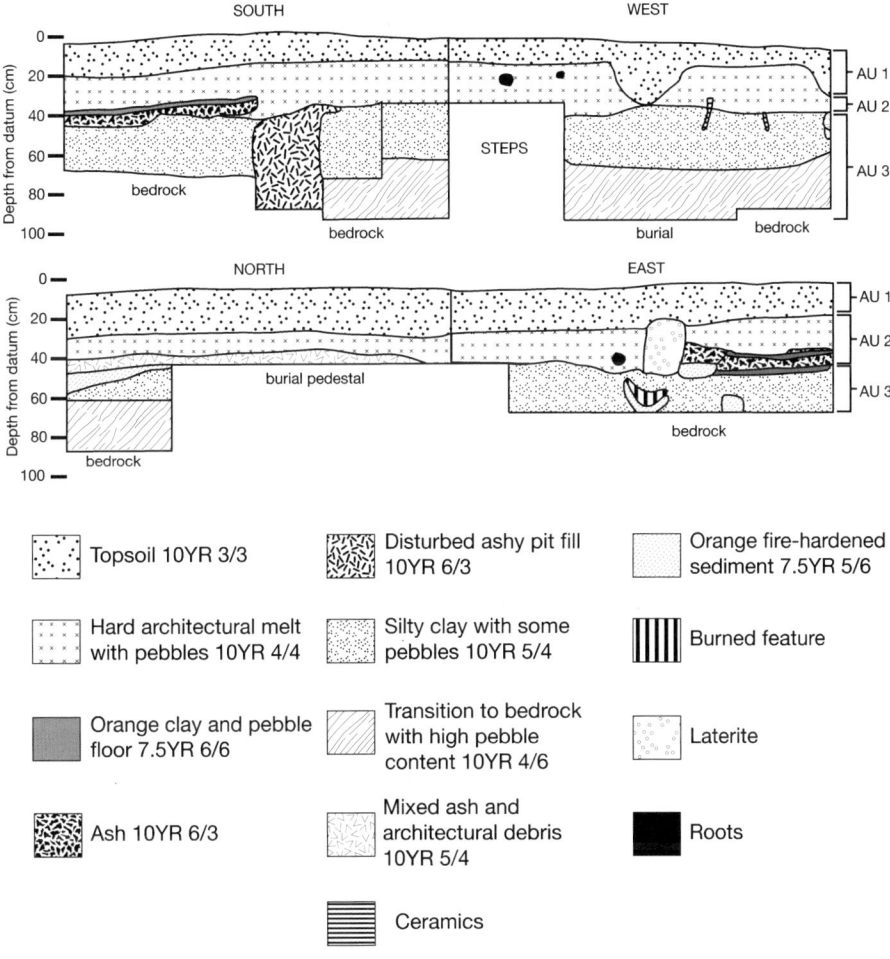

FIGURE 37. Profiles of the stratigraphy of Unit A at site MAS502.3, showing analytical unit (AU) divisions. Soil color designations are from Munsell Color (2009).

ANALYTICAL UNIT 2: STRUCTURE

The only structure in AU2 was identified at 30 to 40 cm depth (stratigraphic levels A04–A12). It had two layers of orange clay and pebble floors that were clearly visible in the profile, although in the unit they were patchy and degraded, making the exact structure boundaries difficult to identify. The lower floor was particularly poorly preserved and a small (40 cm diameter) burned section associated with a large block of laterite (likely a hearth) in the east central unit adjacent to the profile was the only surviving portion. The rest of the unit at this elevation was composed of ashy deposits—perhaps related to the hearth—which contained a variety of animal bones and ceramics. A new floor surface had been laid 5 cm above the hearth, although the laterite block remained in place, suggesting a continuation of the spatial organization of the first floor. The second floor was better preserved and extended from the southeast corner to the center of the unit, where trash deposits with a high ash content had continued to be placed; these yielded animal bones and artifacts. A charcoal sample from the edge of the floors was AMS radiocarbon dated at the 2-sigma range to 890–1025 cal CE (Beta-224995, 1080 ± 40 bp; see Figure 31).

The rim of a pot (stratigraphic level A14) was buried upside-down at the same level in the northwestern part of the unit, to the exterior of the structure; there was no evidence of the vessel base and it was not clear whether the pot was intentionally placed or simply discarded. Pots buried upside-down were identified in the profiles of borrow pits at multiple sites with Siga occupation ceramics, raising the possibility that this was an intrusive feature. An individual was interred in a pit 50 to 60 cm deep and of unknown size in the center and east of the north wall of the unit; the area was pedestaled and the burial was not excavated. This burial was 10 to 20 cm below, and in the same general area, as the upside-down pot and another burial was located 50 cm below the pot, but no clear connection could be made between the upside-down pot and either of the burials.

ANALYTICAL UNIT 1: TOPSOIL
Composed of decayed earthen architecture that dissolved into a shell atop the mound, this deposit in AU1 (stratigraphic levels A01–A03) was compacted and unplowed. The highly fragmented ceramics in this deposit suggested that some degree of trampling or disturbance occurred in the past or that earlier ceramics had been incorporated into the walls of the last structure built at the site. A large grinding stone fragment was recovered from just below the surface.

Material Culture Analyses

Excavations at site MAS502.3 (Unit A) yielded 412 ceramics and we collected an additional 69 sherds from outside the boundaries of the unit (Figures 38 and 39; Table 25). The surface assemblage had more Siga occupation ceramics than found in the Unit A deposits, although the presence of the Siga occupation complicated interpretation, because of the many burial pits that cut through the unit. Unit A ceramics have many similarities to the Unit E assemblage, including a low incidence of red slip and high incidence of polish. Decorations were similarly diverse (eighteen techniques, thirteen of which were also identified in Unit E) and focused on twisted twine, folded strip roulettes, channels, and comb impressions (see Table 20). Decorations were in most cases lightly impressed, although decoration rates were higher and deep impressions more characteristic of the Siga occupation were not uncommon. In contrast to Unit E, Unit A pottery was about 90% grog tempered, with quartz and quartz-grog mixtures represented in low numbers.

Unit A ceramics were less fragmented than those of Unit E, although 47% of sherds were smaller than 4 cm^2. Vessels were slightly larger, with diameters reaching 34 cm, and vessel wall thickness was similar or slightly higher than for Unit E, although the general trend of small, thin vessels essentially held for Unit A as well. The upside-down rim mentioned above (stratigraphic level A14; see Figure 38) was the largest vessel recovered; it was an open, slightly flaring undecorated pot with grog temper, a rim diameter of 34 cm, and a neck diameter of 30 cm.

Like Unit E, ground stone, chert, iron objects, and possible slag were recovered from the excavation (Table 26). The largest piece of ground stone was the lightly used basal grinding stone identified just below the surface. It had been flattened on both sides, but lacked a clear grinding depression. Ground stone was also recovered from AU1 and

TABLE 25. Characteristics of the ceramic assemblages from Unit A at site MAS502.3 and at site MAS902.

Description	MAS502.3				MAS902
	Analytical units				
	AU3	AU2	AU1	Surface	
Average excavated depth (cm)	50–95	25–50	0–25	n/a	n/a
Excavated volume (m^3)	1.15	0.87	0.8	n/a	n/a
Total number of sherds (N)	183	394	462	69	112
Number of sherds per cubic meter (N/m^3)	159	453	578	n/a	n/a
Total mass of sherds (g)	1,740	4,481	1,740	1,167	3,556
Mass of sherds per cubic meter (g/m^3)	1,513	5,150	3,038	n/a	n/a
Number of individually recorded sherds	116	193	103	69	77
Percentage of sherds with:					
Grog temper	94.8	89.1	91.2	81.2	50.6
Quartz temper	5.2	7.3	4.9	17.4	35.1
Grog and quartz temper	0.0	2.1	1.0	1.4	14.2
Mica temper	0.0	1.6	2.9	0.0	0.0
Self-slip, burnished	40.5	32.6	7.8	4.3	12.9
Red slip, burnished	3.4	3.6	8.7	14.5	10.4
Decoration	21.6	19.7	36.9	34.8	31.9
Number of decoration techniques	11	13	10	12	15
Number of decoration techniques per 100 sherds	9.4	6.7	9.7	17.3	19
Mean sherd thickness (mm)	10.7	9.8	9.7	10.8	11.6
Vessel diameters (cm)	17–30	11–34	n/a	26, 19	25, 26

AU3. All three pieces represented the basal portions of grinding stones and were small discarded fragments. Chert debitage was recovered from throughout the unit, with the highest concentrations in the upper levels, although none was recovered from the systematic surface collection.

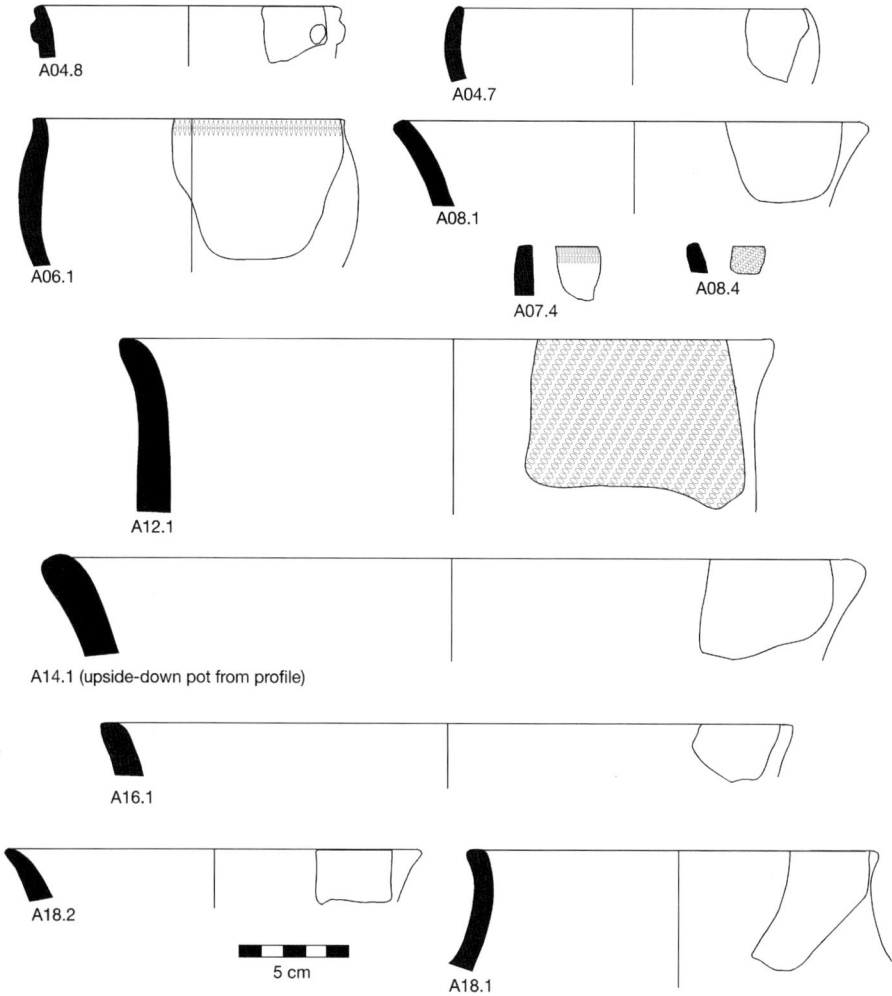

FIGURE 38. Pwoli occupation ceramics from Unit A at site MAS502.3, with excavation levels.

Iron objects, mostly shaft fragments, were present in AU2 and AU3, including two arrowheads or spear points that were found near the bedrock in the eastern half of the unit (see Figure 34). The points and shafts were more similar stylistically to the delicate arrows identified during the Siga occupation (see Chapter 6), than to the large, bulky point from Unit E. Slag was much more common at site MAS502.3 than at MAS541, with multiple pieces recovered in both AU1 and AU3. There was an iron furnace near the site (MAS502.5) with surface pottery dating to the Siga occupation.

Finally, vitrified iron-rich soil was recovered from the AU2 burned feature (described above). This feature initially appeared to be circular, but after the profile was cleaned it did not clearly continue into the wall at both ends and may simply have been an arc. The vitrification, localized in a very small area, suggested burning at a very high tem-

FIGURE 39. Pwoli occupation sherds from Unit A at site MAS502.3, with excavation levels.

perature (or possibly repeatedly over time). No charcoal was recovered during excavation and flotation of the feature and its contents yielded minimal carbonized material.

Faunal and Botanical Analyses

Site MAS502.3 yielded a rich faunal assemblage of 538 fragments, of which 166 could be identified to size class or taxon (Table 27). As at site MAS541, the analysis was carried out by Dueppen (following the methods outlined in Chapter 3 and previously reported in Dueppen and Gallagher [2013]). In general, the mammal and fish assemblages reflected hunting and fishing strategies broadly similar to those at site MAS541, although slightly more locally focused. In contrast, there were significant differences in the use of domesticated animals.

Domesticated cattle and sheep/goat were found throughout Unit A and were likely represented in the medium and large bovid size-classed bones as well. All domesticated livestock were small and comparable in size to those found at Kirikongo in western Burkina Faso (Dueppen 2012c; Dueppen and Gallagher 2013), which was likely indicative of the herding of breeds that had high tolerance for sleeping sickness. Domestic chickens were positively identified from skeletal elements.

Despite the addition of domesticated livestock, hunting remained important at the site. The wild fauna included a range of bovids of several sizes, including both small ones that commonly raid fields and larger ones that could have required more targeted hunting expeditions. Although species like roan antelope and Maxwell's duiker prefer a moister, more forested environment than is found in the region today, these could have been found

TABLE 26. Iron, slag, and stone identified from Unit A at site MAS502.3. For stone, an asterisk (*) indicates a measurement in a fragmented direction.

Analytical unit	Stratigraphic level	Category	Material	Description	Length (cm)	Width (cm)	Height (cm)	Weight (g)
AU1	A01	Chipped stone	Chert	Three pieces of debitage	1–3	—	—	9
AU1	A01	Unworked stone	White sandstone	Unworked	3.2	1.9	1.1	10
AU1	A01	Unworked stone	White sandstone	Unworked	1.5	1.4	1.5	4
AU1	A01	Slag	Slag	One piece	—	—	—	9
AU1	A01	Slag	Slag	Three pieces	—	—	—	16
AU1	A02	Ground stone	White sandtone	Very small basal grinding stone fragment with one worked face	3.9*	2.3*	3.9	37
AU1	A03	Ground stone	White sandstone	Intact basal grinding stone; lightly used	40	20	8	—
AU2	A04	Chipped stone	Chert	Debitage with cortex	>3	—	—	11
AU2	A08	Iron	Iron	Short section of metal wire or shaft fragment with rectangular cross section	3	0.25	0.3	1
AU2	A09	Unworked stone	White sandstone	Unworked	2.7	2.3	1.2	9
AU3	A13	Chipped stone	Chert	Debitage	1–2	—	—	2
AU3	A13	Slag	Slag	One piece	—	—	—	1
AU3	A13	Slag	Slag	Two pieces	—	—	—	8
AU3	A15	Chipped stone	Chert	Debitage	2–3	—	—	4

Continued

TABLE 26 CONTINUED

Analytical unit	Stratigraphic level	Category	Material	Description	Length (cm)	Width (cm)	Height (cm)	Weight (g)
AU3	A16	Iron	Iron	Short section of metal wire of shaft fragment with oval cross section	2.4	0.4	0.35	1
AU3	A17	Iron	Iron	Shaft; potentially a point (has a triangular barb)	3.8	0.5	0.4	3
AU3	A17	Iron	Iron	Metal wire or shaft fragment; bent at a right angle	3.9	3.5	0.4	5
AU3	A18	Chipped stone	Chert	Debitage	—	—	—	1
AU3	A18	Ground stone	White sandstone	Possible basal grinding stone fragment with one slightly smoothed side	4.8*	5.0*	3.4	119
AU3	A18	Iron	Iron	Short section of metal wire or shaft fragment with round cross section	2.4	0.3	0.3	1
AU3	A18	Iron	Iron	Triangular point (flat) with inward curving tang; shaft has been clearly bent	5.3	1.7	0.2	5
AU3	A20	Slag	Slag	Seven pieces	—	—	—	61
AU3	A22	Ground stone	White sandstone	Basal grinding stone fragment with flat surface	13.4*	7	4.4	514
AU3	A22	Iron	Iron	Short section of metal wire of shaft fragment with square cross section	3.1	0.4	0.4	2

TABLE 27. Fauna identified from Unit A at site MAS 502.3. Faunal remains are given as the number of identified specimens (NISP). Analysis by S. Dueppen (Dueppen and Gallagher 2013).

Category	Common name	Scientific name	Analytical units (NISP)			Total
			AU1	AU2	AU3	
Domestic livestock	Cattle	*Bos taurus*	—	1	4	5
	Sheep or goat	*Ovis* or *Capra*		1	3	4
Very small bovid	Maxwell's duiker	*Cephalophus maxwelli*	—	2	2	4
	Unidentified very small bovid		1	—	2	3
Small bovid	Duiker or oribi	*Sylvicapra* or *Ourebia*	1	—	1	2
	Unidentified small bovid		—	11	4	15
Medium bovid	Bohor's reedbuck	*Redunca redunca*	—	1	—	1
	Unidentified medium bovid		—	16	5	21
Large bovid	Roan antelope	*Hippotragus equinus*	—	—	1	1
	Unidentified large bovid		—	9	11	20
Carnivore	Serval cat	*Leptailurus serval*	—	1		1
	White-tailed mongoose	*Ichnemia albicauda*	—	—	1	1
Large rodent	Cane rat	*Thryonomys swinderianus*	—	8	2	10
	Gambian rat	*Cricetomys gambianus*	—	—	1	1
Small rodent	Multimammate rat	*Mastomys* sp.	—	—	4	4
Avian	Domestic chicken	*Gallus gallus*	—	—	1	1
	Chicken or guinea fowl	*Gallus* or *Numida*	—	8	2	10
	Probable domestic chicken (eggshell)		—	1	3	4
	Unidentified galliform		—	5	4	9

Continued

TABLE 27 CONTINUED

Category	Common name	Scientific name	Analytical units (NISP)			Total
			AU1	AU2	AU3	
Reptile and amphibian	Monitor lizard	*Varanus* sp. (*V. niloticus* or *V. exanthematicus*)	—	7	4	11
	Mud turtle	*Pelusios adansonii*	—	6	—	6
	Unidentified turtle		—	1	—	1
	Frog or toad	*Anura* sp.	—	1	1	2
Freshwater bivalve	Bivalve	*Chambardia* sp. or *Spathopsis* sp.	—	5	2	7
	Nile oyster	*Etheria elliptica*	—	—	2	2
	Unidentified bivalve		—	2	1	3
Freshwater mollusk	Snail	*Pila* sp.	—	—	1	1
Fish	Tilapia	Tilapiini	—	1	1	2
	Clarias catfish	*Clarias* sp.	—	—	4	4
	Probable tilapia		—	—	1	1
Total identified			2	87	68	157
Total identified to size class			1	36	22	59
Total identified to taxon			1	51	46	98

near the site during the wetter conditions of the late first millennium CE. Cane rats were once again among the most frequently identified animals. In Unit A another garden pest, the Gambian rat, was also found. A shift toward the local keeping of domesticated animals could also be indicated by the addition of two carnivores, the serval cat and white-tailed mongoose, to the assemblage. Although potentially valued for their skins, these animals could also reflect protective hunting strategies (Dueppen and Gallagher 2013).

In contrast to the assemblage from site MAS541, the aquatic species identified at site MAS502.3 could all have been obtained from nearby seasonal drainages or floodplains, or both. The small size of the fish would indicate some that could even inhabit the remnant pools that last deep into the dry season (see Table 23). There was no evidence of fishing expeditions to larger perennial rivers such as the Pendjari or Kourtiagou.

The botanical assemblage from Unit A, which was significantly more diverse than that of Unit E, was still very small and lacked any direct evidence of domesticated crops (see Table 24). Most of the identified seeds were from weedy or ruderal species such as *Scleria* sp. (which is often found in young fields) and *Trianthema portulacastrum* (which favors inhabited areas). The most common seed was an unknown Leguminosae (subfamily Papilionoideae); its small size makes it likely that it was from a smaller herbaceous or woody plant. Like Unit E, baobab shell was present in every sample.

Surface Survey Evidence of Pwoli Occupation Sites

The Pwoli ceramic assemblage was primarily recovered from subsurface deposits. It was difficult to identify other potential Pwoli sites in the region, in part because there were many Siga occupation sites and these may have been settled on Pwoli locations as was the case at sites MAS541 and MAS502.3. Site MAS902 was the most likely candidate for a Pwoli occupation site as it had several similarities to sites MAS541 and MAS502.3. The site was mounded, with fairly dense ceramics and pebbles on the surface. The ceramics were superficially similar to those of MAS541 and MAS502.3 in that they had high rates of polish for a surface assemblage, low rates of red slip, and a mixture of grog and quartz tempers. Yet the site MAS902 ceramics differed in significant ways as well, including having more diverse decoration and significantly higher average sherd thickness (see Table 25). Site MAS902 was also particularly notable for the high surface density of animal bone, a phenomenon only seen here and at site MAS541.

Dynamics of Pwoli Occupation Lifeways

Settlement and Architecture

Residents of sites MAS541 and MAS502.3 used similar construction techniques. The architectural fill of these mounds was composed of earth mixed with laterite pebbles (typical of the material used to build structures in the region today). No bricks could be identified at either site, which suggested the use of a coursed earth or wet wall technique, in which hand-formed moist earthen balls are used to build up walls in a spiral (Prussin 1969; Geis-Tronich 1991). The higher pebble content and harder texture at site MAS502.3 could be indicative of wall preparation more similar to that used for earthen brick. Floors were made with orange clay, mixed with a low density of laterite pebbles. This mixture was applied in thin strata (1 to 2 cm thick) and pounded to create a durable surface. In some structures, new floors were applied directly over existing surfaces, whereas in other cases, there was a 7 to 10 cm layer of fill between floor surfaces. As is the case at sites in western Burkina Faso and northern Benin, the floors lipped up several centimeters at the walls (Petit 2005; Dueppen 2012a). With small excavation units, degrading floor surfaces, and poor wall preservation, it was not possible to definitively determine the shape or size of structures, although the available evidence suggested round structures.

Curved burned features, neither of which could be associated with floors, were excavated at both sites MAS541 (Unit E) and MAS502.3 (Unit A). In Unit E, the feature was charcoal rich, with the burned surface along the convex side of the arc. In contrast, the Unit A burn feature lacked carbonized material and was burned along the concave side of the arc. Aside from these burn features, a hearth was identified on the interior floor of one structure at site MAS502.3.

Interestingly, both MAS541 and MAS502.3 were used as mortuary sites after abandonment. However, since burials were not excavated, it is not currently possible to assess whether the burials were evidence of continued links to the sites or simply convenient locations on high ground; MAS541 and MAS502.3 were adjacent to both Siga occupation sites and currently occupied residences.

Given the lack of surface evidence for the Pwoli occupation, even at sites like MAS502.3 where it was the primary subsurface component, it was difficult to assess the distribution of habitation in space across the region. The two confirmed Pwoli sites were both located more than 5 km from the Gobnangou escarpment, although the possible Pwoli site MAS902 was much closer. The presence of multiple flooring sequences at MAS541, and at least one instance of reflooring at MAS502.3, suggested repeated or continuous use of these sites through multiple construction episodes. This was in sharp contrast to subsequent occupations (see Chapters 6 and 7).

Potting, Stoneworking, and Smithing

Preserved material culture from the Pwoli occupation included ceramics, ground stone, chipped stone, and forged iron objects. Ceramics and chipped stone were both present in earlier occupations in the region; however, the Pwoli occupation was the first time either ground stone or iron objects were found.

Chipped stone was the primary artifact class of the previous occupations and, although recovered from Pwoli occupation sites, its role in the material culture assemblage diminished significantly. No formal tools were identified in excavations and the debitage recovered could represent waste from production of formal tools, expedient cutting and scraping tools, or fire starting (see the discussions in Chapters 4 and 6). Debitage was slightly more common at site MAS541, which had a stronger emphasis on hunting and logistical expeditions, than at site MAS502.3, but densities overall remained low.

Ceramics have great antiquity in the West African savanna and were present at archaeological sites in the study region by at latest the mid-Holocene (Frank et al. 2001; see Chapter 4). However, the Pwoli occupation was the first occupation in the survey zone in which ceramics were the primary artifact class (although, as discussed in Chapter 4, ceramics were common at earlier sites elsewhere along the escarpment). In attempting to define the Pwoli ceramic assemblage, it was easier to identify what was absent or rare (such as red slip, micaceous or lateritic tempers, large diameter vessels, and sherds over 15 mm thick) than features that could be used to characterize the assemblage. The relative frequency of paste formulas differed significantly between MAS541 and MAS502.3, and although there were strong similarities in the range of decoration techniques in use between the two sites—notably the high frequency of twisted cord roulette and the use of folded strip roulettes and dragged comb or parallel channels (see Table 20)—each site had unique decorations as well. Given the variability between the two assemblages, it is likely that ceramics were produced at the household level. There was no explicit evidence in the assemblage of a shared ceramic tradition between the two sites.

Many researchers argue that the primary factor determining the role of pottery within the material culture assemblage is the functional aspect of diet and food preparation driven by environmental constraints or cultural preferences in cuisine (Rice 1999; Harry and Frink 2009). Ceramic vessels are strongly associated with the consumption of foods that are best processed by boiling or simmering for an extended period, such as grains, shellfish, and nuts (Arnold 1985; Stahl 1993; Rice 1999). For example, in northern Ghana during the second millennium BCE a significant increase in the quantity of pottery between the Punpun and Kintampo phases was associated with more intensive exploitation of oil palm and, potentially, the introduction of pearl millet to the region (Stahl 1993; D'Andrea and Casey 2002). Stahl (1993) suggested that there may have been an accompanying shift in cuisine from "dry" cooking to "wet" cooking of foods available during both phases.

In the MAS study region pottery was in use from at latest the fourth millennium BCE, when it was used by communities that seem to have been relying largely on wild resources (Frank et al. 2001). These uses could have included boiling wild grains or rendering vegetable fat from shea nuts (see Gallagher, Dueppen, and Walsh 2016). Ceramic vessels could have been particularly important for cooking pearl millet and sorghum, which were among the common domesticated resources in the region, as both grains have low gluten content and consequently are typically boiled or steamed rather than baked. In addition, ceramics are also used to brew beer from these grains today, although brewing is typically associated with large vessels. The increased use of ceramics during the Pwoli occupation could indicate a greater reliance on domesticated grains.

Archaeologists have often assumed links between ceramics and mobility and for many years ceramics were particularly associated with sedentary, agricultural lifeways. Although ceramic manufacture and transport posed certain challenges in a mobile environment (for example, weight, durability, and production scale; Arnold 1985), there are several exceptions and mobile groups often use creative strategies, such as caching at locations with predictable seasonal resources, to facilitate ceramic use (Eerkens 2003; Grillo 2014). Although these models were arguably more relevant to understanding the role of ceramics at the Péntènga rockshelter, Pwoli occupation ceramics were thin and vessels tended to be small, qualities that would make them easier to transport. At site MAS541, where the fauna assemblage implied significant seasonal mobility, these trends were more pronounced and quartz temper could have added durability to transported vessels.

Ground stone (represented largely by small basal grinding stone fragments) was usually made from pieces of sandstone, the nearest source for which would have been the Gobnangou escarpment several kilometers away. Given the distance from the source and the labor involved in their preparation, these stones would likely have been used intensively and perhaps moved or repurposed after initial site abandonment, accounting for their fragmentary state. The occurrence of grinding stones in Pwoli occupation sites could be indicative of increasing sedentism or repeated use of the same locations. It is likewise possible that grinding stones were associated with changes in subsistence, in particular increased use of grains, although the limited sample of grinding stones offered little direct insight into diet. Grinding of grains is the most common use, but the stones can also be used to grind sauce ingredients and medicines as well as ceramic tempers and ochres (see the discussions in Chapter 6).

Finally, residents during the Pwoli occupation had access to forged iron objects. Although iron-smelting technology had been both well established and widespread in West Africa for more than one thousand years by the time of the Pwoli occupation (Deme and S. K. McIntosh 2006; Koté 2007; MacDonald et al. 2009; Holl 2014; Junius 2016; Dueppen 2018) and all the raw materials necessary for smelting iron were present in the study region (see Chapter 6), we found no direct evidence that the recovered iron objects were locally produced. More slag was present in the deposits at site MAS502.3 than at MAS541, but the overall quantity was still too low to confirm smelting activity, particularly given the low quality of local ores. In the Fada N'Gourma region, Thiombiano-Ilboudo (2010) interpreted the presence of small amounts of slag without tuyères or furnaces as likely reflecting forging activity.

Although the organization of iron production could not be addressed with the available data, a comparison of recovered iron artifacts from sites MAS541 and MAS502.3 suggested a possible refinement in smithing techniques. The arrow or spear point from Unit E was significantly thicker and heavier than those from Unit A and lacked the delicate tangs of the latter's arrowheads. This difference could also have been a question of function, particularly if the larger point from Unit E was meant for use with a spear and the smaller points from Unit A were intended for projectiles. Although the recovered iron objects from the Pwoli occupation were points, iron is frequently associated with agricultural activity, because it can be used to make axes, hoes, and knives and can facilitate clearing and plowing land as well as the weeding and harvesting of crops (see the discussions in Blench [2014]).

Hunting, Herding, Fishing, Farming, and Collecting

The faunal data from sites MAS541 and MAS502.3 suggested increasingly localized exploitation of wild animal resources and a late adoption of domesticated animals. Hunting patterns were fairly consistent between the two sites: residents seemed to have used a mixed strategy of big game hunting (possibly on organized expeditions) and small game hunting near the site. Ungulates were common targets, yet the potential importance of garden hunting, particularly of cane rats, should not be underestimated (Dueppen 2012a; Dueppen and Gallagher 2013). The increase in species favoring the margins of forests at MAS502.3 could indicate the clearing of land, possibly for cultivation.

The identification of fish at site MAS541 from a distance of at least a day's walk was somewhat of an anomaly, given that the fish recovered both earlier in the sequence, at Péntènga rockshelter, and later in the Pwoli occupation, at site MAS502.3, were all likely locally obtained. Freshwater fish are easily preserved by drying or smoking. Traditionally smoked or dried fish can last for up to nine months, provided they are resmoked or sun-dried every four to six weeks to maintain a low moisture content (FAO 1989). Most likely, these fish would have been caught and preserved at specialized fishing camps near the Pendjari or Kourtiagou River. These types of fishing camps were historically common during the dry season when major channels are easier to access, fish are confined to a smaller area, and preservation by smoking or sun-drying is easier because of low humidity. Nile perch, however, tends to be consumed fresh and its presence in Unit E may indicate direct movements back to the site.

In contrast, fish from floodplains and seasonal drainages require significantly less labor to catch and process, but are on average smaller. Because they are locally obtained, they could have been consumed fresh, although they may also have been preserved. This type of fishing would have occurred during the rainy season, when there was flowing water in the drainage, and at the beginning of the dry season, when fish were stranded in seasonal pools as the water receded.

The faunal evidence from Unit A indicated that domesticated animals became a significant component of the domestic economy during the Pwoli occupation. The dwarf varieties that were identified could have resided in the study region throughout the year and in fact may have inhibited mobility as they do not travel well over long distances and prefer to remain near their residence. The adoption of livestock in the savanna-forest margin was often associated with the intensification of local resource exploitation, notably farming. Because animals were generally consumed infrequently for meat, one of their primary economic roles was as producers of manure, which provides an essential fertilizer (especially when accumulated in pens). Finally, livestock ownership, commonly associated with the accumulation of wealth, can potentially be linked to changing social and economic values (Dueppen and Gallagher 2013).

As described above, the botanical data for the Pwoli occupation were very limited. The single domestic pearl millet grain, from the earliest levels of occupation, could indicate cereal cultivation, although one grain cannot be considered conclusive. This botanical evidence was significantly stronger in the context of the material culture and faunal assemblages. The hunting profiles from both sites MAS541 and MAS502.3 strongly supported the presence of agricultural fields with evidence for the targeting of garden pests, such as cane rats and small bovids, and for changes in the landscape associated with the clearing and development of fallow field systems (Dueppen and Gallagher 2013). Although there was no direct evidence for agriculture in the material culture assemblage, the use of iron, pottery, and grinding stones is consistent with an agricultural economy.

Pearl millet was the only documented domesticated crop plant in use, yet during the wetter climate of the Pwoli occupation the survey zone would have been located near the southern rainfall limit for pearl millet cultivation. A moist climate could have favored sorghum or yam cultivation, the latter of which is very limited in the region today. Pearl millet has been documented archaeologically in forest environments (e.g., Kahlheber, Bostoen, and Newmann 2009; Logan 2016). It is possible that pearl millet was initially grown as a bridging crop, because some varieties can produce grain in as little as seventy days and so provide an important food source early in the rainy season when many wild plants have not yet matured (Swanson 1979b; NRC 1996).

The most commonly identified plant at both sites was the baobab tree. Baobab prefers drier climates and rarely occurs naturally in Guinean forests, although it is an anthropogenic species that is often found near settlements outside its usual distribution. The carbonized seed fragments come from baobab fruits, which are widely consumed. After being soaked to remove the pulp and discarded, as described by Duvall (2007), seeds could have been accidentally burned. Burkill (1985:274) noted that pods can be intentionally burned to make a potash appropriate for soap manufacture. The remaining identified seeds were common weeds, none of which are constrained to a particular microenvironment, although many have ruderal tendencies.

The Pwoli Occupation in Regional Context

Many of the changes that occurred between the Lithic occupation and the Pwoli occupation (that is, increased use of ceramics, cultivation of pearl millet, herding of dwarf livestock, and use of iron implements) were documented at much earlier dates in other parts of the West African savanna and savanna-forest margin (Shinnie and Kense 1989; Watson 2010; Dueppen 2012a, 2018). Given the very small sample size from Frank and colleagues (2001) for the early first millennium CE, it is difficult to make the argument that these resources were not in use before the Pwoli occupation, especially given the light footprint of low-level cultivation. The charcoal sequence from Péntènga showed increased levels of burning from the early first millennium BCE, which could be indicative of clearing land for cultivation or of encouraging fodder growth to attract wild animals (Frank et al. 2001). Perhaps the strongest argument could be made for a late adoption of livestock, since domesticated cattle, sheep, and goats were not present at either Péntènga rockshelter or site MAS541.

By the latter half of the first millennium CE, most archaeologically explored regions of the West African savanna had been settled by sedentary agriculturalists for several hundred years and most sites showed evidence of growth throughout this period (e.g., Dueppen 2012a, 2018; Huysecom et al. 2015; Magnavita 2015; Haour et al. 2016; Haour 2019). Several hundred kilometers to the north, at sites like Kissi and Gao, there is evidence for significant involvement in long-distance trading networks; evidence from sites 140 km northeast of the study region in the Dendi region, including the large site of Birnin Lafiya, suggests that these trading networks may have extended south along the Niger River (Haour et al. 2016; Haour 2019). There is evidence for substantial architectural investment, millet and rice agriculture, the herding of dwarf livestock, hunting, and widespread iron smelting during the first millennium CE at sites in the Dendi region (Haour 2019). Despite the mobility of Pwoli occupation residents (particularly at MAS541), there is currently no evidence that they participated in interregional trade. The MAS sites have no clear similarities in architecture or material culture to those in the Dendi region, aside from the common use of coursed earth techniques (Haour 2019).

In contrast, the Pwoli occupation has several similarities to the sequence described by Petit (2005) and N'Dah (2009) for northern Benin as much as 100 km to the southeast. In both cases, the first mounded settlement sites dated to the mid to late first millennium CE and preserved architecture consisted predominantly of occasional orange plaster floors, although sites in northern Benin were substantially larger than Pwoli occupation sites, with many larger than 2 ha. Although the pottery had some visual similarity to that of sites in the north of the Atakora Mountains (L. P. Petit, personal communication, 2009), it differed in its specifics, including temper, vessel thickness, and decoration techniques. Cord roulettes were not used in northern Benin and twisted cord roulette was the dominant decoration in the MAS study region. Like the Pwoli occupation, iron objects, usually points or shafts, were found at all sites, but there was little evidence for smelting.

In northern Benin, domesticated sheep, goat, and large (not dwarf) cattle were present in the first millennium CE. Although Petit (2005) did not present a complete faunal analysis, preliminary results indicated that hunting was focused on smaller wild animals, such as hares and small ungulates, and fishing was predominantly confined to shallow water. The botanical data indicated the use of pearl millet and sorghum in addition to tree fruits. As in the study region, baobab shell was one of the most frequently recovered carbonized remains.

Early Farmers of the Gobnangou

Archaeological data from before the Pwoli occupation in the Gobnangou region generally indicated a fairly mobile foraging adaptation that used diverse broad-spectrum economic strategies to produce only a limited archaeological signature. By the beginning of the Pwoli occupation a gradual adoption of domesticated crops had likely already begun. This occupation was marked by the first evidence in the survey zone for sedentary settlements and by the use of increasingly localized economic practices over time. At site MAS541, residents incorporated pearl millet and chickens into a still fairly extensive broad-spectrum strategy. Architectural techniques indicated an increasing investment in place, probably derived from the seasonal attachment to crop fields, yet the spectrum of fauna suggests wide-ranging use of the landscape in the procurement of wild resources, notably fish from major rivers. Results from the slightly later site MAS502.3 documented the emergence by the end of the first millennium CE of a domestic economy that could be considered typical of the West African savanna, with likely cultivation of domesticated plants, a full array of domesticated livestock and chickens, and a strong continuing commitment to wild plant and animal resources.

The gradual changes in mobility and economic practices between sites MAS541 and MAS502.3 provide an intriguing glimpse into the ways that agriculture influenced increasing social anchoring and changes in societal strategies leading to ownership systems for land and ultimately livestock. Moreover, the Pwoli occupation attested to general changes in material culture, as architecture, iron, and ceramics became increasingly central to societies in the Gobnangou. These elements of sedentary farming life became foundational to subsequent occupation phases in the Gobnangou that would ultimately result in larger regional populations.

CHAPTER SIX

GENERATIONAL MOBILITY AND HOUSEHOLD NETWORKS
The Siga Occupation

In the early second millennium CE, the relatively rare, stratified, mounded sites of the Pwoli occupation were replaced by hundreds of dispersed, small, shallow sites of the Siga occupation (ca. 1050–1300/1650 CE). The ephemeral nature and spatial distribution of sites, when contextualized with a substantial material culture assemblage of large ceramics, ground stone, and other indicators of sedentism, likely indicates that they are the remnants of farming compounds occupied on a generational basis.

The use of multiple standardized ceramic wares with different pastes, tempers, and decorative elements suggests collective identities and specialized production at the regional level. The common use of this assemblage could reflect a shared practice of food production and consumption related to a regional stylistic and aesthetic tradition. Similarly, iron working may have been specialized, with a significant increase in evidence for iron production in comparison to the Pwoli occupation and spatial clustering of iron smelting sites in a few locations in the landscape.

Because of the lack of stratified deposits, excavations of Siga occupation sites yielded relatively little information. Characterizations of the period were drawn primarily from the analysis of surface artifacts and the nature of the sites themselves. Using limited radiometric dating and comparative analyses of material culture in the greater region, analysis indicates that Siga sites emerged in the early second millennium CE, although temporal precision within the period was challenging (see the discussions below) and the contemporaneity of sites in the survey zone is currently unknown. However, in comparison to the Pwoli occupation, the nature of the sites, their degree of mobility, and their intensified production of material culture bear a closer resemblance to ethnohistorical practices in the region.

The Siga Occupation:
A Cultural Landscape of Small Sites

Siga occupation sites were by far the most numerous in the study region, encompassing 344 of the 517 MAS sites identified (Figures 40 and 41). Sites were assigned to the Siga occupation at two levels of confidence (using the methods described in Chapter 3). Low-

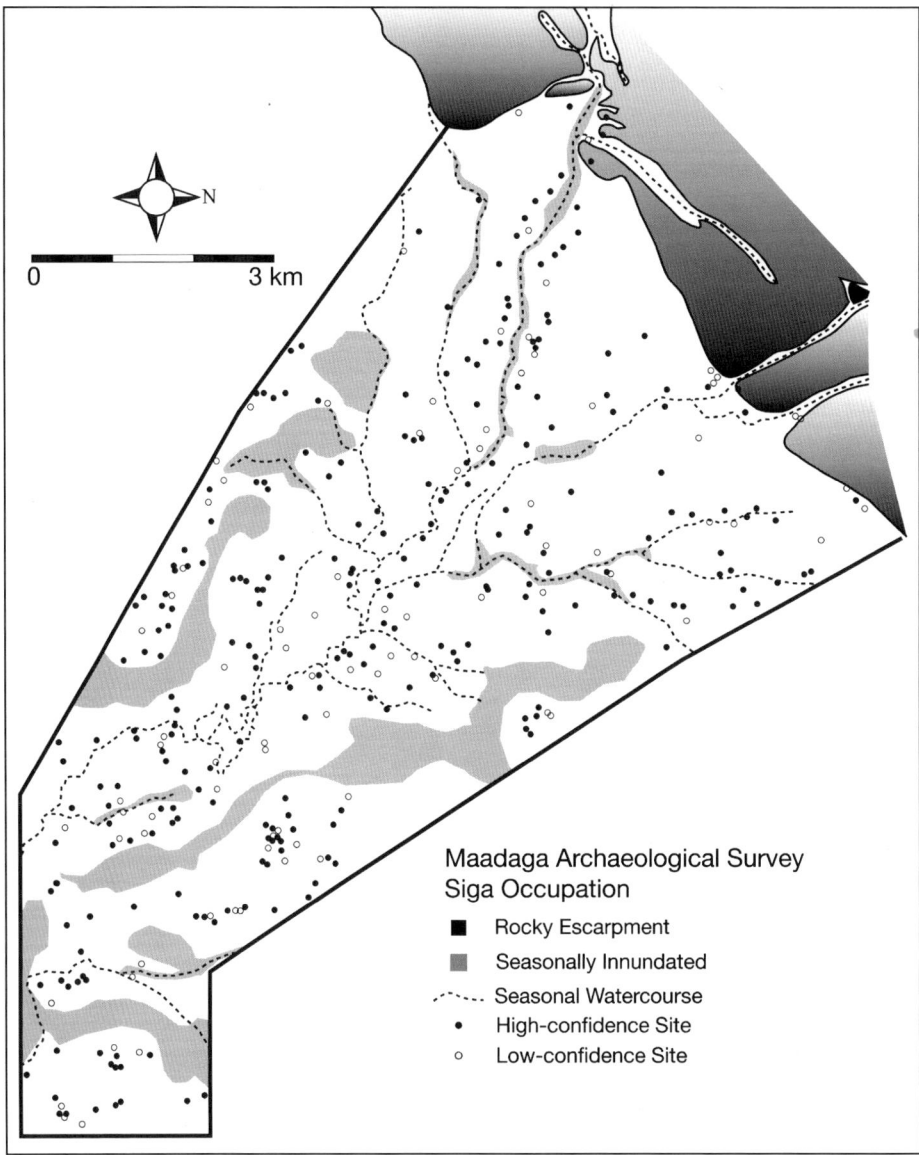

FIGURE 40. Siga occupation sites identified by the Maadaga Archaeological Survey.

confidence sites ($n = 89$) had an almost identical distribution to high-confidence sites ($n = 255$) and are only discussed when they differ significantly. Additionally, several sites ($n = 52$) were identified as having multicomponent ceramic assemblages. Although these sites are included in all discussions of spatial distribution, analyses of artifact frequency and other characteristics of the sites themselves are confined to single-component sites.

Siga Occupation Site Characteristics
Individual sites within the Siga occupation were typically small, shallow, poorly preserved,

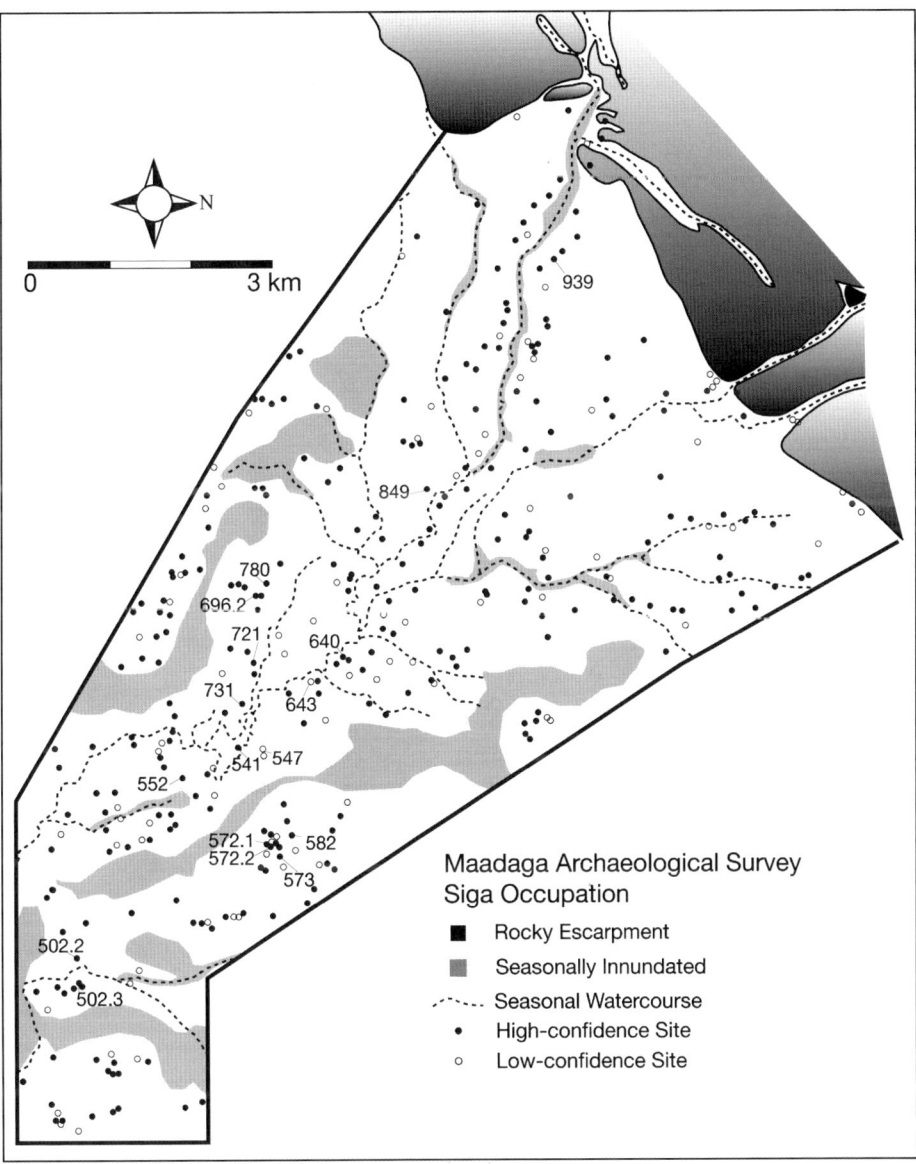

FIGURE 41. Locations of Siga occupation sites mentioned in the text.

and relatively homogenous in their physical characteristics and surface densities. The poor preservation was due not only to their ephemeral nature, but also to the substantial effects of plowing and borrow pits (Table 28).

Several lines of evidence supported the characterization of Siga occupation sites as shallow. Over 75% of sites had an estimated depth of less than 0.5 m, although several examples had estimated depths of over 1 m. However, excavations generally indicated that these figures were too high. For example, sites MAS572.1 and MAS573 were estimated at 2 m and 1.25 m in depth, respectively, but in actuality had less than 0.3 m of cultural

TABLE 28. Characteristics of Siga occupation sites by assigned confidence level for single-component sites.

Site features	High-confidence sites	Low-confidence sites	All sites
Total number of sites	238	54	344
Near baobab trees	29	8	47
Near seasonal drainage	115	22	163
Near seasonal pool	12	6	52
Near seasonal inundation or marsh	40	6	23
Total sites near water	167	34	238
Plowing disturbance present	209	40	296
Borrow pit disturbance present	26	4	46
Chipped stone present	113	27	165
Ground stone present	158	28	219
Slag (rare)	17	4	23
Slag (present)	21	6	30
Iron smelting (small)	8	0	8
Iron smelting (medium)	6	0	8
Iron smelting (very large)	1	0	1

deposits. Likewise, Siga occupations at sites MAS541 and MAS502.3 proved to be entirely superficial and no characteristic pottery from this period was recovered below the plow zone. Site MAS780 was a less extreme case (1.5 m estimated depth, 1.1 m actual depth) but, as will be discussed below, no living surfaces were identified (this site may have been an atypical mortuary location). Finally, we identified no subsurface cultural deposits at any of the forty-six Siga occupation sites with borrow pits. At these sites, which have depth estimates ranging from 0.2 to 1.5 m, examination of scraped pit cuts found only superficial cultural strata that did not extend below the plow zone.

In some cases, Siga occupation cultural materials were identified in borrow pits or eroding from a stratum exposed by a stream cut. In these circumstances, cultural materials were still confined to a single, shallow deposit, albeit one that had been covered by natural processes. These sites tended to occur near main channels and were likely covered and in some cases exposed by the dynamic hydrology of the study region. These sites serve as a cautionary reminder that there may be many subsurface sites in the study region.

Siga occupation sites fell loosely into three size categories (Table 29; Figure 42). The majority of sites were roughly circular with diameters ranging from 10 to 30 m (75 to 625 m^2). These sites were likely individual household compounds with a relatively small range of sizes; the distribution showed minor peaks around 100 and 200 m^2 (11 and 15 m in diameter), which could indicate two size classes within this group. It is possible that this bimodal distribution represents the difference created by the addition of extra structures to a circular compound. Above 200 m^2 the sharply diminishing area distribution suggests either very few larger residences or the effects of plow smearing. These larger sites ($n = 30$, 700 to 3,320 m^2) were not consistent in size and often sprawled along ridgetops over an area that could have included multiple households. Finally, several smaller sites were either nonresidential (for example, small iron smelting locations such as site MAS939) or were poorly preserved (that is, a few sherds pushed to the surface by tree roots or termite mounds). In general, sites of different sizes were proportionately distributed in the landscape, with large sites slightly overrepresented in Zones 1 and 7 (see Figure 16).

The mean and median ceramic densities (measured in grams per square meter) were very similar across site size categories (see Table 29) and differed by less than 2 g. However, removing the upper outliers dropped the average density at small sites in particular from 30.2 to 11.3 g/m^2, whereas medium and large sites experienced significantly smaller declines (to 24.4 and 19.2 g/m^2, respectively). Analyses using different density measures, such as sherds per square meter, and an index that combined both sherds and grams per square meter, yielded similar results. These results indicated that small sites (with one exception) were more ephemeral occupations and large sites were simply more extensive occupations that likely resulted from either multiple simultaneously occupied residences or sequential, slightly overlapping occupations. No regional level spatial patterns could be identified using any of the density measures.

Many of the additional surface characteristics that were recorded proved to be determined largely by local environmental conditions. Soils were those of the surrounding matrix and their color variation reflected the differences between the highly leached sand near the escarpment, the gray clays of the lower Koabu floodplains, and the light brown of the plateaus. Laterite pebble density, although visually striking and almost always higher than the surrounding matrix, correlated with the depth of lateritic bedrock. Thus, sites with dense pebbles were concentrated in Zones B and C, away from the central drainage valley (see Figure 16).

Overall, the size, shape, and cultural surface characteristics of Siga occupation sites were remarkably similar across the survey zone. With the exception of poorly preserved small sites, large sites that were otherwise identical to medium sites, and specialist ironworking sites (discussed below), almost all Siga occupation sites had a circular or oval footprint between 10 and 30 m diameter. This size was consistent with that of twentieth-century residences in the region occupied by an extended or nuclear family. To the north of the Gobnangou escarpment at Yobri, of the fifty-four compounds documented in the 1960s, forty were between 12 and 30 m in diameter (Rémy 1967). These results were similar to those obtained by other twentieth-century studies of house size. For example, most of the compounds Prussin (1969) depicted in her maps of Konkomba, Dagomba, and Tallensi settlements in northern Ghana fell within the 10 to 30 m diameter range.

Ethnohistorically, compounds of similar size could differ significantly in structure density and population (see the discussions in Prussin [1969:43–44]). At Yobri, the forty

TABLE 29. Ceramic assemblage characteristics of Siga occupation sites and location by site size and distance from the Gobnangou escarpment (Zones 1 to 7) and the Koabu drainage (Zones A, B, and C; see also Figure 16).

	Number and size (m^2) of sites		
	Small (1–60)	Medium (75–625)	Large (700–3,320)
Total number of sites	26	171	30
Zone 1	1	3	3
Zone 2	7	37	0
Zone 3	2	36	6
Zone 4	5	33	4
Zone 5	3	33	8
Zone 6	4	18	4
Zone 7	4	11	5
Zone A	19	116	12
Zone B	0	20	6
Zone C	7	35	12
	Ceramic assemblage characteristics		
Mean ceramic density (g/m^3)	27.3	28.5	28.0
Median ceramic density (g/m^3)	17.3	21.6	20.2
Mean number of decoration techniques in use per site	3.0	3.8	5.9
Mean number of decoration techniques in use per 100 sherds	17.8	15.0	13.8

smaller compounds reached seventy residents and the fourteen larger compounds (32 to 52 m diameter) only reached a hundred residents (Remy 1967). Conversely, compounds with thirty residents ranged from 12 to 35 m in diameter. Consequently, although most identified sites likely represent circular household compounds, their similar size does not necessarily imply that houses had similar numbers of residents. Siga occupation sites typically had consistent artifact density throughout, such that internal use of space could not be determined from their surface characteristics.

Excavations at Sites MAS572.1, MAS573, and MAS780

The results of excavations at Siga occupation sites reinforced the site characteristics identified during survey. Cultural deposits tended to be shallow and we found no preserved architecture or floor surfaces. Here, I present descriptions of the excavations at sites MAS572.1, MAS573, and MAS780. Excavation procedures followed the MAS methodolo-

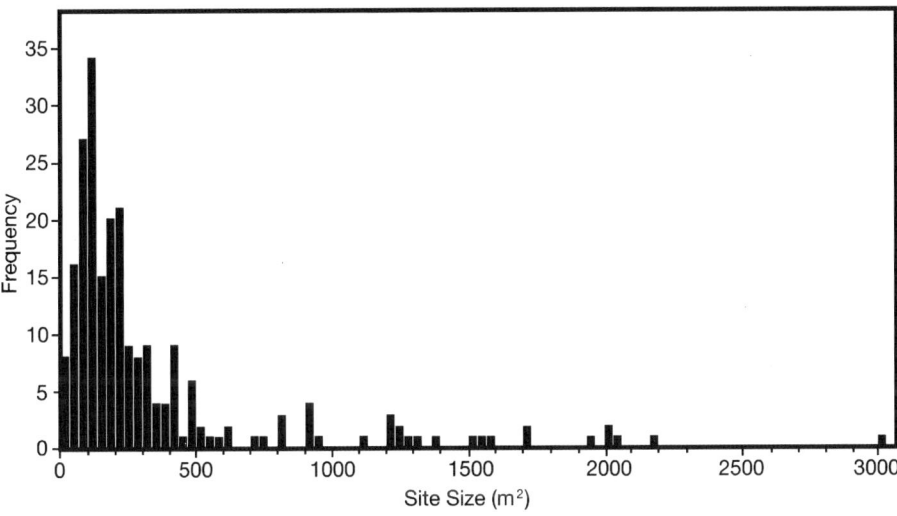

FIGURE 42. Size distribution of Siga occupation sites.

gies (described in Chapter 3). The focus of this section is on site characteristics; artifacts are discussed with survey results in the thematic sections below.

SITE MAS572.1 EXCAVATION AND STRATIGRAPHIC SUMMARY
Site MAS572.1 is part of a small cluster of nine mounded sites (Figure 43). All sites in the cluster date to the Siga occupation; four are approximately the same size as MAS572.1 (910 to 1,260 m^2) and five are significantly smaller (150 to 350 m^2). The sites have similar surface features, including frequent presence of basal grinding stones. There is no evidence of iron working at any site in the cluster. Site MAS572.1 was selected for further study for its size, 2 m estimated depth, and distance from currently occupied households. In 2006, we excavated a 2 by 1.5 m unit (Unit C) at the site.

Unit C contained evidence of a domestic space just below the surface, but we quickly reached sterile soil in a very hard lateritic duracrust (Figure 44). The occupation layer included three large basal grinding stones, a dense concentration of ceramics (including smashed but fairly complete vessels), and a laterite block, all of which seemed to be in situ and below which no artifacts were recovered (Figure 45). The sediment throughout, characterized by local residents as *ubani* because of its exceptional hardness, was incredibly dense and almost impossible to dig through. This hardness likely explained the high degree of preservation in such a thin site; there were slight furrows, but it did not seem that the site had been frequently or deeply plowed.

SITE MAS573 EXCAVATION AND STRATIGRAPHIC SUMMARY
When site MAS572.1 terminated at a shallow depth, we decided to excavate at nearby site MAS573. It had deep, 10 to 15 cm furrows that we hoped indicated softer sediment (see Figure 43). On the ground, the local topography made MAS573 seem distant, but mapping showed it to be within the bounds of the MAS572 site cluster. We excavated a 1 by 1.5 m unit (Unit D) and, although we found a cultural feature just below the surface, we quickly reached sterile soil in a similar hard lateritic duracrust (see Figure 44).

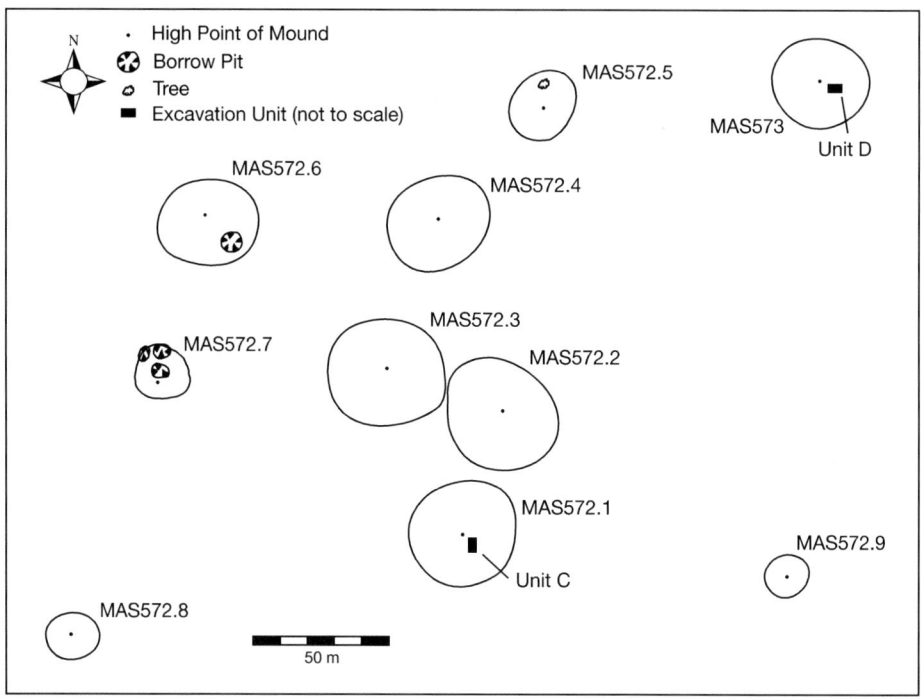

FIGURE 43. The MAS572 site cluster in relation to site MAS573.

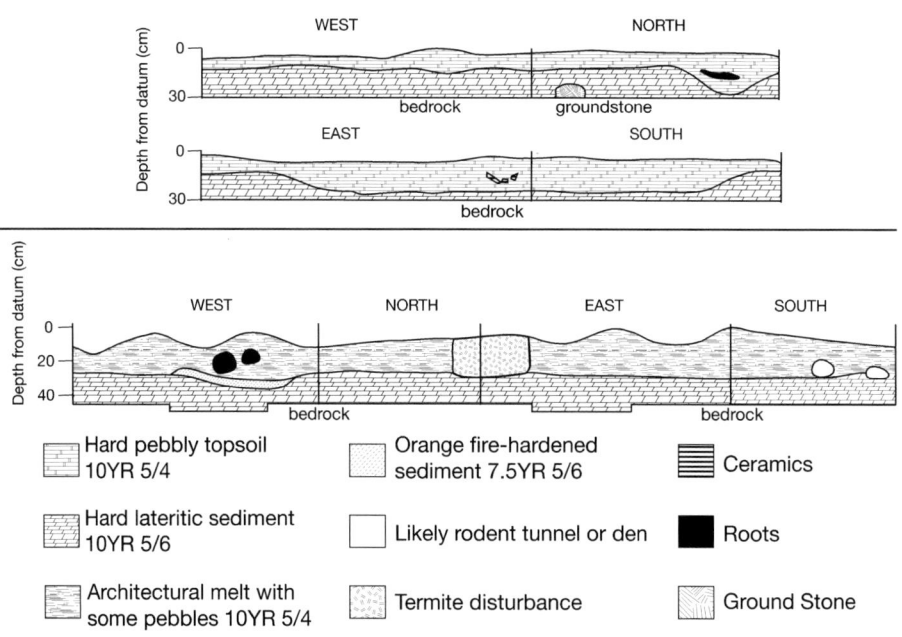

FIGURE 44. Profiles of the stratigraphy of Unit C at site MAS572.1 and Unit D at site MAS573. Soil color designations are from Munsell Color (2009).

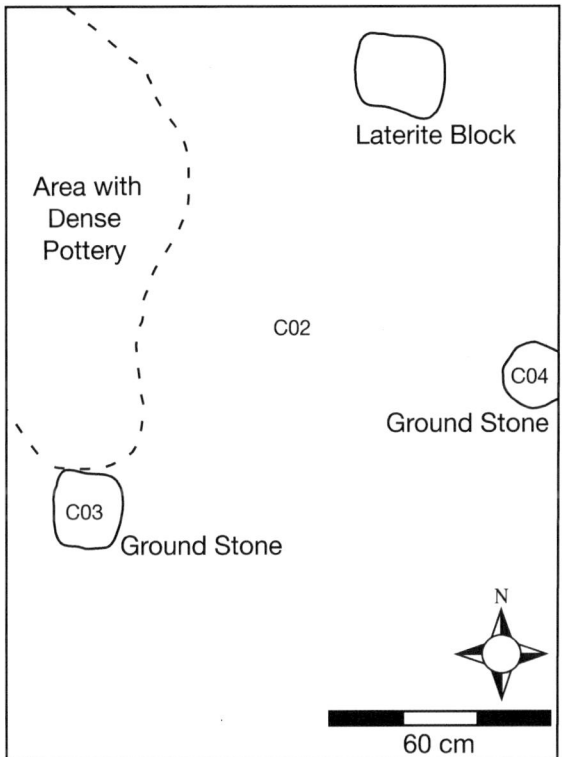

FIGURE 45. Features of Unit C at site MAS572.1 at 12 cm below datum.

The topsoil deposit was looser at site MAS573 from plowing, rodent, and termite disturbance and contained the bulk of artifacts recovered. Below the topsoil we found a roughly elliptical patch of burned earth (100 by 50 cm, 3 to 4 cm thick) likely created by a low-temperature hearth or discard of hot ash. There were some ceramic sherds and ash atop the feature that could substantiate either hypothesis. A fragment of tobacco pipe was found on the surface.

MAS780 Excavation and Stratigraphic Summary

Site MAS780 is on a sandy ridge above a seasonal drainage leading to the Koabu. The site was selected for further study for its size and estimated depth (1,500 m² and 1.5 m, respectively) and its fairly high surface ceramic densities. Amilidi Tindambiga, who lived directly adjacent to the site and farmed the area, reported that he frequently encountered archaeological materials when digging pits, including both ceramics and a burial with iron bracelets (see below). His experience suggested the presence of subsurface archaeological deposits and, in 2006, we excavated a 2 by 1.5 m unit (Unit B) with Tindambiga's participation (Figure 46). Just below the surface of the unit we encountered a 10 to 15 cm deep stratum with few artifacts. Because of this layer the unit was rapidly cut down to 1 by 1.5 m, although deposits ultimately reached a depth of 110 cm.

Archaeological deposits in Unit B differed from those elsewhere in the study region. Rather than clear architectural or activity spaces, the highly compacted deposits had low-

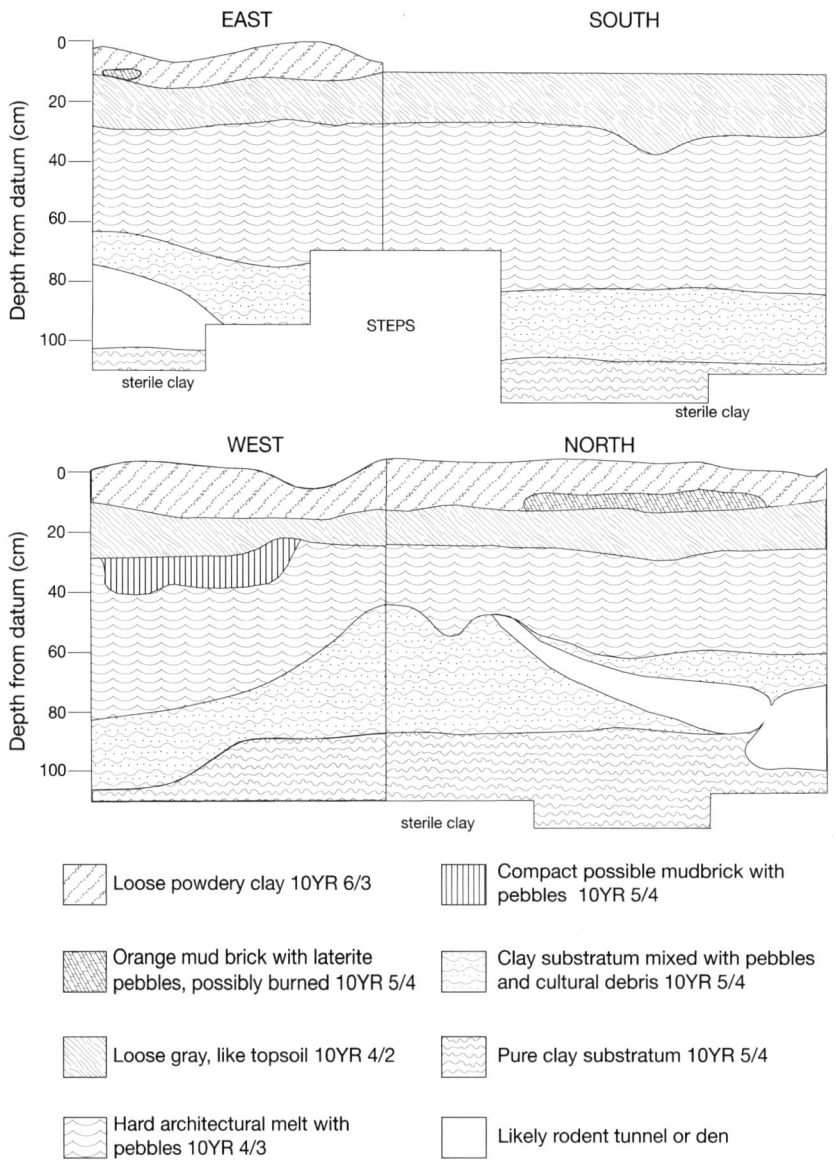

FIGURE 46. Profiles of stratigraphy of Unit B at site MAS780. Soil color designations are from Munsell Color (2009).

density archaeological remains. Strata were not horizontal and included significant bioturbation from rodents and termites. Artifacts were particularly dense from 55 to 110 cm (levels B08 to B12) where most of the iron, animal bones, and ceramics were recovered from a sloping deposit. With such a small sample it was not possible to assess whether this slope was the result of a natural rise, an intentional construction, or a side effect of an activity such as trash dumping, although the underlying sterile clay was fairly flat. Overall, there were no indicators of domestic activity in Unit B, other than the presence of artifacts in the fill. It is possible that site MAS780 (or this particular area of the site) was not residential, particularly given the unique nature of the finds, notably the high densities of iron objects (see below).

Spatial Distribution of Siga Occupation Settlement

Siga occupation sites were evenly distributed throughout the survey region (see Figure 40; Table 30). As described above, larger sites were slightly more likely to be found either close to the Gobnangou escarpment or in the most distant locations, but otherwise no significant spatial patterns could be identified among residential sites (iron-working sites are discussed below). The large number of sites ($n = 344$) likely resulted from an increase in the local population between the Pwoli and Siga occupations. Even though there may have been more sites per household because of the shifting nature of settlement (discussed below), the growth in the number of identified sites seemed unambiguous, even if it is not yet possible to assess the degree of population increase.

Although addressing the relationships between sites was difficult given the challenges of differential site preservation and the palimpsest created by short occupation sites (see the discussion in Chapter 3), the settlement distribution provided insight into spatiosocial choices. Siga sites were frequently located near a water source, an unsurprising observation given the ubiquity of major and minor drainages (including many too ephemeral to be included on the map), seasonal and permanent pools, and seasonally inundated and marshy areas in the survey region (see Table 28). Given the likely historical changes in the hydrology (see Chapter 2), it is very possible that Siga occupation sites not currently near water sources may have been close to them in the past; linear site arrangements may indicate the locations of former seasonal channels, although formal geomorphological study has not taken place. Most sites seem to have been built on natural rises, given the differences in estimated and observed site depths discussed above.

The distribution of sites was such that even close fields extending only a few hundred meters from each site would cover most of the survey area. As a result, virtually all arable land in the survey region was probably farmed at some point during the Siga occupation. With sites located on diverse local soils, Siga occupation farmers clearly had the flexibility and skill to adjust between, for example, the sandy, well-drained soils adjacent to the escarpment and the heavy clays on the edges of seasonal inundations.

In selecting a new household site, residents rarely returned to precisely the same location and most frequently built new compounds at least a hundred meters distant from earlier structures. There were several incidences of closer spacing (within 100 m) that could be indicative of either clustering or repeated use of the same field system. Different sites within clusters often dated to both the Siga and Tuali occupations and currently occupied residential compounds were frequently positioned near archaeological sites such that, if abandoned, they would have appeared to be another site in the cluster. For contemporary farmers, archaeological sites tend to be near good farmland and are an excellent source of building material. It is possible that residents of the region during the Siga occupation valued these qualities as well.

Modeling Residence Length and Population Density during the Siga Occupation

The available data was not sufficient to determine which Siga occupation sites were occupied simultaneously, but it was possible to loosely bracket the number of sites that could

TABLE 30. Spatial distribution of Siga occupation sites by distance from the Gobnangou escarpment (Zones 1 to 7) and the Koabu River drainage (Zones A, B, and C; see also Figure 16). Numbers in parentheses are for single-component high-confidence sites only.

	Number of sites per zone								
	Zone 1	Zone 2	Zone 3	Zone 4	Zone 5	Zone 6	Zone 7	Total number	Total percentage
Zone A	17 (7)	62 (47)	54 (41)	46 (30)	27 (17)	24 (16)	—	230 (158)	66.9 (66.4)
Zone B	—	—	9 (7)	14 (9)	12 (10)	—	—	35 (26)	10.2 (10.9)
Zone C	—	—	—	7 (5)	26 (19)	15 (10)	31 (20)	79 (54)	23.0 (22.7)
Total number	17 (7)	62 (47)	63 (48)	67 (44)	65 (46)	39 (26)	31 (20)	344 (238)	
Total percentage	4.9 (2.9)	18.0 (19.7)	18.3 (20.2)	19.5 (18.5)	18.9 (19.3)	11.3 (10.9)	9.0 (8.4)		

reasonably have been occupied at a given time. This required estimating the duration of occupancy (residence length) and the amount of arable land needed for Siga occupation households.

Ceramics are an unreliable indicator of length of residence at any given site. Surface ceramic density is significantly affected by site preservation (recently plowed sites almost universally had higher densities than undisturbed sites), as well as by the nature and intensity of site use (Cameron and Tomka 1993; Varien 1999). The difficulties of comparing ceramic density at different sites is further complicated by both formation processes (for example, what pottery was left behind when the site was abandoned) and sampling strategies (we took only one systematic surface collection at each site). However, at a population level, material culture densities should reflect significant differences in residence length among households engaged in similar activities using similar material culture. Ceramic densities at 90% of Siga occupation sites fell within one standard deviation of the mean density. Given that most Siga sites have no subsurface deposits, this could indicate that most sites were occupied for roughly the same amount of time.

Although we have no absolute dates for residence length of individual Siga sites, long-term maintenance and reconstruction of earthen architecture produces an accumulation of cultural deposits (see the discussions in R. J. McIntosh [1974] and Dueppen [2012a]). Excavations and observations of borrow pit cuts at Siga occupation sites identified no reflooring or architectural layering (as was present in Pwoli occupation sites), which indicated that houses did not undergo major reconstruction. Ethnohistorically, coursed-earth structures in the West African savanna can last up to five years with no maintenance and simple tasks such as annual plastering and thatching can extend this lifespan significantly (Prussin 1969). Longitudinal studies of house life are rare; however, a thirty- to forty-year time frame before rebuilding is required occurs regularly in the literature (e.g., Blier 1987; Duvall 2006). The occupation length of any given residence was likely driven by historically particular factors, yet this is the best estimate that can be made with the available data. It fits well with the consistent ceramic densities and observed shallow deposits of Siga occupation sites.

Calculating past carrying capacity is an extremely complicated process that requires detailed knowledge of several factors and their average variation through time for reasonable results (e.g., Danielisová et al. 2015). Environmental data for the study region lacks the necessary specificity for construction of a reliable model. In addition, key variables like household size and the importance of cash crops have changed dramatically over the past one hundred years. Despite these limitations, it was possible to create a set of rough estimates using available ethnohistorical data (Table 31).

Average hectares farmed per person and per household were calculated from three different twentieth-century studies, each of which took a different approach. Swanson (1979a, 1979b) conducted a large-scale survey of Gulmance farmers in eastern Burkina Faso, but collected data on the number of fields rather than the area farmed. By combining his results with a much smaller study he completed that included field size, it was possible to derive "average" households. Hough (1989) gave composite figures (total number of inhabitants, households, and hectares farmed) for a small Gulmance community in northern Benin, which were extrapolated to calculate per household and per individual data. In contrast, Barral (1968) presented individual data on compound size and field size for thirty-two Lele households, which were averaged to obtain a composite value. Rémy (1967) and Korbéogo (2013) did not include data on field size and so their studies are not incorporated here.

TABLE 31. Ethnohistorical data from late twentieth-century studies on agricultural land use by Gulmance and Lele households in Burkina Faso (Barral 1968; Swanson 1979b; Marchal 1983) and Benin (Hough 1989).

	Study areas			
	Eastern Burkina Faso[a]	Tanougou, Benin[b]	Tiogo, Burkina Faso[c]	Eastern Burkina Faso[d]
	Gulmance	Gulmance	Lele	Gulmance
Number of households studied	21+	36	23	n/a
Average number of persons per household	7.7	12.2	14.8	—
Average land cultivated per houshold (ha)	7.0	5.7	11.4	5% of land is cultivated[e]
Average land cultivated per person (ha)	1.18	0.47	0.68	—
Average land cultivated per household excluding cash crops (ha)	5.6	4.3	11.4	—
Average land cultivated per person sxcluding cash crops (ha)	—	0.35	0.68	—
Land needed per person with 3:1 fallow ratio (ha)	—	1.4	2.72	—
Estimated number of persons supported in the studied area (75 km²)	—	5,357	2,757	476–928[f]
Estimated number of households supported in the studied area (75 km²)	335	436	165	28–76[f]

[a] Swanson (1979b)
[b] Hough (1989)
[c] Barral (1968)
[d] Marchal (1983)
[e] Determined from aerial photographs. At 5% of land cultivated, the survey area (75 km²) would have included 325 cultivated hectares and 975 fallow hectares.
[f] Estimates for number of persons and households supported on 1,300 ha are based on calculations from Barral (1968), Hough(1989), and Swanson (1979b).

Assuming a three-to-one fallow-to-cropping ratio (that is, four times the land farmed in a given year would be necessary to sustainably support a household; see the discussions in Chapter 2) and assuming for the sake of simplicity that the entire survey zone was arable land, we obtained the number of individuals and households that could be supported in the study region. The wide range of the resulting estimates was indicative of the variability and local circumstances that shape "average" values for farmed territories. However, across the board these numbers suggested that more than half of sites could have been sustainably occupied simultaneously. A counterpoint was provided by Marchal (1983) who, working from aerial photographs, estimated that on average only 5% of land was farmed in Tapoa Province. Using the household requirements calculated from Barral (1968), Hough (1989), and Swanson (1979b), this resulted in a much lower number of simultaneously occupied households.

Overall, every Siga site could have been simultaneously occupied if occupation length was short enough that fallowing was not required. In this extreme scenario, the Siga occupation would have been a brief, high population density florescence followed by rapid movement out of the region. More likely, a subset of households was occupied at any given time and residents moved regularly, creating an extensive archaeological landscape. Although, as will be discussed below, the end date for the Siga occupation is very tentative, if residents moved generationally (every thirty years) for a three-hundred-year period, only thirty to forty households would have been occupied at any given time, with this number fluctuating as households moved in and out, as well as within, the survey zone. Interestingly, this range falls within that calculated using Marchal's (1983) estimate.

If only a subset of sites was occupied at any given time, this raises the question of the spatial arrangement of settlement, as occupied sites could have been scattered throughout the survey zone or clustered in a particular area. The data on this topic were inconclusive. Regular spacing of iron-working installations (discussed below) could suggest changing focal points for the community; however, no spatial patterns were identified in the material culture, as might be expected if different parts of the survey zone were occupied at different times.

The Siga Ceramic Assemblage

The Siga ceramic assemblage was characterized by diversity in temper, decoration, and vessel form (Tables 32 and 33). Some of this diversity could be attributed to the large sample size compared with other occupations ($n = 12,281$, 74% of recorded sherds), but there were high levels of variability at the scale of individual sites. The Siga occupation ceramic assemblage can be divided into two primary categories: (1) sherds that were assigned to sherd types or derived from the same vessels as typed sherds, or both; and (2) those sherds that were from vessels not represented by sherd types (for detailed descriptions and how types were identified, see Chapter 3 and Appendix B). This discussion focuses on the multiple possible sources and implications of the diversity in both typed and untyped sherds.

Typed sherds were of particular interest because they were consistent across several sites. They likely represented widely available vessels used in common tasks that may have had more standardized sets of uses than the many unique vessels present at many sites. Each sherd type (see Appendix B) was striking in its coherence and there was relatively little crossover in tempers, decoration techniques, or vessel forms among them. Ten sherd types were associated with the Siga occupation:, elaborate pedestaled open bowls with channeled decoration and labor-intensive burnished thick red slip (Sherd Type 5, likely with bases of Sherd Types 6 and 7); slightly constricted jars with flared rims and complex decoration (Sherd Type 1); open jars with gently everted simple rims (Sherd Type 2 and likely Sherd Type 3); large open bowls or jars with strongly everted lips (Sherd Type 4); very large open vessels with thick walls and either pinched rims or applied ridges (Sherd Types 8 and 9); and lug handles (Sherd Type 10), which were not associated with any vessel form (Figures 47, 48, and 49; see Table 32). Almost every decoration technique found at

TABLE 32. Characteristics of the ceramic assemblage from the Siga occupation by assigned confidence level for single-component sites. For sherd type descriptions see Appendix B. For full descriptions of decoration techniques see Tables 11–14.

	High-confidence sites	Low-confidence sites	All sites
Number of sherds	7,508	1,368	12,281
Percentage of sherds with:			
Grog temper	76.2	69.3	71.7
Quartz temper	16.3	26.6	21.6
Mica and quartz temper	5.6	2.1	4.4
Decoration	35.3	28.9	32.0
Number of decoration techniques	59	14.2	15.3
Mean number of decoration techniques per 100 sherds	15.6	14.2	15.3
Number of sherds assigned to:			
Sherd Type 1	26	0	32
Sherd Type 2	60	3	78
Sherd Type 3	69	1	83
Sherd Type 4	123	2	157
Sherd Type 5	101	2	141
Sherd Type 6	72	3	84
Sherd Type 7	6	0	9
Sherd Type 8	11	2	16
Sherd Type 9	95	14	125
Sherd Type 10	31	4	45
Sherd Type 11	9	6	24
Sherd Type 12	0	1	2
Sherd Type 13	0	0	7
Sherd Type 14	0	0	21
Sherd Type 15	1	0	14

TABLE 33. Ceramic decoration techniques in use during the Siga occupation at high-confidence single-component sites. For full descriptions of decoration techniques see Tables 11–14.

Decoration category	Technique	Field code	Number of sherds (N = 2,650)	Number of sites (N = 238)	Associated sherd types
Applied	Ridge with finger impressions (double)	R2T	70	51	9
	Ridge with finger impressions (single)	PRT	12	12	9
	Ridge	PR	11	11	9
	Ridge with gouges	PRG	6	6	9
	Plastic button	PB	5	5	—
	Small ridge	MR	3	3	—
	Small ridge with gouges	MRG	1	1	—
Dragged	Channel	CH	162	105	1, 6
	Parallel channels	PC	176	99	1, 5
	Channel comb (single)	CC	36	26	5
	Semicircular channel	SC	20	14	1
	Lip channel	LIPCH	15	12	—
	Channel comb (double)	TC	13	8	5
	Dragged comb	DC	7	7	—
	Incisions	I	5	4	1
	Other channels	IC	4	4	—
	Multiple triangular channels	MCT	4	4	—
	Triangular channel	CT	3	3	1
	"Ladder" channels	LC	3	2	—
	Incisions	MI	2	2	1
	Swirling dragged comb	SDC	2	2	—
	Cross-hatched incisions	XI	4	2	—
	Diagonal incisions	DI	3	1	—
	Gouges	G	1	1	10
	Multiple arching channels	MAC	1	1	—
	Channels	MCH	1	1	—
	Cross-hatched channels	XC	1	1	—
Impressed	Space-filling comb impressions	FCI	32	19	1

Continued

TABLE 33 CONTINUED

Decoration category	Technique	Field code	Number of sherds ($N = 2{,}650$)	Number of sites ($N = 238$)	Associated sherd types
Impressed	Pinched rim	RP	14	14	8
	Braided cord impressions	IB	14	12	2
	Curved comb impressions	CCI	3	3	—
	Rocker comb	COR	3	3	—
	Triangular impressons	TB	3	3	—
	Circular impressions	CI	2	2	—
	Finger impressions	TH	2	2	—
	Comb impressions	COI	1	1	—
	Cord wrapped stick impressions	Cord 12	1	1	—
	Fingernail impressions	FI	1	1	—
	Angular impressions	HC	1	1	—
	Space-filling rocker comb	SCOR	4	1	—
Roulette	Twisted cord roulette	Cord 2	1631	228	2, 4, 9, 10
	Braided cord roulette	Cord 1	157	77	2
	Braided strip roulette	Cord 4	89	65	3
	Twisted knotted cord roulette	Cord 5	70	47	
	Folded strip roulette	Cord 3	69	32	1, 2
	Braided strip roulette	Cord 6	30	23	3
	Twisted cord roulette	Cord 7	15	11	2
	Possible cord wrapped roulette	Cord 8	19	8	2
	Folded strip roulette	Cord 9	15	8	1
	Possible folded strip roulette	R1	6	6	—
	Twisted cord roulette	Cord 13	4	4	—
	Folded strip roulette	Cord 15	5	4	—
	Braided strip roulette	Cord 10	2	2	—
	Cord wrapped roulette	Cord 11	1	1	—
	Cord wrapped roulette	MLI	1	1	—
	Carved wooden roulette	R2	1	1	—
	Carved wooden roulette	R3	1	1	—
	Carved wooden roulette	R5	1	1	—

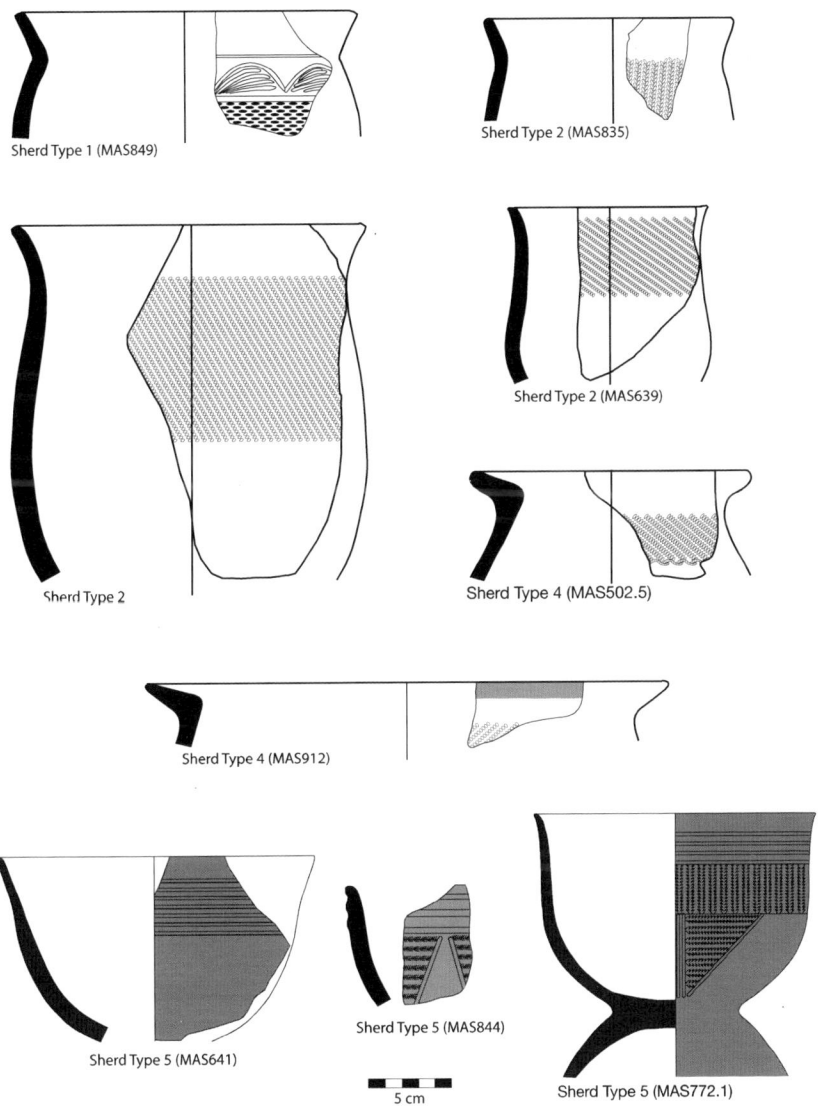

FIGURE 47. Siga occupation ceramics Sherd Types 1 through 5 and associated sites.

more than ten sites (see Table 33) was characteristic of one or more sherd type (although not every incidence was necessarily from a typed sherd or on a vessel represented by typed sherds).

In contrast, untyped sherds added significant variability to household assemblages and were typically found at only a few sites (Figure 50). Thirty-five of the fifty-eight decoration techniques in use during the Siga occupation occurred at five or fewer of the 238 high-confidence single-component sites and sixteen were unique to a single location. Even in these narrow cases, use of decoration techniques was distributed throughout the survey

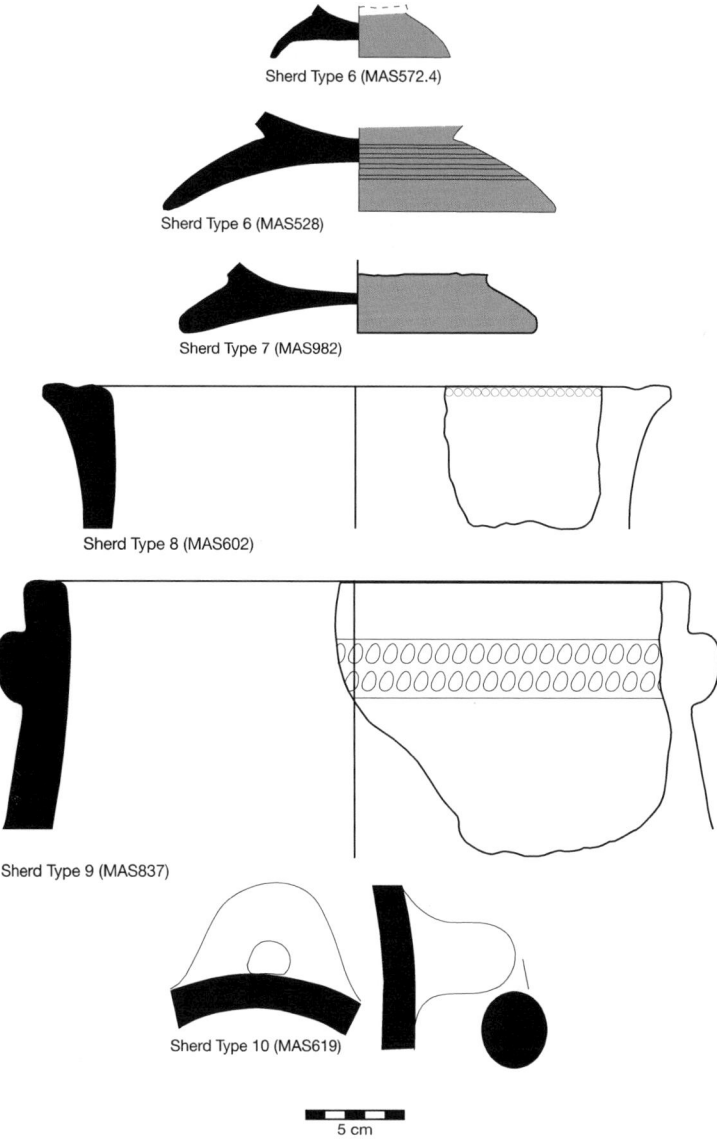

FIGURE 48. Siga occupation ceramics Sherd Types 6 through 10 and associated sites.

area. For example, the swirling dragged comb technique was found at sites in Zones 2A and 4B, ladder channels in Zones 2A and 6C, and curved comb impressions in Zones 2A, 3B, and 4C.

The excavated ceramic assemblages from sites MAS780, MAS572.1, and MAS573 provided a snapshot of the variability in individual site assemblages (Figures 51, 52, and 53; Tables 34 and 35). All three had typical features of the Siga occupation, including: grog, quartz, and mica tempers; decoration with common techniques like twisted cord roulette,

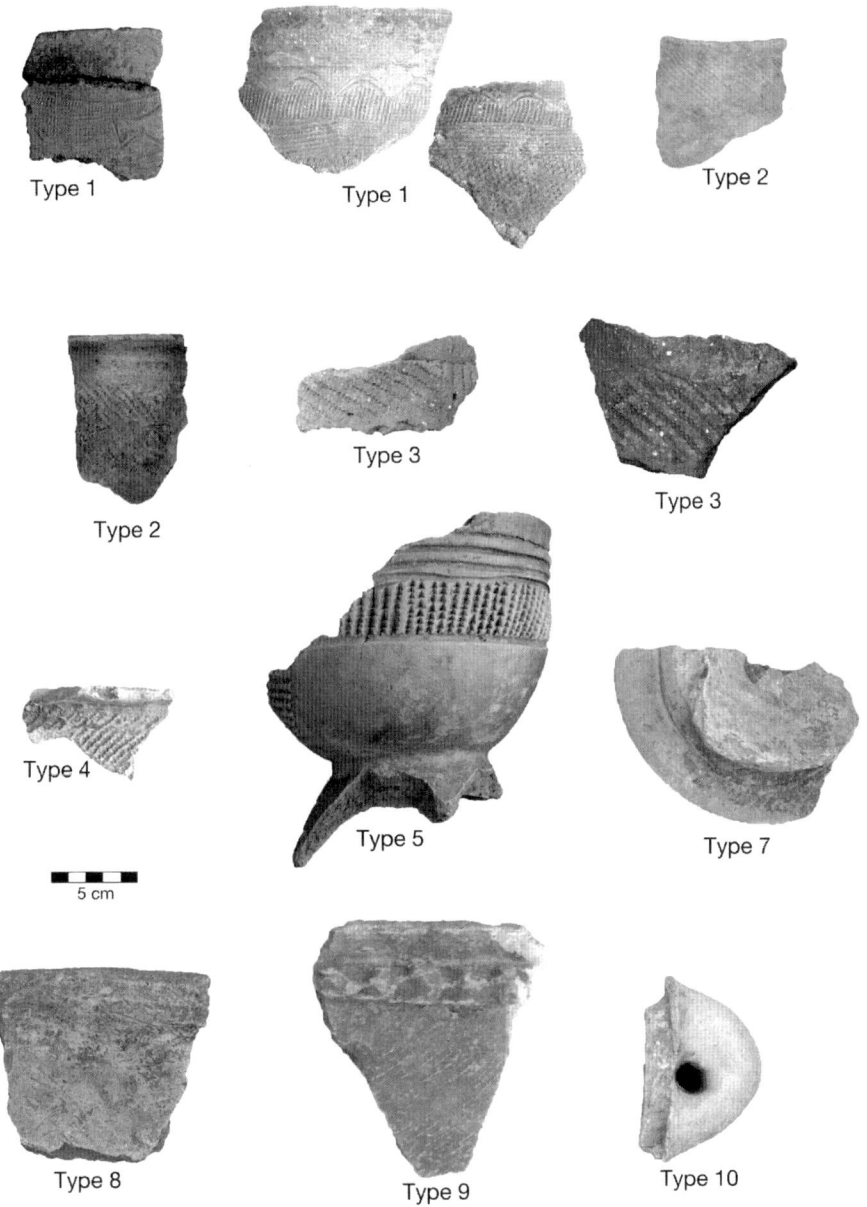

FIGURE 49. Examples of Siga occupation ceramics Sherd Types 1 through 10.

parallel channels, and knotted cord roulette; and typed sherds. At the same time, each assemblage differed in the proportion of sherds represented by particular tempers, in the majority of the decoration techniques in use, and in the particular combination of sherd types present.

Few patterns were detected in comparing individual site assemblages across the sur-

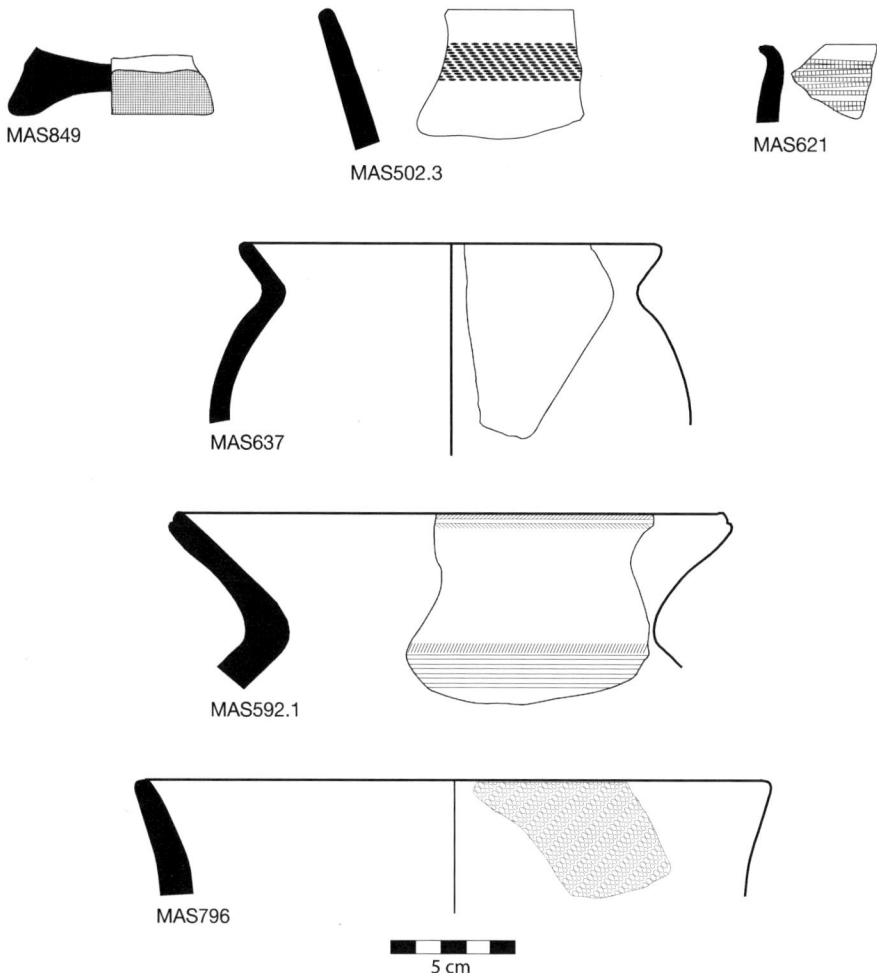

FIGURE 50. Some examples of Siga occupation ceramics not assigned to sherd types, with associated sites.

vey region, particularly as the sample size for any given site was relatively low (on average around thirty-one recorded sherds per site; see Appendix A). Whereas the absolute number of decoration techniques in use at each site decreased with size and density, likely due to smaller samples, the mean index value (techniques per one hundred sherds) remained fairly constant, suggesting that the ceramics at all sites were drawn from the same assemblage, an assertion further supported by the presence of the full range of sherd types at all sizes and densities of sites (see Table 29). No spatial patterns in sherd types, variations within sherd types, untyped sherds, decorations, or tempers could be identified within the Siga occupation assemblage.

Household Assemblages: Exploring Possible Uses for Siga Vessels

Although most vessels are multifunctional, the intended primary use of individual pots influences the potters' choices of raw materials, vessel form, and surface treatment, includ-

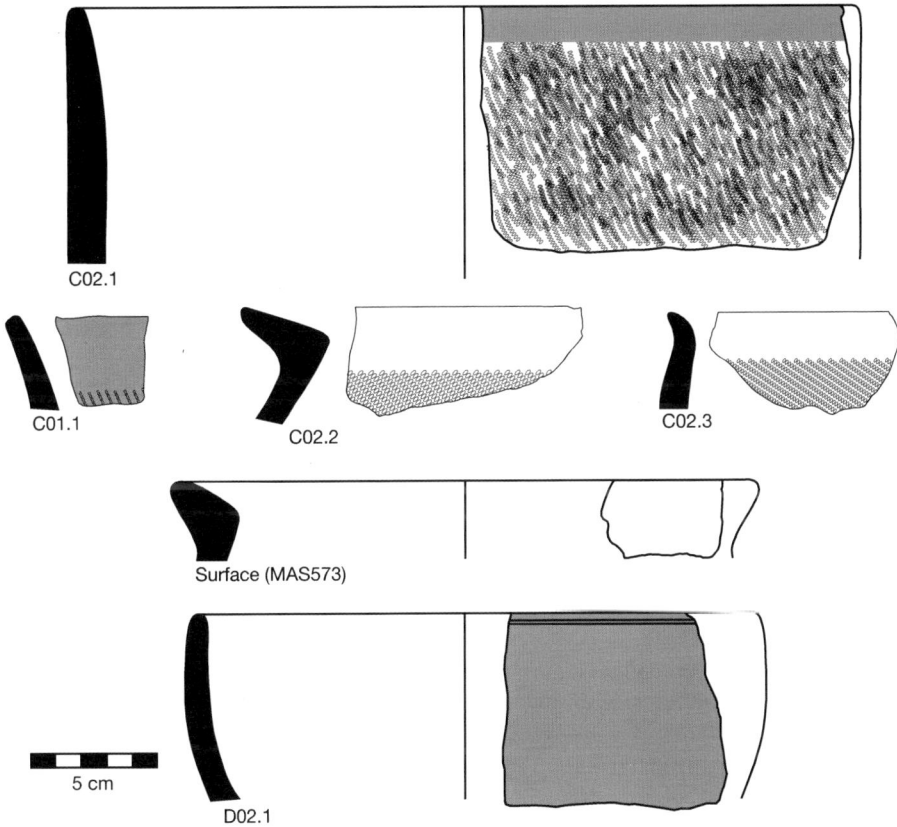

Figure 51. Ceramic assemblages from Unit C at site MAS572.1 (*top*) and Unit D at site MAS573 (*bottom*) showing Sherd Type 2 (levels C02.1, C01.1) and Sherd Type 4 (level C02.2, MAS573 surface).

ing decoration. These choices provide insight into possible activities (Gallay and Huysecom 1989; Gosselain 2000, 2011; Mayor 2011; Dueppen and Gallagher 2016; see the discussions in M'Mbogori [2018] about the role of consumers). Multiple paste formulas were in use at every Siga occupation site, the most common of which were coarse and fine grog-tempered paste, quartz-tempered paste, and a micaceous paste with quartz and possibly additional mica temper (see Table 32). Whereas grog was always an intentional addition, quartz and mica were either added or reflected the clay sources in which they naturally occurred. Regardless, the choice of tempers is often related to vessel use, as they impart different qualities to the ceramic vessels (Rice 2015). For example, the coarse grog and stone temper used in large jars created a very porous fabric, which aids evaporative cooling of stored liquids. Mica is helpful for blocking crack propagation and micaceous vessels are often used for cooking because of their excellent thermal stress properties. The association of different vessel types with different tempers further supports the possibility that tempers varied by use.

However, despite these advantages most tempers were adequate for a normal range of vessel functions. As M'Mbogori (2018) argues, it is important not to overemphasize

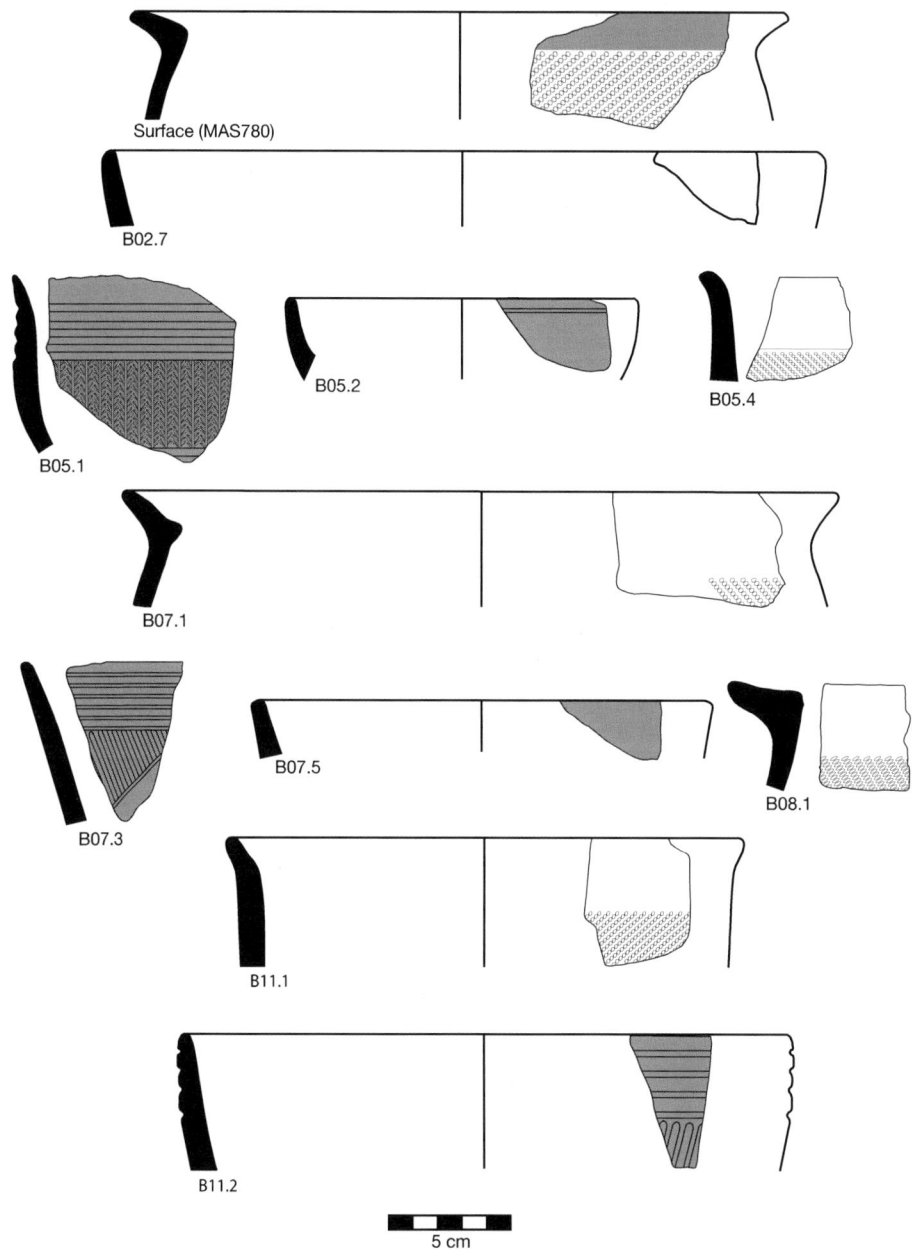

FIGURE 52. Ceramic assemblage from Unit B at site MAS780, showing Sherd Types 2 (levels B05.4, B11.1), Sherd Type 4 (MAS780 surface, levels B07.1, B08.1), and Sherd Type 5 (levels B05.1, B07.3, B11.2).

FIGURE 53. Sherds from Unit B at site MAS780 (*top two rows*), Unit C at site MAS572.1 (*third row*), and Unit D at site MAS573 (*bottom row*), representing Sherd Type 3 (levels B12, B07, C02), Sherd Type 4 (levels B06, C02), and Sherd Type 5 (levels C02, D01).

the significance of minor differences in physical properties. Many current and past potters in West Africa and beyond use similar pastes for all vessels, regardless of size or intended purpose (e.g., S. K. McIntosh 1995; Mayor 2011; Dueppen 2012a). In the study region, the frequent variations on and exceptions to the usual tempers for particular

TABLE 34. Characteristics of the ceramic assemblages from Unit B at site MAS780, Unit C, at site MAS572.1, and Unit D at site MAS573, as well as surface collections at all three sites. See also Appendix B.

	MAS780		MAS572.1		MAS573	
	Unit B	Surface	Unit C	Surface	Unit D	Surface
Number of sherds	587	46	186	40	84	38
Percentage of sherds with:						
Grog temper	61.3	65.2	72.6	80.0	65.5	31.6
Quartz temper	30.7	21.7	12.4	7.5	26.2	68.4
Mica and quartz temper	4.8	8.7	15.1	12.5	8.3	0.0
Red slip, burnished	17.4	23.9	4.8	2.5	14.3	10.5
Decoration	25.2	45.7	40.3	67.5	17.9	13.2
Number of decoration techniques	21	10	10	6	7	3
Number of sherds assigned to:						
Sherd Type 1	1	—	—	—	—	—
Sherd Type 2	2	—	2	—	—	3
Sherd Type 3	2	—	—	—	1	—
Sherd Type 4	8	4	6	—	2	1
Sherd Type 5	12	—	2	1	—	—
Sherd Type 6	—	1	—	1	—	—
Sherd Type 9	—	—	—	2	—	1
Sherd Type 15	—	1	—	—	—	—
Vessel diameters (cm)	14, 18, 20, 20, 21, 25, 29	26, 27	9, 3, 31	10, 36	22, 25	18

sherd types (see Appendix B) suggest that differently tempered vessels could perform the same tasks.

Just as vessel temper is an imperfect measure of intended vessel function, so too is vessel construction and form. Archaeologists and ethnographers, often working in cooperation with local potters, have developed regional models that broadly link vessel form with ranges of common functions (e.g., Gallay and Huysecom 1989; S. K. McIntosh 1995; Mayor 2011; Dueppen and Gallagher 2016). Whereas certain conventions often hold true, multiple forms may be used for the same purpose or, even more common, a single form or even a

TABLE 35. Ceramic decoration techniques in use at sites MAS780, MAS572.1, and MAS573. For full descriptions of decorations techniques see Tables 11–14.

Decoration category	Technique	Field code	Number of sherds					
			MAS780		MAS572.1		MAS573	
			Unit B	Surface	Unit C	Surface	Unit D	Surface
Applied	Small ridge	MR	—	—	1	—	—	—
	Ridge	PR	—	—	—	1	—	—
	Ridge with gouges	PRG	—	—	—	1	—	—
	Ridge with finger impressions (double)	R2T	—	—	—	—	—	1
Dragged	Parallel channels	PC	32	1	2	—	1	1
	Channel	CH	25	1	5	—	4	1
	Cross-hatched incisions	XI	6	—	—	—	1	—
	Multiple triangular channels	MCT	3	—	—	—	—	—
	Incisions	MI	3	—	—	—	—	—
	Channel comb (double)	TC	2	—	2	1	—	—
	Dragged comb	DC	1	1	—	—	—	—
	Other channels	IC	1	—	—	—	1	—
	Channel comb (single)	CC	1	—	—	—	—	—
	Triangular channel	CT	1	—	—	—	—	—
	Diagonal incisions	DI	1	—	—	—	—	—
	Incisions	I	1	—	—	—	—	—
	Cross-hatched channels	XC	1	—	—	—	—	—
	Lip channel	LIPCH	—	1	—	—	—	—
	Semicircular channel	SC	—	—	1	—	—	—

Continued

TABLE 35 CONTINUED

Decoration category	Technique	Field code	Number of sherds					
			MAS780		MAS572.1		MAS573	
			Unit B	Surface	Unit C	Surface	Unit D	Surface
Impressed	Comb impressions	COI	1	—	—	—	—	—
	Space-filling comb impressions	FCI	—	1	—	—	—	—
	Braided cord impressions	IB	—	1	—	—	—	—
	Triangular impressions	TB	—	—	1	—	—	—
Roulette	Twisted cord roulette	Cord 2	52	13	43	24	5	—
	Twisted knotted cord roulette	Cord 5	6	1	5	—	2	—
	Braided strip roulette	Cord 4	6	1	—	—	1	—
	Braided cord roulette	Cord 1	3	1	—	1	—	—
	Possible cord wrapped roulette	Cord 8	1	—	11	1	—	—
	Twisted cord roulette	Cord 7	1	—	—	—	—	—
	Folded strip roulette	Cord 3	1	—	—	—	—	—
	Braided strip roulette	Cord 6	—	—	2	—	—	—

single vessel can be used for multiple purposes. In general, they have found that a combination of vessel height, rim morphology, and orifice size can be used to index diverse tasks. Ultimately, conclusive evidence of vessel function is derived from excavation context or use residues (such as fire blackening), data that is unavailable for the MAS study assemblage.

Certain rare elements in the assemblage (notably handles, bases, and perforations) also provided evidence of possible uses. The handles generally had the form of lug handles (Sherd Type 10). In most cases, these were not very useful for carrying, as they could not support the weight of a filled, large vessel. Instead, lug handles provided a grip for shifting, leaning, or rotating the vessel, a point of attachment for tying down a cover or lid, or both. Bases are often found on serving or drinking vessels, as they provide stability such that the pot can be set on a variety of surfaces. The base types present in the assemblage—pedestal (Type 6), flared (Type 7), ring, and feet— were all plastic additions to the pot and consequently inappropriate for cooking pots because the thermal stress would affect the joints. Finally, several perforated fragments were recovered (n = 38 at 24 sites). Generally undecorated and grog-tempered, but in a range of thicknesses (8 to 24 mm), these sherds had uniform, evenly spaced punctures that ranged in diameter from 0.6 to 1.3 cm, with two outlying examples at 2.3 and 2.8 cm. Perforations of this sort are generally identified with *couscoussières* used to steam pounded millet or sorghum to make a couscous (e.g., Gallay and Huysecom 1989), although perforated vessels may also have been used for other activities, such as leaching vegetable salts or fish smoking.

Finally, the functionality of surface treatment and decoration is particularly complex. Practical considerations can influence decorative choices; slips decrease permeability and plastic ridges or the roughness resulting from many space-filling decoration treatments may make pots easier to grip. However, decoration is also particularly intertwined with the social contexts of production and consumption. In general, vessels with more elaborate decorations are often for use in public, social, and ritually significant settings.

Overall, the vessels represented by typed sherds formed a functionally diverse group (Figure 54). Sherd Type 5 sherds, along with their likely associated bases (Sherd Types 6 and 7), were probably from serving vessels, either for sauce or beer. Their thick, highly burnished slip was one of the most time-intensive techniques among all surface treatments and decorations and they were the most likely of any vessel to have been used in ritual contexts. The other class of elaborately decorated vessels (Sherd Type 1) was of medium-sized jars. The purpose of these flexible forms is unknown, although they were potentially used in the public or ritual sphere given the care that went into their decoration.

The open vessels of Sherd Types 2 and 3, with their smooth curves and simple decoration, were excellent candidates for cooking. This is particularly because Sherd Type 2 came in a range of sizes and because Sherd Type 3 had micaceous temper, with the caveat that many lacked the lipped rims that could aid in lifting the pots from the top (for this reason the larger Sherd Type 4 may also have been a good cooking vessel). With their vertical sides and large diameter, Sherd Types 8 and 9 were good candidates for grain storage, water storage, brewing, or indigo dyeing. Large constricted neck vessels were absent from the assemblage and open vessels were used for water storage in northern Benin (Petit 2005).

Another possible use of large jars is as funerary markers (*ticindi* in Gulmancema; Thiombiano-Ilboudo 2010:484). Jar burials are common throughout eastern Burkina Faso and the jars may either contain or mark the inhumation (see Kiéthéga, Sidibé, and Bedaux 1993; Kiéthéga 2009; Thiombiano-Ilboudo 2010). Kiéthéga (2009, plate 14) even depicts the use of jars with the same pinched ridge decoration characteristic of Sherd Type 9 at Kugribogdo in Oubritenga, near Ouagadougou. This practice of using jars as markers has been documented throughout the Fada N'Gourma region by Thiombiano-Ilboudo (2010) at sites such as Kouaré. A portion of an upside-down jar was identified above a burial in Unit A (see Chapter 5) that may have dated to either the Pwoli or Siga occupations and Breunig and Wotzka (1991) excavated an infant burial in a jar, likely dating to the Tuali-B occupation, near Namounou on the western side of the Gobnangou escarpment.

At six sites, horizontal cross sections of vessels, many of them large Sherd Type 8 or Sherd Type 9 jars, were found inset in the ground. For most it was difficult to tell whether the jar was upright or upside-down, but in at least two cases (a grog-tempered vessel on the surface at site MAS774 and a jar fragment identified in a borrow pit cut at site MAS885) the vessel was upside-down. At site MAS759, a multicomponent Siga and Tuali-A site,

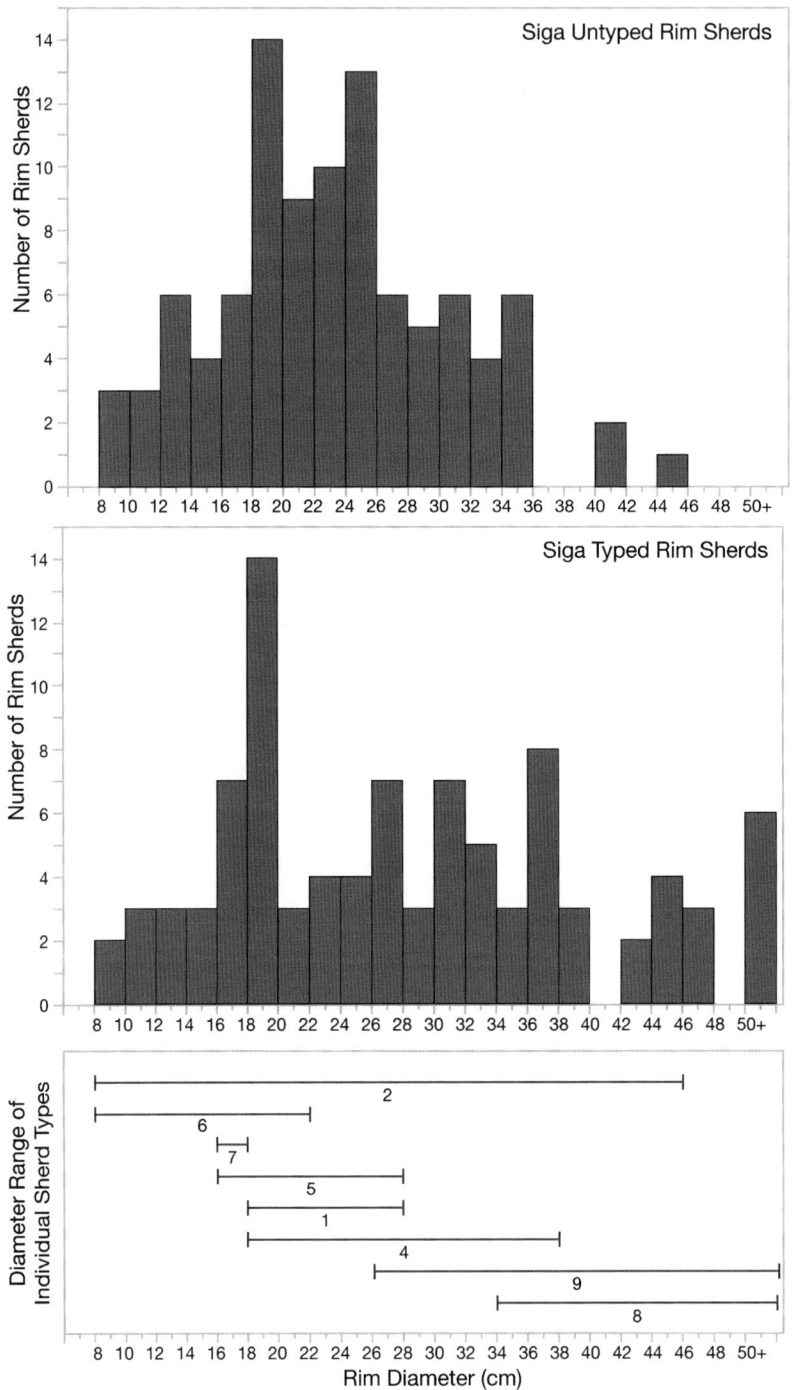

FIGURE 54. Diameter measurements of untyped (*top*) and typed (*center*) rim sherds of Siga occupation vessels compared with ranges for Sherd Types 1, 2, and 4 through 9 (*bottom*).

a small jar eroding from the ground seemed to contain bone fragments and so was left undisturbed. In no cases were large numbers of jars identified at a single site, as has been described at many other jar burial sites in Burkina Faso (Kiéthéga, Sidibé, and Bedaux 1993; Kiéthéga 2009; Thiombiano-Ilboudo 2010).

However, alternate uses for these pots must also be considered. At site MAS557, adjacent horizontal cross sections of Sherd Type 3 and Sherd Type 9 vessels were identified in undisturbed deposits. Ethnohistorically, large and small pots can occur together in several contexts, although the most frequent are cooking installations and water or dry goods storage (daily or weekly grain allotments can be transferred from granaries to these vessels for easier access). Thiombiano-Ilboudo (2010:163) describes the use of a pair of differently sized pots, one 40 cm and the other 25 cm in diameter, as bellows for iron smelting.

Like the typed sherds, the more unique elements of the ceramic assemblage covered a range of pastes, vessel forms, and decorations and fell into the same functional categories as many of the typed sherds (see Figure 54). Among vessels identified at many sites were large, open, thick-sided bowls with cord impressions on the sides and small bowls with narrow strips of decoration at or near the lip (notably folded strip roulette). Ring bases and small legs were generally of an appropriate size for smaller vessels; this could indicate the use of a broad assortment of serving vessels.

Production and Distribution of Siga Ceramics

There are multiple options for pottery vessels regardless of intended use, therefore technological choices are often a result of social factors. These include organization of production and distribution; identity of the potter or intended user of the vessel; and cultural mores, preferences, and restrictions on vessel form and decoration (e.g., David, Sterner, and Gavua 1988; Gosselain 2000, 2008, 2011; Cruz 2011; Guèye 2011; Dueppen 2012a, 2015; M'Mbogori 2018). Given the available data and well-known problems of equifinality in the social processes that lead to choices in ceramic production, these discussions focus on broad patterns and present multiple possible explanations.

Typed sherds showed remarkable consistency across the survey zone. Spatial mappings of their occurrence and the minor variations within them yielded dispersed patterns of sites that were neither bounded nor linked through other commonalities. Given the problems of palimpsest, it is possible that stylistic variance is obscured by the lack of fine-grained chronological control. However, it is more likely that there were no significant differences in access to the vessels represented by typed sherds and that all sites from the Siga occupation were ultimately part of a unified ceramic tradition practiced by potters who supplied the entire study region.

This pattern has implications for specialization and the organization of production. Possibilities include production of the full range of vessels by individual household potters who worked within a common vernacular, production of the full or partial range of vessels by specialized potters, or production of particular vessels by potters who specialized in certain vessel forms. Typed sherds were from distinctive vessels that have many hallmarks of standardization associated with specialized producers. Each group of vessels was made following a consistent, unique *chaîne opertoire* using different techniques for mixing the paste, creating a distinct form, and applying slip and decorations. Minor differences in the paste or decoration (see Appendix B) could be the result of small-batch production or temporal drift.

Within the study region itself, no specialist production centers could be identified.

No sites had a high concentration of typed sherds or evidence of wasters. Polished quartz stones (which could be used for burnishing slip) were recovered from sites MAS552 and MAS582, but whereas at MAS552 an above average 23% of the assemblage was slipped or burnished, or both, there was not a single burnished sherd at MAS582. It is possible that specialist producers were located outside the survey zone, as the distribution of typed sherds in the greater Gobnangou region is poorly understood. Only three of the sherd types are also represented in samples published by the German–Burkinabe team. Of these, Sherd Type 1 is confined to the survey zone and Sherd Types 2 and 4 are documented on both the north and south sides of the escarpment.

Although there was some evidence of specialized production or of a strong common vernacular in the vessels associated with typed sherds, the ceramic assemblage also incorporated a broad variety of rare and unique decoration techniques and vessel forms (see Table 33). Many distinctive rare techniques, such as curved comb impressions or "ladder" channels, were used on sherds with different tempers. This aspect of the assemblage was more typical of idiosyncratic household production. However, if these vessels originated outside the study region, households may have used a set of standardized, specialist-produced ceramics supplemented with different vessels obtained through more extensive trade or kinship networks. Finally, we must consider the possibility that these vessels were produced in low quantities by specialists for a market that valued distinctive and unique pots as supplements to the standardized assemblage.

The number of sherds actually assigned to sherd types underrepresented the frequency of sherds from these vessels in the assemblage (see Chapter 3). By eliminating all sherds with decorations found on typed sherds regardless of whether the individual sherd was assigned, "noise" from these vessels was eliminated. While imperfect, because rare vessels with the same decoration techniques as sherd types were also eliminated, as were undecorated rare vessels, this method provided a sense of the remaining diversity in the assemblage. Of the 238 high-confidence Siga occupation sites, only about one-third ($n = 73$) had sherds with rare decorations. Most of these sites ($n = 68$) had evidence of only one or two vessels with rare decorations. The most diverse site, MAS696.2, had six rare techniques represented, although these may have originated from a slightly higher number of vessels. Interestingly, this site was across a minor drainage from site MAS780 where, as will be seen below, large quantities of iron were recovered. More typically, the presence of sherds with rare decorations did not correlate with any other site features, including the presence of iron-working debris. Large sites were more likely to have sherds with rare decorations than medium or small sites. However, the difference was small enough that it could have been a function of sample size, particularly because large sites tended to have larger opportunistic surface collections.

Given the available regional data, the origin of rare vessels cannot be firmly established, although a few lines of evidence provided some tentative support for importation. Rare vessels had a similar range of orifice diameters to vessels represented by sherd types (see Figure 54), with the exception of very large vessels that would be difficult to transport, and differences were largely stylistic (such as degree of lip eversion) rather than functional (for example, both groups had few closed vessels), suggesting that these vessels did not fulfill unique, necessary functional roles. Only a few sets of vessel decoration had strong similarities to pottery documented in neighboring regions. In comparing decoration techniques, those ubiquitous in West Africa (such as twisted cord roulette) were excluded and the emphasis was on identical use of a given technique; for example, whereas rocker comb was frequently found, it was often applied at a different density and in different locations on the vessel. Vessels decorated with multiple arching channels were found near Kantchari by the German–Burkinabe project (Wotzka and Goedicke 2001) and Petit (2005; L. P. Petit, personal communication, 2009 noted decorations similar to banded dragged comb, diagonal incisions, and "ladder" channels in northern Benin. Finally, Haour and colleagues (2019) identified cross-hatched incisions in the Dendi region. If rare sherds did represent imported vessels, they could indicate that residents of the survey region had extraregional trading or kinship networks. However, decoration similarity can derive from multiple sources (Gosselain 2000, 2008; Guéye 2011) and, consequently, more lines of evidence would be necessary to establish an external origin for these vessels.

Pipes

Smoking pipes constituted a distinct subset of the ceramic assemblages. Pipes in West Africa were typically made using different techniques, decorations, and even clays than the rest of the ceramic assemblage and are consequently assumed to have been produced by different potters in different settings (see the discussions in Stahl [2001], S. K. McIntosh, Gallagher, and R. J. McIntosh [2003], Ogundiran [2007, 2009, 2014], Stahl et al. [2008], Gallagher [2016], and Keita and Coulibaly [2018]). Pipes were very rare at Siga occupation sites; three were recovered from different sites and only one of these was from a site classified as high confidence (Figure 55). Of the three pipes, two were red slipped and decorated bowl fragments. In contrast, the one undecorated stem fragment was only tentatively classed as a pipe, as it is made of rough, unsmoothed clay. In West Africa, the appearance of pipes as a widespread artifact category coincides with introduction of tobacco; the dating implications are discussed below.

Discussion

In conclusion, the Siga occupation ceramic assemblage was composed of a diverse functional set of commonly available household ceramics, supplemented by many often unique vessels. Relocation of households does not seem to have affected access to these different types of ceramics, implying maintenance of economic and social networks and identities (both local and long distance) during moves. If Siga occupation residents were restricted in their ability to relocate within the survey zone, these boundaries were not marked in the ceramic assemblage.

The consistency of vessels represented by the sherd types suggests that they may have been manufactured by specialist potters. We know little about these potters, such as whether they made only one or two types of vessels or the full range, whether they resided within the study region, or whether they were full- or part-time specialists. We do know that they served the entire study region and that there is currently no evidence for restricted access to their products. Ethnographic and archaeological studies of pottery style in West Africa have shown that ceramic traditions may be shared within political, social, or linguistic boundaries (or any combination thereof) depending on the particular local circumstances (Gosselain 2000, 2011; Cruz 2011; Guéye 2011; Mayor 2011; Dueppen 2015; Richard and MacDonald 2015). Thus, the common use of typed vessels could be indicative of some form of social cohesion across the study region. The observed patterns of shared use of a diverse ceramic assemblage in the survey zone further indicates consistency in economic activities requiring pottery, including food preparation and consumption, suggesting a visually identifiable identity experienced and constructed through daily practice.

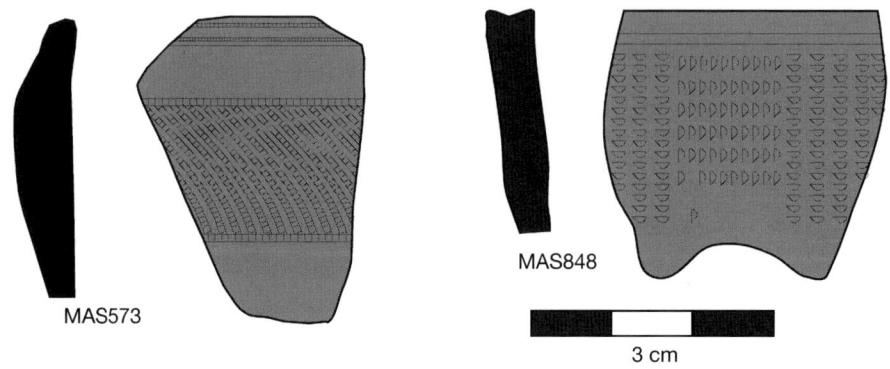

FIGURE 55. Pipe bowls from Siga occupation sites MAS573 and MAS848.

The more unique vessels added significant variability to the Siga ceramic assemblage and may be evidence of long-distance trade or kinship networks or of increased differentiation in access to these networks, or both. Unfortunately, given the limited archaeological research in the greater region, their individuality made interpretation difficult, particularly because their origins (whether regional or local) may have been equally diverse.

Iron Working

The Siga occupation was not the earliest instance of iron use in the survey region, but it was the first occupation for which there was direct evidence of iron production in the form of slag and tuyères. There are two main stages of iron production: smelting and smithing. Each leaves a distinct archaeological signature. Iron smelting is the process by which raw iron is extracted from ore, in this case likely the iron-rich laterite found throughout the region. Smithing involves the processing of both blooms from smelting furnaces and scrap iron to create metal objects. Although the smithing of scrap metal is still a common activity, local smelting traditions all but vanished during the colonial period as local iron was replaced by imported industrial alloys. Consequently, much of our knowledge of West African iron smelting comes from secondary sources (e.g., de Barros 2000), archaeological reconstructions (e.g., Killick 2004, 2015; Coulibaly 2006; Kiéthéga 2009; Thiombiano-Ilboudo 2010; Eichhorn et al. 2013; Iles 2016; Soulignac 2017), and the ethnography of iron workers whose profession had been transformed (e.g., Cline 1937; Saltman, Goucher, and Herbert 1986; Childs 2000; Thiombiano-Ilboudo 2010, 2014, 2016; Soulignac 2017).

Smelting

The smelting process requires access to two primary resources: ore and fuel. Fuelwood must be gathered, dried, and processed before smelting can take place, because the high, sustained temperatures required by iron furnaces can only be achieved with charcoal. Depending on the scale of iron production and local population density, smelting has the potential to strain local fuel supplies (Gordon and Killick 1993; Iles 2016).

In the study region, the most commonly available ore was laterite, a coarse, iron-rich stone. Although no data were available on the iron content of laterite in the region, tests of ore from nearby Park W found iron content of around 12% (Thiombiano-Ilboudo

2010:134), which Thiombiano-Ilboudo notes is on the low end of the ores from throughout Burkina Faso tested by Kiéthéga (2009:217). Lateritic outcrops were found throughout the survey zone and there were veins of laterite in the Gobnangou escarpment itself. In Burkina Faso, laterite mines have been documented in the form of large surface excavations (most common), quarried outcrops, and cylindrical pits (Thiombiano-Ilboudo 2010). No ore mines were located in the surveyed area, although abandoned surface mines can be difficult to identify, particularly if they were not very deep.

Evidence of smelting in the study region during the Siga occupation consisted almost entirely of slag heaps mixed with tuyère fragments (Figure 56; Table 36). No furnaces with intact walls have been identified and none were excavated, making it challenging to assess the furnace technology in use. The measured intact tuyères had internal diameters ranging from 3.2 to 4.5 cm, and a single site often had tuyère diameters from throughout this range. In the Fada N'Gourma region, Thiombiano-Ilboudo (2010) found evidence for multiple types of furnaces.

The quantities of slag present at sites were difficult to measure. Differences in slag pile density from site to site were visually apparent and many areas had been plowed, distributing the slag across a large area. Even if accurate slag volumes could be calculated, they could not be linked to the number or size of smelting events with the available data. However, if the techniques, ore, and fuel were assumed to be fairly constant from site to site, it was possible to compare the relative productivity of different smelting locations. Given the difficulty of producing precise numbers, smelting sites were divided into three categories of increasing production scale. The first group ("small," $n = 8$) consisted of sites with small, isolated slag concentrations that were no more than 5 m in diameter and often of negligible height; the second group ("medium," $n = 6$) included those sites with multiple small slag concentrations or larger slag piles of up to 10 m in diameter; and, finally, the third group was a single site (MAS849) designated as "very large." It had multiple slag concentrations, including one that covered around 300 m². Smelting may have been underrepresented in the survey sample. In comparison to other Siga occupation sites, slag and tuyère concentrations were more likely to be located in subsurface contexts revealed by erosion (e.g., MAS640) or borrow pits (e.g., MAS721).

Sites from the two groups with higher productivity were dispersed throughout the landscape. Site MAS849 was centrally located on the banks of the Koabu and five of the seven sites in the second group were distributed every 2 to 4 km along the Koabu. The remaining two sites were at the heads of major tributaries near the escarpment in the northern section of the study region. In those cases where multiple slag concentrations occurred at a site, the furnaces seem to have been clustered rather than in north-south or east-west alignments, as described by Thiombiano-Ilboudo (2010) for furnace installations in both the Fada N'Gourma region and Park W. The small furnace locations (likely single smelting events) were also scattered along the major drainages (particularly the Koabu) and tended to cluster near the larger sites. Smelting was notably absent from the higher elevation areas at the fringes of the drainage catchment (Zone B and the upper portion of Zone C). These regions did not lack lateritic outcrops; however, they often had deeper water tables and fewer or smaller-sized trees of the preferred fuelwood taxa, many of which favor slightly moister conditions (see Table 4).

Interpretation of this spatial pattern was complicated by the low resolution intra-Siga occupation chronology. However, the preponderance of smelting locations, their distribution, and their infrequent long-term use suggested that iron smelters during this

TABLE 36. Evidence of smelting activity at high-confidence single-component sites during the Siga occupation. Furnace categories are given as "small" (up to 5 m in diameter), "medium" (up to 10 m in diameter), and "very large" (a single site with multiple furnaces that covered around 300 m²). Furnace size is length by width.

Site	Category	Furnace size (m)	Evidence of smelting activity
MAS849	Very large	30 × 10, 4 × 4, 5 × 5	Multiple slag piles with vitrified tuyères, including one very large concentration, organized in a row on the bank of the Koabu
MAS502.5	Medium	5 × 10	Dense slag particularly in northwest of site, but found throughout; many tuyère fragments; interior diameter 3.2 cm on collected tuyère
MAS514	Medium	10 × 10	Dense concentration of slag and vitrified tuyères; interior diameter 4.0 cm on collected tuyère
MAS553	Medium	10 × 5	Dense slag, furnace wall fragments, and tuyères
MAS640	Medium	2 × 2, 2 × 2	At least three furnaces (two measurable) eroding from the bank of a seasonal drainage, dense slag, tuyères, and chipped chert; interior diameter 4.0 cm on collected tuyère
MAS876	Medium	3 × 3, 3 × 3, 1 × 1	Three concentrations of large slag pieces and tuyère fragments
MAS972	Medium	10 × 10	Concentrated slag and tuyères
MAS512	Small	5 × 5	Dense concentration of slag and tuyères pushed to surface by tree roots; very constrained
MAS721	Small	Unknown	Concentration of slag and tuyères around 60 cm below the surface in a borrow pit which was probably the remnants of a smelting installation
MAS730	Small	Unknown	Slag and vitrified tuyères common throughout the site, although not concentrated in any one location
MAS835	Small	1 × 1	Concentration of slag with tuyères located in the northwest of the site, slag scattered throughout; interior diameter 4.5 cm on collected tuyère
MAS856	Small	Unknown	Several large pieces of slag and tuyères
MAS938	Small	Unknown	Slag common throughout the site, although not concentrated in any one location
MAS939	Small	5 × 5	Small slag concentration with tuyères
MAS974	Small	5 × 5	Small slag concentration with tuyères

period, like the general population, moved regularly. Site MAS849 may have been a center where multiple iron smelters came together or a location that was repeatedly revisited for smelting activity. Although it could have been in continuous use by a single iron-working household, its status as a specialized location was supported by the minimal residential debris (although the site was in a high erosion area). Of the other sites, those that seemed to be single furnace locations (regardless of size) tended to be near or part of extensive residential sites. Those with multiple furnaces tended to lack residential debris.

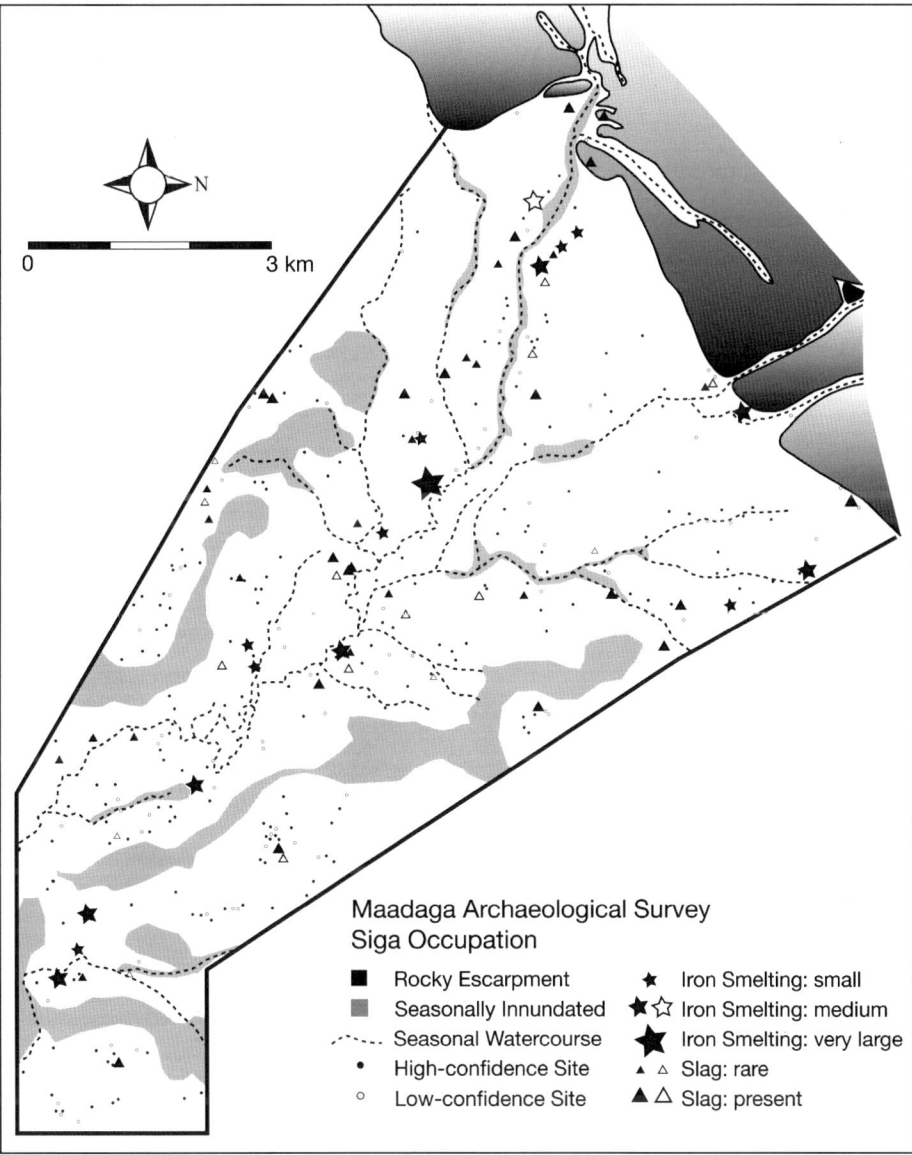

FIGURE 56. Distribution of iron-working activities during the Siga occupation identified by the Maadaga Archaeological Survey. Black dots, stars, and triangles are high-confidence sites; open dots, stars, and triangles are low-confidence sites.

Smithing

Smithing, or the production of iron objects such as hoes, bracelets, and arrowheads, takes place at a small hearth, often augmented with bellows to achieve the necessary heat. The raw iron is heated until softened, then pounded on an anvil. The smithing process produces slag fragments comprised of iron, impurities in the iron, carbon from the fuel, material or sediment from the hearth, and any additional materials added during the

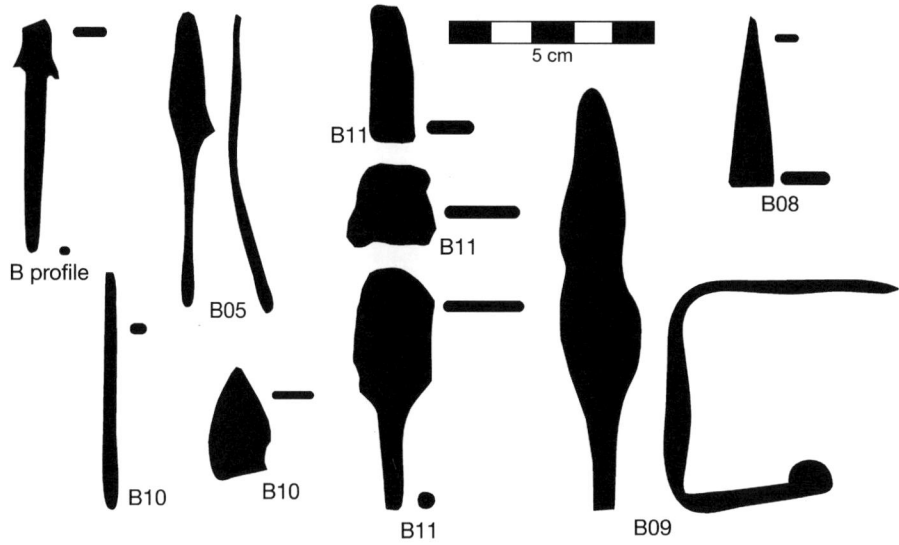

Figure 57. Iron objects from Unit B at site MAS780.

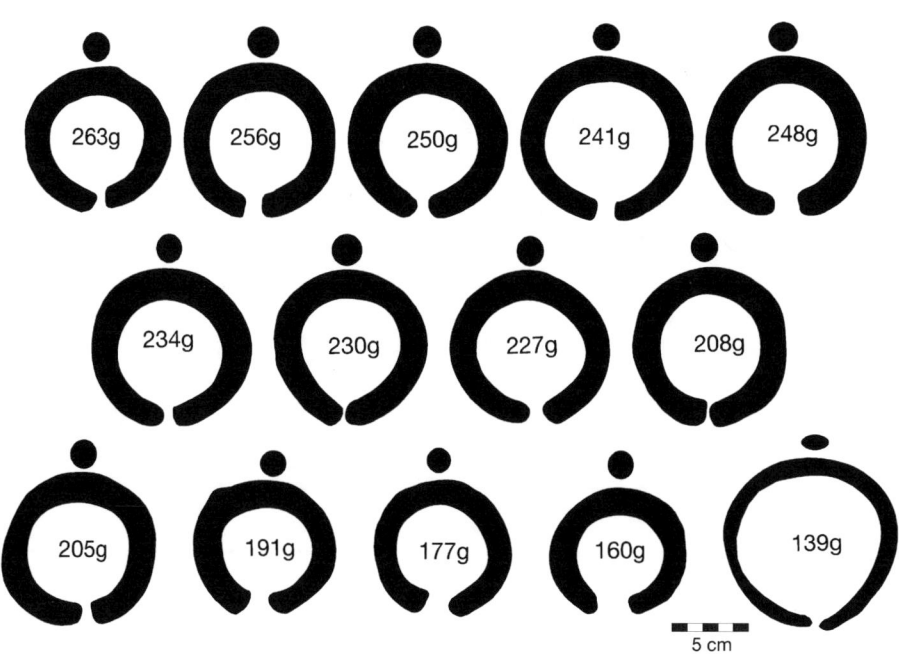

Figure 58. Iron bracelets (outline and profile, with weight) from site MAS780.

smithing process to assist in manipulating or welding the metal (see the discussions in Soulignac [2017]).

Small slag fragments were present at several sites from this phase ($n = 38$). These isolated surface pieces had visible qualities described for smithing slag, although without context or microscopic study their origin was uncertain. However, if even half of the sites at which these slags were observed had smithing activity, then smithing was far more widespread and perhaps more broadly accessible than smelting. Sites with slag were found throughout the study region, but their spatial pattern had little relationship to the pattern of smelting sites. Iron workers may have smelted at specialized locations and smithed in the home, in which case iron workers' residences could have moved more frequently than their smelting locations. However, many of the sites with slag were several kilometers from the nearest smelting location.

Iron Objects

Discarded iron objects rarely find their way into archaeological deposits, since they are normally refashioned into new objects. Their densities at most archaeological sites in West Africa were low, although specific numbers were available for only a few sites: at Jenne-jeno iron densities were on average 10 to 20 g/m^3, with the highest densities reaching 65 g/m^3; similar densities (average 12 g/m^3) were identified at Kirikongo (S. K. McIntosh 1995; Dueppen 2012a). In this context, the quantity of iron recovered from excavations at site MAS780 was high. Seven pieces of metal weighing a total of 42 g and including at least four metal arrow or spear points were recovered from a 35 cm deposit in Unit B, resulting in a density for this deposit of 84 g/m^3 and an overall density for the unit of 30 g/m^3 (Table 37). The points varied in size and shape (see Figure 57) and at least one point was bent twice, possibly intentionally.

The only excavated locations with similarly high numbers of metal objects in West Africa are mortuary sites or large-scale iron reduction sites (e.g., Thilmans, Descamps, and Khayat 1980; Shinnie and Kense 1989; Fabre 2009; Idé 2009; Magnavita 2009, 2015). The former may be the case at site MAS780. About 30 m distant from the project excavations, a local farmer, Amilidi Tindambiga, had dug a large borrow pit (around 15 by 15 by 1.5 m) a few years previously. During this venture he uncovered the burial of an individual wearing several heavy iron bracelets (averaging 216 g each), fourteen of which he still had in his possession and donated to the project (Figure 58). These bracelets are stored with the MAS archaeological materials in the Laboratory of Archaeology at the University of Ouagadougou. Given the spatial dislocation and lack of contextual information, it is unknown whether this burial was contemporaneous with the deposits in Unit B. However, it is possible that the Unit B iron objects were disturbed from a mortuary context.

Iron bracelets were also found at the site of Bandingue at Namoungou in the Fada N'Gourma region by Thiombiano-Ilboudo (2010:461–466). Bandingue is a ritually important site where Labdiédo, the fifth *bado* after Jaba Lompo, was buried. Thiombiano-Ilboudo notes that, ethnohistorically, among the Gulmance iron bracelets play important roles in religion, magic, and medicine and serve a protective function for those who wear them.

TABLE 37. Iron, slag, and stone identified from Unit B at site MAS780, Unit C at site MAS572.1, and Unit D at site MAS573. For stone, an asterisk (*) indicates a measurement in a fragmented direction. Dashes indicate that the measurement was not recorded.

Site	Context	Category	Material	Description	Length (cm)	Width (cm)	Height (cm)	Mass (g)
MAS780	Unit B profile	Iron	Iron	Triangular with slightly flaring tangs (base of point?)	5.2	1	0.2	3
	Unit B surface	Chipped stone	Chert	Three pieces debitage	1–3	—	—	3
	B02	Chipped stone	Chert	One piece debitage	<1	—	—	1
	B02	Chipped stone	Chert	One piece debitage	1–2	—	—	1
	B02	Chipped stone	Chert	One flake	2.2*	—	—	2
	B03	Chipped stone	Chert	One piece debitage	n/a	—	—	1
	B03	Chipped stone	Chert	One flake	1.8	—	—	1
	B04	Ground stone	Green stone?	Very small chip of a rounded smoothed stone	2.9	2.3	1.1	10
	B04	Unworked stone	Red sandstone		3.2	3.8	0.9	16
	B04	Chipped stone	Chert	One piece debitage	>3	—	—	4
	B05	Iron	Iron	Flat, leaf-shaped point with a thin shaft	6.7	0.9	0.2	3
	B05	Ground stone	White sandstone	Basal grinding stone fragment with flat grinding surface	6.1	5.0*	3.0*	137
	B05	Unworked stone	White sandstone		2	2.3	2	16
	B06	Unworked stone	White sandstone		3.6	2.5	1.9	21
	B06	Unworked stone	Green stone		3.6	2.1	0.7	7

Continued

Table 37 continued

Site	Context	Category	Material	Description	Length (cm)	Width (cm)	Height (cm)	Mass (g)
MAS780	B07	Ground stone	White sandstone	Possible edge of basal grinding stone	6.1	4.4	2.2	67
	B07	Ground stone	White sandstone	Possible edge of basal grinding stone	4.5	4.3	2.3	40
	B07	Chipped stone	Chert	One flake	3.1	—	—	7
	B08	Iron	Iron	Elongated isosceles triangle (tip of point?)	3.7	1	0.2	2
	B08	Ground stone	White sandstone	Curved piece; edge of basal or handstone	5.0*	3.5*	2.2*	65
	B08	Ground stone	White sandstone	Basal grinding stone fragment with flat grinding surface	5.6*	5.5*	3.5	165
	B08	Chipped stone	Chert	One piece debitage	1–2	—	—	1
	B08	Chipped stone	Chert	One flake	1.5	—	—	1
	B09	Iron	Iron	Long narrow triangular point, bent in two places (below the base of the point and in the middle of the point) to form three sides of a square	4.7	4.2	—	18
	B09	Slag	Slag	One piece		—	—	13
	B09	Unworked stone	White sandstone		6.1	6.8	1.7	83
	B09	Unworked stone	White sandstone		4.3	3.9	1.9	34
	B10	Iron	Iron	Shaft fragment with round cross section	5.6	0.35	0.35	3

Continued

TABLE 37 CONTINUED

Site	Context	Category	Material	Description	Length (cm)	Width (cm)	Height (cm)	Mass (g)
MAS780	B10	Iron	Iron	Triangular, flat, with slightly rounded sides (tip of point?)	2.4	1.4	0.2	2
	B10	Ground stone	White sandstone	Possible basal grinding stone fragment with flat grinding surface	5.8*	5.4*	3.3	177
	B10	Unworked stone	White sandstone		3.6	1.9	0.9	7
	B10	Chipped stone	Chert	Two pieces debitage	2–3	—	—	3
	B10	Chipped stone	Chert	One flake	2.2	—	—	1
	B10	Chipped stone	Chert	One multi-directional core	5.5	4.4	2.7	83
	B11	Iron	Iron	Short segment of shaft and beginning of a long flat section (base of point?)	5.6	2	0.6	11
	B11	Iron	Iron	Flat trapezoidal piece (midsection of point?)	2	1.9	0.3	3
	B11	Iron	Iron	Elongated flat, slightly tapering rectangle	3.1	0.9	0.3	3
	B11	Slag	Slag	One piece	—	—	—	29
	B12	Chipped stone	Chert	One flake	4	—	—	7
	B13	Ground stone	Gray sandstone	Small chip of a rounded stone, worked?	3.1	1.9	0.6	5

Continued

TABLE 37 CONTINUED

Site	Context	Category	Material	Description	Length (cm)	Width (cm)	Height (cm)	Mass (g)
MAS780	B13	Chipped stone	Quartz	One piece debitage	1–2	—	—	1
MAS572.1	C01	Chipped stone	Chert	One piece debitage	2–3	—	—	2
	C02	Slag	Slag	Two pieces		—	—	525
	C02	Ground stone	Green stone	Small handstone, may be headed toward discoid but is not very worked	4.7	4.6	4	153
	C03	Ground stone	—	Oval basal grinding stone with slightly depressed grinding surface on top and roughly shaped underside	20	17	10	—
	C04	Ground stone	White sandstone	Discoid basal grinding stone with two flat grinding surfaces	15.5	16	4.9	2,950
	C05	Unworked stone	Red sandstone		2.2	1.7	0.5	2
	C05	Chipped stone	Quartz	One piece debitage	1–2	—	—	1
MAS573	D02	Chipped stone	Gray chert	One piece debitage	1–2	—	—	2
	D04	Chipped stone	Gray chert	Possible formal tool	2.2	1.2	0.31	<1
	D05	Iron	Iron	Long narrow shaft, pointed at one end and rectangular at the other		0.5	0.6	6

Ground Stone and Chipped Stone

Chipped stone and ground stone were each found at around half of Siga occupation sites (see Table 28). Chipped stone and small ground stone fragments were collected within the systematic collection area, but load restrictions prevented the collection of most ground stone artifacts. In the opportunistic sample rare items, such as formal chipped stone tools and *hachettes* (small ground stone axe heads), were collected, but debitage and fragmentary ground stone were usually noted and left in place.

Ground Stone

Grinding stones, smoothed pieces of stone used to crush or grind substances, were present at most Siga occupation sites. Stones are most commonly used to grind grains (pearl millet and sorghum), but are also used for preparing sauce ingredients and in some communities for processing shea, as well as for processing medicines, crushing tempers or ochre for pottery, and completing other similar activities (Bascom 1951; Hamon and Le Gall 2013; Korbéogo 2013; Gallagher, Dueppen, and Walsh 2016; Nixon-Darcus and D'Andrea 2017; Shoemaker, Davies, and Moore 2017). Households will often have multiple stones and the use of these may be specialized. For example, the Tallensi in northern Ghana kept a rough and a fine stone for grinding grain and reserved a third stone for other foods (Fortes and Fortes 1936), while the Minyanka of Mali used a larger stone for grain and a smaller stone for condiments (Hamon and Le Gall 2013). However, ethnoarchaeological studies indicate that in practice most grinding stones are used for multiple tasks and are rarely restricted to grinding specific resources (e.g., David 1998; Hamon and Le Gall 2013; Nixon-Darcus and D'Andrea 2017; Shoemaker, Davies, and Moore 2017).

The grinding stones documented during survey and in excavation can be divided into two primary categories: the basal stones (querns) on which grinding takes place (*li naali* in Gulmancema) and the handheld stones used to grind (*u bindu*) (Geis-Tronich 1991). The *u bindu* collected during survey came in several shapes and sizes; most could be classified as trigonal (triangular in cross section), patellar (a smoothed, flattened rhomboid in cross section), or discoid (flat with an oval cross section), but there were several other forms (Figure 59). All shapes of *u bindu* were generally small enough to be held with one hand, as all were less than 10 cm long. Unlike *u bindu,* which were frequently recovered intact, almost all *li naali* were fragmented. *Li naali* require significantly more labor to prepare than *u bindu,* as an appropriate piece of sandstone must be ground down to create both a smooth grinding surface and a stable base. Some of the recovered stones with two flat sides and no grinding depression could have been preforms or been used with *u bindu* that were wider than the stone (e.g., Hamon and Le Gall 2013), although as described above no long *u bindu* were recovered by the project. Geis-Tronich (1991:394) depicted a small flat ground stone as a base on which to separate cotton seeds from their fibers. With very rare exceptions, grinding stones were made from the local sandstones common in the escarpment.

The distribution of grinding stones was difficult to interpret. Production was labor intensive and stones may have been moved rather than left behind when a site was abandoned. The inhabitants of more recent sites in the region may have scavenged stone from older occupations when possible, rather than obtaining new stone from the escarpment. Given their essential function, it was not surprising that grinding stones were distributed evenly throughout the survey zone; although the weight and number of stones per site was

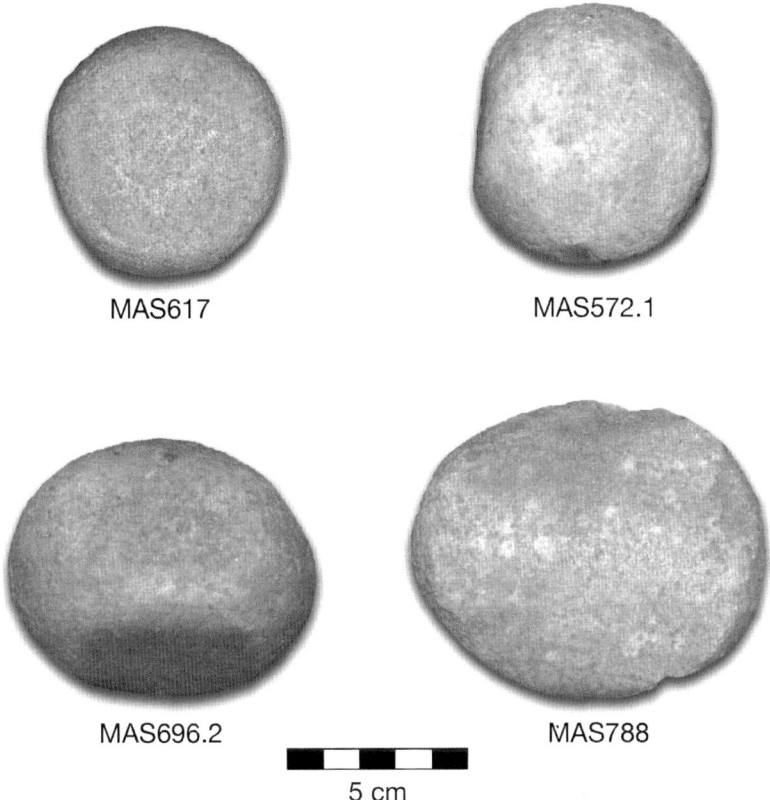

Figure 59. Ground stone objects from Siga occupation sites MAS572.1, MAS617, MAS696.2, and MAS788.

not quantified, sites in Zone 1 were no more likely to have them on the surface than sites in Zone 7. This could be an indicator that the labor involved in preparing stones was a more significant factor than distance from raw material in deciding whether to move stones, leave them behind, or reclaim them from abandoned sites.

At most sites only a single stone or a few fragments were documented, but larger assemblages were occasionally identified (such as the three basal stones at site MAS547; see Figure 14). At site MAS572.1, three grinding stones were recovered from Unit C excavations (see Table 37). One stone was a disk (16 cm in diameter and 5 cm thick) that had been ground flat on both sides. The second was largely unworked on the bottom and had a shallow grinding depression on the top. The third was only visible in the profile. In contrast, at site MAS780, eight small fragments (less than 200 g each) of ground stone were found distributed throughout the unit, along with six unworked sandstone fragments (less than 85 g each).

Four small ground stone *hachettes* were recovered during survey. Three were from high-confidence sites (MAS502.2, MAS572.2, and MAS731) and one from a low-confidence site (MAS643). These *hachettes* ranged in length from 4.8 cm to greater than 10 cm and were variable in width, height, and features, although they were all made of a similar hard stone with a greenish tint, possibly granite (Figure 60). The stone source for these

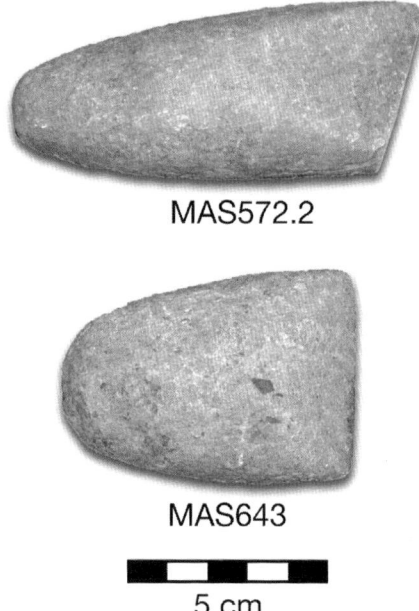

Figure 60. Ground stone *hachettes* from Siga occupation sites MAS572.2 and MAS643.

objects was likely in Birimian deposits to the north or west of the Gobnangou escarpment. There was no residue or evidence of hafting and at least one *hachette* had visible wear along the cutting edge, suggesting that it may have been used in activities in addition to possible ceremonial or symbolic uses. These types of axes, though rare, are not unusual, and their presence was noted by Geis-Tronich (1991) and Breunig and Wotzka (1991). *Hachettes* have been found from at least the mid-Holocene in the West African savanna (see Chapter 4) and, while these may have been produced during the Siga occupation, they could also have been heirloom found objects.

Chipped Stone

Chipped chert occurred at slightly less than half of Siga occupation sites and was recovered in small quantities from the systematic surface collection at only eighty-three sites. In more than 50% of cases, only one piece was found in the 25 m^2 systematic collection area and 90% of sites had fewer than six pieces (the maximum collected was ten). The presence or absence of cores significantly affected sample weight, but over 50% of sites had less than 5 g of chert in the systematic sample (the maximum collected was 120 g). The chert likely came from local sources (see Chapter 4) and as seen from the pieces of unflaked stone collected at twenty-eight Siga occupation sites, it was transported in small rectangular blocks. These blocks were fairly standardized (averaging 4.2 by 3.0 by 1.6 cm with standard deviations of less than 1 cm), which could be a result of natural fracture patterns at the source or a standard unit of exchange. Sites with chipped chert were evenly distributed throughout the study region, although sites ($n = 10$) with particularly high weights or numbers of chipped chert objects were limited to the upper half of the drainage catchment (Zones 1 to 4) closer to the chert sources.

Chipped chert can be used to start fires, a practice described by many local residents although rarely used as matches are now easily available. Chert-on-chert fire-starting is unreliable and usually the stone is sparked with an iron striker. Geis-Tronich (1991) documented the use of this technology by twentieth-century Gulmance, albeit with a piece of quartz rather than chert. The majority of recovered chert— multidirectional cores, flakes, and debitage—could be flaked debris from this activity, although chipped chert was only identified at about half of Siga occupation sites with smelting furnaces or slag. No recovered iron objects have been identified as strikers (see above), but a specific form is not necessary. If chipped chert was in use as a fire starter, some sites consisting only of chert debris could possibly have been activity sites for fire intensive activities such as fish smoking that otherwise leave few surface remains (see the discussions in Chapter 4).

Formal tools were very rare at Siga occupation sites. Only a few backed microliths were identified and most of those occurred at sites near the escarpment or known lithic occupations (where backed microliths were common). The possibility of a continued formalized chipped stone industry cannot be excluded (particularly because the continued use of stone tools despite the availability of iron is well documented in West Africa; MacDonald and Allsworth-Jones 1994; MacDonald 1997; Dueppen and Gokee 2014), but the currently available data did not support this theory in the Gobnangou region (see Chapter 4) and it is most likely that the formal tools recovered from Siga occupation sites were found objects. Regardless, the use of chipped stone as expedient tools should be considered likely, as even unmodified flakes made on this fine-grained chert had very sharp cutting edges. Flakes were recovered almost exclusively from surface contexts, therefore postdepositional effects such as trampling, plowing, and weathering obscured easily identifiable evidence of use wear.

In contrast to chert, quartz was very rare at Siga occupation sites. Chipped quartz was present in the systematic collection at eight sites, and the number only increased to eleven when opportunistic collections were included. Since quartz was a common pottery temper, it is possible that quartz was largely consumed; that is, flakes produced by other activities, such as fire-starting, could have been collected and repurposed. However, sites with chipped quartz actually had significantly lower percentages of quartz-tempered pottery than the complete occupation assemblage. In contrast, of the three sites where unworked pieces of quartz were recovered, two had significantly higher percentages of quartz-tempered pottery.

Farming, Herding, Gathering, and Hunting during the Siga Occupation

There was strong evidence that most sites from the Siga occupation were the remnants of generalized households that moved frequently, likely as part of a program of extensive agriculture. This section presents the limited direct evidence (carbonized plant remains and animal bones) for subsistence, which will then be integrated with the various indirect conclusions on subsistence described above to reconstruct the Siga occupation subsistence economy.

Siga Occupation Faunal and Botanical Analyses
Very little archaeobiological data was available for the Siga occupation. Of the three excavation units, fauna and carbonized botanicals were only recovered from Unit B (MAS780).

Unit C (MAS572.1) and Unit D (MAS573) contained no faunal remains and were too shallow to obtain reliable flotation samples. In Unit B (MAS780), rodent disturbance was so pervasive in the upper layers that flotation samples were only taken from the most intact cultural deposits (levels B09 through B12 at 55 to 110 cm below the surface). Each of these five 2 L samples showed significant evidence of postdepositional intrusion, including uncharred seeds, rootlets, shells, and insect parts. Only one sample (from level B09) yielded identifiable carbonized remains: a seed of *Eleusine indica* (Graminae) and a fragment of shell from *Adansonia digitata* (Bombacaceae). The former is a common ruderal grass that colonizes disturbed areas; it can be found in aging crop fields and other low-nutrient locations. The latter, baobab, is one of the more prominent useful trees in the region (see Chapter 2).

Likewise, Dueppen's faunal analysis found only four identifiable animal bones in the Unit B assemblage: domestic cattle (*Bos taurus*), bushbuck (*Tragalaphus scriptus*), common duiker (*Sylvicapra grimmia*), and catfish (Siluriforme). The three mammals were each represented by a single first phalanx and the catfish by a vertebra. Fragmented, unidentifiable bone, including ribs, long bones, and other body parts consistent with the size classes of these animals, were also recovered.

The three mammals were evidence of three different strategies. Bushbucks are moderately sized animals often found away from human settlements as they prefer areas of thick cover (see Chapter 2; Table 7). They are usually killed during hunting expeditions, particularly during the dry season when they tend to cluster near water sources. In contrast, common duikers live in a variety of habitats and can be common even in fairly populated areas as they breed twice yearly (Spinage 1986). They are known to raid fields and are consequently prime targets for opportunistic hunting. Finally, dimensions of the cattle bone indicated a dwarf breed common in the southern savanna. Dwarf livestock generally fare poorly in transhumant or mobile husbandry strategies and are typically kept near the household. Unfortunately, because different species of catfish live in a wide range of habitats, it is unknown whether this particular fish was caught locally during the wet season or transported (likely in dried or smoked form) from a larger river.

Reconstructing Subsistence during the Siga Occupation
With so little direct evidence, determining the crops under cultivation was challenging. The MAS study region is at the northern limits of yam cultivation and cereals (millet and sorghum) are generally the dominant crops (see Chapter 2). The ubiquity of grinding stones and presence of *couscoussières* during the Siga occupation along with direct evidence for grain agriculture during the Pwoli occupation suggested a reliance on millet or sorghum (or both) as the primary staples, but the potential importance of yams could not be ruled out. Similarly, several varieties of fruits, vegetables, and legumes were likely also cultivated, although again there was no direct evidence.

The settlement pattern outlined above suggests a farming practice that required (or allowed for) the regular relocation of the primary residence. Most likely, residents cultivated a ring of fields directly around their homes (see Chapter 2). Although manure from the dwarf livestock would have been used to fertilize those fields, or more likely vegetable gardens closest to the homes, most of the cultivated area would have been farmed "as is" with few amendments. The usual length of cultivation for a millet or sorghum field is seven years, even with the inclusion of a crop of legumes, after which a fallow period of fifteen to twenty years is required; the decision on how long a farmer would reside in any given location could depend on the quality and extent of easily accessible land from the residence. Conversely, in deciding where to place a residence, a farmer might consider whether the land in that location could support the intended length of occupation.

We presumed that many wild plants played a significant role in Siga occupation diets, although direct evidence was limited. While the presence of edible herbaceous species (such as *Corchorus* spp.) may have been important for choosing residence sites, these plants are easily encouraged, occur widely, and reach harvest within a growing season. More important was access to the crucial useful trees, notably shea, locust bean, and baobab; these orchard crops take years to reach their first harvest, making it unlikely that farmers would see fruit from protected saplings during a short-term occupation. Shea trees bear fruit from around 50 to 250 to 300 years of age and locust bean from around 15 to 100 years of age; the data on baobab are less clear, particularly because intensive harvest of the leaves for sauce on young trees can significantly delay fruiting (Timmer, Kessler, and Slingerland 1996; Duvall 2007; Gallagher, Dueppen, and Walsh 2016). Ethnohistorically, access to trees was often distinct from access to land. In a landscape of cultivation with long fallows, one of the benefits of clearing new territory was often the establishment of tree rights that could be continually exploited. Thus, even if a particular patch of land was not farmed, the trees would be visited and harvested, resulting in an ongoing link to the sites of previous residences and a possible incentive to return to the same general area once the fields have recovered.

Although useful trees were often identified on or near Siga occupation sites, most trees from the first half of the second millennium CE would be deceased and species such as tamarind, locust bean, and shea would have germinated long after the sites were abandoned. The exception is baobab, which can live more than a thousand years (Patrut et al. 2011). However, the unique trunk structure of baobabs makes them very difficult to age by means other than direct radiocarbon dating. In his work in southern Mali, Duvall (2006, 2007) has shown that for baobabs, human activity promoted germination and saplings in settlements were more protected than those in the wild. As a result, baobabs grew in much higher frequencies near settlements, even if they likely reached maturity after settlement abandonment. It is possible, even given conservative estimates for baobab age, that some of the baobabs we recorded germinated during or before the Siga occupation.

Data on hunting and herding was also significantly limited, as we could only rely on the very small animal bone sample. As described above, site MAS780 was fairly unique in the region and may not be representative. Both bushbuck and common duiker could easily have been hunted in thickets near watercourses and an increasingly patchy landscape resulting from extensive agricultural practice may have favored the latter. Cattle are animals that require substantial investment, particularly in the tsetse zone, where even dwarf breeds must be specially cared for. Cattle are almost universally considered a form of storable wealth, therefore their presence could be an indicator of wealth differentials between households.

Dating the Siga Occupation: Absolute Dates, Occupation Length, and Palimpsest

Providing an absolute date for the Siga occupation was challenging because of the ephemeral nature of most of the sites and the lack of a strong regional chronology. Consequently, several dating sources were used, including AMS radiocarbon dates on carbonized wood, direct thermoluminescence (TL) dates on ceramics, and dated artifacts from surrounding

TABLE 38. Associated dates from different sources for the Siga occupation. See also Figure 61.

Sample	Dating technique	Date source	ID number	Conventional radiocarbon age (bp)	Calibrated date range at 2-sigma (cal CE)
Charcoal	AMS radiocarbon	Site MAS780, level B12	Beta–224996	760 ± 40	1190–1294
Six Sherd Type 1 sherds	Thermoluminescence	From surface and near-surface contexts in the study region[a]	45–50[a]	—	320–544
One Sherd Type 1 sherd	Thermoluminescence	From near surface context in the study region[a]	51[a]	—	1055–1267
Three sherds with multiple arching channel decoration (MAC)	Thermoluminescence	From surface contexts in Kantchari[a]	66, 67, 69[a]	—	1122–1222
Sherds with "ladder" channel (LC) and banded dragged comb (BDC) decoration	Associated radiocarbon	From Tchikandou, Benin; charcoal is from lowest levels of excavation unit and may pre-date pottery[b]	ERL 2978	1069 ± 36	894–1023 and later
Smoking pipes	Associated radiocarbon	From sites throughout West Africa[c]	—	—	1600–1900s

[a] Wotzka and Goedicke (2001)
[b] Petit (2005)
[c] See discussions in Chapters 6 and 7.

regions (Table 38; Figure 61). The Siga occupation was initially placed after the Pwoli occupation because of the presence of Siga ceramics on the surfaces of site MAS502.3 (Unit A) and, to a lesser extent, site MAS541 (Unit E). Thus, the Pwoli occupation dates (see Chapter 5) acted as a *terminus post quem*. An AMS radiocarbon sample from the most intact cultural deposits of Unit B (MAS780) yielded a 2-sigma range of 1190–1294 cal CE for the Siga occupation, confirming this chronology.

Further support for an early second millennium CE date for the Siga occupation was provided by the dated use in other regions of the rare decorations "ladder" channels, banded dragged comb, and multiple arching channels. Petit identified several sherds with ladder channel and banded dragged comb decoration at the site of Tchikandou-I in north-

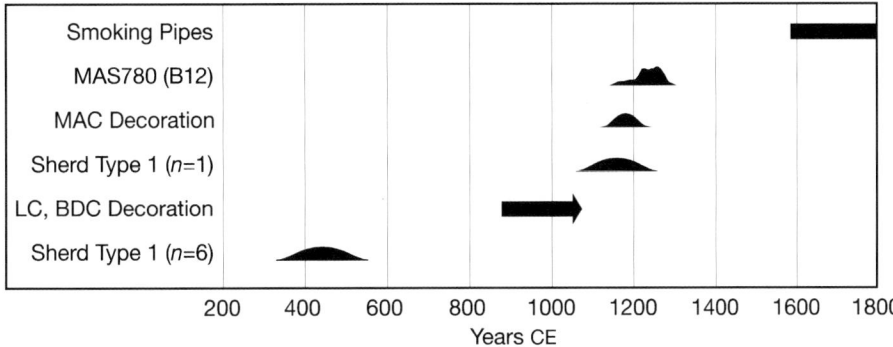

FIGURE 61. Associated dates for datable items of the Siga occupation, from data from site MAS780, Unit B, Wotzka and Goedicke (2001), and Petit (2005), among others. See Table 38 for additional details.

ern Benin. The available radiocarbon date for the site (cal 894–1023 CE) is from the bottom of the 130 cm deep excavation unit in which the relevant pottery was recovered (L. P. Petit, personal communication, 2009). According to Petit (2005:108), the site was abandoned in the twelfth century CE. Sherds with multiple arching channels, collected from several surface sites, including Kantchari by the German–Burkinabe project, were TL dated to 1122–1222 CE (Wotzka and Goedicke 2001).

The German–Burkinabe project also ran TL dates on seven Sherd Type 1 ceramics collected from surface and near-surface contexts in the study region, predominately at Maadaga rockshelter (Wotzka and Goedicke 2001; see Appendix B for more details). Six had similar TL ages that were combined to create a context date of 320–544 CE for the pottery group, earlier than any dates for even the Pwoli occupation. However, the single outlying date, 1055–1267 CE, was consistent with the proposed dates for the Siga occupation. There are several possible explanations for this discontinuity (a return to an earlier ceramic style, errors in dating, and others) that cannot be distinguished with the present data. However, given the total available evidence, we presumed that Sherd Type 1 sherds recovered for this project in association with other Siga occupation ceramics dated to the early second millennium CE.

An upper end for the Siga occupation was suggested by the presence of smoking pipes at a few sites. Although some arguments have been made to the contrary (e.g., Mvondo 1994), the widespread use of smoking pipes generally coincided with the availability of tobacco in the region, usually around 1600 CE (e.g., Shinnie and Kense 1989; S. K. McIntosh, Gallagher, and R. J. McIntosh 2003; Gallagher 2016). Unfortunately, the decorated pipe fragments were bowls, which show the least temporal variation (Shinnie and Kense 1989). However, pipes recovered from Tuali occupation sites likely dated from the seventeenth to the early eighteenth centuries CE (see Chapter 7). While collected on the surface, suggesting a transition between the Siga and Tuali occupations sometime shortly after 1600 CE, it is important to bear in mind that smoking pipes could easily have been deposited after the sites were abandoned. Ethnohistorical and archaeological research indicates that pipes were portable objects, sometimes worn around the neck, and should be considered a highly mobile item that could have been broken or left behind as individuals moved throughout the landscape (e.g., S. K. McIntosh, Gallagher, and R. J. McIntosh 2003;

Gallagher 2016). Pipes were an extremely rare artifact in the survey region, complicating their attribution to a particular occupation.

In summary, most Siga occupation dates clearly clustered in the early second millennium CE (see Figure 61). Although smoking pipes may indicate the temporal extent of the Siga occupation, no other dates were obtained for the fourteenth to the sixteenth centuries CE. Given this currently unresolvable gap and the general mobility of pipes, the end dates for the Siga occupation must remain tentative (further considerations in dating the Siga to Tuali transition are discussed in Chapter 7).

The Siga Occupation in Regional Context

The Siga occupation temporally overlapped with an extremely dynamic period in West African history. In the first quarter of the second millennium CE, the eastern Niger Bend was a vibrant axis of commerce and communication, with large populations stretching from the city of Gao on the Niger River through the villages at Oursi, Kissi, and Saouga in Oudalan Province in northern Burkina Faso (Gado 1993; Czerniewicz 2004; Fabre 2009; Magnavita 2009, 2015; Petit, Pelzer, and Czerniewicz 2011; Takezawa and Cissé 2012, 2017; Cissé et al. 2013). To the northeast of the Gobnangou study region along the Niger River, the mounded site of Birnin Lafiya reached its largest size and provided evidence for trade and even pottery pavements, perhaps reflecting a connection to sites down the Niger River in Nigeria (Haour et al. 2016; Haour 2019). In northern Benin, iron working was common and large complexes have been documented in Park W, the Dendi region, and the Atakora (Petit 2005; Thiombiano-Ilboudo 2010:151; Guemona 2015; Robion-Brunner 2019)

At that time, iron working became a major industry in central Burkina Faso, where very large-scale production areas from the first half of the second millennium CE have been documented (Kiéthéga 2009; Simpore 2009; Serneels 2017). Although there is significantly more evidence for iron production during the Siga occupation than during the Pwoli occupation, furnace installations in the survey zone do not begin to approach the scale documented at these sites. Some locations in Fada N'Gourma Province had iron working closer in scale to the study region, but even there the size of individual installations was frequently larger. For example, the undated clusters of furnaces at Namoungou and Kouare were spaced every 500 m to 1 km and all furnace clusters typically had three to seven or more furnaces (Thiombiano-Ilboudo 2010:151, 2012a; for furnace sites in Fada N'Gourma see also Somda et al. [1985] as cited in Thiombiano-Ilboudo [2010:112]).

As with the Pwoli occupation, there were certain similarities between the sequence described in northern Benin by Petit (2005) and N'Dah (2009) and that of the surveyed area that suggested possible regional scale patterns. From the mid first through early second millennium CE, what is today northern Benin was characterized by fairly sedentary people who created settlement mounds (see above and Chapter 5). In the eleventh to twelfth centuries CE, locations to the north of the Atakora Mountains were abandoned and abandonment of southern mound sites followed approximately three hundred years later. Despite the noted coincidence that northern Benin was possibly depopulated contemporary with or slightly after the beginning of the Siga occupation and its attendant possible increase in population, there was virtually no evidence that suggested a migration to the study region. Petit attributed the changes in settlement strategy to either the effects of the early second millennium CE dry spell, increased insecurity in the region, or both. Sites dating to the mid and late second millennium CE (Petit's [2005] "Historical Period") were few and ephemeral; Petit was not able to subdivide the occupation and most of the described sites had more similarities with the Tuali occupation than the Siga occupation.

There are two ways to interpret these transformations in light of the evidence from the MAS study region. First, residents of northern Benin may have become more mobile, resulting in more ephemeral sites that are difficult to identify, particularly if Petit's and N'Dah's surveyed areas were not extensively plowed like the MAS survey zone. Second, there may in fact have been a depopulation of the region to the north of the Atakora Mountains. In the former case, the basic sequence mirrors that of the study region, where the mounded sites of the Pwoli occupation gave way to the more ephemeral sites of the Siga occupation. This could point to regional level trends that encouraged a shift from more spatially anchored habitations. In the latter case, a depopulation along the banks of the Pendjari would be intriguing given that it was traditionally a southern boundary for the Gulmance kingdoms. The Siga occupation covered the period during which, according to some oral histories, the Gulmance kingdoms were founded and consolidated, and raiding and conflict with peoples to the south was a central part of those narratives (see Chapter 8). Unfortunately, it was not possible to further test these very speculative hypotheses, particularly given the lack of archaeological data for areas directly to the north of the Pendjari River.

Dynamic Landscapes and Complex Materialities

The Siga occupation represented a significant transition from the Pwoli occupation. The basic elements of resource exploitation of the subsistence economy seem to have remained fairly stable, yet the associated farming practices changed dramatically. Residents of the survey region during the Siga occupation lived in household compounds that were widely spaced on the landscape. Occasionally a few may have been adjacent, but the minimum distance between sites was usually over 100 m and often significantly more. During the rainy season, the network of drainages bisecting the landscape would have increased the travel times between sites. Combined with the data suggesting that these sites were not occupied for long periods, residents were likely practicing a form of generational mobility that involved regular relocation of the primary residence.

Given the problems of chronology, it was almost impossible to untangle the complex settlement pattern of the Siga occupation at the regional level. As argued above, the number of households occupied simultaneously could range from a brief florescence of more than two hundred to a more sustained thirty to forty over a period of several hundred years. More likely, population in the region over the course of the Siga occupation fluctuated significantly; the survey boundaries were to a certain extent arbitrary and residents may have been moving within a significantly larger territory. Although the pattern and coordination of moves is unknown, individual households in shifting settlement systems usually have significant autonomy and flexibility in determining when and where they will move, provided they remain within territory controlled by a group (kin-based, political, or cultural) with whom they are identified. In this case, the ceramic data suggested that the entire study region was within one such territory. The transformation in the pottery assemblage between the Pwoli and Siga occupations could indicate migration into the region by at least a subset of the population, although similar pottery has not yet been identified elsewhere. However, it remains likely that the Siga occupation was a period of rapid internal growth.

In making their decisions as to where to locate their residences, and consequently farm (or vice versa), Siga occupation households likely balanced multiple tensions, the foremost of which may have been whether to return to an earlier residence location or move to a previously unoccupied area. The currently available data suggest that reoccupation of sites was rare given the small number of clusters and large sites, although since decayed former residences (and the areas directly surrounding them where trash was deposited) often produced very rich soils, returning to the same field system was likely more common than returning to the same precise residential location.

The data suggested that households during the Siga occupation were fairly generalized; for the most part, they fell within a small range of sizes and were distributed so that each household likely controlled its own field system. They had similar material culture assemblages, suggesting that a similar range of activities took place at each location. There were a few exceptions: at least some ceramics may have been produced by specialists and iron smelting seems to have been carried out at specialized locations, some of which (notably site MAS849) may have been used for extended or high-volume smelting. Additionally, site MAS780 and its environs (including site MAS696.2 less than 350 m distant across a small drainage) had a richer material culture than other sites in the study region. As described above, the densities of iron objects were very high at MAS780 and MAS696.2 had the highest diversity of ceramics in the study region. The burial found by local residents at MAS780, with its iron bracelets, was the only known burial in the study region with grave goods and these objects were likely powerful items with significance that extended beyond adornment. Although the MAS did not excavate burials, these are encountered by farmers who dig borrow pits, wells, and other projects. In our discussions with local residents they considered the MAS780 burial unusual.

It seems as though residents of sites MAS780 and MAS696.2 were differentiated from other households, but there is not yet sufficient data to address whether this translated to political power. Several lines of evidence suggested that, regardless of political organization, residents of the study region during the Siga occupation were not subject to violence or insecurity. Households were able to move freely within the landscape and there was no evidence of settlement concentration near the escarpment. Ceramics, ground stone, flint, and iron objects were likely exchanged throughout the study region. Likewise, the hypothesized small but steady stream of imported ceramics from outside the region could indicate trading relationships with neighboring groups.

Recent analyses of community histories and regional settlement patterns suggest that plague epidemics could be a reason for the end of the Siga occupation in the region if the possible fourteenth-century end date is correct (Dueppen and Gallagher 2016; Chouin 2018; Gallagher and Dueppen 2018). In some regards, the dramatic transformations in the subsequent Tuali period, including potential population loss, reduction in iron smelting, and a decrease in stylistic investment in artifacts, is consistent with the effects of likely plague epidemics seen elsewhere in West Africa at this time.

CHAPTER SEVEN

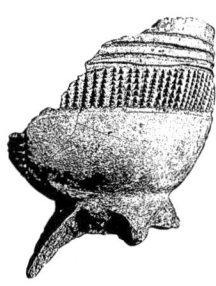

Indigo and the Escarpment
The Tuali Occupation

The Tuali occupation (ca. 1300/1650–1950 CE) consisted almost entirely of small, short-occupation sites consistent with patterns of generational mobility identified during the Siga occupation. This continuity in the basic mode of settlement was accompanied by significant changes in material culture, as seen in the dramatic decrease in the diversity of the ceramic assemblage throughout the Tuali occupation. By the end of the Tuali occupation, settlement shifted toward the Gobnangou escarpment, a site significantly larger than any others in the study region was founded, and several installations of plastered dye pits for large-scale indigo cloth production were constructed.

Tuali occupation sites were divided into two groups, designated here Tuali-A and Tuali-B. Initially separated because of characteristics of the ceramic assemblage, multiple classes of data substantiated this division. Although there were indications that the Tuali-A occupation (ca. 1300/1650–1800 CE) predated the Tuali-B occupation (ca. 1800–1950 CE), no excavation data was available for the Tuali occupation. The Tuali-A and Tuali-B ceramic assemblages were not identified at any stratified sites, leaving open the possibility that their differences were functional or cultural rather than temporal.

Characterizing the Tuali-A Occupation

The Tuali-A occupation produced significantly fewer preserved sites than the preceding Siga occupation (Figures 62 and 63; Table 39). While settlement in the study region continued to be characterized by small sites and generational mobility, the Tuali-A occupation was marked by significant transformations in the ceramic assemblage accompanied by the beginnings of a settlement shift toward the escarpment. Sites were assigned to the Tuali-A occupation at two levels of confidence (see methods described in detail in Chapter 3). Low-confidence sites ($n = 16$) had an almost identical distribution to high-confidence sites ($n = 51$) and are only discussed when they differ significantly. Additionally, several sites ($n = 18$) were identified as having multicomponent ceramic assemblages. Although these sites are included in all discussions of spatial distribution, analyses of artifact frequency and other characteristics of the sites themselves are confined to single-component sites.

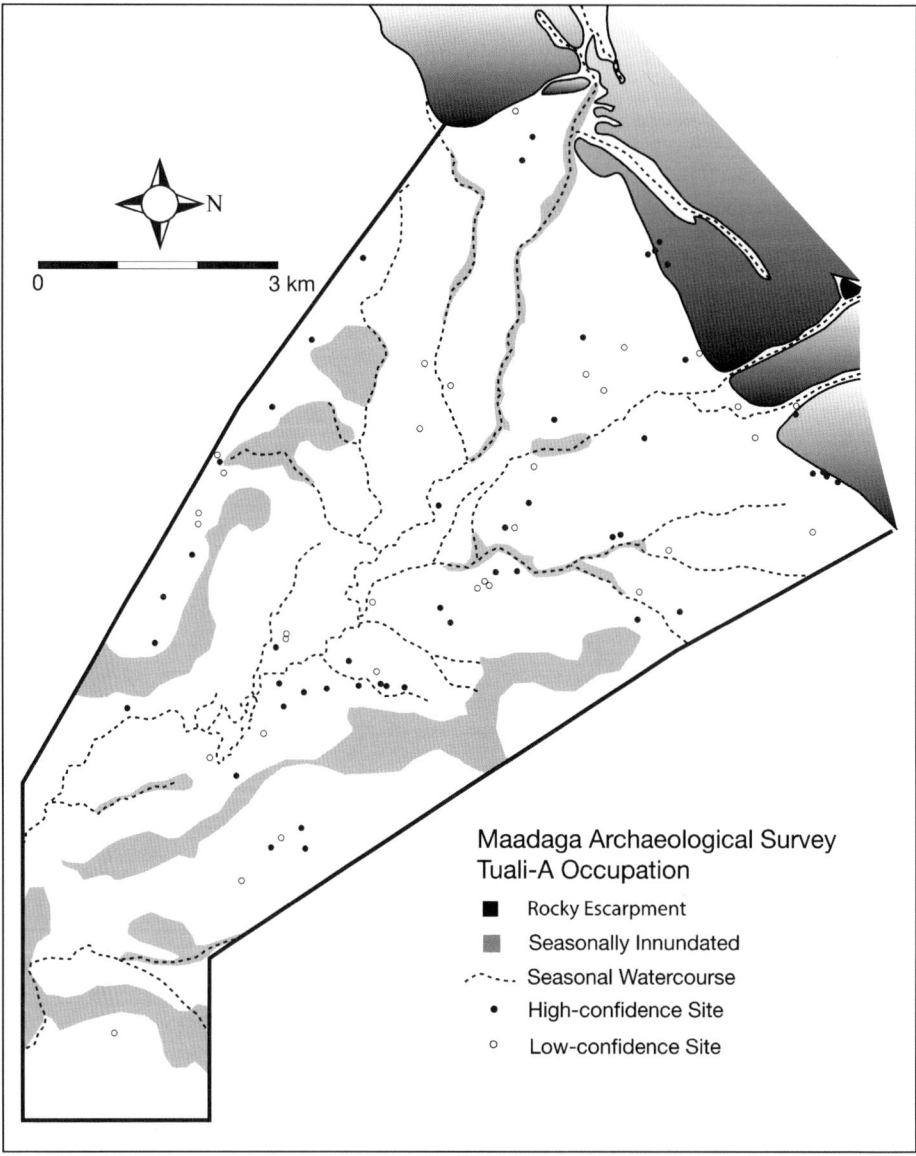

FIGURE 62. Tuali-A occupation sites identified by the Maadaga Archaeological Survey.

Occupation Length and Characteristics

Like Siga occupation sites, Tuali-A occupation sites were shallow and poorly preserved. Tuali-A sites had a mean estimated depth of 0.33 m and, although no Tuali-A sites were excavated, observations at the four sites with borrow pits indicated that the surface-based characterization of them as thin, single-component sites was accurate.

The vast majority of the Tuali-A sites fell within the medium size class defined for the Siga occupation (Table 40) and, like the Siga occupation, the site size histogram showed dual peaks at approximately 11 and 15 m diameters (100 and 200 m², respec-

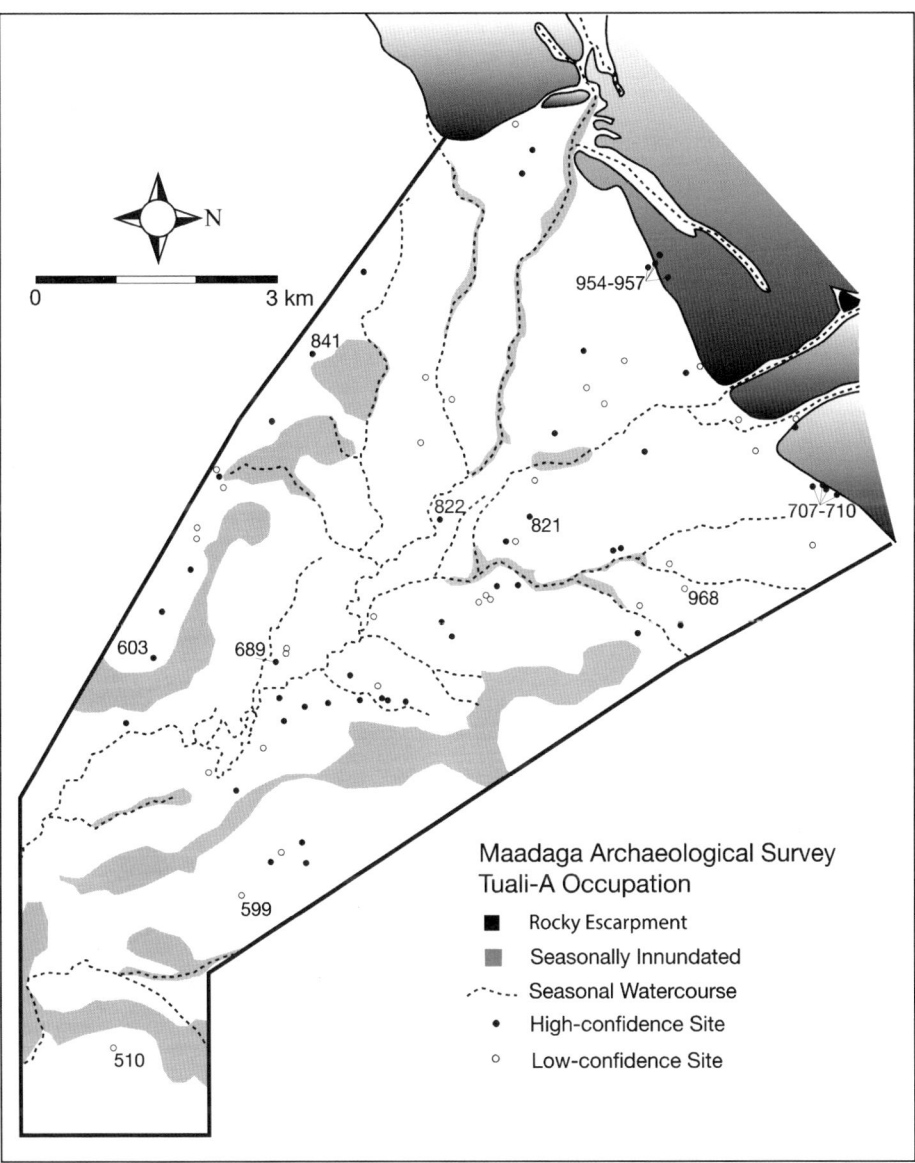

Figure 63. Locations of Tuali-A occupation sites mentioned in the text.

tively; Figure 64). Small sites (less than 70 m²) were slightly more common, but large sites were almost completely absent. For comparison, whereas twenty-eight single-component high-confidence Siga occupation sites were 1,000 to 3,320 m², the largest identified single-component high-confidence Tuali-A site was MAS603 at only 840 m². This pattern suggested lower incidence during the Tuali-A occupation of the multiple compound or close reoccupation phenomenon argued to account for these larger sites (see the discussions in Chapter 6). No relationship could be identified between site size and site location; the largest sites were in Zones 1 and 5 and, although small sites were

TABLE 39. Characteristics of Tuali-A occupation sites by assigned confidence level for single-component sites.

Site features	High-confidence sites	Low-confidence sites	All sites
Total number of sites	51	16	86
Near baobab trees	8	3	13
Near seasonal drainage	19	12	39
Near seasonal pool	0	0	2
Near seasonal inundation or marsh	8	13	50
Total sites near water	27	13	50
Plowing disturbance present	48	16	79
Borrow pit disturbance present	4	0	8
Chipped stone present	25	7	41
Ground stone present	32	11	51
Slag (rare)	6	1	8
Slag (present)	2	1	6
Iron smelting (small)	0	0	0
Iron smelting (medium)	0	0	1
Iron smelting (large)	0	0	0

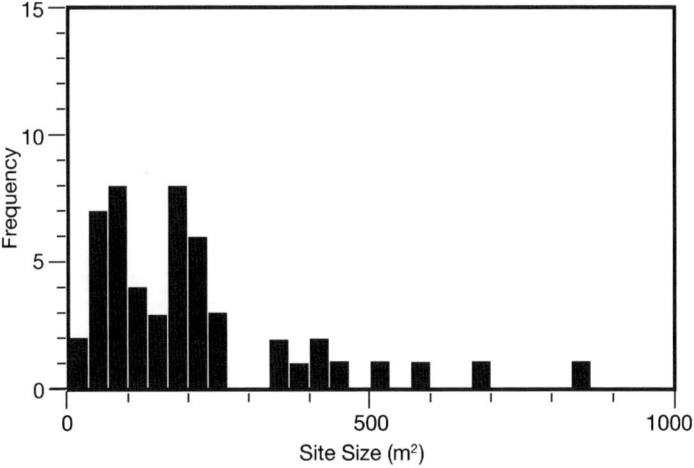

FIGURE 64. Size distribution of Tuali-A occupation sites.

TABLE 40. Ceramic assemblage characteristics of Tuali-A occupation sites and location by site size and distance from the Gobnangou escarpment (Zones 1 to 7) and the Koabu drainage (Zones A, B, and C; see also Figure 16).

	Number and size of sites (m²)		
	Small (20–60)	Medium (75–625)	Large (650–840)
Total number of sites	9	40	2
Zone 1	1	10	1
Zone 2	0	5	0
Zone 3	2	8	0
Zone 4	3	11	0
Zone 5	3	6	1
Zone 6	0	0	0
Zone 7	0	0	0
Zone A	9	30	1
Zone B	0	8	1
Zone C	0	2	0
	Ceramic assemblage characteristics		
Mean ceramic density (g/m³)	24.7	38.3	28.8
Median ceramic density (g/m³)	16.5	20.9	28.8
Mean number of decoration techniques in use per site	1.4	2.1	2.0
Mean number of decoration techniques in use per 100 sherds	5.2	7.3	6.3

slightly more balanced toward Zones 3 to 5, given the low number of sites the effect could be a sampling artifact.

As was the case for the Siga occupation, small Tuali-A occupation sites had lower surface ceramic density, whereas medium and larger sites had similar median surface ceramic density both to each other and to medium and large Siga occupation sites (the Tuali-A average ceramic density by weight was inflated by a few sites that included significant representation of the thick sherds from vessels associated with Sherd Type 9). This could indicate that average length of residence at particular locations remained constant between the Siga and Tuali-A occupations. However, as discussed below, the Tuali-A occupation ceramic assemblage was characterized by a more restricted range of vessels and it is possible that residents used perishable containers in place of ceramic vessels for some tasks. If this was the case, comparable ceramic densities could reflect slightly longer residence length.

Overall, residents of the study region during the Tuali-A occupation produced sites

TABLE 41. Spatial distribution of Tuali-A occupation sites by distance from the Gobnangou escarpment (Zones 1 to 7) and the Koabu drainage (Zones A, B, and C; see also Figure 16). Numbers in parentheses are for single-component, high-confidence sites only.

	Number of sites per zone							Total number	Total percentage
	Zone 1	Zone 2	Zone 3	Zone 4	Zone 5	Zone 6	Zone 7		
Zone A	16 (12)	9 (5)	20 (8)	17 (9)	8 (6)	0 (0)	—	70 (40)	81.4 (78.4)
Zone B	—	—	2 (2)	6 (5)	2 (2)	—	—	10 (9)	11.6 (17.6)
Zone C	—	—	—	0 (0)	4 (2)	1 (0)	1 (0)	6 (2)	7.0 (3.9)
Total number	16 (12)	9 (5)	22 (10)	23 (14)	14 (10)	1 (0)	1 (0)	86 (51)	
Total percentage	18.6 (23.5)	10.5 (9.8)	25.6 (19.6)	26.7 (27.5)	16.3 (19.6)	1.2 (0.0)	1.2 (0.0)		

of similar size, depth, and artifact density to the Siga occupation. Consequently, the social processes that spurred the considerable transformations in material culture described below likely did not significantly affect residential group size, basic architectural layouts, or length of residence.

Spatial Distribution of the Tuali-A Occupation

Only eighty-six Tuali-A sites were identified and of these fifty-one were high-confidence single-component sites (see Table 39). Tuali-A sites were located on the banks of major and minor seasonal drainages, on the highlands near inundated regions, and along the foot of the escarpment (see Figure 62; Table 41). In general, the Tuali-A occupation sites were broadly spaced, but there were two noticeable clusters of sites near the foot of the escarpment (sites MAS707–MAS710 and sites MAS954–MAS957) that could be precursors to the large Tuali-B site discussed below. Although it was not possible to determine whether sites in the cluster were occupied simultaneously, these sites constituted the only evidence for aggregation during the Tuali-A occupation.

The Tuali-A settlement pattern showed a striking shift out of Zones 6 and 7 (see Figure 16). Commonly occupied during Siga (accounting for almost 20% of identified sites), these areas were essentially abandoned during the Tuali-A occupation. Of the two low-confidence multicomponent sites in these zones, MAS510 was the only true outlier given MAS599's position near the edge of Zone 5. The multicomponent assemblage at MAS510 had primarily Siga characteristics, but was also included as a low-confidence Tuali-A site because of the presence of a thin quartz-tempered sherd with braided strip roulette (similar to Sherd Type 12).

The boundary between the unoccupied Zone 6 and the occupied Zone 5 was fairly abrupt. Sites were evenly distributed among Zones 1 to 5 and Zone 5 was as likely to have a Tuali-A occupation site as Zone 1. There was no obvious environmental reason for the transition as the soils and topography of Zones 4 and 5 and Zones 6 and 7 were similar, which suggests that social factors motivated the decision to avoid areas farther downstream. What was less clear was whether residents were gravitating toward the escarpment or away from the unoccupied area.

As will be discussed below, during the Tuali-B occupation households clustered near the escarpment. The Tuali-A settlement pattern could be the first evidence for this shift. Movements toward highlands were common in neighboring regions during the latter part of the second millennium CE (e.g., Petit 2005; Swanepoel 2005, 2009; N'Dah 2009; MacEachern 2011). While often attributed to the security afforded by highlands in the event of raiding or other forms of unrest, in the case of the Tuali-A occupation settlement remained common in Zones 3, 4, and 5, out of sight of the escarpment. Settlement could also have been moving away from the southeast in response to events outside the survey area rather than toward the escarpment. Finally, since the Tuali-A occupation had significantly fewer sites than the Siga occupation, it is possible that this change in settlement pattern was simply an artifact of the particular group of sites occupied at that time; that is, it is a snapshot of a continual trend of movement toward and away from the escarpment that was obscured in the Siga occupation site distribution.

The Tuali-A Ceramic Assemblage

The Tuali-A ceramic assemblage was less than 20% the size of the Siga ceramic assemblage, with 1,708 sherds from high-confidence single-component sites (Figures 65 and 66; Table

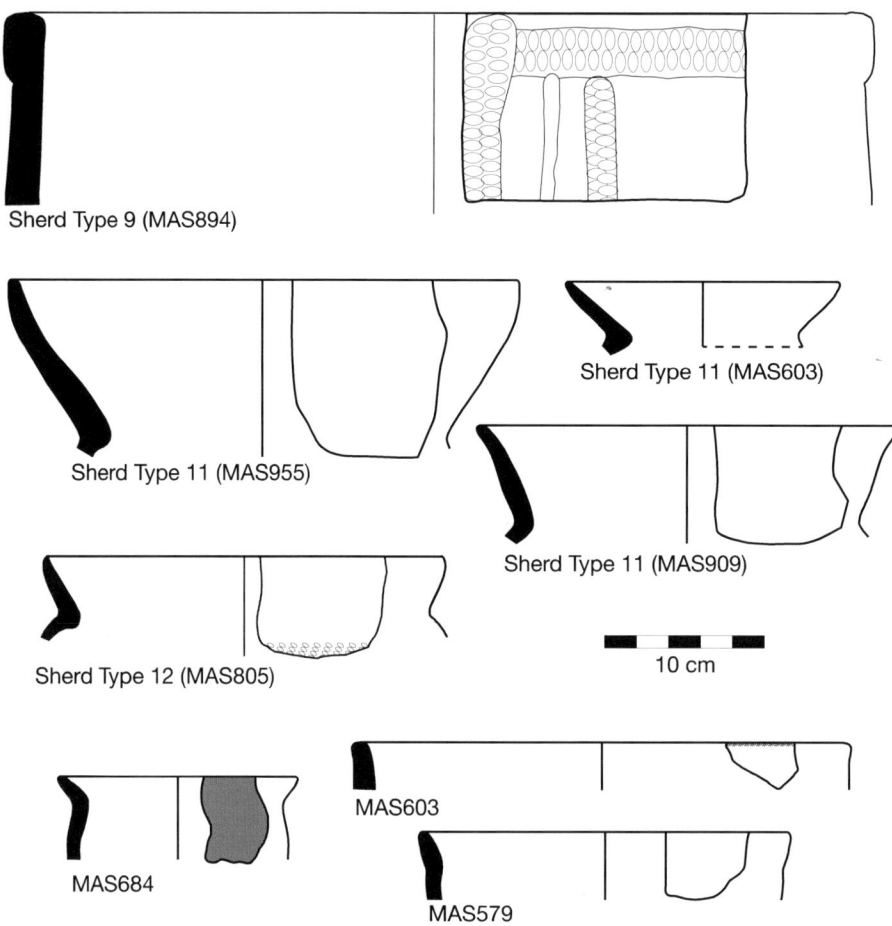

FIGURE 65. Tuali-A occupation ceramics Sherd Types 9, 11, and 12 and untyped ceramics with their associated sites.

42). Even with this smaller sample, there were well-defined changes in the nature of the assemblage. Quartz-tempered vessels increased in importance and constituted the majority of recovered sherds. Grog-tempered vessels were still common, particularly the large grog- and laterite-tempered vessels associated with Sherd Type 9 (see below); however, mica-tempered sherds virtually disappeared from the assemblage. Functionally, quartz temper creates a very strong paste that can be used to create large, thin-walled vessels, a property that was clearly favored by the potters of the Tuali-A occupation since over 50% of quartz-tempered sherds were less than 8 mm thick.

Household Assemblages during the Tuali-A Occupation

The Tuali-A ceramic assemblage was also marked by a significant decrease in the diversity of vessel forms. Slightly restricted jars with large flaring necks (usually quartz-tempered) emerged as by far the most common vessel shape and accounted for a large percentage of the assemblage (Figures 65 and 66). Sherd Type 11 was the archetypical example of these

FIGURE 66. Tuali-A and Tuali-B occupation Sherd Types 11, 12, and 13.

vessels and these quartz-tempered rims occur in a wide range of sizes (vessel diameters were evenly distributed from 16 to 40 cm, although throat diameters clustered at 9 to 18 cm and 26 to 36 cm). The vessels associated with Sherd Type 12 were a subset of those associated with Sherd Type 11; the rim was identical, but Sherd Type 12 was marked by the presence of a braided strip roulette decoration (usually Cord 6) on the shoulder of the vessel. These vessels had particularly thin walls onto which a slightly thicker rim had been applied. Similarly, the roughing treatment that distinguished Sherd Type 14 was universally found on thick quartz-tempered sherds. The same roughing treatment was documented on the base of large flared jars by Geis-Tronich (1989) and was a common feature of the bases of jars available for sale at local markets in 2004 and 2006. Sherd Type 9 was the only other sherd type common in the Tuali-A ceramic assemblage; these very large, open grog- and laterite-tempered vessels with coarse ridges were also present in the Siga assemblage and were the primary point of continuity between the two assemblages. The persistence of these vessels could indicate a specialized function. These vessels may have been used to mark burials, but also could have had diverse household functions (such as for water storage, brewing, and dyeing; see Chapter 6).

Among untyped rim sherds, half were quartz-tempered simple rims and, although likely from the upper sections of Sherd Type 11 or 12 flared vessels, they were not assigned to these sherd types because the inflection point was not present. The remaining untyped rims were grog-tempered. Most were small fragments, but the majority of larger examples came from slightly everted open vessels (see Figure 65). As was the case during

TABLE 42. Characteristics of the ceramic assemblage from the Tuali-A occupation by assigned confidence level for single-component sites. See also Appendix B.

	High-confidence sites	Low-confidence sites	All sites
Number of individually recorded sherds	1,708	558	2,720
Percentage of sherds with:			
Grog temper	31.2	46.1	36.2
Quartz temper	65.5	50.2	60.4
Grog and quartz temper	4.7	4.8	4.4
Mica and quartz temper	0.8	1.0	0.8
Red slip	10.2	13.2	11.6
Decoration	12.2	25.8	17.0
Number of decoration techniques	16	19	31
Mean number of decoration techniques per 100 sherds	6.8	9.9	9.0
Number of sherds assigned to:			
Sherd Type 1	0	0	1
Sherd Type 2	2	1	3
Sherd Type 3	3	0	3
Sherd Type 4	0	3	4
Sherd Type 5	0	0	7
Sherd Type 7	0	1	1
Sherd Type 8	0	0	2
Sherd Type 9	26	14	50
Sherd Type 10	0	3	4
Sherd Type 11	34	3	43
Sherd Type 12	13	2	15
Sherd Type 13	0	1	1
Sherd Type 14	57	3	81

the Siga occupation, the untyped Tuali-A rim assemblage was comprised predominantly of medium and small vessels.

In comparing the Siga occupation and Tuali-A occupation ceramic assemblages, the elimination of most vessels that would likely be used for serving was striking. The Sherd Type 11 and 12 vessels could easily have taken on the roles performed by Sherd Types 2,

3, and 4 during the Siga occupation, but there were no equivalents for Sherd Types 5, 6, and 7. Indeed, bases of all kinds (pedestals, rings, and feet) were largely absent from the Tuali-A assemblage; only three were identified. The best possibilities for serving vessels were the untyped, everted, grog-tempered rims, which occurred in the assemblages of at least half of high-confidence single-component sites. This pattern could indicate a change in the social context of food and beverage consumption (see the discussions in Gijanto and Walshaw [2014]), but also a shift in the role of ceramics. Preferred serving vessels during the Tuali-A occupation could have been manufactured using materials that did not preserve in the archaeological record, such as carved wooden bowls or decorated calabashes (gourds).

The decline in the diversity and complexity of ceramic decoration during the Tuali-A occupation may also be indicative of the lessening importance of ceramics as loci of social signaling. The great majority of vessels, including the untyped, everted grog-tempered rims (mentioned above) possible serving vessels, were undecorated. Decoration rates fell to 12% from 35% during the Siga occupation. The total number of decoration techniques in use declined as well to only sixteen and a few techniques—twisted cord roulette (Cord 2), braided strip roulette (Cord 6), and the plastic ridges associated with Sherd Type 9—accounted for more than 75% of decorated sherds (Table 43). Standardized complex design grammars such as those associated with Sherd Types 1 and 5 during the Siga occupation were completely absent. Even the surface treatments indicated less investment in ceramic production. Red slip decreased in frequency, although this could be in part due to weathering, the effects of which are more pronounced when slip is applied in a thin layer and only lightly burnished. Burnishing was almost completely absent in the Tuali-A assemblage.

Like the Siga occupation, there was no direct evidence for pottery production at any sites (with the possible exception of a broken burnishing stone recovered from site MAS957) and the lack of ceramic data for the greater region complicated assessments of the organization of production. However, the lower per pot investment in finishing and decoration, as well as the standardization of pastes and forms, could suggest an increase in the scale of production, a reduction in the number of active potters and pottery workshops, or both.

Pipes and Other Clay Objects

Although still a rare class of artifact, clay pipes became relatively more common during the Tuali-A occupation, with five pipe stems recovered from three sites (Figure 67). Pipemakers in West Africa typically used different production techniques, decoration, and clay sources than were used for ceramic vessels (Stahl 2001, 2007; S. K. McIntosh, Gallagher, and R. J. McIntosh 2003; Ogundiran 2007, 2009, 2014; Stahl et al. 2008; Gallagher 2016; Keita and Coulibaly 2018; see Chapter 6). There is as yet no broadly established pipe chronology for West Africa, however, some temporal trends have been noted at particular sites. Morphologically, the pipe from site MAS603 had a double-angle base, which Shinnie and Kense (1989) considered among the earliest pipe forms in stratified deposits from northern Ghana. It was also found among the earliest pipes at the Djenné Museum Site in Mali (S. K. McIntosh, Gallagher, and R. J. McIntosh 2003). If pipes in the study region follow the same temporal trends, the pipe from MAS603 can be dated to the seventeenth to eighteenth centuries CE. Two of the pipes from site MAS968 had squared tips (the third was an undecorated cylinder). Collared pipe tips were common in West Africa, but this precise morphology has not to date been identified at other sites.

TABLE 43. Ceramic decoration techniques in use during the Tuali-A occupation at high-confidence single-component sites. For sherd type descriptions see Appendix B. For full descriptions of decoration techniques see Tables 11–14.

Technique	Field code	Number of sherds ($N = 208$)	Number of sites ($N = 51$)	Associated sherd types
Twisted cord roulette	Cord 2	110	33	9, 12
Ridge with finger impressions (double)	R2T	27	17	9
Braided strip roulette	Cord 6	19	16	12
Channel	CH	12	10	—
Braided strip roulette	Cord 4	7	6	—
Folded strip roulette	Cord 3	6	3	—
Parallel channels	PC	5	5	—
Lip channel	LIPCH	4	4	—
Braided cord roulette	Cord 1	3	3	—
Other channels	IC	2	2	—
Diagonal incisions	DI	1	1	—
Braided cord impressions	IB	1	1	—
Small ridge	MR	1	1	9
Ridge	PR	1	1	9
Ridge with gouges	PRG	1	1	9
Pinched rim	RP	1	1	—

An undecorated partial bead or spindle whorl made of roughly smoothed clay was recovered from the surface of site MAS841 (see Figure 67). If this artifact is a spindle whorl, it would be the first direct evidence for the manufacture of cloth in the region; as will be shown below, the dyeing of cloth became a significant specialist enterprise during the Tuali-B occupation. Spindle whorls are a common artifact of second millennium CE West Africa and were used as weights on the end of drop spindles when making cotton thread. This method was still practiced in the study region in 2004 and 2006. The resulting thread was usually woven into narrow strips (Geis-Tronich 1991; Kriger 2006). Cotton, while very hard on the soil, grows well in the study region and may have been cultivated locally; its inclusion in the farming economy could have expanded the area under cultivation during particular growing seasons and more rapidly drained nutrients from the soil, resulting in more extensive field systems.

Iron Working

Unlike the Siga and Tuali-B occupations, there was no clear evidence for iron smelting during the Tuali-A occupation (Figure 68). The single smelting site associated with Tuali-A was a low-confidence site that was also assigned at a high-confidence level to the Siga occupation. The absence of evidence for iron-smelting activity at Tuali-A sites as

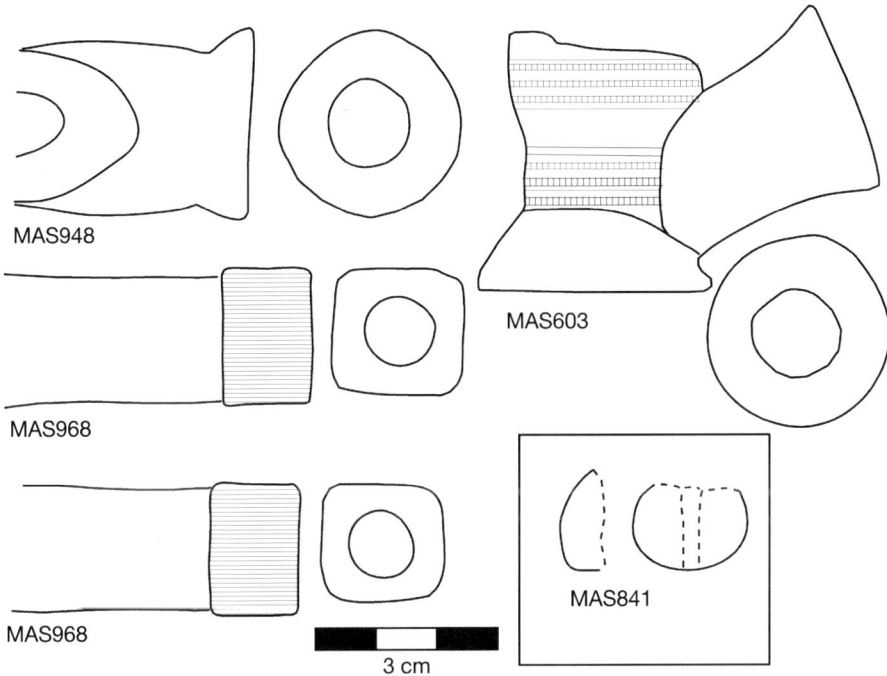

FIGURE 67. Pipes from Tuali-A occupation sites MAS603, MAS948, MAS968; and partial bead or spindle whorl from MAS841.

compared with Tuali-B was the strongest line of evidence for temporal overlap between the two occupations.

In contrast, slag was found at Tuali-A sites throughout the region in similar proportions to its occurrence during other occupations (16.0%, 15.7%, and 15.6% of high-confidence single-component sites during the Siga, Tuali-A, and Tuali-B occupations, respectively). This distribution suggested some continuity in the organization of iron production from the Siga to the Tuali-A occupations. However, compared with Siga and Tuali-B sites, Tuali-A occupation sites were much more likely to have only rare instances of slag.

Ground Stone and Chipped Stone

Like Siga occupation sites, ground stone and chipped stone were the most common classes of artifacts besides ceramics. Ground stone continued to be an essential item, as evidenced by its even distribution throughout the study region; sites in Zone 5 were only slightly less likely than those in Zone 1 or 2 to have ground stone present and, given the small number of sites, the differences may be insignificant. The grinding stones recovered from Tuali-A sites were essentially similar to those recovered from Siga sites and showed the same range of variability in their handstones (*u bindu*). The querns (*li naali*) again tended to be left in place during survey because of load restrictions, although identified fragments included those with both flat and depressed grinding surfaces. Sites directly along the edge of the escarpment frequently contained blocks of unworked sandstone, even though it was no more common at sites than at areas along the escarpment edge with no other cultural materials.

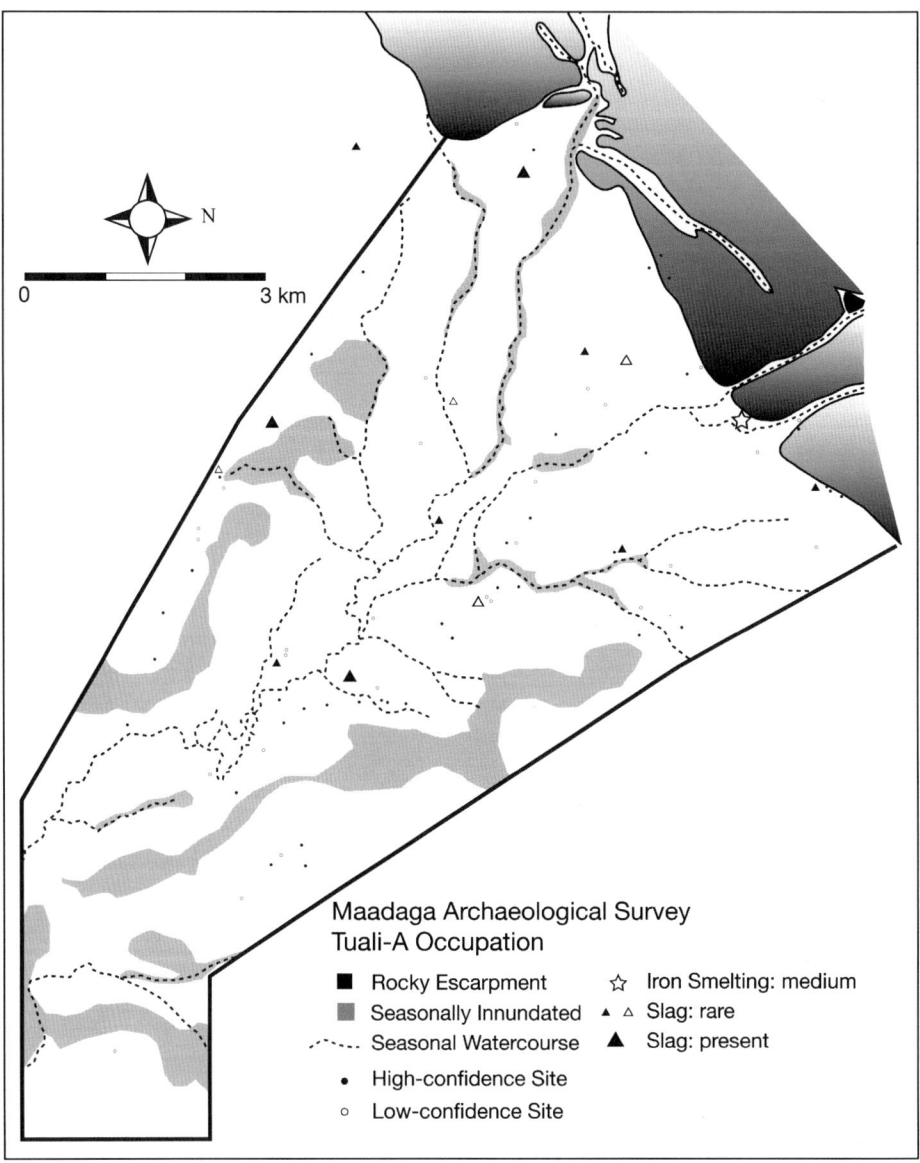

FIGURE 68. Distribution of iron-working activities during the Tuali-A occupation identified by the Maadaga Archaeological Survey. Black dots, stars, and triangles are high-confidence sites; open dots, stars, and triangles are low-confidence sites.

Chipped chert likewise was common throughout the study region at Tuali-A occupation sites. As with the Siga occupation, in most cases chert was found in very low densities; typically only one to two flakes or debitage fragments were present in the systematic collection. The exceptions were site MAS689 (two flakes and a core) and site MAS822 (two flakes and two pieces of debitage) with only slightly higher occurrence. Interestingly, half of the possible formal microlithic tools found during the survey were from Tuali-A sites (Figure 69). These were distributed throughout the surveyed area and two occurred

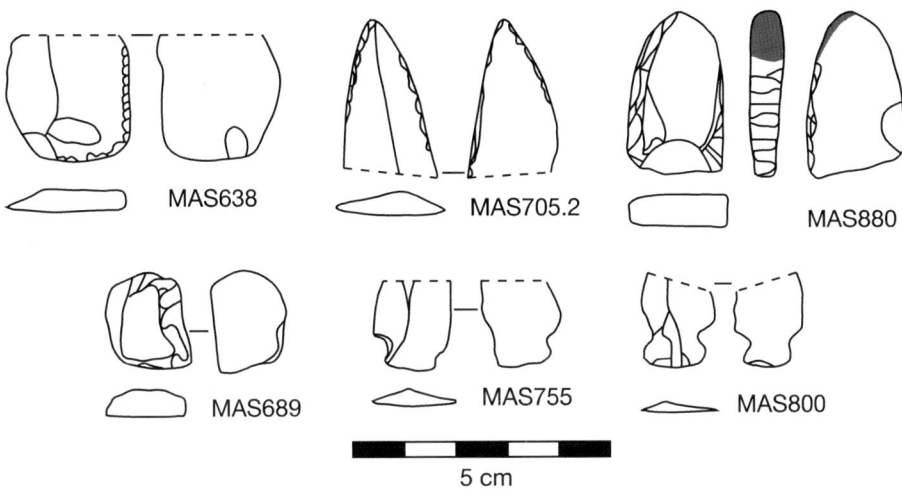

FIGURE 69. Formal chipped stone tools from Tuali-A occupation sites MAS638, MAS689, MAS705.2, MAS755, and MAS880.

in Zone B, where few sites with large chipped stone assemblages had been identified. Unworked pieces of chert, present at six sites, had the same standardized dimensions noted during the Siga occupation and likely were from the same source. In contrast to chert, quartz was very rare at Tuali-A occupation sites. One 151 g unworked piece was recovered from site MAS821 and a single piece of debitage was found at site MAS708.

Characterizing the Tuali-B Occupation

During the Tuali-B occupation (Figures 70 and 71; Table 44) many of the trends identified during the Tuali-A occupation intensified. Settlement shifted even more strongly toward the escarpment base and the range of variability in ceramic vessel forms and decoration decreased further. These changes were accompanied by the founding of the largest site recorded by the survey (MAS937), an increase in iron production, and, for the first time, the construction of specialized pits used for large-scale indigo dyeing. Despite these transformations, basic farming practices, as indicated by settlement patterns and site characteristics, remained remarkably stable.

I assigned sites to the Tuali-B occupation at two levels of confidence (see the methods described in detail in Chapter 3). Low-confidence sites ($n = 5$) had an almost identical distribution to high-confidence sites ($n = 32$) and are only discussed when they differ significantly. Additionally, several sites ($n = 13$) with multicomponent ceramic assemblages were identified. These sites are included in all discussions of spatial distribution, but analyses of artifact frequency and other characteristics of the sites themselves are confined to single-component sites.

Occupation Length and Characteristics
Consistent with previous occupations, most sites during the Tuali-B occupation were generally the size of household compounds and typically had only surface artifacts. As

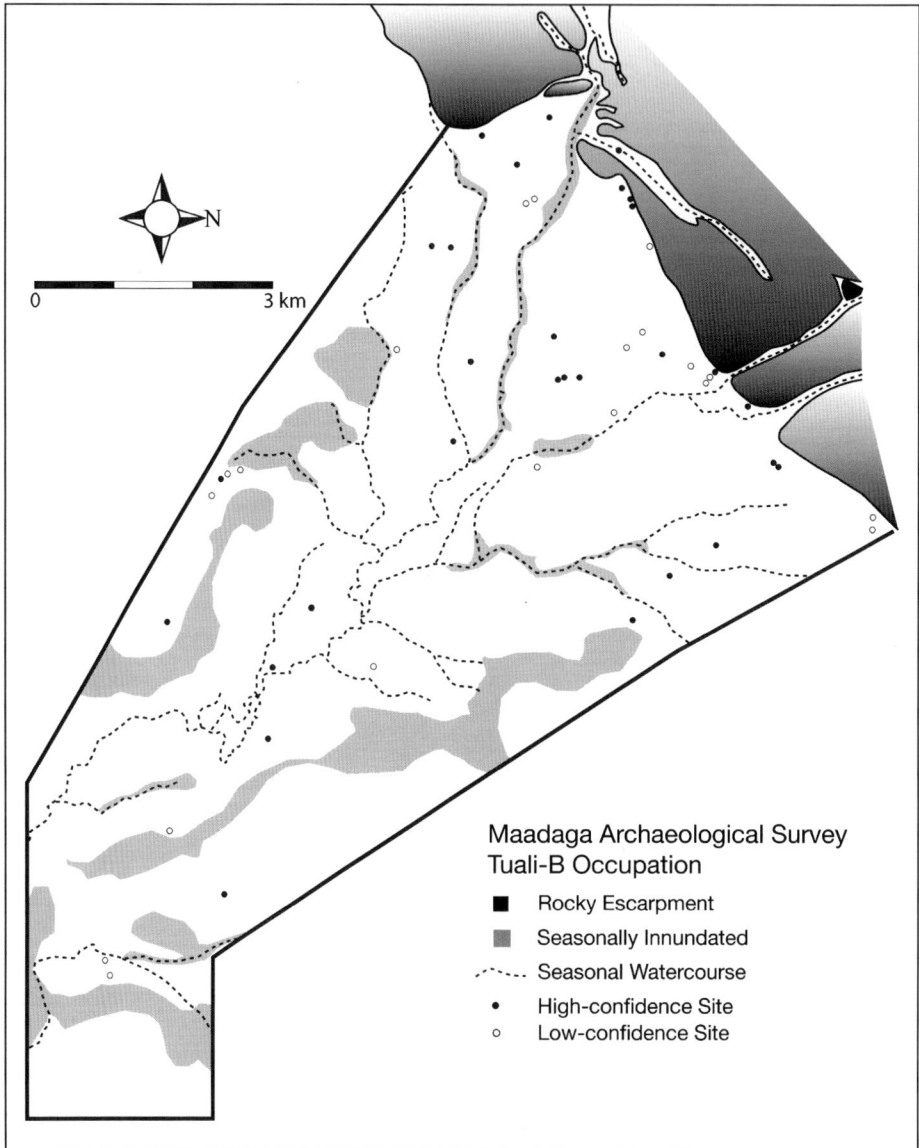

Figure 70. Tuali-B occupation sites identified by the Maadaga Archaeological Survey.

with the Tuali-A occupation, the estimated site depth was shallow and averaged less than 0.3 m. Seven shovel tests at site MAS937 in 2004 identified no subsurface deposits, even in areas with dense surface pottery, and we observed no subsurface deposits at the two sites with borrow pits.

With the exception of MAS937, site size during the Tuali-B occupation was overall even more tightly clustered than in the Tuali-A occupation, with twenty-two of the thirty-two high-confidence single-component sites measuring between 80 and 250 m². Of the three slightly larger sites (415 to 615 m²), two were indigo-dyeing installations; among the

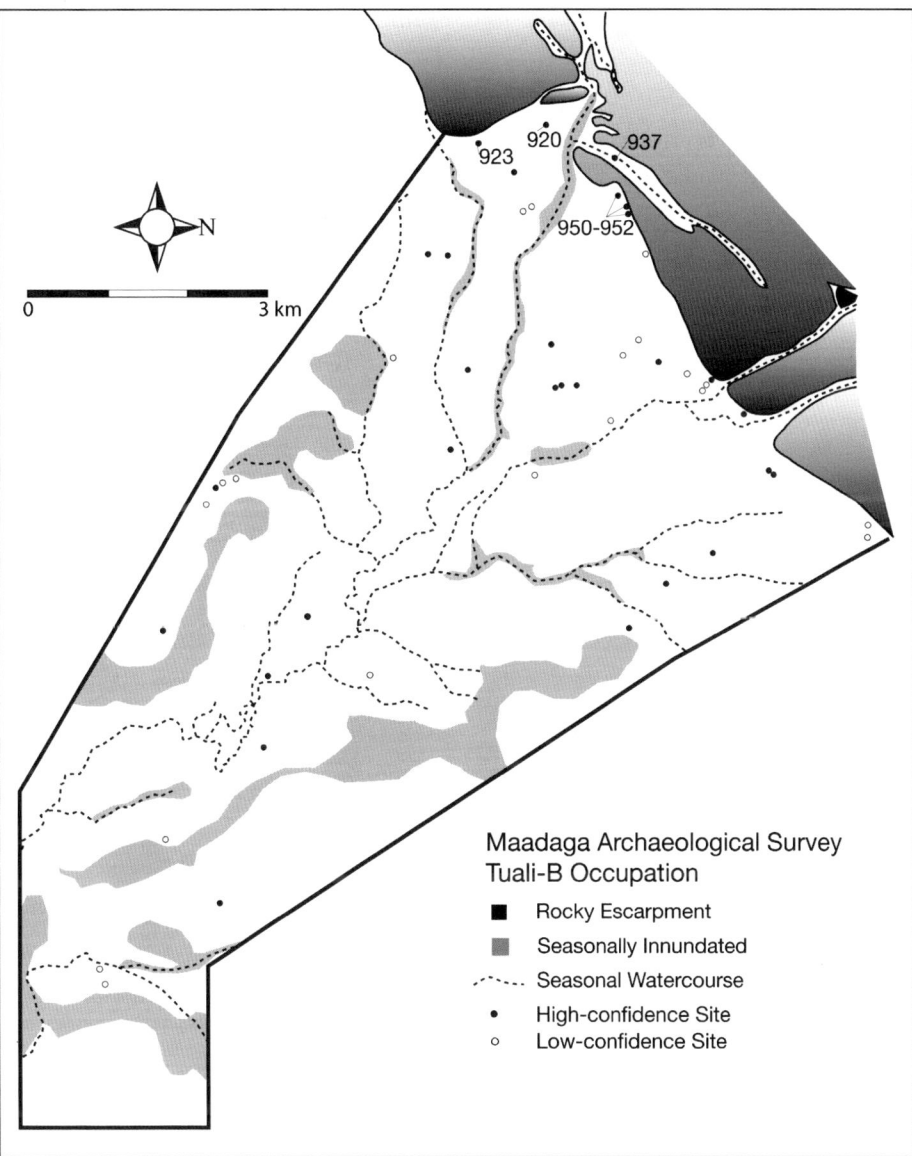

FIGURE 71. Locations of Tuali-B sites mentioned in the text.

six smaller sites, two were iron furnaces. Site MAS937 was a clear outlier at a conservative 10,000 m² and was the sole site with evidence for iron smelting, indigo dyeing, and residential activities in the same location.

The ceramic densities at Tuali-B sites were also consistent with the Tuali-A occupation, with medium sites having a lower mean of 24.5 g/m², due to the lack of high-density outliers and an almost identical median of 19.8 g/m². Site MAS937 had the median ceramic density, suggesting that despite its unique size and features, occupation length and residential activities may have been similar to other sites.

TABLE 44. Characteristics of Tuali-B occupation sites by assigned confidence level for single-component sites.

Site features	High-confidence sites	Low-confidence sites	All sites
Total number of sites	32	5	50
Near baobab trees	1	1	6
Near seasonal drainage	10	2	15
Near seasonal pool	1	0	2
Near seasonal inundation or marsh	3	0	5
Total sites near water	14	2	22
Plowing disturbance present	24	4	38
Borrow pit disturbance present	2	0	4
Chipped stone present	7	1	14
Ground stone present	18	3	25
Slag (rare)	2	0	3
Slag (present)	3	0	6
Iron smelting (small)	2	0	2
Iron smelting (medium)	1	1	3
Iron smelting (large)	1	0	1
Indigo dye pits	3	0	3

Unlike other sites identified in the survey region, site MAS937 was likely occupied by multiple households. Although sequential residence at many closely spaced households remains a possibility, no other example of similarly dense reoccupation was identified in the surveyed area (the closest analog is the site MAS572 Siga occupation cluster, which had clear spacing between households and no evidence of iron smelting). All ceramics from the site fell clearly within the Tuali-B assemblage, such that sequential occupation would have happened over a very short period. Activity areas (for iron and indigo) were easily identifiable, but ceramic concentrations seemed more linked to erosional processes than residences and the locations of individual households within the site could not be identified.

The founding of site MAS937 represents a significant shift toward nucleation, yet notably it was accompanied by maintenance of key characteristics that had persisted

TABLE 45. Ceramic assemblage characteristics of Tuali-B occupation sites and location by site size and distance from the Gobnangou escarpment (Zones 1 to 7) and the Koabu drainage (Zones A, B, and C; see also Figure 16).

	Number and size of sites (m^2)		
	Small (5–20)	Medium (75–615)	Large (>10,000)
Total number of sites	6	25	1
Zone 1	4	5	1
Zone 2	2	7	0
Zone 3	0	6	0
Zone 4	0	3	0
Zone 5	0	2	0
Zone 6	0	2	0
Zone 7	0	0	0
Zone A	6	21	1
Zone B	0	3	0
Zone C	0	1	0
	Ceramic assemblage characteristics		
Mean ceramic density (g/m^3)	37.8	24.7	19.8
Median ceramic density (g/m^3)	27.06	22.1	19.8
Mean number of decoration techniques in use per site	2.0	1.0	2.0
Mean number of decoration techniques in use per 100 sherds	10.9	4.7	6.4

from the Siga occupation onward. Sites the size of individual households remained common and even at MAS937, current evidence suggests occupation length did not increase significantly.

Spatial Distribution of the Tuali-B Occupation

The settlement pattern during the Tuali-B occupation showed a clear shift toward the base of the escarpment (see Figure 70; Tables 45 and 46). Although the entire study region was still occupied and settlement expanded once more into Zone 6 and possibly Zone 7, site occurrence decreased rapidly with distance. For the first time in the sequence sites were significantly more likely to be located in Zones 1 and 2 than in any other part of the surveyed area. This pattern was particularly pronounced for specialist activity sites, as they tended to be directly at the base of the escarpment. The shift was even more dramatic when

TABLE 46. Spatial distribution of Tuali-B occupation sites by distance from the Gobnangou escarpment (Zones 1 to 7) and the Koabu drainage (Zones A, B, and C; see also Figure 16). Numbers in parentheses are for single-component high-confidence sites only.

	Number of sites per zone							Total number	Total percentage
	Zone 1	Zone 2	Zone 3	Zone 4	Zone 5	Zone 6	Zone 7		
Zone A	17 (10)	13 (9)	6 (6)	2 (1)	2 (1)	2 (1)	—	42 (28)	84 (87.5)
Zone B	—	—	0 (0)	4 (2)	1 (1)	—	—	5 (3)	10 (9.4)
Zone C	—	—	—	0 (0)	0 (0)	1 (1)	2 (0)	3 (1)	6 (3.1)
Total number	17 (10)	13 (9)	6 (6)	6 (3)	3 (2)	3 (2)	2 (0)	50 (32)	
Total percentage	34 (31.3)	26 (28.1)	12 (18.8)	12 (9.4)	6 (6.3)	6 (6.3)	4 (0)		

the size of MAS937 was taken into account. Tucked into a small canyon running parallel to the escarpment face, its location would have been largely hidden from view to casual travelers through the region.

The spatial pattern of Tuali-B sites had some similarity to historical patterns described by Rémy (1967) for the community of Yobri on the north side of the escarpment. According to local oral histories collected by Rémy and Cartry, Yobri residents lived in dispersed households at some distance from the escarpment until the mid-nineteenth century, when raiding in the region forced them to move into nucleated villages against the edge of the escarpment. According to Rémy, an ethos of mobility was retained and Yobri's location moved four times over the course of forty years (possibly an increase in frequency due to the effects of nucleation on soil fertility). The potentially defensive position of site MAS937 could support the occurrence of similar security concerns in the surveyed area and, like Yobri, there was evidence that creation of larger settlements was not accompanied by significant changes in length of residence.

The relationship of the dispersed Tuali-B households to site MAS937 is currently unknown. In the Yobri case, during the colonial era administrators fixed community locations and forced farmers to maintain residence in these sedentary communities (Rémy 1967; Swanson 1979a). In response, farmers developed a system of dispersed seasonal residences adjacent to their fields (*kwadiegu*), where they lived during the rainy season. If the Tuali-B occupation extended into the colonial era, the single household sites could have been part of this system. Alternatively, perhaps the degree of nineteenth-century nucleation was not constant and during periods of greater security people returned to more dispersed settlement practices.

The Tuali-B Ceramic Assemblage

Like Tuali-A, the Tuali-B ceramic assemblage was relatively small in comparison to the Siga assemblage (only 767 sherds from high-confidence single-component sites; Figures 66 and 72; Table 47). In general, the Tuali-B occupation continued the trend toward greater homogeneity in pottery; the assemblage was almost entirely quartz-tempered and the range of vessel forms narrowed even further, with the elimination of large Sherd Type 9 vessels and a reduction in the diversity of untyped forms.

More than 80% of Tuali-B ceramics were quartz-tempered, with most of the remaining grog-tempered sherds from medium or small vessels. Although decoration rates dropped even more, the incidence of red-slipping increased, possibly in part due to better preservation of more recently produced vessels. Vessel form, characterized by primarily large flared jars (Sherd Type 11), remained consistent with the Tuali-A ceramic assemblage and the incidence of basal roughing (Sherd Type 14) almost doubled. The vessels associated with Sherd Type 11 remained consistent in size range (15 to 45 cm in diameter), as did untyped quartz-tempered rims (16 to 40 cm in diameter), which once again were most were likely from broken flare fragments from Sherd Type 11 jars. Among the much smaller set of untyped grog-tempered rims, vessel diameters covered a similar range (13 to 32 cm) and the forms were typically flared, similar to the quartz-tempered vessels. Only one example of the slightly everted open vessels found at Tuali-A sites was identified, although the sample size of grog-tempered rims was small.

Particularly notable in the Tuali-B assemblage was the introduction of wooden roulette decoration (Sherd Type 13) on the shoulders of vessels. This decoration was in the same location as braided strip roulette (Cord 6) on Sherd Type 12 vessels and seemed to

TABLE 47. Characteristics of the Tuali-B occupation ceramic assemblage by assigned confidence level for single-component sites. See also Appendix B.

	High-confidence sites	Low-confidence sites	All sites
Number of individually recorded sherds	767	80	1,207
Percentage of sherds with:			
Grog temper	15.8	37.5	20.2
Quartz temper	83.3	58.8	76.2
Grog and quartz temper	3.4	5.0	3.2
Mica and quartz temper	0.5	2.5	1.2
Red slip	19.6	8.8	20.4
Decoration	8.7	25.0	11.5
Number of decoration techniques	13	11	25
Mean number of decoration techniques per 100 sherds	5.9	22.9	10.1
Number of sherds assigned to:			
Sherd Type 1	0	1	2
Sherd Type 2	0	1	3
Sherd Type 3	0	1	3
Sherd Type 4	2	0	4
Sherd Type 5	0	0	3
Sherd Type 8	0	0	1
Sherd Type 10	0	0	2
Sherd Type 11	16	0	19
Sherd Type 12	0	0	2
Sherd Type 13	15	2	23
Sherd Type 14	60	0	81

replace it as a preferred decoration. Only thirteen decoration techniques were in use during the Tuali-B occupation. Of these, only carved wooden roulettes, twisted cord roulettes, and parallel channels were found at multiple sites (Table 48). Aside from wooden roulettes, most decorations occurred on grog-tempered sherds; 24% of untyped grog-tempered sherds were decorated as compared with only 2% of untyped quartz-tempered sherds.

In general, the Tuali-B ceramic assemblage can be interpreted in much the same way as the Tuali-A assemblage, with a narrow set of vessel forms used for a diverse set of

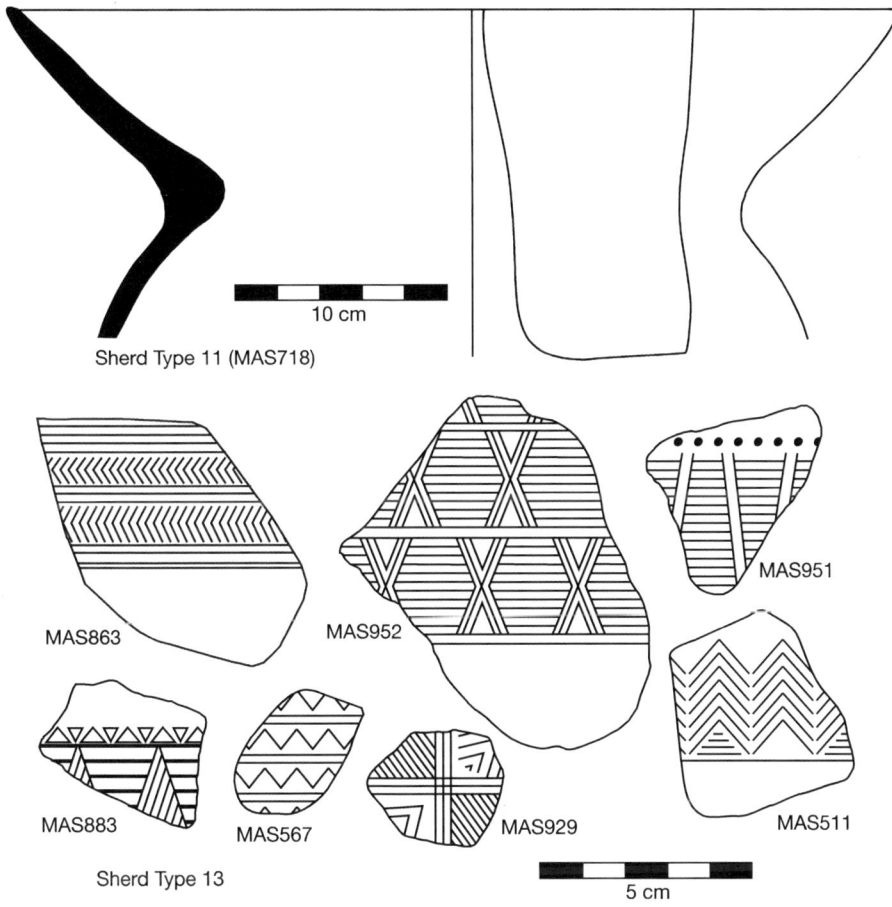

FIGURE 72. Tuali-B occupation ceramics Sherd Types 11 and 13 and associated sites.

functions. The elimination of Sherd Type 9 could be either due to replacement by vessels in another medium (unlikely given their size), expansion of the role of large flared jars, or a phasing out of their particular task. Large open basins were typically used for tasks involving large quantities of liquids, such as for water storage, brewing, dyeing, and tanning (see Chapter 6). During the 2004 and 2006 seasons, large flared jars similar in form to vessels associated with Sherd Type 11 were observed in use by contemporary households for water storage and brewing, a practice that could have originated during Tuali-B. Alternatively, in addition to their potential use as funerary jars, Sherd Type 9 pots may have been used for indigo dyeing and been phased out as dyers in the region began using pit technology (discussed below).

Iron Working

The Tuali-B occupation had the highest ratio of smelting sites to nonsmelting sites of any occupation in the study region and almost all were either large furnaces or complexes of multiple furnaces (Figure 73; Table 49). Unlike the Siga occupation, when furnace

TABLE 48. Ceramic decoration techniques in use during the Tuali-B occupation at high-confidence single-component sites. For sherd type descriptions see Appendix B. For full descriptions of decoration techniques see Tables 11–14.

Technique	Field code	Number of sherds (N = 67)	Number of sites (N = 32)	Associated sherd types
Twisted cord roulette	Cord 2	36	13	9, 12
Carved wooden roulette	TDC	13	6	13
Parallel channels	PC	6	4	
Carved wooden roulette	VC	5	5	13
Twisted knotted cord roulette	Cord 5	1	1	4
Channel	CH	1	1	
Circular impressions	CI	1	1	13
Rocker comb	COR	1	1	
Folded strip roulette	Cord 3	1	1	
Braided strip roulette	Cord 4	1	1	
Braided strip roulette	Cord 6	1	1	12
Other channels	IC	1	1	
Lip channel	LIPCH	1	1	15

sites (6.5% of high-confidence single-component sites) were distributed primarily along the Koabu, during the Tuali-B occupation furnaces (12.5% of high-confidence single-component sites) were clustered by the foot of the escarpment near the Koabu headwaters, creating a high density of smelting activity within a fairly constrained area. Although these furnaces could have been used sequentially or simultaneously, the concentration of activity suggests lower mobility of smelters, more intensive production, or a higher degree of specialization in production.

The positioning of smelting installations near the base of the escarpment could be indicative of widespread cultivation. As described in the previous chapter, smelting requires large quantities of wood charcoal. In general, the rocky slopes and proximal portions of the escarpment plateau within the study region have relatively little woody vegetation; it is necessary to travel several hundred meters or more into the escarpment to gather fuel. However, the escarpment also has shallow soils, which are rarely cultivated, and a position near the escarpment with access to this relatively stable wood source could have been favored for a charcoal-intensive task like iron smelting. None of the smelting sites were located directly adjacent to current primary drainage channels or permanent pools, but it is possible that water courses have shifted.

The possible evidence for smithing activity (that is, small quantities of slag at residential sites; see the Tuali-A discussion above) was much more consistent with previous occupations. Slag was present at a similar percentage of high-confidence single-component sites (approximately 15%) and was recovered from sites throughout the survey zone, including at sites in Zones B and C where there was no evidence of smelting activity during any occupation. This continuity in both the density and distribution of sites with slag is particularly interesting in light of the shifts in the organization of smelting activity.

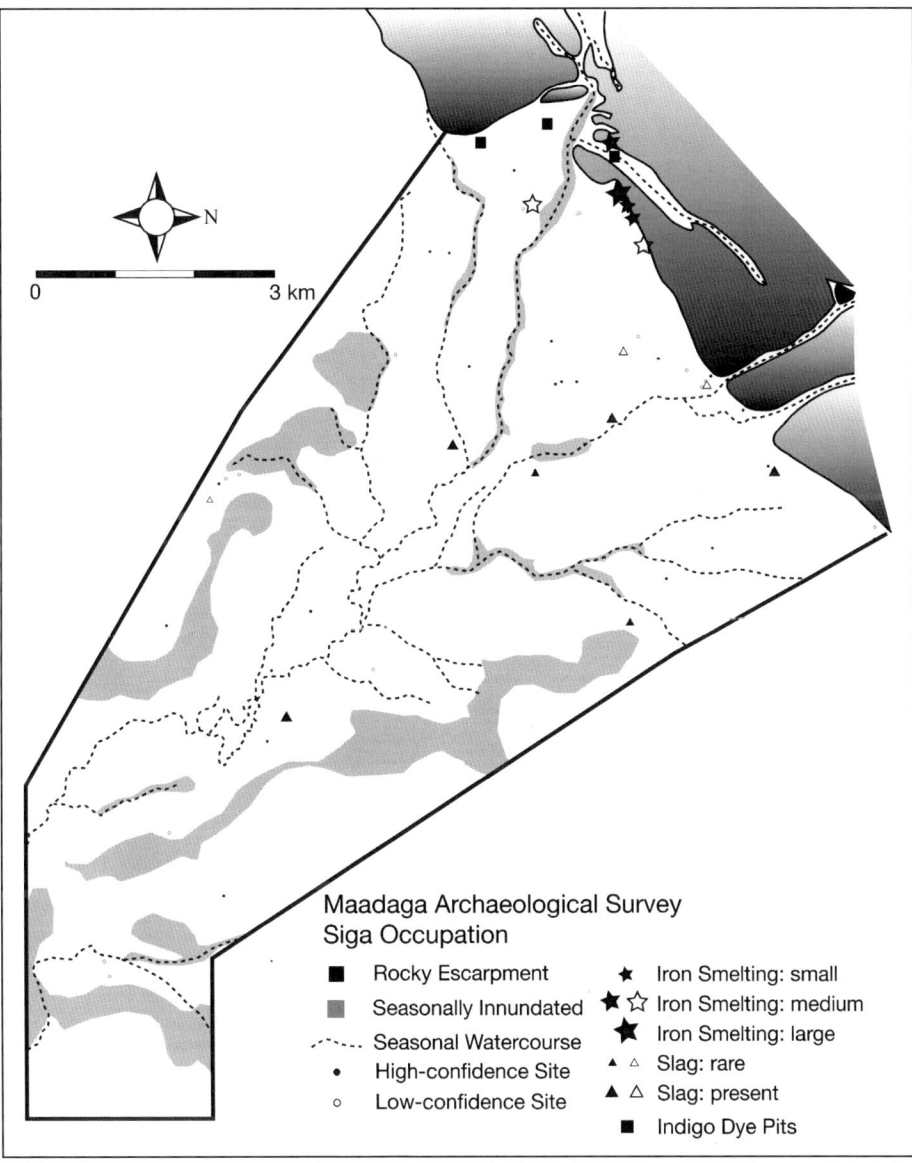

FIGURE 73. Distribution of iron-working and indigo dyeing activities during the Tuali-B occupation identified by the Maadaga Archaeological Survey. Black dots, stars, and triangles are high-confidence sites; open dots, stars, and triangles are low-confidence sites.

Ground Stone and Chipped Stone

Despite most sites being located closer to the escarpment, the observed ground stone remained consistent with both the Siga and Tuali-A occupations. Stones had a similar morphology and there were no indications of either an increase or a decrease in frequency. This regularity from throughout the sequence could suggest a relatively stable economic role for grinding and, therefore, potentially for the role of cereals in the local economy.

TABLE 49. Evidence of smelting and indigo dyeing activity at high- and low-confidence single-component sites during the Tuali-B occupation. Furnace categories are given as "small" (up to 5 m in diameter), "medium" (up to 10 m in diameter or multiple small furnaces), and "large" (greater than 10 m diameter or multiple small and medium furnaces). Furnace size is length by width.

Site	Category	Furnace size (m)	Evidence of smelting activity
MAS950	Large	19 × 8	A very large slag heap at least 1 m high, on a high bank overlooking a depressed area that can flood seasonally; there is a very large tuyère (interior diameter 8 cm, exterior diameter 19 cm)
MAS937	Medium	2 × 2, 3 × 3, 6 × 6	Several dense concentrations of slag
MAS953	Medium	7 × 9	Large, very dense slag pile with many vitrified tuyère fragments; interior diameter 3.8 cm for collected tuyère
MAS951	Small	4 × 4	Dense slag concentration disturbed by plowing
MAS952	Small	3 × 3	Dense slag concentration mixed with sandstone pieces

Site	Category	Number of dyeing pits	Evidence of indigo dyeing activity
MAS937	Indigo pits	>4 pits	Ash pile overgrown with small trees and brush; poorly visible, but edges of at least four pits identified
MAS920	Indigo pits	>4 pits	Large ash piles reaching 1.5 to 2 m in height, largely obscuring indigo pits; the four visible pits are 1 m in diameter and filled with ash
MAS923	Indigo pits	>12 pits	Lightly mounded ash surrounding and filling a complex of at least twelve pits; each around 1 m in diameter; plastered shallow pit may have been used for crushing indigo
None	Indigo pits	>22 pits	Large pit complex located along the escarpment north of Maadaga, 1.3 km outside survey zone; minimal ash present; pit diameters 1.25 to 1.5 m; pit depths 1.5 to 2.0 m

Several large *li naali* were found at the-iron smelting site MAS951; one was fairly flat with a 45 by 35 cm grinding surface and the other had a narrow 30 by 60 cm grinding hollow.

In contrast, the frequency of chipped stone decreased dramatically during the Tuali-B occupation; it was present at less than 25% of sites even though chipped stone was generally more common near the escarpment where most Tuali-B sites were located. If, as has been hypothesized in previous chapters, the role of chipped stone was as a firestarter or as an expedient sharp tool, the decrease in chipped stone use could possibly point to the availability of other tools, such as imported European products like steel blades and

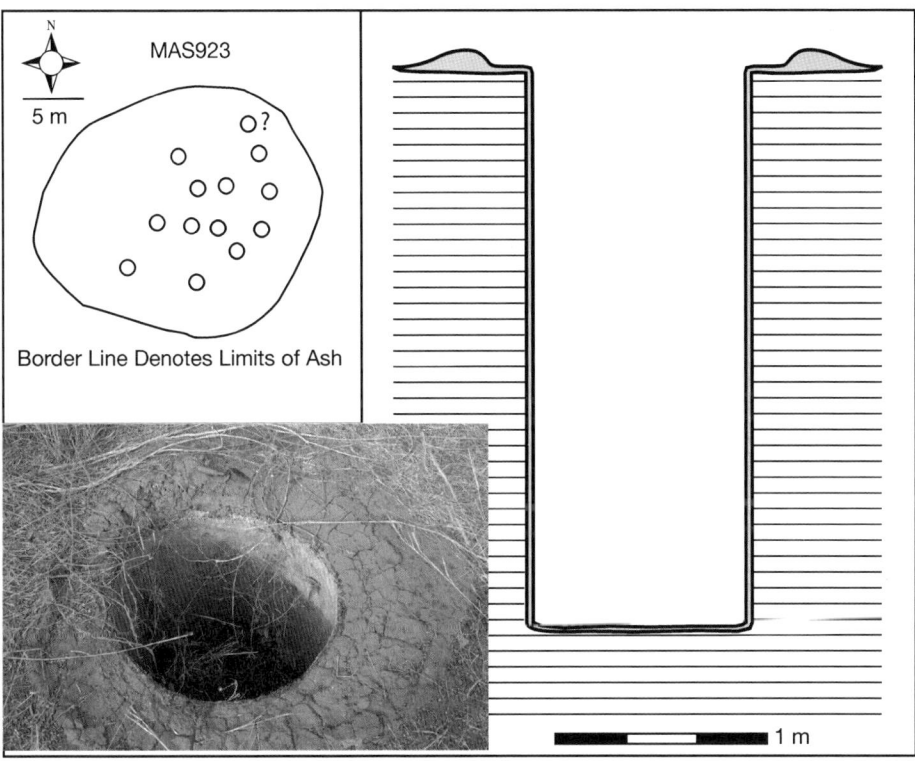

FIGURE 74. Indigo dye pit features. *Upper left*, plan of site MAS923; *lower left*, dye pit from a site north of Maadaga (1.3 km from the survey zone); *at right*, cross section of a dye pit from a site north of Maadaga (1.3 km from the survey zone).

matches. Although we have very little evidence for when European trade goods reached the interior, matches became popular in Europe in the mid-1800s and were for sale in Mossi markets by at the latest the early twentieth century (Mangin 1914; Pyne 2001).

Indigo Dyeing

Three large indigo-dyeing complexes consisting of plastered pits in mounds of ash were associated with the Tuali-B occupation (see Figure 73; Table 49). The pits were flush with the ground, around 1 m in diameter, and at least 2.5 m deep, if not more (Figure 74). The walls were finished with multiple layers of plaster, described by Geis-Tronich (1991) as a mixture of sediment drawn primarily from termite mounds, and in all cases the pits were surrounded by mounds of discarded potash. Of the three sites identified, MAS937 was overgrown with trees and brush, MAS920 was surrounded by very large ash piles over 2.0 m tall that likely obscured many of the dye pits (only four were visible), and MAS923 was deflated such that the rims of at least fourteen pits could be mapped (see Figure 74). There was a plastered, shallow depression at the edge of MAS923 that may have been used for crushing indigo. Another example, with twenty-two dye pits, was noted just outside the study region, at the north end of the currently occupied community of Maadaga. This site was deflated and unlike other sites, where the pits were filled to the rim with ash, many of these contained only some trash at their bottoms, which allowed better measurements of interior dimensions.

With the exception of site MAS937, the identified pit installations were not in association with household debris or adjacent to residential sites, which is unsurprising given the pungent smell of the dyes. Indigo dye pits are often considered an early nineteenth-century innovation, although their precise origin is unknown, and were associated with intensive cloth production (Shea 1975a, 1975b; Candotti 2010). If the large basins associated with Sherd Type 9 were previously used for dyeing, their replacement by pit complexes could represent a shift from a household-based practice to a specialist activity or at least one carried out collectively at common sites. The practical and social implications of these features are discussed in detail below.

Dating the Tuali-A and Tuali-B Occupations

Dating the Tuali-A and Tuali-B occupations was particularly challenging. No datable organic materials were recovered from these sites and they were not found in, or in association with, any stratified deposits. Of the two occupations, Tuali-A was considered likely to be the oldest, given the continuity of large open vessels with ridges (Sherd Type 9) from the Siga occupation. Tuali-B sites had significant similarity in ceramics with Tuali-A sites, but stopped using the large open vessels and replaced braided strip roulette with wooden roulettes (Sherd Type 13). The use of the latter decoration is documented in the twentieth-century ethnohistorical record (Geis-Tronich 1991) and also occurs in eighteenth- and nineteenth-century CE sites in the Dendi region (Haour 2019; see the discussion in Appendix B). It is possible that there was overlap between the Tuali-A and Tuali-B occupations, in which case the observed variability in the ceramic assemblages could represent different facets or variations of a single ceramic assemblage rather than temporal change.

The two most unique aspects of the Tuali-B occupation were the founding of a large residential site (MAS937) and the construction of indigo-dyeing pits. If events in the surveyed area followed the same timeline described in oral histories from Yobri, nucleation dated to the nineteenth century. Pit dyeing techniques may have spread to the study region from northern Nigeria in response to increasing demand for dyed cloth in the nineteenth-century Sokoto Caliphate or from central Burkina Faso, where indigo dyeing was of significance in Mossi and other Gulmance kingdoms. Thiombiano-Ilboudo (2010:269) argues that in the region near Fada N'Gourma dye pits date from the eighteenth century onward. Dye pits are still common in northern Nigeria, but in the study region there were no pit complexes in active use; however, older adults in Maadaga said that dye pits had been used by the previous generation. Together, these lines of evidence suggested a date for Tuali-B sites between 1800 and 1960 CE. If chipped stone was indeed in use primarily as a firestarter, its decrease in frequency further supports nineteenth- and twentieth-century dates for Tuali-B sites. The end of Tuali-B was bracketed by the Ring occupation sites (see Appendix C), which because of the presence of plastic and bottle glass likely dated to after 1960 CE.

There were fewer lines of evidence available with which to date the Tuali-A occupation, although it was bracketed by the Siga occupation, which could have ended as early as 1300–1400 CE or as late as 1650 CE (see the discussions in Chapter 6), and by the Tuali-B occupation, which likely began in the early nineteenth century. Pipes were more common during the Tuali-A occupation, which suggests a post-1600 CE date for these sites, although the same concerns about the use of isolated surface finds of these easily lost portable objects (discussed in Chapter 6) applied to the Tuali-A occupation as well. Although tobacco pipes can be heirlooms, the double-angle pipe (1600–1800 CE?) from site MAS603 did fit the proposed chronology. Finally, as discussed in more detail below, the simplification of ceramic decoration was a widespread phenomenon in the fifteenth- to seventeenth-century West African savanna and could potentially be considered a proxy indicator in and of itself. Whereas the timing of the Siga to Tuali-A transition remains uncertain, the Tuali-A occupation may date from 1300–1650 to 1800 CE.

The Tuali Occupation in Regional Context

The Tuali occupation encompassed a period of dramatic transformations to the north and south. In the south, European trade along the coast began in the fifteenth century and expanded rapidly, reorienting the flow of exchange within West Africa. By the sixteenth century, large forest-belt states were trading enslaved people and both manufactured and natural products (cloth, animal products, and gold) for European tradewares such as cloth, metal goods, ceramics, and glass (Alpern 1995). The ways in which this trade affected areas as far north as the study region is unknown. At a material level, by the sixteenth century European-manufactured ceramics were a major artifact class at sites on the coast, along with European-made clay pipes, gunflints, and beads (e.g., DeCorse 2001; Kelly 2009; Norman 2009; Monroe and Ogundiran 2012; Monroe 2014), while in central Ghana, Benin, and Nigeria European trade goods were not as immediately prominent and remained rare, although they gradually become more common through the seventeenth to nineteenth centuries CE (e.g., York 1973; Stahl 2001, 2002; Ogundiran 2009; Gurstelle, Labiyi, and Agani 2015; Compton 2017; Haour 2019). The influence of the Atlantic exchange at these inland locations is seen in the widespread ubiquity of African-made smoking pipes, as well as in the trade of particular cowrie species (see the discussions in Haour and Christie [2019]). Neither necessitated direct access to Atlantic coast markets.

Although direct material evidence of inland influence of the Atlantic exchange was scarce (many of the primary products, such as gold, kola, metals, and cloth, did not preserve well in the material record), the social and political changes caused by the reorientation of trade routes and the consequences of both external and internal trade in enslaved people were profound. For example, in northern Ghana there was evidence from the seventeenth to nineteenth centuries for the construction of defensive walls, for the movement to defensive locations such as inselbergs and caves, and for the creation of new marketplaces and the enrichment of merchant families (Kankpeyeng 2009; Swanepoel 2009).

To the north and west, large and diverse dynamic political entities covered much of northern Ghana and Burkina Faso. As discussed in previous chapters, although it is possible that many of the Voltaic states and empires (e.g., Mossi, Dagomba, Nunumba, and Gulmance) had already been founded during the preceding Siga occupation, many scholars place their origins closer to the middle of the second millennium CE (e.g., Madiéga 1982, 2009; Madiéga et al. 1983; Izard 2003; N'Dah 2009; Thiombiano-Ilboudo 2010). Nungu (Fada N'Gourma), the center of the Gulmance kingdoms, may have been founded in the eighteenth century CE (Madiéga 1982). The study region would have been buffered by the other Gulmance kingdoms and the Mossi kingdoms from events farther to the north, including the rise and fall of the Songhai empire. In comparison to the forest states to the south, there has been less archaeological research in the territory of the Mossi, with the exception of research on iron working north of Ouagadougou (Kiéthéga 2009; Simpore 2009; Thiombiano-Ilboudo 2012b; Serneels 2017) and survey in the far northwestern corner of the Mossi empire (Marchal 1978; Lingané 1995). In northern Ghana, excavations at Yendi Dabari, a sixteenth- and seventeenth-century CE capital of Dagomba, revealed large, multistoried structures and dense material remains at a 2 ha site (Shinnie and Ozanne 1962). Regardless, Mossi and Gulmance both persisted as independent political entities until the early twentieth century and their leaders continue to fulfill important public roles in Burkina Faso today. Consequently, during the Tuali occupation the study region was almost certainly incorporated into the Gulmance kingdoms, although the nature of the political and economic obligations to the center at Nungu (Fada N'Gourma) likely varied over time (see Chapter 8).

Thiombiano-Ilboudo's (2010) research at multiple sites in the Fada N'Gourma region provides a point of comparison to the investigations in the Gobnangou region. Most of these sites likely date to the same period covered by the Tuali occupation. Her work found thriving complex communities with dense settlement, significantly larger-scale iron working than has been observed in the Gobnangou region for any period, and an investment in indigo dyeing. Thiombiano-Ilboudo also documented many laterite fortifications and defensive structures (*bilnu*), which she describes as present throughout the Gulmance territories, although these are particularly common (or well documented) in the northeast in Gnaga Province and in eastern Fada N'Gourma Province (Madiéga et al. 1983; Thiombiano-Ilboudo 2010).

The pottery illustrated in Thiombiano-Ilboudo's published work has very few similarities to those recovered by the Maadaga Archaeological Survey (with the exception of a possible Sherd Type 9 vessel). However, Thiombiano-Ilboudo does note the use of specific decorations found on sherds collected by Frank and colleagues (2001) and Wotzka and Goedicke (2001), notably comb impressions and twisted cord roulettes, that are not among those common in Tuali-B assemblages. There is no clear evidence for the wooden roulettes characteristic of Tuali-B (although see the discussions in Appendix B).

To the northeast of the study region, archaeological and oral history research in the Dendi region describes a complex mosaic of communities located near a major crossing point along the Niger River (Haour 2019; see especially Gosselain and Haour [2019], Gosselain and Smolderen [2019], and Haour and Nixon [2019]). After what may have been a brief hiatus in the mid-second millennium CE with the abandonment of tell sites such as Birnin Lafiya, many new settlements were founded in the seventeenth, eighteenth, and nineteenth centuries. These settlements did not accumulate the depth of cultural deposits present at earlier sites and many of them relocated several times for a variety of reasons, among them regional violence. During this time, communities included members of trading diasporas from both the Mande region (evidenced by oral histories, family names, and the introduction of *Blepharis* sp. roulettes after 1600 CE) and both northern and potentially southern Nigeria in addition to more local groups, among them Gulmance. Although the ceramic assemblage was very different from both the Tuali-A and Tuali-B ceramic assemblages, wooden roulette decorations identical to those from Tuali-B were identified at multiple nineteenth-century sites (see the discussion in Appendix B).

Farther east, in what is today northeastern Nigeria, there were Hausa city states from at least the mid-second millennium CE until 1804 CE, when Sheikh Uthman dan Fodio unified the region under the Sokoto Caliphate (Effah-Gyamfi 1986; Kuba 2009; Haour and Rossi 2010; Sule and Haour 2014). Despite the political changes, evidence suggests that the major urban centers (e.g., Kano, Katsina, and Zaria) continuously maintained their economic centrality. There has likewise been little archaeological research in the western part of this region, although excavations at mounded sites near the Sokoto River, such as Birnin Leka, have found potsherd pavements, glass bracelets and beads, clay beads or spindle whorls, clay tobacco pipes, and marine shells in addition to domestic pottery and animal bone (Obayemi 1973; Sule and Haour 2014). These sites had striking material indicators of wealth and access to trade items when compared to sites from this time in the Gobnangou region. The potential links between this region and the study area based on the use of plastered dye pits is discussed in detail in the next section.

More locally, in northern Benin the Atakora region is thought to have been outside the control of not only the Gulmance kingdoms, but also the complex polities (e.g., Bariba) to the south and the Hausa states to the east (Petit 2005; N'Dah 2009). N'Dah (2009) argues that throughout the second half of the second millennium CE the region may have been a refuge for diverse populations seeking to avoid the influence of these expanding states. As described in previous chapters, settlement mounds in northern Benin were abandoned between the twelfth and fifteenth centuries CE, at which point the population became more mobile, resulting in more ephemeral sites. These more ephemeral sites were also characterized by intensive iron smelting (evidenced by large slag heaps and tuyères) and had high densities of ground stone. Petit (2005) divided this period into two groups according to their ceramics. The carved roulette group was confined to the mountains and the northern plains of his study area. Unlike the Gulmance, local communities in northern Benin did not use carved wooden roulettes nor remember their use in the past. For this reason, Petit assigned these sites to 1400–1800 CE. The second, more widespread group was characterized by the use of rocker stamping and cord and strip roulettes and had strong similarities with early twenty-first-century pottery in the region.

There were points of both articulation and contradiction between the Gobnangou and northern Benin sequences. Ephemeral sites with evidence of iron working were found in both regions and there was some evidence of a move toward the highlands, similar to the shift in residence toward the escarpment during the Tuali occupation. Petit's carved roulette group had clear parallels to the Tuali-B assemblage. However, the dating, particularly for the carved wooden roulette group, was different than that proposed for the Gobnangou region and his rocker stamped group has no clear analog in Tuali-A or Tuali-B ceramics. While the rocker stamped group did include deeply impressed strip roulettes as in the Tuali-A assemblage, it lacked large open vessels analogous to Sherd Type 9 and its primary decoration techniques (rocker stamping) were absent in the Tuali-A assemblage. Once again, although similar on a macroscale, the particulars are distinct enough that the trajectories seemed to be largely independent.

Indigo Dyeing during the Tuali Occupation: Techniques and Social Implications

Cotton cloth has a long history in West Africa and, as evidenced by fragments from cave sites in Mali dating to the eleventh to twelfth centuries CE, it has been produced for hundreds of years by weaving handspun cotton thread, often dyed dark blue with indigo, into narrow strips (Geis-Tronich 1989, 1991; Kriger 2006). In the study region, the first potential direct evidence for weaving and dyeing of cotton cloth was a possible partial spindle whorl recovered from a Tuali-A site. More definitely, during the Tuali-B occupation three major indigo-dyeing installations were constructed, each consisting of multiple plastered dye pits surrounded by mounds of ash. Given the sparse evidence for weaving, the discussion here will focus primarily on indigo dyeing.

Indigo Dye: The Technical Process

Indigo dye is typically made from the leaves of many species of *Indigofera*, which differ widely in their indigotin content. *Lonchocarpus cyanescens,* or Yoruba indigo, which produces a dye on a par with many *Indigofera* species, has not been identified in botanical surveys of the study region, although it is commonly used in northern Nigeria (Burkill 1995; Küppers 1996; Kriger 2006; Ouédraogo et al. 2011). Its relative, *Lonchocarpus laxiflorus,* does grow wild in the region, but the quality of its dye is considered inferior.

According to Geis-Tronich (1991), *Indigofera tinctoria,* a domesticated species originating in India but possibly with great antiquity in West Africa, was the only indigo cultivated in the study region in the 1980s. The same species is also described by Thiombiano-Ilboudo (2010:264) as in use in the early twentieth century near Fada N'Gourma. Leaves were collected at the end of the rainy season in November, pounded, mixed with ash, and formed into balls or logs that were left to dry for over a year (Geis-Tronich 1991; Thiombiano-Ilboudo 2010). These balls could be traded and Kriger (2006) has suggested that in some cases their standardization may have contributed to an increase in the scale of production for indigo cloth by facilitating the consistent production of effective dyes.

Indigo is not water soluble and its preparation requires an alkaline solution that is usually made with salts, particularly potash (Kriger 2006; Thiombiano-Ilboudo 2010). Potash production begins by carbonizing a carefully chosen wood; Geis-Tronich (1991) recorded the use of *Sclerocarya birrea* and Thiombiano-Ilboudo (2010) mentions *Vitellaria paradoxa,* but several species have been documented in other regions of West Africa (Portères 1950). The resulting ash is leached once using a filtration process that can involve using two-pot perforated strainers or baskets, or simply pouring ash mixed with water through a layer of fibers (Portères 1950; Geis-Tronich 1991; Folorunso 2002; Kriger 2006). Perforated pots, which may be for steaming or straining, were regularly identified during the Siga occupation and occurred very occasionally at Tuali-A and Tuali-B sites. None of the perforated sherds from Tuali occupation sites had the larger holes (more than 2 cm) associated with specialized potash straining pots that I saw in use in western Burkina Faso in the early 2000s.

To mix the dye, indigo and potash are combined with water to form a clear solution, which is then allowed to rest, covered, for approximately one week to ten days (Shea 1975a; Geis-Tronich 1991). The cloth is dipped or soaked in the dye, sometimes transferred to a second pit for rinsing, then left to dry in the sun. It is only at this stage that the dye oxidizes and the cloth takes on its characteristic dark blue color. There is significant room for error throughout the process, as the deepness and permanence of the color depends on the species, the preparation of the indigo, the type of potash or salt added to the dye, and the timing of the dye process (Kriger 2006). Thiombiano-Ilboudo (2010:266) describes two colors produced ethnohistorically in the Fada N'Gourma region: *wanuama* (light black), which is made by quickly dyeing and washing the cloth, and *libonbonli* (black), created by dyeing the cloth two or three times. Geis-Tronich (1991) and Shea (1975a) both described dyers tasting the indigo solution to test its alkalinity.

The indigo dye solution is usually prepared in large clay pots or in plastered pits. Although the basic process is the same in both cases, pits are associated with larger-scale production. Monteil (1927:85) went even further, suggesting that dye pits were used by "professionals"; that is, full- or part-time specialists. Some specialists used pots (e.g., Folorunso 2002), but no examples could be found in the West African ethnohistorical record of occasional dyers constructing pit complexes. Descriptions of dye pits suggested that they are remarkably standardized across the savanna zone of West Africa, with those identified in the study region falling well within the normal range of variation according to both ethnographic and archaeological research (Monteil 1927; Shea 1975a; Geis-Tronich 1991; Kriger 2006; Sule Sani 2010; Thiombiano-Ilboudo 2010; Giade 2016).

Social and Historical Implications of Weaving and Dyeing

While it is possible, even likely, that cotton cloth was woven and dyed during the Siga occupation (possibly in the large Sherd Type 9 vessels), the dye pit installations of the Tuali occupation indicate a significant expansion of the economic role of cloth production. The scale of production suggests involvement in commercial relationships.

The West African cloth trade is thought to have expanded throughout the latter half of the second millennium CE; historical records from the coast clearly show the importance of cloth for export by European traders to markets outside West Africa, as well as among indigenous coastal polities throughout the seventeenth and eighteenth centuries CE (Kriger 2006). Most of this cloth was produced on vertical looms in the south, but the cotton thread may have come from areas farther to the north. In the nineteenth century, when the price of cloth produced in Europe and the Americas decreased dramatically because of the innovations of the industrial revolution, the export market for West African cloth largely disappeared. However, it was replaced by a robust internal market for traditionally produced cloth. The local demand for this cloth was sufficiently great that several colonial attempts throughout the latter half of the nineteenth into the twentieth century to funnel raw cotton from West Africa into European markets met with almost total failure (Roberts 1996).

In the Fada N'Gourma region, Thiombiano-Ilboudo (2010:254) describes dye pits (*siébuogu* in Gulmancema) as common and studied multiple installations in depth. For example, at Yiendéni at Kouaré she documented a group of seven clay-plastered pits dug 65 to 70 cm into laterite for stability with evidence of a superstructure that added depth (Thiombiano-Ilboudo 2010:254–255). Pits at several sites were similar to those at Yiendéni; however, near Kouaré she described a more recent installation that had a more complex plastering, but also used an above-ground structure to increase the depth of the pit (Thiombiano-Ilboudo 2010:256). These latter pits were more similar to those at Fada N'Gourma, where the presence of ashes made it difficult to determine whether above-ground structures were in place (Thiombiano-Ilboudo 2010:262). She ascribes these different dye pit forms to the influence of different populations, including those from the south, from Mali, and from the Hausa region of Nigeria. Thiombiano-Ilboudo suggests that the demand for cloth was high in this densely populated area and that these installations largely produced cloth for a local market.

Cloth production in the Gobnangou region may also have been affected by the creation of the Sokoto Caliphate in 1804, which actively promoted an increase in cloth production in northern Nigeria (Candotti 2010). According to Shea (1975a) in his history of cloth production in the Kano Emirate (the main center of cloth production within the

Sokoto Caliphate), the shift to the use of plastered dye pits in the nineteenth century was strongly associated with increased production of dyed cloth. Nast (2008) has argued that indigo dyeing in Kano was traditionally done by women, who controlled this symbolically potent craft and pioneered a transition from above-ground pots to inset pots. She places the nineteenth-century expansion in commercial cloth production and construction of pits in the context of changing gender relations under the Sokoto Caliphate and argues that the state facilitated male appropriation of this increasingly economically important and commoditized activity.

In the first half of the nineteenth century most commercial cloth production in northern Nigeria took place near major centers such as Sokoto, Kano, and Zaria, but by the second half of that century the need for more land for cotton cultivation had pushed production into rural areas. At the same time, increased taxes on production caused many merchants and artisans to move to the periphery of the caliphate (Candotti 2010:204). Although the eastern boundary of the Sokoto Caliphate is typically drawn near the Niger River, more than 125 km east of the study region, according to twentieth-century ethnographers and historians the Gobnangou region was integrated into Hausa trading networks (Rémy 1967; Madiéga 1982).

Dye pit complexes were common at eighteenth- and nineteenth-century sites in the Dendi region, where indigo dyeing activities were closely associated not only with trade, but also with migrants along these trade routes (Gosselain and Haour 2019; Gosselain and Smolderen 2019). According to oral traditions, indigo dyeing centers in the region had strong links to Mande and other Niger Bend dyeing traditions. Gosselain and Haour (2019) suggest that the role of Hausa in the indigo cloth trade to the west of Sokoto may be overemphasized. The dye pits are not described, so it is difficult to determine whether they have the same structure as those found in the Gobnangou region.

Although historically the Gulmance political context differed significantly in both concentration of state power and its religious underpinnings, the transition toward pit dyeing during the Tuali-B occupation could be linked to changes in the assignment of gender roles to this craft, as Nast (2008) has argued for Sokoto. Notably, the construction of dye pits was likely accompanied by movement of indigo dyeing out of the household. The distribution of these pit complexes in locations distant from residences mirrored that of iron smelting (a universally male activity in the West African ethnohistorical record), although practical considerations (such as heat and smells) may also have been behind this spatial arrangement. In the ethnohistorical record of the Gobnangou region, twentieth-century dyers who used pits were male (Geis-Tronich 1991). In contrast, Gosselain and Haour (2019:303) discuss oral histories in the Dendi region that describe dye pit technology as imported from Mali and enthusiastically adopted, which points to different potential histories for this technology.

Shea (1975a:163) estimated that construction of an individual pit took about twenty days (a timeline that could include waiting for the plaster to dry), but once completed an individual dyer could dye more cloth with significantly less effort. There were thousands of pits within the Kano Emirate at its peak, but "prosperous dyers" within the city itself generally controlled only five to ten pits at the most (Shea 1975a:165; Candotti 2010:200). By this measure, the fourteen pits from site MAS923 alone were indicative of a large dye center, particularly for a rural area. In the Fada N'Gourma region, Thiombiano-Ilboudo's (2010:262) discussions with elders about the construction of dye pits also described a labor-intensive process, albeit one that seems to have taken less time.

Dye pits in rural areas were generally located where indigo could be locally grown and water was plentiful during the dry season. Shea noted that a single batch of dye used more than 65 kg of fresh indigo. This figure could be high for dye pits in the Gobnangou region, because Shea did not specify the size of the pit (pits in Kano could reach 6 m deep, although most were 2.5 to 3.5 m deep) or the intensity of the desired color. In this sense, the Gobnangou region would have been ideal for indigo cloth production: surface water was available year-round and the low-lying swampy areas favored by indigo were common, as were the well-drained soils favored by cotton.

Given the necessary capital investment (dye pit construction, indigo and cotton farming, and the weaving or purchase of cotton cloth) and the rapid increase in scale of indigo cloth production suggested by the archaeological sites in the study region, it is reasonable to assume that dyers were serving markets outside the local community, whether through direct trade or middlemen. The Gobnangou region had links to Hausa trade routes and the dye pits have more structural similarities to those from northern Nigeria than those described near Fada N'Gourma by Thiombiano-Ilboudo. However, demand for indigo cloth was also high from the political centers of the Gulmance and Mossi polities (Shea 1975a; Skinner 1989; Thiombiano-Ilboudo 2010) and it is equally likely that the cloth trade was focused on the north and west.

Iron and Indigo in the Gobnangou

Settlement during the Tuali occupation showed significant continuity with previous occupations. Most sites are approximately the same size and are similarly thin. There was no evidence of a decrease in mobility and, particularly during the Tuali-A occupation, people were likely still living in dispersed household compounds that moved regularly. There is evidence of settlement nucleation with the founding of site MAS937 and a shift toward the escarpment in the Tuali-B occupation. Before the MAS, researchers had long noted the settlement trend of movement toward the escarpment in the Gobnangou during the past several hundred years. This move has been almost universally attributed to the need to seek refuge from raiders: Rémy (1967) described previously dispersed households aggregating near the escarpment for security; Millogo and Koté (2000) noted the appearance of "hidden" granaries built into caves (see also Appendix D); and Frank and colleagues (2001) reported local oral traditions to this effect.

Thiombiano-Ilboudo (2010) documented a variety of fortifications near Fada N'Gourma, including laterite wall foundations and large rocks placed to provide shelter from arrows. In the Gobnangou region, Madiéga and colleagues (1983) mention the influence of raids leading to the construction of fortifications at Partiaga and Namounou on the western side of the escarpment (see the discussion in Thiombiano-Ilboudo [2010]). In regions such as northern Ghana, where there was also clear evidence for insecurity and raiding, communities not only constructed fortifications, but also moved into defensive locations (e.g., Swanepoel 2009). In contrast, in the Dendi region where there was significant unrest and several communities were burned in the 1800s, there is little surviving evidence for formal fortifications (largely made of wood and coursed earth) and oral histories describe the dense bushy vegetation as having offered significant security (Brunfaut and Pinet 2019).

In the survey region the evidence was slightly more ambiguous. The move toward the escarpment was not absolute. Although MAS937 was perhaps located defensively in a small hidden canyon, many sites were still several hundred, if not thousands, of meters from the shelter of its canyons and ravines. As will be seen below, the settlement shift was accompanied by a significant expansion in craft production and likely greater participation in regional trade, a trade that was probably relatively stable given the high levels of investment in indigo dye pits.

With no direct evidence, it was difficult to assess changes in farming, gathering, hunting, and herding practices during the Tuali-A or Tuali-B occupation. The distribution of sites and maintenance of mobility practices suggested that the basic practices of farming remained the same; there was no evidence for intensification of production or increased length of residence at individual sites. The narrow distribution of site size (aside from MAS937) and lack of differentiation in the ceramic assemblage suggested generalized site purpose; there was no evidence for the use of field huts or other seasonal occupation strategies that might have been indicated by an increase in the number of small or low-density sites. It is possible that increased cultivation of millet, cotton, or groundnuts favored occupation in areas closer to the escarpment (as these plants prefer well-drained soils).

Likewise, it is important to consider the potential consequences of the adoption of new crop plants originating in the Americas (see Table 6). It is unquestionable that introduced foods—including maize, peanuts, tomatoes, and peppers—have become essential in the local diet, yet the process, speed, and timing of their incorporation is still largely unknown in inland areas of West Africa (Gallagher 2016; for an exception see Logan [2016]). Because New World plants likely spread to the study region from the coast, varieties that were probably first used favored moister climates and may have been initially grown primarily near drainages.

Presumably, residents continued their gathering and hunting activities, but herding of domesticated animals, particularly cattle, was rarely documented among Gulmance populations of the study region during the twentieth century (Rémy 1967; Swanson 1979b). Instead, the local residents obtained access to these animals through trade with Fulani herders who moved into the region during the dry season. This represented a significant change from the Pwoli and Siga occupations, when dwarf cattle were raised locally. Although the MAS project collected no evidence that could be used to assess the timing of this transition, it is possible that these arrangements were first negotiated during the Tuali occupation.

A major feature of the Tuali-A and Tuali-B occupations was the simplification of pottery traditions. This phenomenon was not confined to the study region, but has been noted during the latter half of the second millennium CE at archaeological sites throughout the West African savanna region (e.g., S. K. McIntosh, Gallagher, and R. J. McIntosh 2003; Petit 2005; Dueppen and Gallagher 2016). Several arguments have been made for the reasons behind simplification in ceramic traditions, including: restricted access to elaborate material culture in contexts of increasing social and political stratification (Wengrow 2001; Pollock 2013); changes in labor priorities due to shortages (Logan and Cruz 2014), increasing consumer demand (Sinopoli 2003), or the effects of plague (Dueppen and Gallagher 2016; Gallagher and Dueppen 2018); shifts in aesthetic expression (Dueppen and Gallagher 2016); and changes in the social role of ceramics (Ashley 2010; Dueppen and Gallagher 2016).

As mentioned above, the apparent decline in social investment in ceramics could correspond with increasing importance of another class of vessel, possibly the bottle gourd or calabash (*Lagenaria siceraria*). As a serving vessel, the calabash had several advantages over ceramic vessels: it was lighter, less breakable, easily repaired, and could be decorated by individuals other than the potter. Although the calabash has great antiquity on the African subcontinent, we have relatively little knowledge of the development of the varieties in use today. The sweeping change in ceramics could be related to the spread of a new calabash varietal, either indigenously developed or introduced from the Americas, that was perhaps stronger, larger, or easier to grow than extant varieties (Gallagher 2016).

Although there are a few key differences between the Tuali-A and Tuali-B ceramic assemblages, notably a significant reduction in large and small grog-tempered pots, the occupations differed most dramatically in their specialist activity. The Tuali-A occupation has comparatively little evidence for iron working, whereas the Tuali-B occupation not only shows evidence of increased iron working, but also of intensive dyed cloth production. The distinct economic character of the two occupations raises the possibility that they could be contemporary components of a single diversified community. The evidence suggests iron smelting may have been more intensive during the Tuali-B occupation than in the Siga occupation, but production was likely still for local consumption, as iron smelting activity did not remotely approach that of the early second millennium CE large-scale furnace complexes identified in other parts of Burkina Faso (e.g., Fabre 2009; Kiéthéga 2009; Thiombiano-Ilboudo 2012a; Serneels 2017). In contrast, as discussed above, the scale and density of dye pit complexes almost certainly reflected production of indigo cloth for extra-local use (either as trade or tribute).

Unlike many excavated trading centers of the eighteenth and nineteenth centuries elsewhere in West Africa, European metal objects, glass, and pipes of African manufacture were rare or absent at sites in the Gobnangou region. While this does not eliminate the possibility of participation in exchange networks, particularly given the evidence for cloth production, it does suggest that durable exotic goods may not have had the same social role they held elsewhere.

In conclusion, the clustering of dispersed, shifting settlements at the base of the Gobnangou escarpment was the combined result of multiple settlement influences. Involvement in regional trade networks may have encouraged the construction of high-investment production centers (dye pits), which would have tied residents to a location and potentially pushed them toward the escarpment where they could exploit the year-round water sources for indigo dyeing and more easily access trade routes. At the same time, the hidden location and nucleation of site MAS937 provides possible evidence for regional insecurity in the nineteenth century, similar to that described for Yobri and elsewhere in the southern savanna region (Rémy 1967; Netting 1968; Norris 1986; Swanepoel 2005, 2009; Usman 2007; Kankpeyeng 2009; Thiombiano-Ilboudo 2010; MacEachern 2011; MacDonald 2012; Gosselain and Haour 2019; Gosselain and Smolderen 2019). Despite these changes, as well as significant transformation in material culture, many aspects of the basic mode of settlement documented during the Siga occupation persisted, albeit within a more limited area, illustrating the continued importance of generational mobility to Gobnangou society.

CHAPTER EIGHT

SITUATING THE ARCHAEOLOGY
OF SOUTHEASTERN BURKINA FASO

The Gulmance practice of generational mobility derived primarily from its political milieu and was deeply intertwined with complex historically rooted dynamics. Regular movements in Gulmance communities allowed the politics of territory to be activated, perhaps underwriting the power and authority of elites and reinforcing cultural values regarding natural resources. The research presented in this book has addressed the antiquity of these practices and shed light on the historical circumstances leading to this cultural setting in the Gobnangou region on the southern edge of the ethnohistorical Gulmance territory. Our fieldwork documented hundreds of sites, spanning several millennia, although most were ephemeral sites from the past thousand years that resulted from this system of generational mobility. As described previously, the sequence spans centuries of spatial and social choices and incorporates periods of both profound transformation and remarkable continuity.

Overall, the Maadaga Archaeological Survey has built on earlier research in the region to contribute a previously unknown sequence focused on non-urban complexity to archaeological research in West Africa. Major changes identified include a late adoption of agriculture in the late first millennium CE, the development of spatial correlates of generational mobility with material indicators of complexity in the early second millennium CE, and an increase in interregional connectivity despite the continuation of spatial strategies over the past five hundred years. In the process, the MAS project has provided archaeological insights into the history of Gulmance and questioned common and persistent narratives of the African past.

Contributions to the Archaeology of the Gobnangou Region

The Gobnangou is a favored location with rich natural resources. As established by previous research and confirmed by the results of the MAS project, foraging populations occupied the Gobnangou region by at the latest the mid-Holocene. These populations used broad-spectrum economic strategies and practiced a highly mobile lifestyle at both rockshelter and open-air sites, the latter found at both the foot of the escarpment and several kilometers away in the adjacent plains. With the evidence of the diverse fauna recovered from the Péntènga and Yobri rockshelters (Millogo 1993a; Frank et al. 2001) and the availability of permanent water at escarpment springs, it is possible that foragers stayed in the region year-round, although the lack of identified hearths, structures, or middens dating to this period suggests frequent movement.

By taking advantage of local, high-quality chert sources Gobnangou foragers made a variety of backed microlithic tools, with micropoints most common at all sites with large assemblages (Frank et al. 2001). Evidence from Péntènga and Yobri rockshelters also indicates the use of ceramics from at least the fourth millennium BCE, a practice common among middle to late Holocene foragers throughout the West African savanna (Millogo 1993a, 1993b; MacDonald 1997; Frank et al. 2001; Wotzka and Goedicke 2001; Huysecom et al. 2009). Interestingly, ground stone adzes, axes, and *hachettes* were absent from middle to late Holocene foraging sites, despite being frequently found with microlith assemblages in other regions of Burkina Faso (Andah 1978; Millogo and Koté 2000; Fontana et al. 2010). Gobnangou sites, like those in northern Benin and elsewhere in Burkina Faso, also lacked the distinctive material correlates of the second millennium BCE Kintampo complex in nearby northern Ghana (Andah 1978, 1980; Breunig and Neumann 2002; Petit 2005; N'Dah 2009; Watson 2010).

The Gobnangou region is notable for its relatively late adoption of an agricultural economy during the late first millennium CE Pwoli occupation. In the West Africa savanna both animal and plant domesticates were widely available by the second and first millennia BCE, sedentary iron-using farming communities were common by the first few centuries CE, and village communities had developed widely by the mid-first millennium CE (see the reviews in Kahlheber and Neumann [2007] and Dueppen [2018]). Given the few early sites with organic preservation, use of domesticates possibly occurred in the region before it was first documented at site MAS541, around 650 CE. However, even if there was low level use of domesticates, there is no evidence for any cultural transformations associated with subsistence change or agricultural lifeways earlier than the Pwoli occupation. A similar late chronology of agricultural adoption was identified in the Atakora region of Benin (Petit 2005; N'Dah 2009), raising the possibility that foraging persisted as a primary economic strategy until the mid-first millennium CE throughout the Pendjari basin.

Pwoli occupation sites represent a stark shift in the archaeology of the region. These were sedentary farming homesteads, located 3 to 5 km apart, that used new technologies, subsistence strategies, and cultural practices. Pwoli occupation households lived in earthen structures with pounded clay floors that were remodeled and reconstructed multiple times in the same location, creating tells through accumulation of architectural melt and trash. Based on size, each site was likely home to only one or two extended family household compounds.

During the Pwoli occupation ceramics became the most common artifact class and a broad diversity of vessels was recovered from each excavated site. The ceramics found at sites MAS541 and MAS502.3 represented independent household traditions with some shared decorations and forms, but many unique ones as well. Interestingly, they had no clear affinities to ceramics used by earlier foragers in the Gobnangou region or by contemporary populations in neighboring regions (Frank et al. 2001; Wotzka and Goedicke 2001; Petit 2005; Haour et al. 2019). The use of grinding stones, made with sandstone likely obtained several kilometers away at the escarpment, became common and further supported the shift toward a reliance on cultivated grains, although these could have been used for processing wild plants such as shea. The Pwoli occupation also marked the introduction of iron tools, typically points or spearheads. Unlike first millennium CE farming communities to the north in Oudalan and to the east along the Niger River (Magnavita 2015; Haour et al. 2016; Haour 2019), Pwoli sites yielded no evidence of participation in interregional trading networks (including a complete lack of glass and stone beads and cowries). In this respect, Pwoli occupation sites are more similar to those in western Burkina Faso, where politics were rooted in localized sources of power and wealth (Dueppen 2012a).

Economic practices during the Pwoli occupation included cultivating pearl millet, collecting wild tree fruits, keeping domestic fowl (and in some cases livestock), and using a variety of hunting and fishing strategies (Dueppen and Gallagher 2013). The dating of sites MAS541 and MAS502.3 was not precise enough to be definitive, yet there were indications of a socioeconomic transition over time within the Pwoli occupation. Whereas millet was cultivated, chickens were kept, and localized hunting and fishing occurred at both sites, at the likely earlier MAS541 these were supplemented by long-distance hunting and fishing expeditions to the Kourtiagou or Pendjari Rivers. In contrast, residents of MAS503.2 focused on a more localized foodshed and invested more deeply in domesticated resources by adopting livestock. This transition may have been linked to a shift from maintenance of regional social relations through shared activities in the dry season to the use of domesticates as a durable transferable resource to facilitate social relations between increasingly locally oriented communities (see Dueppen and Gallagher 2013). Overall, the highly dispersed spatial arrangement and lack of evidence for specialized tasks (with a possible exception of iron working) suggest economically independent homesteads like those found in the initial agricultural periods that occur earlier elsewhere in Burkina Faso (Dueppen 2012a).

The Siga occupation marked a second dramatic transformation in both the nature and distribution of archaeological sites in the Gobnangou region. The survey identified hundreds of ephemeral Siga occupation sites throughout the survey zone, all of which had little evidence for depositional stratification despite architecture and material culture indicative of sedentary settlement. The vast majority were 11 to 15 m diameter surface scatters of ceramics and likely represent individual household compounds. According to multiple measures of ceramic density, these sites were occupied for roughly the same length of time, with the large number of sites the result of complex sequential histories of abandonment and construction of new residences in new locations. Most sites had been disturbed by plowing and features such as smelting furnaces or inset pot bases were rare.

Although this shallow distributed settlement pattern has some similarities to the archaeological record of the southern Senegambia (Lawson 2003; Richard 2009, 2018; Donnay 2016), the Siga occupation contrasts starkly with other documented early second millennium CE sites in central West Africa, which tend to be either deeply stratified or large-scale specialist complexes (e.g., Holl and Koté 2000; Koté 2007; Simporé 2009; Thiombiano-Ilboudo 2010; Dueppen 2012a, 2018; Holl 2014; Magnavita 2015; Serneels 2017; Haour 2019). The exception is a similar shift toward regular site abandonment and movement that occurred in the Atakora Mountains in the early second millennium CE, although that change likely happened during or near the end of the Siga occupation (Petit 2005; N'Dah 2009).

The residents of Siga occupation sites had a shared complex ceramic tradition. Anchored by a diverse set of standardized vessels that included open bowls with pedestal bases, open and slightly restricted jars, and large open vessels, this assemblage incorporated a range of pastes, surface treatments, and decoration techniques that were used in consistent combinations. All of the common vessels were rarely found together at a single site, but components of this assemblage were present at almost every site. These standardized vessels likely accounted for the majority of sherds collected. Residents at a third of Siga occupation sites supplemented their household assemblage with rare or unique vessels, many decorated using techniques found at fewer than five sites. Currently, there is very little evidence for the organization of ceramic production during the Siga occupation, although the level of standardization may reflect specialization.

Ground stone, chipped stone, and slag were also present at a more limited number of Siga occupation sites (66%, 47%, and 22% of sites, respectively). Very few intact basal grinding stones were identified, perhaps because these labor-intensive tools were moved or later repurposed, and most ground stone at sites consisted of small fragmentary pieces. Handheld grinding stones were more frequently found intact and a few ground stone *hachettes* were also collected. Chipped stone was typically rare at Siga occupation sites and may have been used for expedient tools or for starting fires. In contrast, evidence for iron smelting (in the form of dense concentrations of slag and tuyères) was found at only fifteen Siga occupation sites. Smelting sites during the Siga occupation were distributed along the banks of the Koabu and its major tributaries and ranged in size from small isolated furnaces to the large iron-working complex at site MAS849. Small amounts of slag were found at an additional thirty-eight sites (16%) throughout the survey zone, raising the possibility that either smithing was more widely practiced or that blacksmiths moved their residences more frequently than their smelting locations. The scale of iron smelting identified was consistent with production for local markets and even the largest sites were orders of magnitude smaller than the early to mid-second millennium CE complexes documented in northern Burkina Faso (Fabre 2009; Kiéthéga 2009; Simporé 2009; Serneels 2017)

A few Siga occupation sites yielded evidence for the possible presence of elites in the region. At site MAS780, excavations near an elite burial found by local residents recovered high densities of iron objects. Nearby, site MAS696.2 contained the most diverse ceramic assemblage identified in Siga survey sites, with a particularly high frequency of rare or uncommon decoration techniques, although it was typical in size and surface density. Even in the case of these potential elite habitations and cemeteries, Siga occupation sites continued to lack evidence for common trade items such as glass and semiprecious stone beads, cowries, or copper despite the likely development of major exchange networks along the Niger River only 150 km to the east (Haour et al. 2016; Haour 2019).

While the lack of chronological control within the Siga occupation was limiting, there were clearly major differences with the preceding Pwoli occupation. First, regional populations increased, potentially significantly, as simultaneous occupation of even 5% of high-confidence Siga occupation sites would represent a four- to six-fold increase from the Pwoli occupation. Second, stratified sites disappeared and a cultural landscape derived from the practice of generational mobility appeared. Third, the emergence of a shared material culture likely indicates the development of a common identity (political, economic, or social) within the region and could be evidence of specialized production. If indeed generational mobility was correlated with increasing complexity (that is, facilitated by a secure landscape and encouraged by political imperatives for its practice), then the settlement pattern further supports the argument for increasing social differentiation during the Siga occupation.

The transition from the Siga to the Tuali occupation is currently one of the more poorly understood aspects of the sequence, due to the lack of temporal data. However, the apparent population reduction and simplification of ceramic traditions that occur at the Siga–Tuali transition resemble processes that occur elsewhere in the West African savanna in the fourteenth to fifteenth centuries CE (e.g., S. K. McIntosh, Gallagher, and R. J. McIntosh 2003; Petit 2005; Dueppen and Gallagher 2016; Gallagher and Dueppen 2018). Often attributed to factors such as environmental change, plague, or simply changing cultural practices, these events farther west were associated with population movements and interregional economic transformations, in particular the expansion of Mande trading diasporas (Kiéthéga 1983; Brooks 1993; Millogo 1998; Wilks 2000; Insoll 2003; Phliponeau 2010; Somé and Simporé 2014; Dueppen and Gallagher 2016; Gallagher and Dueppen 2018). Whereas there is historical evidence for Mande diasporas to the east of the study region along the Niger River corridor (Kuba 2009; Gosselain and Haour 2019; Gosselain and Smolderen 2019), there is currently no mid-second millennium CE archaeological evidence for Mande influence in the study region. Until the dating is refined, the linking of trends in the Gobnangou region to these broader regional phenomena remains tentative.

The Tuali occupation (divided into Tuali-A and Tuali-B) was characterized by the reorientation of settlement toward the Gobnangou escarpment, changes in material culture, and the addition of new activities. At the same time, clear continuities were present, including ongoing use of some elements of the Siga occupation ceramic assemblage during the Tuali-A occupation and, more significantly, the maintenance of a dispersed settlement pattern and the persistence of generational mobility. The balance of evidence indicates that the Tuali-A predates the Tuali-B, yet the possibility remains that the distinct characteristics of these occupations represent different facets of society rather than temporal change.

As in the Siga occupation, the majority of residential Tuali occupation sites were the size of individual household compounds, although there was one particularly large Tuali-B site at the base of the escarpment (MAS937). Tuali occupation sites were located throughout much of the survey zone, with the exception of a notable decrease in sites more than 8 km from the escarpment. During Tuali-A, settlement was evenly distributed across the remainder of the survey zone. In contrast, Tuali-B settlement shifted and for the first time sites became much more likely to be located within sight of the escarpment, mirroring settlement patterns in the region today. This change could be related to increasing insecurity in the region, necessitating access to highlands, or could be related to localization of settlement near major trade routes.

Tuali ceramic traditions were significantly less elaborate than those dating to the Siga occupation, perhaps reflecting changes in identity or material expression (see Dueppen and Gallagher 2016). The assemblage became significantly more homogenous along every axis of analysis with fewer pastes, vessel forms, and decoration techniques in use and the clear majority of Tuali pots were quartz-tempered flared jars in a variety of sizes. Small open bowls that could have been used for serving largely disappeared from the assemblage and, as opposed to the complex design grammars found on some vessels during the Siga occupation, Tuali ceramic decoration was typically confined to a roulette on the vessel shoulder.

Ground stone remained common at Tuali sites, suggesting continuity in subsistence practices including grain processing. In contrast, whereas chipped stone was present at 49% of Tuali-A sites, it was found at only 22% of Tuali-B sites, despite their frequent location in areas with Lithic occupation sites. This decrease could indicate the availability of imported alternatives for cutting or fire-starting tasks. The archaeological record for iron working during the Tuali occupation is particularly confusing. Although small amounts of slag were found in identical proportions of Siga, Tuali-A, and Tuali-B sites, evidence for iron smelting was virtually absent during Tuali-A and particularly common during Tuali-B. Tuali-B furnace sites were on average larger than Siga iron-working sites (although none reached the size at site MAS849) and located at the base of the escarpment rather than along major drainages.

During the Tuali-B occupation, construction of multiple dye pit complexes marked a major intensification in the production of indigo cloth. Like iron furnaces, these installations were located exclusively near the escarpment base. While indigo dyeing may have taken place earlier at a household level in large pots, the pits indicate a move toward specialist production at a much larger scale, possibly for extra-local consumption. The adoption of dye pits could indicate links to the extensive cloth manufacturing network developed by the nineteenth-century Sokoto Caliphate (Candotti 2010). At the same time, cloth trade could also be indicative of closer ties to Gulmance political centers to the north and west (Thiombiano-Ilboudo 2010). Aside from the dye pits, there is very little direct evidence for engagement in interregional exchange networks during the Tuali occupation. Glass beads, cowries, and European trade goods were not found and even objects like African-made smoking pipes, common in seventeenth- to nineteenth-century sites elsewhere in West Africa, were very rare.

In conclusion, survey and excavation data indicate a unique archaeological sequence in the Gobnangou compared with those described for other investigated areas of the savanna. Foraging persisted as the primary mode of subsistence much longer and the first direct evidence for agriculture dated to the mid-first millennium CE. These early farmers were locally anchored, but in the early second millennium CE their use of the landscape changed to one of generational mobility. Households likely moved only two or three times on the scale of an individual lifetime, yet the long-term accumulative effect created an extensive archaeological landscape. A shared material culture tradition linked the region and multiple lines of evidence suggest the presence of elites. Simplification of ceramics, intensification of cloth production, and a shift in settlement toward the escarpment characterized the second half of the second millennium CE. However, the settlement pattern indicative of generational mobility continued, connecting the use of space in the past to the ethnohistorical record.

These patterns are most similar to those documented in the Atakora Mountains and Pendjari River basin of northern Benin (Petit 2005; N'Dah 2009). However, despite having similar broad outlines (such as a late adoption of agriculture and replacement of tells with an extensive landscape), the timing of the sequences did not always align and there was no evidence of shared material culture traditions between them. Ethnohistorically, the Pendjari River basin has functioned as a southern border to the Gulmance polities and scholars have described northern Benin as a refuge for those fleeing the influence of hierarchical rulers in Gulmance, Mossi, and other polities (N'Dah 2009). Overall, from the perspective of the archaeological data, the Gobnangou sequence indicates major societal transformations over time in a rich environmental setting and provides important data for outlining local histories and addressing regional debates.

Contributions to the History of Gulmance

The archaeological sequence presented here is a contribution in and of itself, but this research has the potential to provide archaeological insights on the Gulmance kingdoms as well. Although often coterminus, there is frequently a divide between the history of an ethnic or linguistic group (a socially cohesive group of people), the history of a political entity (a group united under a system of governance), and the history of place (a geographical locale). The nature of archaeological data inherently results in a narrative of transformation in a place, while oral traditions are more commonly oriented around social or political units. As Andah (1995a) has made explicit, ignoring ties between modern ethnic groups, the history of places, and the archaeological record results in what he calls "fragmentation syndrome" in which the past and the present are irrevocably split. Further, the issue cannot be sidestepped, because, as Trouillot (1995) made clear, silences are as powerful as mentions.

Like the value in analyzing the simultaneous truth of distinct oral historical narratives, the archaeological record is most useful as a complementary material perspective (Robertshaw 2000; Stahl 2001; DeCorse and Chouin 2003; Schmidt 2006, 2015; Thiombiano-Ilboudo 2010). As described in Chapter 1, the published oral histories for eastern Burkina Faso are oriented around a political structure—the Gulmance kingdoms—and primarily collected hundreds of kilometers from the study region (Chantoux 1966; Madiéga 1982, 2009; Madiéga et al. 1983). While this poses significant methodological challenges, it is equally problematic to separate the archaeological record from the strong identification of most people in the Gobnangou region today with linguistic, cultural, and political Gulmance identities.

Given the distances involved, this project takes as its locus of analysis macrolevel themes around population and governance documented in Gulmance oral history (Chantoux 1966; Madiéga 1982, 2009; Madiéga et al. 1983; Thiombiano-Ilboudo 2010; Korbéogo 2013). Most accounts characterize Gulmance territory as originally inhabited by egalitarian indigenous communities; however, different scholars ascribe different temporalities to subsequent events. Some suggest that the twelfth- to thirteenth-century arrival of Jaba Lompo, who intermarried with the Woba (hunters) and Tindamba (earth priests), created the foundations of a new Gulmance identity within a new political entity (e.g., Chantoux 1966). In these versions, expansion and consolidation of local political units continued until the late fourteenth century CE, when the development of a larger political and military confederation occurred. In contrast, other scholars compress this timeline, with both the initial intermarriage of outsider elites with indigenous peoples and the creation of the confederation occurring in the fifteenth to sixteenth centuries CE (e.g., Madiéga 1982, 2009; Thiombiano-Ilboudo 2010). According to different traditions, these elites traveled to the region from Gambaga in northern Ghana or from Bornu near Lake Chad and, in some cases, from Gobir in northwestern Nigeria.

The collected oral histories agree that regional Gulmance polities maintained significant autonomy until the eighteenth century, when the thirteenth dynasty *Nunbado* Yendabri consolidated power at his new capital of Nungu. During this period, the *Nunbado* held significant ideological influence over the regional polities, demanding tributes and maintaining a military. By the nineteenth century, this highly centralized influence waned as conflict with neighboring Fulani and Mossi populations increased (Korbéogo 2016). In the southeast, this period may have also seen greater economic connectivity as

Hausa merchants in the Sokoto Caliphate developed extensive trade networks. By the late nineteenth century, Gulmance had fragmented and the *Nunbado* had fled the capital after a succession dispute. Shortly thereafter the region came under French colonial control.

The Gobnangou region is typically mentioned in passing in these histories as one of the independent kingdoms within the confederation and at the southern borders where some conflicts may have occurred. However, it was presumably subjected to some of the same processes as other Gulmance kingdoms that have been the focus of more academic research. At the level of archaeological visibility, the oral histories describe the creation of a more homogenous cultural entity from multiple diverse populations, the development of linked independent local kingdoms before the consolidation of a more centralized Gulmance confederacy, and a general process of increasing regional connectivity over time with complex societies to the west and east. These processes could be expressed through broader similarities and differences in material culture and other social practices over time. It is well established that the materialization of the complex relationships between various social and political groupings can produce diverse equifinality in the archaeological record (see the discussions in Cruz [2011], Guèye [2011], and Richard and MacDonald [2015]). At the same time, it was unlikely that dramatic transformations in settlement and material culture had no correlation with social or political change. These moments of change provided an entry point for analysis.

The contrast between the Pwoli and Siga occupations suggests holistic shifts in society in the Gobnangou region that were most likely associated with the establishment of new ideologies. Pwoli occupation sites were widely distributed, likely multigenerational, homesteads with little evidence for specialization in economic activities or inequalities between homesteads. In many ways they resemble early agricultural settlements in other parts of the Voltaic region (e.g., Dueppen 2012a). The subsequent Siga phase indicated a very different cultural setting, as settlement became less anchored, material culture traditions became more complex and unified, and evidence for the presence of elites strengthened.

The Siga occupation data are compatible with the development of a ranked polity in the Gobnangou in the early second millennium CE, as suggested in oral traditions. Given the strong evidence for population growth and clear substantial cultural change that accompanied the Siga occupation, it is very possible that this shift was associated with the arrival of at least some part of the population from elsewhere, although the Siga occupation ceramics have at best weak links to described late first or early second millennium CE ceramic traditions elsewhere in West Africa. At the same time, there is little material evidence for regional exchange networks, perhaps reflecting a more localized focus.

The timing of the transition between the Siga and Tuali occupations is poorly understood chronologically. However, the shift in ceramic style and possible population drop could reflect major changes in the region. Many outside factors, including climate change, plague, or the influence of newly introduced plant species could have been behind these changes. They also could have resulted from a changing relationship between the Gobnangou and the *Nunbado*, although there is no clear evidence for strong affinities between the Gobnangou ceramics and those studied at sites near Fada N'Gourma by Thiombiano-Ilboudo (2010).

Although conflicts with populations in northern Benin are described in Gulmance oral traditions, there was little direct evidence of insecurity in the survey zone aside from the undated presence of hidden granaries in the escarpment (see Appendix D) and shifts in settlement toward the escarpment during the Tuali-B occupation. This stands in contrast to the fortifications (*bilni*) documented by Madiéga and colleagues (Madiéga 1982; Madiéga et al. 1983) throughout much of Gulmance territory (although particularly in the west) and by Thiombiano-Ilboudo (2010) in Fada N'Gourma Province in particular. Interestingly, despite many parallels in their archaeological sequences, there were very few similarities between Tuali occupation ceramics and those from northern Benin (Petit 2005; N'Dah 2009). Wooden roulettes similar to those used during the Tuali-B occupation do occur earlier in the Benin sequence, such that the dating does not align. While closely interacting populations frequently maintain distinct material culture, the archaeological evidence does not contradict the presence of a social boundary near the Pendjari River throughout the past millennium.

One of the strongest indicators for the long-term continuity of complex polities in the Gobnangou was the system of generational mobility, which persisted for almost the entire second millennium CE. In the ethnohistorical record, generational mobility was ideologically central in Gulmance communities, to the point where, when the colonial administration forbid the movement of villages in the early 1900s, Yobri responded by increasing the distances between residences along the escarpment and by significantly expanding the use of field huts, thus maintaining regular access to new land as well as a degree of mobility (Rémy 1967). It is possible that the adoption or maintenance of this settlement strategy was linked to broader Gulmance political and cultural integration.

Contributions to the Reevaluation of Colonial and Postcolonial Narratives

In West Africa, where colonialism has shaped not only the present, but also the construction of historical narratives, archaeological research has proven transformative for our understandings of both colonial and precolonial history (see the discussions in Andah [1995a, 1995b], Thiaw [2010], Ogundiran [2013], and Anquandah [2014]). The results of this project directly address two common narratives of the Burkinabe past and present: environmental degradation and the peripheral political and economic status of the Gobnangou region. These narratives have their roots in the colonial era and require reevaluation in the context of the data presented.

Environmental Degradation

Throughout much of the twentieth century environmental degradation was a significant concern of anthropologists, ecologists, and agronomists in West Africa. Based in very real concerns about increased population density and exacerbated by the Sahel drought in the 1970s, this narrative suggests that traditional agricultural practices in the savanna region are systematically destroying the natural environment. Deforestation and desertification remain continuing foci in the literature (e.g., UNEP 2008). Over the past twenty-five years a series of innovative studies by geographers, historians, and ecologists systematically deconstructed this narrative (e.g., Fairhead and Leach 1996; Leach and Mearns 1996; Mortimore 1998; Baker 2000; Bassett and Crummey 2003; Guyer et al. 2007). Armed with new concepts of savanna ecology and a long-term perspective that recognized colonial bias, they found that traditional agricultural practices were remarkably robust in the context of the unpredictable yet resilient savanna environment.

Archaeologically, the long-term sustainability of traditional farming practices in the savanna has been well established. Sites like Sadia (750–1270 CE) and Kirikongo (100–1700 CE) were occupied for hundreds of years, yet archaeobiological analyses have to date identified no evidence for environmental degradation in their sequences despite population growth, intensification of iron working, and other processes that have been suggested as potentially damaging to local environments (Dueppen 2012a; Huysecom et al. 2015). In the southern Senegambia (e.g., at Payoungou, at the latest 1200 CE to the present), evidence from sites where short-distance moves resulted in shallow but continuous and extensive occupations has likewise showed successful long-term management of field systems in a relatively fixed location (Lawson 2003; Donnay 2016). As households that move longer distances produce smaller, even more ephemeral sites with poor preservation and stratigraphic integrity of archaeobiological samples, the long-term sustainability of traditional strategies in a spatially extensive landscape has been more difficult to address.

The Gobnangou is therefore a unique and important case example. In the study region, the archaeological data indicated that residents have been practicing a form of generational mobility for nearly a millennium, during which populations likely rose and fell, agricultural production expanded and decreased, and various cash and subsistence crops came into and went out of favor. During the Tuali occupation, it is likely that farming activities increased as the region became more engaged in regional cloth production networks. Many of the specifics of farming practices remain unknown, yet this extensive strategy could not have persisted if it was not effective within the local environment. Although it is important not to minimize the potential effects of recent dramatic increases in both population and cotton cultivation in southeastern Burkina Faso and, consequently, the possible need for innovations in agricultural strategies (see the discussions in Korbéogo [2015] and Knauer et al. [2017]), the demonstrated long-term sustainability of generational mobility suggests potential for further research.

Centering Gulmance

The Gulmance kingdoms of Burkina Faso have been peripheralized in historical accounts since the precolonial period. Arabic descriptions of West African societies over the course of the second millennium CE tend to focus on Islamic peoples or large trading entrepôts, or both. The Gulmance kingdoms had neither (although Islamization of some northern communities has increased over the course of the twentieth century). The peripheralization of this part of West Africa was further exacerbated by colonial and postcolonial borders, as southeastern Burkina Faso, and in particular the Gobnangou region, tended to stay on the margins of administrative units (between 1897 and 1960 it was administered by Dahomey, French Sudan, Niger, and Upper Volta). Moreover, the Gobnangou region's geographical isolation was enhanced by the creation of several parks and reserves, resulting in a buffer zone largely absent of population to the south, east, and west (Figure 75). The pioneering oral historical research of Madiéga (1982) and its inclusion in the UNESCO *General History of Africa* (Izard and Ki-Zerbo 1992) brought the history of the Gulmance kingdoms to a larger audience, yet these kingdoms remain absent from most maps of precolonial complex societies in West Africa.

Despite their prominence in oral histories in central West Africa, areas that would ultimately be controlled by different Mossi states are only beginning to be included in systematic archaeological research (see Lingané 1995; Simporé 2009; Serneels 2017) similar to the research histories on the Dagbon and Mamprusi polities in northern Ghana.

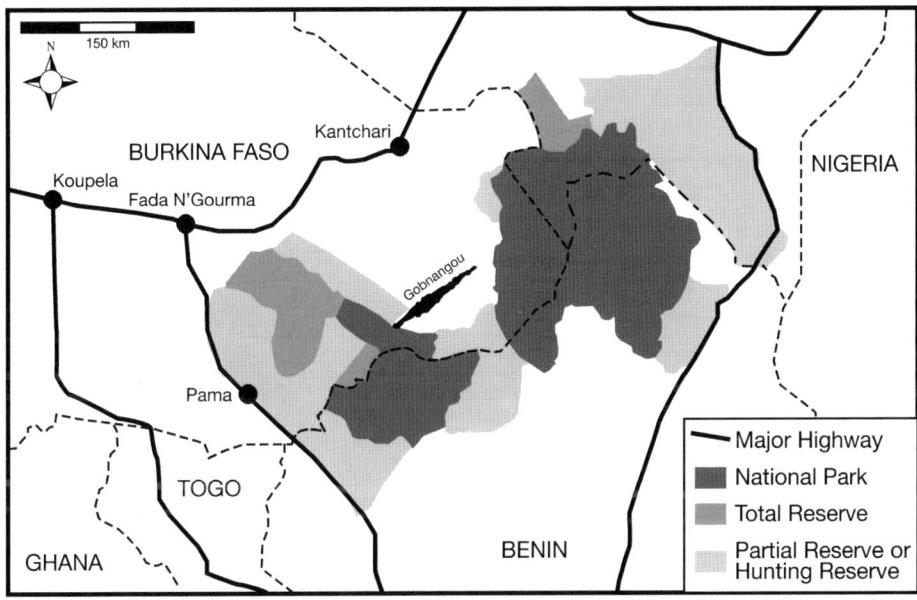

FIGURE 75. Major roads and locations of parks and reserves in the Burkina–Benin–Niger border region of southeastern Burkina Faso.

In southeastern Burkina Faso, aside from the Maadaga Archaeological Survey, the only archaeological research within the territory encompassed by the Gulmance kingdoms is exploratory surveys by Kiéthéga, Millogo, and Koté, the German–Burkinabe fieldwork in the Gobnangou on mid-Holocene foragers, and most significantly, recent survey and excavations of multiple sites near Fada N'Gourma by Thiombiano-Ilboudo (2010, 2012a).

This is likely in part because of the nature of the archaeological sites themselves. As the results presented in this volume show, the settlement patterns of the Gulmance produced large numbers of ephemeral sites rather than the urban sites and stratified tells common in other parts of the Niger Bend. The limited results to date from archaeological research elsewhere in Mossi, Dagbon, and Mamprusi areas likewise have yet to identify deeply stratified residential sites (although given the lack of survey coverage their potential presence cannot be excluded). However, as increasingly shown by archaeological research around the world, analysis of ephemeral sites can provide insight into complex political and social phenomena (e.g., Varien 1999; Stahl 2001; Ogundiran 2002, 2016; Langlois 2007; Swanepoel 2008; Richard 2009, 2015, 2018; Lavachery et al. 2010; Usman 2012; Insoll, MacLean, and Kankpeyeng 2013; Lindsay and Greene 2013; Honeychurch 2014; Ashley, Antonites, and Fredrikson 2016; Donnay 2016).

Documentation of extensively used spaces requires a landscape approach to identify patterning and recognition of more subtle archaeological signatures of complex political processes. The movement of households in Gulmance communities was historically enabled by a complex system of assured access to farmland at the community level across a broad spatial region (Madiéga 1982; Korbéogo 2013). This access was maintained not through physical continuity in a particular place, but rather through communal security, a shared ethos of access to land, and recognition of hierarchical authority.

According to ethnohistorical accounts, generational mobility also acted against the interests of nonchiefly social segments, as these were constantly shifting their sociospatial settings while the chiefly lineage remained spatially stable (Korbéogo 2013). We identified no equivalent anchored residence among the shifting households in the archaeological record of the survey zone. However, whereas Tuali occupation sites tended to be flat, many Siga occupation sites seemed to be small tells (see Appendix A). Although excavation and examination of borrow pit cuts found only ephemeral Siga cultural deposits over either natural sediment or Pwoli habitation, the possibility of a stratified Siga occupation site cannot be ruled out. In addition, the size of these precolonial territories is unknown and an elite leader could have lived outside the survey zone, as the *bado* for that area does today.

It is clear that a complex sociopolitical landscape emerged with subsequent dynamic changes throughout the second millennium CE, yet the historical articulation of the Gobnangou within the Gulmance political sphere remains poorly understood. However, the regional sequence exemplifies the diversity of societies that inhabited the precolonial West African savanna and points toward the dynamic social, economic, and political pathways and cultural choices that future archaeological research will uncover.

APPENDIX A

Maadaga Archaeological Survey Site Catalog

This appendix presents a condensed tabular catalog of sites (Table A.1) identified by the Maadaga Archaeological Survey; see the column descriptions below. For a descriptive catalog with site locations and site-by-site discussions of deposits, environmental setting, sources of disturbance, and finds, see Gallagher (2010:274–353).

Key to Table

A consecutive *site number* was assigned to individual sites; see Chapter 3 for details of this site numbering system. *Occupation* and *confidence level* (L, low confidence; H, high confidence) were assigned using the methodologies described in Chapter 3. *Area* and *estimated height* are based on site maps drawn during the survey.

The *ceramic sample size* includes only individually recorded sherds. It does not include small sherds that were counted and weighed following the protocols described in Chapter 3. For sites that were surveyed in both 2004 and 2006, the 2006 sample size is listed first, followed by the 2004 sample size. If no ceramics were found at the site, the sample is recorded as "none present." If ceramics were observed but left in place (as they were at a rock art site), the sample is recorded as "none collected." If ceramics were present and collected, but none were individually recorded since all sherds were small, the sample size is "0."

Ceramic density is based on the systematic surface collection and encompasses the entire collection, including sherds that were not individually recorded. Both volume (sherds per square meter) and weight (grams per square meter) are given; "n/a" indicates that only an opportunistic surface collection was made. The number of unique impressed, dragged, applied, and roulette *decoration techniques* in use at the site is given for the 2006 sample; surface treatments (such as red slip and intentional roughing) are not included in this category. All *sherd types* present at each site are listed; see Appendix B for full descriptions of each sherd type.

Chipped stone is listed as "common" when it was a primary artifact class at the site, "present" when it occurred regularly at the site but was not a primary artifact class (according to both field notes and systematic surface collections), and "rare" when only isolated examples were found. Ground stone was primarily mentioned in field notes and only small examples were collected. *Ground stone* is recorded only as "present" or absent.

Slag includes all evidence of iron working. Slag is recorded as "rare" when only one or two pieces were identified and "present" when its occurrence is more frequent. Probable furnaces (dense concentrations of slag with vitrified tuyères) are recorded as "small" when less than 5 m in diameter, "medium" when 5 to 10 m in diameter or when two to three small furnaces occur at the same site, "large" when more than 10 m in diameter or multiple small and medium furnaces were present, and "extra large" in one case that had a slag concentration over 300 m^2 (see the discussion in Chapter 6).

Other finds and features include significant objects or features identified during the survey.

APPENDIX A

TABLE A.1. Catalog of sites documented by the Maadaga Archaeological Survey.

	Site description			Ceramic assemblages					Other artifacts			
Site number	Occupation (confidence level)	Area (m^2)	Estimated height (m)	Sample size 2006 (2004)	Ceramic density (sherds per m^2)	Ceramic density (g/m^2)	Number of decoration techniques	Sherd types	Chipped stone presence	Ground stone presence	Slag presence	Other finds and features
MAS500	Siga (L)	1,550	1.3	35	0.88	10.56	3	3, 15	Rare	—	Rare	—
MAS501	Tuali-B (L), Ring (L)	450	0.5	25	0.84	5	2	14	Rare	—	—	—
MAS502.1	Siga (H)	1,700	2	115	2.72	18.56	11	5	Rare	Present	Rare	—
MAS502.2	Siga (H)	1,550	3	34 (10)	0.6	22.48	7	3	Rare	Present	—	—
MAS502.3	Pwoli (H), Siga (H)	7,200	6	481	2.08	19.76	24	2, 4, 5, 10	—	Present	—	—
MAS502.4	Siga (H)	900	1	51	1.56	22.08	4	2, 4, 7, 9	—	—	—	—
MAS502.5	Siga (H)	600	1	41 (11)	1.32	18.32	3	4	Rare	Present	Medium furnace	—
MAS503	Siga (H)	300	0.75	23	1	29.32	3	3, 4, 6	—	—	—	—
MAS504	Siga (L)	125	0.75	22	0.92	7.2	2	None	—	—	—	—
MAS505	Siga (H)	2,040	0.75	24	0.64	13.36	4	4, 5, 6, 7	Rare	Present	—	Animal teeth
MAS506	Siga (H)	2,000	1.5	60	1.84	43.84	6	4, 5	Rare	Present	—	—
MAS507	Siga (H)	425	0.5	32	0.56	72.72	3	9	—	—	—	—
MAS508	Siga (H)	350	1	15	0.52	51.04	1	None	Rare	Present	Present	—
MAS509	Siga (L)	2,025	1.5	25	0.76	11.84	7	5, 9	Rare	Present	—	—
MAS510	Siga (L), Tuali-A (L)	125	0.8	13	0.12	1	4	8, 9	Rare	—	—	—
MAS511	Siga (L), Tuali-B (H)	300	0.8	23	0.68	16.12	6	3, 13	—	—	—	—

Continued

TABLE A.1 CONTINUED

	Site description				Ceramic assemblages					Other artifacts			Other finds and features
Site number	Occupation (confidence level)	Area (m²)	Estimated height (m)	Sample size 2006 (2004)	Ceramic density (sherds per m²)	Ceramic density (g/m²)	Number of decoration techniques	Sherd types	Chipped stone presence	Ground stone presence	Slag presence		
MAS512	Siga (H)	20	0.2	28 (1)	0.56	4.84	3	4, 7, 15	Rare	—	Small furnace	—
MAS513	Siga (H)	5,700	2	67 (19)	1.92	33.84	12	3, 4, 5, 10	Rare	Present	—	—
MAS514	Siga (H)	1,290	0.8	47	1.32	37.2	6	9, 10	Rare	—	Medium furnace	—
MAS515	Siga (L), Ring (H)	4,000	0	26 (4)	0.88	13.88	3	15	—	Present	—	—
MAS516	Siga (H)	50	0.4	16	n/a	n/a	6	4, 8, 10	—	—	—	—
MAS517	Not assigned	100	0.5	6	n/a	n/a	1	9	Rare	—	—	—
MAS518	Siga (L)	255	0.6	4	0.08	4.8	1	8, 10	—	Present	Rare	—
MAS519	Siga (H)	175	0.4	38	0.92	22.36	5	4, 9	—	Present	—	—
MAS520	Siga (H)	350	0.4	35	0.6	8.24	4	4, 6	—	Present	—	—
MAS521	Siga (H)	50	0.5	30	2.28	162.04	7	4, 6, 8, 9	—	Present	—	—
MAS522	Tuali-B (H)	80	0.5	12	0.08	1.6	2	None	—	—	—	—
MAS523	Siga (H)	50	0.6	18	0.4	28	1	2	Rare	—	—	—
MAS524	Siga (L)	1,950	2.5	23	n/a	n/a	7	None	—	Present	—	—
MAS525	Siga (H)	1,250	2	55	2.2	124.52	6	4, 9	—	—	—	—
MAS526	Siga (L)	2,150	0.8	74	2.52	29.56	8	n/a	Rare	—	—	—
MAS527	Siga (H)	150	0.5	33	2.36	10.2	5	3, 5, 6	—	—	—	—
MAS528	Siga (H)	130	0.4	43	1.52	59.6	3	4, 6	—	—	—	—

Continued

TABLE A.1 CONTINUED

Site number	Site description				Ceramic assemblages					Other artifacts			
	Occupation (confidence level)	Area (m²)	Estimated height (m)	Sample size 2006 (2004)	Ceramic density (sherds per m²)	Ceramic density (g/m²)	Number of decoration techniques	Sherd types	Chipped stone presence	Ground stone presence	Slag presence	Other finds and features
MAS529	Siga (H)	50	0.45	22	0.96	11.32	3	3, 11	Rare	Present	—	—
MAS530	Siga (H)	30	0.1	20	n/a	n/a	4	4, 9	—	—	—	—
MAS531.1	Siga (L)	225	0.5	29	1.8	12.68	5	None	Rare	Present	—	—
MAS531.2	Siga (H)	275	0.8	36	2	21.6	5	4, 5	—	Present	—	—
MAS531.3	Siga (H)	150	0.6	28	1.28	14.56	2	None	—	Present	—	—
MAS531.4	Siga (L)	310	0.5	48	4.68	100.84	4	9	Rare	—	—	—
MAS531.5	Siga (L)	310	0.6	105	9.28	89.8	7	9, 10, 11	—	—	—	—
MAS532	Siga (L)	20	0.3	19	1.12	19.12	5	None	Rare	—	—	—
MAS533	Siga (H)	70	0.3	41	2.12	22.2	3	4	—	—	—	—
MAS534	Siga (H)	300	0.8	49	2.12	189.68	6	2, 3, 9	Rare	Present	—	—
MAS535	Siga (H)	280	0.8	7	n/a	n/a	5	3, 9	—	Present	—	—
MAS536	Siga (H)	50	0.4	30	1.76	51.44	4	4	Rare	—	—	—
MAS537	Siga (H)	150	0.6	31	1.48	34.04	3	4	Rare	Present	—	—
MAS538	Ring (H)	750	0.4	25	0.76	8.28	1	None	—	—	—	—
MAS539	Siga (H)	150	0.5	33	0.76	4.12	4	2, 4	—	Present	—	—
MAS540	Siga (H)	130	0.6	15	0.4	49.16	2	5, 10	—	Present	—	—
MAS541	Pwoli (H), Siga(H)	1,375	3.5	708 (33)	8.8	75.08	21	2, 10	Rare	Present	—	—
MAS542	Lithic	n/a	n/a	None present	n/a	n/a	n/a	n/a	Common	—	—	—

Continued

TABLE A.1 CONTINUED

Site description					Ceramic assemblages					Other artifacts			
Site number	Occupation (confidence level)	Area (m²)	Estimated height (m)	Sample size 2006 (2004)	Ceramic density (sherds per m²)	Ceramic density (g/m²)	Number of decoration techniques	Sherd types	Chipped stone presence	Ground stone presence	Slag presence	Other finds and features
MAS543	Siga (H), Tuali-A (L)	850	1.25	48	2.24	30.08	6	1, 8, 9	Rare	Present	—	Remnant of mud brick structure from recent reoccupation
MAS544	Siga (L)	1,590	2	53	3.04	48.6	10	None	Rare	Present	—	Pipe?
MAS545	Not assigned	80	0.2	21	0.8	24.6	0	None	Rare	—	—	—
MAS546	Not assigned	310	0.4	8	0.12	1.2	0	None	—	Present	—	—
MAS547	Siga (L), Tuali-A (L)	1,140	2.5	33 (10)	2.44	26.36	0	4	—	Present	—	—
MAS548	Siga (L)	300	0.25	22	0.68	54.32	3	6	Rare	Present	—	—
MAS549	Siga (L), Ring (L)	900	0.6	21	0.88	12.72	4	6	—	Present	—	—
MAS550	Siga (L)	700	2	44 (0)	1.84	59.28	8	None	Rare	Present	—	—
MAS551	Siga (H)	1,000	1.25	50 (11)	2.64	22.72	6	2, 4, 5, 9	Rare	Present	—	—
MAS552	Siga (H)	80	0.5	56 (0)	2.4	18.96	4	4, 5	Rare	—	—	Polishing stone
MAS553	Siga (H)	100	0.5	21	1.04	12.68	3	4	Rare	Present	Medium furnace	—
MAS554	Siga (H)	275	0.4	31	1.4	39.56	1	5	—	Present	—	—
MAS555	Siga (H)	110	0.2	18	0.28	4.4	5	3, 5, 14	—	Present	—	—

Continued

APPENDIX A

TABLE A.1 CONTINUED

	Site description				Ceramic assemblages					Other artifacts			
Site number	Occupation (confidence level)	Area (m²)	Estimated height (m)	Sample size 2006 (2004)	Ceramic density (sherds per m²)	Ceramic density (g/m²)	Number of decoration techniques	Sherd types	Chipped stone presence	Ground stone presence	Slag presence	Other finds and features
MAS556	Siga (H)	80	0.6	48	2	30.84	2	2, 4	Rare	Present	—	—
MAS557	Siga (H)	180	0.4	27	1.4	22.6	3	5, 9	—	—	—	—
MAS558	Siga (L)	110	0.4	24	0.68	5.36	1	2	—	—	—	—
MAS559	Siga (H)	90	0.6	24	1.48	45.36	4	3, 8	—	—	—	—
MAS560	Tuali-B (L), Ring (L)	50	0.7	2	n/a	n/a	1	None	—	—	—	—
MAS561	Siga (H)	410	0.6	10	0.04	1.52	3	4, 6, 10, 11	—	—	—	—
MAS562	Siga (L)	200	0.5	24	0.68	19.6	3	15	—	—	—	—
MAS563	Tuali-A (H)	60	0.3	38	2	35.6	2	None	Rare	—	—	—
MAS564	Not assigned	80	0.2	1	n/a	n/a	0	None	—	—	—	—
MAS565	Siga (L)	510	0.6	29	1.32	11.64	3	None	Rare	Present	—	—
MAS566	Siga (L)	660	0.6	46	2.44	58.48	4	None	—	—	—	—
MAS567	Tuali-B (H), Ring (H)	525	0.6	20	0.48	9.08	3	13, 15	—	—	Present	—
MAS568	Tuali-A (H)	420	0.6	45	1.56	148.24	4	9	Rare	—	—	—
MAS569	Ring (H)	60	n/a	10	n/a	n/a	1	None	—	—	—	Well
MAS570	Siga (H)	375	0.3	60	2.2	22	5	3	Rare	Present	—	—
MAS571	Not assigned	60	0.2	None collected	n/a	n/a	n/a	None	—	—	—	Ceramics on surface but no collection in records

Continued

TABLE A.1 CONTINUED

Site number	Site description			Ceramic assemblages					Other artifacts			
	Occupation (confidence level)	Area (m²)	Estimated height (m)	Sample size 2006 (2004)	Ceramic density (sherds per m²)	Ceramic density (g/m²)	Number of decoration techniques	Sherd types	Chipped stone presence	Ground stone presence	Slag presence	Other finds and features
MAS572.1	Siga (H)	1,130	2	226	2.16	47.76	13	2, 4, 5, 6, 9	Rare	Present	—	—
MAS572.2	Siga (H)	1,260	2	20	0.96	10.8	4	n/a	Rare	Present	—	—
MAS572.3	Siga (L)	1,200	1.5	22	1.28	14.92	4	None	—	—	—	—
MAS572.4	Siga (H)	960	1.5	44	1.16	17.68	6	3, 4, 6	Rare	Present	—	Pipe?
MAS572.5	Siga (H)	350	0.75	13	0.4	9.72	2	n/a	—	Present	—	—
MAS572.6	Siga (L)	910	1.25	33	1.72	86.12	5	4, 11	Rare	—	—	—
MAS572.7	Siga (H)	200	1	19	0.52	5.56	7	5	Rare	—	—	—
MAS572.8	Siga (H)	150	0.6	17	1	7.24	4	5	Rare	—	—	—
MAS572.9	Siga (L)	180	0.6	13	0.96	4.68	2	None	Rare	—	—	—
MAS573	Siga (H)	800	1.25	122	1.96	25.84	8	3, 4, 9	Rare	Present	Present	Pipe?
MAS574	Tuali-A (L)	415	0.7	31	2	23.6	2	9	—	—	—	—
MAS575	Siga (H)	415	0.7	25	1.32	11.68	1	None	Rare	Present	—	—
MAS576	Siga (H)	110	0.2	16	1.28	7.6	4	3, 4, 5	Rare	Present	—	—
MAS577	Tuali-A (H)	110	0.25	17	0.16	11.32	1	9	—	—	—	—
MAS578	Siga (L)	60	0	22	0.96	8.44	2	5	Rare	—	Present	—
MAS579	Tuali-A (H)	180	0.1	57	3.84	36.2	2	11, 12	Rare	Present	—	—
MAS580	Siga (L), Tuali-A (H)	80	0.3	17	0.72	9.96	1	None	—	—	—	—
MAS581	Siga (L)	325	0.4	37	1.32	15.68	3	None	Rare	Present	—	—
MAS582	Siga (H)	110	0.3	40	1.8	35.84	2	3	Rare	Present	—	Polishing stone

Continued

TABLE A.1 CONTINUED

Site description				Ceramic assemblages					Other artifacts			
Site number	Occupation (confidence level)	Area (m^2)	Estimated height (m)	Sample size 2006 (2004)	Ceramic density (sherds per m^2)	Ceramic density (g/m^2)	Number of decoration techniques	Sherd types	Chipped stone presence	Ground stone presence	Slag presence	Other finds and features
MAS583	Siga (H)	620	0.5	47	2.68	25.72	3	4, 5, 6	Rare	Present	—	—
MAS584	Siga (H)	310	0.3	62	3.16	29.72	4	None	Rare	Present	—	—
MAS585	Ring (H)	410	0.5	15	0.16	1.04	1	None	Rare	Present	—	—
MAS586	Ring (H)	340	0.5	18	0.28	3.84	2	15	—	Present	—	—
MAS587	Siga (L)	310	0.4	43	2.04	43.36	2	6	—	Present	—	—
MAS588	Siga (H)	230	0.4	37	1.4	29.92	5	3, 4	—	—	—	—
MAS589	Siga (H)	490	0.4	53	2.4	29.48	7	5, 6, 8, 9	—	—	—	—
MAS590	Siga (H)	60	0.4	23	1.16	17.32	3	4, 9	—	—	—	—
MAS591	Siga (H)	150	0.4	17	0.88	10.8	5	3, 5, 9	—	—	—	—
MAS592.1	Siga (H)	3,320	1.5	39	0.8	17.84	13	1, 3, 4, 5, 7	Rare	—	—	—
MAS592.2	Siga (L)	510	0.6	22	0.84	9.56	4	None	Rare	—	—	—
MAS592.3	Siga (H)	710	0.5	27	0.76	21.56	4	5, 7	Rare	Present	—	—
MAS592.4	Siga (H)	1,960	0.7	32	1.44	11.52	2	6	—	—	—	—
MAS593	Not assigned	n/a	n/a	None present	n/a	n/a	n/a	n/a	—	—	—	—
MAS594	Siga (H)	80	0.4	12	0.56	4.72	1	2	—	Present	—	—
MAS595	Tuali-B (H)	250	0.5	59	2.4	13.88	3	13	Rare	—	—	—
MAS596	Siga (L)	350	1	32	1.2	9.64	4	None	Rare	Present	—	—
MAS597	Siga (L)	130	0.6	26	1.8	32.56	2	11	—	—	—	—
MAS598	Siga (H)	350	0.3	31	1.16	47.4	6	3, 4, 6, 8, 9	Rare	—	—	—
MAS599	Siga (L), Tuali-A (L)	200	0.4	19	0.24	17	3	None	Rare	—	—	—

Continued

TABLE A.1 CONTINUED

Site number	Site description			Ceramic assemblages						Other artifacts			Other finds and features
	Occupation (confidence level)	Area (m²)	Estimated height (m)	Sample size 2006 (2004)	Ceramic density (sherds per m²)	Ceramic density (g/m²)	Number of decoration techniques	Sherd types	Chipped stone presence	Ground stone presence	Slag presence	
MAS600	Siga (H)	175	0.2	21	1.44	12.92	3	3, 5	—	—	—	—
MAS601	Siga (H)	130	0.3	36	2.12	9.48	2	3	—	—	—	—
MAS602	Siga (H)	325	0.3	30	1.64	112.28	6	5, 8	Rare	Present	—	—
MAS603	Tuali-A (H)	840	0.3	36	1.52	37.8	3	11	Rare	—	—	Pipe
MAS604	Siga (H)	310	0.6	47	3.12	24.64	7	2, 3, 4, 5, 9	—	Present	—	—
MAS605	Not assigned	80	0.2	15	0.88	12.8	0	None	Rare	—	—	—
MAS606	Siga (L)	80	0.3	14	n/a	n/a	3	2	—	Present	—	—
MAS607	Siga (H)	400	0.3	80	4	55.88	6	2, 5	Rare	Present	—	—
MAS608	Siga (H)	130	0.4	26	0.96	39.56	2	9	Rare	—	—	—
MAS609	Siga (H)	90	0.5	22	0.72	7.96	4	4, 9	—	—	—	—
MAS610	Siga (H)	50	0.2	34	1.16	22.4	3	4	—	—	Rare	—
MAS611	Siga (H)	80	0.5	60	3.28	45.24	6	3, 4, 6, 9	—	—	—	—
MAS612	Siga (H)	80	0.2	18	0.76	6.56	4	3, 6	Rare	—	Rare	—
MAS613	Siga (H)	125	0.4	22	1.04	18.16	1	4	—	—	Rare	—
MAS614	Siga (H)	175	0.4	21	0.68	8.6	2	None	—	—	—	—
MAS615	Tuali-A (H)	430	2	27	0.8	8.88	2	3, 12	—	—	—	—
MAS616	Siga (H)	130	0.6	52	1.72	64.52	6	4, 6, 8, 9	—	Present	—	—
MAS617	Siga (H)	220	0.4	33	0.96	117.12	7	3, 5, 9	—	Present	—	—
MAS619	Siga (H)	1,730	3	26 (16)	0.52	21.92	4	8, 9, 10	—	—	—	—
MAS620	Siga (H)	110	0.6	34	1.96	21.6	4	4, 5, 6, 9	—	—	—	—
MAS621	Siga (L)	380	0.4	37 (0)	1.32	23.08	5	None	—	—	—	—

Continued

APPENDIX A 271

TABLE A.1 CONTINUED

	Site description			Ceramic assemblages					Other artifacts			Other finds and features
Site number	Occupation (confidence level)	Area (m²)	Estimated height (m)	Sample size 2006 (2004)	Ceramic density (sherds per m²)	Ceramic density (g/m²)	Number of decoration techniques	Sherd types	Chipped stone presence	Ground stone presence	Slag presence	
MAS622	Siga (L)	175	1	23	0.76	10.88	2	None	—	—	—	—
MAS623	Siga (H)	450	0.7	13	0.48	7.08	5	10	—	—	—	—
MAS624	Siga (H)	270	0.2	17	0.56	25.64	3	6	—	Present	—	—
MAS625	Siga (H)	175	0.4	16	0.64	5	4	5	Rare	—	—	—
MAS626	Siga (H)	175	0.5	13	0.48	2.36	2	4, 10	—	—	—	—
MAS627	Not assigned	115	0.4	14	0.48	3.96	5	9	Rare	—	—	—
MAS628	Siga (H)	115	0.5	29	1.8	13.68	3	6	Rare	—	—	—
MAS629	Siga (H)	80	0.4	13	0.68	6.8	1	None	Rare	Present	—	—
MAS630	Siga (H)	80	0.3	23	1.12	56.56	3	5, 9	Rare	—	—	—
MAS631	Not assigned	50	0.4	15	1	12.08	2	14	—	—	—	—
MAS632	Tuali-A (H)	20	0	14	0.64	8.72	1	None	—	Present	—	—
MAS633	Not assigned	50	0.3	4	n/a	n/a	2	None	—	—	—	—
MAS634	Tuali-A (H)	60	0.2	54	3.76	71.6	5	9	Rare	—	—	—
MAS635	Siga (H)	750	1.5	94	7.04	66.36	9	3, 4, 5, 6, 9	Present	Present	—	—
MAS636	Siga (H)	140	0.2	62	3.08	45.48	4	2, 4	Rare	Present	—	—
MAS637	Siga (H)	80	0.2	46	1.88	26	6	3, 4, 9	Rare	—	—	—
MAS638	Tuali-A (L)	50	0	19 (0)	0.64	17.64	1	10, 11	Rare	Present	Rare	—
MAS639	Siga (H)	490	0.3	24	1.04	12.32	3	2	Rare	—	Medium furnace	—
MAS640	Siga (H)	n/a	n/a	7	n/a	n/a	3	None	Rare	—	—	—
MAS641	Siga (H)	1	0	45	2.84	44.04	4	3, 5	Rare	—	—	—
MAS642	Siga (H)	180	0.3	25	0.36	15.32	3	3	Rare	—	—	—

Continued

TABLE A.1 CONTINUED

	Site description			Ceramic assemblages					Other artifacts			Other finds and features
Site number	Occupation (confidence level)	Area (m²)	Estimated height (m)	Sample size 2006 (2004)	Ceramic density (sherds per m²)	Ceramic density (g/m²)	Number of decoration techniques	Sherd types	Chipped stone presence	Ground stone presence	Slag presence	
MAS643	Siga (L)	50	0.3	13	0.52	8.24	3	n/a	Rare	Present	—	—
MAS644	Siga (H)	1,200	0	10	0.36	13.8	3	10	Rare	—	—	—
MAS645	Tuali-A (H)	20	0.2	11	0.64	16.52	1	11	—	—	—	—
MAS646	Ring (H)	400	0.5	4	n/a	n/a	0	None	—	—	—	—
MAS647	Siga (L)	20	0.2	7	0.16	2.36	1	None	—	Present	—	—
MAS648	Siga (H)	30	0.5	24	0.92	47.84	2	2, 9	Rare	Present	—	—
MAS649	Siga (H)	310	0.3	18	0.96	18.52	4	5	Rare	Present	—	—
MAS650	Siga (H)	175	0.2	33	2.56	18.16	3	5	Rare	Present	—	—
MAS651	Siga (H)	50	0.1	41	2.84	13.52	1	5	Rare	Present	—	—
MAS652	Not assigned	175	0.3	8	n/a	n/a	1	None	Rare	Present	—	—
MAS653	Siga (H)	1,590	0.5	42	2	14.4	7	2, 3, 4, 6, 9, 10	Rare	Present	Rare	—
MAS655	Siga (L)	80	0.2	16	0.56	15.8	2	9	—	—	—	—
MAS656	Ring (H)	255	0.3	8	0.12	3.8	1	11, 15	Rare	Present	—	—
MAS657	Siga (L)	410	0.4	50	2.96	35.32	3	2, 15	Rare	Present	Present	—
MAS658	Siga (H)	20	0.1	14	0.44	12.32	5	4	—	—	—	—
MAS659	Siga (H)	290	0.3	61	3.08	95.92	7	3, 4, 6, 8, 9	—	Present	—	—
MAS660	Ring (H)	20	0.4	14	0.52	6.76	1	14	Rare	—	—	—
MAS661	Siga (H)	113	0.2	30	1.92	17.28	4	5, 9	Rare	Present	—	—
MAS662	Not assigned	400	0.3	27	1.48	17.68	2	11	Rare	Present	—	—
MAS663	Siga (H)	425	0.4	51	3.08	42.56	4	1, 2, 5	Rare	Present	—	—

Continued

TABLE A.1 CONTINUED

	Site description			Ceramic assemblages						Other artifacts			Other finds and features
Site number	Occupation (confidence level)	Area (m²)	Estimated height (m)	Sample size 2006 (2004)	Ceramic density (sherds per m²)	Ceramic density (g/m²)	Number of decoration techniques	Sherd types	Chipped stone presence	Ground stone presence	Slag presence		
MAS664	Ring (H)	260	0.3	12	0.32	2.44	3	None	—	—	—	—
MAS665	Siga (L), Tuali-A (H)	325	0.3	52	3.32	31.92	6	5, 10	Rare	Present	Present	—
MAS666	Siga (H)	115	0.3	33	1.44	27.56	3	None	—	Present	Present	—
MAS667	Tuali-A (H)	50	0.1	20	0.68	38.2	1	9, 11	—	Present	—	—
MAS668	Tuali-A (H)	175	0.3	59	3.68	172.48	4	9, 14	Rare	—	—	—
MAS669	Siga (H)	240	0.4	5	0.08	0.92	2	4	—	—	—	—
MAS670	Siga (L)	75	0.4	29	1.2	17.12	3	9	—	—	—	—
MAS671	Ring (H)	500	0.3	None present	n/a	n/a	n/a	n/a	—	—	—	—
MAS672	Siga (L)	325	0.3	82	1.28	19.28	6	2, 5, 9, 10	—	Present	Rare	—
MAS673	Not assigned	840	0.4	13	0.76	7.08	3	9	Rare	Present	Rare	—
MAS674	Siga (L)	160	0	9	0.52	4.2	1	None	Rare	—	—	Vitrified ceramic
MAS675	Siga (L)	80	0.1	14	0.4	21.84	2	9	—	—	—	—
MAS676	Siga (L)	95	0.3	28	1.28	40.24	4	3, 9, 11	—	—	—	—
MAS677	Tuali-A (L)	150	0.1	15	0.8	9.16	1	None	—	—	—	—
MAS678	Tuali-B (L)	95	0.2	7	0.12	1.24	0	None	Rare	—	—	—
MAS679	Tuali-A (H)	80	0.1	28	0.76	31.52	1	11	—	Present	—	—
MAS680	Tuali-A (H)	50	0.2	15	0.28	4.44	0	None	Rare	—	—	—
MAS681	Siga (H)	75	0.4	29	1.88	16.24	1	6, 11	Rare	Present	—	—
MAS682	Tuali-A (H)	175	0.3	67	3.68	41.28	2	11, 12	Rare	—	—	—

Continued

TABLE A.1 CONTINUED

	Site description				Ceramic assemblages					Other artifacts			Other finds and features
Site number	Occupation (confidence level)	Area (m²)	Estimated height (m)	Sample size 2006 (2004)	Ceramic density (sherds per m²)	Ceramic density (g/m²)	Number of decoration techniques	Sherd types	Chipped stone presence	Ground stone presence	Slag presence	
MAS683	Siga (H)	125	0.4	25	1.68	9.8	3	5	—	—	—	—
MAS684	Tuali-A (H)	595	0.6	39	0.36	26.2	0	11, 14	Rare	—	—	—
MAS685	Tuali-A (H)	115	0.4	47	1.92	27.12	4	9	Rare	Present	—	—
MAS686	Siga (H)	80	0.3	20	0.52	19.12	4	None	Rare	Present	—	—
MAS687	Tuali-A (L)	300	0.2	32	1.08	25.92	3	7, 9	Rare	Present	—	—
MAS688	Siga (L), Tuali-A (L)	95	0.2	20	1.16	22.76	5	4, 5, 11	—	—	—	—
MAS689	Tuali-A (H)	440	0.2	163	18.96	186.56	6	9, 11, 12, 14	Rare	Present	Rare	—
MAS690	Siga (L)	115	0.3	40	2.28	41.04	5	8	Rare	Present	—	—
MAS691	Not assigned	20	0	11	1.24	7.44	0	None	—	—	Rare	—
MAS692	Siga (H)	210	0.4	9	1.48	11.36	4	1, 6	Rare	—	—	—
MAS693	Not assigned	80	0.2	23	1.52	14.12	3	1, 14	Rare	Present	Rare	—
MAS694.1	Not assigned	260	0.3	13	0.76	5.16	5	8	Rare	Present	—	—
MAS694.2	Siga (H)	510	0.3	33	2.32	21.6	6	1, 6, 9	—	Present	—	—
MAS694.3	Siga (H)	175	0.4	14	0.84	12.12	1	2	Rare	—	—	—
MAS695	Not assigned	50	0.1	7	0.2	2.08	1	4, 11	—	Present	—	—
MAS696.1	Siga (H)	260	0.4	42	2.48	49.76	1	4, 6, 11	Rare	Present	Rare	—
MAS696.2	Siga (H)	510	0.8	96	6.36	75.76	16	1, 4, 5, 6, 11	Rare	Present	—	—
MAS697	Siga (H)	135	0.4	51	4.48	29.12	7	1, 2, 3, 4	Rare	Present	—	—
MAS698	Siga (H)	310	0.6	16	0.44	10.44	2	3	—	Present	—	—
MAS699.1	Tuali-A (H)	175	0.6	15	0.92	11.52	3	None	—	Present	—	—

Continued

TABLE A.1 CONTINUED

Site description				Ceramic assemblages					Other artifacts			
Site number	Occupation (confidence level)	Area (m²)	Estimated height (m)	Sample size 2006 (2004)	Ceramic density (sherds per m²)	Ceramic density (g/m²)	Number of decoration techniques	Sherd types	Chipped stone presence	Ground stone presence	Slag presence	Other finds and features
MAS699.2	Not assigned	490	0.6	23	1.12	54	4	None	Rare	Present	—	—
MAS699.3	Siga (H)	705	0.8	6	0.2	3.6	1	None	Rare	Present	—	—
MAS699.4	Siga (L)	855	1	47	2.92	29.88	6	2, 4, 5	Rare	—	—	—
MAS700	Siga (H)	380	0.5	41	2.24	20.12	5	3, 6	Rare	—	—	—
MAS701	Siga (H)	315	0.5	23	1.64	37.56	5	4	Rare	Present	—	—
MAS702	Siga (H)	390	0.5	42	3.92	38.84	4	3, 4, 5	Rare	Present	—	—
MAS703	Siga (H)	380	0.4	41	1.64	86.08	5	9	Rare	Present	—	—
MAS704	Siga (H)	490	0.5	36	2.16	53.6	5	2	Rare	Present	—	—
MAS705.1	Siga (H)	1,200	1.25	66	4.96	38.6	7	3, 4, 7	Rare	Present	—	—
MAS705.2	Tuali-A (H)	225	0.4	26	1.56	31.92	6	3, 9, 11, 14	Rare	Present	—	—
MAS706	Siga (L)	490	0.7	25	1.12	9.52	6	4, 15	—	Present	—	—
MAS707	Siga (L), Tuali-A (H)	310	0.2	14 (2)	0.52	6.24	2	9, 11	Rare	Present	—	—
MAS708	Tuali-A (H)	360	0.2	107	10.44	134.2	5	9, 11, 12, 14	Rare	—	—	Vitrified tuyère fragment
MAS709	Tuali-A (H)	675	0.2	24	1.2	19.96	1	11	—	Present	—	—
MAS710	Tuali-A (H)	380	0.3	110	7.4	108.92	6	14	—	Present	Rare	—
MAS711	Not assigned	240	0.2	26	2	10.92	2	2, 11	—	—	Present	—
MAS712	Not assigned	310	0	13 (4)	1.92	6.8	2	None	Rare	—	—	—
MAS713	Siga (L)	310	0.3	18	1.68	10.52	4	2, 10	Rare	—	—	—
MAS714	Tuali-A (L)	310	0	11	0.12	5.6	2	4, 10	—	—	—	—

Continued

TABLE A.1 CONTINUED

	Site description				Ceramic assemblages					Other artifacts			
Site number	Occupation (confidence level)	Area (m²)	Estimated height (m)	Sample size 2006 (2004)	Ceramic density (sherds per m²)	Ceramic density (g/m²)	Number of decoration techniques	Sherd types	Chipped stone presence	Ground stone presence	Slag presence	Other finds and features
MAS715	Siga (L)	490	0.5	28	1.6	30.12	3	11	—	Present	—	Two sandstone circles (2 m diameter)
MAS716	Tuali-A (H)	160	0.1	25	2.04	16.68	1	None	Rare	—	—	—
MAS717	Tuali-A (H)	80	0.3	21	0.8	9.92	1	14	—	Present	—	—
MAS718	Tuali-B (H)	50	0.2	38	1.52	87.48	1	11, 14	—	—	—	—
MAS719	Tuali-B (H)	115	0.3	47	1.84	48.72	0	11, 14	—	Present	Present	—
MAS720	Tuali-B (H)	30	0	21	0.48	9.96	2	None	—	—	—	—
MAS721	Siga (H)	n/a	n/a	13	0.52	12.36	3	None	—	Present	Small furnace	—
MAS722	Siga (H)	90	0	23	1.24	18.04	4	3	Rare	—	—	—
MAS723	Lithic (L)	120	0	0	0.16	0.6	n/a	n/a	Common	—	—	—
MAS724	Not assigned	80	0.3	60	2.32	32.88	5	4, 9	Rare	—	—	—
MAS725	Siga (H)	2,190	0.5	47	2.88	23.36	5	3, 4, 5	Rare	Present	—	—
MAS726	Siga (H)	225	0.3	45	1.72	51.6	3	4	—	Present	—	—
MAS727	Tuali-B (H)	80	0.2	38	2.16	18.8	1	11	Rare	Present	—	—
MAS728	Siga (L)	400	0.5	37	2.72	34.12	3	9	—	Present	Present	—
MAS729	Siga (H)	65	0.3	35	1.2	13.96	3	2	—	—	—	—
MAS730	Siga (H)	415	0.4	38	1.8	49.76	4	2, 3	—	Present	Small furnace	—
MAS731	Siga (H)	175	0.3	48	4.48	38.72	9	4, 5, 9	Rare	Present	—	—

Continued

TABLE A.1 CONTINUED

Site description				Ceramic assemblages					Other artifacts			Other finds and features
Site number	Occupation (confidence level)	Area (m^2)	Estimated height (m)	Sample size 2006 (2004)	Ceramic density (sherds per m^2)	Ceramic density (g/m^2)	Number of decoration techniques	Sherd types	Chipped stone presence	Ground stone presence	Slag presence	
MAS732	Siga (H)	115	0.2	36	2.2	47.52	3	2	—	—	—	—
MAS733	Not assigned	350	0.5	31	2.04	26.84	3	None	Rare	Present	Small furnace	—
MAS734	Siga (L)	415	0.5	30	1.32	16.56	3	10	Rare	Present	—	—
MAS735	Siga (L)	280	0.5	27	1.72	17.24	5	3	Rare	Present	—	—
MAS736	Siga (H)	115	0.4	9	0.56	17.52	2	4, 9	—	Present	Present	—
MAS737	Tuali-A (H)	80	0.1	31	1.16	20.88	1	9	—	—	—	—
MAS738	Tuali-B (H)	175	0.1	36	2.16	25.4	0	14	—	Present	Rare	—
MAS739	Siga (H)	115	0.5	30	1.52	43.84	3	3, 9	—	Present	—	—
MAS740	Siga (L), Tuali-A (H)	80	0	19	0.52	10.4	1	2, 12	—	—	—	—
MAS741	Siga (H)	250	0.3	16	1.04	12.52	1	10	—	Present	—	—
MAS742	Siga (H)	115	0.2	29	2.08	12.12	5	11	Rare	Present	Present	—
MAS743	Siga (H)	40	0	19	0.84	4.64	2	None	—	—	—	—
MAS744	Not assigned	80	0.2	24	1.6	10.12	1	None	—	Present	—	—
MAS745	Siga (H)	415	0.3	32	1.24	46.88	3	2, 3, 4, 6	Rare	Present	—	—
MAS746	Siga (H)	175	0.3	29	1.24	37.72	1	6	Rare	Present	Rare	—
MAS747	Siga (L)	130	0.3	32	1.4	30.4	3	9	—	Present	—	—
MAS748	Siga (H)	200	0.3	17	0.6	57.88	2	6	—	Present	—	—
MAS749	Siga (L)	65	0.3	40	2.16	23.92	2	None	—	Present	—	—
MAS750	Not assigned	615	0.4	16	0.4	6.12	3	None	Rare	Present	—	—

Continued

TABLE A.1 CONTINUED

	Site description				Ceramic assemblages					Other artifacts			Other finds and features
Site number	Occupation (confidence level)	Area (m²)	Estimated height (m)	Sample size 2006 (2004)	Ceramic density (sherds per m²)	Ceramic density (g/m²)	Number of decoration techniques	Sherd types	Chipped stone presence	Ground stone presence	Slag presence		
MAS751	Siga (H)	805	0.5	22	0.64	33.64	0	2, 10	—	Present	—	—
MAS752	Siga (H)	900	0.3	33	1.6	10.36	5	4	Rare	Present	Present	Vitrified tuyère fragment
MAS753	Siga (H)	285	0.6	57	3.08	33.6	11	2, 3, 4, 5, 6, 9, 11	—	Present	Rare	—
MAS754	Siga (H)	20	0.05	31	1.16	10.44	2	None	Rare	—	—	—
MAS755	Tuali-A (H)	350	0.4	30	2.56	15.96	1	11	Rare	Present	Present	—
MAS756	Siga (H)	910	1.25	32	1.8	13.6	5	4	Rare	Present	Present	—
MAS757	Siga (H)	115	0.3	25	0.72	6.92	5	4, 5, 9	Rare	—	—	—
MAS758	Siga (L)	95	0.3	19	0.8	7.16	5	None	—	—	—	—
MAS759	Siga (L), Tuali-A (L)	140	0.1	15	1	7.48	5	5, 9	—	—	Rare	Infant burials in pots eroding from surface; left undisturbed
MAS760	Tuali-A (H)	240	0.5	19	2.32	14.8	0	None	Rare	Present	—	—
MAS761	Tuali-A (L)	95	0.1	16	0.96	4.8	1	None	—	Present	—	—
MAS762	Siga (L), Tuali-B (L)	175	0.5	36	1.72	17.8	4	5, 12, 14	—	Present	—	—

Continued

TABLE A.1 CONTINUED

	Site description			Ceramic assemblages					Other artifacts			
Site number	Occupation (confidence level)	Area (m²)	Estimated height (m)	Sample size 2006 (2004)	Ceramic density (sherds per m²)	Ceramic density (g/m²)	Number of decoration techniques	Sherd types	Chipped stone presence	Ground stone presence	Slag presence	Other finds and features
MAS763	Tuali-B (H)	200	0.2	34	1.12	27.72	2	4	—	Present	—	—
MAS764	Siga (H)	200	0.5	17	0.48	6.64	2	3	—	Present	Rare	—
MAS765	Siga (L), Tuali-B (L)	215	0.4	72	4.52	36.44	4	3, 4, 5, 14	Rare	Present	Rare	—
MAS766	Tuali-A (H)	80	0.2	38	1.52	15.28	1	11	—	Present	—	—
MAS767	Tuali-A (H)	200	0.5	47	3.88	27.48	2	2, 12, 14	—	Present	—	—
MAS768	Siga (H)	910	1.25	38	3.08	26.44	4	6, 9	—	Present	Present	—
MAS769	Siga (H)	95	0.2	66	3.24	41	6	2, 5, 6	Rare	Present	Rare	—
MAS770	Tuali-B (H)	500	0	18	0.48	4.88	0	None	—	Present	—	—
MAS771	Tuali-A (H)	176	0.3	8	n/a	n/a	1	None	Rare	—	—	—
MAS772.1	Siga (H)	70	n/a	5	n/a	n/a	6	1, 5	—	—	Present	Deposits 35 cm below surface
MAS772.2	Siga (H)	215	n/a	5(8)	n/a	n/a	2	4, 9	—	—	Present	Deposits 35 cm below surface
MAS773	Siga (H)	225	0.1	16	0.48	9.8	5	3, 5, 6, 15	—	Present	Present	—
MAS774	Siga (H)	550	1.75	70	4.32	61.32	8	1, 4	—	—	—	Whole pot eroding from surface similar to Sherd Type 9

Continued

TABLE A.1 CONTINUED

Site number	Site description					Ceramic assemblages					Other artifacts			
	Occupation (confidence level)	Area (m²)	Estimated height (m)	Sample size 2006 (2004)	Ceramic density (sherds per m²)	Ceramic density (g/m²)	Number of decoration techniques	Sherd types	Chipped stone presence	Ground stone presence	Slag presence	Other finds and features
MAS775	Siga (H)	200	0.3	31	2.52	22.08	8	2, 5	—	Present	—	—
MAS776	Siga (H)	315	1.25	22	0.32	3.68	5	4, 5, 15	—	—	—	—
MAS777	Ring (H)	490	0.5	None present	n/a	n/a	n/a	n/a	—	Present	—	—
MAS778	Siga (H)	290	0.5	24	0.84	7.92	6	1, 4	Rare	Present	—	—
MAS779	Siga (L)	225	0.5	14	0.64	17.92	1	11	—	Present	—	—
MAS780	Siga (H)	1,500	1.5	633	2.4	32.68	24	1, 2, 3, 4, 5, 6, 15	Rare	Present	—	—
MAS781	Not assigned	120	0.3	23	2.08	42.44	1	None	—	Present	Present	—
MAS782	Siga (L)	375	0.3	41	2	251.92	2	9	—	Present	Present	—
MAS783	Siga (H)	50	0.25	26 (2)	0.8	17.6	3	8	Rare	Present	Rare	—
MAS784	Siga (L)	240	0.3	13	0.32	6.2	5	4, 9	—	Present	—	—
MAS785	Not assigned	175	0.3	22	1.2	50.56	6	1, 5	Rare	Present	—	—
MAS786	Not assigned	80	0.1	10	0.68	13.8	3	None	Rare	Present	—	—
MAS787	Siga (H)	115	0.2	21	0.96	48.24	1	2, 6	—	Present	—	—
MAS788	Siga (H)	85	0.4	34	1.76	14.04	5	3, 4	Rare	Present	—	—
MAS789	Tuali-A (H)	115	0.3	28	1.32	13.76	2	9, 11	Rare	Present	—	—
MAS790	Tuali-A (H)	80	0.2	22	0.56	13.92	1	None	—	Present	—	—
MAS791	Siga (L), Tuali-A (L)	65	0.3	22	0.64	17.84	2	4	—	Present	—	—
MAS792	Siga (H)	115	0.25	58	3.08	49.12	6	2, 5, 6, 9, 10	Rare	Present	—	—
MAS793	Siga (H)	175	0.4	29	2.32	45.56	3	6, 9	—	Present	—	—

Continued

APPENDIX A

TABLE A.1 CONTINUED

Site number	Site description				Ceramic assemblages					Other artifacts			Other finds and features
	Occupation (confidence level)	Area (m²)	Estimated height (m)	Sample size 2006 (2004)	Ceramic density (sherds per m²)	Ceramic density (g/m²)	Number of decoration techniques	Sherd types		Chipped stone presence	Ground stone presence	Slag presence	
MAS794	Tuali-A (L)	275	0.2	86	10.76	87.92	7	None		Rare	Present	—	—
MAS795	Siga (L), Tuali-A (L)	855	0.2	51	4.64	59.96	9	5, 11		Rare	Present	Present	—
MAS796	Siga (H)	225	0.4	20	0.76	41.8	8	3, 6, 9		—	Present	—	—
MAS797	Not assigned	145	0.4	14	0.36	3.6	5	None		—	Present	—	—
MAS798	Siga (L)	215	0.5	30	0.72	16.2	5	4, 14, 15		—	—	—	—
MAS799	Tuali-A (H)	40	0	49	2.2	23.44	2	11, 12		Rare	Present	Rare	—
MAS800	Tuali-A (H)	175	0.2	20	0.32	9.12	1	12		Rare	Present	Rare	—
MAS801	Siga (H)	140	0.15	47	2.72	30.4	3	5, 6		—	Present	—	—
MAS802	Siga (H)	80	0.3	16	0.84	9.8	3	3		Rare	—	—	—
MAS803	Siga (H)	200	0.4	26	1.52	19.48	6	5		—	Present	—	—
MAS804	Tuali-A (L)	1,134	1	36	1.72	30.76	8	9, 13		—	Present	—	—
MAS805	Tuali-A (H)	513	1	21	0.92	16.4	3	9, 12, 14		—	Present	—	—
MAS806	Siga (H)	120	0.5	20	0.44	11.8	4	6		—	Present	—	—
MAS807	Siga (H)	300	0.4	34 (7)	1.4	18	5	9		—	Present	—	—
MAS808	Siga (L)	80	0.25	16	0.72	23.72	1	6		—	—	—	—
MAS809	Siga (L)	227	0.4	28	1.16	18.92	5	11		Rare	Present	—	—
MAS810	Siga (H)	177	0.5	30	1.16	132.48	3	6		—	Present	—	—
MAS811	Tuali-A (H)	175	0.4	23	0.84	20.88	2	9, 11		—	Present	—	—
MAS812	Tuali-A (L), Tuali-B (L)	80	0.1	50	2.08	54.88	2	11, 14		—	Present	Present	—
MAS813	Tuali-A (L)	175	0.3	39	2.24	19.92	2	10, 11		Rare	Present	Present	—

Continued

TABLE A.1 CONTINUED

	Site description			Ceramic assemblages					Other artifacts			
Site number	Occupation (confidence level)	Area (m²)	Estimated height (m)	Sample size 2006 (2004)	Ceramic density (sherds per m²)	Ceramic density (g/m²)	Number of decoration techniques	Sherd types	Chipped stone presence	Ground stone presence	Slag presence	Other finds and features
MAS814	Siga (H)	113	0.2	11	0.2	33.64	1	2	—	Present	—	—
MAS815	Siga (H)	189	0.4	49	2.56	17.48	5	3, 4, 6	Rare	Present	—	—
MAS816	Tuali-B (H)	250	0.7	45	2.24	41.2	3	4, 14	—	Present	Present	—
MAS817	Not assigned	227	0.5	15	0.72	11.08	2	9	Rare	Present	Rare	—
MAS818	Tuali-B (H)	225	0.3	18	0.36	6.92	0	14	—	Present	Rare	—
MAS819	Tuali-A (L)	315	0.6	19	0.68	13.96	4	9	Rare	Present	—	—
MAS820	Ring (L)	175	0.4	16	0.28	7.44	1	None	—	Present	—	—
MAS821	Tuali-A (H)	113	0.4	11	0.32	1.96	3	3, 14	—	Present	—	—
MAS822	Tuali-A (H)	254	0.3	16	0.84	18.48	1	9, 11	Present	Present	Rare	—
MAS823	Siga (H)	201	0.3	27 (11)	1.56	30.4	3	2	Present	Present	—	—
MAS824	Siga (H)	225	0.3	24 (0)	1.16	36.92	4	2, 5	Present	Present	—	—
MAS825	Siga (H)	315	0.3	24	1	26.76	3	5	Rare	Present	—	—
MAS826	Siga (H)	315	0.3	10	0.44	34.96	2	5, 10	Rare	Present	—	—
MAS827	Siga (L)	425	0.6	24	2.12	24.88	3	5, 6, 14	—	Present	—	—
MAS828	Tuali-A (H)	80	0.3	17	0.8	17.88	1	9, 11, 14	Rare	Present	—	—
MAS829	Siga (H)	115	0.4	26	1.16	55.36	1	6	Rare	Present	—	—
MAS830	Siga (H)	225	0.3	47	2.68	131.88	5	3, 5, 9	Rare	Present	—	—
MAS831	Siga (H)	95	0.1	66	3.44	58.68	4	2, 3, 5, 10	Rare	Present	—	—
MAS832	Not assigned	80	0.1	17	0.64	20	1	None	Rare	Present	—	—
MAS833	Not assigned	80	0.1	15	0.48	7.32	3	14	Rare	—	—	—
MAS834	Siga (H)	175	0.3	45	1.64	32.76	3	4, 6	—	Present	Rare	—

Continued

TABLE A.1 CONTINUED

Site number	Site description			Ceramic assemblages					Other artifacts			
	Occupation (confidence level)	Area (m²)	Estimated height (m)	Sample size 2006 (2004)	Ceramic density (sherds per m²)	Ceramic density (g/m²)	Number of decoration techniques	Sherd types	Chipped stone presence	Ground stone presence	Slag presence	Other finds and features
MAS835	Siga (H)	175	0.3	58	2.84	50.64	6	1, 2	Rare	Present	Small furnace	—
MAS836	Siga (L), Tuali-A (L)	150	0.4	17	n/a	n/a	2	14	—	—	—	—
MAS837	Siga (H)	225	0.3	23	0.72	59.6	3	2, 4, 9	—	—	Present	—
MAS838	Tuali-B (H)	115	0.5	40	2.24	77.44	1	None	—	Present	—	—
MAS839	Ring (H)	175	0.5	None present	n/a	n/a	n/a	n/a	—	—	—	—
MAS840	Tuali-A (H)	80	0.3	22	0.72	4.08	4	None	—	—	—	Spindle or bead
MAS841	Tuali-A (H)	200	0.3	13	0.64	5.04	2	11, 12	—	Present	—	—
MAS842	Siga (H)	80	0.1	20	1.24	8.32	2	None	—	—	—	—
MAS843	Siga (H)	175	n/a	28	2.56	14.88	5	4, 10	Rare	—	—	—
MAS844	Siga (H)	1,500	1.5	90	5.4	48.4	15	1, 3, 4, 5, 11	Rare	Present	Present	—
MAS845	Siga (H)	255	0.7	21	0.84	8.96	4	9	—	Present	—	—
MAS846	Not assigned	345	1	22	1.44	13.16	6	3, 5, 9, 11	—	Present	—	—
MAS847	Siga (H)	175	0.6	18	0.76	9.32	2	None	—	Present	—	—
MAS848	Siga (L)	225	0.7	11	0.32	12.12	1	12	Rare	Present	—	Pipe
MAS849	Siga (H)	1,000	0.9	74 (10)	7	78.56	11	1, 5, 10	Present	Present	Very large furnace	—
MAS850	Siga (H)	255	0.6	30	1.6	26.08	7	2, 3, 4	—	Present	—	—

Continued

TABLE A.1 CONTINUED

	Site description			Ceramic assemblages					Other artifacts			
Site number	Occupation (confidence level)	Area (m²)	Estimated height (m)	Sample size 2006 (2004)	Ceramic density (sherds per m²)	Ceramic density (g/m²)	Number of decoration techniques	Sherd types	Chipped stone presence	Ground stone presence	Slag presence	Other finds and features
MAS851	Siga (H)	150	0.3	26	1.16	32.64	3	4	Rare	Present	—	—
MAS852	Siga (H)	125	0.3	19	0.48	4.88	1	2	—	Present	—	—
MAS853	Ring (H)	200	0.3	5	n/a	n/a	0	None	—	—	—	—
MAS854	Ring (H)	150	0.3	None present	n/a	n/a	n/a	n/a	—	—	—	—
MAS855	Siga (H)	1,300	0.3	38	0.96	14.08	3	2, 4, 6	Rare	Present	—	—
MAS856	Siga (H)	400	0.3	15 (5)	0.4	10.04	3	2, 4	—	Present	Small furnace	—
MAS857	Siga (L)	150	0.3	34	2.52	47.04	6	9	Rare	Present	—	—
MAS858	Tuali-A (H)	50	0.2	15	0.68	14.96	1	12	Rare	—	—	—
MAS859	Siga (L)	80	0.3	24	0.52	10.76	4	None	—	Present	—	—
MAS860	Siga (H)	80	0.2	16	0.56	4.2	2	15	Present	Present	Present	—
MAS861	Not assigned	240	0.6	33	1.24	19.16	4	5	—	Present	—	—
MAS862	Tuali-A (L)	80	0.3	20	1.16	29.68	2	9, 11	—	Present	Rare	—
MAS863	Tuali-B (H)	240	0.4	17	0.2	6.68	4	11, 13	Rare	Present	Present	—
MAS864	Lithic (L), Siga (L)	95	0	2	0.2	1	0	None	Common	—	—	—
MAS865	Siga (L)	115	0.2	12	0.52	2.76	4	3, 13	—	Present	—	—
MAS866	Siga (H)	50	0	19	0.72	9.88	1	None	Rare	Present	—	—
MAS867	Lithic (H), Siga (L)	15	0	2	n/a	n/a	0	None	Common	—	—	—
MAS868	Siga (L)	225	0.4	15 (1)	0.76	72.6	5	5, 13	Rare	Present	Present	—

Continued

APPENDIX A 285

TABLE A.1 CONTINUED

Site number	Site description			Ceramic assemblages					Other artifacts			
	Occupation (confidence level)	Area (m²)	Estimated height (m)	Sample size 2006 (2004)	Ceramic density (sherds per m²)	Ceramic density (g/m²)	Number of decoration techniques	Sherd types	Chipped stone presence	Ground stone presence	Slag presence	Other finds and features
MAS869	Siga (H)	200	0.3	15	0.2	1.68	6	2, 5, 9	—	Present	—	—
MAS870	Siga (H)	200	0.1	19	1.36	23.52	3	5, 10	Present	Present	—	—
MAS871	Siga (H)	490	0.1	4	n/a	n/a	2	2, 3	—	—	—	—
MAS872	Siga (H)	490	0.1	22	1.6	10.04	5	None	Rare	Present	—	—
MAS873	Siga (H)	270	0.3	27 (3)	1.96	51.68	4	2, 5, 9, 10	Rare	Present	—	—
MAS874	Not assigned	315	0.3	24	1.36	24.12	5	1	Rare	Present	—	—
MAS875	Siga (L)	200	0.3	16	0.6	4.92	2	None	—	Present	Present	—
MAS876	Siga (H)	200	0	11	0.24	15.64	1	None	—	—	Medium furnace	—
MAS877	Not assigned	80	0.1	7	0.24	3.64	1	None	—	Present	—	—
MAS878	Siga (H)	150	0	18 (6)	0.56	15.84	5	5, 6, 7, 9	Rare	Present	Rare	One piece of vitrified tuyère
MAS879	Siga (H), Tuali-A (L)	350	0.5	51	2.64	70.4	4	5, 9, 11	Present	Present	Medium furnace	—
MAS880	Tuali-B (H)	30	0.1	26	1.24	21.16	2	11, 13	Rare	—	—	—
MAS881	Not assigned	350	0.4	16	n/a	n/a	2	6, 7, 14, 15	—	—	—	—
MAS882	Siga (H)	30	0.3	20	0.8	10.08	2	9	Rare	—	—	—
MAS883	Siga (L), Tuali-B (H)	115	0.3	27 (2)	1.24	39.04	2	2, 8, 13, 14	—	—	—	—
MAS884	Siga (L), Tuali-B (L)	80	0.1	39	1.52	126.56	2	10, 13	—	Present	Present	—

Continued

TABLE A.1 CONTINUED

	Site description				Ceramic assemblages					Other artifacts			
Site number	Occupation (confidence level)	Area (m²)	Estimated height (m)	Sample size 2006 (2004)	Ceramic density (sherds per m²)	Ceramic density (g/m²)	Number of decoration techniques	Sherd types	Chipped stone presence	Ground stone presence	Slag presence	Other finds and features
MAS885	Siga (H)	285	0.5	27	1.08	16.6	6	3, 8, 9	Rare	Present	Rare	Upside-down pot in borrow pit profile
MAS886	Siga (L), Tuali-B (L)	175	0.3	25	0.96	11.92	3	1, 11	—	—	—	—
MAS887	Tuali-A (L)	275	0	20	0.88	46.56	2	9	—	Present	—	—
MAS888	Tuali-B (L)	80	0	18	0.92	15.32	3	2	Rare	Present	—	—
MAS889	Tuali-A (H)	50	0	14	0.8	8.84	0	11	—	—	—	—
MAS890	Tuali-B (H)	80	0.2	20	0.48	5.88	2	14	—	—	—	One piece of vitrified tuyère
MAS891	Tuali-B (H)	80	0.2	35	1.8	39.72	1	11, 14	Rare	Present	—	—
MAS892	Siga (L), Tuali-A (L)	160	0.3	28	1.12	28	3	5, 9	Rare	Present	—	—
MAS893	Tuali-A (L)	115	0.3	25	0.52	26.68	4	9	Rare	Present	—	—
MAS894	Siga (L), Tuali-A (H)	225	0.4	13	0.36	6.28	2	2, 9, 11	Rare	Present	—	—
MAS895	Siga (L)	80	0	21	0.56	4.56	4	14	Rare	—	—	—
MAS896	Siga (H)	250	0.3	20	1.12	14.76	3	4, 6, 10	Rare	Present	Present	—
MAS897	Siga (H)	250	0.4	20	0.8	27.32	4	1, 6, 10	Rare	Present	Rare	—
MAS898	Siga (H)	115	0.1	19	0.68	18.88	3	3	Present	Present	—	—
MAS899	Siga (H)	205	0.1	26	1.52	17.36	3	2, 9, 10	Present	Present	—	—

Continued

TABLE A.1 CONTINUED

Site number	Site description			Ceramic assemblages					Other artifacts			Other finds and features
	Occupation (confidence level)	Area (m²)	Estimated height (m)	Sample size 2006 (2004)	Ceramic density (sherds per m²)	Ceramic density (g/m²)	Number of decoration techniques	Sherd types	Chipped stone presence	Ground stone presence	Slag presence	
MAS900	Siga (H)	265	0.2	73 (11)	5.52	55.76	12	1, 2, 4, 5, 10	Present	Present	—	—
MAS901	Not assigned	490	0.3	40	2.36	29.44	10	1	Rare	Present	—	—
MAS902	Pwoli (L), Siga (L)	380	1	77	n/a	n/a	14	2, 6, 10	Rare	Present	—	Animal bone
MAS903	Siga (H)	575	0.8	15	0.76	21.72	6	4, 6, 10	—	Present	—	Several large, intact basal grinding stones
MAS904	Siga (H)	115	0.3	29	1.68	29.6	5	1, 5	—	Present	Rare	—
MAS905	Siga (H)	95	0.2	24	1.52	19.72	3	5	Rare	Present	—	—
MAS906	Siga (L)	50	0.1	9 (2)	0.6	24.44	1	None	Present	—	—	—
MAS907	Lithic (L), Siga (L)	330	0.1	11	0.4	1.6	1	None	Common	—	—	—
MAS908	Siga (H)	230	0.1	30	0.76	11	3	5, 6	Rare	Present	—	—
MAS909	Tuali-B (H)	200	0.3	18	0.68	25.56	0	11	—	Present	—	—
MAS910	Siga (H)	80	0.3	11	0.24	2.52	3	3	Rare	Present	Rare	—
MAS911	Siga (H)	80	0.1	15	0.48	5.08	3	1, 2, 4, 5	—	Present	—	—
MAS912	Siga (H)	115	0.2	20	0.8	14.96	3	3, 4, 6	—	Present	—	—
MAS913	Tuali-B (H)	80	0.1	19	0.84	25.88	1	None	—	—	—	—
MAS914	Not assigned	65	0.2	15	0.64	52.6	1	9	—	Present	—	—
MAS915	Siga (H)	190	0.4	16	0.44	8.4	2	6, 10	—	Present	—	—

Continued

TABLE A.1 CONTINUED

Site description				Ceramic assemblages					Other artifacts			Other finds and features
Site number	Occupation (confidence level)	Area (m²)	Estimated height (m)	Sample size 2006 (2004)	Ceramic density (sherds per m²)	Ceramic density (g/m²)	Number of decoration techniques	Sherd types	Chipped stone presence	Ground stone presence	Slag presence	
MAS916	Tuali-B (H)	80	0.1	14	0.36	3.56	1	14	—	Present	—	—
MAS917	Siga (H)	n/a	n/a	9	n/a	n/a	5	1	—	—	—	—
MAS918	Tuali-B (H)	230	0.25	26	0.8	65.28	3	13, 14	—	—	—	—
MAS919	Tuali-A (H)	157	0.3	19	0.64	22.6	1	11, 12, 14	Rare	Present	Present	—
MAS920	Tuali-B (H)	615	0	4	n/a	n/a	0	11	—	—	—	Indigo dye pits
MAS921	Not assigned	n/a	n/a	None present	n/a	n/a	n/a	n/a	—	—	—	Rock art site
MAS922	Siga (L), Tuali-A (L)	1,470	0	0	22	0.68	27.6	6	11	Rare	Present	—
MAS923	Tuali-B (H)	415	0.6	6	n/a	n/a	1	13	—	—	—	Indigo dye pits
MAS924	Tuali-A (H)	200	0.2	12	0.48	9.8	0	14	—	Present	—	—
MAS925	Not assigned	n/a	n/a	None collected	n/a	n/a	n/a	n/a	—	—	—	Rock art site
MAS926	Siga (H)	1,200	0	50 (45)	6.48	34.52	5	4, 5, 10	Rare	Present	Present	—
MAS927	Siga (H)	150	0.5	30	1.16	34.68	4	9	—	—	Present	—
MAS928	Siga (H)	115	0.2	28 (7)	0.96	20.8	3	3	—	Present	—	—
MAS929	Siga (L), Tuali-B (L)	625	0	20 (15)	0.84	15.76	5	2, 13	Rare	—	Medium furnace	—
MAS930	Tuali-B (L)	200	0.2	8	0.2	3	1	13	—	Present	—	—
MAS931	Siga (H)	125	0.1	26	0.96	27.56	7	1	—	Present	—	—

Continued

TABLE A.1 CONTINUED

	Site description				Ceramic assemblages					Other artifacts			
Site number	Occupation (confidence level)	Area (m^2)	Estimated height (m)	Sample size 2006 (2004)	Ceramic density (sherds per m^2)	Ceramic density (g/m^2)	Number of decoration techniques	Sherd types	Chipped stone presence	Ground stone presence	Slag presence	Other finds and features
MAS932	Siga (H)	65	0.2	16	0.4	5.96	3	2, 3, 9	—	Present	—	—
MAS933	Siga (H)	1,375	2	19 (8)	0.4	12.88	4	6, 7, 9	—	Present	Present	—
MAS934	Siga (L)	175	0.2	24	0.96	16.2	2	10	—	Present	—	—
MAS935	Siga (H)	275	0	38 (10)	1.84	16.28	3	2, 5	Rare	Present	Present	—
MAS936	Siga (H)	805	0	54 (36)	4.44	48.12	3	2	Rare	—	—	—
MAS937	Tuali-B (H)	>10,000	0.2	31 (56)	1.08	19.8	2	13, 14	Rare	Present	Medium furnace	Indigo dye pits
MAS938	Siga (H)	190	0.2	27 (10)	0.76	23.52	5	5, 10	—	Present	Small furnace	—
MAS939	Siga (H)	50	0	10	n/a	n/a	1	4, 6	—	—	Small furnace	—
MAS940	Siga (H)	20	0.05	15	0.6	9.72	3	2, 5, 9	—	Present	—	Inset sandstone arrangements
MAS941	Tuali-A (H)	150	0.4	21	0.64	25.36	1	14	—	Present	—	—
MAS942	Tuali-B (H)	200	0.4	12	0.28	32.16	0	14	—	Present	—	—
MAS943	Tuali-B (H)	80	0.2	13	0.4	12.68	0	11, 14	—	Present	—	—
MAS944	Tuali-B (H)	115	0.4	12	0.32	7.64	0	11, 14	—	Present	—	—
MAS945	Siga (H)	150	0.4	18	0.84	11.52	4	2, 5, 9	—	Present	Present	—
MAS946	Not assigned	705	0	24	1.16	10.68	5	9	—	—	—	—
MAS947	Lithic (L)	115	0	None present	n/a	n/a	n/a	n/a	Common	—	—	—

Continued

TABLE A.1 CONTINUED

Site description					Ceramic assemblages					Other artifacts			
Site number	Occupation (confidence level)	Area (m^2)	Estimated height (m)	Sample size 2006 (2004)	Ceramic density (sherds per m^2)	Ceramic density (g/m^2)	Number of decoration techniques	Sherd types	Chipped stone presence	Ground stone presence	Slag presence	Other finds and features
MAS948	Tuali-A (H)	175	0.4	24	0.96	19.48	2	9, 11, 14	Rare	Present	Rare	Pipe
MAS949	Tuali-B (H)	80	0.2	23	1	39.16	0	14	—	—	—	—
MAS950	Tuali-B (H)	90	0.5	11	n/a	n/a	0	n/a	—	—	Large furnace	—
MAS951	Tuali-B (H)	13	0.4	15	n/a	n/a	4	13	—	Present	Small furnace	—
MAS952	Tuali-B (H)	7	0.4	13	n/a	n/a	2	13	—	—	Small furnace	—
MAS953	Tuali-B (L)	50	0.8	3	n/a	n/a	2	None	—	—	Medium furnace	—
MAS954	Tuali-A (H)	95	0.3	27	0.96	47.52	2	9	—	Present	—	—
MAS955	Tuali-A (H)	200	0.4	27	3.08	23.6	2	11, 14	Rare	Present	—	Circular stone arrangement
MAS956	Tuali-A (H)	250	0.3	50	4.52	54.2	2	14	Rare	Present	—	Pipe, polishing stone
MAS957	Tuali-A (H)	200	0.4	48	4.68	72.24	2	11, 12, 14	—	—	—	—
MAS958	Siga (H)	150	0.3	24	1	23.88	3	4, 13	—	Present	—	—
MAS959	Siga (H)	80	0	8	0.32	14.16	2	3	—	Present	—	—
MAS960	Not assigned	175	0	8	n/a	n/a	1	None	—	Present	—	—
MAS961	Siga (H)	80	0.1	22	0.44	7.48	3	2, 5, 6	—	Present	—	—

Continued

APPENDIX A   291

TABLE A.1 CONTINUED

Site number	Site description			Ceramic assemblages						Other artifacts				
	Occupation (confidence level)	Area (m²)	Estimated height (m)	Sample size 2006 (2004)	Ceramic density (sherds per m²)	Ceramic density (g/m²)	Number of decoration techniques	Sherd types	Chipped stone presence	Ground stone presence	Slag presence	Other finds and features
MAS962	Siga (H)	125	0.3	22	1.16	8.36	4	5, 10, 14	Rare	—	—	—
MAS963	Tuali-A (L)	150	0.4	35	1.56	60.2	5	9	—	Present	—	—
MAS964	Tuali-B (H)	50	0.05	25	1.44	32.96	1	14	—	—	—	—
MAS965	Siga (H)	255	0.4	22	0.84	11.2	2	None	—	Present	—	—
MAS966	Siga (H)	925	0.5	26	2.28	13.04	3	5, 6, 10	—	Present	Present	—
MAS967	Siga (L), Tuali-A (H)	80	0.5	29	0.56	18.72	1	14	—	—	—	—
MAS968	Tuali-A (L)	200	0.2	20	0.68	6.04	1	6	—	Present	—	Three pipes
MAS969	Siga (H)	490	0.5	24	1	37.84	4	9, 10	—	Present	—	—
MAS970	Siga (L)	175	0.4	23	0.84	24.16	3	6, 9	—	Present	—	—
MAS971	Siga (H)	95	0.4	36	1.44	66.36	2	2, 9	—	Present	—	—
MAS972	Siga (H)	90	0.1	11	0.08	3.28	4	None	—	Present	Medium furnace	—
MAS973	Siga (H)	490	1.25	24	0.8	33.12	6	1, 6, 9	—	Present	—	—
MAS974	Siga (H)	20	0.1	8	n/a	n/a	2	5	—	—	Small furnace	—
MAS975	Siga (H)	105	0.3	23	1.2	25.56	2	None	—	—	—	—
MAS976	Siga (H)	115	0.4	20	0.68	6.36	1	None	—	Present	—	—
MAS977	Tuali-A (L)	660	1.25	41	2.68	32.28	2	9, 14	Rare	Present	—	—
MAS978	Siga (H)	145	0.5	32	2.08	36.32	4	2, 9	—	Present	—	—
MAS979	Siga (H)	50	0.3	22	0.84	31.88	2	2	—	—	—	—

Continued

TABLE A.1 CONTINUED

Site description					Ceramic assemblages				Other artifacts			
Site number	Occupation (confidence level)	Area (m²)	Estimated height (m)	Sample size 2006 (2004)	Ceramic density (sherds per m²)	Ceramic density (g/m²)	Number of decoration techniques	Sherd types	Chipped stone presence	Ground stone presence	Slag presence	Other finds and features
MAS980	Siga (H)	225	0.4	27	1.88	28.76	5	9, 11	—	Present	—	—
MAS981	Siga (H)	105	0.3	19	0.64	11.76	4	5	—	Present	—	—
MAS982	Siga (H)	50	0.1	25	0.68	26.96	3	4, 7	—	Present	—	—
MAS983	Siga (H)	115	0.4	30	1.16	15.2	3	None	—	Present	—	—
MAS984	Siga (L)	1,350	0.7	38	1.68	15.96	6	1, 2, 14	—	Present	—	—
MAS985	Tuali-B (H)	175	0.4	16	0.68	14.6	0	11, 14	Rare	Present	—	Pipe
MAS986	Siga (L)	80	0.1	10	0.2	4.56	1	None	—	—	—	—
MAS987	Siga (H)	225	0.7	18	0.8	6.52	2	None	—	Present	—	—
MAS988	Siga (L), Tuali-B (L)	450	0	20	0.6	8.84	4	5, 10	Rare	Present	—	—
MAS989	Tuali-B (L)	80	0	21	0.32	5.04	4	1	Rare	—	—	—
MAS990	Siga (H)	400	0	15	0.76	5.32	3	1, 5, 11	Rare	Present	Present	—
MAS991	Not assigned	225	0.2	84	6.76	58.76	2	11, 14	Rare	—	Rare	—

APPENDIX B

Ceramic Tempers, Decorations, and Sherd Types

This appendix provides additional details on the ceramic analysis presented in Chapter 3 and elaborated on in Chapters 6 and 7. It includes additional data on temper variability (Table B.1) and decoration groups (Table B.2), as well as full descriptions of the sherd types used to seriate surface assemblages ($N = 1{,}149$ sherds [7% of the study assemblage and 25% of decorated sherds]) from the Maadaga Archaeological Survey. See Tables 11–14 for definitions of decoration field codes.

Full Descriptions of Sherd Types

Sherd Type 1 ($n = 38$)
Figures 19A, 21, 47, and 49

Temper: The majority of these sherds (87%) had quartz-dominant temper and 13% had grog-dominant temper. Additional temper inclusions were rare.

Vessel Form: These vessels were spheroids with slightly constricted throats and flaring necks. Diameters could be obtained from only four vessels: three were almost exactly the same size (neck/rim: 14/18 cm, 15/19 cm, x/19 cm) and one was slightly larger (22/26 cm). As was apparent from the neck and rim diameters, the angle and length of the neck flare were also very consistent, resulting in a standard 4 cm diameter differential. The walls had a fairly narrow thickness distribution (range 5 to 14 mm, mean 10.0 mm, standard deviation 2.3 mm).

Surface Treatment: Of the few vessels that were not weathered, all were self-slipped. The only instance of red slip was on a single sherd with a burnished red slip on the interior of the rim.

Decoration: These vessels had a fairly standardized and complex design grammar, described as Decoration Group C (see Table B.2). The relative frequency of the different decoration techniques in the assemblage was a function of the parts of the vessel represented, not of their relative prominence. The only pattern noted in the design variability was in the use of semicircular channels rather than angular incisions. The former were used on both grog-tempered and quartz-tempered sherds, whereas angular incisions were found only on quartz-tempered sherds.

Firing: These vessels had exceptionally high levels of complete reduction (33%). Smudging techniques may have been in use by some producers or at certain times.

Regional Similarities: Wotzka and Goedicke (2001) classified very similar vessels with identical form and design grammar as Group 13. However, their group consisted entirely of examples with semicircular channels; the variations with angular incisions were absent.

TABLE B.1. Frequency of dominant and regularly occurring temper combinations in the Maadaga Archaeological Survey ceramic assemblage.

Number of sherds	Percentage of assemblage	Field code	Dominant and regular tempers					
			Organic	Grog	Quartz	Mica	Laterite	Slag
7,423	44.9	16	—	×	—	—	—	—
5,088	30.8	28	—	—	×	—	—	—
1,405	8.5	2	—	×	—	—	×	—
920	5.6	1	×	×	—	—	×	—
614	3.7	21	—	—	×	×	—	—
582	3.5	5	—	×	×	—	—	—
172	1.0	15	×	×	—	—	—	—
63	0.4	10	—	×	—	×	—	—
38	0.2	24	—	—	×	×	—	×
36	0.2	4	—	×	×	×	—	—
31	0.2	3	—	×	×	—	×	—
28	0.2	32	—	—	—	×	—	—
27	0.2	20	—	—	×	×	×	—
22	0.1	30	×	—	—	—	—	—
20	0.1	25	—	—	×	—	×	—
16	0.1	22	×	—	×	—	—	—
15	0.1	14	×	×	×	—	—	—
9	0.1	19	—	×	—	—	—	×
4	<0.1	6	—	×	×	×	×	—
2	<0.1	7	—	×	×	—	—	×
2	<0.1	9	×	×	—	×	—	—
8	<0.1	11	—	×	—	×	×	—
1	<0.1	12	×	×	—	—	×	×
3	<0.1	13	×	×	×	—	×	—
2	<0.1	18	×	×	×	×	—	—
1	<0.1	23	×	—	×	×	—	—
1	<0.1	26	—	—	×	—	×	×
7	<0.1	27	—	—	×	—	—	×
1	<0.1	29	×	—	—	—	×	—
3	<0.1	31	—	—	—	×	×	—
1	<0.1	33	—	—	—	—	—	×

Wotzka and Goedicke described the temper of their Group 13 as feldspar, rather than quartz. Their analysis of temper was made in a laboratory setting and the two minerals are visually very similar, therefore it is possible that Sherd Type 1 ceramics were likewise feldspar-tempered. If so, this would have some interesting implications for the temper sourcing, as feldspars are volcanic in origin and more likely found in Birimian deposits to the north and west of the Gobnangou region rather than in the Voltaic sandstones of the escarpment. Thermoluminescence dates on six sherds from Group 13 yielded a 2-sigma date range of 320–544 CE, although one outlier sherd dated to 1055–1267 CE.

Linked Sherds: No other sherd types were likely to derive from the same vessels as Sherd Type 1. Untyped sherds that could derive from the same vessels included quartz-tempered folded strip roulette sherds (Decoration Groups I and N; see Table B.2; in particular, those that were fired in a reduced atmosphere) and undecorated small rim fragments from flared vessels with the same temper and firing conditions. The upper body decoration (incisions and space-filling comb impressions) was distinctive enough that sherds from this part of the vessel were likely to have been assigned to Sherd Type 1.

Sherd Type 2 (n = 83)
FIGURES 21, 47, 49, 51, AND 52

Temper: The bulk of sherds (85%) had grog temper. There were seven quartz-tempered sherds and three tempered primarily with mica. The latter might be a better fit with Sherd Type 3 despite lacking a braided strip roulette (Cord 4) decoration.

Vessel Form: These sherds were from ovoid vessels with open orifices and slightly flaring walls. The vessels were evenly represented across a wide range of diameters with no evidence of size classes (interior range 8 to 34 cm, mean 19.2 cm, standard deviation 7.3 cm; exterior range 10 to 44 cm, mean 22.4 cm, standard deviation 7.8 cm). The vessels had a moderate wall thickness (range 6 to 17 mm, mean 10.3 mm, standard deviation 2.4 mm), although there were significant fluctuations in the vessel wall due to the curvature.

Surface Treatment: The bulk of sherds (60%) were weathered, but the remainder was divided equally between slipped and self-slipped sherds. About half the sherds in each category were burnished.

Decoration: The majority (60%) of sherds had a cord roulette in a wide band on the body of the vessel. Most vessels had twisted cord roulette decoration (Cord 2), although braided cord roulette (Cord 1) was also present on multiple sherds. Folded strip roulette (Cord 3), loosely twisted cord roulette (Cord 7), cord wrapped roulette (Cord 8), and impressed braided cord (IB) were present on one to two sherds for each decoration. Analysis of other vessel characteristics suggested that these cords were used interchangeably. Sherds in this group decorated with braided cord roulette (Cord 1) and sherds with twisted cord roulette (Cord 2) co-occurred at site MAS885.

Firing: Black coring, complete oxidation, and full reduction proportions were generally in line with those of the complete assemblage.

Regional Similarities: Some similar vessels were included in Frank and colleagues' (2001) extremely diverse Group 3. Petit (2005) found vessels with this form throughout the Iron Age in northern Benin, although cord roulette decoration was limited to the latter part of the sequence. In the Dendi region, vessels with similar form (although slightly more defined eversions) and a band of cord roulette decoration were identified at Kwara zeno (site KAZ-14-SI), a site that dates to the late eighteenth century (see Amoussou, Amoussou et al. 2019; Haour 2019:613, plate 12). Finally, Thiombiano-Ilboudo (2010:311) identified vessels with a similar form and possibly banded decoration at Kouaré.

Linked Sherds: No other sherd types were likely to derive from the same vessels as Sherd Type 2. Untyped body sherds from Decoration Groups G and H (see Table B.2) could have

TABLE B.2. Common decorative groups identified in the Maadaga Archaeological Survey ceramic assemblage. See Tables 11–14 for definitions of decoration field codes.

Decoration group	Number of sherds	Percentage of decorated sherds ($N = 4,569$)	Description	Comments
A	196	4.29	Plastic ridges (including R2T, PR, PRG, PRT, MR, MRG); these ridges usually occur in a band near the neck, but may also occur in vertical or circular motifs; the ridges may or may not have twisted cord roulette (Cord 2) on the body below the ridge; straw impressions are frequent	Tend to be thick sherds (mean 17.9 mm) with large, coarse grog and laterite temper. Undecorated surface is usually roughly smoothed and self-slipped.
B	144	3.15	Channel comb (CC or TC) in co-occurrence with parallel channels (PC) in one or two different directions; may have triangular channels (CT) or channels (CH) separating zones of decoration; parallel channels were made by a dragged comb and have distinctive depth and spacing	Tend to be thin sherds (mean 8.7 mm) with grog temper. Interior and exterior surfaces usually with red slip and often polished.
C	38	0.83	Zoned decoration consisting of upper bounding channel or parallel channels at the neck with a band of incised shapes below (CT, I, MI, or SC), the space around which is often filled with comb impressions (FCI); these are then separated from a zone of folded strip roulette (Cord 3 or 9) that covers the base of the vessel by additional parallel channels	Tend to be thin sherds (mean 10.1 cm) with quartz temper.
D	94	2.06	Twisted knotted cord roulette (Cord 5); may occur in a single band or in a block, often together with twisted cord roulette (Cord 2)	Tend to be thin sherds (mean 9.0 mm) with grog temper.

Continued

TABLE B.2 CONTINUED

Decoration group	Number of sherds	Percentage of decorated sherds ($N = 4{,}569$)	Description	Comments
E	26	0.57	Carved wooden roulettes with TDC or VC patterns; may have occasional additional decorative motifs (CI, MCT, PC). TDC and VC can co-occur	Sherds are thin (mean 10.1 mm) and all have quartz temper.
F	14	0.31	Triangular channels, either single (CT) or nested (MCT) with parallel channels or single channels (PC, CH)	This is a highly variable group. Although a few sherds have red slip with a coarse quartz temper, there are no consistent patterns.
G	230	5.03	Braided cord roulette (Cord 1)	This is a highly variable group with a wide range of thicknesses, tempers, and surface treatments.
H	2443	53.47	Twisted cord roulette (Cord 2), occasionally with single channels (CH)	This is a highly variable group with a wide range of thicknesses, tempers, and surface treatments.
I	132	2.89	Folded strip roulette (Cord 3)	This is a highly variable group with a wide range of thicknesses, tempers, and surface treatments.
J	127	2.78	Braided strip roulette (Cord 4) alone or with bounding channel	Of these sherds, 60% have mica temper with weathered surfaces (thickness mean 11.3 mm). The remainder have significant variability in temper, thickness, and surface treatment.
K	79	1.73	Braided strip roulette in chevron pattern (Cord 6)	Of these sherds, 55% are very thin (mean 8.9 mm) with quartz temper. The remainder have significant variability in temper, thickness, and surface treatment. A few examples with mica temper have cord spacing more consistent with Group J.

Continued

TABLE B.2 CONTINUED

Decoration group	Number of sherds	Percentage of decorated sherds ($N = 4{,}569$)	Description	Comments
L	17	0.37	Twisted cord roulette (Cord 7)	This is a highly variable group with a wide range of thicknesses, tempers, and surface treatments.
M	26	0.57	Possible cord wrapped roulette (Cord 8)	All sherds have grog temper; twelve of these sherds were excavated from site MAS572.3 and are likely from the same pot.
N	41	0.90	Folded strip roulette (Cord 9)	This is a fairly variable group; fourteen sherds are from the excavations at sites MAS541 (likewise variable) and MAS572.3 (all with grog temper).
P	20	0.44	Impressed braided cord (IB)	This is a highly variable group with a wide range of thicknesses, tempers, and surface treatments.
Q	26	0.57	Possible folded strip roulette (R1)	Predominantly with grog temper and weathered surfaces. The sherds are concentrated at only thirteen sites.
U	34	0.74	Lip channels (LIPCH)	Those sherds that are not weathered are all red slipped and polished. Although most have quartz temper, about 30% have grog temper.

derived from these vessels, particularly if the sherds were grog-tempered and there was evidence that the roulette decoration occurred in a band. However, twisted cord roulette (Cord 2) was the most common decoration in the assemblage and was found on multiple types of vessels.

Sherd Type 3 ($n = 88$)

FIGURES 17J, 21, 49, AND 53

Temper: These sherds were all made with clay containing dense particles of mica. It is unknown to what extent additional mica may have been added to any that occurred naturally. Of these sherds, 92% had quartz temper, usually recorded as codominant with the mica. In the other 8%, small quantities of crushed slag had been added to the standard quartz–mica mix.

Vessel Form: The curvature of the larger sherds seems to indicate that the vessels had essentially the same open, flaring jar shape as Sherd Type 2. No rim data was available for this group, primarily due to the friable nature of these sherds; all edges, including lips, were heavily eroded. One micaceous vessel with a diameter of 15 cm was identified inset in the ground at site MAS557, although because of the hardness of the sediment no information aside from fabric and diameter could be obtained. Vessel thickness was relatively standardized (range 7 to 15 mm, mean 11.3 mm, standard deviation 1.7 mm).

Surface Treatment: All sherds (including those from excavation) were weathered on both the interior and exterior. These vessels were possibly neither burnished nor slipped, although micaceous slips could have been applied to the exteriors of several sherds that had particularly bright surfaces.

Decoration: All sherds had braided strip roulette decoration, usually in a horizontal band on the neck or body of the vessel, or both. In most cases potters had applied the braided strip roulette along a single diagonal, but in eight cases the roulette was applied in two directions to create a diamond crosshatch pattern. Six sherds had alternate braided strip roulette in a chevron pattern (Cord 6). In some cases a bounding channel demarcated the zone of decoration.

Firing: Black coring, complete oxidation, and full reduction proportions were generally in line with those of the complete assemblage.

Regional Similarities: Micaceous clay is common in the area south of the Atakora Mountains and similar vessels with strip roulettes have been found throughout northwestern Benin (L. P. Petit, personal communication, 2009). Haour and colleagues (2019:165) mention the use of a micaceous fabric in conjunction with a knotted strip roulette at the Phase 4 (early second millennium CE) site of Kantoro (Champion, Haour, and Filippini 2019) in the Dendi region. Possible knotted strip roulettes were very rare in the Maadaga Archaeological Survey assemblage and did not occur on vessels with micaceous fabric.

Linked Sherds: No other sherd types were likely to derive from the same vessels as Sherd Type 3. Untyped sherds that could be from the same vessels included undecorated sherds with the same temper and thickness as Sherd Type 3, as there was evidence the decoration was zoned.

Sherd Type 4 (n = 155 and 9 necks)
FIGURES 17C, 17D, 21, 47, 49, 51, 52, AND 53

Temper: Grog was the primary temper in this group, as it was dominant in 146 (94%) sherds, only 21 of which included additional tempers (mica, quartz, grog, or laterite). The remaining 9 sherds had an assortment of tempers, among them quartz-dominant and mica-dominant sherds. Eighty-nine percent of sherds had medium temper and the remainder had primarily small temper.

Vessel Form: These sherds were from open vessels with only very slightly restricted rims (the fragments were too small to determine whether they were bowls or jars). The rims were very sharply everted with short necks and consequently diameters were taken at both the edge of the lip and at the throat. Rim diameters (n = 32, range 18 to 36 cm, mean

28.3 cm, standard deviation 4.9 cm) were 4 to 8 cm larger than the throat diameters, although the throats were not more consistent than the rims ($n = 26$, range 13 to 32 cm, mean 22.3 cm, standard deviation 5.0 cm). In both cases, the diameters were distributed across the range, rather than clustered. Vessel walls were fairly thin, especially considering that the thickness was likely skewed by the large number of rim sherds (range 5 to 16 mm, mean 9.6 mm, standard deviation 2.2 mm). The significance of neck form was recognized in the field after the completion of primary coding. Nine necks were identified in the body sherd assemblages and recorded by site. However, it was not always possible to match neck data with the primary coding information, as most were undecorated. Consequently, necks were not included in discussions of other variables.

Surface Treatment: As with the assemblage, a large percentage of the sherd interiors (40%) were weathered. Of the remaining sherds, 69 were self-slipped, 27 of which had been burnished. Twenty-three were slipped with a lightly applied, often streaky, orange-red slip. The exteriors were mostly decorated and only 12% had the same very lightly applied orange-red slip as the vessel interiors. This slip may be underrepresented in the coding because of its superficial nature.

Decoration: The majority of sherds were decorated with cord roulettes on the exterior. Almost all decorated sherds (61%) had a variation on twisted knotted cord roulette (Cord 5), either in multiple rows (cord with multiple knots) or in single rows (single knot). Twisted cord roulette (Cord 2) rarely occurred without the knots. When it did it was often from near the neck and may have had knots below on the vessel body. Three examples had twisted cord roulette (Cord 2) on the interior of the neck, such that it would have been visible from above.

Firing: These sherds were more oxidized than the general assemblage. There were no examples of fully reduced sherds and only 60% had black coring. The vessels from which these sherds derived may have been fired at a higher temperature or in a more open atmosphere, but it is also possible this result was due to thin body walls, more porous textures, or a less organic clay source.

Regional Similarities: These sherds were similar to those described as Group 7 by Frank and colleagues (2001). The vessel forms and decorative techniques in use were essentially identical. However, grog was not mentioned as a temper and no dates were given for this group.

Linked Sherds: No other sherd types were likely to derive from the same vessels as Sherd Type 4. Some untyped sherds with twisted cord roulette (Cord 2) could be from these vessels, particularly if they were thin and grog-tempered.

Sherd Type 5 ($n = 144$)
Figures 18A, 18B, 18C, 21, 47, 49, 52, and 53

Temper: The temper for this group was particularly homogenous; 142 sherds were grog dominant and only one had a regularly occurring temper other than grog. The remaining sherds were both quartz dominant: one was an unambiguous example of the definitive double channel comb (TC) decoration and the other had only parallel channels (PC). Of these sherds 85% had medium-sized temper and the remainder had small temper.

Vessel Form: These sherds were from simple open bowls. However, the only nearly complete vessel profile (from site MAS780; see Figure 49) was of a double, hourglass-shaped open bowl. Whether this shape was typical or an anomaly was not certain, although the frequency of similar pedestal bases (see Sherd Type 6) would seem to suggest that Sherd Type 5 was often from double-bowl vessels. Diameters could be obtained from seventeen sherds and were distributed evenly (range 16 to 26 cm, mean 20.2 cm, standard deviation 2.8 cm). The vessels had thin walls (range 5 to 12 mm, mean 8.6 mm, standard deviation 1.6 mm).

Surface Treatment: Sherds of this type were usually completely covered with a thick, highly burnished layer of red slip. Of these sherds, 75% had slip on the interior surface and an additional 20% were weathered. Only seven examples had a self-slipped interior, and only two of these were burnished. We recorded 68% with red slip on the exterior. The remaining 32% were recorded as weathered or decorated and weathered. There were no confirmed examples of sherds with exterior self-slipping.

Decoration: These sherds generally had a zone of decoration of variations on the dragged comb techniques extending from the rim to the mid to lower body (see Decoration Group B, Table B.2). Parallel channels (PC) were almost always present (often in two directions) and single channel comb (CC) decoration was present on 32% of vessels. In contrast, double channel comb (TC) occurred on only 10% of sherds and never co-occurred with single channel comb (CC), although otherwise the sherds were very similar. This minor variation did not pattern spatially and could be the result of production by multiple potters and workshops, a temporal shift in technique, or simply artistic license. At site MAS780 double channel comb (TC) sherds were found in the deep excavation levels, whereas single channel comb (CC) examples occurred in the plow zone, which could suggest a temporal relationship. However, the single channel comb (CC) example was a very small, trampled sherd that may have been dug up from the deep borrow pit nearby. The single and double channel comb (CC and TC) technique co-occurred on the surface at one site (MAS502.7). Parallel channels on sherds assigned to this type had a very standardized spacing of approximately 5 to 7 mm.

Firing: Black coring, complete oxidation, and full reduction proportions were generally in line with those of the complete assemblage, although the reduction proportions were at slightly higher levels than normal.

Regional Similarities: Thiombiano-Ilboudo (2010) documents the frequent use of multiple well-defined parallel channels in the Fada N'Gourma region, but they do not seem to be on the same types of vessels, have the same spacing and design grammar, or use the same very thick red slip. A vessel with a similar hourglass shape was recovered by Petit in northern Benin at the site of Yohongou-I; however, this vessel was decorated with a strip roulette (Petit 2005; L. P. Petit, personal communication, 2009). Petit also identified similar decorative techniques, but never in combination. As described in the Sherd Type 6 discussion below, hourglass vessels with central stems are more widely known. In the Dendi region, burnished bowls of a similar size with incised decorations were identified (Haour et al. 2019:167), but there was no evidence for the hourglass form or the same distinctive use of channels.

Linked Sherds: The association of Sherd Type 5 with Sherd Type 6 bases was presumed from the single example from site MAS780 that combines both types (illustrated in Figure 49). However, it was neither certain that all Sherd Type 5 vessels had a pedestal base nor could it be assumed that all Sherd Type 6 pedestal bases were associated with Sherd Type 5 vessel forms and decoration. Sherd Type 7 had temper and surface treatment consistent with Sherd Type 5 and could be an alternative base form for these vessels. Among untyped sherds, thin grog-tempered sherds with thick red slip on both the interior and exterior could be associated with Sherd Type 5 vessels, but could also come from Sherd Type 6 bases.

Sherd Type 6 ($n = 86$)
Figures 21 and 48

Temper: All but one example had grog-dominant temper and of these only six sherds contained additional temper. There was a single example of a mica-tempered sherd, but while clearly a base of a similar sort, it was heavily eroded and could not be firmly assigned to this sherd type.

Vessel Form: These sherds were high, arching pedestal bases. Joined directly to the rounded base of a vessel, these sherds had the form of small, shallow, upside-down bowls. The base maintained an even or slightly narrowing wall thickness and usually had a clear point of contact with the ground (as opposed to the gradual slope of the underside in Sherd Type 7). The interior arch was at least 1.5 cm, but was often significantly more, possibly 4 to 5 cm or greater. The bases ranged in diameter from 8.5 to 22 cm, with no clear peaks (mean 15.6 cm, standard deviation 4.4 cm). When the diameter could also be taken at the attachment point with the pot, it was generally 50% to 60% of the diameter of the base.

Surface Treatment: These sherds had three distinct zones of surface treatment: the exterior of the vessel (including the visible portion of the base), the interior of the vessel, and the underside of the base. All except for two of the vessel exteriors were slipped and burnished. The vessel interiors likewise were usually slipped and burnished, although a few sherds were self-slipped or weathered. In contrast, the undersides of the bases were only slipped and burnished on 21% of the sherds. Instead, self-slipping was the usual treatment, present on 70% of sherds. The remaining base undersides are weathered or in one case burnished. While it was possible that cases with slipping on the underside may actually have been be lid handles (such that this area would be visible), the one intact Sherd Type 5 or 6 vessel had slipping on the underside of the base.

Decoration: There were channels on about one-third of these sherds, usually about 2 to 4 cm from the base of the sherd. Some intact examples did not have channels and many sherds were missing the areas where channels would usually occur.

Firing: Black coring, complete oxidation, and full reduction proportions were generally in line with those of the complete assemblage.

Regional Similarities: The most frequently cited pedestal bases in West Africa are those of the tripod bowls common archaeologically throughout the contemporary Mande region and neighboring areas (e.g., Mayor et al. 2005; Mayor 2011; Dueppen 2015). This is mentioned here only to emphasize that Sherd Type 6 bases lacked the characteristic three-pillar stem of those vessels. Geis-Tronich (1991) depicted pedestal bases on some twentieth-century vessels. In the Dendi region, bases were rare and the one example of a similar base (B3) was thicker and unslipped (Amoussou, Livingstone Smith et al. 2019:550; Haour et al. 2019).

Linked Sherds: The association of Sherd Type 5 with these bases was presumed from the single example from site MAS780 that combined both types (illustrated in Figure 49). However, it was neither certain that all Sherd Type 5 vessels had a pedestal base nor could it be assumed that all Sherd Type 6 pedestal bases were associated with Sherd Type 5 vessel forms and decoration. Among untyped sherds, as discussed above, thin grog-tempered sherds with thick red slip on both sides could come from either Sherd Type 5 or Sherd Type 6, whereas those with red slip on one side would be more likely to be associated with Sherd Type 6.

Sherd Type 7 (n = 11)
FIGURES 21, 48, AND 49

Temper: Over 90% of sherds were grog-tempered and only one example was quartz-tempered.

Vessel Form: These sherds were flat, flaring pedestal bases. Joined directly to the rounded pot base, they flared outward to create a stable foundation for the pot. The edges of the pedestal were rounded and, at the edge, the underside lay nearly flat against the ground. There may have been a slight depression in the center of the base, but it reached no more than 1 cm above the ground. Although these were likely the bases of open bowls, no sherds of this type were recovered with the upper vessel intact. Because the edges of the pedestals were frequently highly eroded, diameters could be taken on only a few bases; these ranged from 6 to 17.5 cm with a tendency toward the larger bases. These figures were in concordance with the diameters taken at the pedestal–body junction (range 9 to 13 cm, mean 10.1 cm, standard deviation 1.9 cm).

Surface Treatment: These sherds had three distinct zones of surface treatment: the exterior of the vessel (including the visible portion of the base), the interior of the vessel, and the underside of the base. In all cases the exterior of the vessel was slipped and burnished. The same was true of the interior in most cases (although, unlike the exterior, the interiors were frequently weathered). The underside of the base was left unslipped or self-slipped.

Decoration: None present on either the base or the few basal portions of the vessel body present.

Firing: Black coring, complete oxidation, and full reduction proportions were generally in line with those of the complete assemblage.

Regional Similarities: As discussed for Sherd Type 6, bases are generally rare. No bases with this form were identified in the Dendi region (Haour et al. 2019).

Linked Sherds: Sherd Type 7 had temper and surface treatment consistent with Sherd Type 5 and could be an alternative base form for Sherd Type 5 vessels.

Sherd Type 8 (n = 17)
FIGURES 19C, 22, 48, AND 49

Temper: The majority of sherds (88%, $n = 15$) were grog dominant. Of these, thirteen had only grog or organics. Laterite inclusions were more rare. Two sherds were quartz dominant.

Vessel Form: These vessels were open (jars or bowls) with a somewhat similar shape to Sherd Type 9 vessels, although the rims were extruded and pinched to create a faceted appearance. They had a comparable range of diameters (interior range 31 to 48 cm, mean 38.1 cm, standard deviation 5.9 cm; exterior range 34 to 52 cm, mean 43.9 cm, standard deviation 5.9 cm), but they were neither as large nor as small as Sherd Type 9. The vessels were thick, but thinned away from the rim, leading to a relatively flat thickness distribution (range 12 to 25 mm, mean 17.8 mm, standard deviation 4.1 mm).

Surface Treatment: This group of sherds had exceptionally diverse surface treatment; on both the interior and exterior approximately half were self-slipped, with the remainder equally divided among burnished, slipped, slipped and burnished, and weathered. Particularly notable was the high instance of burnishing on both red-slipped and self-slipped vessels (25% of the sherds in this group). Approximately 60% of vessels had straw impressions on the interior, exterior, or both.

Decoration: Pinched rims (RP) were present on all sherds. There were no other decorations on these sherds; if the vessels these sherds are from had additional decoration, it was confined to an area well below the rim.

Firing: No sherds were completely oxidized.

Regional Similarities: Vessels of similar size are common throughout the greater region, although they lack the characteristic rim treatment.

Linked Sherds: No other sherd types likely derived from the same vessels as Sherd Type 8. Among untyped sherds, thick (more than 15 mm) grog-tempered sherds could have come from the same vessels as Sherd Type 8 sherds, particularly if they had burnished exteriors, although there may be some overlap with sherds from Sherd Type 9 vessels.

Sherd Type 9 (n = 175)
Figures 20A, 20B, 20C, 22, 48, 49, and 65

Temper: One hundred sixty-one (92%) of these sherds had dominant grog temper. Of these, 128 also contained laterite and 94 also contained organics. Only 12 sherds were quartz dominant and several of them co-occurred at sites with grog-dominant versions of this type. The remaining sherds had variations on grog, laterite, and organic temper. The majority of sherds (59%) had large temper and the remainder had medium temper.

Vessel Form: These vessels had very thick walls and relatively straight sides. According to a similar vessel drawn by Geis-Tronich (1991:154), they may have been elongated jars with rounded bases, although since no large fragments were recovered from which to reconstruct a vessel profile, they could also have been large open basins. There may have been two size classes: the first a minor group (3 vessels) with interior diameters of 19 to 25 cm and the second the dominant class (33 vessels) with interior diameters from 30 to 50 cm or larger. These vessels had very thick walls (range 9 to 37 mm, mean 18.9 mm, standard deviation 4.6 mm).

Surface Treatment: These sherds were predominantly weathered or self-slipped. Only 5% of sherds had interior slip and a mere 2% had exterior slip. Isolated straw impressions were common; 25% of interiors and 21% of exteriors had them. These impressions were not regular and seemed accidental. It was not apparent whether they were the result of large organic fragments in the clay or from surface impressions made during manufacture (for example, from rotating the pot on a surface during construction).

Decoration: All vessels had a large plastic ridge, usually in a horizontal band either directly on or just below the square rims (ridge placement did not pattern spatially). Occasionally vertical columns or other patterns had been made with the ridge. Ridges most commonly had double-finger impressions (R2T), which were present on 77% of sherds. The remainder was split fairly evenly among the other large ridge forms (PRG, PRT, and PR). The only other decoration on these vessels was twisted cord roulette (Cord 2), a large version of which occurred below the ridge on 13% of sherds. Given the size of these vessels, the bulk of sherds from a given pot were undecorated or had only twisted cord roulette. Although these sherds were not specifically assigned, thick grog- and laterite-tempered sherds were considered in context when seriating site assemblages.

Firing: All sherds were mixed or oxidized. The lack of fully reduced sherds in this case may have been due to the particularly coarse temper.

Regional Similarities: Vessels of similar size were common throughout the greater region. The characteristic ridged rim treatment has been identified at several sites. In Burkina Faso, Kiéthéga (2009, plate 13) depicts a large open vessel with identical decoration in use as a funerary jar at Kugribogdo in Oubritenga. A potentially similar vessel is present at Kouaré in the Fada N'Gourma region (Thiombiano-Ilboudo 2010:307).

In northern Nigeria, Sieber (1992:296, 299) depicted similar rims from sites near Kano. Several examples were found at the Fallau site (I1401-1), which dated to the late first and early second millennia CE. In northern Ghana, Insoll and colleagues (Insoll et al. 2011; Insoll, MacLean, and Kankpeyeng 2013) identified similar ridges (described as "embossed appliqué strip") at the site of Zandoya (1000–1500 CE, with an emphasis on 1300–1500 CE). Interestingly, finger-impressed plastic ridges were not identified in the Dendi region (Haour et al. 2019).

Linked Sherds: No other sherd types were likely derived from the same vessels as Sherd Type 9. Among untyped sherds, thick (more than 15 mm) grog and laterite, as well as grog-tempered, sherds that were either undecorated or decorated with twisted cord roulette (Cord 2) could have been from the same vessels as Sherd Type 9 sherds.

Sherd Type 10 ($n = 49$)
FIGURES 22, 48, AND 49

Temper: The largest temper group consisted of grog-dominant sherds (85%), a quarter of which also had laterite temper. The remaining examples were quartz dominant.

Vessel Form: The intact handles were hemispherical loops with the two ends attaching to the vessel only 1 to 3 cm apart. Many had a central core that extended into the vessel body with the outer layer of the handle smoothed to create a seamless bond with the vessel surface. In a few cases, the handle was recovered with a fragment of the vessel body. In one instance, the handle was perpendicular to the attachment surface and in three other cases it was at a 45° angle. The handles were roughly round in cross section (vertical and horizontal dimensions were usually within 0.5 cm), and were within a fairly small range of diameters (range 1.5 to 4.5 cm, mean 3.2 cm, standard deviation 0.5 cm). Decoration and temper crosscut the diameter spread. We had no information on the type of vessel to which these handles may have been attached, although two handles were associated with perforated vessel walls, a feature that is generally associated with steamers or *couscoussières* (S. K. McIntosh 1995; Mayor 2011). Geis-Tronich (1991) only depicted handles that extended in a gentle arc from the middle of the vessel body to the rim or throat on vessels in a pitcher style. Some of the handle fragments may have been of this variety.

Surface Treatment: Approximately 40% of all lug handles were red slipped and about half of these were also burnished. The remainder was weathered, with the exception of five examples of self-slip.

Decoration: Only three handles were decorated. One was covered with a twisted cord roulette (Cord 2) and the other two had gouges in a V pattern along the handle exterior.

Firing: Black coring, complete oxidation, and full reduction proportions were generally in line with those of the complete assemblage.

Regional Similarities: Variations on lug handles were found in most regional ceramic assemblages that included large vessels.

Linked Sherds: Given the limited understanding of how lug handles were associated with full vessels, it was not possible at this time to assess whether these sherds were derived from the same vessels as other typed or untyped sherds.

Sherd Type 11 (n = 86 and 7 necks)
Figures 22, 65, 66, and 72

Temper: All sherds had quartz as a dominant temper. Only seven (8%) had another temper (six with grog and one with mica); 97% of sherds had medium temper.

Vessel Form: These sherds were from jars with large flaring necks, similar (although not necessarily identical) to the jars found in Gobnangou region markets in 2004 and 2006. For a few jars ($n = 15$) it was possible to take a diameter at the throat (range 9 to 36 cm, mean 11.8 cm, standard deviation 2.9 cm). The throat diameters clustered into two size classes: 9 to 18 cm and 26 to 36 cm. Given the long and variable necks, diameter at the rim varied widely ($n = 31$, range 15 to 50 cm or more, mean 27.3 cm, standard deviation 8.8 cm). The size classes present in the throat diameter data were obscured by the variability in neck length. Because all these sherds were rims with strong, thickened inflection points, thickness measures were strongly influenced by how far below the neck the measurement was taken (range 7 to 23 mm, mean 11.8 mm, standard deviation 2.9 mm).

Surface Treatment: These sherds had a particularly high instance of weathering (61%) on both the interior and exterior. Of those that were not weathered, approximately half were red slipped and the other half were self-slipped. On the red-slipped sherds the pigment covered both the interior and exterior surfaces completely.

Decoration: No decorations were recorded for any sherd in this group. However, the sherds rarely extended past the neck and no data were available on shoulder and body decoration or lack thereof.

Firing: Black coring, complete oxidation, and full reduction proportions were generally in line with those of the complete assemblage.

Regional Similarities: Frank and colleagues (2001) included a rim similar to these in their Group 5. Group 5 also contained Sherd Type 9 sherds. While large flared rims are common in northern Burkina Faso (Czerniewicz 2004), central Burkina Faso (Thiombiano-Ilboudo 2010), and to the east along the Niger River (Haour et al. 2016, 2019), they were not known to the south in northern Benin (L. P. Petit, personal communication, 2009). There is no current evidence that the flared vessels identified in neighboring regions were similar in any respect other than form.

Linked Sherds: These sherds were potentially from the same kind of vessels (or, although unlikely, even literally from the same pot if sherds are from the same site) as many other typed sherds. Sherd Type 12 sherds were characterized by thin-walled bodies and braided strip roulette (Cord 6) decoration on the shoulder, but were identical above the neck to Sherd Type 11 sherds, such that Sherd Type 12 sherds broken at the neck would be classified with Sherd Type 11. Geis-Tronich (1989, 1991) depicted vessels with Sherd Type 11 rims, Sherd Type 13 shoulder decoration, and Sherd Type 14 basal roughing. Consequently, Sherd Type 11 likely incorporates significant variability in vessels. Among untyped sherds, quartz-tempered sherds with or without red slip could have derived from the same vessels as Sherd Type 11, but could also be from Sherd Type 12, 13, 14, or 15.

Sherd Type 12 (n = 6 and 12 necks)
Figures 17K, 22, 65, and 66

Temper: All sherds had exclusively quartz temper. Temper size was predominantly medium.

Vessel Form: These were jars with large flaring necks, similar to those from which Sherd Type 11 sherds were drawn. The two vessels on which rim diameters could be taken both fell within the small diameter category of Sherd Type 11 (neck/rim: 10/15.5 cm and 20/27 cm). The primary distinguishing vessel form characteristic between the two was the extremely thin body walls of Sherd Type 12. Because the sample was very small and these sherds were primarily located near the rim, the difference between the two types was not as clear in the data as it was visually (range 7 to 12 mm, mean 9.5 mm, standard deviation 2.2 mm).

Surface Treatment: These sherds were generally weathered. A gray surface treatment (possibly underfired red slip) was present on some sherds of this group, but it was not consistently recorded.

Decoration: The sherds were from vessels with a crisp, deeply impressed version of braided strip roulette in a chevron pattern (Cord 6) on the shoulder; in some cases, where not enough of the decoration was present to see the full motif, it was recorded as a twisted cord roulette (Cord 2), because braided strip roulette was not recognized in the field. Some thin, quartz-tempered, braided strip roulette (Cord 6) body sherds should almost certainly be included here, but it was clear from the assemblage that these sherds were also associated with other types of vessels. Consequently, only sherds associated with the appropriate vessel form are assigned, although all thin, quartz-tempered, braided strip roulette (Cord 6) sherds were considered in context when seriating the site assemblages.

Firing: There were no completely reduced sherds; however, the sample size was small.

Regional Similarities: None, other than those described generally for Sherd Type 11 jars above.

Linked Sherds: As described above, these sherds could have been considered a subset of Sherd Type 11 sherds. There were likely sherds from the same vessels as Sherd Type 12 grouped with Sherd Type 11, as many Sherd Type 11 sherds lacked the characteristic shoulder portion of the vessel. Sherd Type 13 sherds had the same temper as Sherd Type 12. It is possible that this technique was used on these vessels, although the very thin shoulder walls would have needed to thicken substantially toward the base. It is more likely that the decorations characteristic of Sherd Type 12 and Sherd Type 13 were applied to different vessels and not used in conjunction with each other. Among untyped sherds (as noted under Decoration above), very thin braided strip roulette (Cord 6) and twisted cord roulette (Cord 2) (and undecorated) quartz-tempered sherds could have derived from the same vessels as Sherd Type 12 sherds. However, there was likely overlap (particularly among undecorated sherds) with sherds deriving from the vessels associated with Sherd Types 11, 13, 14, and 15.

Sherd Type 13 (n = 26)
FIGURES 17L, 17M, 22, 66, AND 72

Temper: All sherds in this group were tempered exclusively with quartz.

Vessel Form: As this type was represented only by body sherds, no archaeological vessel form data were available. Geis-Tronich (1989, 1991) depicted several vessels decorated with very similar roulettes. In all cases, these vessels were ovoid jars with constricted throats (*cuali*) and flaring necks. The roulette was applied to the shoulder or upper body of the vessel, or both. The vessel walls had relatively standardized thickness, perhaps in part because all sherds may have been from the same part of the vessel (range 8 to 13 mm, mean 10.2 mm, standard deviation 1.3 mm).

Surface Treatment: Of the two sherds that were not weathered on the interior, one was self-slipped and one was red slipped and burnished. (This could indicate a more open vessel orifice if the decoration was on the shoulder. Slipping and burnishing rarely occurred beyond the neck on the interiors of highly constricted vessels.) On the exterior, approximately 25% of sherds were red slipped. In many cases, the red slip was primarily in undecorated areas, possibly from zonal application or because these areas retained slip during weathering, since they could be burnished for better adhesion. In either case, the incidence of red slip depended in part on whether the decoration filled the sherd.

Decoration: These vessels all had carved wooden roulette decoration (see Decoration Group E, Table B.2). These roulettes fell into two categories: those with closely spaced parallel channels in overlapping triangular arrangements and those with raised V motifs in nested or linear patterns. In two cases both types of roulettes occurred on the same sherd. Other decorative techniques were occasionally applied over or around these roulettes, including small circular impressions or channels in parallel or triangular designs.

Firing: Black coring, complete oxidation, and full reduction proportions were generally in line with those of the complete assemblage.

Regional Similarities: Frank and colleagues (2001) classified this type of wooden roulette, quartz- or feldspar-tempered sherd as Group 5 and noted the similarity of these sherds to the contemporary Gulmance pottery described by Geis-Tronich (1989, 1991). Many of the examples they described were also red slipped. These vessels were presumed to date to the latter second millennium CE (Wotzka and Goedicke 2001). Thiombiano-Ilboudo (2010:322) includes a drawing of a zigzag triangle roulette from Bandingue at Namoungou that could be similar to that found in the Gobnangou region and, more significantly, indicates that the forms and decorations she identified at Yiendéni at Kouaré are similar to those in Frank and colleagues' (2001) Groups 3 and 5 (Thiombiano-Ilboudo 2010:409).

According to Petit, wooden roulettes, some similar to those described here, were found north of the Atakora Mountains throughout the historical period (fourteenth to eighteenth century CE). They were often associated with iron production (Petit 2005; L. P. Petit, personal communication, 2009). In the MAS area, we recovered Sherd Type 13 sherds from at least two smelting sites, but we also found these at habitations and in association with dye pits.

In the Dendi region, an identical roulette was identified at the site of Boyeri (Haour 2019:612, plate 11, sherd 1), which according to oral histories was occupied between the 1850s and the 1880s (Nikis, Livingstone Smith, and Gosselain 2019). Sherds with identically coded decoration were also found at Kwara zeno (late eighteenth century CE), Torouway (eighteenth to nineteenth century CE), and Bokorobu (undated, but late second millennium CE) (Amoussou, Amoussou et al. 2019; Haour et al. 2019; Livingstone Smith and Gosselain 2019; Takpara 2019).

Linked Sherds: These sherds potentially derived from the same vessels as Sherd Types 11 and 14 sherds. As described above, Geis-Tronich (1989, 1991) depicted vessels with Sherd Type 11 or 15 rims, Sherd Type 13 shoulder decoration, and Sherd Type 14 basal roughing. Among untyped sherds, quartz-tempered sherds with or without red slip could have been from the same vessels as Sherd Type 13, but could also derive from Sherd Type 11, 12, 14, or 15. Interestingly, at Boyeri this sherd also co-occurs with large flared rims (Haour 2019:612, plate 11).

Sherd Type 14 (n = 166)

Temper: All sherds had quartz-dominant temper and only four examples contained any additional type of temper.

Vessel Form: Because the basal roughing treatment characteristic of this type was normally applied to the rounded base of the vessel, virtually no vessel form information could be derived from the archaeological sherd assemblage. Geis-Tronich's (1989, 1991) illustrations suggested that this treatment was used primarily on large constricted-neck storage jars or water jars, although it was present on a range of vessels. The example of interior red slip (see below) indicated that at least some open vessels had this treatment. Sherds were fairly thick, as they likely came from the basal portion of the pot (range 8 to 20 mm, mean 13.0 mm, standard deviation 2.5 mm).

Surface Treatment: Of these vessels, 90% were weathered on the interior. Of the remaining 10%, approximately half were self-slipped and half were red slipped. All vessels had a roughing layer applied to the exterior and none had red slip.

Decoration: None.

Firing: Black coring, complete oxidation, and full reduction proportions were generally in line with those of the complete assemblage.

Regional Similarities: Geis-Tronich (1989, 1991) described the use of this technique by contemporary Gulmance potters (see discussion above).

Linked Sherds: These sherds are potentially from the same vessels as Sherd Types 11, 13, and 15 sherds. As described above, Geis-Tronich (1989, 1991) depicted vessels with Sherd Type 11 or 15 rims, Sherd Type 13 shoulder decoration, and Sherd Type 14 basal roughing. Among untyped sherds, quartz-tempered sherds with or without red slip derived from the same vessels as Sherd Type 13, but could also be from Sherd Type 11, 12, 14, or 15.

Sherd Type 15 (n = 19)
FIGURES 22 AND C.1

Temper: All sherds had exclusively quartz temper.

Vessel Form: In general, only small rim segments were available for this group; however, most of them seemed to be the flaring necks of constricted jars. It was possible to measure rim diameter on only five vessel. These ranged evenly from 14 to 44 cm, suggesting that this sherd type covered a whole class of vessels. Sherd thickness was moderate (range 7 to 15 mm, mean 11.1 mm, standard deviation 2.1 mm).

Surface Treatment: All sherds were completely red slipped on both the interior and the exterior. Burnishing was ubiquitous on the exterior, but only 63% of sherds had burnishing on the interior.

Decoration: All vessels had a channel along the top of the lip (LIPCH). This channel was possibly made using a technique documented by Geis-Tronich (1989, 1991), in which a leaf of *Ficus gnaphalocarpa* was wrapped around the rim of the pot, with its prominent midrib aligned along the top of the lip and dragged in a circle to smooth, channel, and otherwise finish the rim.

Firing: Black coring, complete oxidation, and full reduction proportions were generally in line with those of the complete assemblage.

Regional Similarities: Geis-Tronich (1989, 1991) described the use of this technique by contemporary Gulmance potters (see discussion above). These rims were identical to those of jars for sale at the Nampuansiga market in 2004 and 2006, but those vessels also had mica in the paste, which differentiated them from these archaeological examples.

Linked Sherds: These sherds are potentially from the same vessels as Sherd Type 13 and 14 sherds. As described above, Geis-Tronich (1989, 1991) depicted vessels with Sherd Type 11 or 15 rims, Sherd Type 13 shoulder decoration, and Sherd Type 14 basal roughing. Among untyped sherds, quartz-tempered sherds could have derived from the same vessels as Sherd Type 15, particularly if they had red slip, but could also be from Sherd Type 11, 12, 13, or 14.

APPENDIX C

Ring Occupation Sites

The Maadaga Archaeological Survey documented every location with evidence of human occupation that lacked standing architecture, therefore some recorded sites dated to the recent past (within the last fifty years). Some of these sites were easily identifiable by artifacts that included bottle glass and plastics, wooden bases of granaries still in place, and visible individual round hut locations. Huts were typically arranged on the edges of a circle with a gap (entry area) to the west and an open, often ashy central courtyard, thus the moniker "Ring" (Table C.1; see sketch map of site MAS864 in Figure 14). Like the sites of the previous occupations, Ring occupation sites were typically the size of a household compound, were shallow, and lacked depth of deposit. The material culture of these more well-preserved sites was used as a baseline to identify other very recent sites that were less well preserved.

In general, the Ring sites had very few artifacts and, in particular, very few ceramics (in several cases none could be located). In the five cases where a systematic surface collection was taken, the average density was only 4.36 g/m², significantly lower than previous occupations. The highest density site (MAS538 at 8.28 g/m²) would be in the bottom 15% of other occupations. This paucity of ceramic artifacts is likely the result of several factors. First, ceramics have been replaced in many daily tasks by metal and plastic containers (Geis-Tronich 1991). Second, the increased availability of donkeys and donkey carts in the latter half of the twentieth century would have made moving ceramic vessels, particularly large ones, a much easier task (Swanson 1979b). Finally, the significant increase in cotton cultivation over the past twenty-five years has dramatically transformed the landscape. Farmers are cultivating significantly larger areas and soil nutrients are more quickly depleted with this demanding crop. More rapid soil exhaustion combined with increases in the area cultivated around the household compound in a given year could easily result in shorter average occupation length.

Ring occupation sites had a more constrained ceramic assemblage than the Tuali occupation (Tables C.2 and C.3; Figure C.1). More than 95% of sherds were tempered with quartz and rates of red slipping were significantly higher (over 50%), although the latter could be simply a function of a shorter period of exposure to the elements. Other than slip, sherds were generally undecorated, with the exception of an occasional cord roulette or

TABLE C.1. Characteristics of Ring occupation single-component sites assigned a high level of confidence.

Site features	High-confidence sites
Total number of sites	13
Near neem trees	2
Near seasonal drainage	3
Near seasonal pool	0
Near seasonal inundation or marsh	0
Total sites near water	3
Plowing disturbance present	7
Borrow pit disturbance present	0
Chipped stone present	3
Ground stone present	4

TABLE C.2. Characteristics of the ceramic assemblage from the Ring occupation by assigned confidence level for single-component sites.

Site features	High-confidence sites
Number of sherds	112
Percentage of sherds with:	
Grog temper	6.3
Quartz temper	93.7
Grog and quartz temper	—
Mica and quartz temper	—
Red slip	70.5
Decoration	8.9
Number of decoration techniques in use	6
Mean number of decoration techniques in use per 100 sherds	13.5
Number of sherds assigned to:	
Sherd Type 11	1
Sherd Type 14	1
Sherd Type 15	3

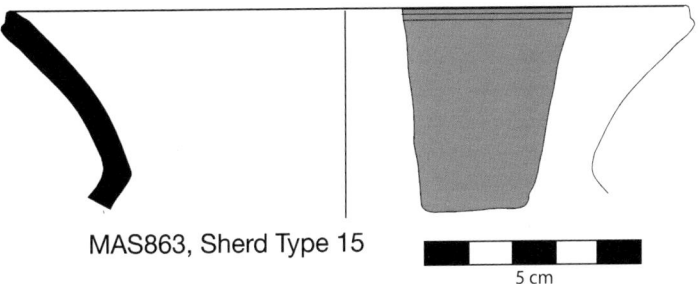

FIGURE C.1. Ring occupation ceramics Sherd Type 15 from site MAS863.

TABLE C.3. Decorations in use in the Ring occupation ceramic assemblage at high-confidence single-component sites. For sherd type descriptions see Appendix B. For full descriptions of decoration techniques see Tables 11–14.

Technique	Field code	Number of sherds ($n=112$)	Number of sites ($n=13$)	Associated sherd types
Twisted cord roulette	Cord 2	3	3	
Lip channel	LIPCH	4	2	15
Multiple triangular channels	MCT	3	2	
Parallel channels	PC	2	2	
Cord wrapped roulette	Cord 11	1	1	
Channel	CH	1	1	

incised triangular channels. Flared jars with channels on the lip (Sherd Type 15) were the most common vessel form and, in one case, Sherd Type 14 was also present.

Ring sites are limited in their interpretive value because they represent a small, transitional sample toward current occupation patterns. They were fairly substantial for seasonal occupation sites, as they had multiple structures and were likely inhabited as the primary residence. Over the past thirty years, as population has expanded in the study region, more and more farmers have moved from nucleated villages to more distant areas, an effect clearly seen in comparisons of satellite images from the early 1970s and early 2000s (UNEP 2008; see also the discussions in Casti [2015]). In the earlier images, the boundaries of the national parks and other protected areas could not be distinguished and most intensive cultivation was concentrated near communities. In contrast, the images from 2000 show evidence of extensive cultivation and park boundaries are visible as crisp transitions. The increase in land under cultivation in the study region can even be seen between 2004 and 2006. In the first season several parts of the survey area were uncultivated, but by 2006 cotton farming had increased to the point where no arable land was left fallow.

APPENDIX D

Rock Art and Hidden Granary Sites

The Maadaga Archaeological Survey identified two rock art sites and one hidden granary site (Figure D.1). Although significant, these sites are undated and could not be fully incorporated into the primary text of this book.

Rock Art in the Gobnangou Region

The MAS documented two rock art sites (MAS921 and MAS925). Both sites are well known to local residents, who encouraged us to visit them. The shelters seem to have been used for painting over many years, with many overlapping motifs. Characterization of these complex palimpsests was further complicated by the poor condition of the paintings. Not only were spalls common at both shelters, but the paint itself was faded or flaking in many places.

Similar sites have been identified near Yobri and presumably occur throughout the Gobnangou region (Millogo and Koté 2000:50). Millogo and Koté (2000:50) describe the motifs at Yobri as drawn from the signs used in Gulmance geomancy. Although no pictures of the Yobri rock art have been published, Cartry (1963) documented signs used by mid-twentieth-century Yobri geomancers.

Site MAS921 (Figure D.2) was a small cave approximately 12 m across and 4 m deep with a roof height of 2 to 3 m. Located an easy climb up a gentle rock face, the cave had a clean rock floor and, aside from the dense, overlapping paintings that seem to have originally covered the walls and ceiling, no cultural artifacts were found. The paintings at this site were particularly poorly preserved and heavily affected by spalling, although we were able to identify several motifs, including dots with short lines extending from them, rows of small dots, parallel lines, chains, and lines and zigzags.

In contrast to the small enclosed MAS921, MAS925 was a large, airy overhang (Figure D.2). The platform measured 20 m across and 6 m deep, with the flat, angled rock face that formed the rear wall of the shelter rising up at least 20 m to its roof. The shelter was high on the escarpment face and access required both navigating the talus slope and scrambling up a sheer portion of the escarpment. The rear wall was painted with an as-

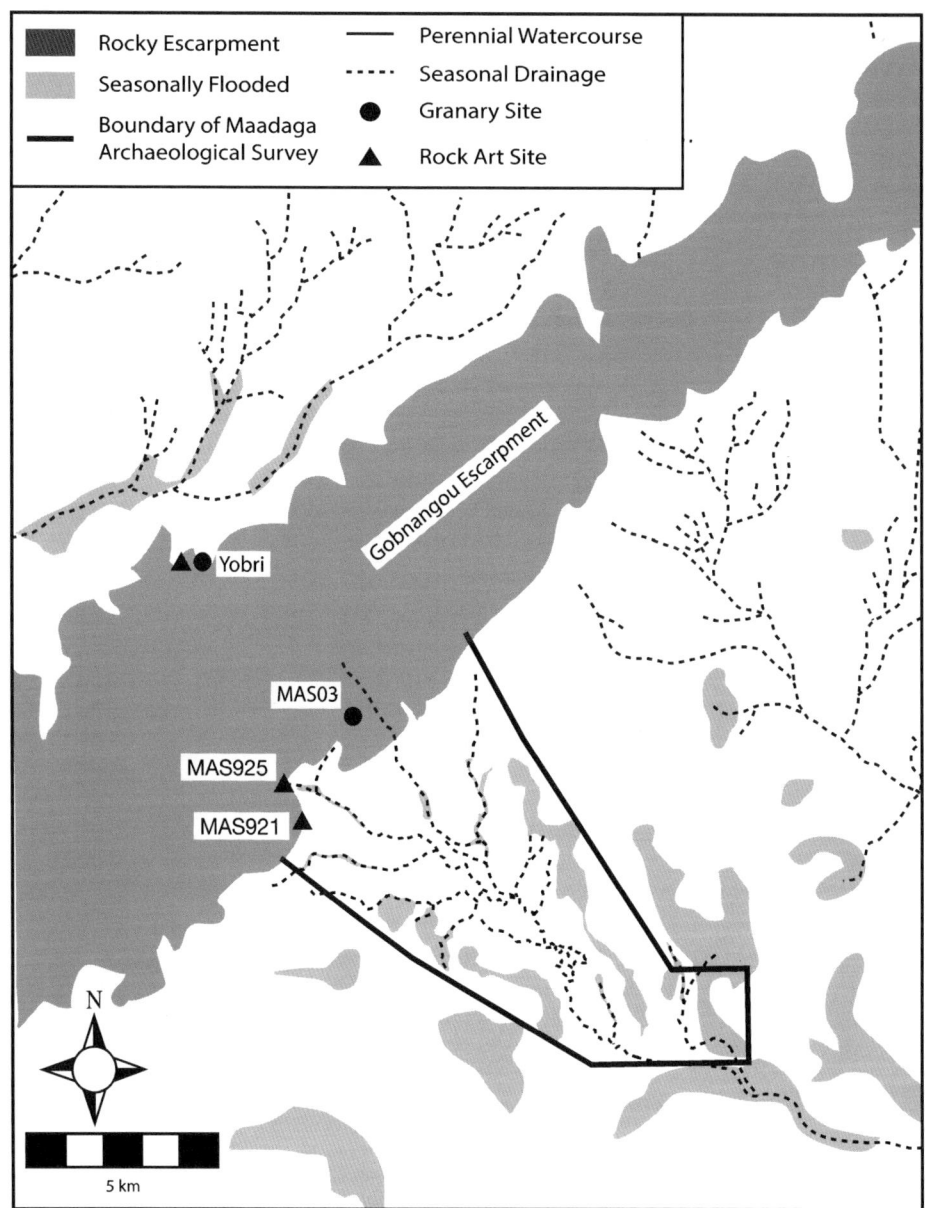

FIGURE D.1. Rock art (MAS921 and MAS925) and hidden granary (MAS03) sites in the Gobnangou region.

sortment of motifs, including chains, groups of small dots, and circles containing dots (Figures D.3 and D.4).

Ceramics were present in some degraded sandstone pockets at the north end of the overhang. We left them undisturbed because of the symbolic significance of the site, but noted the presence of decorations, including twisted cord roulette, cross-hatched incisions, and V-shaped incisions (see Wotzka and Goedicke [2001, fig. 7.3] for a similar sherd).

Figure D.2. Rock art sites MAS921 (*at left*) and MAS925 (*at right*) seen from the base of the Gobnangou escarpment.

The MAS921 and MAS925 rock art sites shared similarities in painting method and motifs. Both sites were decorated primarily with orange and red pigments, with occasional use of black pigment (possibly charcoal). The line widths were consistent with the use of fingers to apply the colors. Several motifs, including lines, chains, groups of dots, and messy space-filling lines and zig-zags, were present at both shelters, although each also had unique motifs. The clearest analogs to the geomancy symbols described by Cartry (1963) were the dots with short lines found at MAS921; however, many other symbols could also derive from geomancy. Casti (2015) described rockshelters in the escarpment as being used for ritual purposes, including *bado* investitures and divination by geomancers.

Hidden Granary Sites in the Gobnangou Region

In 2004, the MAS visited and documented a hidden granary site on top of the escarpment. Like the rock art sites, it is well known to local residents, who suggested that we visit it. As the site was outside the survey boundaries, it was not revisited in 2006 and therefore not included in the MAS site numbering system (see Chapter 3). Because it was the third site visited in 2004, it will be referred to as MAS03.

Site MAS03 was a small, low rockshelter located on the edge of an interior valley near the middle of the escarpment. The shelter entrance was difficult to see from the ground and high enough to have a good view of the valley, although the gentle slope made

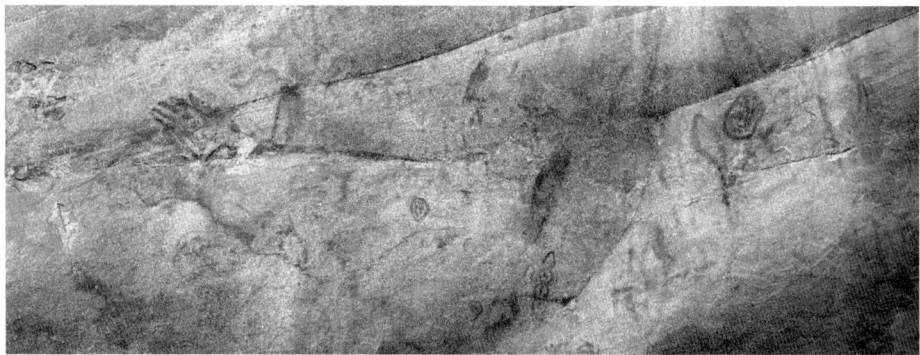
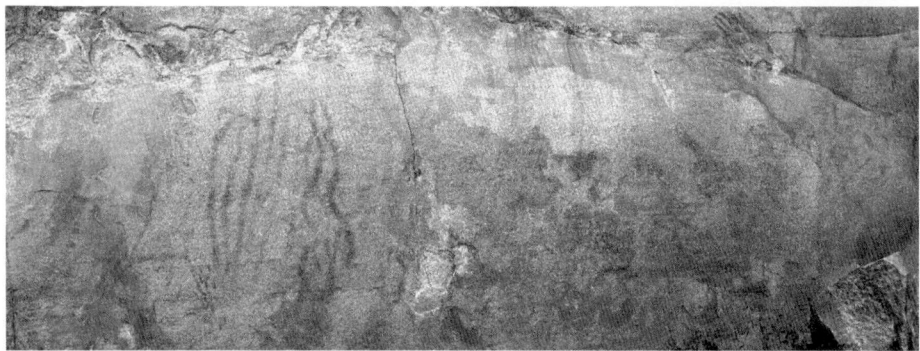

Figure D.3. Paintings at rock art site MAS925. Contrast has been increased in the photographs to make the markings more visible. See Figure D.4.

it easy to reach. The shelter itself was small and low, with the interior height ranging from 50 to 90 cm (Figures D.5 and D.6). Within the shelter were eleven small clay structures, located 1 to 3 m from the drip line so that they could not be seen from below even if the entrance was spotted.

These structures, seven round and four square, were made of organic-tempered clay with pure clay layers on the interior and exterior to smooth them. In several cases ceramics or pieces of rock built on the rock floor of the shelter were used to create level bases, presumably for coiling given the wall thickness of around 3 to 5 cm. A few ceramics from the site were documented, most of which had quartz and grog temper, although one was

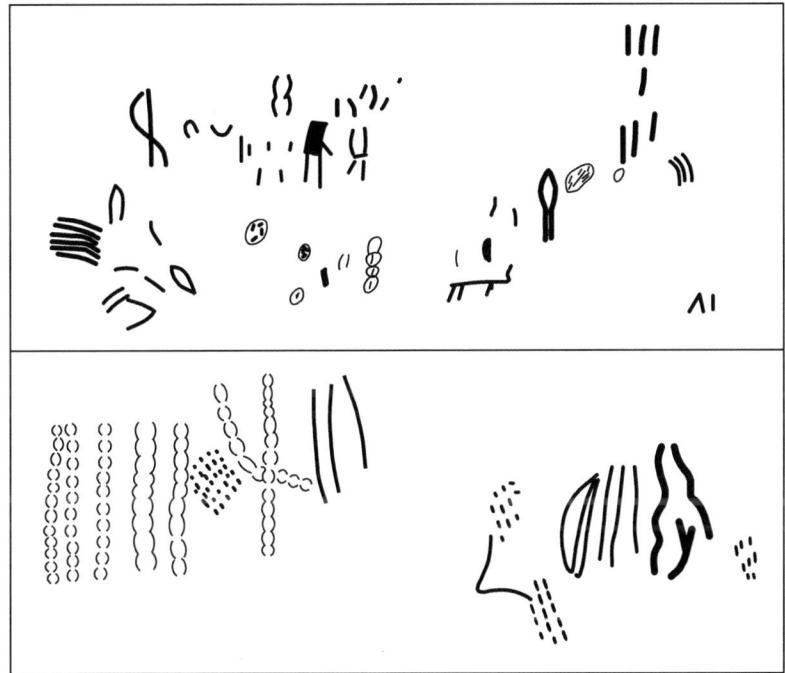

FIGURE D.4. The rock art motifs at site MAS925 (see Figure D.3; spatial arrangement of the drawings is approximate).

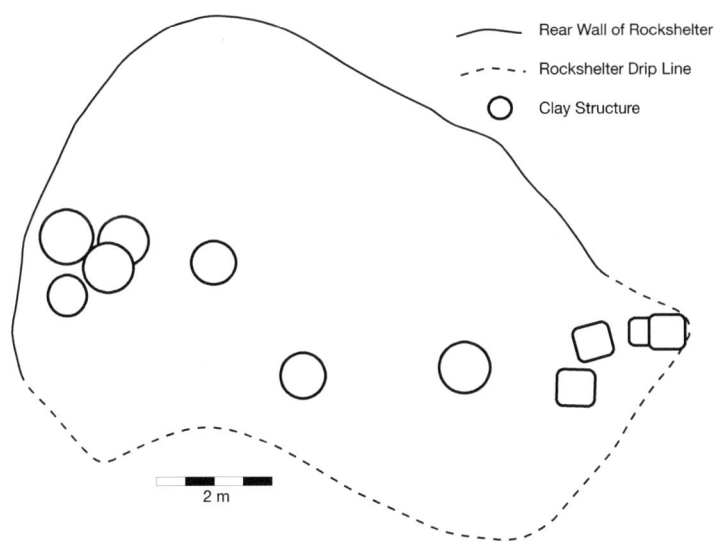

FIGURE D.5. Plan of hidden granary rockshelter site MAS03 showing the locations of clay structures.

FIGURE D.6. Circular (*top*) and square (*bottom*) structures at hidden granary rockshelter site MAS03.

micaceous. Most sherds were undecorated; twisted cord roulette and a carved wooden roulette that produced dense small squares were the only decorations observed. According to local residents, the structures at the site were constructed during an old war, one which took place before guns were available. They explained that the round structures were used for storing millet and the square ones were for baobab fruits. They noted that, on occasion, people would sleep at the site for safety.

Similar structures hidden in rockshelters, all also described as granaries, have been documented by Millogo on the north side of the escarpment (Millogo and Koté 2000:54–56) and noted in additional locations north of the escarpment by Casti (2015). At

Yobri, the granaries were large (more than 4 m tall) and part of what Millogo characterized as a defensive structure. In contrast, those at Pagou were much more similar to those at site MAS03, as they were less than a meter tall and in an elevated cave with a low ceiling. Millogo associated these with refuge rather than defense. Millogo documented local oral histories indicating that the granaries were used until the sixteenth century, when the arrival of the Gulmance caused people to flee to the Atakora Mountains. Thiombiano-Ilboudo (2010) likewise documented small rockshelters, some of which had been dug out to increase their size, including one near Kouaré with a fortified entrance.

REFERENCES

ADAMS, WILLIAM Y., AND ERNEST W. ADAMS. 1991. *Archaeological Typology and Practical Reality.* Cambridge: Cambridge University Press. 427 pp.

AGORSAH, E. KOFI. 1985. Archeological implications of traditional house construction among the Nchumuru of northern Ghana. *Current Anthropology* 26(1):103–115.

AHN, PETER M. 1970. *West African Soils.* 3rd ed. Oxford: Oxford University Press. 332 pp. (West African Agriculture 1.)

ALLSWORTH-JONES, PHILLIP. 1987. The earliest settlement in West Africa and the Sahara. *West African Journal of Archaeology* 17:87–129.

—2019. *The Middle Stone Age of Nigeria in Its West African Context.* Oxford: Archaeopress. 240 pp.

ALPERN, STANLEY B. 1995. What Africans got for their slaves: A master list of European trade goods. *History in Africa* 22:5–43.

ALVES, JOÃO PEDRO GALHANO. 2012. *Anthropologie et écosystèmes au Niger: humains, lions et esprits de la forêt dans la culture gourmantché.* Paris: Editions L'Harmattan. 444 pp.

AMBROSE, STANLEY H. 2002. Small things remembered: Origins of early microlithic industries in sub-Saharan Africa. *Archaeological Papers of the American Anthropological Association* 12(1):9–29. https://doi.org/10.1525/ap3a.2002.12.1.9.

AMES, KENNETH M. 1991. Sedentism: A temporal shift or a transitional change in hunter-gatherer mobility patterns? In: Susan A. Gregg, ed. *Between Bands and States.* Carbondale: Center for Archaeological Investigations, Southern Illinois University at Carbondale. pp. 108–134. (Occasional Paper 9.)

AMOUSSOU, PASCAL GNANKPO, INÈS COROLIN AMOUSSOU, NICOLAS NIKIS, OLIVIER GOSSELAIN, AND ALEXANDRE LIVINGSTONE SMITH. 2019. Kwara zeno (KAZ-14-SI & II). In: Anne Haour, ed. *Two Thousand Years in Dendi, Northern Benin: Archaeology, History and Memory.* Leiden: Brill. pp. 373–378. (Journal of African Archaeology Monograph Series 13.) https://doi.org/10.1163/9789004376694.

AMOUSSOU, PASCAL GNANKPO, ALEXANDRE LIVINGSTONE SMITH, NICOLAS NIKIS, AND ANNE HAOUR. 2019. Tomboutou (TOU-14-S1). In: Anne Haour, ed. *Two Thousand Years in Dendi, Northern Benin: Archaeology, History and Memory.* Leiden: Brill. pp. 546–550. (Journal of African Archaeology Monograph Series 13.) https://doi.org/10.1163/9789004376694.

ANDAH, BASSEY W. 1978. Excavations at Rim, Upper Volta. *West African Journal of Archaeology* 8:75–138.

—1980. Excavations at Rim, north-central Upper Volta: A paleoecological study. In: B. K. Swartz, Jr., and Raymond E. Dumett, eds. *West African Culture Dynamics: Archaeological and Historical Perspectives.* The Hague: Mouton. pp. 41–66. https://doi.org/10.1515/9783110800685.41.

—1995a. Studying African societies in cultural context. In: Peter R. Schmidt and Thomas C. Patterson, eds. *Making Alternative Histories: The Practice of Archaeology and History in Non-Western Settings*. Santa Fe, NM: School of American Research Press. pp. 149–181.

—1995b. European encumbrances to the development of relevant theory in African Archaeology. In: Peter J. Ucko, ed. *Theory in Archaeology: A World Perspective*. London: Routledge. pp. 116–128.

ANQUANDAH, JAMES. 2014. Trends in the development of archaeology and heritage studies in Ghana. In: Samuel Agyei-Mensah, Joseph Atsu Ayee, and Abena D. Oduro, eds. *Changing Perspectives on the Social Sciences in Ghana*. Dordrecht: Springer. pp. 11–31.

ARAZI, NOÉMIE, AND KATIE MANNING. 2010. Twisted cord roulettes. In: Anne Haour, Katie Manning, Noémie Arazi, Olivier Gosselain, Ndèye Sokhna Guèye, Daouda Keita, Alexandre Livingstone Smith, et al., eds. *African Pottery Roulettes Past and Present: Techniques, Identification and Distribution*. Oxford: Oxbow Books. pp. 134–143.

ARNOLD, DEAN E. 1985. *Ceramic Theory and Cultural Process*. Cambridge: Cambridge University Press. 268 pp.

ASHLEY, CERI Z. 2010. Towards a socialised archaeology of ceramics in Great Lakes Africa. *African Archaeological Review* 27(2):135–163. https://doi.org/10.1007/s10437-010-9074-0.

ASHLEY, CERI Z., ALEXANDER ANTONITES, AND PER DITLEF FREDRIKSEN. 2016. Mobility and African archaeology: An introduction. Special Issue: Mobility and African Archaeology. *Azania: Archaeological Research in Africa* 51(4):417–434. https://doi.org/10.1080/0067270X.2016.1233766.

ASHLEY, CERI Z., AND KATHERINE M. GRILLO. 2015. Archaeological ceramics from eastern Africa: Past approaches and future directions. *Azania: Archaeological Research in Africa* 50(4):460–480. https://doi.org/10.1080/0067270X.2015.1102939.

ASSÉ, RAINER, AND JAMES P. LASSOIE. 2011. Household decision-making in agroforestry parklands of Sudano-Sahelian Mali. Agroforestry Systems 82:247–261. https://doi.org/10.1007/s10457-011-9395-2.

AUBRÉVILLE, ANDRÉ. 1949. *Climats, Forêts, et Désertification de l'Afrique Tropicale*. Paris: Société d'Editions de Géographiques, Maritimes et Coloniales. 351 pp.

BAKER, KATHLEEN M. 2000. *Indigenous Land Management in West Africa: An Environmental Balancing Act*. Oxford: Oxford University Press. 271 pp.

BALANDIER, GEORGES, AND GILLES SAUTTER. 1963. Mission M. Cartry-G. Remy en Haute-Volta (1962). *Cahiers d'Etudes Africaines* 3(11):435–442. https://www.jstor.org/stable/4390842.

BARHAM, LARRY, AND PETER MITCHELL. 2008. *The First Africans: African Archaeology from the Earliest Toolmakers to Most Recent Foragers*. New York: Cambridge University Press. 601 pp.

BARNARD, HANS, AND WILLEKE WENDRICH, EDS. 2008. *The Archaeology of Mobility: Old World and New World Nomadism*. Los Angeles: Cotsen Institute of Archaeology at UCLA. 617 pp. (Cotsen Advanced Seminars Series 4.)

BARRAL, HENRI. 1968. Tiogo: *Étude Géographique d'un Terroir Léla (Haute-Volta)*. Paris: Mouton. 72 pp. (Atlas des structures agraires au sud du Sahara 2.)

BASCOM, WILLIAM. 1951. Yoruba cooking. *Africa: Journal of the International African Institute* 21(2):125–137. https://www.jstor.org/stable/1156465.

BASSETT, THOMAS J., AND DONALD CRUMMEY, EDS. 2003. *African Savannas: Global Narratives and Local Knowledge of Environmental Change*. Oxford: James Currey. 270 pp.

BAYALA, JULES, J. SANOU, ZEWGE TEKLEHAIMANOT, SIBIRI JEAN OUEDRAOGO, ANTOINE KALINGANIRE, RICHARD COE, AND MEINE VAN NOORDWIJK. 2015. Advances in knowledge of processes in soil–tree–crop interactions in parkland systems in the West African Sahel: A review. *Agriculture, Ecosystems and Environment* 205:25–35. https://doi.org/10.1016/j.agee.2015.02.018.

BEAUDRY, MARY C., AND TRAVIS G. PARNO, EDS. 2013. Archaeologies of Mobility and Movement. New York: Springer. 265 pp.

BECKER, MARK, AND FRED WENDORF. 1993. A microwear study of a Late Pleistocene Qadan assemblage from southern Egypt. *Journal of Field Archaeology* 20(4):389–398. https://www.jstor.org/stable/530070.

BEDAUX, ROGET, JEAN POLET, KLENA SANOGO, AND ANNETTE SCHMIDT, EDS. 2005. *Recherches Archéologiques à Dia dans le Delta Intérieur du Niger (Mali): Bilan des Saisons de Fouilles 1998–2003*. Leiden: Research School of Asian, African, and Amerindian Studies, Leiden University. (Mededelingen van het Rijksmuseum voor Volkenkunde 33.) 544 pp.

BELEMSOBGO, URBAIN, PIERRE KAFANDO, BASILE A. ADOUABOU, SOMANEGRÉ NANA, SIA COULIBALY, ASSAN GNOUMOU, AND TILLMANN KONRAD. 2010. Le réseau d'aires protégées [Network of protected areas]. In: Adjima Thiombiano and Dorothea Kampmann, eds. *Atlas de la Biodiversité de l'Afrique de l'Ouest [Biodiversity Atlas of West Africa]*. Volume 2, Burkina Faso. Ouagadougou and Frankfurt am Main: BIOTA. pp. 354–363 [in French and English]. https://www.uni-frankfurt.de/47616989/BIOTA-Atlas-BF.

BERELOV, ILYA. 2006. Signs of sedentism and mobility in an agro-pastoral community during the Levantine Middle Bronze Age: Interpreting site function and occupation strategy at Zahrat adh-Dhrá 1 in Jordan. *Journal of Anthropological Archaeology* 25(1):117–143. https://doi.org/10.1016/j.jaa.2005.09.001.

BINFORD, LEWIS R. 1980. Willow smoke and dogs' tails: Hunter-gatherer settlement systems and archaeological site formation. *American Antiquity* 45(1):4–20. https://doi.org/10.2307/279653.

—1982. The archaeology of place. *Journal of Anthropological Archaeology* 1(1):5–31. https://doi.org/10.1016/0278-4165(82)90006-X.

BINNEMAN, JOHAN N. F. 1997. Usewear traces on Robberg bladelets from Rose Cottage Cave. *South African Journal of Science* 93(10):479–481. http://search.ebscohost.com/login.aspx?direct=true&db=aph&AN=278789&site=ehost-live&scope=site.

BINNEMAN, JOHAN N. F., AND PETER J. MITCHELL. 1997. Usewear analysis of Robberg bladelets from Sehonghong Shelter, Lesotho. *Southern African Field Archaeology* 6(1):42–49.

BLANTON, RICHARD E. 2016. *How Humans Cooperate: Confronting the Challenges of Collective Action*. With Lane F. Fargher. Boulder: University Press of Colorado. 435 pp. https://muse.jhu.edu/book/48975.

BLENCH, ROGER. 2014. African agricultural tools: Implications of synchronic ethnography for agrarian history. In: Chris J. Stevens, Sam Nixon, Mary Anne Murray, and Dorian Q. Fuller, eds. *Archaeology of African Plant Use*. Walnut Creek, CA: Left Coast Press. pp. 243–257. (Publications of the Institute of Archaeology, University College of London 61.)

BLIER, SUZANNE PRESTON. 1987. *The Anatomy of Architecture: Ontology and Metaphor in Batammaliba Architectural Expression*. Chicago: University of Chicago Press. 332 pp.

BOFFA, JEAN-MARC. 1999. *Agroforestry Parklands in Sub-Saharan Africa*. Rome: FAO. 230 pp. (FAO Conservation Guide 34.)

BOHANNAN, PAUL. 1954. *Tiv Farm and Settlement*. London: Her Majesty's Stationery Office. 87 pp. (Colonial Research Studies 15.)

BOND, WILLIAM J. 2008. What limits trees in C4 grasslands and savannas? *Annual Review of Ecology, Evolution, and Systematics* 39:641–659. https://www.jstor.org/stable/30245180.

BOULET, RENÉ, AND JEAN-CLAUDE LEPRUN. 1969. *Étude Pédologique de la Haute-Volta, Région Est*. Dakar: Centre ORSTOM. 331 pp.

BOUSMAN, C. BRITT. 2005. Coping with risk: Later Stone Age technological strategies at Blydefontein Rock Shelter, South Africa. *Journal of Anthropological Archaeology* 24(3):193–226. https://doi.org/10.1016/j.jaa.2005.05.001.

BREUNIG, PETER, AND KATHERINA NEUMANN. 2002. From hunters and gatherers to food producers: New archaeological and archaeobotanical evidence from the West African Sahel. In: Fekri A. Hassan, ed. *Droughts, Food and Culture: Ecological Change and Food Security in Africa's Later Prehistory*. New York: Kluwer Academic/Plenum Publishers. pp. 123–156.

BREUNIG, PETER, AND HANS-PETER WOTZKA. 1991. Archäologische Forschungen im Südosten Burkina Fasos 1989/90: Vorbericht über die erste Grabungskampagne des Frankfurter Sonderforschungsbereichs 268 "Westafrikanische Savanne." *Beiträge zur Allgemeinen und Vergleichenden Archäologie* 11:145–187.

BRONK RAMSEY, CHRISTOPHER. 2017. Methods for summarizing radiocarbon datasets. *Radiocarbon* 59(2):1809–1833. https://doi.org/10.1017/RDC.2017.108.

BROOKS, GEORGE E. 1993. *Landlords and Strangers: Ecology, Society, and Trade in Western Africa, 1000–1630*. Boulder: Westview Press. 360 pp.

BRUNFAUT, VICTOR, AND JEAN-FRANÇOIS PINET. 2019. Architecture and settlements today. In: Anne Haour, ed. *Two Thousand Years in Dendi, Northern Benin: Archaeology, History and Memory*. Leiden: Brill. pp. 58–72. (Journal of African Archaeology Monograph Series 13.) https://doi.org/10.1163/9789004376694.

BURKILL, HUMPHREY MORRISON. 1985. *The Useful Plants of West Tropical Africa*. 2nd ed. Volume 1, Families A–D. Kew: Royal Botanic Gardens. 976 pp.

—1994. *The Useful Plants of West Tropical Africa*. 2nd ed. Volume 2, Families E–I. Kew: Royal Botanic Gardens. 636 pp.

—1995. *The Useful Plants of West Tropical Africa*. 2nd ed. Volume 3, Families J–L. Kew: Royal Botanic Gardens. 857 pp.

—1997. *The Useful Plants of West Tropical Africa*. 2nd ed. Volume 4, Families M–R. Kew: Royal Botanic Gardens. 969 pp.

—2000. *The Useful Plants of West Tropical Africa*. 2nd ed. Volume 5, Families S–Z, Corrigenda, Addenda, Cryptogamata. Kew: Royal Botanic Gardens. 686 pp.

—2004. T*he Useful Plants of West Tropical Africa*. 2nd ed. Volume 6, General Index. Kew: Royal Botanic Gardens. 1,263 pp.

CAMERON, CATHERINE M., AND STEVE A. TOMKA, EDS. 1993. *The Abandonment of Settlements and Regions: Ethnoarchaeological and Archaeological Approaches*. Cambridge: Cambridge University Press. 201 pp. (New Directions in Archaeology.)

CANDOTTI, MARISA. 2010. The Hausa textile industry: Origins and development in the precolonial period. In: Anne Haour and Benedetta Rossi, eds. *Being and Becoming Hausa*. Leiden: Brill. pp. 187–212. (African Social Studies Series 23.)

CAPRON, JEAN. 1973. *Communautés Villageoises Bwa: Mali, Haute Volta*. Paris: Musée de l'Homme, Institut d'Ethnologie. 379 pp. (Mémoires de l'Institut d'Ethnologie 9.)

CARTRY, MICHEL. 1963. Notes sur les signes graphiques du géomancien Gourmantché. *Journal de la Société des Africanistes* 33(2):275–306. https://doi.org/10.3406/jafr.1963.1373.

—1966. Clans, lignages et groupements familiaux chez les Gourmantché de la région de Diapaga. *L'Homme* 6(2):53–81. https://www.jstor.org/stable/25131229.

—1968. La calebasse de l'excision en pays Gourmantché. *Journal de la Société des Africanistes* 38(2): 189–225.

—1987. Le suaire du chef. In: Michel Cartry, ed. *Sous le Masque de l'Animal: Essais sur le Sacrifice en Afrique Noire*. 1st ed. Paris: Presses Universitaires de France. pp 131–232.

CASTI, EMANUELA. 2015. *Reflexive Cartography: A New Perspective on Mapping*. Amsterdam: Elsevier. 288 pp. (Modern Cartography 6.)

CASTI, EMANUELA, AND SAMUEL YONKEU, EDS. 2009. *Le Parc national d'Arly et la falaise du Gobnangou (Burkina Faso)*. Paris: L'Harmattan. 270 pp.

CHAMPION, LOUIS, AND DORIAN FULLER. 2019. Archaeobotanical remains. In: Anne Haour, ed. *Two Thousand Years in Dendi, Northern Benin: Archaeology, History and Memory*. Leiden: Brill. pp. 216–233. (Journal of African Archaeology Monograph Series 13.) https://doi.org/10.1163/9789004376694.

CHAMPION, LOUIS, ANNE HAOUR, AND ANNE FILIPPINI. 2019. Kantoro (KRO-14). In: Anne Haour, ed. *Two Thousand Years in Dendi, Northern Benin: Archaeology, History and Memory*. Leiden: Brill. pp. 551–574. (Journal of African Archaeology Monograph Series 13.) https://doi.org/10.1163/9789004376694.

CHANTOUX, ALPHONSE. 1966. *Histoire du pays Gourma: Traditions orales*. Fada N'Gourma, Burkina Faso: Éditions Ti Dogu. 62 pp.

CHENORKIAN, ROBERT. 1983. Ivory Coast prehistory: Recent developments. *African Archaeological Review* 1:127–142. https://doi.org/10.1007/BF01116775.

CHEVRIER, BENOÎT, ÉRIC HUYSECOM, SYLVAIN SORIANO, MICHEL RASSE, LAURENT LESPEZ, BRICE LEBRUN, AND CHANTAL TRIBOLO. 2018. Between continuity and discontinuity: An overview of the West African Paleolithic over the last 200,000 years. *Quaternary International* 466(Part A):3–22. https://doi.org/10.1016/j.quaint.2017.11.027.

CHILDS, S. TERRY. 2000. Traditional iron working: A narrated ethnoarchaeological example. In: Michael S. Bisson, Terry S. Childs, Philip De Barros, and Augustin F. C. Holl. Joseph O. Vogel, eds. *Ancient African Metallurgy: The Sociocultural Context*. Walnut Creek, CA: Altamira. pp. 199–254.

CHIRIKURE, SHADRECK, TAWANDA MUKWENDE, ABIGAIL J. MOFFETT, ROBERT T. NYAMUSHOSHO, FOREMAN BANDAMA, AND MICHELLE HOUSE. 2017. No big brother here: Heterarchy, Shona political succession and the relationship between Great Zimbabwe and Khami, southern Africa. *Cambridge Archaeological Journal* 28(1):45–66. https://doi.org/10.1017/S0959774317000555.

CHOUIN, GÉRARD. 2018. Reflections on plague in African history (14th–19th c.). *Afriques: Débats, Méthodes et Terrains d'Histoire* 9 [with French abstract]. https://doi.org/10.4000/afriques.2228.

CISSÉ, MAMADOU, SUSAN KEECH MCINTOSH, LAURE DUSSUBIEUX, THOMAS FENN, DAPHNE GALLAGHER, AND ABIGAIL CHIPPS SMITH. 2013. Excavations at Gao Saney: New evidence for settlement growth, trade, and interaction on the Niger Bend in the first millennium CE. *Journal of African Archaeology* 11(1):9–37. https://www.jstor.org/stable/43135595.

CLARK, COLIN, AND MARGARET HASWELL. 1966. *The Economics of Subsistence Agriculture*. 2nd ed. New York: St. Martin's Press. 216 pp.

CLARK, J. DESMOND. 1969. *Kalambo Falls Prehistoric Site*. Volume 1, The Geology, Palaeoecology and Detailed Stratigraphy of the Excavations. Cambridge: Cambridge University Press. 253 pp.

CLINE, WALTER. 1937. *Mining and Metallurgy in Negro Africa*. Menasha, WI: George Banta Publishing Company. 155 pp. (General Series in Anthropology 5.)

CLOSE, ANGELA E., AND C. GARTH SAMPSON. 1998. Backed microlith clusters in Late Holocene rock shelters of the Upper Karoo. *The South African Archaeological Bulletin* 53(168):63–72. https://doi.org/10.2307/3889181.

COLE, MONICA M. 1986. *The Savannas: Biogeography and Geobotany*. London: Academic Press. 438 pp.

COMPTON, ANNE M. 2017. *Excavations at Kranka Dada: An Examination of Daily Life, Trade, and Ritual in the Bono Manso Region*. Oxford: BAR Publishing. 189 pp. (BAR International Series 2857.)

CONKLIN, HAROLD C. 1954. Section of Anthropology: An ethnoecological approach to shifting agriculture. *Transcripts of the New York Academy of Sciences* 17(2):133–142. https://doi.org/10.1111/j.2164-0947.1954.tb00402.x.

—1963. *El estudio del cultivo de roza [The Study of Shifting Cultivation]*. Washington, DC: Unión Panamerica. 185 pp. (Estudios y Monografías 11; Studies and Monographs 6.) [In Spanish and English.]

COULIBALY, ÉLISÉE. 2006. *Savoirs et Savoir-faire des Anciens Métallurgistes d'Afrique occidentale: Procédés et Techniques de la Sidérurgie Directe dans le Bwamu (Burkina Faso et Mali)*. Paris: Éditions Karthala. 422 pp. (Archéologies Africaines.)

CRUZ, MARIA DORES. 2011. "Pots are pots, not people": Material culture and ethnic identity in the Banda Area (Ghana), nineteenth and twentieth centuries. *Azania: Archaeological Research in Africa* 46(3):336–357 [with French abstract]. https://doi.org/10.1080/0067270X.2011.629525.

CZERNIEWICZ, MAYA VON. 2004. "Studien zur Chronologie der Eisenzeit in der Sahel-Zone von Burkina Faso, Westafrika" [dissertation]. Frankfurt am Main: Goethe-Universität. 378 pp. http://publikationen.ub.uni-frankfurt.de/files/5231/CzerniewiczMayavon.pdf.

D'ANDREA, A. CATHERINE, AND JOANNA CASEY. 2002. Pearl millet and Kintampo subsistence. *African Archaeological Review* 19(3):147–173 [abstract in English and French]. https://doi.org/10.1023/A:1016518919072.

DANIELISOVÁ, ALŽBĚTA, KAMILA OLŠEVIČOVÁ, RICHARD CIMLER, AND TOMÁŠ MACHÁLEK. 2015. Understanding the Iron Age economy: Sustainability of agricultural practices under stable population growth. In: Gabriel Wurzer, Kerstin Kowarik, and Hans Reschreiter, eds. *Agent-based Modeling and Simulation in Archaeology*. Cham, Switzerland: Springer. pp. 183–216. (Advances in Geographic Information Science.) https://doi.org/10.1007/978-3-319-00008-4_9.

DAVID, NICHOLAS. 1998. The ethnoarchaeology and field archaeology of grinding at Sukur, Adamawa State, Nigeria. *African Archaeological Review* 15(1):13–63. https://www.jstor.org/stable/25130640.

DAVID, NICHOLAS, JUDY STERNER, AND KODZO GAVUA. 1988. Why pots are decorated. *Current Anthropology* 29(3):365–389. https://www.jstor.org/stable/2743453.

DAVIES, OLIVER. 1967. *West Africa before the Europeans: Archaeology and Prehistory*. London: Methuen. 364 pp.

DAVY, P. 1952. *Histoire du pays Gourmantché*. Paris: Centre des Hautes Études d'Administration Muselmane. 108 pp. (Mémoire 1964.)

DE BARROS, PHILIP. 2000. Iron metallurgy: Sociocultural context. In: Michael S. Bisson, Terry S. Childs, Philip de Barros, and Augustin F. C. Holl. eds. *Ancient African Metallurgy: The Sociocultural Context*. Foreword by Joseph O. Vogel. Walnut Creek, CA: Altamira Press. pp. 147–198.

DECORSE, CHRISTOPHER R. 2001. *An Archaeology of Elmina: Africans and Europeans on the Gold Coast, 1400–1900*. Washington, DC: Smithsonian Institution Press. 286 pp.

DECORSE, CHRISTOPHER R., AND GÉRARD L. CHOUIN. 2003. Trouble with siblings: Archaeological and historical interpretation of the West African past. In: Toyin Falola and Christian Jennings, eds. *Sources and Methods in African History: Spoken, Written, Unearthed*. Rochester, NY: University of Rochester Press. pp. 7–15.

DEME, ALIOUNE, AND SUSAN KEECH MCINTOSH. 2006. Excavations at Walaldé: New light on the settlement of the Middle Senegal Valley by iron-using peoples. *Journal of African Archaeology* 4(2): 317–347. http://www.jstor.org/stable/43135410.

DONKIN, ROBIN A. 1991. *Meleagrides, an Historical and Ethnogeographical Study of the Guinea Fowl*. London: Ethnographica. 157 pp.

DONNAY, SIRIO CANÓS. 2016. Shifting sedentism in the Upper Casamance (Senegal). *Azania: Archaeological Research in Africa* 51(4):453–468 [abstract in English and French]. https://doi.org/10.1080/0067270X.2016.1249588.

DUEPPEN, STEPHEN A. 2011. Early evidence for chickens at Iron Age Kirikongo (c. AD 100–1450), Burkina Faso. *Antiquity* 85(327):142–157. https://doi.org/10.1017/S0003598X00067491.

—2012a. *Egalitarian Revolution in the Savanna: The Origins of a West African Political System*. London: Equinox. 344 pp. (Approaches to Anthropological Archaeology.)

—2012b. From kin to great house: Inequality and communalism at Iron Age Kirikongo, Burkina Faso. *American Antiquity* 77(1):3–39. https://doi.org/10.7183/0002-7316.77.1.3.

—2012c. Cattle in the West African savanna: Evidence from 1st millennium CE Kirikongo, Burkina Faso. *Journal of Archaeological Science* 39(1):92–101. https://doi.org/10.1016/j.jas.2011.09.005.

—2015. Expressing difference: Inequality and house-based potting in a first-millennium AD community (Burkina Faso, West Africa). *Cambridge Archaeological Journal* 25(1):17–43. https://doi.org/10.1017/S0959774314000687.

—2018. The archaeology of political complexity in West Africa through 1450 CE. Oxford Research Encyclopedia of African History. https://doi.org/10.1093/acrefore/9780190277734.013.140.

DUEPPEN, STEPHEN A., AND DAPHNE E. GALLAGHER. 2013. Adopting agriculture in the West African savanna: Exploring socio-economic choices in first millennium CE southeastern Burkina Faso. *Journal of Anthropological Archaeology* 32(4):433–448. https://doi.org/10.1016/j.jaa.2013.08.001.

—2016. Changing crafts in the spaces between states: Formal, functional, and decorative transformations in fifteenth-century CE ceramics at Kirikongo, Burkina Faso (West Africa). *African Archaeological Review* 33(2):129–161 [abstract in English and French]. https://doi.org/10.1007/s10437-016-9219-x.

DUEPPEN, STEPHEN A., AND CAMERON GOKEE. 2014. Hunting on the margins of medieval West African states: A preliminary study of the zooarchaeological record at Diouboye, Senegal. *Azania:*

Archaeological Research in Africa 49(3):354–385 [abstract in English and French]. https://doi.org/10.1080/0067270X.2014.931628.

DUNNELL, ROBERT C. 1992. The notion site. In: Jacqueline Rossignol and LuAnn Wandsnider, eds. *Space, Time, and Archaeological Landscapes*. New York: Plenum Press. pp. 21–42.

DUVALL, CHRIS S. 2006. "Villages, Vegetation, Bedrock, and Chimpanzees: Human and Non-Human Sources of Ecosystem Structure in Southwestern Mali" [dissertation]. Madison, WI: University of Wisconsin–Madison, Department of Geography. 305 pp. ProQuest Dissertations & Theses Global, order no. 3245661; https://search.proquest.com/dissertations-theses/villages-vegetation-bedrock-chimpanzees-human-non/docview/304975273/se-2.

—2007. Human settlement and baobab distribution in south-western Mali. *Journal of Biogeography* 34(11):1947-1961. https://doi.org/10.1111/j.1365-2699.2007.01751.x.

EERKENS, JELMER W. 2003. Residential mobility and pottery use in the western Great Basin. *Current Anthropology* 44(5):728–738. https://doi.org/10.1086/379262.

EFFAH-GYAMFI, KWAKU. 1986. Ancient urban sites in Hausaland. *West African Journal of Archaeology* 16:117–134.

EICHHORN, BARBARA, AND KATHARINA NEUMANN. 2014. Holocene vegetation change and land use at Ounjougou, Mali. In: Chris J. Stevens, Sam Nixon, Mary Anne Murray, and Dorian Q. Fuller, eds. *Archaeology of African Plant Use*. Walnut Creek, CA: Left Coast Press. pp. 83–96. (Publications of the Institute of Archaeology, University College of London 61.)

EICHHORN, BARBARA, CAROLINE ROBION-BRUNNER, VINCENT SERNEELS, AND SÉBASTIEN PERRET. 2013. Fuel for iron: Wood exploitation for metallurgy on the Dogon Plateau, Mali. In: Jane Humphries and Thilo Rehren, eds. *The World of Iron*. London: Archetype. pp. 435–443.

EPSTEIN, HELLMUT. 1971. *The Origin of the Domestic Animals of Africa*. New York: Africana Publishing. 2 volumes.

ESTES, RICHARD DESPARD. 1991. *The Behavior Guide to African Mammals: Including Hoofed Mammals, Carnivores, Primates*. 1st ed. Berkeley: University of California Press. 611 pp.

FABRE, JEAN-MARC. 2009. La métallurgie du fer au Sahel Burkinabé à la fin du 1er millénaire AD. In: Sonja Magnavita, Lassinà Koté, Peter Breunig, and Oumarou A. Idé, eds. *Crossroads: Cultural and Technological Developments in First Millennium bc/ad West Africa [Carrefour Sahel: développements culturels et technologiques pendant le premier millénaire bc/ad dans l'Afrique de l'Ouest]*. Frankfurt am Main: Africa Magna. pp. 167–178. (Journal of African Archaeology Monograph Series 2.)

FAIRHEAD, JAMES, AND MELISSA LEACH. 1996. *Misreading the African Landscape: Society and Ecology in a Forest-Savanna Mosaic*. Cambridge: Cambridge University Press. 354 pp. (African Studies Series 90.)

[FAO] FOOD AND AGRICULTURE ORGANIZATION OF THE UNITED NATIONS. 1989. *Report of the FAO Expert Consultation on Fish Technology in Africa: Abidjan, Côte d'Ivoire, 25–28 April 1988 [Rapport de la Consultation d'Experts FAO sur la Technologie du Poisson en Afrique: Abidjan, Côte d'Ivoire, 25–28 avril 1988]*. Rome: FAO. 45 pp. (FAO Fisheries Report 400.) [In English and French.]

FOLORUNSO, C. A. 2002. The archaeology and ethnoarchaeology of soap and dye making at Ijaye, Yorubaland. *African Archaeological Review* 19(3):127–145. https://doi.org/10.1023/A:1016535202233.

FONTANA, ALESSANDRO, PAOLO MOZZI, ALDINO BONDESAN, ARMANDO DE GUIO, AND LASSINA KOTÉ. 2010. Late prehistory and environmental changes along the Débé River in the lower Sourou Valley (Burkina Faso, West Africa). *Il Quaternario: Italian Journal of Quaternary Sciences* 23(2):199–216. http://www.aiqua.it/index.php/the-journal/il-quaternario-1988-2011/volume-23-2/167-late-prehistory-and-environmental-changes-along-the-debe-river-in-the-lower-sourou-valley-burkina-faso-west-africa.

FORSSMAN, TIM. 2015. A macro-fracture investigation of the backed stone tools from Dzombo Shelter, eastern Botswana. *Journal of Archaeological Science: Reports* 3:265–274. https://doi.org/10.1016/j.jasrep.2015.06.020.

FORTES, MEYER, AND SONIA L. FORTES. 1936. Food in the domestic economy of the Tallensi. *Africa: Journal of the International African Institute* 9(2):237–276. https://www.jstor.org/stable/1155627.

Frank, Barbara E. 1998. *Mande Potters and Leather-workers: Art and Heritage in West Africa.* Washington, DC: Smithsonian Institution Press. 192 pp.

Frank, Tenney, Peter Breunig, Peter Müller-Haude, Katherina Neumann, Wim van Neer, Ralf Vogelsang, and Hans-Peter Wotzka. 2001. The Chaîne de Gobnangou, SE Burkina Faso: Archaeological, archaeobotanical, archaeozoological and geomorphological studies. *Beiträge zur Allgemeinen und Vergleichenden Archäologie* 21:127–190. [In English, French, and German.]

Gado, Boube. 1993. Un "village des morts" à Bura en République du Niger. In: Jean Devisse, ed. *Vallées du Niger* [exhibition catalog]. Paris: Éditions de la Réunion des Musées Nationaux. pp. 365–374. (Petit Journal des Grandes Expositions 250.)

Gallagher, Daphne E. 2010 "Farming Beyond the Escarpment: Society, Environment, and Mobility in Precolonial Southeastern Burkina Faso" [dissertation]. Ann Arbor: University of Michigan, Department of Anthropology. 390 pp. http://hdl.handle.net/2027.42/75953 .

—2016. American plants in sub-Saharan Africa: A review of the archaeological evidence. *Azania: Archaeological Research in Africa* 51(1):24–61. https://doi.org/10.1080/0067270X.2016.1150081.

Gallagher, Daphne E., and Stephen A. Dueppen. 2018. Recognizing plague epidemics in the archaeological record of West Africa. *Afriques: Débats, Méthodes, et Terrains d'Histoire* 9. https://doi.org/10.4000/afriques.2198.

—2019. Households and plant use at Kirikongo, Burkina Faso: Seeds and fruits from Mound 1 (450–1450 AD). In: Barbara Eichhorn and Alexa Höhn, eds. *Trees, Grasses and Crops—People and Plants in Sub-Saharan Africa and Beyond.* Bonn: Verlag Dr. Rudolf Habelt GmbH. (Frankfurt Archaeological Studies 37.) pp. 141–156.

Gallagher, Daphne E., Stephen A. Dueppen, and Rory Walsh. 2016. The archaeology of shea butter (Vitellaria paradoxa) in Burkina Faso, West Africa. *Journal of Ethnobiology* 36(1):150–171. https://doi.org/10.2993/0278-0771-36.1.150.

Gallagher, Daphne E., Susan Keech McIntosh, and Shawn S. Murray. 2018. Agriculture and wild plant use in the Middle Senegal River Valley, c. 800 BC–1000 AD. In: Anna Maria Mercuri, A. Catherine D'Andrea, Rita Fornaciari, and Alexa Höhn, eds. *Plants and People in the African Past: Progress in African Archaeobotany.* Cham: Springer. pp. 328–361. https://doi.org/10.1007/978-3-319-89839-1_16.

Gallagher, Daphne E., and Shawn S. Murray. 2016. Paleoethnobotanical analysis of seeds and fruits from Unit C3A. In: Roderick J. McIntosh, Susan Keech McIntosh, and Hamady Bocoum, eds. *The Search for Takrur: Archaeological Excavations and Reconnaissance along the Middle Senegal River Valley.* New Haven: Yale University Department of Anthropology and Yale Peabody Museum of Natural History. pp. 299–310. (Yale University Publications in Anthropology 93.)

Gallay, Alain, and Eric Huysecom. 1989. *Ethnoarcheologie africaine: un programme d'étude de la céramique récente du Delta Intérieur du Niger (Mali, Afrique de l'Ouest).* Geneva: University of Geneva. 252 pp. (Document du Département d'Anthropologie et d'Ecologie de l'Université de Genève 14.)

Geis-Tronich, Gudrun. 1989. *Les Métiers Traditionnels des Gulmance [Bi Gulmanceba Maasuagu Tuonbuoli].* Stuttgart: Franz Steiner-Verlag Wiesbaden GmbH. 109 pp. (Sonderschriften des Frobenius-Instituts 6.) [In French and Gulmancema.] http://publikationen.ub.uni-frankfurt.de/files/55606/464312094_ocrf.pdf.

—1991. *Materielle Kultur der Gulmance in Burkina Faso.* Stuttgart: Franz Steiner Verlag. 522 pp. (Studien zur Kulturkunde 98.)

Giade, Asma'u Ahmed. 2016. "An Archaeological Investigation in Shira Region, Bauchi, Northeast Nigeria" [dissertation]. Norwich, England: University of East Anglia. 474 pp. https://ueaeprints.uea.ac.uk/63062/

Gijanto, Liza, and Sarah Walshaw. 2014. Ceramic production and dietary changes at Juffure, Gambia. *African Archaeological Review* 31(2):265–297. https://doi.org/10.1007/s10437-014-9150-y.

GOKEE, CAMERON D. 2016. Assembling the Village in Medieval Bambuk: An Archaeology of Interaction at Diouboye, Senegal. Sheffield, UK: Equinox Publishing. 318 pp. (New Directions in Anthropological Archaeology.)

GOLDSTEIN, STEVEN T., AND CHRISTOPHER M. SHAFFER. 2017. Experimental and archaeological investigations of backed microlith function among Mid-to-Late Holocene herders in southwestern Kenya. *Archaeological and Anthropological Sciences* 9(8):1767–1788. https://doi.org/10.1007/s12520-016-0329-9.

GORDON, ROBERT B., AND DAVID J. KILLICK. 1993. Adaptation of technology to culture and environment: Bloomery iron smelting in America and Africa. *Technology and Culture* 34(2):243–270. https://doi.org/10.2307/3106536.

GOSSELAIN, OLIVIER P. 2000. Materializing identities: An African perspective. *Journal of Archaeological Method and Theory* 7(3):187–217.

—2008. Mother bella was not a bella: Inherited and transformed traditions in southwestern Niger. In: Miriam T. Stark, Brenda J. Bowser, and Lee Horne. eds. *Cultural Transmission and Material Culture: Breaking Down Boundaries*. Tucson, AZ: University of Arizona Press. pp. 150–177.

—2011. Pourquoi le décorer? Quelques observations sur le décor céramique en Afrique. *Azania: Archaeological Research in Africa* 46(1):3–19. https://doi.org/10.1080/0067270X.2011.553356.

GOSSELAIN, OLIVIER P., AND ANNE HAOUR. 2019. The site within West African political and craft history. In: Anne Haour, ed. *Two Thousand Years in Dendi: Archaeology, History and Memory, Northern Benin*. Leiden: Brill. pp. 294–306. (Journal of African Archaeology Monograph Series 13.) https://doi.org/10.1163/9789004376694.

GOSSELAIN, OLIVIER P., AND LUCIE SMOLDEREN. 2019. Crossing archaeology and oral tradition: Approaching Dendi history from sites of memory. In: Anne Haour, ed. *Two Thousand Years in Dendi, Northern Benin: Archaeology, History and Memory*. Leiden: Brill. pp. 6–19. (Journal of African Archaeology Monograph Series 13.) https://doi.org/10.1163/9789004376694.

GRAHAM, MARTHA. 1994. *Mobile Farmers: An Ethnoarchaeological Approach to Settlement Organization among the Raramuri of Northwestern Mexico*. Ann Arbor, MI: International Monographs in Prehistory. 113 pp. (Ethnoarchaeological Series 3.)

GRILLO, KATHERINE M. 2014. Pastoralism and pottery use: An ethnoarchaeological study in Samburu, Kenya. *African Archaeological Review* 31(2):105–130. https://doi.org/10.1007/s10437-014-9147-6.

GROVE, ALFRED T., AND FRANCES M. G. KLEIN. 1979. *Rural Africa*. Cambridge: Cambridge University Press. 122 pp. (Cambridge Topics in Geography.)

GUEMONA, DJIMET. 2015. "Reconnaissance archéologique et enquêtes historiques sur la métallurgie ancienne du fer dans la région de Kandi (nord-est du Bénin): Cas de site métallurgique de Lolo" [mémoire de master 1]. Toulouse, France: University of Toulouse. 100 pp. http://dante.univ-tlse2.fr/id/eprint/413.

GUÈYE, NDÈYE SOKHNA. 2011. Dis-moi quel pot tu as et je te dirai qui tu es! Matérialiser les identités sociales dans les décors céramiques de la moyenne vallée du fleuve Sénégal (nord du Sénégal) [Tell me what you pot and I'll tell you who you are! Materializing social identities in the ceramics decoration of the middle valley of the Senegal River (northern Senegal)]. *Azania: Archaeological Research in Africa* 46(1):20–35. [In French with English abstract.] https://doi.org/10.1080/0067270X.2011.553397.

GUINKO, SITA. 1984. "Végétation de la Haulte-Volta" [dissertation]. Pessac, France: Université Bordeaux 3, Michel de Montaigne. 2 volumes.

GURSTELLE, ANDREW W., NESTOR LABIYI, AND SIMON AGANI. 2015. Settlement history and chronology in the Savè area of central Bénin. *Azania: Archaeological Research in Africa* 50(2):227–249. https://doi.org/10.1080/0067270X.2015.1020631.

GUYER, JANE I., ERIC F. LAMBIN, LISA CLIGGETT, PETER WALKER, KOJO AMANOR, THOMAS BASSETT, ELIZABETH COLSON, ET AL. 2007. Temporal heterogeneity in the study of African land use: Interdisciplinary collaboration between anthropology, human geography and remote sensing. *Human Ecology* 35(1):3–17. https://doi.org/10.1007/s10745-006-9085-2.

HAMON, CAROLINE, AND VALERIE LE GALL. 2013. Millet and sauce: The uses and functions of querns among the Minyanka (Mali). *Journal of Anthropological Archaeology* 32(1):109–121. https://doi.org/10.1016/j.jaa.2012.12.002.

HAOUR, ANNE. 2013. Mobilité et archéologie le long de l'arc oriental du Niger: Pavements et percuteurs [Mobility and archaeology along the eastern bend of the Niger River: Pottery pavements and pounders]. *Afriques: Débats, Méthodes et Terrains d'Histoire* 4. [In French with English abstract.] https://doi.org/10.4000/afriques.1134.

— ED. 2019. *Two Thousand Years in Dendi, Northern Benin: Archaeology, History and Memory.* Leiden: Brill. 802 pp. (Journal of African Archaeology Monograph Series 13.) https://doi.org/10.1163/9789004376694.

HAOUR, ANNE, AND ANNALISA CHRISTIE. 2019. Cowries in the archaeology of West Africa: The present picture. *Azania: Archaeological Research in Africa* 54(3):287–321. https://doi.org/10.1080/0067270X.2019.1648726.

HAOUR, ANNE, AND DAOUDA KEITA. 2010. Folded strip roulette [Roulette de fibre plate pliée]. In: Anne Haour, Katie Manning, Noémie Arazi, Olivier Gosselain, Ndèye Sokhna Guèye, Daouda Keita, Alexandre Livingstone Smith, et al., eds. *African Pottery Roulettes Past and Present: Techniques, Identification and Distribution.* Oxford: Oxbow Books. pp. 169–176.

HAOUR, ANNE, AND KATIE MANNING. 2010. Introductory note: How archaeologists work. In: Anne Haour, Katie Manning, Noémie Arazi, Olivier Gosselain, Ndèye Sokhna Guèye, Daouda Keita, Alexandre Livingstone Smith, et al., eds. *African Pottery Roulettes Past and Present: Techniques, Identification and Distribution.* Oxford: Oxbow Books. pp. 131–133.

HAOUR, ANNE, KATIE MANNING, NOÉMIE ARAZI, OLIVIER GOSSELAIN, NDÈYE SOKHNA GUÈYE, DAOUDA KEITA, ALEXANDRE LIVINGSTONE SMITH, ET AL., EDS. 2010. *African Pottery Roulettes Past and Present: Techniques, Identification and Distribution.* Oxford: Oxbow Books. 196 pp.

HAOUR, ANNE, AND SAM NIXON. 2019. Birnin Lafiya within West African archaeology. In: Anne Haour, ed. *Two Thousand Years in Dendi, Northern Benin: Archaeology, History and Memory.* Leiden: Brill. pp. 283–293. (Journal of African Archaeology Monograph Series 13.) https://doi.org/10.1163/9789004376694.

HAOUR, ANNE, SAM NIXON, ALEXANDRE LIVINGSTONE SMITH, NICOLAS NIKIS, AND DAVID K. KAY. 2019. The pottery. In: Anne Haour, ed. *Two Thousand Years in Dendi, Northern Benin: Archaeology, History and Memory.* Leiden: Brill. pp. 139–173. (Journal of African Archaeology Monograph Series 13.) https://doi.org/10.1163/9789004376694.

HAOUR, ANNE, SAM NIXON, DIDIER N'DAH, CARLOS MAGNAVITA, AND ALEXANDRE LIVINGSTONE SMITH. 2016. The settlement mound of Birnin Lafiya: New evidence from the eastern arc of the Niger River. *Antiquity* 90(351):695–710. https://doi.org/10.15184/aqy.2016.7.

HAOUR, ANNE, AND BENEDETTA ROSSI. 2010. Hausa identity: Language, history and religion. In: Anne Haour and Benedetta Rossi, eds. *Being and Becoming Hausa.* Leiden: Brill. pp. 1–34.

HAOUR, ANNE, VICKY WINTON, OUMAROU A. IDÉ, HELEN RENDELL, AND MICHÈLE CLARKE. 2006. The Projet SAHEL 2004: An archaeological sequence in the Parc W, Niger. *Journal of African Archaeology* 4(2):299–315. https://www.jstor.org/stable/43135409.

HAPPOLD, DAVID C. D. 1987. *The Mammals of Nigeria.* Oxford: Clarendon Press. 402 pp.

HARRY, KAREN, AND LIAM FRINK. 2009. The arctic cooking pot: Why was it adopted? *American Anthropologist* 111(3):330–343. https://doi.org/10.1111/j.1548-1433.2009.01136.x.

HASWELL, MARGARET. 1953. *Economics of Agriculture in a Savannah Village: Report on Three Years' Study in Genieri Village and Its Lands, the Gambia.* London: H. M. Stationery Office for the Colonial Office. 142 pp. (Colonial Research Studies 8.)

HIEN, PIERRE CLAVER, AND MOUSTAPHA GOMGNIMBOU, EDS. 2009. *Histoire des royaumes et chefferies au Burkina Faso précolonial.* Ouagadougou: Editeur Scientific DIST (CNRST). 405 pp.

HISCOCK, PETER, CHRIS CLARKSON, AND ALEX MACKAY. 2011. Big debates over little tools: Ongoing disputes over microliths on three continents. *World Archaeology* 43(4):653–664. https://doi.org/10.1080/00438243.2011.624755.

HÖHN, ALEXA, AND KATHERINA NEUMANN. 2012. Shifting cultivation and the development of a cultural landscape during the Iron Age (0–1500 AD) in the northern Sahel of Burkina Faso, West Africa: Insights from archaeological charcoal. *Quaternary International* 249:72–83. https://doi.org/10.1016/j.quaint.2011.04.012.

HOLL, AUGUSTIN F. C. 2014. *Archaeology of Mound-clusters in West Africa*. Oxford: Archaeopress. (BAR International Series 2660.)

HOLL, AUGUSTIN F. C., AND LASSINA KOTÉ. 2000. Settlement patterns, food production, and craft specialization in the Mouhoun Bend (NW Burkina Faso): Preliminary results of the MOBAP 1997–1999 field seasons. *West African Journal of Archaeology* 30(1):69–107.

HONEYCHURCH, WILLIAM. 2014. Alternative complexities: The archaeology of pastoral nomadic states. *Journal of Archaeological Research* 22(4):277–326. https://doi.org/10.1007/s10814-014-9073-9.

HOPKINS, BRIAN. 1974. Forest and Savanna: *An Introduction to Tropical Terrestrial Ecology with Special Reference to West Africa*. 2nd ed. Ibadan, Nigeria: Heinemann. 154 pp.

HOUGH, JOHN LAURENCE. 1989. "National Park–Local People Relationships: Case Studies from Northern Benin, West Africa and the Grand Canyon, USA" [dissertation]. Ann Arbor: University of Michigan, Natural Resources. 300 pp. http://hdl.handle.net/2027.42/162319.

HUGHES, RALPH H., AND JANE S. HUGHES. 1992. *A Directory of African Wetlands*. Cambridge and Nairobi: Gland, Switzerland: IUCN–World Conservation Union; Nairobi, Kenya: United Nations Environment Programme; Cambridge: World Conservation Monitoring Centre. 820 pp. https://portals.iucn.org/library/sites/library/files/documents/1992-007.pdf

HURLEY, WILLIAM M. 1979. *Prehistoric Cordage: Identification of Impressions on Pottery*. Washington, DC: Taraxacum. 154 pp. (Aldine Manuals on Archeology 3).

HUYSECOM, ERIC, SYLVAIN OZAINNE, CHRYSTEL JEANBOURQUIN, ANNE MAYOR, MARIE CANETTI, SERGE LOUKOU, LOUIS CHAIX, ET AL. 2015. Towards a better understanding of sub-Saharan settlement mounds before AD 1400: The tells of Sadia on the Seno Plain (Dogon Country, Mali). *Journal of African Archaeology* 13(1):7–38. https://www.jstor.org/stable/44291850.

HUYSECOM, ERIC, SYLVAIN OZAINNE, FRANCESCO RAELI, AZIZ BALLOUCHE, MICHEL RASSE, AND STEPHEN STOKES. 2004. Ounjougou (Mali): A history of Holocene settlement at the southern edge of the Sahara. *Antiquity* 78(301):579–593. https://doi.org/10.1017/S0003598X00113237.

HUYSECOM, ERIC, MICHEL RASSE, LAURENT LESPEZ, KATHARINA NEUMANN, AHMED FAHMY, AZIZ BALLOUCHE, SYLVAIN OZAINNE, MARINO MAGGETTI, CH. TRIBOLO, AND SYLVAIN SORIANO. 2009. The emergence of pottery in Africa during the tenth millennium cal BC: New evidence from Ounjougou (Mali). *Antiquity* 83(322):905–917. https://doi.org/10.1017/S0003598X00099245.

IDÉ, OUMAROU A. 2009. La question du fer dans la vallée de la Mékrou, Niger méridional. In: Sonja Magnavita, Lassina Koté, Peter Breunig, and Oumarou A. Idé, eds. *Crossroads: Cultural and Technological Developments in First Millennium bc/ad West Africa [Carrefour Sahel: développements culturels et technologiques pendant le premier millénaire bc/ad dans l'Afrique de l'Ouest]*. Frankfurt am Main: Africa Magna. pp. 157–166. (Journal of African Archaeology Monograph Series 2.)

ILES, LOUISE. 2016. The role of metallurgy in transforming global forests. *Journal of Archaeological Method and Theory* 23(4):1219–1241. https://www.jstor.org/stable/26748544.

INSOLL, TIMOTHY. 2003. *The Archaeology of Islam in Sub-Saharan Africa*. Cambridge: Cambridge University Press. 470 pp.

INSOLL, TIMOTHY, RACHEL MACLEAN, CERI ASHLEY, AND BENJAMIN W. KANKPEYENG. 2011. The Iron Age ceramics from the Tong Hills, northern Ghana. Sequence and comparative perspective. *Journal of African Archaeology* 9(1):15–39. https://www.jstor.org/stable/43135532.

INSOLL, TIMOTHY, RACHEL MACLEAN, AND BENJAMIN KANKPEYENG. 2013. *Temporalising Anthropology: Archaeology in the Talensi Tong Hills, Northern Ghana*. Frankfurt am Main: Africa Magna. 270 pp. (Journal of African Archaeology Monograph Series 10.)

IZARD, MICHEL. 1985 *Gens du Pouvoir, Gens de la Terre: Les Institutions Politiques de l'Ancien Royaume du Yatenga (Bassin de la Volta Blanche)*. Cambridge: Cambridge University Press. 594 pp.

—2003. *Moogo: L'émergence d'un Espace Étatique Ouest-Africain au XVIe Siècle*. Paris, France: Éditions Karthala. 394 pp.

Izard, Michel, and Joseph Ki-Zerbo. 1992. From the Niger to the Volta. In: Bethwell A. Ogot, ed. *General History of Africa*. Volume 5, Africa from the Sixteenth to the Eighteenth Century. Berkeley: University of California Press. pp. 327–367.

Junius, Henrik. 2016. Nok early iron production in central Nigeria—New finds and features. *Journal of African Archaeology* 14(3):291–311. https://www.jstor.org/stable/44295243.

Kaboré, Alexis. 2018. Revendications religieuses sur les aires protégées chez les Gourmantché du Burkina Faso: Des obligations sacrificielles à la résistance. *VertigO: La revue électronique en sciences de l'environnement* 18(1). https://id.erudit.org/iderudit/1058446ar.

Kahlheber, Stefanie. 2004. "Perlhirse und Baobab—Archäobotanische Untersuchungen im Norden Burkina Fasos" [dissertation]. Frankfurt am Main: Johann Wolfgang Goethe University. 296 pp. http://publikationen.ub.uni-frankfurt.de/frontdoor/index/index/docId/4965.

Kahlheber, Stefanie, Koen Bostoen, and Katharina Neumann. 2009. Early plant cultivation in the Central African rain forest: First millennium BC pearl millet from South Cameroon. *Journal of African Archaeology* 7(2):253–272. https://doi.org/10.3213/1612-1651-10142.

Kahlheber, Stefanie, and Katharina Neumann. 2007. The development of plant cultivation in semi-arid West Africa. In: Tim Denham, José Iriarte, and Luc Vrydaghs, eds. *Rethinking Agriculture: Archaeological and Ethnoarchaeological Perspectives*. Walnut Creek, CA: Left Coast Press. pp. 320–346. (One World Archaeology 51.)

Kankpeyeng, Benjamin W. 2009. The slave trade in northern Ghana: Landmarks, legacies and connections. *Slavery and Abolition* 30(2):209–221. https://doi.org/10.1080/01440390902818930.

Keay, Ronald W. J. 1959. Derived savanna—derived from what? *Bulletin de l'Institut Français d'Afrique Noire, Série A, Sciences Naturelles* 21(2):427–438.

Keita, Daouda, and Nafogo Coulibaly. 2018. Les pipes du Delta Interieur du Niger: Typologie et diffusion. *Revue Africaine d'Anthropologie, Nyansa-Pô* 27:7–30.

Kelly, Kenneth G. 2009. Controlling traders: Slave Coast strategies at Savi and Ouidah. In: Caroline A. Williams, ed. *Bridging the Early Modern Atlantic World People, Products, and Practices on the Move*. Farnham, England: Ashgate Publishing. pp. 151–172.

Kelly, Robert L. 1992. Mobility/sedentism: Concepts, archaeological measures, and effects. *Annual Review of Anthropology* 21:43–66. https://www.jstor.org/stable/2155980.

Kiéthéga, Jean-Baptiste. 1983. *L'or de la Volta Noire: Archéologie et histoire de l'exploitation traditionelle, Région de Poura, Haute-Volta*. Paris: Éditions Karthala, Centre de Recherches Africaines. 247 pp. (Archéologies Africaines 1.)

—2009. *La Métallurgie Lourde du Fer au Burkina Faso: Une Technologie à l'Époque Précoloniale*. Paris: Éditions Karthala. 500 pp.

Kiéthéga, Jean-Baptiste, Samuel Sidibé, and Rogier Bedaux. 1993. Vallee du Niger on funerary practices. In: Jean Devisse, ed. *Vallées du Niger*. Paris: Réunion des Musées Nationaux. pp. 425–439. (Petit Journal des Grandes Expositions 250.)

Killick, David. 2004. What do we know about African iron working? [review essay]. *Journal of African Archaeology* 2(1):97–113. https://www.jstor.org/stable/43135336.

—2015. Invention and innovation in African iron-smelting technologies. *Cambridge Archaeological Journal* 25(1):307–319. https://doi.org/10.1017/S0959774314001176.

Killion, Thomas W. 1990. Cultivation intensity and residential site structure: An ethnoarchaeological examination of peasant agriculture in the Sierra de los Tuxtlas, Veracruz, Mexico. *Latin American Antiquity* 1(3):191–215. https://doi.org/10.2307/972161.

Kingdon, Jonathan. 1997. *The Kingdon Field Guide to African Mammals*. San Diego: Academic Press. 464 pp.

—2004. *The Kingdon Pocket Guide to African Mammals*. Princeton: Princeton University Press. 272 pp.

Knauer, Kim, Ursula Gessner, Rasmus Fensholt, Gerald Forkuor, and Claudia Kuenzer. 2017. Monitoring agricultural expansion in Burkina Faso over 14 years with 30 m resolution time series: The role of population growth and implications for the environment. *Remote Sensing* 9(2):132. https://doi.org/10.3390/rs9020132.

KOECHLIN, JEAN. 1997. Ecological conditions and degradation factors in the Sahel. In: Claude Raynaut, ed. *Societies and Nature in the Sahel*. Translated by Dominique Simon and Hilary Koziol. London: Routledge. pp. 12–36. (Routledge/SEI Global Environment and Development Series.)

KORBÉOGO, GABIN. 2013. *Pouvoir et accès aux ressources naturelles au Burkina Faso: La topographie du pouvoir*. Paris: Éditions L'Harmattan. 298 pp.

—2015. Reinventing new systems of crop production in time of agro-ecological change in Burkina Faso. *African Journal of Environmental Science and Technology* 9(5):464–472. https://doi.org/10.5897/AJEST2012.046.

—2016. Variabilité socio-écologique, crise du pastoralisme et résilience des Peuls pasteurs du Gourma rural (Burkina Faso). *VertigO: La revue électronique en sciences de l'environnement* 16(1). https://doi.org/10.4000/vertigo.17241.

KOSTER, STANLEY H. 1982. "A Survey of the Vegetation and Ungulate Populations in Park W, Niger" [master's thesis]. Ann Arbor: Michigan State University, Department of Fisheries and Wildlife. 146 pp. ProQuest Dissertations & Theses Global, order no. 1318482; https://search.proquest.com/dissertations-theses/survey-vegetation-ungulate-populations-park-w/docview/303215178/se-2.

KOTÉ, LASSINA. 2007. *Deux mille [2000] ans au bord du Mouhoun: du VIIème siècle avant Jésus Christ au XIVème siècle après Jésus Christ; Recherches archéologiques à Douroula Province du Mouhoun—Burkina Faso*. Ouagadougou: Imprimerie Arts Graphiques. 48 pp.

KOWAL, JAN M., AND A. H. KASSAM. 1978. *Agricultural Ecology of the Savanna: A Study of West Africa*. Oxford: Clarendon Press. 403 pp.

KRIGER, COLLEEN E. 2006. *Cloth in West African History*. Lanham, MD: AltaMira Press. 214 pp.

KUBA, RICHARD. 2009. Cultural contacts between the savannah and the forest: Trade along the eastern Niger. In: Sonja Magnavita, Lassina Koté, Peter Breunig, and Oumarou A. Idé, eds. *Crossroads: Cultural and Technological Developments in First Millennium bc/ad West Africa [Carrefour Sahel: développements culturels et technologiques pendant le premier millénaire bc/ad dans l'Afrique de l'Ouest]*. Frankfurt am Main: Africa Magna. pp. 147–156. (Journal of African Archaeology Monograph Series 2.)

KÜPPERS, KARIN. 1996. "Die Vegetation der Châine de Gobnangou: Verbreitung und floristische Zusammensetzung von Savannen in Abhängigkeit von den natürlichen Standortverhältnissen und der Art und Intensität des menschlichen Einflusses" [dissertation]. Frankfurt am Main: Goethe-Universität. 216 pp.

LAL, RATTAN. 1974. Soil erosion and shifting agriculture. In: FAO, Soil Resources, Development and Conservation Service, Land and Water Development Division. *Shifting Cultivation and Soil Conservation in Africa: Papers Presented at the FAO/SIDA/ARCN Regional Seminar Held at Ibadan, Nigeria, 2–21 July 1973*. Rome: Food and Agriculture Organization of the United Nations. pp. 48–71. (FAO Soils Bulletin 24.)

LANGLOIS, OLIVIER. 2007. Intrasite feature distribution as a source of social information: The case of Djaba-Hosséré (Northern Cameroon). *Journal of Anthropological Archaeology* 26(2):172–197. https://doi.org/10.1016/j.jaa.2006.08.001.

LANKOANDE, SALIF TITAMBA. 2008. *Les Gourmantché*. Ouagadougou, Burkina Faso: Presses Africaines du Burkina. 211 pp.

LAVACHERY, PHILIPPE. 2001. The Holocene archaeological sequence of Shum Laka rock shelter (Grassfields, western Cameroon). *African Archaeological Review* 18(4):213–247. https://doi.org/10.1023/A:1013114008855.

LAVACHERY, PHILIPPE, SCOTT MACEACHERN, TCHAGO BOUIMON, AND CHRISTOPHE MBIDA MINDZIE. 2010. *Komé-Kribi: Rescue Archaeology along the Chad–Cameroon Oil Pipeline, 1999–2004*. Frankfurt am Main: Africa Magna. 192 pp. (Journal of African Archaeology Monograph Series 4.)

LaViolette, Adria J. 2000. *Ethno-Archaeology in Jenné, Mali: Craft and Status among Smiths, Potters and Masons.* Oxford: Archaeopress. 156 pp. (BAR International Series 838.)

Lawson, Amy. 2003. "Megaliths and Mande States: Sociopolitical Change in the Gambia Valley over the Past Two Millennia" [dissertation]. Ann Arbor: University of Michigan, Department of Anthropology. 858 pp. ProQuest Dissertations & Theses Global, order no. 3079483; https://search.proquest.com/dissertations-theses/megaliths-mande-states-sociopolitical-change/docview/305323476/se-2.

Lawson, George W., ed. 1986. *Plant Ecology in West Africa: Systems and Processes.* New York: John Wiley and Sons. 357 pp.

Leach, Melissa, and Robin Mearns, eds. 1996. *The Lie of the Land: Challenging Received Wisdom on the African Environment.* Oxford: International African Institute in association with James Curry; Portsmouth, NH: Heinemann. 240 pp.

Lentz, Carola. 2006. Land rights and the politics of belonging in Africa: An introduction. In: Richard Kuba and Carola Lentz, eds. *Land Rights and the Politics of Belonging in West Africa.* Boston: Brill. pp. 1–34. (African Social Studies Series 9.)

—2013. *Land, Mobility, and Belonging in West Africa: Natives and Strangers.* Bloomington: Indiana University Press. 348 pp. https://www.jstor.org/stable/j.ctt16gh6b4.

Lindsay, Ian, and Alan Greene. 2013. Sovereignty, mobility, and political cartographies in Late Bronze Age southern Caucasia. *Journal of Anthropological Archaeology* 32(4):691–712. https://doi.org/10.1016/j.jaa.2013.04.003.

Lingané, Zakaria. 1995. "Sites d'anciens villages et organisation de l'espace dans le Yatenga (Nord-Ouest du Burkina Faso)" [dissertation]. Paris: Université de Paris-1, Panthéon-Sorbonnes. 1,256 pp.

Livingstone Smith, Alexandre, and Olivier Gosselain. 2019. Torouwey (TRO-14-S1). In: Anne Haour, ed. *Two Thousand Years in Dendi, Northern Benin: Archaeology, History and Memory.* Leiden: Brill. pp. 333–335. (Journal of African Archaeology Monograph Series 13.) https://doi.org/10.1163/9789004376694.

Livingstone Smith, Alexandre, Olivier Gosselain, Anne Mayor, and Ndèye Sokhna Guèye. 2010. Modern roulettes in sub-Saharan Africa. In: Anne Haour, Katie Manning, Noémie Arazi, Olivier Gosselain, Ndèye Sokhna Guèye, Daouda Keita, Alexandre Livingstone Smith, et al., eds. *African Pottery Roulettes Past and Present: Techniques, Identification and Distribution.* Oxford: Oxbow Books. pp. 36–114.

Logan, Amanda L. 2016. "Why can't people feed themselves?": Archaeology as alternative archive of food security in Banda, Ghana. *American Anthropologist* 118(3):508–524. https://doi.org/10.1111/aman.12603.

Logan, Amanda L., and M. Dores Cruz. 2014. Gendered taskscapes: Food, farming, and craft production in Banda, Ghana in the eighteenth to twenty-first centuries. *African Archaeological Review* 31(2):203–231. https://doi.org/10.1007/s10437-014-9155-6.

Lombard, Marlize, and Justin Pargeter. 2008. Hunting with Howiesons Poort segments: Pilot experimental study and the functional interpretation of archaeological tools. *Journal of Archaeological Science* 35(9):2523–2531. https://doi.org/10.1016/j.jas.2008.04.004.

Lombard, Marlize, and Isabelle Parsons. 2008. Blade and bladelet function and variability in risk management during the last 2000 years in the Northern Cape. *The South African Archaeological Bulletin* 63(187):18–27. https://www.jstor.org/stable/20474988.

Lombard, Marlize, Lyn Wadley, Janette Deacon, Sarah Wurz, Isabelle Parsons, Moleboheng Mohapi, Joane Swart, and Peter Mitchell. 2012. South African and Lesotho Stone Age sequence updated. *The South African Archaeological Bulletin* 67(195):123–144. https://www.jstor.org/stable/23631399.

Lüning, Sebastian, Mariusz Gałka, Iliya Bauchi Danladi, Theophilus Aanuoluwa Adagunodo, and Fritz Vahrenholt. 2018. Hydroclimate in Africa during the Medieval Climate Anomaly. *Palaeogeography, Palaeoclimatology, Palaeoecology* 495:309–322. https://doi.org/10.1016/j.palaeo.2018.01.025.

MacDonald, Kevin C. 1997. Korounkorokalé revisited: The *Pays Mande* and the West African microlithic technocomplex. *African Archaeological Review* 14(3):161–200. https://doi.org/10.1007/BF02968406.

—2012. "The least of their inhabited villages are fortified": The walled settlements of Segou. *Azania: Archaeological Research in Africa* 47(3):343–364. https://doi.org/10.1080/0067270X.2012.707478.

MacDonald, Kevin C., and Philip Allsworth-Jones. 1994. A reconsideration of the West African macrolithic conundrum: New factory sites and an associated settlement in the Vallée du Serpent, Mali. *African Archaeological Review* 12(1):73–104. https://doi.org/10.1007/BF01953039.

MacDonald, Kevin C., and Katie Manning. 2010. Cord-wrapped roulettes. In: Anne Haour, Katie Manning, Noémie Arazi, Olivier Gosselain, Ndèye Sokhna Guèye, Daouda Keita, Alexandre Livingstone Smith, et al., eds. *African Pottery Roulettes Past and Present: Techniques, Identification and Distribution*. Oxford: Oxbow Books. pp. 144–156.

MacDonald, Kevin C., Robert Vernet, Marcos Martinón-Torres, and Dorian Q. Fuller. 2009. Dhar Néma: From early agriculture to metallurgy in southeastern Mauritania. *Azania: Archaeological Research in Africa* 44(1):3–48. https://doi.org/10.1080/00671990902811330.

MacEachern, Scott. 2011. Enslavement and everyday life: Living with slave raiding in the northeastern Mandara Mountains of Cameroon. In: Paul J. Lane and Kevin C. MacDonald, eds. *Slavery in Africa: Archaeology and Memory*. Oxford: Oxford University Press. pp. 109–124. (Proceedings of the British Academy 168.)

Madiéga, Y. Georges. 1982. *Contribution à l'Histoire Précoloniale du Gulma (Haute Volta)*. Wiesbaden: Franz Steiner. 260 pp. (Studien zur Kulturkunde 62.)

—2009. Approche historique des royaumes (diemamba) du Gulmu à la fin du XIXe siècle. In: Pierre Claver Hien and Moustapha Gomgnimbou, eds. *Histoire des royaumes et chefferies au Burkina Faso précolonial*. Ouagadougou, Burkina Faso: Editeur Scientific DIST (CNRST). pp. 281–291.

Madiéga, Y. Georges, Benoit Bendi Ouoba, Oger Kabore, and Nurukyor Claude Somda. 1983. *Projet Gulma: Histoire du Peuplement du Gulma par la Tradition Orale*. Ouagadougou, Burkina Faso: Institut de Recherche en Sciences Sociales et Humaines (Haute Volta). 140 pp.

Magnavita, Sonja. 2009. Sahelian crossroads: Some aspects on the Iron Age sites of Kissi, Burkina Faso. In: Sonja Magnavita, Lassina Koté, Peter Breunig, and Oumarou A. Idé, eds. *Crossroads: Cultural and Technological Developments in First Millennium bc/ad West Africa [Carrefour Sahel: développements culturels et technologiques pendant le premier millénaire bc/ad dans l'Afrique de l'Ouest]*. Frankfurt am Main: Africa Magna. pp. 79–104. (Journal of African Archaeology Monograph Series 2.)

—2015. *1500 Jahre am Mare de Kissi: Eine Fallstudie zur Besiedlungsgeschichte des Sahel von Burkina Faso*. Frankfurt: Africa Magna. 421 pp.

Maley, Jean, and Robert Vernet. 2015. Populations and climatic evolution in north tropical Africa from the end of the Neolithic to the dawn of the modern era. *African Archaeological Review* 32(2):179–232. https://doi.org/10.1007/s10437-015-9190-y.

Mangin, P. Eugène. 1914. Les Mossi. Essai sur les us et coutumes du peuple Mossi au Soudan Occidental. Livre Troisieme. Vie active et industrielle. *Anthropos* 9(5–6):705–736. https://www.jstor.org/stable/40443130.

Marchal, Jean-Yves. 1978. Vestiges d'occupation ancienne au Yatenga (Haute Volta): Une reconnaissance du pays Kibga. *Cahier ORSTOM, Séries Science Humaine* 15(4):449–484. https://api.semanticscholar.org/CorpusID:210069068.

Marchal, Monique. 1983. *Les Paysages Agraires de Haute-Volta: Analyse Structurale par la Méthode Graphique*. Paris: ORSTOM. 115 pp. (Atlas des Structures Agraires au Sud du Sahara 18.)

Mayor, Anne. 2010. Braided strip roulettes. In: Anne Haour, Katie Manning, Noémie Arazi, Olivier Gosselain, Ndèye Sokhna Guèye, Daouda Keita, Alexandre Livingstone Smith, et al., eds. *African Pottery Roulettes Past and Present: Techniques, Identification and Distribution*. Oxford: Oxbow Books. pp. 181–186.

—2011. *Traditions céramiques dans la Boucle du Niger: Ethnoarchéologie et histoire du peuplement au temps des empires précoloniaux*. Frankfurt am Main: Africa Magna. 292 pp. (Journal of African Archaeology Monograph Series 7.)

MAYOR, ANNE, ERIC HUYSECOM, ALAIN GALLAY, MICHEL RASSE, AND AZIZ BALLOUCHE. 2005. Population dynamics and paleoclimate over the past 3000 years in the Dogon Country, Mali. *Journal of Anthropological Archaeology* 24(1):25–61. https://doi.org/10.1016/j.jaa.2004.08.003.

MCINTOSH, RODERICK J. 1974. Archaeology and mud wall decay in a West African village. *World Archaeology* 6(2):154–171. https://doi.org/10.1080/00438243.1974.9979599.

—1998. *The Peoples of the Middle Niger: The Island of Gold*. Malden, MA: Blackwell Publishers. 346 pp.

—2005. *Ancient Middle Niger: Urbanism and the Self-Organizing Landscape*. Cambridge: Cambridge University Press. 261 pp. (Case Studies in Early Societies 7.)

—2015 Alternative polities. In: Robert A. Scott, Stephen M. Kosslyn, and Marlis Buchmann, eds. *Emerging Trends in the Social and Behavioral Sciences: An Interdisciplinary, Searchable, and Linkable Resource [electronic resource]*. Hoboken, NJ: John Wiley and Sons. pp. 1–10. https://doi.org/10.1002/9781118900772.etrds0008.

MCINTOSH, RODERICK J., SUSAN KEECH MCINTOSH, AND HAMADY BOCOUM, EDS. 2016. *The Search for Takrur: Archaeological Excavations and Reconnaissance along the Middle Senegal Valley*. New Haven: Yale University Department of Anthropology and the Yale Peabody Museum of Natural History. 578 pp. (Yale University Publications in Anthropology 93.)

MCINTOSH, SUSAN KEECH, ED. 1995. *Excavations at Jenné-jeno, Hambarketolo, and Kaniana (Inland Niger Delta, Mali), the 1981 Season*. Berkeley: University of California Press. 605 pp. (University of California Publications in Anthropology 20.)

—1999. Pathways to complexity: An African perspective. In: Susan Keech McIntosh, ed. *Beyond Chiefdoms: Pathways to Complexity in Africa*. Cambridge: Cambridge University Press. pp. 1–30.

—2020. Long-distance exchange and urban trajectories in the first millennium AD: Case studies from the middle Niger and middle Senegal River valleys. In: Martin Sterry and David J. Mattingley, eds. *Urbanisation and State Formation in the Ancient Sahara and Beyond*. Cambridge: Cambridge University Press. pp. 521–563. (Trans-Saharan Archaeology 3.)

MCINTOSH, SUSAN KEECH, DAPHNE GALLAGHER, AND RODERICK MCINTOSH. 2003. Tobacco pipes from excavations at the Museum Site, Jenne, Mali. *Journal of African Archaeology* 1(2):171–199. https://doi.org/10.3213/1612-1651-10008.

MCINTOSH, SUSAN KEECH, AND NDÈYE SOKHNA GUÈYE. 2010. Braided cord roulettes. In: Anne Haour, Katie Manning, Noémie Arazi, Olivier Gosselain, Ndèye Sokhna Guèye, Daouda Keita, Alexandre Livingstone Smith, et al., eds. *African Pottery Roulettes Past and Present: Techniques, Identification and Distribution*. Oxford: Oxbow Books. pp. 157–168.

MENAUT, JEAN-CLAUDE, AND JACQUES CESAR. 1982. The structure and dynamics of a West African savanna. In: Bruce L. Huntley and Brian H. Walker, eds. *Ecology of Tropical Savannas*. New York: Springer. pp. 80–100. (Ecological Studies 42.)

MENJAUD, HENRI. 1932. Documents ethnographiques sur le Gourma. *Journal de la Société des Africanistes* 2(1):35–47.

MILLOGO, JEAN BLAISE. 1998. "Histoire du peuplement précolonial du pays Bobo-Sogokire (Burkina Faso)" [dissertation]. Paris: Université Paris I, Department of History. 522 pp.

MILLOGO, K. ANTOINE. 1993a. Résultats des premiers sondages dans l'Abri de Yobri (Sud-Est du Burkina Faso). *L'Anthropologie* 97(1):119–30.

—1993b. Recherches préhistoriques au Burkina Faso. *L'Anthropologie* 97(1):97–118.

MILLOGO, K. ANTOINE, AND LASSINA KOTÉ. 2000. Éléments d'archéologie ouest-africaine I: Burkina Faso. Nouakchott: CRIAA; Paris: Éditions Sépia. 71 pp.

MITCHELL, PETER J. 2017. Discontinuities in hunter-gatherer prehistory in southern African drylands. *Journal of Anthropological Archaeology* 46:40–52. https://doi.org/10.1016/j.jaa.2016.07.001.

M'Mbogori, Freda Nkirote. 2018. Ethnographic clay sourcing practices: Insights for archaeological assemblage interpretations. *African Archaeological Review* 35(4):597–608. https://doi.org/10.1007/s10437-018-9316-0.

Monroe, J. Cameron. 2013. Power and agency in precolonial African states. *Annual Review of Anthropology* 42(1):17–35. https://doi.org/10.1146/annurev-anthro-092412-155539.

———2014. *The Precolonial State in West Africa: Building Power in Dahomey*. New York: Cambridge University Press. 265 pp.

Monroe, J. Cameron, and Akinwumi Ogundiran, eds. 2012. *Power and Landscape in Atlantic West Africa: Archaeological Perspectives*. New York: Cambridge University Press. 390 pp.

Monteil, Charles. 1927. *Le Coton chez les Noirs*. Paris: Librairie Emile LaRose. 99 pp.

Moody, Keith. 1974. Weed control in shifting cultivation. In: FAO, Soil Resources, Development and Conservation Service, Land and Water Development Division. *Shifting Cultivation and Soil Conservation in Africa: Papers Presented at the FAO/SIDA/ARCN Regional Seminar Held at Ibadan, Nigeria, 2–21 July 1973*. Rome: Food and Agriculture Organization of the United Nations. pp. 155–166. (FAO Soils Bulletin 24.)

Moritz, Timo, and Philippe Lalèyè. 2018. Fishes of the Pendjari National Park (Benin, West Africa). *Bulletin of Fish Biology* 18(1/2):1–57.

Mortimore, Michael. 1998. *Roots in the African Dust: Sustaining the Sub-Saharan Drylands*. Cambridge: Cambridge University Press. 219 pp.

Muller, Jocelyn, and Astier M. Almedom. 2008. What is "famine food"? Distinguishing between traditional vegetables and special foods for times of hunger/scarcity (Boumba, Niger). *Human Ecology* 36(4):599–607. https://doi.org/10.1007/s10745-008-9179-0.

Müller-Haude, Peter. 1995. *Landschaftsökologie und Traditionelle Bodennutzung in Gobnangou (SE-Burkina Faso, Westafrika)*. Frankfurt am Main: Institut für Physische Geographie. 170 pp. (Frankfurter Geowissenschaftliche Arbeiten, Serie D 19, Physische Geographie.)

Munsell Color. 2009. *Munsell Soil-Color Charts* [loose-leaf]. Rev. ed. Grand Rapids, MI: Munsell Color. 1 volume.

Murray, Shawn S. 2005. "The Rise of African Rice Farming and the Economic Use of Plants in the Upper Middle Niger Delta (Mali)" [dissertation]. Madison: University of Wisconsin, Department of Anthropology. 539 pp. ProQuest Dissertations & Theses Global, order no. 3175547; https://search.proquest.com/dissertations-theses/rise-african-rice-farming-economic-use-plants/docview/305389548/se-2.

Nacoulma, Blandine Marie Ivette, Katharina Schumann, Salifou Traoré, Markus Bernhardt-Römermann, Karen Hahn, Rüdiger Wittig, and Adjima Thiombiano. 2011. Impacts of land-use on West African savanna vegetation: A comparison between protected and communal area in Burkina Faso. *Biodiversity and Conservation* 20(14):3341–3362. https://doi.org/10.1007/s10531-011-0114-0.

Nash, David J., Gijs De Cort, Brian M. Chase, Dirk Verschuren, Sharon E. Nicholson, Timothy M. Shanahan, Asfawossen Asrat, Anne-Marie Lézine, and Stefan W. Grab. 2016. African hydroclimatic variability during the last 2000 years. *Quaternary Science Reviews* 154:1–22. https://doi.org/10.1016/j.quascirev.2016.10.012.

Nast, Heidi J. 2008. Women, royalty, and indigo dyeing in northern Nigeria, circa 1500–1807. In: Anne Walthall, ed. *Servants of the Dynasty: Palace Women in World History*. Berkeley: University of California Press. pp. 232–260. (California World History Library 7.)

N'Dah, Didier. 2009. Contribution de l'archéologie à la connaissance de l'histoire du peuplement de l'Atakora entre le premier et le second millénaire après Jésus-Christ. In: Sonja Magnavita, Lassina Koté, Peter Breunig and Oumarou A. Idé, eds. *Crossroads: Cultural and Technological Developments in First Millennium bc/ad West Africa [Carrefour Sahel: développements culturels et technologiques pendant le premier millénaire bc/ad dans l'Afrique de l'Ouest]*. Frankfurt am Main: Africa Magna. pp. 179–191. (Journal of African Archaeology Monograph Series 2.)

Netting, Robert M. 1968. *Hill Farmers of Nigeria: Cultural Ecology of the Kofyar of the Jos Plateau*. Seattle: University of Washington Press. 259 pp.

Neumann, Katherina. 1999. Early plant food production in the West African Sahel: New evidence. In: Marjike van der Veen, ed. *The Exploitation of Plant Resources in Ancient Africa*. New York: Kluwer/Plenum. pp. 73–80.

Nikis, Nicolas, Alexandre Livingstone Smith, and Olivier Gosselain. 2019. Boyeri (BOY-14-SI & II). In: Anne Haour, ed. *Two Thousand Years in Dendi, Northern Benin: Archaeology, History and Memory*. Leiden: Brill. pp. 359–365. (Journal of African Archaeology Monograph Series 13.) https://doi.org/10.1163/9789004376694.

Nixon-Darcus, Laurie, and A. Catherine D'Andrea. 2017. Necessary for life: Studies of ancient and modern grinding stones in highland Ethiopia. *African Archaeological Review* 34(2): 193–223. https://doi.org/10.1007/s10437-017-9252-4.

Norman, Neil L. 2009. Hueda (Whydah) country and town: Archaeological perspectives on the rise and collapse of an African Atlantic kingdom. *The International Journal of African Historical Studies* 42(3):387–410. http://search.ebscohost.com/login.aspx?direct=true&db=hft&AN=509894519&site=ehost-live&scope=site.

Norris, Edward Graham. 1986. Atakora Mountain refuges systems of exploitation in Northern Togo. *Anthropos* 81(1/3):109–136. https://www.jstor.org/stable/40462028.

[NRC] National Research Council, Board on Science and Technology for International Development. 1996. *Lost Crops of Africa*. Volume 1, Grains. Washington, DC: National Academy Press. 383 pp.

—2006. *Lost Crops of Africa*. Volume 2, Vegetables. Washington, DC: National Academy Press. 378 pp.

—2008. *Lost Crops of Africa*. Volume 3, Fruits. Washington, DC: National Academy Press. 380 pp.

Nye, Peter Hague, and Dennis J. Greenland. 1960. *The Soil Under Shifting Cultivation*. Farnham Royal, Bucks, England: Commonwealth Agricultural Bureau. 156 pp. (Technical Communication 51.)

Oas, Sarah E., A. Catherine D'Andrea, and Derek J. Watson. 2015. 10,000 year history of plant use at Bosumpra Cave, Ghana. *Vegetation History and Archaeobotany* 24(5):635–653. https://doi.org/10.1007/s00334-015-0514-2.

Obayemi, Ade. 1973. A note on test excavations at Leka and Soro, Sokoto Province. *Studies in Nigerian Culture: Occasional Papers of the Centre for Nigerian Cultural Studies, Ahmadu Bello University* 1(1):110–116.

Ogundiran, Akinwumi. 2002. *Archaeology and History in Ìlàrè District (Central Yorubaland, Nigeria), 1200–1900 AD*. Oxford: Archaeopress. 163 pp. (BAR International Series 1090.)

—2007. Living in the shadow of the Atlantic world: History and material life in a Yoruba–Edo hinterland, ca. 1600–1750. In: Akinwumi Ogundiran and Toyin Falola, eds. *Archaeology of Atlantic Africa and the African Diaspora*. Bloomington: Indiana University Press. pp. 77–99.

—2009. Material life and domestic economy in a frontier of the Oyo Empire during the Mid-Atlantic Age. *The International Journal of African Historical Studies* 42(3):351–385. https://www.jstor.org/stable/40646774.

—2013. The end of prehistory? An Africanist comment. *The American Historical Review* 118(3): 788–801. https://doi.org/10.1093/ahr/118.3.788.

—2014. The making of an internal frontier settlement: Archaeology and historical process in Osun Grove (Nigeria), seventeenth to eighteenth centuries. *African Archaeological Review* 31(1):1–24. https://doi.org/10.1007/s10437-014-9152-9.

—2016. Movementality: A reflection on the experience of mobility. *Azania: Archaeological Research in Africa* 51(4):534–539. https://doi.org/10.1080/0067270X.2016.1233765.

Okigbo, Bede N. 1984. Shifting cultivation in tropical Africa: Definition and description. In: A. H. Bunting and Edward Bunting, eds. *The Future of Shifting Cultivation in Africa and the Task of Universities: proceedings of the International Workshop on Shifting Cultivation: Teaching and Research at University Level, 4–9 July 1982, Ibadan, Nigeria*. Rome: Food and Agriculture Organization of the United Nations. pp. 18–36.

OSBORNE, COLIN P., TRISTAN CHARLES-DOMINIQUE, NICOLA STEVENS, WILLIAM J. BOND, GUY MIDGLEY, AND CAROLINE E. R. LEHMANN. 2018. Human impacts in African savannas are mediated by plant functional traits. *New Phytologist* 220(1):10–24. https://doi.org/10.1111/nph.15236.

OSSAH MVONDO, J. P. 1994. La question des pipes archéologiques en Afrique: les nouvelles évidences. *West African Journal of Archaeology* 24:1–19.

OUÉDRAOGO, ISSAKA, BLANDINE MARIE IVETTE NACOULMA, KAREN HAHN, AND ADJIMA THIOMBIANO. 2014. Assessing ecosystem services based on indigenous knowledge in south-eastern Burkina Faso (West Africa). *International Journal of Biodiversity Science, Ecosystem Services and Management* 10(4):313–321. https://doi.org/10.1080/21513732.2014.950980.

OUÉDRAOGO, OUMAROU, MARCO SCHMIDT, ADJIMA THIOMBIANO, KAREN HAHN, SITA GUINKO, AND GEORG ZIZKA. 2011. Magnoliophyta, Arly National Park, Tapoa, Burkina Faso. *Check List* 7(1):85–100. https://doi.org/10.15560/7.1.85.

PARGETER, JUSTIN. 2011. Assessing the macrofracture method for identifying Stone Age hunting weaponry. *Journal of Archaeological Science* 38(11):2882–2888. https://doi.org/10.1016/j.jas.2011.04.018.

PARGETER, JUSTIN, AND JUSTIN BRADFIELD. 2012. The effects of Class I and II sized bovids on macrofracture formation and tool displacement: Results of a trampling experiment in a southern African Stone Age context. *Journal of Field Archaeology* 37(3):238–251. https://doi.org/10.1179/0093469012Z.00000000022.

PATRUT, ADRIAN, KARL R. VON REDEN, ROBERT VAN PELT, DIANA H. MAYNE, DANIEL A. LOWY, AND DRAGOS MARGINEANU. 2011. Age determination of large live trees with inner cavities: Radiocarbon dating of Platland tree, a giant African baobab. *Annals of Forest Science* 68(5):993–1003. https://dx.doi.org/10.1007/s13595-011-0107-x.

PÉLISSIER, PAUL. 1966. *Les Paysans du Sénégal: Les Civilisations Agraires du Cayor à Casamance.* Saint-Yrieix (Haute-Vienne): Imprimerie Fabrégue. 941 pp.

PETIT, LUCAS P. 2005. *Archaeology and History in North-Western Benin.* Oxford: Archaeopress. 171 pp. (BAR International Series 1398.)

PETIT, LUCAS P., MAYA VON CZERNIEWICZ, AND CHRISTOPH PELZER, EDS. 2011. *Oursi Hu-beero: A Medieval House Complex in Burkina Faso, West Africa.* Leiden: Sidestone Press. 282 pp.

PHILLIPSON, DAVID W. 1976. *The Prehistory of Eastern Zambia.* Nairobi: British Institute in Eastern Africa. 229 pp. (Memoir 6.)

PHLIPONEAU, MARIE. 2010. Micro-histoire de la diffusion de l'islam en Afrique de l'Ouest: Création de réseaux et de chaînes d'enseignement en Bwamu (Burkina Faso). *Cahiers d'Études Africaines* 49(196):969–1000. https://www.jstor.org/stable/40380045.

PIERI, CHRISTIAN J. M. G. 1992. *Fertility of Soils: A Future for Farming in the West African Savannah* [*Fertilité des terres de savannes*]. Translated by Philip Gething. Berlin: Springer. 348 pp. (Springer Series in Physical Environment 10.)

PIGEONNIÈRE, ANNE LEREBOURS, AND SYLVIE JOMNI. 1998. *Atlas du Burkina Faso.* 3rd ed. Paris: Éditions Jeune Afrique. 54 pp.

POLLOCK, SUSAN. 2013. Commensality, public spaces and Handlungsräume in ancient Mesopotamia. In: John Robb and Timothy Pauketat, eds. *Big Histories, Human Lives: Tackling Problems of Scale in Archaeology.* 1st ed. Santa Fe, NM: School for Advanced Research Press. pp. 145–170.

PORTÈRES, ROLAND. 1950. *Les Sels Alimentaires, Cendres d'Origine Végétale, Sels de Cendres comme Succédanés du Chlorure de Sodium Alimentaire et Catalogue des Plantes Salifères en Afrique Intertropicale et à Madagascar.* Dakar: Gouvernement Général de l'Afrique Occidentale Française, Direction Générale de la Santé Publique. 77 pp.

PRUDENCIO, COFFI Y. 1993. Ring management of soils and crops in the West African semi-arid tropics: The case of the Mossi farming system of Burkina Faso. *Agriculture, Ecosystems and Environment* 47(3):237–264. https://doi.org/10.1016/0167-8809(93)90125-9.

PRUSSIN, LABELLE. 1969. *Architecture in Northern Ghana: A Study of Forms and Functions.* Berkeley: University of California Press. 120 pp.

Pullan, Robert Allen. 1974. Farmed parkland in West Africa. *Savanna* 3(2):119–151.

Pyne, Stephen J. 2001. *Fire: A Brief History*. Seattle, WA: University of Washington Press. 204 pp.

Rémy, Gerard. 1967. *Yobri: Étude Géographique du Terroir d'un Village Gourmantché de Haute-Volta*. Paris: Mouton. 100 pp. (Atlas des Structures Agraires au Sud du Sahara 1.)

—1972. *Donsin: Les structures agraires d'un village Mossi de la région de Nobéré (Cercle de Manga)*. Paris: CNRS; Ouagadougou, Burkina Faso: Centre Voltaïque de la Recherche Scientifique. 144 pp. (Recherches Voltaïques 15.) https://horizon.documentation.ird.fr/exl-doc/pleins_textes/divers11-02/05694.pdf.

Rice, Prudence M. 1999. On the origins of pottery. *Journal of Archaeological Method and Theory* 6(1):1–54. https://doi.org/10.1023/A:1022924709609.

—2015. *Pottery Analysis: A Sourcebook*. 2nd ed. Chicago: University of Chicago Press. 592 pp.

Richard, François G. 2009. Historical and dialectical perspectives on the archaeology of complexity in the Siin-Saalum (Senegal): Back to the future? *African Archaeological Review* 26(2):75–135. https://doi.org/10.1007/s10437-009-9050-8.

—2015. The African state in theory: Thoughts on political landscapes and the limits of rule in Atlantic Senegal (and elsewhere). In: Stephanie Wynne-Jones and Jeffrey Fleisher, eds. *Theory in Africa, African in Theory: Locating Meaning in Archaeology*. New York: Routledge. pp. 201–231.

—2018. *Reluctant Landscapes: Historical Anthropologies of Political Experience in Siin, Senegal*. Chicago: University of Chicago Press. 414 pp.

Richard, François G., and Kevin C. MacDonald, eds. 2015. *Ethnic Ambiguity and the African Past: Materiality, History, and the Shaping of Cultural Identities*. Walnut Creek, CA: Left Coast Press. 296 pp. (Publications of the Institute of Archaeology, University College London 65.)

Roberts, Benjamin W., and Marc Vander Linden, eds. 2011. *Investigating Archaeological Cultures: Material Culture, Variability, and Transmission*. New York: Springer. 393 pp.

Roberts, Richard L. 1996. *Two Worlds of Cotton: Colonialism and the Regional Economy in the French Soudan, 1800–1946*. Stanford, CA: Stanford University Press. 381 pp.

Robertshaw, Peter. 2000. Sibling rivalry? The intersection of archaeology and history. *History in Africa* 27:261–286. https://doi.org/10.2307/3172117.

Robion-Brunner, Caroline. 2019. Ironworking. In: Anne Haour, ed. *Two Thousand Years in Dendi, Northern Benin: Archaeology, History and Memory*. Leiden: Brill. pp. 174–192. (Journal of African Archaeology Monograph Series 13.) https://doi.org/10.1163/9789004376694.

Sahlins, Marshall D. 1957. Land use and the extended family in Moala, Fiji. *American Anthropologist* 59(3):449–462. https://doi.org/10.1525/aa.1957.59.3.02a00040.

Saltman, Carlyn, Candice L. Goucher, and Eugenia W. Herbert. 1986. *The Blooms of Banjeli: Technology and Gender in African Ironmaking*. Videocassette (VHS); approx. 30 min. Watertown, MA: Documentary Educational Resources. Available from Kanopy Streaming, 2014; http://www.kanopystreaming.com/node/48891.

Sankaran, Mahesh, Niall P. Hanan, Robert J. Scholes, Jayashree Ratnam, David J. Augustine, Brian S. Cade, and Jacques Gignoux, et al. 2005. Determinants of woody cover in African savannas. *Nature* 438(7069):846–849. https://doi.org/10.1038/nature04070.

Sattran, Vladimir, and Urbain Wenmenga. 2002. *Géologie du Burkina Faso [Geology of Burkina Faso]*. 1st ed. Praha: Czech Geological Survey. 136 pp. [In English and French.]

Savonnet, Georges. 1959. Un système de culture perfectionné, pratiqué par les Bwaba–Bobo-Oulé de la région de Houndé (Haute-Volta). *Bulletin de l'Institut Français d'Afrique Noire. Série B, Sciences Humaines* 21(3–4):425–458. https://horizon.documentation.ird.fr/exl-doc/pleins_textes/divers20-05/010027418.pdf

—1970. *Pina: Étude d'un Terroir de Front Pionnier en Pays Dagari (Haute-Volta)*. Paris: Mouton. 63 pp. (Atlas des Structures Agraires au Sud du Sahara 4.)

—1976. *Les Birifor de Diépla et sa Région, Insulaires du Rameau Lobi (Haute-Volta)*. Paris: Mouton. 169 pp. (Atlas des Structures Agraires au Sud du Sahara 12.)

SAVONNET-GUYOT, CLAUDETTE. 1986. *État et Sociétés au Burkina: Essai sur le Politique Africain.* Paris: Éditions Karthala. 232 pp. (Hommes et Sociétés.)

SCERRI, ELEANOR M. L., JAMES BLINKHORN, HUW S. GROUCUTT, AND KHADY NIANG. 2016. The Middle Stone Age Archaeology of the Senegal River Valley. In: James Blinkhorn, Eleanor Scerri, Huw Groucutt, and Anne Delagnes, eds., special issue, *The Middle Palaeolithic in the Desert II. Quaternary International* 408(Part B):16–32. https://doi.org/10.1016/j.quaint.2015.09.025.

SCERRI, ELEANOR M. L., JAMES BLINKHORN, KHADY NIANG, MARK D. BATEMAN, AND HUW S. GROUCUTT. 2017. Persistence of Middle Stone Age technology to the Pleistocene/Holocene transition supports a complex hominin evolutionary scenario in West Africa. *Journal of Archaeological Science: Reports* 11:639–646. https://doi.org/10.1016/j.jasrep.2017.01.003.

SCHIFFER, MICHAEL B. 1987. *Formation Processes of the Archaeological Record.* 1st. ed. Albuquerque: University of New Mexico Press. 428 pp.

SCHMIDT, MARCO, SALIFOU TRAORÉ, AMADÉ OUÉDRAOGO, ELISÉE MBAYNGONE, OUMAROU OUÉDRAOGO, ALEXANDER ZIZKA, IVANA KIRCHMAIR, ET AL. 2013. Geographical patterns of woody plants' functional traits in Burkina Faso. *Candollea* 68:197–207. https://doi.org/10.15553/c2012v682a3.

SCHMIDT, PETER R. 2006. *Historical Archaeology in Africa: Representation, Social Memory, and Oral Traditions.* Lanham, MD: Altamira Press. 316 pp.

—2015. Historical archaeology in East Africa: Past practice and future directions. *The Journal of African History* 57(2):183–194. https://doi.org/10.1017/S0021853715000791.

SCHWAHN, JOACHIM. 2003. *Zur Fischfauna des Pendjari-Nationalparks in Benin (Westafrika). Deutsche Gesellschaft für Limnologie (DGL)—Tagungsbericht 2002 (Braunschweig).* 6 pp. https://www.yumpu.com/de/document/read/6863331/bericht-uber-die-fischfauna-des-pendjari-np.pdf.

SELLET, FRÉDÉRIC, RUSSELL D. GREAVES, AND PEI-LIN YU, EDS. 2006. *Archaeology and Ethnoarchaeology of Mobility.* Gainesville: University Press of Florida. 290 pp.

SERNEELS, VINCENT. 2017. The massive production of iron in the Sahelian belt: Archaeological investigations at Korsimoro (Sanmatenga–Burkina Faso). *Materials and Manufacturing Processes* 32(7–8):900–908. https://doi.org/10.1080/10426914.2016.1244842.

SHANAHAN, TIMOTHY M. 2018 April 26. Quaternary Climate Variation in West Africa. *Oxford Research Encyclopedia of Climate Science.* 39 pp. https://doi.org/10.1093/acrefore/9780190228620.013.526.

SHAW, THURSTAN. 1985. The prehistory of West Africa. In: J. F. Ade Ajayi and Michael Crowder, eds. *History of West Africa,* Volume 1. 3rd ed. New York: Longman. pp. 48–86.

SHEA, PHILIP J. 1975a. "The Development of an Export Oriented Dyed Cloth Industry in Kano Emirate in the Nineteenth Century" [dissertation]. Madison: University of Wisconsin–Madison, Department of Anthropology. 592 pp. ProQuest Dissertations & Theses Global, order no. 7602506; https://search.proquest.com/dissertations-theses/development-export-oriented-dyed-cloth-industry/docview/302807578/se-2.

—1975b. Responses to changing economic conditions in the indigo-dyeing industry in Kano in the nineteenth century. *African Economic History Review* 2(1):30–32. https://doi.org/10.2307/3601082.

SHINNIE, PETER L., AND FRANÇOIS J. KENSE. 1989. *Archaeology of Gonja, Ghana: Excavations at Daboya.* Calgary: University of Calgary Press. 369 pp.

SHINNIE, PETER L., AND PAUL C. OZANNE. 1962. Excavations at Yendi Dabari. *Transactions of the Historical Society of Ghana* 6:87–118. https://www.jstor.org/stable/41405754.

SHOEMAKER, ANNA C., MATTHEW I. J. DAVIES, AND HENRIETTA L. MOORE. 2017. Back to the grindstone? The archaeological potential of grinding-stone studies in Africa with reference to contemporary grinding practices in Marakwet, northwest Kenya. *African Archaeological Review* 34(3):415–435. https://doi.org/10.1007/s10437-017-9264-0.

SIEBER, ELLEN. 1992. "Iron Age Archaeology in Kano State, Nigeria" [dissertation]. Bloomington: Indiana University, Department of Anthropology. 390 pp. ProQuest Dissertations & Theses Global, order no. 9301474. https://search.proquest.com/dissertations-theses/iron-age-archaeology-kano-state-nigeria/docview/304006823/se-2.

SIMPORÉ, LASSINA. 2009. La métallurgie traditionnelle du fer et la fondation du Royaume de Wogdogo (Ouagadougou, Burkina Faso). In: Sonja Magnavita, Lassina Koté, Peter Breunig, and Oumarou A. Idé, eds. *Crossroads: Cultural and Technological Developments in First Millennium bc/ad West Africa [Carrefour Sahel: développements culturels et technologiques pendant le premier millénaire bc/ad dans l'Afrique de l'Ouest]*. Frankfurt am Main: Africa Magna. pp. 251–258. (Journal of African Archaeology Monograph Series 2.)

SINOPOLI, CARLA M. 2003. *The Political Economy of Craft Production: Crafting Empire in South India, c. 1350–1650*. Cambridge: Cambridge University Press. 354 pp.

SKINNER, ELLIOTT PERCIVAL. 1989. *The Mossi of Burkina Faso: Chiefs, Politicians and Soldiers*. Prospect Heights, IL: Waveland Press. 279 pp.

SLINGERLAND, MAJA, AND MOUGA MASDEWEL. 1996. Mulching on the Central Plateau of Burkina Faso: Widespread and well adapted to farmers' means. In: Chris Reij, Ian Scoones and Camilla Toulmin, eds. *Sustaining the Soil: Indigenous Soil and Water Conservation in Africa*. London: Earthscan Publications. pp. 85–89.

SOMÉ, MAGLOIRE, AND LASSINA SIMPORÉ. 2014. Lieux de mémoire, patrimoine et histoire en *Afrique de l'Ouest: Aux origines des Ruines de Loropéni, Burkina Faso*. Paris: Éditions des Archives Contemporaines. 291 pp.

SOPER, ROBERT. 1985. Roulette decoration on African pottery: Technical considerations, dating and distributions. *African Archaeological Review* 3(1):29–51. https://doi.org/10.1007/BF01117454.

SORIANO, SYLVAIN, MICHEL RASSE, CHANTAL TRIBOLO, AND ERIC HUYSECOM. 2010. Ounjougou: A long middle Stone Age sequence in the Dogon country (Mali). In: Philip Allsworth-Jones, ed. *West African Archaeology: New Developments, New Perspectives*. Oxford: Archaeopress. pp. 1–14. (BAR International Series 2164.)

SOULIGNAC, RAPHAËLLE. 2017. *Les Scories de Forge du Pays Dogon (Mali): Entre Ethnoarchéologie, Archéologie Expérimentale, et Archéométrie*. Basel: Librum Publishers. 208 pp.

SPINAGE, CLIVE A. 1986. *The Natural History of Antelopes*. London: Croom Helm. 203 pp.

STAHL, ANN BROWER. 1993. Intensification in the West Africa Late Stone Age: A view from central Ghana. In: Thurstan Shaw, Paul Sinclair, Bassey Andah, and Alex Okpoko, eds. *The Archaeology of Africa: Foods, Metals and Towns*. London: Routledge. pp. 261–273. (One World Archaeology 20.)

—2001. *Making History in Banda: Anthropological Visions of Africa's Past*. Cambridge: Cambridge University Press. 270 pp. (New Studies in Archaeology.)

—2002. Colonial entanglements and the practices of taste: An alternative to logocentric approaches. *American Anthropologist* 104(3):827–845. https://doi.org/10.1525/aa.2002.104.3.827.

—2007. Entangled lives: The archaeology of daily life in the Gold Coast hinterlands, AD 1400–1900. In: Akinwumi Ogundiran and Toyin Falola, eds. *Archaeology of Atlantic Africa and the African Diaspora*. Bloomington: Indiana University Press. pp. 49–76.

STAHL, ANN B., MARIA DAS DORES CRUZ, HECTOR NEFF, MICHAEL D. GLASCOCK, ROBERT J. SPEAKMAN, BRETTON GILES, AND LEITH SMITH. 2008. Ceramic production, consumption and exchange in the Banda area, Ghana: Insights from compositional analyses. *Journal of Anthropological Archaeology* 27(3):363–381. https://doi.org/10.1016/j.jaa.2008.04.001.

STAVER, A. CARLA, SALLY ARCHIBALD, AND SIMON LEVIN. 2011. Tree cover in sub-Saharan Africa: Rainfall and fire constrain forest and savanna as alternative stable states. *Ecology* 92(5):1063–1072. https://doi.org/10.1890/10-1684.1.

STEBBING, EDWARD PERCY. 1935. The encroaching Sahara: the threat to the West African colonies. *The Geographical Journal* 85(6):506–519. https://doi.org/10.2307/1785870.

STONE, GLENN DAVIS. 1996. *Settlement Ecology: The Social and Spatial Organization of Kofyar Agriculture*. Tucson: University of Arizona Press. 257 pp. (Arizona Studies in Human Ecology.)

SULE SANI, ABUBAKAR. 2010. Kirfi, Bauchi: An archaeological investigation of the Hausa landscape. In: Anne Haour and Benedetta Rossi, eds. *Being and Becoming Hausa: Interdisciplinary Perspectives.* Leiden: Brill. pp. 165–186. https://doi.org/10.1163/ej.9789004185425.i-310.52.

SULE SANI, ABUBAKAR, AND ANNE HAOUR. 2014. The archaeology of northern Nigeria: Trade, people and polities, 1500 BP onwards. *Azania: Archaeological Research in Africa* 49(4):439–462. https://doi.org/10.1080/0067270X.2014.968330.

SWANEPOEL, NATALIE. 2005. Socio-political change on a slave-raiding frontier: War, trade and 'Big Men' in nineteenth century Sisalaland, northern Ghana. *Journal of Conflict Archaeology* 1(1):265–293. https://doi.org/10.1163/157407705774928999.

—2008. View from the village: Changing settlement patterns in Sisalaland, northern Ghana. *The International Journal of African Historical Studies* 41(1):1–27. https://www.jstor.org/stable/40282454.

—2009. Every periphery is its own center: Sociopolitical and economic interactions in nineteenth-century northwestern Ghana. *The International Journal of African Historical Studies* 42(3):411–432. https://www.jstor.org/stable/40646776.

SWANSON, RICHARD A. 1979a April 15. *Gourmantché Agriculture.* Part 1, Land tenure and field cultivation [typescript]. USAID, Mission to Upper Volta. Contract AID-686-049-78; document no. 7. Fada N'Gourma [Upper Volta: s.n.]. 77 pp. https://pdf.usaid.gov/pdf_docs/PNAAT306.pdf.

—1979b April 30. *Gourmantché Agriculture.* Part 2, Cultivated plant resources and field management [typescript]. USAID, Mission to Upper Volta. Contract AID-686-049-78; document no. 8. Fada N'Gourma, [Upper Volta: s.n.]. 205 pp. https://pdf.usaid.gov/pdf_docs/PNAAT307.pdf.

—1985. *Gourmantche Ethnoanthropology: A Theory of Human Being.* Lanham, MD: University Press of America. 464 pp.

SWIFT, JEREMY. 1996. Desertification: Narratives, winners, and losers. In: Melissa Leach and Robin Mearns, eds. *The Lie of the Land: Challenging Received Wisdom on the African Environment.* Oxford: International African Institute in association with James Curry; Portsmouth, NH: Heinemann. pp. 73–90.

TAKEZAWA, SHOICHIRO, AND MAMADOU CISSÉ. 2012. Discovery of the earliest royal palace in Gao and its implications for the history of West Africa [Découverte du premier palais royal à Gao et ses implications pour l'histoire de l'Afrique de l'Ouest]. *Cahiers d'Études Africaines* (52):813–844 [in English with French abstract]. https://doi.org/10.4000/etudesafricaines.17167.

—2017. *Sur les Traces des Grands Empires: Recherches Archéologiques au Mali.* Paris: L'Harmattan. 309 pp.

TAKPARA, FRANK N'PO. 2019. Bokorobu (BOK). In: Anne Haour, ed. *Two Thousand Years in Dendi, Northern Benin: Archaeology, History and Memory.* Leiden: Brill. pp. 421–426. (Journal of African Archaeology Monograph Series 13.) https://doi.org/10.1163/9789004376694.

TAUXIER, LOUIS. 1912. *Le Noir du Soudan, Pays Mossi et Gourounsi:. Documents et analyses.* Paris: Larose. 796 pp. https://hdl.handle.net/2027/mdp.35112105256970.

THIAW, IBRAHIMA. 2010. Histoire, espace, et identités sénégambiennes. In: Ibrahima Thiaw, ed. *Espaces, Culture Matérielle et Identités en Sénégambie.* Dakar: CODESRIA. pp. 4–17.

THILMANS, GUY, CYR DESCAMPS, AND BERNARD KHAYAT. 1980. *Protohistoire du Sénégal: Recherches Archéologiques.* Volume 1, Les sites megalithiques. Dakar: Institut Fondamental d'Afrique Noire. 158 pp. (Mémoires 91.)

THIOMBIANO, ADJIMA, MARCO SCHMIDT, SYLVESTRE DA, KAREN HAHN-HADJALI, GEORG ZIZKA, AND RÜDIGER WITTIG. 2010. Les plantes vasculaires: Les plantes à fleurs [Vascular plants: Flowering plants]. In: Adjima Thiombiano and Dorothea Kampmann, eds. *Atlas de la Biodiversité de l'Ouest [Biodiversity Atlas of West Africa].* Volume 2, Burkina Faso. Ouagadougou and Frankfurt am Main: BIOTA. pp. 184–192 [in French and English]. https://www.uni-frankfurt.de/47616989/BIOTA-Atlas-BF.

THIOMBIANO-ILBOUDO, ELISE FONIYAMA. 2010. "Les vestiges de l'occupation humaine ancienne dans la province du Gourma, des origines à la pénétration coloniale (cas de Kouaré et de

Namoungou)" [dissertation]. Ouagadougou; Université de Ouagadougou, Burkina Faso, UFR/SH, département d'Histoire et Archéologie. 671 pp.

—2012a. La métallurgie ancienne du fer à Namoungou, Province du Gourma, Burkina Faso. *Cahiers du CERLESHS* 26(41):106–129.

—2012b. Impact de la culture maraîchere sur les sites metallurgiques du Sanmatenga: Cas de Korsimoro. *Annales de l'Université de Ouagadougou, Série A* 15:139–169.

—2014. L'activité du Koudougou ou de la forge à Sadaba (Province de l'Oubritenga, Burkina Faso): La transmission d'une technique entre méthodes anciennes et innovations [The activity of Koudougou or mine in Sadaba (Oubritenga Province, Burkina Faso): The transmission of a technique between old methods and innovations]. *e-Phaïstos* 3(1):59–72 [In French with English abstract]. https://doi.org/10.4000/ephaistos.581.

—2016. Mutations techniques dans le domaine de la fonderie à Kolonkani-Ba (Province de la Kossi, Burkina Fasso) [Technical changes in the field of foundry in Kolonkani-Ba (province of Kossi, Burkina Faso)]. *e-Phaïstos* 5(1):92–102 [in French with English abstract]. https://doi.org/10.4000/ephaistos.5867.

TIMMER, L. A., J. J. KESSLER, AND MAJA SLINGERLAND. 1996. Pruning of Néré trees (*Parkia biglobosa* (Jacq.) Benth.) on the farmlands of Burkina Faso, West Africa. *Agroforestry Systems* 33(1): 87–98. https://doi.org/10.1007/BF00122891.

TROCHAIN, JEAN-LOUIS. 1940. *Contribution à l'étude de la végétation du Sénégal.* Paris: Librairie Larose. 433 pp. (Mémoires de l'Institut Français d'Afrique Noire 2.)

TROUILLOT, MICHEL-ROLPH. 1995. *Silencing the Past. Power and the Production of History.* Boston: Beacon Press. 191 pp.

[UNEP] UNITED NATIONS ENVIRONMENT PROGRAMME. 2008. *Africa: Atlas of our Changing Environment.* Nairobi, Kenya: UNEP. 374 pp.

USMAN, ARIBIDESI. 2007. The landscape and society of northern Yorubaland during the era of the Atlantic slave trade. In: Akinwumi Ogundiran and Toyin Falola, eds. *Archaeology of Atlantic Africa and the African Diaspora.* Bloomington: Indiana University Press. pp. 140–159.

—2012. *The Yoruba Frontier: A Regional History of Community Formation, Experience, and Changes in West Africa.* Durham, NC: Carolina Academic Press. 249 pp.

VANSINA, JAN. 1965. *Oral Tradition: A Study in Historical Methodology.* Translated by H. M. Wright. Reprint ed. London: Routledge and Keegan Paul. 226 pp.

VARIEN, MARK D. 1999. *Sedentism and Mobility in a Social Landscape: Mesa Verde and Beyond.* Tucson: University of Arizona Press. 276 pp.

VERNET, ROBERT. 1996. *Le Sud-Ouest du Niger de la Préhistoire au Début de l'Histoire.* Niamey: Institut de Recherches en Sciences Humaines; Paris: Editions SÉPIA. 394 pp. (Études Nigériennes 56.)

WALKER, BRIAN H., AND IMANUEL NOY-MEIR. 1982. Aspects of the stability and resilience of savanna ecosystems. In: Brian J. Huntley and Brian H. Walker, eds. *Ecology of Tropical Savannas.* New York: Springer. pp. 556–590. (Ecological Studies 42.)

WATSON, DEREK J. 2010. Within savanna and forest: A review of the Late Stone Age Kintampo Tradition, Ghana. *Azania: Archaeological Research in Africa* 45(2):141–174. https://doi.org/10.1080/0067270X.2010.491361.

—2017. Bosumpra revisited: 12,500 years on the Kwahu Plateau, Ghana, as viewed from "On top of the hill." *Azania: Archaeological Research in Africa* 52(4):437–517. https://doi.org/10.1080/0067270X.2017.1393925.

—2018. Akyekyema Bour and Apreku rock shelters: Lithics, pottery and society at the forest's edge during the second millennium cal. AD, Kwahu Plateau, Ghana. *African Archaeological Review* 35(1): 21–55. https://doi.org/10.1007/s10437-018-9288-0.

WENGROW, DAVID. 2001. The evolution of simplicity: Aesthetic labour and social change in the Neolithic Near East. *World Archaeology* 33(2):168–188. https://doi.org/10.1080/00438240120079235.

WHALLON, ROBERT, AND JAMES A. BROWN, EDS. 1982. *Essays on Archaeological Typology.* Evanston, IL: Center for American Archaeology Press. 200 pp. (Kampsville Seminars in Archeology 1.)

WILKS, IVOR. 2000. The Juula and the expansion of Islam into the forest. In: Nehemia Levtzion and Randall L. Pouwels, eds. *The History of Islam in Africa*. Athens: Ohio University Press. pp. 93–116.

WILLS, J. BRIAN, ED. 1962. *Agriculture and Land Use in Ghana*. London: Published for the Ghana Ministry of Food and Agriculture by the Oxford University Press. 503 pp.

WITTIG, RÜDIGER, AND REGINA MARTIN. 1995. Krautige Wildpflanzen in der Provinz Tapoa (Burkina Faso) und ihre Nutzung für die menschliche Ernährung. In: Herausgegeben von Karsten Brunk and Ursula Greinert-Byer, eds. *Mensch un Natur in Westafrika: Eine interdisziplinäre Festschrift für Günter Nagel*. Frankfurt am Main: SFB 268. pp. 203–214. (Berichte des Sonderforschungsberiechs 268, "Kulturentwicklung und Sprachgeschichte im Naturraum Westafrikanishe Savanne" 5.)

WOTZKA, HANS-PETER, AND CHRISTIAN GOEDICKE. 2001. Thermoluminescence dates on Late Stone Age and later ceramics from Tapoa Province (southeastern Burkina Faso) and Konduga (Borno, northeastern Nigeria). *Beiträge zur Allgemeinen und Vergleichenden Archäologie* 21:75–126.

WYLIE, ALISON. 2002. *Thinking from Things: Essays in the Philosophy of Archaeology*. Berkeley: University of California Press. 339 pp.

YORK, RICHARD N. 1973. Excavations at New Buipe. *West African Journal of Archaeology* 3:1–189.

Index

A

Acacia macrostachya, 50
Acacia spp., 59
accelerator mass spectrometry (AMS) analysis, 125, 205
Adansonia digitata (baobab trees) *See* baobab trees (*Adansonia digitata*)
adzes
 artifact associations, 119
 foraging populations, 250
African Archaeobotany Laboratory (Frankfurt), 78
African Archaeology Lab (Oregon), 77
African hunting dogs, 62
agricultural practices
 anthropological research, 14–16
 cultivated plants, 52, 59–61
 ecological characteristics, 51
 environmental degradation, 257–258
 fallow fields, 14–15, 23–24, 25, 50, 60
 faunal destruction, 62
 generational mobility, 1, 7, 8, 9, 11, 13–15, 204–205, 259–260
 Gobnangou region, 52, 59–61, 156, 246, 250–251
 Gulmance farming strategies, 1, 7, 8, 14–15, 60–61
 introduced foods, 246
 iron artifacts, 153
 Lithic Occupation, 105
 MAS502.3, 150
 MAS541, 250, 251
 occupation length estimates, 169–171
 Pwoli occupation sites, 123–124, 154, 250–251
 rainfall, 13–14, 28–29
 Ring occupation sites, 311, 313
 savannas, 1, 10–11, 13–16, 52, 155
 Siga occupation sites, 167, 204–205
 socioeconomic evolution, 156
 soil characteristics, 13–14, 23–25, 50
 spatial data analyses, 75
 spatial distribution, 52, 59
 Tuali-B occupation sites, 231
 See also domesticated animals
Alcelaphus buselaphus, 62
Allophylus sp., 111
Amaranthaceae, 139
amphibians, 62, 138
anchored residences, 254, 256, 260
Andropogon spp., 60
animal bone assemblages
 MAS502.3, 145, 149–150, 153
 MAS541, 135, 138
 MAS902, 150
 northeastern Nigeria, 241
 Péntènga rockshelter, 109, 112–113, 250
 Pwoli occupation sites, 153–154
 Siga occupation sites, 203–205
 Yobri rockshelter, 113, 250
animal husbandry, 31, 62, 63, 69, 246
 See also livestock
Annona senegalensis, 70
Anogeissus leiocarpus, 60, 111
Antaris africana, 50
antelopes, 62, 135, 145
applied decorations, 86
aquatic resources
 MAS502.3, 145, 150, 153
 MAS541, 135, 138
 northern Benin, 155–156
 Péntènga rockshelter, 112–113, 153
 Pwoli occupation sites, 153–154
 Yobri rockshelter, 113
aquifers, 18–19
arching channel decorative technique, 206–207
architectural features
 households, 9
 MAS502.3, 141–142, 150–151
 MAS541, 125–127
aridification, 69–70, 111–112
Arly, 119
Arly National Park, 51, 52
arrow barbs, 120
arrowheads
 MAS502.3, 144, 153
 MAS780, 195
artifacts
 analysis and curation procedures, 77–78
 excavation methodologies, 74
 generational mobility, 9–10
 spatial data analyses, 75–76
 survey methodologies, 72–73
ash deposits
 indigo-dyeing activities, 242
 MAS502.3, 140, 141–142
 MAS541, 125, 126
 MAS573, 165
 Tuali-B occupation sites, 237
Atakora Mountains, 19, 79, 107, 155, 208, 209, 241, 251, 254, 321
Atlantic trade exchange, 239
Auchenoglanis sp., 138
axes (stone tools), 119, 201–202, 250

B

baagu, 24, 25
backed microliths, 108, 111, 117, 120, 121, 203, 250
bado (Gulmance chief), 3, 6, 8, 260, 317
Bamako, Mali, 120
banded dragged comb decorations, 189, 206–207
Bandingue, 195
Bantchande, 6
baobab trees (*Adansonia digitata*)
 dietary role, 31, 59
 foundational stories, 5
 MAS03, 320
 MAS502.3, 150
 MAS541, 139
 northern Benin, 156
 Pwoli occupation sites, 154
 Siga occupation sites, 204, 205
bark cloth, 50
basal grinding stones, 200, 201
base forms, 83, 84–85, 184–185, 221, 252, 301–303
batieba (Gulmance chiefs), 6
beads, 239, 241, 251, 252, 254
beakers, 84
Bemba peoples, 5
Benin, 2, 51, 78–79, 155–156, 169, 239
bifacial flaking techniques, 107, 119
bilharzia, 20
bilnu, 239, 240, 245–256, 257
birds, 62
Birimian deposits, 80, 202
Birnin Lafiya, 155, 208, 240
Birnin Leka, 241
bivalves, 63
black clay (*u yoagboanu*), 80
blades/bladelets
 Maadaga rockshelter, 117
 Péntènga rockshelter, 111
Blepharis sp., 240
boanbala, 24, 25
bobli, 83
Bokorobu archaeological site, 309
Bombacaceae, 204
Bombax costatum, 50
bone artifacts
 funerary markers, 185, 187
 MAS502.3, 145, 149–150, 153
 MAS541, 135, 138
 MAS902, 150
 northeastern Nigeria, 241
 Siga occupation sites, 203–205
bone temper, 81
bonfire firing technique, 89–90
Bornu, 5, 255
borrow pits
 Pwoli occupation sites, 142
 research methodologies, 72, 75, 98

Siga occupation sites, 159, 160, 169, 185, 191, 195, 210, 260
 smelting activity, 191
 Tuali-A occupation sites, 212
 upside-down pots, 185
Bos taurus (cattle)
 See cattle (*Bos taurus*)
Bosumpra, Ghana, 119
botanical assemblages
 MAS502.3, 150
 MAS541, 139
 northern Benin, 156
 Pwoli occupation sites, 154
 Siga occupation sites, 203–205
bottle gourds, 246–247
bovids, 135, 145, 154
bowls
 Siga occupation ceramics, 252
 vessel formation techniques, 83, 84
 vessel function, 187
Boyeri, 309
bracelets, 195, 210, 241
Brachiaria villosa, 60
braided strip roulette decorations
 Tuali-A occupation ceramics, 219, 221
 Tuali-B occupation ceramics, 231–232, 238
brush fires, 111–112
buffalo, 62
bulo (shrines), 7
burial artifacts, 185, 187, 210
burial pits
 excavation methodologies, 75
 iron artifacts, 195, 210
 MAS502.3, 139–140, 142
 MAS541, 128
 Pwoli occupation sites, 151
Burkea africana, 50, 51
Burkina–Benin–Niger border region, 2
Burkinabe savanna, 10–11
burned features
 MAS502.3, 140, 141, 144–145, 151
 MAS541, 125–126, 151
 MAS573, 165
burnished vessels
 MAS502.3 ceramics, 142
 MAS541 ceramics, 129
 Siga occupation ceramics, 171
 spatial distribution, 188
 surface treatments and decoration, 85
 Tuali-A occupation ceramics, 221
 vessel function, 185
bushbucks, 204
bush field system, 61
button feet, 85

C

cabbage, 59
calabash, 246–247
Cameroon, 119
cancanli, 83
cane rats, 62, 135, 149, 153, 154
Canis familiaris (dogs)
 See dogs (*Canis familiaris*)
Capra hircus (goats)
 See goats (*Capra hircus*)
carbonized seeds and fruits
 Pwoli occupation sites, 145, 151, 154, 156
 Siga occupation sites, 203–204, 205
carinated vessels, 84
carnivores, 62, 149
carrots, 59
carved wooden roulette decorations
 MAS03 ceramics, 320
 northern Benin, 241
 Tuali-B occupation ceramics, 231–232, 238
Casamance villages, 15
catfish, 63, 204
cats, 62
cattle (*Bos taurus*)
 importance, 69
 MAS502.3, 145
 MAS541, 138
 northern Benin, 155
 prevalence, 63
 Siga occupation sites, 204, 205
 Tuali occupation sites, 246
caves, 315
 See also rockshelter sites
Celtis integrifolia, 50
ceramic assemblages
 analysis and curation procedures, 77–78
 analytical methodologies, 78–79
 chronological uncertainties, 119–120
 clay characteristics, 79–82
 comparison studies, 256–257
 decoration techniques, 85–86
 defining typologies, 93–94, 96
 Dendi region, 79, 84, 189, 208, 238, 295, 299, 302, 309
 European trade goods, 239
 excavation methodologies, 74
 Fada N'Gourma, 301, 305
 firing techniques, 89–90
 foraging populations, 111, 250
 Ghana, 152, 250
 local occupation sequence, 99, 102–104
 MAS03, 318, 320
 MAS502.3, 142, 250
 MAS541, 128–129, 131, 135, 250
 MAS573, 165

MAS780, 176, 188, 301
MAS902, 150
MAS925, 316
MAS archaeological sites, 117
northern Benin, 155, 189, 207, 241
Péntènga rockshelter, 109, 111
Pwoli occupation sites, 98, 102, 117, 123, 128–129, 131, 135, 150, 151–152, 250
rare vessels/decorations, 188, 206–207, 252
research methodologies, 261–262
Ring Occupation, 98, 104, 311, 313
roughing treatments, 85, 219, 231
seriation process, 93, 96
settlement patterns, 208–209, 254
simplification of traditions, 246–247, 253
site density analyses, 169, 215, 227–228, 238
site-occupation attribution, 96–99, 117
surface treatments, 85
survey methodologies, 72–73
temper materials, 80–82
thermoluminescence (TL) dating, 108, 111
Tuali-A occupation sites, 211, 215, 217–221, 238, 246–247, 253
Tuali-B occupation sites, 227–228, 231–233, 246–247, 253
vessel formation techniques, 82–85, 182, 184–185
vessel function, 152, 178–179, 181–182, 184–185, 187, 218–221, 232–233
Yobri rockshelter, 108, 113
See also Siga occupation ceramics; temper materials
Ceratotheca sesamoides, 50
chaîne opertoire research approach, 78, 85, 187
channeled decorative techniques
MAS502.3 ceramics, 142
MAS541 ceramics, 131
Pwoli occupation sites, 151
Ring occupation ceramics, 313
Siga occupation ceramics, 171, 176, 177, 188, 189, 206
surface treatments and decoration, 86
Tuali-B occupation ceramics, 232
charcoal
Siga occupation sites, 190
Tuali-B occupation sites, 234

charcoal dating studies, 69–70, 108, 111, 123, 142
cherts, 17, 25, 28, 121
chert tools and artifacts
foraging populations, 250
Kidikanbou, 113
Lithic occupation sites, 105
MAS502.3, 142, 143
MAS541, 135
MAS542, 113, 115–116, 117
MAS archaeological sites, 117, 119
Siga occupation sites, 202–203
site-occupation attribution, 117, 119
Tuali-A occupation sites, 224–225
chickens (*Gallus gallus*), 69, 138, 145, 251
chili peppers, 59
chipped stone tools
analysis and curation procedures, 77
dating challenges, 119, 120
Lithic Occupation, 99
MAS archaeological sites, 117, 119, 135
Middle Stone Age (MSA), 107
Pwoli occupation sites, 151
Siga occupation sites, 202–203, 252
site-occupation attribution, 117, 119
Tuali-A occupation sites, 223–225, 254
Tuali-B occupation sites, 235–237, 254
chisels, 120
circular household compounds, 7
Cissus populnea, 50
Citrullus spp., 59
Clarias spp., 63, 138
clay deposits, 24, 25, 79–82, 161
clay pipes, 221, 238–239, 241
See also pipes/pipe fragments; smoking pipes; tobacco pipes
clay surfaces
MAS03, 318
MAS502.3, 141, 150
MAS541, 125–127
Pwoli occupation sites, 155
climate, 28–29
climate change research, 69
cloth production and trade, 222, 239, 242–245, 254
clustered households, 14, 167
coiling formation techniques, 82, 83
colonial narratives, 4, 257, 258
comb decorations
MAS502.3 ceramics, 142
MAS541 ceramics, 131

Pwoli occupation sites, 151
Siga occupation ceramics, 176, 188–189, 206
surface treatments and decoration, 86
Tuali occupation sites, 240
Combretum glutinosum, 50, 60, 70
Combretum paniculatum, 52
Combretum spp., 51, 60
common duikers, 135, 204, 205
construction woods, 31, 50, 51, 60
cooking vessels, 83, 184–185
copper artifacts, 252
Corchorus spp., 205
cord decorative techniques
MAS03 ceramics, 320
MAS541 ceramics, 129, 131
MAS925 ceramics, 316
northern Benin, 155, 241
occurrences, 240
Pwoli occupation sites, 151
Ring occupation ceramics, 311
Siga occupation ceramics, 177, 187
surface treatments and decoration, 86
Tuali-A occupation ceramics, 221
Tuali-B occupation ceramics, 232
core tools
analysis and curation procedures, 77
Lithic occupation sites, 115, 117, 121
Maadaga rockshelter, 107
Siga occupation sites, 202–203
Tuali-A occupation sites, 224
cotton cloth, 241–242
cotton cultivation, 59, 222, 244, 245, 246, 258, 311, 313
couscoussières, 185, 204, 305
cowpeas, 69
cowrie shells, 239, 251, 252, 254
crescents
hafted tools, 121
Kidikanbou, 113
Maadaga rockshelter, 117
MAS542, 116
Péntènga rockshelter, 111
prevalence, 121
Yobri rockshelter, 113
crocodiles, 62, 138
Crocodylus spp., 62
Crocuta crocuta, 62
crop rotation, 13–14
crops
See agricultural practices
cross-hatched incised designs, 189, 316
Crossopteryx febrifuga, 52
Crossroads of Empires project, 79
crushed mineral tempers, 80

cuali, 83
Cucumis spp., 59
cultivated plants, 52, 59–61
cultural deposits
　analysis and curation procedures, 77–78
　excavation methodologies, 74–75
　generational mobility, 9–10
　survey methodologies, 72
cultural landscapes
　agricultural practices, 14–16, 52, 59–61
　climate, 28–29, 69–70
　ecological characteristics, 31, 50–52
　environmental perspective, 17–21, 23–25, 28
　faunal species, 62–63, 69
　mineral resources, 25, 28, 121
　plant communities, 23–25, 29–31, 50–52, 69–70
curved comb decorations, 188
cutting implements, 120–121
cylindrical feet, 85

D

Dactyloctenium aegyptium, 60
Dagbon, 258, 259
Dagomba, 161, 239, 240
Damaliscus lunatus, 62
Daniella oliveri, 50
Dapaong–Boumbouaka Group, 17
debitage
　Maadaga rockshelter, 105
　MAS502.3, 143, 151
　MAS541, 135, 151
　MAS542, 117
　Péntènga rockshelter, 111
　Siga occupation sites, 203
　Tuali-A occupation sites, 224, 225
decoration techniques
　characterizations, 85–86
　frequency decline, 221
　MAS03 ceramics, 320
　MAS502.3, 142
　MAS541 ceramics, 129, 131, 135
　MAS925 ceramics, 316
　northern Benin, 241
　production and distribution patterns, 188
　Pwoli occupation sites, 151–152
　rare decorations, 188–189, 206–207, 252
　research methodologies, 93, 261–262
　Ring occupation ceramics, 311, 313
　Siga occupation ceramics, 175–177, 252

simplification of traditions, 246, 253
Tuali-A occupation ceramics, 218–219, 221
Tuali-B occupation ceramics, 231–232
Tuali occupation ceramics, 253
vessel function, 185
defensive fortifications, 239, 240, 245, 256–257
deflation, 9
deforestation, 257
Dendi region
　ceramic assemblages, 79, 84, 189, 208, 238, 295, 299, 302, 309
　defensive fortifications, 245
　hunting activities, 155
　indigo-dyeing activities, 244
　settlement patterns, 240
　trading networks, 155
denticulates, 107
derived savannas, 15
desertification, 257
Detarium microcarpum, 50
diagonal incised designs, 189
Dialium guineense, 52
discoidal fabrication techniques, 107
discoid grinding stones, 200, 201
diseases, 20
dispersed households, 14
Djenné, Mali, 9
Djenné Museum Site, 221
dogs (*Canis familiaris*), 62, 69
domesticated animals
　Gobnangou region, 63, 69, 250
　MAS502.3, 145, 149
　MAS541, 138
　northern Benin, 155
　Pwoli occupation sites, 123–124, 153, 154, 155, 251
　rockshelter sites, 155
　Siga occupation sites, 204
　socioeconomic evolution, 156
　Tuali occupation sites, 246
donkeys (*Equus asinus*), 69, 311
double-angle pipes, 239
double-bowl vessels, 301
double channel comb decorations, 301
double simple open bowls, 84
dragged decorations, 86, 151, 176, 189, 206–207, 301
drainage systems, 19–21, 23
drawn formation techniques, 82, 85
drought, 257
dry forests, 70
duikers, 135, 145, 204, 205
duricrusts, 140, 163
dwarf livestock, 63, 69, 154, 155, 204, 205, 246

dye pits, 211, 237–238, 241–247, 254
　See also indigo-dyeing activities
dye plants, 31, 242, 245

E

earthen architectural features, 9
earth priests (*tindano*), 7, 8
edible plants, 31, 50, 52, 59, 60
egusi, 59
Egypt, 120
elephants, 62
Eleusine indica, 204
elite populations, 252
enslaved peoples, 239
environmental degradation, 257
ephemeral sites, 9–10, 249, 251, 258, 259, 260
Equus asinus (donkeys)
　See donkeys (*Equus asinus*)
eroded surface deposits, 116–117
escarpment
　See Gobnangou escarpment
European trade goods, 239, 247, 254
eutrophic soils, 24
everted necks, 84
everted rims/lips
　Siga occupation ceramics, 171
　Tuali-A occupation ceramics, 219, 221
　Tuali-B occupation ceramics, 231

F

Fada N'Gourma
　archaeological research, 4, 79, 259
　ceramic assemblages, 301, 305
　defensive fortifications, 245, 257
　elite populations, 255
　funerary markers, 185
　indigo-dyeing activities, 238, 242, 244, 245
　iron artifacts, 195
　iron-working activities, 208
　political organization, 6
　rainfall, 28
　smelting activity, 153, 191
　sociopolitical change, 239–240
Fallau archaeological site, 305
fallow fields, 14–15, 23–24, 25, 50, 60, 154, 204
farming strategies
　See agricultural practices
faunal assemblages
　MAS502.3, 145, 149–150, 153
　MAS541, 135, 138
　northern Benin, 155
　Péntènga rockshelter, 109, 112–113, 250

Pwoli occupation sites, 153–154
Siga occupation sites, 203–205
Yobri rockshelter, 113, 250
faunal species, 62–63, 69
feet bases, 184, 221
feldspar temper, 80, 294
ferruginous soils, 24
fiber plants, 31
Ficus gnaphalocarpa, 310
Field Museum of Natural History (Chicago, Illinois), 78
fire starters, 203, 238, 254
firewood, 31, 50, 60, 70
firing techniques, 89–90
fish/fishing activities
MAS502.3, 145, 150, 153
MAS541, 135, 138
northern Benin, 155–156
Péntènga rockshelter, 112–113, 153
preservation techniques, 153
Pwoli occupation sites, 153–154, 251
Siga occupation sites, 204
species, 63
flaked stone tools
analysis and curation procedures, 77
artifact associations, 119
MAS542, 115–116, 117
Siga occupation sites, 202–203
Tuali-A occupation sites, 224
Yobri rockshelter, 113
flapshell turtle, 138
flared bases, 184
flared necks/rims
Ring occupation ceramics, 313
Tuali-A occupation ceramics, 218–219
Tuali-B occupation ceramics, 231, 233
Tuali occupation ceramics, 253
typologies, 83, 84
floors
MAS502.3, 141–142, 150–151
MAS541, 125–127
Pwoli occupation sites, 155
flotation samples, 78
fluvisols, 25
fodder plants, 31, 50, 51, 60
folded strip decorative techniques, 131, 142, 187, 295
fonio, 13
food cooking and preservation, 152, 153
foraging populations
ceramic assemblages, 111, 250
Gobnangou region, 105–106, 108, 156, 249–250, 254, 259
Late Stone Age (LSA), 108
Lithic Occupation, 105–106
microlithic tools, 105–106, 120, 250

mobility influences, 120–122, 123, 250
rockshelter sites, 123, 249–250
stone tools and artifacts, 250
forest crops, 52
forests, 52, 62, 70, 111–112
forged iron objects, 153
formal chipped stone tools
Siga occupation sites, 203
Tuali-A occupation sites, 224–225
fortifications and defensive structures (*bilnu*), 239, 240, 245–246, 257
fragmentation syndrome, 255
frequency of movement, 9–10
freshwater bivalves, 63
freshwater mollusks, 113
fruit trees, 50, 60
fuelwood, 190, 191
Fulani herders, 2, 63, 246, 255
funerary markers, 185, 187, 233, 305
furnaces
Fada N'Gourma, 153, 191
regional patterns, 208
Siga occupation sites, 190, 191, 192, 254
Tuali-B occupation sites, 227, 233–234, 254

G

gallery forests, 52, 62
Gallus gallus (chickens)
See chickens (*Gallus gallus*)
Gambaga, Ghana, 255
Gambia, 15
Gambian rats, 149
Gao, 155, 208
garden eggs, 52, 59
garden hunting, 62, 153, 154
gardens, 52, 59
gathering activities, 246
generational mobility
agricultural practices, 1, 7, 8, 9, 11, 13–15, 204–205, 259–260
archaeological research, 8–11, 254
ethnohistorical perspective, 259–260
Gobnangou region, 249, 252–254, 257, 258, 259–260
Gulmance kingdoms, 1, 15, 249, 257, 259–260
importance, 247
occupation length estimates, 169–171
settlement patterns, 254
Siga Occupation, 209–210, 252–253
sociopolitical perspectives, 7–8, 239–240, 249

Tuali occupation sites, 253
geomancy, 315, 317
geometric microlith assemblages
artifact associations, 119
dating challenges, 119–120
foraging populations, 105–106, 120, 250
fracture studies, 122
hafted tools, 120–121
Kidikanbou, 113
Lithic occupation sites, 99
MAS542, 113, 115–116, 117
mineral source proximity, 121–122
open-air sites, 108
Péntènga rockshelter, 108, 109, 111–113
prevalence, 108
Yobri rockshelter, 108, 113
German–Burkinabe project, 11, 71, 72, 104, 105, 123, 188, 207, 259
Ghana
archaeological research, 258
artifact associations, 119
ceramic assemblages, 152, 250
clay pipes, 221
defensive fortifications, 245
elite populations, 255
European trade goods, 239
grinding stones, 200
household site distribution and characteristics, 161
settlement patterns, 240
sociopolitical change, 239–240
glacial activity, 17
glass beads, 251, 252, 254
Gnaga Province, 240
goats (*Capra hircus*), 63, 69, 138, 145, 155
Gobir, Nigeria, 255
Gobnangou escarpment, 10–11, 17–21, 23–31, 50, 123, 247
See also Tuali-A occupation sites; Tuali-B occupation sites; Tuali Occupation
Gobnangou region
agricultural practices, 52, 59–61, 156, 246, 250–251
archaeological research, 4, 78–79, 254, 255–259
chronological uncertainties, 119–120
climate, 28–29, 69–70
cloth production, 243–244, 245, 258
cultivated plants, 52, 59–61, 222, 244, 245, 246, 258
defensive fortifications, 240, 245–246, 256–257
ecological characteristics, 31, 50–52
environmental degradation, 257–258

ethnohistorical perspective,
    4–8, 255–257, 259–260
faunal species, 62–63, 69
foraging populations, 105–106,
    108, 156, 249–250, 254, 259
generational mobility, 249,
    252–254, 257, 258, 259–260
geological characteristics, 10,
    17–19, 24
geometric microlith
    assemblages, 108
hydrological characteristics,
    19–21, 23
indigo-dyeing activities, 240,
    245
Lithic Occupation, 74, 98, 99,
    105–106
mineral resources, 25, 28, 121
oral histories, 255–257
plant communities, 23–25,
    29–31, 50–52, 69–70
regional settlement patterns,
    240, 245–246, 254
rock art, 10, 315–317
socioeconomic evolution, 156
sociopolitical perspectives,
    255–256, 260
sociospatial systems, 1–2, 7, 8
soil classification systems, 24–25
trading networks, 247
Goethe University (Frankfurt), 10,
    78, 105
gold, 239
gourds, 246–247
Gourmantche
    See Gulmance kingdoms
Gourma Plains, 79
grains, 31, 59, 60, 152–153
Gramineae, 139, 204
granary sites, 10, 245, 256,
    317–318, 320–321
grasses, 52, 60, 113, 204
grasslands, 51
gray clay, 125
grinding stones
    analysis and curation
        procedures, 77
    household functions, 200–201
    MAS502.3, 142–143
    MAS541, 135
    MAS572.1, 163
    Pwoli occupation sites, 152–153,
        250–251
    Siga occupation sites, 200–201,
        204, 252
    Tuali-A occupation sites, 223
    Tuali-B occupation sites,
        235–236
grog temper
    characteristics, 80
    MAS03 ceramics, 318
    MAS502.3 ceramics, 142
    MAS541 ceramics, 129

MAS902 ceramics, 150
    prevalence, 81
    Siga occupation ceramics, 176,
        179
    Tuali-A occupation ceramics,
        218, 219, 221, 247
    Tuali-B occupation ceramics,
        231, 232, 247
    upside-down pots, 185
groundnuts, 246
ground stone tools
    analysis and curation
        procedures, 77, 78
    foraging populations, 250
    MAS502.3, 142–143
    northern Benin, 241
    Pwoli occupation sites, 152–153
    Siga occupation sites, 200–201,
        252
    Tuali-A occupation sites,
        223–225, 253–254
    Tuali-B occupation sites,
        235–236, 253–254
Guiera senegalensis, 70
guinea fowl, 69
Guinean forests, 52
gulmanceba, 2, 5
Gulmance kingdoms
    agricultural practices, 1, 7, 8,
        14–15, 60–61
    archaeological research, 4,
        255–259
    characteristics, 1–4
    colonial narratives, 4, 257, 258
    conflicts and disputes, 6, 8
    defensive fortifications, 257
    elite populations, 255
    ethnohistorical perspective,
        4–8, 255–257, 259–260
    foundational stories, 5
    generational mobility, 1, 15, 249,
        257, 259–260
    indigo-dyeing activities, 238
    iron artifacts, 195
    occupation length estimates,
        169–171
    oral histories, 255–257
    political organization, 3–7, 260
    ritual practices, 16
    settlement patterns, 7, 209, 254,
        259
    sociopolitical perspectives,
        239–240, 249, 255–256,
        259–260
Gulmance soil classification
    systems, 24–25
gunflints, 239

H

hachettes, 77, 119, 201–202, 250,
    252
hafted tools, 120–121

handheld grinding stones,
    200–201, 223
handles, 171, 184, 305, 306
handspun cotton thread, 242, 243
hares, 155
hartebeests, 62, 113, 135
Hausa city states, 2, 240, 241,
    243–244, 245, 256
hearths
    foraging populations, 250
    MAS502.3, 140, 141, 151
    MAS573, 165
herbaceous plants, 31, 50, 52, 205
herding practices, 63, 69, 246
hidden granary sites, 10, 245, 256,
    317–318, 320–321
hippopotamus, 62
Hippopotamus amphibius, 62
Hippotragus equinus, 62
Holocene
    ceramic assemblages, 151
    foraging populations, 106, 111,
        123, 250, 259
    geometric microlith
        assemblages, 108, 121
    Pleistocene–Holocene
        transition, 107
    rainfall, 70
    stone tools and artifacts, 107,
        111
hourglass-shaped vessels, 84, 300,
    301
households
    agricultural practices, 14–15,
        61, 231
    archaeological research, 9–10,
        254, 259
    architectural features, 9
    ceramic assemblages, 178–179,
        181–182, 184–185, 218–221
    generational mobility, 7, 8,
        9–10, 14–15, 209–210, 254,
        259–260
    grinding stones, 200–201
    occupation length estimates,
        169–171
    settlement patterns, 155–156,
        208–210, 225, 229, 231, 238,
        250, 254
    site distribution and
        characteristics, 157–162,
        167, 169
    spatial data analyses, 75–76, 167,
        171, 228–229, 231, 253
    Tuali occupation sites, 253
humus, 23–24, 50, 60
hunting activities
    animal bone assemblages,
        112–113
    animal species, 62, 135, 145
    Dendi region, 155
    geometric microlith
        assemblages, 121

hunting strategies, 153
implement repair, 122
Kidikanbou, 113
MAS502.3, 145, 149
MAS541, 135, 151
national parks, 51
northern Benin, 155
Pwoli occupation sites, 153–154, 251
Siga occupation sites, 204, 205
Tuali occupation sites, 246
hyaenas, 62

I

impressed decorations
  MAS502.3 ceramics, 142
  MAS541 ceramics, 129, 131, 135
  Siga occupation ceramics, 176, 188
  surface treatments and decoration, 86
incised designs, 189, 295, 316
indigo, 59
indigo-dyeing activities
  Fada N'Gourma, 238, 242, 244, 245
  gender roles, 244
  Gobnangou region, 240, 245
  Nigeria, 238, 242, 243, 245
  sociohistorical implications, 242–245
  technical process, 242–243
  Tuali-B occupation sites, 226, 227, 237–238, 241–242, 244, 247, 254
Indigofera, 242
Indigofera tinctoria, 242
Inland Niger Delta, 13
Institut Français de l'Afrique Noire, 105
introduced foods, 246
iron artifacts
  analysis and curation procedures, 77
  chronological uncertainties, 120
  MAS502.3, 142, 144, 153
  MAS541, 135, 153
  MAS780, 165–167, 195, 210
  northern Benin, 155
  Pwoli occupation sites, 153
  Siga occupation sites, 195, 210
iron ore, 25, 190–191
iron-working activities
  archaeological research, 4
  Gobnangou region, 240
  northern Benin, 155, 241
  Pwoli occupation sites, 153, 208, 251
  regional patterns, 208
  Siga occupation sites, 190–193, 195, 210, 252, 254

smelting processes, 190–192, 222–223, 227, 233–234, 241, 247, 252, 254
smithing processes, 190, 193, 195, 234, 252
Tuali-A occupation sites, 222–223, 247, 254
Tuali-B occupation sites, 223, 227, 233–234, 247, 254
Iwo Eleru, Nigeria, 121

J

Jaba Lompo, 5, 195, 255
jars
  Ring occupation ceramics, 313
  Siga occupation ceramics, 171, 252
  Tuali-A occupation ceramics, 218, 219
  Tuali-B occupation ceramics, 231, 233
  Tuali occupation ceramics, 253
  vessel formation techniques, 83, 84
  vessel function, 185, 187, 233

K

Kano Emirate, 243–244, 305
Kantchari, 83, 189
Kantoro archaeological site, 299
Kenya, 120
Kidikanbou
  archaeological research, 71
  chert deposits, 121
  dating challenges, 119–120
  geometric microlith assemblages, 108, 113, 121, 122
  kinship networks, 189, 190
Kintampo phase, 152, 250
Kirikongo, 195
Kissi, 155, 208
knotted decorative techniques, 86, 177, 299, 300
Koabu drainage
  aquatic resources, 63, 138
  archaeological research, 10, 123
  archaeological sites, 113, 116, 117
  drainage characteristics, 21, 23
  sandy deposits, 24
  smelting activity, 191, 234, 252
  spatial data analyses, 75–76
  survey methodologies, 71
Kodjari, 24, 52, 121
kola, 239
Konduga, Nigeria, 119
Konkomba settlements, 161
Korounkorokalé, Mali, 119, 120
Kouaré, 185, 208, 243, 295, 305, 321

Kourtiagou Reserve, 51
Kourtiagou River, 20, 21, 138, 153, 251
Kudiaboangu, 5
Kugribogdo, 185, 305
kwadiegu system, 61, 231
Kwara zeno archaeological site, 295, 309

L

Labdiédo, 195
Laboratory of Archaeology (Ouagadougou), 77, 195
ladder channel decorative technique, 176, 188, 189, 206
Lagenaria siceraria, 247
Lake Chad, 69
land rights, 7–8
landscape archaeology
  climate, 28–29, 69–70
  cultivated plants, 52, 59–61
  ecological characteristics, 31, 50–52
  environmental perspective, 17–21, 23–25, 28
  faunal species, 62–63, 69
  plant communities, 23–25, 29–31, 50–52, 69–70
  sociospatial systems, 1–2
land tenure system, 7–8, 61
Lannea acida, 59
Lannea microcarpa, 50, 59
laterite dye pits, 243
laterite fortifications, 245
laterite ore deposits, 25, 190–191
laterite pebbles
  MAS502.3, 140, 141, 150
  MAS541, 125, 150
  Siga occupation sites, 161
laterite tempers
  characteristics, 81
  Tuali-A occupation ceramics, 218
Lates niloticus (Nile perch)
  See Nile perch (*Lates niloticus*)
Late Stone Age (LSA), 108
leafy greens, 31, 50
legumes, 52, 204
Leguminosae, 150
Lele households, 169
Levallois cores, 107
libobili, 83
libonbonli (black), 242
likwali, 83
li naali, 200, 223, 236
lisanli, 83
Lithic Occupation
  ceramic assemblages, 98, 99
  excavation methodologies, 74
  microlithic tools, 99, 105–106
  See also foraging populations

livestock
  fodder plants, 31
  MAS502.3, 145
  MAS541, 138
  northern Benin, 155
  prevalence, 63
  Pwoli occupation sites, 153, 154, 155, 251
  rainy season, 69
  Siga occupation sites, 204, 205
  Tuali occupation sites, 246
  wild animal competition, 62
lizards, 138
local occupation sequence, 99, 102–104
locust bean, 31, 59, 205
Logobou, 28
Lonchocarpus cyanescens, 242
Lonchocarpus laxiflorus, 242
Loudetia togoensis, 51
low-fertility soils, 13–14, 23–24
lug handles, 171, 184, 306
Lycaon pictus, 62

M

Maadaga, 5, 10, 28, 71, 237, 238
Maadaga Archaeological Survey
  analysis and curation procedures, 77–78
  excavation methodologies, 74–75
  research background, 1, 10–11, 15, 71
  spatial data analysis, 75–76, 249
  survey methodologies, 72–73
Maadaga rockshelter
  archaeological research, 10, 71
  dating uncertainties, 108, 119, 207
  eroded surface deposits, 116–117
  Lithic Occupation, 105
  stone tools and artifacts, 107–108, 117
maize agriculture, 246
Makwe, Zambia, 120
Mali
  artifact associations, 119
  clay pipes, 221
  dye pits, 243
  grinding stones, 200
Malvaceae, 139
mammals, 62, 113, 145, 204
Mamprusi, 258, 259
Mande region, 240, 244, 253
Mandinka villages, 15
MAS03, 317–318
MAS502.2, 201
MAS502.3
  agricultural practices, 251
  base materials, 140
  botanical assemblages, 150
  ceramic assemblages, 142, 250

cultural fill, 140
excavation methodologies, 75, 123, 139–140
faunal assemblages, 145, 149–150, 153
iron artifacts, 142, 144, 153
material culture assemblages, 142–145
radiocarbon dating, 206
socioeconomic perspective, 251
stratigraphic analyses, 140–142
structural features, 141–142
surface/topsoil characteristics, 142
MAS502.7, 301
MAS541
  agricultural practices, 250, 251
  architectural features, 125–127
  base materials, 125
  botanical assemblages, 139
  ceramic assemblages, 128–129, 131, 135, 250
  cultural fill, 127–128
  excavation methodologies, 75, 123, 125
  faunal assemblages, 135, 138
  iron artifacts, 135, 153
  material culture assemblages, 128–129, 131, 135
  radiocarbon dating, 206
  stone artifacts, 135
  stratigraphic analyses, 125–128
  surface/topsoil characteristics, 128
  survey methodologies, 72
MAS542
  dating challenges, 119, 120
  excavation methodologies, 74, 113, 115
  geometric microlith assemblages, 113, 115–116, 117
  mineral source proximity, 121
MAS547, 201
MAS552, 188
MAS557, 187
MAS572
  household distribution, 228
  survey methodologies, 72
MAS572.1
  ceramic assemblages, 176
  excavation methodologies, 75, 162–163
  faunal and botanical assemblages, 204
  grinding stones, 201
  stratigraphic analyses, 163
  survey methodologies, 72
MAS572.2, 201
MAS573
  ceramic assemblages, 176
  excavation methodologies, 75, 162–163

faunal and botanical assemblages, 204
stratigraphic analyses, 163, 165
MAS582, 188
MAS603, 221, 231
MAS640, 191
MAS643, 201
MAS689, 224
MAS696.2, 188, 210
MAS707, 217
MAS708, 225
MAS710, 217
MAS721, 191
MAS723
  dating challenges, 119, 120
  mineral source proximity, 121
  stone tools and artifacts, 117
MAS731, 201
MAS759, 185
MAS774, 185
MAS780
  ceramic assemblages, 176, 188, 301
  excavation methodologies, 75, 162–163, 165
  faunal and botanical assemblages, 203–205
  grinding stones, 201
  iron artifacts, 165–167, 195, 210
  material culture assemblages, 210
  stratigraphic analyses, 165–167
MAS821, 225
MAS822, 224
MAS841, 222
MAS849, 119, 191, 192, 210, 252, 254
MAS864
  dating challenges, 119, 120
  mineral source proximity, 121
  stone tools and artifacts, 117
MAS867
  dating challenges, 119, 120
  mineral source proximity, 121
  stone tools and artifacts, 117
MAS885, 185
MAS902, 123, 150, 151
MAS907
  dating challenges, 119, 120
  mineral source proximity, 121
  stone tools and artifacts, 117
MAS920, 237
MAS921, 315, 317
MAS923, 237, 244
MAS925, 315–317
MAS929, 119
MAS937
  ceramic density analyses, 227
  characteristics, 225
  excavation methodologies, 74
  household distribution, 228–229, 231, 238, 253
  indigo-dyeing activities, 237

settlement patterns, 245–246, 247
subsurface deposits, 226
MAS947
  dating challenges, 119, 120
  mineral source proximity, 121
  stone tools and artifacts, 117
MAS951, 236
MAS954, 217
MAS957, 217
MAS968, 221
matches, 237
material culture assemblages
  comparison studies, 256–257
  Gobnangou region, 255–256
  northern Benin, 250
  Pwoli occupation sites, 151–153, 256
  Siga occupation sites, 157, 160, 161–162, 169, 210, 252, 256
Maxwell's duiker, 145
medicinal plants, 31, 52
melons, 59, 62
metal artifacts, 77, 239
  See also iron artifacts
metamorphic rocks, 17
mica temper
  characteristics, 80
  MAS03 ceramics, 320
  prevalence, 81
  Siga occupation ceramics, 176
  Siga occupation sites, 179
  Tuali-A occupation ceramics, 218
Microchloa indica, 51
microlithic tools
  dating challenges, 119–120
  foraging populations, 105–106, 120, 250
  fracture studies, 122
  hafted tools, 120–121
  Kidikanbou, 113
  Lithic occupation sites, 99, 105–106
  MAS542, 113, 115–116, 117
  mineral source proximity, 121–122
  Péntènga rockshelter, 109, 111–113
  Siga occupation sites, 203
  Tuali-A occupation sites, 224
  Yobri rockshelter, 113
  See also geometric microlith assemblages
micropoints
  chronological uncertainties, 120
  foraging populations, 250
  Kidikanbou, 113
  Péntènga rockshelter, 111
  prevalence, 121
  Yobri rockshelter, 113
midden deposits, 250
Middle Stone Age (MSA), 107–108

millet
  Dendi region, 155
  faunal destruction, 62
  MAS03, 320
  MAS541, 139, 156
  mulching practices, 23
  northern Benin, 156
  Pwoli occupation sites, 152, 154, 251
  rainfall requirements, 52
  Siga occupation sites, 204
  staple crops, 13, 59, 70
  Tuali occupation sites, 246
mineral resources, 25, 28, 121
minimally anthropogenic savannas, 51, 52, 60, 70
mining activities, 191
Minyanka peoples, 200
miscellaneous use plants, 31, 50
mobility
  See generational mobility
mobility influences, 120–122, 123, 249–250
Mogho Naba, 6
molding formation techniques, 82–83
mollusks, 113
mongoose, 149
monitor lizards, 138
Moringa olifera, 51
mortuary sites, 195, 210
Mossi Plateau, 17
Mossi society
  archaeological research, 4, 258, 259
  elite populations, 5, 8, 255
  food preparation, 50
  indigo-dyeing activities, 238
  political organization, 6
  settlement patterns, 14, 254
  sociopolitical perspectives, 5, 239–240
mounded settlements, 155, 208–209, 241, 260
mulching practices, 23, 28–29, 59

N

Namoungou, 195, 208
Namounou, 245
National Museum of Natural History, 78
national parks, 51, 313
neck form, 299–300, 306, 309
nere, 31, 59
New World plants, 246
Niger, 2, 51, 78, 79, 208
Niger Bend, 2, 69, 208, 244, 259
Nigeria
  artifact associations, 119, 241
  cloth production, 243–244
  elite populations, 255
  European trade goods, 239

  indigo-dyeing activities, 238, 242, 243, 245
  sociopolitical change, 240–241
Niger River, 2, 5, 6, 208, 240, 244, 251, 252
Nile perch (*Lates niloticus*), 63, 138, 153–154
northern Benin
  ceramic assemblages, 155, 189, 207, 241, 295
  faunal and botanical assemblages, 155–156
  hidden granary sites, 256
  iron-working activities, 155, 241
  material culture assemblages, 250
  occupation length estimates, 169
  settlement patterns, 208–209, 241, 254
notched stone tools, 107
Numida meleagris, 69
Nunbado, 5–7, 255, 256
Nungu, 6, 239, 255
  See also Fada N'Gourma
Nunumba, 239
nuts, 152

O

occupation length, 9–10, 169–171, 212–213, 215, 217, 225–229
Odundo spring and pool, 21
oil palm, 59, 152
okra, 52, 59, 61
onchocerciasis, 20
open-air firing technique, 89–90
open-air sites
  archaeological research, 10–11, 123
  foraging populations, 250
  geometric microlith assemblages, 108
  Lithic Occupation, 105
  Middle Stone Age (MSA), 107
  stone tools and artifacts, 108
open vessels
  Siga occupation ceramics, 171, 252
  Tuali-A occupation ceramics, 219, 238
  Tuali-B occupation ceramics, 231, 233
  vessel function, 83, 84, 185, 187
oral histories, 255–257
orange clay, 125–126, 141, 150, 155
orange-red slipped vessels, 300
organic temper, 81, 303, 304, 318
oribi, 113
Osteolaemus spp., 62
Ouagadougou, 240
Oubritenga, 185, 305
Oudalan Province, 208, 251
Ouédraogo, 5

O

Ounjougou, Mali, 107, 119, 185
Oursi, 208
out-turned lips, 84
Ovis aries (sheep)
    See sheep (*Ovis aries*)
oxen, 63

P

Pagou, 321
Paliboa, 71
Pama, 5, 28, 119
Paniceae, 139
Papilionoideae, 150
parallel channel decorative
    technique
    Siga occupation ceramics,
        177
    Tuali-B occupation ceramics,
        232
Parkia biglobosa, 31, 59
parks and reserves, 51, 258
Park W
    See W National Park
Partiaga, 245
pastes, 82, 151, 179, 181, 252
    See also potting clay
patas monkeys, 135
patellar grinding stones, 200
Payoungou, 258
peanuts, 246
pearl millet (*Pennisetum glaucum*),
    13, 52, 139, 152, 154, 156, 251
pedestal bases, 83, 84–85, 171, 184,
    221, 252, 301–303
Pendjari National Park, 51
Pendjari/Oti Group, 17
Pendjari River, 5, 19–21, 52, 63,
    138, 153, 209, 251, 254
Pennisetum glaucum (pearl millet)
    See pearl millet (*Pennisetum glaucum*)
Péntènga rockshelter
    animal bone assemblages, 109,
        112–113, 250
    archaeological research, 10–11,
        123
    dating challenges, 119–120
    domesticated animals, 155
    foraging populations, 123
    geometric microlith
        assemblages, 108, 109,
        111–113, 121, 122
    paleoclimate research, 69
    stone tools and artifacts, 108
peppers, 246
perforated vessels, 184, 185, 242
permanent fields, 13, 14
pigments, 317
pigs, 69
Piliostigma sp., 83, 85
Piliostigma spp., 60
Piliostigma thonningii, 60

pipes/pipe fragments
    analysis and curation
        procedures, 77
    European trade goods, 239
    northeastern Nigeria, 241
    occurrences, 247
    Siga occupation sites, 165, 189,
        207–208
    Tuali-A occupation sites, 221,
        238–239
plague epidemics, 210, 253, 256
plant communities, 23–25, 29–31,
    50–52, 59, 69–70, 205
    See also botanical assemblages
plastic ridges, 221
Pleistocene–Holocene transition,
    107
points
    hafted tools, 120
    MAS780, 195
    northern Benin, 155
    Pwoli occupation sites, 251
polished stone artifacts, 119
polishing stones, 77
potash, 237, 242
potting clay, 79–82
    See also clay deposits
precipitation
    See rainfall
preserved floors
    MAS502.3, 141–142, 150–151
    MAS541, 125–127
    Pwoli occupation sites, 155
primates, 62
Procavia capensis, 62
pseudogleys, 24
Pterocarpus cf. *erinaceus*, 111
Punpun phase, 152
Pwoli Occupation
    agricultural practices, 123–124,
        250–251
    architectural characteristics,
        150–151, 155
    botanical assemblages, 154
    ceramic assemblages, 98, 123,
        131, 135, 150, 151–152, 250
    excavation methodologies, 74
    faunal assemblages, 153–154
    iron-working activities, 153,
        208, 251
    material culture assemblages,
        128–129, 151–153, 256
    radiocarbon dating, 206
    seasonal mobility, 152
    settlement patterns, 155–156,
        250, 256
    sherd typologies, 102
    site-occupation attribution,
        117
    socioeconomic evolution, 156,
        251
    sociopolitical characteristics,
        251

stone tools and artifacts, 119,
    120, 151, 250–251
    See also MAS502.3; MAS541

Q

quartzite, 17, 107, 121
quartz temper
    characteristics, 80
    MAS03 ceramics, 318
    MAS502.3 ceramics, 142
    MAS541 ceramics, 129
    MAS902 ceramics, 150
    prevalence, 81
    Ring occupation ceramics, 311
    Siga occupation ceramics, 176,
        179, 203
    Tuali-A occupation ceramics,
        218, 219
    Tuali-B occupation ceramics,
        231, 232
    Tuali occupation ceramics, 104,
        253
quartz tools
    Siga occupation sites, 203
    Tuali-A occupation sites, 225
querns, 200

R

radiocarbon dating
    charcoal assemblages, 108, 111,
        123
    chronological uncertainties,
        119–120, 205–208
    Maadaga rockshelter, 108, 119
    MAS502.3, 142
    MAS541, 125, 126
    Siga occupation sites, 205–208
rainfall
    agricultural practices, 13–14,
        28–29, 52
    annual patterns and
        distribution, 28–29
    climate and vegetation histories,
        69–70
    Gobnangou escarpment, 18–21
    savanna systems, 15–16
    seasonality, 18
rare vessels/decorations, 188–189,
    206–207, 252
red clay (*u yoagpienu*), 80
red ochre, 25, 135
red-slipped ware
    frequency decline, 221
    MAS502.3 ceramics, 142
    MAS541 ceramics, 129, 135
    MAS902 ceramics, 150
    Ring occupation ceramics, 311
    Siga occupation ceramics, 171,
        189
    surface treatments and
        decoration, 85

Tuali-B occupation ceramics, 231
reptiles, 62, 113, 138
residential mobility, 7–8
   See also generational mobility; households; settlement patterns
restricted vessels, 83, 84, 218–219
rice, 52, 59
ridge decorations, 86, 221, 304–305
Rim, 113
rims
   decoration techniques, 85
   MAS541 ceramics, 129
   research methodologies, 93
   Siga occupation ceramics, 171
   Tuali-A occupation ceramics, 218–220
   Tuali-B occupation ceramics, 231
   upside-down pots, 142
   vessel formation techniques, 83–84
ring bases, 84–85, 184, 221
Ring Occupation
   ceramic assemblages, 98, 311, 313
   settlement patterns, 313
   sherd typologies, 104
   site characteristics, 311
riparian environments, 52
ritual practices
   ceramic assemblages, 185, 187
   Gulmance kingdoms, 16
   rockshelter sites, 317
river blindness, 20
riverine corridors, 52
river systems, 19–21, 23
roan antelopes, 62, 135, 145
rock art, 10, 315–317
rocker comb decorations, 188–189
rocker stamped decorations, 241
rock hyrax, 62
rockshelter sites
   archaeological research, 10–11, 71, 123
   ceramic assemblages, 99, 250
   cultural artifacts, 315–317
   dating challenges, 119–120
   domesticated animals, 155
   excavation methodologies, 107
   foraging populations, 123, 249–250
   functional role, 320–321
   geometric microlith assemblages, 108, 111–113, 121, 122
   Lithic occupation sites, 105
   paleoclimate research, 69
   stone tools and artifacts, 107–108, 121
   See also specific rockshelter
rodents, 62, 135, 149, 153, 154, 204

roselle, 59
rotating fields, 13, 14, 15
roughing treatments
   surface treatments and decoration, 85
   Tuali-A occupation ceramics, 219
   Tuali-B occupation ceramics, 231
roulette decorations, 151, 187
   MAS03 ceramics, 320
   MAS502.3 ceramics, 142
   MAS541 ceramics, 129, 131, 135
   MAS925 ceramics, 316
   northern Benin, 155, 241
   occurrences, 240, 257
   Ring occupation ceramics, 311
   Siga occupation ceramics, 176
   surface treatments and decoration, 86
   Tuali-A occupation ceramics, 219, 221
   Tuali-B occupation ceramics, 231, 238
   Tuali occupation ceramics, 253
royaumes (kingdoms), 3–4

S

Sahel drought, 257
Sahel zone, 13, 14
salty soils, 28
sandstones, 10, 17–19, 24, 107, 152–153, 200
   See also grinding stones
sand temper, 80, 81
sanli, 83
Saouga, 208
savannas
   agricultural practices, 1, 10–11, 13–16, 52, 155
   architectural features, 9
   climate, 69–70
   ecological characteristics, 15–16, 29–30, 51
   environmental degradation, 257–258
   faunal species, 62–63, 69
   geological characteristics, 10
   microlithic tools, 121
   parkland vegetation, 51
   plant communities, 29–31, 51, 69–70
   soil characteristics, 13–14, 23–24
schistosomiasis, 20
Scleria sp., 150
Sclerocarya birrea, 50, 242
scrapers
   hafted tools, 120–121
   MAS542, 116
   Middle Stone Age (MSA), 107

seasonal drainage
   aquatic species, 63, 113, 138, 150, 154
   clay deposits, 25, 79
   Gobnangou region, 20–21
   MAS502.3, 139
   MAS541, 138
   MAS780, 165
   riverine plants, 52
   Siga occupation sites, 167
   survey methodologies, 71
   Tuali-A occupation sites, 217
seasonal mobility, 9, 14–15, 121–122, 123, 152, 167, 231, 246
sedges, 52
sedimentary materials, 17
seed stock, 52
self-slipped vessels, 85
semiprecious stone beads, 252
Senegalese flapshell turtle, 138
Senegal River valley, 13
Senegambia, 251, 258
Senna obtusifolia, 50
serial sedentism, 15
serval cats, 149
serving vessels, 184, 185, 187, 220–221, 246–247
settlement patterns
   generational mobility, 254
   Gulmance kingdoms, 7, 209, 254, 259
   MAS937, 245–246, 247
   northern Benin, 208–209, 241, 254
   Pwoli occupation sites, 155–156, 250, 256
   Ring occupation sites, 313
   seasonal mobility, 14–15
   Siga occupation sites, 208–210, 251, 252–253
   Tuali-B occupation sites, 225, 229, 231, 253
   Tuali occupation sites, 211, 217, 253
shafts
   MAS502.3, 144
   northern Benin, 155
shales, 24
shea/shea butter (*Vitellaria paradoxa*), 31, 59, 60, 152, 205, 242
sheep (*Ovis aries*), 63, 69, 138, 145, 155
shell artifacts, 241
shellfish, 63, 152
shell temper, 81
sherds/sherd typology
   analytical methodologies, 78–79
   characterizations, 293–310
   dating challenges, 207
   decoration techniques, 85–86
   defining components, 93–94, 96
   firing techniques, 89–90

local occupation sequence, 99, 102–104
MAS502.3, 142
MAS541, 128–129, 131, 135, 250
MAS573, 165
MAS archaeological sites, 117
research methodologies, 261–262
seriation process, 93, 96
site-occupation attribution, 96–99, 117
surface treatments, 85
survey methodologies, 73
Tuali-A occupation ceramics, 171, 211, 215, 217–221, 246–247
Tuali-B occupation ceramics, 231, 240, 246–247
typed vs. untyped sherds, 175, 177, 187, 219–221, 231–232
vessel formation techniques, 83–84
See also Siga occupation ceramics
shifting sedentism, 15
shrubs, 29–31, 50, 60, 70
Shum Laka, Cameroon, 119, 121
siébuogu (dye pits), 243
Siga Occupation
agricultural practices, 204–205
burial artifacts, 185, 187
dating challenges, 205–208, 252
elite populations, 252
excavation methodologies, 159–160, 162–163, 165
faunal and botanical assemblages, 203–204
generational mobility, 209–210, 252–253
iron artifacts, 195, 210
iron-working activities, 190–193, 195, 208, 210, 222–223, 252, 254
material culture assemblages, 157, 160, 161–162, 169, 210, 252, 256
occupation site distribution and characteristics, 157–162, 167, 169–171
research methodologies, 157
settlement patterns, 208–210, 251, 252–253
Siga-Tuali transition, 253, 256
stone tools and artifacts, 119, 120, 200–203, 204, 252
stratigraphic analyses, 163, 165–167
Siga occupation ceramics
burial artifacts, 185, 187
decorative characteristics, 171, 175–178, 221
household functions, 178–179, 181–182, 184–185, 187

iron artifacts, 144
material culture assemblages, 128–129, 142
production and distribution patterns, 187–190
sherd typologies, 103–104
site-occupation attribution, 97, 98, 117
smoking pipes, 189, 207–208
typed vs. untyped sherds, 171, 175–176
vessel form and function, 189, 251–252
Siluriforme, 204
simple open bowls, 84
single channel comb decorations, 301
Singou Reserve, 51
slag
analysis and curation procedures, 78
MAS502.3, 142, 144
MAS541, 135
northern Benin, 241
Pwoli occupation sites, 153
Siga occupation sites, 190, 191, 193, 195, 223, 252
temper materials, 81, 299
Tuali-A occupation sites, 223
Tuali-B occupation sites, 223, 234, 254
sleeping sickness, 31
slipped vessels, 295, 300
surface treatments and decoration, 85
See also red-slipped ware
slow wheel formation techniques, 83
slurries, 85
smelting activity
northern Benin, 155, 241
Pwoli occupation sites, 153
Siga occupation sites, 190–192, 222, 252
Tuali-A occupation sites, 222–223
Tuali-B occupation sites, 227, 247, 254
smithing activity
Siga occupation sites, 190, 193, 195, 252
Tuali-B occupation sites, 234
Smithsonian Institution (Washington, DC), 78
smoking pipes
European trade goods, 239
northeastern Nigeria, 241
occurrences, 247
Siga occupation sites, 165, 189, 207–208
Tuali-A occupation sites, 221, 238–239
Tuali occupation sites, 254

social networks, 189, 190
socioeconomic evolution, 156, 251
sociopolitical change, 239–240
soils
classification systems, 24–25
ecological characteristics, 31, 50–52
fertility, 13–14, 23–24
Gobnangou escarpment, 23–25
Sokoto, 244
Sokoto Caliphate, 238, 240, 243–244, 254, 256
Sokoto River, 241
Songhai empire, 239
sorghum, 13, 59, 152, 154, 156, 204
South Africa, 120
spear points
MAS502.3, 144, 153
MAS780, 195
Pwoli occupation sites, 251
specialized plant communities, 52
spindle whorls
analysis and curation procedures, 77
northeastern Nigeria, 241
Tuali-A occupation sites, 222
stamped decorations, 241
staple crops, 13–14, 28, 31, 59, 61, 70
steel blades, 236
stone temper
See temper materials
stone tools and artifacts
analysis and curation procedures, 77–78
dating challenges, 119–120
foraging populations, 105–106, 120, 250
fracture studies, 122
MAS502.3, 142
MAS541, 135
Middle Stone Age (MSA), 107–108
mineral source proximity, 121–122
Pwoli occupation sites, 119, 120, 151, 250–251
Siga occupation sites, 119, 120, 200–203, 204, 252
Tuali-A occupation sites, 223–225, 253–254
Tuali-B occupation sites, 234–236, 253–254
See also geometric microlith assemblages; microlithic tools
storage vessels, 83, 185, 187, 233, 309
strip decorative techniques
MAS502.3 ceramics, 142
MAS541 ceramics, 131
northern Benin, 241
Pwoli occupation sites, 151

surface treatments and
  decoration, 86
Tuali-A occupation ceramics,
  219, 221
Tuali-B occupation ceramics,
  231–232, 238
sub-Saharan West Africa, 119–120
sugar cane, 59
surface treatments
  decoration techniques, 85
  research methodologies, 93
  Siga occupation ceramics, 252
  See also decoration techniques
Sus scrofa, 69
sustainable agricultural practices,
  13–15
Sylvicapra grimmia, 135, 204, 205
Syncerus caffer, 62
Synodontis sp., 138

T

Taaba peoples, 5
Takamba peoples, 5
Tallensi settlements, 14, 161, 200
tamarind trees, 5, 205
Tamarindus indicus, 59
Tanbaga, 82
Tapoa Province, 28, 171
Tchikandou-I archaeological site,
  206–207
tell formation, 2, 9, 15
  See also mounded settlements
temperature patterns, 28
temper materials
  characterizations, 80–82
  MAS03 ceramics, 318
  MAS502.3 ceramics, 142
  MAS541 ceramics, 129
  MAS902 ceramics, 150
  research methodologies, 93
  Ring occupation ceramics, 311
  Siga occupation ceramics,
    176–177, 179
  Tuali-A occupation ceramics,
    218, 219
  vessel function, 179, 181–182
  wall thickness, 80
Terminalia spp., 51, 60, 111
thermoluminescence (TL) dating,
  108, 111, 205, 207
Thryonomys swinderianus, 62
ticindi, 185
tilapia, 63, 138
tillites, 17
tinboanga, 24
Tindamba peoples, 5, 255
Tindambiga, Amilidi, 165, 195
tindanos (earth priests), 7, 8
tinmoanga, 24
tinpienga, 24
Tiv settlements, 14
tobacco, 59, 207

tobacco pipes
  European trade goods, 239
  MAS573, 165
  northeastern Nigeria, 241
  occurrences, 247
  Siga occupation sites, 165, 189,
    207–208
  Tuali-A occupation sites, 221,
    238–239
tomatoes, 246
topi, 62, 135
Torouway archaeological site, 309
trading networks
  cloth production and trade, 243,
    245, 247, 254
  Dendi region, 244
  diasporas, 240, 253
  European trade goods, 237, 239,
    254
  Hausa city states, 244, 245, 254,
    256
  mounded settlements, 241
  Pwoli occupation sites, 155, 251
  Siga occupation sites, 188, 189,
    190, 208, 210, 252
  Tuali occupation sites, 237, 239,
    246, 254
Tragalaphus scriptus, 204
trapezes
  Kidikanbou, 113
  Péntènga rockshelter, 111
trees, 29–31, 50, 59–60, 205
triangles
  Kidikanbou, 113
  Maadaga rockshelter, 117
  Péntènga rockshelter, 111
  prevalence, 121
  Ring occupation ceramics, 313
Trianthema portulacastrum, 150
trigonal grinding stones, 200
tripod bowls, 302
truncated flake tools, 107
trypanosomiasis, 31
tsetse flies, 31, 63, 205
Tuali-A occupation sites
  agricultural practices, 246
  ceramic assemblages, 211, 215,
    217–221, 238, 246–247, 253
  characteristics, 211–213
  clay pipes, 221
  dating challenges, 238
  household assemblages, 218–221
  iron-working activities,
    222–223, 247, 254
  occupation length and site size,
    212–213, 215, 217
  settlement patterns, 217,
    245–246, 253
  spatial distribution, 217, 253
  stone tools and artifacts,
    223–225, 253–254
Tuali-B occupation sites
  agricultural practices, 246

ceramic assemblages, 227–228,
  231–233, 238, 246–247, 253
dating challenges, 238
household distribution,
  228–229, 231, 253
indigo-dyeing activities, 226,
  227, 237–238, 241–242, 244,
  247, 254
iron-working activities, 223, 227,
  233–234, 247, 254
occupation length and site size,
  225–229
settlement patterns, 225, 229,
  231, 238, 245–246, 253
spatial distribution, 229, 231,
  253
stone tools and artifacts,
  234–236, 253–254
Tuali Occupation
  burial artifacts, 185, 187
  ceramic assemblages, 97–98
  characterizations, 253
  excavation methodologies, 74
  generational mobility, 253
  regional settlement patterns,
    211, 217, 225, 229, 231, 238,
    239–241, 245–246, 253
  sherd typologies, 104
  Siga–Tuali transition, 253, 256
  site-occupation attribution, 117
  smoking pipes, 207, 254
  sociopolitical change, 239–240
  stone tools and artifacts, 119, 120
  trading networks, 254
tubers, 31
tubes, ceramic, 77
turtles, 138
tuyères
  analysis and curation
    procedures, 77, 78
  Fada N'Gourma, 153, 191
  northern Benin, 241
  Siga occupation sites, 190, 191
twisted cord decorative techniques
  MAS03 ceramics, 320
  MAS502.3 ceramics, 142
  MAS541 ceramics, 129
  MAS925 ceramics, 316
  northern Benin, 155
  occurrences, 240
  Pwoli occupation sites, 151
  Siga occupation ceramics, 176
  surface treatments and
    decoration, 86
  Tuali-A occupation ceramics,
    221
  Tuali-B occupation ceramics,
    232
twisted twine decorative
  techniques, 142
typed sherds
  Siga occupation ceramics, 171,
    175, 177

spatial distribution, 187–188
Tuali-B occupation ceramics, 231
vessel function, 187

U

ubani, 163
u bindu, 200, 223
ungulates, 62, 153, 155
University of Michigan Museum of Anthropological Archaeology, 78
University of Oregon, 77
University of Ouagadougou, 10, 77, 105, 195
untyped sherds
 Siga occupation ceramics, 175
 Tuali-A occupation ceramics, 219–221
 Tuali-B occupation ceramics, 231–232
upside-down pots, 142, 185, 302
useful plants, 31, 50, 59
Uthman dan Fodio (Sheikh), 240
u yoagboanu (black clay), 80
u yoagpienu (red clay), 80

V

vegetables, 52, 59, 62
vegetation
 See plant communities
verticle vessel walls, 84
vertisols, 24
vessel formation techniques, 82–85, 129, 142, 182, 184–185
vessel thickness
 See wall thickness
village drift, 9, 15
Vitellaria paradoxa (shea/shea butter)
 See shea/shea butter (*Vitellaria paradoxa*)
Vitex doniana, 50
vitrification, 77
volcanic materials, 17
Volta Basin, 17, 19, 24, 89, 239, 256
V-shaped incised designs, 316

W

wall thickness
 research methodologies, 93
 temper materials, 80
wanuama (light black), 242
water jars, 82–83, 309
waterlogged soils, 24
watermelon, 59
weaving activities, 242–245
 See also cloth production and trade
weed control, 23–24
white-tailed mongoose, 149
wild plants
 See plant communities
W National Park, 51, 190, 208
Woba peoples, 5, 255
wooden roulette decorations
 MAS03 ceramics, 320
northern Benin, 241
Tuali-B occupation ceramics, 231–232, 238, 240, 257
woody vegetation, 50, 51, 60
 See also plant communities

Y

yams, 52, 59, 61, 154, 204
yellow-backed duikers, 135
yellow clay, 126–127
Yendabri, 255
Yendi Dabari, 240
Yiendéni, 243
Yobri, 7–8, 28, 161–162, 231, 247, 321
Yobri rockshelter
 animal bone assemblages, 113, 250
 archaeological research, 10, 123
 artifact associations, 119
 geometric microlith assemblages, 108, 113, 121
 rock art, 315
 stone tools and artifacts, 107–108
Yoruba indigo, 242

Z

Zambia, 120
Zandoya archaeological site, 305
Zaria, 244
zoned decorations, 129, 299